1 MONTH OF
FREE
READING

at

www.ForgottenBooks.com

By purchasing this book you are
eligible for one month membership to
ForgottenBooks.com, giving you
unlimited access to our entire
collection of over 1,000,000 titles via
our web site and mobile apps.

To claim your free month visit:
www.forgottenbooks.com/free1123267

ISBN 978-0-331-43289-3
PIBN 11123267

Ward 11–Precinct 1

CITY OF BOSTON

LIST OF RESIDENTS
20 YEARS OF AGE AND OVER

(NON-CITIZENS INDICATED BY ASTERISK)
(FEMALES INDICATED BY DAGGER)

AS OF

JANUARY 1, 1941

JOSEPH F. TIMILTY, *Chairman*
FREDERIC E. DOWLING, *Secretary*
WILLIAM A. MOTLEY, JR.
FRANCIS B. McKINNEY
HILDA HEDSTROM QUIRK
Listing Board.

CITY OF BOSTON PRINTING DEPARTMENT

Anita Terrace

A	Heald Doris—†	5	housekeeper	30	38 Wensley
B	Heald John F	5	chauffeur	59	38 "
C	Kelly Annie—†	5	housekeeper	63	here
D	Kelly Ellen M—†	5	at home	72	"
E	DuPrey Ethel—†	5	housewife	61	"
F	DuPrey William R	5	foreman	69	
G	Ericson Albert	6	laborer	54	
H	Ericson Sophie—†	6	housewife	43	"
K	Fleming Estelle—†	6	"	35	
L	*Fleming James	6	mechanic	42	"
M	Dorsey Joseph	6	salesman	42	265 Roxbury
N	Morley Charles E	6	clerk	24	here
O	Morley Marjorie—†	6	housewife	24	"
P	Hillcoat Jeanne—†	7	"	64	"
R	Hillcoat Robert	7	machinist	68	"
S	Hillcoat Robert, jr	7	salesman	36	"
T	Hillcoat William N	7	laborer	27	Somerville
U	Moore Catherine—†	7	housewife	49	here
V	Moore William S	7	painter	59	"
W	Gipper Louisa—†	7	laundress	54	"
X	Popp Paulina—†	7	clerk	63	
Y	Prassa Emelia—†	7	housekeeper	85	"
Z	Rose Frederick	8	laborer	33	57 Lamartine

2

A	Rose Rita B—†	8	housewife	23	57 "
B	Grant Thomas	8	bartender	56	here
C	Brennan James	8	retired	74	"
D	McCarten Dudley	15	shoeworker	48	"
E	McCarten Gertrude—†	15	clerk	49	
F	McCarten Harry	15	laster	50	"
G	Erickson Joseph	17	mechanic	45	"
H	Becker Adolph	17	baker	55	
L	Skinner Lester M	19	toolmaker	43	"
M	Skinner Marian E—†	19	housewife	38	"
N	Eldridge Mary E—†	19	clerk	61	
O	Eldridge William	19	retired	56	"
P	Fiebelkorn Berhart	19	laborer	36	"
R	*Feibelkorn Martha—†	19	housekeeper	43	"
S	Swain Albert	20	waiter	42	"
T	Swain Helen—†	20	housewife	35	"

Page.	Letter.	FULL NAME.	Residence, Jan. 1, 1941.	Occupation.	Supposed Age.	Reported Residence, Jan. 1, 1940. Street and Number.

Anita Terrace—Continued

u	Curley Malcolm	20	laborer	48	here
v	Rooney Florence—†	21	housekeeper	34	1242 Tremont
w	Rooney James	21	laborer	31	1242 "
x	Anderson Abbie—†	21	housewife	32	Saugus
y	*Anderson John	21	laborer	39	"
z	Croke Harriet J—†	21	housekeeper	32	here

3

a	Croke John	21	seaman	30	"
b	*Finn Beatrice—†	22	housewife	30	"
c	Finn Patrick J	22	chauffeur	32	"
d	LeBlanc Leopold P	22	laborer	30	1491 Col av
e	LeBlanc Mary—†	22	housewife	58	1491 "
f	Craig Charles	22	laborer	53	52 Elmwood
g	Skidmore Amy—†	22	housewife	52	52 "
h	Skidmore John	22	clerk	22	52 "
k	Tucker Theresa—†	23	housewife	25	here
l	Tucker William	23	laborer	24	"
m	Moshak John	23	carpenter	64	"
n	*Sorpewitz Andrew	23	"	63	
o	*Sorpewitz Elizabeth—†	23	housewife	60	"

Carnes Place

p	Carey Dorothy—†	1	housewife	23	1219 Tremont
r	Carey Paul	1	laborer	27	1219 "
s	Grant Harry	1	"	24	8 Malbon pl
t	Grant Louise—†	1	housewife	24	8 "
u	Grant Horatio H	1	retired	69	here
v	O'Donnell Helen V—†	2	housewife	32	"
w	O'Donnell James A	2	packer	32	"
x	Major Agnes M—†	2	housewife	34	"
y	Major George	2	laborer	36	"
z	O'Connor Bridget—†	2	housewife	40	21 Anita ter

4

a	O'Connor Cornelius	2	laborer	45	21 "
b	Amadoony Peter	3	"	48	here
d	Gutgesell Alfred W	3	painter	36	"
e	Gutgesell Frances A—†	3	housewife	40	"
f	*Gutgesell William	3	retired	79	"
g	Eno Angie E—†	4	housewife	41	58 Bromley
h	Eno Henry J	4	laborer	53	58 "

3

Carnes Place—Continued

K	Hogan Edna M—†	4	housewife	31	here
L	Hogan William P	4	carpenter	31	"
M	Creighton James F	4	operator	38	"
N	Creighton Rose M—†	4	housewife	41	"
O	Gill James A	5	retired	66	
P	Gill Mary—†	5	housewife	68	"
R	Gill William J	5	laborer	52	
S	Girten Charles S	5	upholsterer	41	"
T	Girten Esther A—†	5	clerk	20	
U	Girten Lydia E—†	5	housewife	40	"

Cedar Park

W	Nichols Edith—†	5	housewife	33	9 Cliff
X	Nichols Jesse	5	watchman	50	9 "
Z	Liolin Edna—†	7	housewife	50	775 Tremont

5

A	Liolin Thomas G	7	waiter	49	775 "
B	Carter Mary E—†	8	housewife	53	here
C	Carter Rita P—†	8	secretary	23	"
D	Philbrook Claude	9	chauffeur	45	"
E	Philbrook Clayton	9	U S A	21	
F	Philbrook Lillian—†	9	housewife	39	"
G	Moreau Irene—†	10	assessor	31	
H	Moreau Leonard	10	meatcutter	25	"
K	Moreau Louise—†	10	housewife	58	"
L	Coakley Cornelius	11	clerk	29	57 Minden
M	Coakley Helen—†	11	housewife	27	57 "
N	McClellan Elizabeth F—†	12	"	54	here
O	McClellan John J	12	laborer	22	"
P	Grady Frank	14	salesman	30	"
R	Starrs Bernard	14	finisher	59	
S	Starrs Bernard F, jr	14	machinist	23	"
T	Starrs Catherine—†	14	housewife	49	"
U	Starrs Charles J	14	clerk	28	
V	Starrs Mary—†	14	operator	25	
W	Starrs Walter	14	"	21	
X	Doolan Anna—†	16	housekeeper	49	"
Y	Middless Harry	16	laborer	39	"
Z	Schoen Dorothy—†	16	domestic	28	"

6
Cedar Park—Continued

A	Schoen Jacob	16	laborer	67	here
B	Schoen Sophie—†	16	sorter	38	"
C	Campbell John	18	engineer	42	"
D	Campbell Mary—†	18	housewife	34	"
E	Allen John H	20	mechanic	42	204 Heath
F	Allen Mary E—†	20	housewife	36	204 "
G	Schoen Barbara—†	22	"	35	here
H	Schoen John J	22	chauffeur	47	"
K	*McDonald Donald	24	mechanic	29	79 Fort av
L	*McDonald Mary—†	24	housewife	29	79 "
M	Runge George	24	brewer	47	here
N	Runge Olga—†	24	housewife	44	"
O	Coit Mabel—†	26	"	33	"
P	Coit Thomas	26	laborer	42	"
R	Foley Gladys—†	26	waitress	37	"
S	*McLeod Donald	26	chauffeur	62	"
T	*McLeod Jeanette—†	26	housewife	62	"
U	McLeod Pearl—†	26	waitress	26	
V	Capone Caroline—†	28	operator	41	
W	Dowd Agatha—†	28	housekeeper	39	"
X	Dowd Hazel K—†	28	clerk	42	"
Y	Dowd Lauretta B—†	28	secretary	35	"
Z	Dowd Lottie B—†	28	housewife	64	"

7

A	Dowd William T	28	clerk	36	

Cedar Street

B	Freeman Irving	99	janitor	44	here
C	Freeman Laurena—†	99	housewife	44	"
D	McDonald Charles B	99	laborer	49	"
E	*McDonald Rosetta—†	99	housewife	45	"
F	McGill John	99	waiter	36	"
G	McGill Susan—†	99	housewife	31	"
H	Bryant David R	101	laborer	33	
K	Bryant Ida—†	101	housewife	33	"
L	Bryant Verona—†	101	domestic	44	"
M	Abbott Caroline—†	101	hairdresser	59	"
N	Abbott Earlie—†	101	housewife	48	"

Cedar Street—Continued

o	Abbott Lenora—†	101	domestic	25	here
p	Davis Clara M—†	101	housewife	64	"
r	Diggs Washington	101	retired	77	"
s	McHallam Mary—†	103	housewife	39	8 Heath av
t	McHallam Peter	103	inspector	43	8 "
u	*MacDonald Agnes—†	103	housewife	35	39 Laurel
v	*MacDonald John J	103	laborer	38	39 "
w	Ahl Effie M—†	103	housewife	54	here
x	Ahl Leslie	103	laborer	45	"
y	Lee Chester A	103	"	34	"
z	Moran Frances—†	103	operator	33	"

8

a	*Lelle Maria—†	104	housewife	61	"
b	Lelle Philip	104	machinist	58	"
c	Sullivan Anna—†	104	housewife	26	82 Cedar
d	Sullivan William	104	painter	32	82 "
e	Tebeau Mary—†	104	teacher	46	here
f	*Welsh Mary—†	104	domestic	60	"
l	Burns Clarence E	106	retired	64	"
m	Burns Madeline V—†	106	clerk	28	"
n	Burns Thomas L	106	patternmaker	21	"
o	McGlynn Frank	106	laborer	62	
p	McGlynn Nellie—†	106	housewife	58	"
r	Crimmins Bessie—†	107	teacher	38	
s	*Crimmins Susan—†	107	housewife	76	"
t	Hurley Joseph	107A	conductor	35	"
u	Hurley Josephine—†	107A	housewife	32	"
v	McDonald Betty—†	107A	secretary	22	"
w	McDonald John H	107A	conductor	49	"
x	*McDonald Lucy—†	107A	housewife	47	"
y	Pender John	108	porter	40	
z	Pender Ruth—†	108	housewife	30	"

9

a	MacDonald Mary—†	108	"	67	
b	MacDonald William J	108	carpenter	65	"
c	Brockman Grace L—†	109	housewife	48	"
d	Brockman William E	109	painter	51	
e	Tufankjian Catherine—†	109	housewife	46	"
f	Tufankjian Leon	109	cabinetmaker	51	"
g	Patriquin Catherine—†	109	housewife	52	"
h	Patriquin Charles L	109	mechanic	39	"

Cedar Street—Continued

K	Patriquin Eleanor R—†	109	clerk	24	here
L	Russo James	rear 109	retired.	47	"
M	Russo Margaret—†	" 109	saleswoman	40	"
N	Russo Theresa—†	" 109	housewife	46	"
o	*Brown Eleanor—†	110	"	47	
P	Brown William	110	fisherman	47	"
R	*Jackson Bernice—†	110	domestic	45	2 Orchard pk
S	Mayer Agnes—†	110	housewife	27	here
T	Mayer Carlton	110	foreman	27	"
X	*Manifase Earl	112	laborer	40	"
Y	*Manifase Mary—†	112	housewife	38	"
Z	McLean Charles A	112	printer	40	
	10				
A	McLean George W	112	shipper	36	
B	McLean Veronica—†	112	housewife	65	"
C	Cameron David F	112	chauffeur	39	"
D	Cameron Helen R—†	112	housewife	36	"
F	Gray Leo	113	clerk	42	
G	Gray Ralpha—†	113	housewife	35	"
H	Barbour Alice M—†	113	stenographer	30	"
K	Barbour Carl L	113	shipper	27	"
L	Crimmins Catherine E—†	114	housewife	42	"
M	Crimmins John M	114	ironworker	46	"
N	Crimmins Marie R—†	114	clerk	20	
o	Franzen Joseph	114	retired	69	
P	Lewald Fritz	114	laborer	59	
R	*Lewald Margaret—†	114	housewife	62	"
S	Carlson Anne—†	114	clerk	21	
T	Pearson Albert	114	counterman	20	"
U	Pearson Robert	114	longshoreman	24	"
V	Jellon Joseph	115	laborer	40	"
W	Jellon Mary—†	115	housewife	33	"
X	Brady Betty—†	115	stitcher	46	1 Fuller
Y	Brady Michael	115	laborer	45	1 "
Z	Hartin Henry	115	operator	22	here
	11				
A	Hartin Mary—†	115	housewife	49	"
B	Hartin William A	115	laborer	47	
C	Naugler Esther J—†	115	domestic	24	"
D	Naugler Ethel M—†	115	housewife	61	"
E	Naugler Marion T—†	115	folder	22	

Page.	Letter.	FULL NAME.	Residence, Jan. 1, 1941.	Occupation.	Supposed Age.	Reported Residence, Jan. 1, 1940. Street and Number.

Cedar Street—Continued

F	Meyer John	117	chauffeur	25	here
G	Meyer Marie—†	117	housewife	24	"
H	Beck Joseph G	117	clerk	34	"
K	Beck Margaret—†	117	housewife	24	"
L	Beck Sadie J—†	117	"	53	
M	Eaton Flora E—†	117	stitcher	40	
N	Hanna Eunice E—†	118	attendant	23	"
O	Hanna Frederick T	118	painter	46	
P	Hanna Marion A—†	118	housewife	42	"
R	Goudis Penelope—†	118	"	45	
S	Goudis Thomas	118	barber	55	"
T	McSherry James	118	laborer	61	56 Day
U	McSherry James J, jr	118	manager	28	here
V	McSherry Margaret—†	118	housewife	44	56 Day
W	Overton Alice—†	119	"	57	here
X	Overton Florence—†	119	attendant	21	"
Y	Hogan John E	119	retired	67	"
Z	Hogan William H	119	painter	58	

12

A	Maguire Lillian—†	119	packer	21	
B	Maguire Louis	119	carpenter	56	"
C	Maguire Marie—†	119	housewife	50	"
D	Maguire Walter	119	mechanic	23	"
E	MacNeil Mary L—†	120	housewife	42	"
F	MacNeil Ralph M	120	chauffeur	58	"
G	MacNeill Ralph M, jr	120	U S A	21	
H	*Kroposky Joseph	120	operator	53	
K	*Kroposky Pauline—†	120	housewife	43	"
L	Kelley Agnes E—†	120	"	51	
M	Kelley Charles E	120	laborer	21	"
N	Foley Michael	121	"	36	32 Erie
O	Foley Sarah—†	121	housewife	35	32 "
P	Beaudoin Marion—†	121	"	24	here
R	Beaudoin Rudolph	121	shoeworker	29	"
S	Beauregard Harry W	121	chemist	36	"
T	O'Brien Annie M—†	121	housekeeper	69	"
U	Cass Catherine—†	121	housewife	29	"
V	Cass John	121	mechanic	28	"

13

B	Bridges Jessie—†	123	domestic	50	"
C	Martin Charles	123	musician	32	"

8

Page.	Letter.	FULL NAME.	Residence, Jan. 1, 1941.	Occupation.	Supposed Age.	Reported Residence, Jan. 1, 1940. Street and Number.

Cedar Street—Continued

	D	Martin Naomi—†	123	entertainer	26	here
	E	Wade Henry	123	porter	55	"
	F	*Edwards Olwen—†	124	housewife	31	"
	G	Edwards William	124	dyemaker	31	"
	H	Small Ethel L—†	124	housewife	51	"
	K	Small Horace C	124	mechanic	49	"
	L	Mattler Minna—†	125	housewife	23	19 Moseley
	M	Mattler Ralph	125	grillman	24	19 "
	N	Pierce Andrew J	125	fireman	44	here
	O	Pierce Helen G—†	125	housewife	43	"
	P	*Sarian Mary—†	125	"	39	"
	R	*Sarian Rose—†	125	clerk	30	
	S	*Sarian Stephen	125	salesman	41	"
	T	*Marino Theresa—†	126	housewife	41	"
	U	Marino Thomas	126	tilesetter	46	"
	Y	Cadagan Catherine A—†	129	housewife	46	"
	Z	Cadagan John J	129	chauffeur	46	"
14						
	A	MacLeod Harriet—†	129	housekeeper	42	"
	B	Smilewicz Joseph	129	laborer	22	..
	C	Smilewicz Raymond	129	"	25	
	D	*Smilewicz Ursula—†	129	housewife	61	"
	E	*Smilewicz Vincent	129	laborer	52	
	F	Smilewicz Walter	129	counterman	29	"
	G	Murray Kathleen—†	131	housewife	34	"
	H	Murray Thomas	131	laborer	38	"
	K	*Creehan Catherine—†	131	housewife	30	"
	L	Creehan Mark	131	porter	38	
	M	Buechs Herman	131	chauffeur	36	"
	N	*Buechs Jessie—†	131	housewife	26	"
	O	Manning Mary H—†	133	"	39	
	P	Manning Peter	133	chauffeur	47	"
	R	*MacQuarrie Margaret—†	133	housewife	40	18 Vale
	S	MacQuarrie Murdock	133	salesman	38	18 "
	T	Disco Catherine—†	133	housewife	23	here
	U	Disco Michael	133	laborer	26	"
	V	Ross Bessie—†	133	housewife	61	"
	W	Ross Chester M	133	laborer	33	
	X	MacLean Laughlin	135	janitor	44	"
	Y	Carley Ralph	135	laborer	27	Connecticut
	Z	Endey Frank	135	houseman	32	15 Newark

9

15
Cedar Street—Continued

A	Sweeney Sara—†	135	housewife	49	here
B	*Kraston Emily—†	135	"	50	88 Thornton
C	Laiweneek Mildred—†	135	"	26	82 Cedar
D	Laiweneek Robert	135	machinist	26	82 "
E	Stroup Lillian—†	135	hairdresser	26	38 Thornton
F	Lynch Josiah	139	painter	39	here
G	*Lynch Stella—†	139	housewife	35	"
H	*Keskula Mathilda—†	139	"	49	"
K	Keskula Madis	139	mechanic	48	"
L	Grover Anna—†	139	housewife	39	49 Fulda
M	Grover Earl F	139	chauffeur	38	49 "
N	Haverty Helen—†	139	housewife	21	here
O	Haverty Richard	139	clerk	23	"
P	Caulfield Reta—†	140	housewife	21	51 Walden
R	Caulfield Thomas	140	laborer	25	51 "
S	Greenberg Andrew	140	painter	69	here
T	*Greenberg Lizzie—†	140	housewife	68	"
U	*Reisner Helen—†	140	"	48	"
V	Reisner Jacob	140	engineer	61	
W	Hart Agnes M—†	141	housewife	69	"
X	Hart Joseph A	141	retired	79	
Y	Hart Joseph E, jr	141	laborer	29	
Z	Hart Kathryn C—†	141	nurse	33	

16

A	Gatt George R	141	chauffeur	43	"
B	Gatt Gertrude C—†	141	clerk	20	
C	Gatt Marie S—†	141	housewife	43	"
D	Joslyn Charles	141	retired	48	
E	Smith Alexander A	141	carpenter	51	"
F	Smith Augusta—†	141	housewife	43	"
G	McCormack Thomas H	143	laborer	36	
H	Turner Edward S	143	retired	76	
K	Turner Maud—†	143	housewife	58	"
L	Fink Richard S	143	laborer	45	
M	Rothwell James, jr	143	foreman	55	
N	Rothwell Mary—†	143	housewife	57	"
S	Fenton Herbert	145–147	bartender	33	"
T	Fenton Mary M—†	145–147	housewife	33	"
U	Carrigg Catherine—†	145–147	"	65	"
V	Carrigg Esther—†	145–147	boxmaker	25	"

10

Page.	Letter.	Full Name.	Residence, Jan. 1, 1941.	Occupation.	Supposed Age.	Reported Residence, Jan. 1, 1940. Street and Number.

Cedar Street—Continued

	w	Curry Arthur	145–147	stonecutter	32	here
	x	Curry Catherine—†	145–147	baker	32	"
	y	LePage Irene—†	146	housewife	50	"
	z	LePage Robert L	146	mechanic	53	"
17						
	a	Greene Anna—†	146	housewife	31	"
	b	Greene Paul S	146	fisherman	32	"
	c	Stephens Anne E—†	146	forewoman	46	"
	d	Sacks Edgar	146	woodcarver	41	"
	e	Brown Gertrude—†	146	housekeeper	52	"
	f	Hawes Florence B—†	153	housewife	58	"
	g	Snell Charles N	153	engineer	55	
	h	Snell Frances O—†	153	housewife	39	"
	k	Belfiore Domonic	155	bartender	42	"
	l	Belfiore Lillis—†	155	housewife	36	"
	m	Leonard Christine—†	157	"	31	126 Bay State rd
	n	Leonard Peter	157	chauffeur	31	47 E Dedham
	o	Richardson George	159	foreman	51	here
	p	Richardson Isabelle—†	159	forewoman	49	"
	s	*Lowe Helen—†	162	housewife	36	134 Cedar
	t	*Lowe Thomas	162	watchman	38	134 "
	u	Mills James E	162	meatcutter	23	here
	v	Mills Marjorie A—†	162	housewife	22	"
	w	Horgan Frances L—†	162	"	49	"
	x	Horgan Patrick J	162	engineer	50	
	y	Carter Louise M—†	164	housewife	49	"
	z	Carter Walter A	164	laborer	27	
18						
	a	Kilgannon Michael J	164	policeman	45	38 Dunreath
	b	Kilgannon Mildred M—†	164	housewife	34	38 "
	c	Adler Evelyn—†	164	laundress	22	Norwood
	d	Bauer Dorothy L—†	164	housewife	39	193 Dudley
	e	Bauer Otto	164	painter	42	193 "
	f	Killarney Mary—†	166	housewife	22	52 Atherton
	g	Killarney William J	166	laborer	24	54 Bickford
	h	Whalen Caroline—†	166	housewife	21	894 Hunt'n av
	k	Whalen Joseph	166	timekeeper	25	894 "
	l	Webber Annette—†	166	housewife	24	here
	m	Webber George	166	laborer	26	"
	o	Kijewski Felix	168A	manager	47	"
	p	Kijewski Helen—†	168A	housewife	38	"

Page.	Letter.	FULL NAME.	Residence, Jan. 1, 1941.	Occupation.	Supposed Age.	Reported Residence, Jan. 1, 1940. Street and Number.

Cedar Street—Continued

	R	Monahan Cornelius	172	laborer	55	here
	S	Monahan John	172	"	23	"
	T	Monahan Julia—†	172	housewife	51	"
	U	Monahan Julia—†	172	clerk	21	
	v	*Brown Catherine—†	174	housekeeper	48	"
	x	Regan Catherine—†	174	"	57	"

Centre Place

	Y	Apsit Annie—†	1	clerk	25	here
	z	Apsit John	1	machinist	62	"
19						
	A	Apsit John	1	superintendent	45	"
	B	Apsit Minna—†	1	housewife	58	"
	D	Muise John	1	operator	40	"
	E	Muise Mary—†	1	housewife	32	"
	F	Grube Alice—†	2	"	35	"
	G	Grube August	2	breweryworker	48	3 Centre pl
	H	Missin Charles	2	machinist	50	here
	K	Sawitzky Frank	2	"	60	6 Romar ter
	L	Bloomberg Henry	2	clerk	23	6 "
	M	Bloomberg John	2	machinist	48	6 "
	N	Bloomberg Julia—†	2	housewife	49	186 Bay State rd
	O	*Blossman Mary—†	3	"	60	here
	P	*Stroupe Alma B—†	3	clerk	31	"
	R	Sugar Edward J	3	painter	54	"
	S	Johnson Dorothy G—†	3	housewife	26	79 Centre
	T	Johnson Ralph	3	clerk	31	115 Cabot
	U	Schultz Elizabeth J—†	3	housewife	35	here
	V	Schultz Hans A	3	clerk	32	"
	w	Lyman John	4	carpenter	58	"
	x	Lyman Lucy—†	4	housewife	59	"
	Y	Sanerib Lydia—†	4	houseworker	50	"
	z	Herlihy Bertha—†	4	housewife	47	"
20						
	A	Herlihy Leo J	4	policeman	51	"
	B	Lamb Henry J	4	accountant	29	"
	C	Lamb Margaret F—†	4	housewife	27	"
	D	Lertner Clara—†	5	stitcher	49	
	E	Prichard Charles	5	laborer	33	

Page.	Letter.	FULL NAME.	Residence, Jan. 1, 1941.	Occupation.	Supposed Age.	Reported Residence, Jan. 1, 1940. Street and Number.

Centre Place—Continued

	F	Prichard Lilly—†	5	housewife	30	here
	G	Elias Delia J—†	5	"	28	5090 Wash'n
	H	Elias Thomas	5	laborer	27	5090 "
	K	Procopio Anna—†	5	housewife	33	here
	L	Procopio Louis	5	foreman	35	4031 Wash'n
	M	Hoefling Anton	6	retired	83	here
	N	Hoefling Francka—†	6	housewife	81	"
	O	Campbell Bridget—†	6	retired	72	"
	P	Timmins Mary M—†	6	houseworker	66	"

Centre Street

	¹s	Gillard Alfreda—†	51	housewife	39	here
	U	Carey Joseph	53	laborer	34	"
	V	Carey Mary—†	53	housewife	29	"
	W	Mardney Beatrice—†	53	housekeeper	49	1 Kemble
	X	Dempsey Helen—†	53	operator	23	here
	Y	Dempsey James	53	laborer	20	"
	Z	Dempsey Marie—†	53	housewife	53	"
21						
	A	Gorman Mary—†	55	housekeeper	62	"
	B	Maguire Edward	55	laborer	25	
	C	Maguire James	55	painter	24	
	D	Maguire Susannah—†	55	housekeeper	52	"
	E	Maguire Thomas	55	baker	22	"
	F	Buechs Anna—†	55	packer	29	
	G	Buechs Florence—†	55	laundress	22	"
	H	Buechs Leopold	55	retired	67	
	K	Capozzi Rose—†	57	stitcher	32	
	L	Johnson Carl R	57	retired	68	"
	M	Barry Helen—†	57	"	66	"
	N	Reid David T	57	"	62	"
	O	Looney Hannah M—†	59	"	66	
	P	McGonagle Catherine—†	59	"	70	
	R	Norton Martin	59	"	65	
	T	Lomas Catherine—†	61	housekeeper	73	"
	U	Lomas John	61	grocer	39	"
	V	Ecker Gustav	63	operator	37	
	W	Ecker Helen S—†	63	housekeeper	66	"
	X	*Pezzano Dominic	63	operator	42	128 Heath

Page.	Letter.	FULL NAME.	Residence, Jan. 1, 1941.	Occupation.	Supposed Age.	Reported Residence, Jan. 1, 1940. Street and Number.

Centre Street—Continued

	Y	Pezzano Erna—†	63	stitcher	41	128 Heath
22						
	A	Brooks Alice—†	65	housewife	34	here
	B	Brooks Arthur	65	laborer	35	"
	D	*Robash Dora—†	67	housewife	63	"
	E	Robash Fred	67	machinist	64	"
	F	Lanigan Bridget—†	67	housekeeper	41	"
	G	Lanigan Robert	67	laborer	41	"
	H	*McGuiness Ellen—†	67	nurse	57	1250 Tremont
	K	Martin Guilford	69	mechanic	41	here
	L	Martin Myrtle—†	69	housewife	34	"
	M	McAtee Madeline—†	69	cook	27	"
	N	Hughes Anthony	71	realtor	39	
	O	Hughes Gerald	71	chauffeur	35	"
	P	Hughes Marie—†	71	housewife	68	"
	R	Campbell Catherine—†	71	"	42	68 Centre
	S	Campbell James J	71	accountant	43	68 "
	T	Campbell Paul	71	laborer	22	68 "
	U	Rowan Mary—†	71	housekeeper	60	68 "
	V	Harkins Edward J	71	retired	60	here
	W	Harkins Mary A—†	71	housekeeper	55	"
	X	Anzello Hortense—†	73	housewife	24	"
	Y	Anzello Salvatore	73	woodworker	28	"
	Z	Tavano Constantino	73	laborer	27	
23						
	A	*Tavano Gino—†	73	housewife	50	"
	B	Tavano Valentino	73	manager	52	"
	C	Boyle Olive V—†	73	housewife	52	"
	D	Boyle Patrick J	73	fireman	58	
	E	Hansen Dorothy M—†	73	stenographer	24	"
	F	Hansen Raymond	73	clerk	22	,,
	G	Jessen Mabel C—†	73	maid	55	
	H	Canavin Helen T—†	73	"	33	
	K	Canavin James J	73	packer	39	
	L	Canavin Mary A—†	73	housewife	68	"
	M	Wallace Hazel—†	75	laundress	35	180 Centre
	N	Perkins Jennie L—†	75	housewife	79	here
	O	Perkins Susie B—†	75	bookkeeper	57	"
	P	Richards Louise K—†	75	housekeeper	60	"
	R	Hansen Mary—†	75	housewife	32	"
	S	Hansen Richard	75	printer	35	

14

Page.	Letter.	FULL NAME.	Residence, Jan. 1, 1941.	Occupation.	Supposed Age.	Reported Residence, Jan. 1, 1940. Street and Number.

Centre Street—Continued

	T	Curran Anna R—†	77	housewife	39	here
	U	Curran William H	77	painter	40	"
	V	Lamb John	77	clerk	23	"
	W	Craig Agnes—†	77	housewife	57	"
	X	Craig Evelyn—†	77	clerk	27	
	Y	Craig Harry	77	shipper	22	
	Z	Craig James	77	printer	24	
24						
	A	Craig Thomas	77	clerk	25	
	B	Woods Manuel	77	painter	36	
	C	Woods Sophie—†	77	housewife	44	"
	D	*Barrett Ellen—†	79	"	29	
	E	*Barrett Thomas	79	clerk	29	
	F	Perry Clara E—†	79	housewife	52	"
	G	Perry Roscoe F	79	merchant	64	"
	H	McCarroll Walter	79	packer	23	85 Minden
	K	Youngdahl Althea B—†	79	housewife	46	85 "
	L	Youngdahl Ernest	79	laborer	41	85 "
	M	Mallon Annie—†	81	shoeworker	38	here
	N	Mallon Edward	81	retired	74	"
	O	Mallon Ellen—†	81	shoeworker	39	"
	P	Mallon Margaret—†	81	candyworker	36	"
	R	Hackett Mary—†	81	housekeeper	69	"
	S	Wheeler Alice—†	81	housewife	30	"
	T	Hovhannesian Annie—†	81	"	29	
	U	Hovhannesian Sahag	81	printer	41	
	W	Peterson Alfred	93	engineer	22	
	X	Peterson Annette—†	93	housewife	51	"
	Y	Peterson Jacob	93	seaman	58	
	Z	Peterson Jacob	93	laborer	20	"
25						
	A	Jaunklavin Vera—†	93	clerk	33	4 Oakland
	B	Zepurneek Frederick	93	laborer	21	Wellesley
	C	Zepurneek Lucy—†	93	housewife	60	here
	D	Lynch Frances—†	93	clerk	39	"
	E	Lynch Hannah —†	93	housewife	64	"
	F	Lynch Vincent—†	93	electrician	25	"
	G	Mahar Agnes T—†	94	operator	49	"
	H	Mahar Mary A—†	94	housewife	82	"
	K	Lally John F	96	retired	69	
	L	Lally Julia—†	96	housewife	64	"

Page.	Letter.	FULL NAME.	Residence, Jan. 1, 1941.	Occupation.	Supposed Age.	Reported Residence, Jan. 1, 1940. Street and Number.

Centre Street—Continued

	M	Glennon Ann M—†	98	housewife	37	here
	N	Glennon Walter J	98	chauffeur	35	"
	O	Demetriades George	100	clerk	50	"
	P	Demetriades Mae—†	100	housewife	47	"
	R	O'Rourke Lula—†	100	clerk	43	
	S	Lyons James	107	laborer	47	
	T	McArdle Nellie—†	107	shoeworker	45	"
	U	Gaffney Joseph F	107	painter	63	
	V	Gaffney Mary A—†	107	housewife	52	"
	W	Gaffney Rita—†	107	nurse	22	"
	X	Gaffney Ruth A—†	107	bookkeeper	27	"
	Y	Kelly John	107	B F D	43	
	Z	Quinn Mary—†	107	dietitian	42	

26

	A	Francis Ann—†	109	laundress	25	"
	B	Francis Annie—†	109	housewife	66	"
	C	Francis Mary—†	109	operator	27	"
	D	Doyle Cecelia—†	109	secretary	29	"
	E	McHugh Nellie—†	109	housewife	63	"
	F	McHugh Thomas J	109	millwright	65	"
	G	McHugh Thomas H	109	chauffeur	38	"
	H	Colby Effie M—†	109	housewife	50	"
	K	Colby Merle F	109	millwright	49	"
	L	Ela Florence—†	109	shoeworker	55	"
	M	Burns James J	111	mortician	46	"
	N	Burns Mary—†	111	housewife	45	"
	O	Daylor Daniel H	111	machinist	63	"
	P	Daylor Mary—†	111	housewife	61	"
	R	Milne May—†	111	housekeeper	56	"
	S	Owens Carrie—†	111	maid	34	"
	T	Skelly Margaret—†	111	laundress	50	"
	U	Galvin Mary L—†	117	housewife	60	"
	V	Galvin Thomas E—†	117	physician	65	"
	W	Gorham Rena—†	117	housekeeper	35	"
	X	O'Neil Catherine F—†	117	"	71	"
	Y	O'Neil Elizabeth A—†	117	teacher	69	

27

	A	DeSemone Angeline—†	121	housewife	48	121 Marcella
	B	DeSemone Clara—†	121	operator	23	121 "
	C	DeSemone Edward	121	laborer	22	121 "
	D	DeSemone Perseo	121	carpenter	50	121 "

Centre Street—Continued

E	DeSemone Virgil	121	waiter	27	121 Marcella
F	DeSemone William	121	wrapper	21	121 "
O	Roach Edward	123	clerk	38	here
P	Wise Theresa—†	123	housekeeper	62	"
R	Coffey Sarah J—†	125	housewife	70	106 Marcella
S	Ginnetty Velma—†	125	waitress	24	5 Mark
T	Kolusky Irene—†	125	housewife	48	28 Albion
U	Kolusky Paul J	125	painter	47	28 "
V	*Gillen Catherine A—†	125	housekeeper	72	7 Regent ct
W	Gillen Elizabeth J—†	125	stitcher	57	7 "
X	Gillen Ellen T—†	125	housewife	66	7 "
Y	Jones Emma—†	127	"	55	here
Z	Jones James	127	mechanic	28	"

28

A	Jones Wilma—†	127	housewife	27	"
B	Patrick Helena I—†	129	"	64	
C	Patrick Thomas W	129	physician	68	"
D	Greene Edith E—†	131	clerk	37	
E	Dooner Helen—†	131	housewife	70	"
F	Dooner John P	131	retired	82	
G	Doherty Owen	131	laborer	38	"
L	Connelly Agnes V—†	137	stitcher	42	2 Terry
M	Connelly Joseph	137	inspector	43	107 Rosseter
N	Walsh Mary—†	137	housewife	34	here
O	Walsh Francis	137	chauffeur	35	"
P	Reynolds George M	137	mechanic	41	"
R	Reynolds Sadie C—†	137	housewife	39	"
S	Reynolds Theresa A—†	137	supervisor	42	"
T	Misilo John	139	cook	41	
U	*Misilo Mary—†	139	housewife	40	"
V	Lane Mary—†	139	"	54	
W	Lane Michael J	139	laundryman	55	"
X	McHugh Thomas	139	retired	63	"
Y	Nolan Anna F—†	139	housewife	40	8 Ward
Z	Nolan Francis	139	chauffeur	43	8 "

29

A	Nolan Robert E	139	clerk	23	8 "
B	Galvin Celia—†	141	housewife	59	here
C	Galvin Dorothy—†	141	librarian	21	"
D	Russell Margaret J—†	141	domestic	70	137 Centre
E	Godsoe Mary—†	141	housewife	23	34 Highland av

Page.	Letter.	FULL NAME.	Residence, Jan. 1, 1941.	Occupation.	Supposed Age.	Reported Residence, Jan. 1, 1940. Street and Number.

Centre Street—Continued

	F	Godsoe William	141	clerk	29	34 Highland av
	G	Stockinger Charles A	141	watchman	61	here
	H	Stockinger Helen C—†	141	clerk	27	"
	K	Stockinger Mary A—†	141	housewife	59	"

30 Columbus Avenue

	D	Holman Arthur	1263	mechanic	32	here
	E	Holman Greta—†	1263	housewife	32	"
	F	Bird John	1265	retired	76	"
	G	Bird Mary A—†	1265	housewife	63	"
	H	Laird Clara—†	1267	maid	62	
	K	*Golleski Olga—†	1267	housewife	46	"
	L	*Golleski William	1267	laborer	56	..
	M	Rhode Charles	1267	clerk	21	
	N	Rhode Edmund	1267	salesman	23	"
	R	Carnation Bernadette—†	1271	housewife	29	"
	S	Carnation Joseph	1271	laborer	25	
	T	Walsh John I	1271	chauffeur	39	"
	U	Walsh Mary A—†	1271	housewife	38	"
	V	Walsh Patrick L	1271	shipper	37	
	W	Davis Irene—†	1275	housewife	33	"
	X	*Estrella Anna—†	1275	"	41	
	Y	*Estrella Thomas	1275	retired	48	
	Z	Langer Conrad C	1275	baker	49	
	31					
	B	Giovaniello James	1279	laborer	48	5 Minden
	C	Giovaniello Rose—†	1279	housewife	39	5 "
	D	Tabbi Joseph	1279	factoryhand	24	7 "
	E	Tabbi Josephine—†	1279	housewife	46	7 "
	F	Tabbi Leo	1279	clerk	20	7 '
	G	Tabbi Mary—†	1279	shoeworker	23	7 "
	H	Tabbi Salvatore	1279	laborer	52	7 "
	L	Sinclair Hannah—†	1283	housewife	41	12 Ritchie
	M	Sinclair Herbert	1283	chauffeur	43	1513 Col av
	P	Carpenter Josephine—†	1299	at home	65	here
	32					
	F	*Mroz Elizabeth—†	1362	housewife	40	"
	G	Mroz Michael	1362	molder	47	"
	H	Cyr Charles	1362	painter	25	112 Amory
	K	Cyr Jesse	1362	"	57	112 "

Columbus Avenue—Continued

	L	Cyr Mary—†	1362	housewife	55	112 Amory
	M	Dipasquo Carradino	1362	laborer	44	here
	N	Dipasquo Virginia—†	1362	housewife	38	"
	O	*Kyle Greta—†	1362	"	26	134 Terrace
	R	Byrne Margaret C—†	1368	"	54	here
	S	Byrne William A	1368	lithographer	70	"
	T	Byrne William A, jr	1368	shipfitter	23	"
	U	*Juzefowicz Stanley	1368	retired	68	
	V	Parsons Charles	1368	clerk	46	
33						
	B	Carter Winifred—†	1378	housewife	28	239 Highland
	C	Cummings John	1378	laborer	32	239 "
	D	Cummings Joseph	1378	shoeworker	36	239 "
	E	Cummings Patrick J	1378	retired	67	239 '
	F	*Cummings Winifred—†	1378	housewife	68	239 "
	G	Lawlor Margaret—†	1378	"	30	34 Whitney
	H	Shields Dorothy—†	1378	"	26	3 Fellows
	K	Shields Francis	1378	salesman	26	3 "
	L	Havey John L	1378	mechanic	57	here
	M	Kenney John T	1378	laborer	57	"
	N	Kenney Mary—†	1378	housekeeper	67	"
	O	Rodgers Cecelia—†	1384	housewife	42	"
	P	Rodgers Walter	1384	shipper	43	"
	R	Scheffler Ella—†	1384	housewife	47	8 New Heath
	S	Scheffler John J	1384	laborer	21	8 "
	T	Scheffler Walter L	1384	upholsterer	23	8 "
	U	*Giannini Maria—†	1384	housewife	57	here
	V	Giannini Vincent	1384	mechanic	21	"
	W	LaFreniere Diana—†	1386	stitcher	41	"
	X	*LaFreniere Narcisse	1386	retired	74	
	Y	Famularo Angelo	1386	merchant	58	"
	Z	Famularo Onofrio	1386	"	38	
34						
	B	Hamilton Harry	1390	metal buffer	45	2498 Wash'n
	C	Hamilton Jeannie—†	1390	housewife	46	2498 "
	D	Earner John T	1390	chauffeur	34	here
	E	Earner Margaret—†	1390	housewife	65	"
	G	Aprille Lucy—†	1392	"	28	5 Albert
	H	Aprille Vito	1392	laborer	32	5 "
	K	*Donahue Ellen—†	1392	housewife	40	150 Lamartine
	L	*Donahue Patrick	1392	laborer	60	150 "

Columbus Avenue—Continued

	Letter	Full Name	Res. 1941	Occupation	Age	Reported Residence 1940
	M	Fallon Mary—†	1392	housekeeper	39	here
	N	Fallon Patrick	1392	retired	84	"
	R	Chiarino Inez—†	1394	housewife	36	160 Heath
	S	Chiarino Lorenzo	1394	laborer	50	160 "
	Y	Dee Mabel—†	1400	housewife	37	here
	Z	Dee Maurice	1400	laborer	42	"

35   Decatur Avenue

	Letter	Full Name	Res. 1941	Occupation	Age	Reported Residence 1940
	C	Suddard Albertine—†	4	housewife	53	1392 Col av
	D	Suddard Clayton	4	ironworker	59	1392 "
	E	Curtis Edwin	6	retired	63	1326 Tremont
	F	Curtis Leroy	6	shoeworker	26	Maine
	G	Smith Charles E	6	chauffeur	27	1326 Tremont
	H	Smith Ella—†	6	housewife	23	1326 "

Fort Avenue

	Letter	Full Name	Res. 1941	Occupation	Age	Reported Residence 1940
	K	Arnoff Louis	17	clerk	20	here
	L	*Ashman Harry	17	carpenter	64	"
	M	Ashman Mary—†	17	saleswoman	21	"
	N	Ashman Nathan	17	clerk	26	
	O	*Ashman Rebecca—†	17	housewife	54	"
	P	Ashman Rose—†	17	bookkeeper	31	"
	R	Francis George B	17	retired	76	Dedham
	S	Hill Ethel—†	17	housewife	48	"
	T	Hill Wilfred	17	conductor	55	"
	U	Cahill Delia—†	19	housekeeper	57	here
	V	Cahill Jeremiah	19	paperhanger	32	"
	W	Cahill John	19	laborer	21	"
	X	*Walsh John	19	"	58	
	Z	Judson Ida—†	23	housewife	42	"
36						
	A	Judson Mortimer J	23	molder	45	
	B	Williams James	23	cook	42	
	C	Williams Rose—†	23	housewife	41	"
	F	Foley John	27	bartender	23	"
	G	Foley William	27	chauffeur	30	"
	H	Jenkins Mary—†	27	housewife	28	"
	K	Jenkins William	'27	chauffeur	31	"
	L	Simond George	27	"	36	

Page.	Letter.	FULL NAME.	Residence, Jan. 1, 1941.	Occupation.	Supposed Age.	Reported Residence, Jan. 1, 1940. Street and Number.

Fort Avenue—Continued

M	Simond Mary—†	27	housewife	35	here
N	*Mara Margaret I—†	27	"	35	"
O	Mara Philip J	27	laborer	40	"
R	Segien George	29	painter	35	
S	Segien Wilma—†	29	housewife	32	"
T	Damschkaln Anna—†	29	seamstress	23	"
U	Damschkaln Elizabeth—†	29	domestic	50	"
V	Bloom Reginald	29	laborer	25	
W	Boitman Elizabeth—†	29	domestic	45	"
X	Anderson Anna—†	29	cook	48	
Y	Anderson Gordon	29	laborer	20	
Z	Anderson Norman	29	"	20	

37

A	Potter Earl	31	ironmolder	42	"
B	Potter Helen—†	31	housewife	38	"
D	Tanner Rita—†	31	"	21	11 Sheridan
E	*Tanner Roderick	31	printer	23	4 Romar ter
F	Lowd John E	31	laborer	24	22 Buswell
G	Lowd Margaret—†	31	housewife	26	22 "
H	Murphy Charles	35	shipper	46	here
K	Murphy Margaret—†	35	housewife	45	"
L	*Dann August	35	watchman	59	"
M	Dann Carl	35	operator	24	"
N	Dann Edward	35	steamfitter	22	"
O	*Dann Martha—†	35	housewife	53	"
P	Dann Oscar	35	laborer	25	
R	Glennon Anna—†	35	laundress	33	"
S	McLaughlin Edward	35	porter	51	"
T	Allen Vernon	37	laborer	22	15 King
U	Williamson Elizabeth—†	37	housewife	59	here
V	Williamson Hans	37	cabinetmaker	60	"
W	Kahps Fritz	37	carpenter	52	"
X	*Kahps Lena—†	37	seamstress	48	"
Y	Stevens Lillian—†	37	housewife	22	"
Z	Stevens Raymond L	37	machinist	26	"

38

A	Jacobs Janice—†	39	housewife	20	"
B	Jacobs Jerry	39	laborer	23	"
C	Hanlon John	39	"	26	17 Herman
D	Hanlon Olga—†	39	housewife	26	17 "
E	O'Neil Edna—†	39	"	37	here

Page.	Letter.	FULL NAME.	Residence, Jan. 1, 1941.	Occupation.	Supposed Age.	Reported Residence, Jan. 1, 1940. Street and Number.

Fort Avenue—Continued

F	O'Neil Franklin D	39	janitor	42	here
H	*Karagozian Mary—†	41	housekeeper	56	"
K	Karagozian Reuben	41	pedler	43	"
L	*Karagozian Siranoush—†	41	housewife	31	"
M	Mouradian Annie—†	41	waitress	22	
N	Mouradian Arakel	41	laborer	24	
O	Mouradian Margaret—†	41	waitress	20	
P	*Mouradian Mary—†	41	housewife	50	"
R	*Kayajanian Helen—†	41	"	34	
S	Kayajanian John	41	laborer	47	
T	Smith Charles R	41	carpenter	57	"
U	Smith Lena—†	41	housewife	55	"
V	Quant Lena—†	43.	seamstress	28	"
W	Frisoni Dolores—†	43	housekeeper	21	537 Mass av
X	Call Margaret—†	43	seamstress	38	3135A Wash'n
Y	Wescott Mary—†	43	housekeeper	39	1378 Col av
Z	*Doucet Bridget J—†	45	housewife	69	here

39

A	Doucet Frank E	45	metalworker	31	"
B	Doucet John S	45	clerk	36	
C	Doucet Peter G	45	operator	30	
D	Englar Martha C—†	45	librarian	30	
E	Englar Rudolph	45	janitor	60	
F	*Parel John	45	carpenter	45	"
G	*Timmerman Minnie—†	45	housekeeper	44	"
H	Harwood Albert W	45	garageman	60	35 Worcester
K	Harwood Esther F—†	45	laundress	47	35 "
L	McCormick Effie—†	47	housewife	66	2991 Wash'n
M	McCormick Joseph	47	chauffeur	42	2991 "
N	Koughan Marie—†	47	housewife	22	139 Centre
O	Koughan William P	47	laborer	24	139 "
P	Koughan Anna—†	47	housewife	60	139 "
R	Koughan Martin	47	machinist	21	139 "
S	Morgan Margaret—†	47	housekeeper	74	here
T	Morgan William J	47	retired	66	31 Glenwood
U	Titus Doris—†	49	housewife	23	35 Paul Gore
V	Titus James	49	salesman	28	6 Columbus sq
W	Sargent Albert	49	welder	26	162 Lambert
X	Sargent Elizabeth—†	49	housewife	60	162 "
Y	McMahon Catherine—†	49	clerk	29	here
Z	McMahon Louise—†	49	housewife	70	57 Regent

Fort Avenue—Continued

A	Gagnon Alfred	51	baker	24	3 Whittier
B	Harper Alexander A	51	painter	34	here
C	Harper Barbara E—†	51	housewife	77	"
D	Shields Joseph	51	salesman	45	"
E	Bransfield Angela J—†	53	housekeeper	31	"
F	King Lillian—†	53	housewife	38	"
G	King Thomas	53	laborer	40	
H	Humphrey Ann—†	53	housewife	32	"
K	Humphrey David	53	painter	34	
L	Mahoney Catherine W—†	55	housewife	33	"
M	Mahoney Francis V	55	laborer	35	
N	McCarthy Florence—†	55	housewife	38	"
O	McCarthy George	55	laborer	39	
P	Reece Gordon W	55	steamfitter	45	"
R	*Reece Margaret—†	55	housewife	40	"
S	Schlitz Catherine—†	57	leatherworker	22	12 Cherokee
T	Schlitz Helen—†	57	housekeeper	20	12 "
U	*Schlitz Joseph	57	laborer	56	here
V	*Balbolewski Helen—†	57	housewife	52	"
W	Balbolewski Joseph	57	laborer	56	"
X	Torigian Arakiel	57	merchant	29	"
Y	*Torigian Bulbel—†	57	housewife	62	"
Z	Rubin Benjamin	59	electrician	33	"

41

A	*Rubin Dora—†	59	housewife	63	"
B	*Rubin Edward	59	laborer	24	
C	Rubin George	59	welder	21	
D	Rubin Max F	59	tailor	64	
E	Karklin Emily—†	59	housekeeper	50	"
F	Postell Irene—†	61	laundress	53	"
G	Postell Thomas	61	cook	28	
H	Goodrich John	61	laborer	43	
K	Mendes Rose—†	61	musician	33	"
M	Tierney John	63	clerk	29	4 Weld av
N	Tierney Lucille—†	63	waitress	20	4 "
O	Richardson Mary J—†	63	clerk	45	here
P	Belongie Alexander	65	janitor	58	8 Whitney
R	*Belongie Irene—†	65	housewife	55	8 "
S	Ierubino Angelina—†	65	"	26	here
T	Ierubino Pasquale	65	clerk	26	"

Fort Avenue—Continued

u	*Limbo Angelo	65	laborer	30	13 Harvard
v	Limbo Theresa—†	65	housewife	28	13 "
w	Perry Harry	65	laborer	58	1 Linwood
x	Waters Harry S	65	chauffeur	23	1 "
y	Arching Claire—†	67	housewife	28	Cambridge
z	Arching Edward J	67	laborer	33	"

42

a	Dooley Edward	67	counterman	32	here
b	Dooley Mary—†	67	housewife	27	"
c	Timilty Florence—†	67	"	24	1048 Col av
d	Timilty Harold	67	laborer	28	1048 "
e	Sullivan Delia J—†	69	housekeeper	60	here
f	Halley Howard	69	laborer	60	"
g	Colnan Joseph	69	"	60	"
h	Colnan Josephine—†	69	housewife	60	"
k	Mooradian Kay—†	73	clerk	28	
l	*Mooradian Mary—†	73	housewife	64	"
m	Rogers Helen—†	73	"	52	
n	Rogers John J	73	salesman	48	"
o	Woodworth Anna G—†	75	housewife	31	"
p	Woodworth David H	75	metalworker	38	"
r	Carpenter Marjorie—†	79	housewife	24	"
s	Carpenter Reginald	79	mechanic	27	"
t	Mawn Francis	79	bookkeeper	34	58 Boynton
u	Mawn Regina—†	79	housewife	31	58 "
v	Woodward Lydia—†	79	housekeeper	41	here
w	Mulvey Annie L—†	81	"	58	"
x	Norris Mary P—†	81	clerk	62	"
y	Reynolds Edwin A	81	retired	71	53 Prince
z	Dooley Joseph E	83	laborer	26	43 Fort av

43

a	Dooley Melvina—†	83	housewife	20	Somerville
b	McCormick George	83	painter	44	9 Norfolk
c	Moore Charles	83	bartender	50	9 "
d	Shaw Catherine—†	83	housewife	54	9 "
e	Shaw George	83	clerk	20	9 "
f	Sweeney Edward J	83	laborer	41	here
g	Sweeney Mary A—†	83	housewife	29	"
h	Weniger Ernest	85	laundryman	32	"
k	*Weniger Gertrude—†	85	domestic	33	"
l	Harrington Charles A	85	clerk	33	41 Congreve

Fort Avenue—Continued

M	Harrington Mary J—†	85	housewife	52	41 Congreve
N	Foley Catherine A—†	85	presser	29	35 Boylston
O	Foley Delia T—†	85	housekeeper	30	35 "
P	Ross Edna B—†	87	bookkeeper	30	here
R	Ross Hugh	87	chauffeur	36	"
S	Bellew Margaret—†	87	housekeeper	66	"
T	Ward Mary A—†	87	housewife	30	714 E Fourth
U	Ward Thomas G	87	mechanic	28	11 Bancroft
V	Carroll Josephine C—†	89	housekeeper	68	here
W	Clarke Gertrude M—†	89	secretary	68	"
X	Farina Louise—†	91	housewife	45	"
Y	Farina Salvatore	91	tailor	64	
Z	Donahue Catherine—†	91	laundress	45	"
	44				
A	Donahue Thomas	91	laborer	23	
B	*Burke Josephine—†	91	housewife	62	"
C	Burke Mary A—†	91	clerk	34	
D	Shefchuk Frank	93	tailor	46	
E	Kopps Anna—†	93	housekeeper	49	"
F	Kopps George	93	laborer	54	".."

Gardner Street

R	Cashman John	rear 10	laborer	27	here
S	Cashman Louise—†	" 10	housewife	24	"
T	MacDonald Ernest	" 10	accountant	36	"
U	MacDonald Evelyn—†	" 10	housewife	30	"
V	Jones Evan	" 10	mechanic	45	20 Halleck
W	Jones Mary—†	" 10	housewife	46	20 "
X	Zahlit Arnold	12	painter	39	here
Y	Zahlit Melanie—†	12	housewife	34	"
Z	*Feldman Annette—†	12	"	63	"
	45				
A	Curley James M	16	laborer	24	
B	Curley Margaret T—†	16	hairdresser	23	"
C	Curley Mary A—†	16	housewife	41	"
D	Curley Patrick J	16	laborer	52	
E	Curley Thomas J	16	clerk	20	"
F	Dawson Hugh	18	mechanic	41	7 Elmwood pl
G	*Dawson Rose—†	18	housewife	42	7 "
H	Pieroway Elvira—†	22	"	46	here

Gardner Street—Continued

	K	McClellan Charles	22	mechanic	65	5 Norfolk
	L	McClellan Lillian—†	22	housewife	47	5 "
	M	Casey Catherine—†	22	shoeworker	48	here
	N	Casey James	22	letter carrier	38	"
	O	Casey Lillian—†	22	shoeworker	46	"
	P	*King Laura—†	24	housekeeper	41	"
	R	Lauder Charles	24	cook	23	15A Alleghany
	S	Lauder Florence—†	24	housewife	23	15A "
	T	Devlin Albert A	26	laborer	37	here
	U	Devlin Anna M—†	26	housewife	72	"
	V	Baldwin Anthony	26	steamfitter	48	"
	W	Baldwin Pearl—†	26	housewife	38	"
	X	Adams Armina—†	26	housekeeper	58	"

Harrington Avenue

	Y	McCarthy Dorothy—†	1	laundress	20	here
	Z	McCarthy Frank	1	laborer	52	"
46						
	A	McCarthy Susan A—†	1	housewife	55	"
	B	Whitney Frances—†	1	clerk	22	
	C	Cashman John H	1	laborer	43	
	D	Corcoran Helen B—†	1	housewife	44	"
	E	Corcoran Helen B—†	1	operator	21	
	F	Corcoran Margaret—†	1	clerk	20	"

Highland Street

	K	Hennessey Lawrence	63	barber	34	Foxboro
	L	Hennessey Monica—†	63	housewife	29	"
	M	Hill Edith H—†	63	"	53	here
	N	Hill John H	63	steward	61	"
	O	Duzant Louis J	63	waiter	52	"
	P	Meegan Bridget—†	63	housewife	78	"
	R	Meegan Joseph	63	painter	40	
	S	Meegan Marie—†	63	housewife	36	"
	T	O'Keefe Donald	65	bartender	23	53 Vale
	U	O'Keefe Edmund	65	laborer	22	9 Minden
¹	U	O'Keefe Gertrude—†	65	housewife	21	9 "
	V	O'Keefe Mary—†	65	"	22	53 Vale
	W	Roche Joseph	65	metalworker	44	here

Page	Letter	Full Name	Residence, Jan. 1, 1941.	Occupation	Supposed Age	Reported Residence, Jan. 1, 1940. Street and Number.

Highland Street—Continued

	Letter	Full Name	Res. 1941	Occupation	Age	Reported Residence
	x	Roche Mary—†	65	housewife	42	here
	y	Roche Mary H—†	65	clerk	20	"
	z	Bailey Francis	65	machinist	21	15 Weston pl
47						
	a	Duprey Harriet—†	65	housewife	41	15 "
	b	Duprey Raymond	65	chauffeur	29	5 Anita ter
	c*Dunn Helen—†	67	housewife	29	here	
	d	Dunn John F	67	waiter	28	"
	e	Hart Bridget—†	67	housewife	70	"
	f	Hart James M—†	67	laborer	36	
	g	Hart Mary E—†	67	clerk	38	
	h	Hart Timothy	67	retired	70	"
	k	Reid Edward R	67	welder	29	83 Dakota
	l	Reid Johina—†	67	clerk	20	83 "
	m*Reid Margaret—†	67	housewife	49	83 "	
	n	Wharton Clifton R	69	executive	42	here
	o	Wharton Harriett B—†	69	housewife	40	"
	p	Hicks Mary M—†	69	"	59	"
	r	Hicks Thomas H	69	janitor	66	"
	s	Gaynor Josiah	69	laborer	44	65 Camden
	t	Gaynor Loretta—†	69	housewife	40	65 "
	u	Reid Gaston O	69	chauffeur	23	65 "
	v	Boone Charles	71	steward	46	here
	w	Boone India R—†	71	housewife	42	"
	x	Forsyth Clementine—†	71	clerk	22	"
	y	Forsyth Mary—†	71	housewife	49	"
	z	Lawrence Alfred	71	laborer	30	
48						
	a	Lawrence Kathleen—†	71	housewife	26	"
	b	Garrett Anna—†	71	clerk	45	
	c	Ridgeley Aldas	71	engineer	42	
	d	Ridgeley Mayme—†	71	housewife	43	"
	e	Townes John	71	porter	65	"
	f	Thomas James M	73	cleaner	71	121 Warwick
	g	Thomas Jessie T—†	73	housewife	55	121 "
	h	Merritt Mary F—†	73	"	33	here
	k	Williamson Henry L	73	waiter	67	"
	l	Williamson Lucinda J—†	73	housewife	58	"
	m	Selden Edgar	75	chauffeur	42	44 Guild
	n	Selden Tamar—†	75	housewife	38	44 "
	o	Silva Cynthia—†	75	clerk	20	44 "

Page.	Letter.	Full Name.	Residence, Jan. 1, 1941.	Occupation.	Supposed Age.	Reported Residence, Jan. 1, 1940. Street and Number.

Highland Street—Continued

P	Norwood Dorothy—†	75	housewife	40	here
R	Norwood John	75	porter	39	"
S	Wilder Lena—†	75	domestic	42	"
T	Graham Stanley	75	cleaner	21	750 Col av
U	Robinson Alberta—†	75	housewife	39	750 "
V	Robinson George	75	porter	42	750 "
W	Sullivan Estelle N—†	77	housewife	31	here
X	Sullivan Ethelbert	77	seaman	41	"
Y	White Armada—†	77	maid	36	"
Z	White Frank G	77	custodian	55	"

49

A	Fubler Mary V—†	77	housewife	62	"
B	Fubler Nathaniel T	77	porter	63	"
C	Rigney Joseph	79	nurse	28	692 Mass av
D	Rigney Josephine—†	79	"	25	692 "
E	Cooper Harry	79	leatherworker	51	here
F	Gerraghty Ethel—†	79	housewife	33	"
G	Tobin James	79	machinist	37	"
H	*Tobin Joyce—†	79	housewife	35	"
K	Campbell Donald W	81	machinist	21	119 Dale
L	Campbell Dorothy E—†	81	housewife	20	119 "
M	*Johnson Bertha—†	81	"	48	here
N	Johnson Norman E	81	watchman	49	4 Dabney pl
O	Agym Marguerite—†	81	clerk	25	here
P	Arorian Jacob	81	"	45	"
R	Arorian John	81	repairman	22	"
S	*Arorian Mary—†	81	housewife	43	"
T	*Lew Charlie	83	laundryman	60	"
U	Rogers Bertha—†	85	housekeeper	48	"
V	Wall Mary—†	85	housewife	59	"
W	Wall Sarsfield	85	polisher	31	
X	*Clark Mary—†	85	housekeeper	51	"
Y	Egan William	85	roofer	58	

50

A	Raftes Charles	101	retired	76	17 Vancouver
B	*Raftes Mary—†	101	housewife	64	17 "
C	Vasconcellos Theodora-†	101	"	23	17 "
D	Vasconcellos Walter H	101	baker	25	17 "
E	Needham Mary—†	101	secretary	39	here
F	*Needham Nora—†	101	housewife	72	"
G	Needham Thomas	101	mechanic	40	"

H	Carosella Anthony	101	engineer	27	5 Estey
K	Carosella Valeria—†	101	housewife	27	5 "
L	Daniels Ann—†	101	clerk	20	41 Minden
M	Malkowski Adam	101	knitter	49	41 "
N	Prisby Catherine—†	101	clerk	21	41 "
O	Prisby Frances—†	101	checker	24	41 "
P	Prisby Walter	101	packer	22	41 "
R	Strungis Ann—†	101	housewife	28	41 "
S	Strungis William	101	packer	28	41 "
W	Bentley Anna—†	125	at home	75	here
X	Breen Maria—†	125	"	70	"
Y	Clarke Anna M—†	125	superintendent	55	"
Z	Curtis Katherine—†	125	maid	75	

51

A	*Downes Mary E—†	125	at home	75	Cambridge
B	Edney Julia S—†	125	"	70	here
C	Fairman Susan—†	125	"	80	"
D	Fields Rita—†	125		59	"
E	*Finch Annie—†	125		78	
F	Gardner Fannie—†	125		90	"
G	Hooper Helena—†	125		60	459 Park Drive
H	Lee Emily—†	125		89	here
K	Lee Sadie—†	125	"	71	36 Symphony rd
L	Mathews Lillie N—†	125	housekeeper	44	65 Ruggles
M	Newell Frances G—†	125	"	64	here
N	Olney Mary A—†	125	"	32	17 Louisburg sq
O	*Reid Annie—†	125	at home	75	here
P	Sawyer Catherine—†	125	"	80	80 Sterling
R	Taylor Amanda—†	125	"	75	here
S	White Rosa—†	125		82	"
T	Williams Georgiana—†	125	"	67	"
U	Gewenor Albert S	133	retired	65	160 Highland
V	Schulz Oscar	133	"	69	here
W	Kahle Omar	133	manager	52	123 Marcella
X	Waters Grace—†	133	housewife	22	here
Y	Waters Thomas F	133	chauffeur	27	"
Z	Parker Verna—†	135	housekeeper	27	184 Eustis

52

A	Azevdo Helen A—†	135	housewife	42	here
B	Azevdo Helen M—†	135	housekeeper	23	"
C	Azevdo Manuel	135	painter	44	"

Highland Street—Continued

D	*Caudle Arthur	135	porter	37	here
E	*Caudle Margaret—†	135	housewife	27	"
K	Barr Catherine E—†	139	teacher	46	"
L	McLain Edith H—†	139	housekeeper	62	"
M	Spaline Mary H—†	139	secretary	63	"
N	Crowley David F	141	timekeeper	45	"
O	Crowley David F, jr	141	clerk	22	..
P	Crowley Margaret M—†	141	housewife	46	"
R	*Urquhart Margaret—†	141	"	35	
S	*Urquhart Trueman	141	laborer	39	
T	Brune Emma—†	141	housewife	23	"
U	Breene Francis L	141	cleaner	28	
V	Cephas Charles	143	porter	64	"
W	Otway Alfonso	143	"	31	88 Harrishof
X	Otway Mildred—†	143	housewife	26	88 "
Y	Orman Mildred—†	145	"	37	23 Dorr
Z	Goldman Joseph	145	grocer	52	here

53

A	Goldman Lizza—†	145	housewife	49	"
B	Goldman Sarah—†	145	saleswoman	21	"

Highland Park Avenue

C	Rafferty Mary T—†	5	housewife	50	here
D	Rafferty Thomas J	5	clerk	54	"
E	*Berweiler Bridget C—†	5	housekeeper	68	"
F	Berweiler Nicholas	5	waiter	62	"
G	Stanley Mary A—†	5	housewife	23	29 Union ter
H	Stanley Walter V	5	machinist	23	29 "
K	Littlefield Beulah—†	7	housewife	25	6 Linwood
L	Littlefield Robert F	7	salesman	27	6 "
M	Gately Birdie A—†	7	waitress	32	here
N	Gately Elizabeth—†	7	"	34	305 Beacon
O	Gately John J	7	carpenter	44	here
P	Gately Mary A—†	7	housewife	39	"
R	Craik Eleanor C—†	7	"	27	694 Metropolitan av
S	Craik Norman B	7	manager	27	694 "
T	Dansereau Addie—†	8	housewife	62	here
U	Dansereau Alfred C	8	attendant	20	"
V	Goodell Henry P	8	machinist	59	"
W	Kucher Michael	8	pinboy	22	..

Page.	Letter.	FULL NAME.	Residence, Jan. 1, 1941.	Occupation.	Supposed Age.	Reported Residence, Jan. 1, 1940. Street and Number.

Highland Park Avenue—Continued

x	Kucher Pauline—†	8	cleaner	45	here
y	Kucher Samuel	8	laborer	47	"
z	Wynohradnyk Annie—†	8	housewife	23	"
	54					
a	Wynohradnyk John	8	laborer	24	
b	Slaughter Edward	9	cook	50	
c	Slaughter Elizabeth—†	9	domestic	47	"
d	Slaughter Ernest	9	baker	31	
e	Allen May—†	11	domestic	64	"
f	Chappells Nora—†	11	maid	51	
g	Davis Norris	11	mortician	30	"
h	Davis Rosa—†	11	housewife	54	"
k	Smith Margaret E—†	13	housekeeper	66	75 Sterling
l	Husband Ina—†	13	domestic	52	here
m	Smith Chester	13	watchman	26	223 W Springfield
n	Smith Muriel—†	13	stenographer	24	47 Symphony rd
o	Kupchyk John	14	bartender	47	here
p	*Kupchyk Tina—†	14	housewife	47	"
r	Sanerib Ollie—†	14	waitress	21	"
s	Sanerib Richard A	14	metalworker	23	"
t	Curran Mary A—†	15	housekeeper	72	197 Vernon
u	Tucker Harlan C—†	15	pedler	60	here
v	Tucker Russell	15	clerk	21	"
w	Wiswell Doris E—†	15	housewife	26	Revere
x	Wiswell John M	15	electrician	41	"
y	Whycoff George	16	waiter	46	here
z	Whycoff Lena—†	16	clerk	20	"
	55					
a	Whycoff Olympia—†	16	housewife	44	"
b	*Bordna Eva—†	16	"	60	
c	Bordna Peter	16	mechanic	62	"
d	Bordna Walter	16	student	23	"
e	Popowich Helen—†	16	cook	45	".."
f	Popowich Mary—†	16	student	25	
h	Aki Eleanor E—†	17	housewife	44	"
k	McLellan Lucy E—†	17	"	39	
l	Frieberg Anna—†	18	laundress	54	"
m	Frieberg William	18	carpenter	57	"
n	Toorks Alice K—†	18	librarian	24	".."
o	Toorks Peter	18	carpenter	54	"
p	Toorks Wilhelmina—†	18	housewife	52	"

Highland Park Avenue—Continued

R	Wassman Helen—†	18	at home	70	here
s	Page Helen M—†	19	housewife	31	"
T	Page Joseph M	19	laborer	31	"
u	Riley Ellen M—†	19	housewife	68	"
v	Riley Patrick	19	retired	74	"
w	Korp Sarah—†	20	housewife	64	293½ Highland
x	Stimson Karl L	20	U S A	25	New York
y	Boure Edward N	20	clerk	40	here
z	Boure Mildred L—†	20	housewife	36	"

56

A	Chavers Sarah—†	21	housekeeper	65	"
B	Washington Clara—†	21	seamstress	25	"
c	Washington George	21	clerk	30	34 Claremont pk
D	Coffin Daniel W	22	seaman	30	4 Alvah Kittredge pk
E	Coffin Gertrude L—†	22	housewife	29	4 "
F	Hunter Charles E	23	guard	43	here
G	Hunter Thomas	23	shoecutter	57	"
H	*Caulfield Anna B—†	24	housewife	39	"
K	Caulfield Lawrence T	24	steamfitter	40	"
L	Barrow Joseph A	25	porter	70	
M	West Marion B—†	25	housewife	41	"
N	Caulfield James G	26	clerk	34	
O	Kelley Alice J—†	26	housewife	46	"
P	Kelley Peter J	26	custodian	48	"
R	*Cochis Nicholas	27	merchant	64	"
s	*Cochis Sophie—†	27	housewife	46	"
T	*Palazzi Aldo	28	shoeworker	26	"
u	Palazzi Justine—†	28	housewife	21	"
v	Poleet George F	28	draftsman	41	414 Col av
w	Poleet Thelma A—†	28	housewife	34	414 "
x	*Szemeta Joseph	28	laborer	63	here
y	*Szemeta Mary—†	28	housewife	59	"
z	LaFargue Lillian—†	29	"	38	"

57

A	LaFargue Vivian	29	porter	43	
B	Weldon Maybelle—†	29	nurse	39	
c	*Gittins Alice J—†	31	housewife	42	"
D	Gittins Herbert	31	operator	64	
E	Dempsey Arthur	31	porter	36	
F	Dempsey Theresa—†	31	waitress	33	
G	McManus Francis	32	laborer	30	

Highland Park Avenue—Continued

H	McManus Margaret—†	32	housewife	28	here
K	Riley Catherine—†	32	"	59	"
L	Riley Helen—†	32	clerk	24	"
M	Riley John	32	retired	64	
N	Ross Alexander	34	chauffeur	37	"
O	Ross Elizabeth—†	34	housewife	34	"
P	Assatly Margaret—†	34	"	27	
R	Assatly William A	34	laborer	28	"
S	Daley Edward	34	"	28	25 Lambert av
T	Wadsemeek Andrew	34	"	59	here
V	Short Alfred	36	janitor	36	"
W	Short Catherine—†	36	housewife	32	"
X	Harper Russell	36	salesman	45	"
Y	Harper Ruth—†	36	housewife	40	"

58

A	Lang Anna M—†	38	"	32	
B	Lang George J	38	policeman	34	"
C	Begee Benjamin	38	painter	44	
D	Begee Mary—†	38	housewife	43	"
E	Begee Mary—†	38	student	20	
G	Boyd Juanita M—†	41	stenographer	54	"
H	Walker Mattie V—†	41	hairdresser	61	"

Highland Park Street

K	Moroz Mary—†	40	housewife	45	here
L	Moroz Peter	40	laborer	39	"
M	Zwaryck George	40	porter	47	"
N	*Zwaryck Margaret—†	40	housewife	44	"
O	Franquer Benjamin	40	shoeworker	62	"
P	Franquer Elizabeth—†	40	housewife	60	"

Linwood Street

R	Carroll Daniel A	2	longshoreman	35	here
S	Carroll Mary—†	2	housewife	56	"
T	Carroll Mary D—†	2	winder	26	"
U	Hantis Costas G	2	cook	49	
V	*Hantis Pauline—†	2	housewife	44	"
W	Hurley Thomas	4	laborer	68	Rockland
X	Fromouth George	4	ironworker	63	here

Linwood Street—Continued

Page.	Letter.	Full Name.	Residence, Jan. 1, 1941.	Occupation.	Supposed Age.	Reported Residence, Jan. 1, 1940. Street and Number.
	Y	Fromouth Lena—†	4	housewife	55	here
	Z	Grant Mary—†	4	housekeeper	67	"
59						
	A	Downey Elizabeth—†	6	housewife	55	"
	B	Downey John F	6	salesman	28	"
	C	Governor William F	6	operator	41	160 Highland
	D	Murphy George	6	engineer	61	1048 Col av
	E	Murphy Lucy—†	6	typist	20	1048 "
	F	Murphy Rose—†	6	housewife	60	1048 "
	G	Washburn George L	10	manager	38	here
	H	Washburn Katherine—†	10	housewife	32	"
	K	Brown George	10	retired	74	"
	L	Brown Samuel	10	janitor	42	"
	M	Collins Kathleen—†	10	typist	20	
	N	Collins Louise—†	10	housewife	41	"
	O	Collins Timothy F	10	operator	43	"
	P	*Guinta Sautina—†	10	housewife	47	16 Linwood
	R	Guinta Santo	10	mechanic	60	16 "
	S	Sechovicz Frank	14	laborer	60	here
	T	Sechovicz Helen—†	14	stitcher	30	"
	U	Sechovicz John	14	mechanic	28	"
	V	Sechovicz William	14	clerk	24	
	W	Bergen Henry	14	inspector	49	"
	X	Bergen Mary A—†	14	housewife	47	"
	Y	Aylward Jennie—†	14	housekeeper	72	18 Linwood
	Z	Birt Pearl E—†	14	housewife	43	18 "
60						
	A	Birt Reuben L	14	operator	43	18 "
	B	White Cecil	16	chauffeur	31	82 Cedar
	C	White Florence—†	16	housewife	30	82 "
	D	Themmen Alfred	16	printer	47	here
	E	Themmen Frances—†	16	housewife	42	"
	F	Sawizky Alfred	16	machinist	22	"
	G	*Sawizky Olga—†	16	housewife	52	"
	H	Thompson Helen—†	16	operator	24	
	L	Caulfield Parker	18	painter	36	
	M	Shine James	18	finisher	34	
	N	Shine Nora—†	18	housewife	31	"
	O	Winslow Jesse	18	welder	25	"
	P	Vaccaro George	18	agent	55	120 Dartmout
	R	Vaccaro Olga—†	18	housewife	55	120 "

Linwood Street—Continued

s	Keeley Agnes—†	20	housewife	35	here
T	Keeley James	20	chauffeur	36	"
u	Manning Francis D	20	broker	41	"
v	Manning Winifred E—†	20	housewife	37	"
w	Kontanis Anna—†	20	clerk	20	
x	Kontanis Leonadas	20	"	21	
y	Kontanis Nicholas	20	laborer	58	
z*	Kontanis Stella—†	20	housewife	43	"
	61				
A	Larkin Helen—†	24	"	60	
B	Larkin William B	24	salesman	65	
c	Cavanaugh Bridget—†	26	housewife	40	"
D	Cavanaugh Henry	26	electrician	50	"
E	Lewis Fannie—†	32	housekeeper	43	"
F	Lewis Irving	32	attorney	39	::
G	Lewis Josiah	32	clerk	35	
H	Lewis Rose S—†	32	saleswoman	36	"
K	Lewis Samuel M	32	clerk	47	
L	Lewis Solomon	32	electrician	45	"
M	Curran Bessie—†	34	housewife	60	"
N	Curran James P	34	retired	70	
o	Curran Philip J	34	accountant	27	"
P	Fitts Clara E—†	40	housewife	66	"
R	Fitts Frederick W	40	clergyman	68	"
s	Hyland Ellen—†	40	domestic	40	"
T	Curratto Gregory	44	retired	76	
u	Parodi Theresa—†	44	housekeeper	81	"
v	Shea Harry F	44	policeman	51	"
w	Shea Isabella V—†	44	housewife	39	73 Centre
x	Dame Claudia B—†	46	at home	75	here
y	Hayes John F	46	letter carrier	50	2 Linwood sq
z	Reilly John F	46	"	59	here
	62				
A	Reilly Mary A—†	46	housewife	58	"
B	Crowe Ella J—†	50	retired	88	
c	Fisher Henry D	50	electrician	57	"
D	Fisher Maria A—†	50	housewife	56	"
E	Dabol Alma—†	54	waitress	26	
F	Dabol Elizabeth—†	54	housewife	55	"
G	Dabol John	54	painter	55	
H	Dabol Lillian—†	54	clerk	21	"

Page.	Letter.	FULL NAME.	Residence, Jan. 1, 1941.	Occupation.	Supposed Age.	Reported Residence, Jan. 1, 1940. Street and Number.

Linwood Street—Continued

	K	Johns John W	54	carpenter	45	here
	L	Downey Arthur G	56	social worker	31	"
	M	Downey Ethel C—†	56	teacher	29	"
	N	Downey Mary E—†	56	stenographer	39	"
	O	Downey Philip J	56	steamfitter	37	"
	P	Downey Walter C	56	clerk	35	

Merton Place

	R	*Kelly John	1	painter	30	283 Highland
	S	*Kelly Mary—†	1	housewife	31	283 "
	T	*Pugsley Frederick	1	mechanic	58	here
	U	Rose Rose—†	2	housewife	35	3 Howard av
	V	Kalpowsky Emily—†	2	"	56	here
	W	Kalpowsky Jacob	2	carpenter	61	"
	X	Schneider Henry	2	laborer	34	"
	Y	Schneider Sally—†	2	housewife	32	"
	Z	Ritz Frank	rear 2	attendant	26	127 Marcella
63						
	A	Ritz Irene—†	" 2	housewife	31	127 "
	B	Pothier Florence—†	" 2	"	23	here
	C	Pothier Lester	" 2	manager	26	"
	D	Crane Agnes J—†	" 2	operator	57	"
	E	MacNeil Doris G—†	" 2	housewife	25	"
	F	MacNeil Louis F	" 2	auditor	28	
	H	Veligar Anthony	3	mover	24	
	K	*Veligor Mary—†	3	housewife	35	"
	L	Veligor Vincent	3	shoeworker	47	"
	M	Crockett Elmer	4	porter	27	
	N	Crockett Mary—†	4	housewife	26	"
	O	Brooks Irene—†	4	seamstress	54	1 Glenwood
	P	Cummings Barbara—†	4	waitress	22	82 E Newton
	R	*Steinhart Maria—†	4	housewife	44	here
	S	*Steinhart Warren	4	metalworker	52	"

Newark Street

	T	Fish Elizabeth—†	1	housewife	56	here
	U	Fish Walter	1	laborer	23	"
	V	Inglis Robert	1	"	56	"
	W	Desmarais Cecilia—†	1	housewife	29	"

Page.	Letter.	Full Name.	Residence, Jan. 1, 1941.	Occupation.	Supposed Age.	Reported Residence, Jan. 1, 1940. Street and Number.

Newark Street—Continued

	x	Desmarais Charles	1	clerk	31	here
	y	Walsh James	1	laborer	39	135 Williams
	z	Broadbent James B	1	retired	69	here
64						
	b	Healey Mary—†	3	housewife	65	"
	c	Healey Thomas W	3	retired	67	
	d	Gurley Ellen M—†	3	housewife	46	"
	e	Gurley William H	3	laborer	54	
	f	Kodad Francis	3	"	43	"
	g	Good Charles	5	"	54	177 Centre
	k	Richardson Lorena—†	5	at home	73	here
	l	Clifford Daniel	6	laborer	65	"
	m	Long Theodore	6	"	22	124 Terrace
	n	Paylor Florence G—†	6	housewife	50	124 "
	p	Linden Thomas	7	chauffeur	41	here
	r	Boyajian Mardiros	7	laborer	44	"
	s*	Boyajian Rosa—†	7	housewife	39	"
	t	Healey Ellen—†	7	"	66	
	u	Healey Michael	7	laborer	59	
	v	O'Brien Mary—†	7	clerk	28	"
	w	Donlon James F	8	waiter	24	7 Texas
	x	Golden William A	8	chauffeur	28	7 "
	y	Thomas Lewis E	8	laborer	39	7 "
	z	Thomas Margaret A—†	8	housewife	37	7 "
65						
	a	Vartanian Sarah—†	8	"	38	here
	b	Vartanian Setrag	8	painter	48	"
	c	Pugsley Amory	8	laborer	27	1 Merton pl
	d	Pugsley Donald	8	"	21	1 "
	e	Pugsley Dora—†	8	housewife	65	1 "
	g	Deshamps Herman	11	laborer	36	here
	h	Deshamps Ruth—†	11	housewife	28	"
	k	Ridge Charles	11	painter	40	34 Hanson
	l	Ridge Florence L—†	11	housewife	50	here
	m	McCune James	13	laborer	37	"
	n	McCune Rose—†	13	housewife	24	"
	o	McLain Marias	13	laborer	29	
	p	McLain Mary—†	13	housewife	23	"
	r	Hayward Daniel	13	packer	30	
	s*	Hayward Estelle—†	13	housewife	27	"
	t*	Galanian Samuel	15	shoemaker	48	368 Centre

Page.	Letter.	FULL NAME.	Residence, Jan. 1, 1941.	Occupation.	Supposed Age.	Reported Residence, Jan. 1, 1940. Street and Number.

Newark Street—Continued

	u	Reilly Loretta—†	15	housewife	25	13 Newark
	v	Basabe Catherine—†	15	housekeeper	30	here
	w	Shirley Neal	17	laborer	40	"
	x	*Shirley Pansy—†	17	housewife	36	"
	y	Hagopian Arman	17	barber	46	
	z	Hagopian Isabelle—†	17	housewife	32	"
66						
	a	Nahabedian George	17	laborer	58	
	b	*Nahabedian Katherine—†	17	housewife	55	"
	c	Corcoran James	19	chauffeur	23	125 Cedar
	d	Corcoran Justine—†	19	housewife	20	125 "
	e	*Dognazzi Edward	19	laborer	40	here
	f	*Dognazzi Julia—†	19	housewife	30	"
	g	Nahabedian Dorothy—†	19	housekeeper	41	"
	h	Libby Ruth—†	21	housewife	28	1 Merton pl
	k	Libby Sherwood	21	chef	25	1 "
	l	Shulakovksy Josephine-†	21	housewife	47	132 Marion
	m	Shulakovsky Stanley	21	laborer	20	132 "
	n	Dunigan Charles	21	motorman	32	here
	o	Dunigan Ruth—†	21	housewife	31	"
	p	Higgins Edith—†	23	domestic	41	"
	r	O'Tool James	23	laborer	28	"
	s	O'Tool Martha—†	23	housekeeper	27	"
	t	Whalen Mary A—†	23	housewife	43	"
	u	Whalen William J	23	laundryman	40	"
	v	Crockett Elma	32	retired	72	144 W Concord
	w	York Grace—†	32	housewife	57	1 Glenwood
	x	Brooks Irene—†	32	cutter	55	1 "
	y	Cummings Barbara—†	32	waitress	22	here
	z	McNulty Margaret G—†	32	housewife	38	"
67						
	a	McNulty William P	32	laborer	40	

New Heath Street

	b	Cryan Mary—†	1	housewife	52	here
	c	Cryan William M	1	clerk	61	"
	d	Davin Peter	1	laborer	34	"
	e	Doherty John	1	clerk	45	
	f	*Doherty Monica—†	1	housewife	42	"
	g	*Durkin Nellie—†	1	housekeeper	46	414 Market

New Heath Street—Continued

H	Kilroy James J	3	manager	38	here	
K	Kilroy Margaret J—†	3	housewife	36	"	
L	Lees Mary E—†	3	"	68	"	
M	Kideas Allison	5	"	45	23 Schiller	
N	Kideas George	5	salesman	46	23 "	
O	Oliver Joseph H	5	laborer	59	here	
P	Oliver Lilas—†	5	housewife	64	"	
R	Chausse Exilda—†	5	housekeeper	47	"	
S	Murray Bernard T	5	clerk	47	"	
T	Kelly Mary E—†	7	housewife	84	"	
U	Kelly Teresa J—†	7	housekeeper	65	"	
V	Kelly William L	7	retired	63	"	
W	Pelletier Olive—†	9	waitress	28		
X	Pelletier Wilfred	9	embalmer	33	"	
Y	Baumister Ellen M—†	9	housekeeper	90	"	
Z	Foley Elizabeth—†	11	housewife	45	"	

68

A	Foley Hugh	11	roofer	45	"	
B	Miley Annie—†	11	laundress	49	New York	
C	Uva Angeline—†	13	housewife	29	10A New Heath	
D	Uva William	13	cleaner	39	10A "	
E	Dermody Mary V—†	13	housewife	36	14 "	
F	Dermody William A	13	chauffeur	43	14 "	
G	Finneran Margaret—†	15	housewife	57	here	
H	Sullivan James	15	retired	74	"	
K	Pray Aurora—†	17	housewife	37	"	
L	Pray Charles	17	painter	36		

Romar Terrace

M	*Noseworthy Mary—†	4	waitress	35	here	
N	*Noseworthy Mathias	4	fireman	48	"	
O	*Larson John	4	carpenter	34	"	
P	*Larson Margaret—†	4	housewife	35	"	
R	*Tanner Owen	4	shipper	43		
S	*Tanner Thirza—†	4	saleswoman	21	"	
T	*Tanner Violet—†	4	housewife	43	"	
U	Poplawsky Eugene		salesman	31	"	
V	Poplawsky Genevieve—†		housewife	29	"	
W	*Estefano Amelia—†	6	trimmer	25	218 Parker Hill av	
X	Hajjar Joseph	6	broker	36	218 "	

Page.	Letter.	FULL NAME.	Residence, Jan. 1, 1941.	Occupation.	Supposed Age.	Reported Residence, Jan. 1, 1940. Street and Number.

Romar Terrace—Continued

	Y	*Hajjar Julia—†	6	housewife	27	here
	Z	Burnett Agnes—†	6	clerk	21	"
69						
	A	Lataites Katherine—†	6	housewife	55	"
	B	Duke John	8	carpenter	58	"
	C	Duke Mary—†	8	housewife	57	"
	D	*Dosenberg Alida—†	8	houseworker	45	"
	E	VanAlderstine Elsie—†	8	housewife	34	104 Minden
	F	Van Alderstine Harry	8	plumber	34	104 "
	G	*Abolin Mary—†	8	retired	76	9 Anita ter

Roxbury Street

	H	White Eleanor—†	292	saleswoman	23	here
	K	White Mary C—†	292	dietitian	46	"
	L	Nehiley Adeline—†	292	housewife	51	"
	M	Nehiley Joseph	292	laborer	56	
	N	Norton George J	292	insulator	28	"
	O	Norton Martha E—†	292	housewife	65	"
	P	McIntyre Albert	292	painter	58	"
	R	Kirk Ralph M	294	mechanic	31	42 Woodbine
	S	Kirk Teresa—†	294	housewife	29	42 "
	T	Gillis Mary—†	294	"	27	here
	U	Gillis Roy J	294	chauffeur	30	"
	V	Keegan Bertha—†	294	housekeeper	57	"
	W	Malcolm Catherine V—†	294	housewife	44	"
70						
	A	Moriarty Matilda—†	298	"	30	4 Pine Grove ter
	B	Sullivan Nora M—†	298	at home	73	here
	C	Keegan Florence—†	300	housewife	27	228 Highland
	D	Keegan William	300	salesman	30	228 "
	E	Gibbons Ann—†	300	housekeeper	22	here
	F	Gibbons Mary A—†	300	housewife	51	"
	G	Gibbons Thomas J	300	clerk	53	"
	L	Stevens Eleanor—†	308	housekeeper	38	243 Roxbury

Ward 11—Precinct 2

CITY OF BOSTON

LIST OF RESIDENTS
20 YEARS OF AGE AND OVER

(NON-CITIZENS INDICATED BY ASTERISK)
(FEMALES INDICATED BY DAGGER)

AS OF

JANUARY 1, 1941

JOSEPH F. TIMILTY, *Chairman*
FREDERIC E. DOWLING, *Secretary*
WILLIAM A. MOTLEY, Jr.
FRANCIS B. McKINNEY
HILDA HEDSTROM QUIRK

Listing Board.

CITY OF BOSTON PRINTING DEPARTMENT

200
Amory Street

A	DeRosa Frances—†	32	housewife	32	here
B	DeRosa Ralph	32	painter	29	"
C	Hickey George	32	retired	67	"
D	Hickey Marion—†	32	housewife	54	"
E	Wilkins Charles	32	porter	22	
F	Wilkins Lillian—†	32	stenographer	23	"
G	Devin Sadie—†	32	housekeeper	44	19 Fort av
H	Grubbs Blanche—†	34	housewife	43	here
K	Grubbs Charles	34	chauffeur	44	"
M	Lyle Eunice—†	36	housewife	27	"
N	Lyle Wilbur	36	machinist	29	"
P	Ehret Bernhard	42	retired	78	
R	Ehret Harold B	42	embalmer	30	"
S	Ehret Louise—†	42	housekeeper	36	"
T	Gahn Christian	42	banker	40	"
U	Hudlin Herman J	42	machinist	62	"
V	Hudlin Sophie M—†	42	housewife	60	"
X	Bronhurst Mary—†	44	housekeeper	61	"
Y	McGrath Doris N—†	46	stitcher	45	"
Z	McGrath James	46	salesman	48	"

201

A	Murphy Francis B	46	clerk	53	
B	Rich Louis C	48	watchman	67	"
C	Rich Sarah E—†	48	housewife	56	"

Batchelder Terrace

E	Dacey Catherine A—†	1	cleaner	44	here
F	Dacey James	1	retired	76	"
G	Dacey Mary—†	1	housewife	41	"
H	Ready Joseph	2	printer	21	
K	Ready Mary—†	2	maid	35	
L	Sussan Catherine—†	2	housewife	40	"
M	Sussan David	2	manager	48	
N	Crehan Helen G—†	3	housewife	29	"
O	Crehan Matthew	3	inspector	36	"
P	Gurney Joseph P	3	laborer	52	
R	Gurney Margaret M—†	3	housewife	52	"
S	Joyce Julia M—†	4	cleaner	42	

Page.	Letter.	Full Name.	Residence, Jan. 1, 1941.	Occupation.	Supposed Age.	Reported Residence, Jan. 1. 1940. Street and Number.

Batchelder Terrace—Continued

	t	*Peters George	5	pressman	32	71 Brighton
	u	Peters Laura—†	5	housewife	32	71 "

Beech Glen Street

	w	Jordan Aurelia R—†	1	housewife	57	here
	x	Jordan George R	1	engineer	33	"
	y	Jordan Orlando	1	clerk	30	"
	z	Jordan Oswald	1	student	26	
202						
	a	Yagian George	21	baker	30	
	b	Yagian Mary—†	21	clerk	25	
	c	Yagian Richard	21	retired	60	
	d	Yagian Rose—†	21	housewife	55	"
	e	Abrahamian Elmas—†	21	"	40	
	f	Abrahamian Michael	21	clerk	51	
	g	Argoomanian Lakar	21	"	63	
	h	Ryan Catherine—†	21	housewife	37	"
	k	Ryan Edward J	21	laborer	26	
	l	Ryan Frederick	21	watchmaker	38	"
	m	Ryan John	21	chemist	34	
	n	Bersan Alexander	25	retired	45	
	o	Darles Helen—†	25	housewife	45	"
	p	Darles Waldemar	25	machinist	27	"
	r	Pehda Emily—†	25	laundress	40	"
	s	Alaimo Eleanor—†	25	housewife	28	"
	t	Alaimo Joseph	25	shipper	28	"
	u	Seeley Robert	27	laborer	64	
	v	McCarthy Mary A—†	27	housekeeper	61	"
	w	Richardson Florence—†	27	housewife	25	29 Dean
	x	Richardson Walter	27	laborer	25	29 "
	y	Ellis Virginia—†	29	housewife	25	117 Dale
	z	Lang Leo	29	baker	22	189 Highland
203						
	a	Lang Rose—†	29	housewife	19	1857 Col av
	c	Lovejoy Freedland	29	attendant	24	10 Salman
	b	Lovejoy Grace—†	29	housewife	21	10 "
	d	O'Leary Catherine—†	31	"	50	here
	e	O'Leary Charles T	31	mechanic	23	"
	f	O'Leary Dennis J	31	letter carrier	53	"
	g	O'Leary John J	31	operator	27	"

3

Beech Glen Street—Continued

H	Battles Kathleen—†	31	housewife	25	here
K	Battles William E	31	laborer	23	"
L	Nelson Dorothy—†	31	housewife	28	"
M	*Nelson Harry	31	mason	40	
N	Fallon Daniel E	33	paver	61	
O	Fallon Daniel J	33	mechanic	22	"
R	Fitzgerald Harold C	43	pharmacist	50	"
S	Fitzgerald Helen T—†	43	housewife	50	"
T	Fitzgerald Mildred—†	43	clerk	24	
U	Tjaerlis Anthony	43	mechanic	20	"
V	Tjaerlis Constantine	43	chef	51	
W	Tjaerlis George	43	U S A	31	
X	Tjaerlis Sophia—†	43	housewife	49	"
Y	Eggers Clarence G	43	machinist	31	64 St James
Z	Eggers Ruby—†	43	housewife	37	64 "
	204				
A	Colleran Patrick	45	laborer	52	here
B	Colleran Sarah—†	45	housewife	43	"
C	Zepurneck Edward	45	machinist	32	"
D	Zepurneck Nellie—†	45	housewife	30	"
E	Hinderschidt Bertrand	45	baggagemaster	43	"
F	Hinderschidt Irene—†	45	housewife	40	"
G	*Galvin Emily—†	47	housekeeper	63	"
H	Grundman John	47	laborer	62	..
K	*Orchard Elizabeth—†	47	housekeeper	65	"
L	Dunford James E	47	retired	44	Somerville
M	Dunford Mary—†	47	housewife	33	181 Highland
N	Dunford Michael J	47	laborer	53	181 "
O	Schievink Gertrude—†	47	housewife	44	45 School
P	Schievink Joseph	47	painter	47	45 "
S	Coffey Anna T—†	49	clerk	26	here
T	Coffey Bridget—†	49	housewife	62	"
U	Coffey John F	49	coppersmith	27	"
V	Coffey Mary A—†	49	clerk	24	
W	Hadden Elizabeth H—†	49	housewife	39	"
X	Hadden John	49	gasmaker	35	"
Y	Hogan Jane—†	49	housewife	41	"
Z	Hogan John	49	chauffeur	45	"
	205				
A	Vivavorian Hripsime—†	51	housekeeper	60	"
B	Laughlin John	51	engineer	30	''

Page.	Letter.	Full Name.	Residence, Jan. 1, 1941.	Occupation.	Supposed Age.	Reported Residence, Jan. 1, 1940. Street and Number.

Beech Glen Street—Continued

	c	Laughlin Marguerite—†	51	housewife	28	25 Highland
	d	O'Leary James A	51	B F D	41	here
	e	O'Leary Rita E—†	51	housewife	37	"
	f	Morris Alice—†	53	hairdresser	30	"
	g	Morris Elizabeth—†	53	housewife	50	"
	h	Morris John H	53	U S N	29	
	k	Morris John J	53	steward	62	
	l	Morris Olive P—†	53	saleswoman	22	"
	m	Cunningham Elizabeth—†	53	housekeeper	28	"
	n	Cunningham Josephine—†	53	housewife	54	"
	o	Cunningham Mary—†	53	laundress	32	"
	p	Cunningham Thomas	53	laundryman	24	"
	r	Schoffer Rose—†	53	housewife	43	"
	s	Schoffer Siegfried	53	engineer	46	"
	t	*Whyte Delia—†	55	housewife	36	17 Fort av
	u	Whyte Henry T	55	salesman	42	17 "
	v	Mules George	55	chauffeur	35	39 Dudley
	w	Mules Violet—†	55	housewife	37	here
	x	Lynch Mary—†	55	housekeeper	50	"
	y	*Becherer Charles	57	foreman	67	"
	z	Becherer Elizabeth—†	57	housewife	67	"
		206				
	a	Duffey Gertrude—†	57	"	40	
	b	Duffey Hugh F	57	printer	46	"
	c	Kelly Jennie A—†	59	housewife	44	55 Beech Glen
	d	Kelly William	59	steamfitter	45	55 "
	e	Reidy Mary—†	59	nurse	42	55 "
	f	Lazarou Nikita	59	laborer	51	here
	g	Lazarou Rita—†	59	housewife	27	"
	h	DeRoche Ellen—†	61	"	40	"
	k	DeRoche John	61	investigator	39	"
	l	Rooney Margaret—†	61	packer	21	319 Warren
	m	Schell Edward	61	printer	50	here
	n	Schell Edward J	61	mechanic	27	"
	o	Schell Mary—†	61	housewife	53	"
	p	Schell Mary—†	61	clerk	21	
	r	Schell Walter J	61	machinist	23	"
	s	White Frank	61	janitor	42	319 Warren
	t	Seegraber Andrew	63	batteryman	56	here
	u	Seegraber Emma—†	63	housewife	49	"
	v	Seegraber Frank	63	clerk	24	"

Page.	Letter.	FULL NAME.	Residence, Jan. 1, 1941.	Occupation.	Supposed Age.	Reported Residence, Jan. 1, 1940. Street and Number.

Beech Glen Street—Continued

	w	Seegraber Theresa—†	63	clerk	27	here
	x	Crowley Catherine—†	65	housewife	44	"
	y	Crowley Francis	65	accountant	40	260 Parker Hill av
	z	Crowley Genevieve—†	65	housewife	39	260 "
207						
	A	Crowley Joseph F	65	clerk	45	here

Centre Street

	c	Flaherty Anna C—†	149	waitress	22	here
	D	Flaherty Helen M—†	149	clerk	24	"
	F	Flaherty Michael J	149	operator	52	"
	E	Flaherty Rita—†	149	saleswoman	20	"
	G	Robinson Catherine B—†	149	housekeeper	65	13 Bromley pk
	H	Dolan Annie C—†	151	housewife	53	here
	K	Kilduff Mary—†	151	cashier	61	"
	L	Dimitrakis Custos	151	restaurateur	50	"
	M	Dimitrakis Mary—†	151	housewife	40	"
	N	Burham Grace—†	151A	"	45	Cambridge
	o	Burham Jerome	151A	painter	57	"
	P	Rose Harriet G—†	153	housewife	66	here
	R	Rose Harry V	153	retired	72	"
	s	Greene Mary—†	153	housewife	54	"
	T	Greene Michael M	153	watchman	54	"
	U	Greene William P	153	laborer	58	
	v	Traynor Andrew J	153A	chauffeur	35	"
	w	Traynor Helen—†	153A	housewife	31	"
	x	Kelly Catherine—†	155	clerk	20	
	y	Kelly James	155	laborer	62	
	z	Kelly Mary—†	155	housewife	62	"
208						
	A	Kelly Michael	155	clerk	24	
	B	Mulligan Alice—†	155	retired	50	"
	c	Mulligan Edward	155	chauffeur	45	"
	D	Mulligan Helen—†	155	housewife	43	"
	E	Linehan Mary—†	155	"	38	
	F	Linehan Thomas	155	bartender	36	"
	G	Murray James	158	laborer	34	
	H	Normile Annie—†	158	housekeeper	65	"
	K	Murphy Annie—†	158	housewife	71	"
	L	Murphy James S	158	retired	67	"

6

Centre Street—Continued

M	Boivin Helen—†	158	housewife	27	here
N	Boivin Windon	158	printer	35	"
O	*Kenney Effie—†	158	housewife	40	"
P	*Kenney Robert	158	pinboy	23	
R	Delvental Catherine—†	160	housekeeper	69	"
S	Delvental Matthew	160	metalworker	32	"
T	*Burkman John	160	retired	80	
U	*Burkman Mary—†	160	housewife	73	"
V	Wilds Mary E—†	160	"	37	
W	Wilds William B	160	mechanic	40	"
X	Donelan Anne—†	162	housewife	22	"
Y	Donelan John	162	waiter	26	
Z	McRae Andrew	162	laborer	39	

209

A	McRae Arthur	162	chauffeur	36	"
B	McRae James	162	laborer	40	
C	McRae John	162	attendant	47	"
D	Splaine Elizabeth—†	162	housewife	28	"
E	Splaine Richard	162	chauffeur	30	"
F	Crowley Anna—†	165	maid	52	"
G	Doherty Mary—†	165	cook	60	Newton
H	Marks Richard	165	clergyman	37	Wellesley
K	O'Brien Margaret—†	165	housekeeper	65	here
L	Sullivan Edward	165	clergyman	45	"
M	Sullivan Mark	165	"	76	"
P	Piggreno Hattie—†	168	housekeeper	65	"
R	Bevere Louis	168	laborer	31	"
S	Bevere Sadie—†	168	housewife	30	"
U	Sarno Alfonzo	168	shoeworker	30	"
T	Sarno Anna—†	168	housewife	26	"
W	*McLellan C James	169	chauffeur	39	"
V	McLellan Celia—†	169	housewife	37	"
X	Delaney Joseph	169	ironworker	50	"
Y	Delaney Mary—†	169	housewife	57	"
Z	Hall Jennie—†	169A	"	53	

210

A	Hall Robert L	169A	coppersmith	53	"
C	Burns Frank J	171½	rigger	38	
D	Nugent Frank H	171½	painter	63	
E	Nugent Mary—†	171½	housewife	59	"
F	Garrity Charles A	171½	boilermaker	53	"

Centre Street—Continued

Page.	Letter.	FULL NAME.	Residence, Jan. 1, 1941.	Occupation.	Supposed Age.	Reported Residence, Jan. 1, 1940. Street and Number.
	G	Garrity Mabel—†	171½	housewife	51	here
	H	White Bridget—†	171½	"	62	"
	K	White Dorothy—†	171½	laundress	23	"
	L	White Eleanor—†	171½	"	20	
	M	Finneran Anne—†	173	housekeeper	60	"
	N	Finneran Thomas	175	retired	84	"
	O	Finneran Thomas	173	"	25	"
	P	Friggell Ernest	173	laborer	27	Burlington
	R	*Friggell John C	173	shipper	49	"
	S	Friggell John C, jr	173	laborer	21	"
	T	Friggell Marie R—†	173	housekeeper	23	"
	U	*Friggell Mary—†	173	housewife	47	"
	V	Foley Dennis	173	steamfitter	42	1431 Col av
	W	Foley Dorothy J—†	173	housewife	38	1431 "
	X	Waters Alice—†	173	forewoman	32	1431 "
	Y	Favreau Edmund	174	laborer	24	here
	Z	Favreau Ruth—†	174	housewife	22	"
211						
	A	Glynn Margaret—†	174	"	40	
	D	Finneran Joseph	175	bartender	26	"
	E	Finneran Julia—†	175	housewife	25	"
	F	Wolfe Max	175	merchant	68	"
	H	Basili Rocco	176	shoemaker	54	"
	K	Basili Rose—†	176	housewife	46	"
	L	Del Grasso Josephine—†	176	factoryhand	45	11 Merriam
	N	Buckley Elizabeth-†1st r	177	housekeeper	66	1414 Col av
	O	Costello Christina-† 1st "	177	housewife	35	305 Highland
	P	Costello John 1st "	177	roofer	45	305 "
	R	Travers Agnes—† 2d "	177	housewife	32	92 Heath
	S	Travers John 2d "	177	inspector	29	92 "
	T	Martin Helen—† 2d "	177	housewife	46	1119 Harrison av
	U	Martin Herbert 2d "	177	laborer	59	1119 "
	V	Martin John 2d "	177	mechanic	21	1119 "
	W	*Tate Agnes—† 2d "	177	housewife	37	1414 Col av
	X	Tate Harold 2d "	177	plumber	37	1414 "
	Y	Berrigan Bernard	178	laundryman	35	here
	Z	Berrigan Margaret—†	178	housewife	32	"
212						
	A	D'Amico Margaret—†	178	"	48	14 Albert

Centre Street—Continued

	B	D'Amico Peter	178	barber	53	14 Albert
	c	*Scordino Antonette—†	178	housewife	38	here
	D	Scordino Charles	178	painter	42	"
	E	McRae Anna—†	179	housekeeper	46	11½ Gainsboro
	F	McRae Anna—†	179	clerk	23	11½ "
	G	McRae Kathryn—†	179	housekeeper	26	11½ "
	H	Belfiore Joseph	179	shoemaker	47	here
	K	*Belfiore Josephine—†	179	housewife	45	"
	M	Romano Eleanora—†	180	attendant	27	"
	N	Romano Julia—†	180	packer	22	
	O	Romano Mary—†	180	"	25	"
	P	Weber Anna—†	180	housewife	27	136 Heath
	R	Weber Charles, jr	180	attendant	27	136 "
	S	De Fronzo Anthony	180	tilesetter	44	here
	T	De Fronzo Mary—†	180	housewife	41	"
	U	Morse Walter	181	engineer	54	"
	v	*Robidoux Marie—†	181	entertainer	32	"
	w	*Robidoux Rose—†	181	housekeeper	53	"
	X	Lampro Margaret—†	181	"	64	34 Walden
	Y	Weiler Edward	181	painter	30	34 "
	z	Weiler Margaret—†	181	housewife	29	34 "
		213				
	A	Corcoran Edward J	182	watchman	55	here
	B	Corcoran Nora—†	182	housewife	50	"
	c	Engeian Mary—†	182	stitcher	35	"
	D	*Bevere Lorenzo	182	barber	60	
	E	Bevere Louise—†	182	housewife	53	"
	F	Bevere Mario	182	sprayer	25	
	G	Piscatelli Helen—†	183	housewife	34	"
	H	Piscatelli John J	183	clerk	35	"
	K	Scarlatta Esther—†	183	housewife	26	"
	L	Scarlatta James	183	laborer	30	"
	M	Packer Albert J	184	"	27	
	N	Packer Marie—†	184	housewife	32	"
	O	Vitale Gaetano	184	laborer	73	1495 Col av
	P	Vitale Mary—†	184	housewife	56	1495 "
	R	Palumbo Eleanor—†	184	"	23	1495 "
	S	Palumbo Frank	184	laborer	27	3 Wiggin
	z	Lopez Manuel	197	manager	60	here

214

Centre Street—Continued

A	Lopez Sarah J—†	197	housewife	63	here
B	Melone Louis	197	laborer	31	5 Bromley

Centre Street Terrace

E	Gamboa Anthony	1	chauffeur	36	here
F	Gamboa Emma—†	1	housewife	29	"
G	Harris Edgar	1	painter	42	"
H	Harris Eva L—†	1	housewife	42	"
K	Florio Alfred	1	attendant	26	"
L	*Florio Domenic	1	janitor	63	
M	*Florio Giuditta—†	1	housewife	60	"
N	Powers Helen R—†	1	"	41	
O	Powers James A	1	B F D	42	
P	Lennon Anna—†	1	housekeeper	45	"
R	Lennon Florence—†	1	shoeworker	43	"
S	McLellan Dorothy—†	1	housewife	28	"
T	McLellan Edward	1	pressman	28	"
U	Amero Jean M—†	1	housekeeper	24	"
V	Barletto Louis	1	electrician	31	"
W	Barletto Mary—†	1	housewife	28	"
X	Hogan Mattie—†	1	cutter	51	
Y	Ferris Freedman	1	mechanic	35	"
Z	Ferris Lydia—†	1	housewife	25	"

215

A	Rea Eleanor—†	1	housekeeper	24	"
B	*Rea Mary—†	1	housewife	65	"
C	Rea William	1	painter	63	
D	Rea William T	1	mechanic	21	"
E	Blasi Anthony	1	barber	28	
F	Blasi Eva—†	1	housewife	25	"
G	Goulet Charles	1	laborer	32	
H	Goulet Monica—†	1	housewife	31	"
K	Hagerup Peter	2	painter	50	
L	Hall Albert	2	engineer	27	"
M	Hall Mary—†	2	housewife	23	"
N	Coviello Joseph	2	attorney	35	"
O	Coviello Mae—†	2	housewife	33	"
P	Farrell Hugh	2	clerk	29	
R	Farrell Margaret—†	2	housewife	29	"

10

Centre Street Terrace—Continued

	s	Gaffney Josephine—†	2	housewife	26	here
	t	Gaffney Stephen L	2	manager	26	"
	u	Correia Myrtle—†	2	waitress	27	"
	v	Riveiro Antone	2	welder	37	"
	w	Riveiro Elizabeth—†	2	housewife	32	"
	x	Nicsosio Guy	2	factoryhand	33	"
	y	Nicsosio Mary—†	2	housewife	29	"
	z	Orlando Jean—†	2	"	31	
216						
	a	Orlando Michael	2	laborer	31	
	b	Leahy Catherine—†	2	clerk	35	
	c	Leahy John E	2	painter	39	
	d	Leahy Mary—†	2	shoeworker	40	"
	e	Leahy Patrick	2	retired	69	
	f	Leahy Timothy	2	clerk	42	
	g	Leahy William	2	painter	36	

Columbus Avenue

	l	Britt Frederick W	1407	chef	52	here
	m	Britt Margaret M—†	1407	housewife	75	"
	n	Sheeran Elizabeth L—†	1407	cook	47	"
	o	Moylan Delia—†	1407	housewife	71	192 Amory
	p	Moylan John J	1407	retired	71	192 "
	r	Moylan John J	1407	chauffeur	44	192 "
	s	Moylan Robert	1407	laborer	36	192 "
	u	Simeone Guy B	1410	"	23	here
	v	Simeone Mary C—†	1410	housewife	40	"
	w	Simeone Salvatore	1410	storekeeper	51	"
	x	Freeman Arline—†	1410	secretary	22	"
	y	Freeman Frederick	1410	mechanic	25	"
	z	Freeman John	1410	carpenter	51	"
217						
	a	Arnold Agnes—†	1413	housewife	42	"
	b	Arnold Walter H	1413	electrician	47	"
	c	Kehl Carl J	1413	usher	26	"
	d	Nichols Frances R—†	1413	chauffeur	35	1477 Col av
	e	Nichols Josephine M—†	1413	housewife	33	1477 "
	f	Montgomery Josephine-†	1413	housekeeper	47	here
	g	Tully James F	1414	chauffeur	39	38 Heath av
	h	Tully Mabel A—†	1414	housewife	36	38 "

Page.	Letter.	FULL NAME.	Residence, Jan. 1, 1941.	Occupation.	Supposed Age.	Reported Residence, Jan. 1, 1940. Street and Number.

Columbus Avenue—Continued

K	Armstrong Josephine—†	1414	housewife	32	83 Marcella
L	*Armstrong Paul	1414	laborer	32	83 "
M	McElaney Ann—†	1414	housewife	50	10 Minden
N	McElaney Edward	1414	laborer	56	10 "
O	Dandrea Alfred	1415	"	22	here
P	*Dandrea Anna—†	1415	housewife	59	"
R	Dandrea Eleanor—†	1415	domestic	21	"
S	Newton Joseph	1415	laborer	44	
T	Newton Sadie—†	1415	housewife	42	"
U	Kelly Annie—†	1415	"	72	
V	Kelly William C	1415	painter	37	
X	Maggi Angelina—†	1419	operator	46	
Y	Maggi Frances—†	1419	seamstress	23	"
Z	Maggi Peter	1419	barber	26	

218

A	Kennealy Mary—†	1419	housewife	71	"
B	Kennealy William P	1419	retired	73	
C	Mudge Robert	1419	chauffeur	43	"
D	Vierkant Charles A	1420	retired	63	"
E	Landry Helen J—†	1421	housewife	33	970 Parker
F	Landry Joseph W	1421	laborer	38	970 "
G	Flanagan James J	1421	retired	77	here
H	Flanagan James J, jr	1421	constable	39	"
K	Hughes Bertha—†	1421	housewife	39	58 Bickford
L	Hughes James	1421	laborer	45	58 "
M	*Canning Mary—†	1422	housekeeper	54	here
N	Cody Marie—†	1422	maid	54	"
O	Manning Katherine B–†	1422	housewife	55	"
P	Manning Wilfred J	1422	retired	61	
R	Vierkant Peter	1422	laborer	38	
S	Farrell Annie—†	1422	housewife	42	"
T	Farrell William M	1422	mechanic	50	"
V	Little James J	1425	laborer	29	
W	Little Mary—†	1425	housewife	59	"
X	Little Patrick	1425	retired	73	
Y	Soper Ada A—†	1425	attendant	24	"

219

A	Soper Geneva M—†	1425	maid	21	
B	Soper Theresa R—†	1425	housewife	55	"
C	Ruiz Anna—†	1425	"	32	6 Albert
D	Belfiore Edith—†	1426	housewife	22	here

Columbus Avenue—Continued

E	Belfiore Michael	1426	bartender	26	here
G	Kennedy Helen—†	1427	housewife	40	"
H	Kennedy William J	1427	clerk	38	"
K	Walker Chester L	1427	laborer	49	41 Codman pk
L	Walker Olivia—†	1427	housewife	44	41 "
P	Mize Helen—†	1431	housekeeper	37	864 Col av
R	Linnehan Anna F—†	1431	housewife	42	here
S	Linnehan James	1431	painter	40	"
U	Barter Carrie—†	1433	housekeeper	65	1 Penryth
V	Belfiore Ralph	1433	shoeworker	46	2049 Wash'n
W	Puzo Angelo M	1433	chef	28	4 Penryth
X	Murta William	1433	plumber	48	here

220

A	Scardino Domenic	1436	manager	49	"
B	Scardino Rose—†	1436	housewife	48	"
C	Scardino Rose M—†	1436	hairdresser	24	"
D	De Gregorio Catherine-†| 1436	housewife	26	"
E	De Gregorio Louis	1436	bartender	30	"
F	DeMinico Charles	1438	shoemaker	50	"
G	DeMinico Elvira—†	1438	housewife	47	"
H	Marcella Joseph	1438	baker	21	"
K	*Marcella Mary—†	1438	housewife	50	"
L	*Marcella Samuel	1438	laborer	51	
M	Marcella Sarafino	1438	painter	25	

221

T	Fortin Bessie—†	1471	housewife	41	"
U	Fortin Ernest	1471	painter	36	
X	Cyr Elinor—†	1473	housewife	25	"
Y	Cyr John	1473	painter	27	

222

D	Keliher Anna G—†	1475	housewife	69	"
E	Keliher James W	1475	clerk	35	
F	Keliher William J	1475	salesman	66	"
L	Curtis Florence—†	1477	housekeeper	47	18 Burnett
P	Beloise Sarah E—†	1479	"	68	39 Bickford
R	*De Angelis Antoinette-†	1479	housewife	50	here
S	*De Angelis John	1479	baker	56	"
T	De Angelis Mary—†	1479	shoeworker	25	"
U	Prizio John	1479	laborer	33	
V	Prizio Rose—†	1479	housewife	31	"
Z	Tedeschi Genevieve—†	1483	"	27	

223
Columbus Avenue—Continued

A	Tedeschi Thomas	1483	cutter	27	here
B	Messina Esther—†	1483	housewife	43	"
C	Messina Mauro	1483	student	20	"
D*| Messina Thomas	1483	laborer	44	
E	Flavin Charlotte—†	1483	housewife	28	"
F	Flavin John	1483	inspector	35	"
G	D'Amore Adeline—†	1484	housewife	22	"
H	D'Amore Anthony	1484	cobbler	21	
K	Ferrera Alvira—†	1484	housewife	25	"
L	Ferrera Raymond	1484	shoeworker	32	"
O*| De Gregorio Antoinette—†	1487	housewife	62	"
P*| De Gregorio Fred	1487	barber	62	
R	De Gregorio Fred, jr	1487	chemist	23	
S	De Gregorio Josephine—†	1487	clerk	31	
T	De Gregorio Susan—†	1487	shoeworker	27	"
U	Fecteau Gerard J	1487	mechanic	22	"
V*| Fecteau Theresa—†	1487	housewife	24	"
W	O'Brien Elizabeth—†	1487	seamstress	52	"

224

A	Hickey Constance—†	1491	housewife	31	32 Heath av
B	Hickey John J	1491	laborer	34	32 "
G	Di Gregorio Florence—†	1495	housewife	23	here
H	Di Gregorio Louis	1495	chauffeur	24	"
K	Flavin Edward	1495	laborer	40	"
L	Flavin Frances—†	1495	housekeeper	23	"
M	Da Pota Mario	1495	barber	28	"
N	Da Pota Marion—†	1495	housewife	25	"
P	Lorenzetti Ethel—†	1495	"	31	6 Oakland
R	Lorenzetti Victor	1495	molder	46	here

225

A	Ryan Arthur C	1545	shipper	25	
B	Ryan Arthur J	1545	laborer	59	
C	Ryan Bernard	1545	clerk	23	
D	Ryan Evelyn—†	1545	housewife	24	"
E	Ryan Raymond	1545	clerk	37	
F	Molino Antonio	1545	laborer	57	
G*| Molino Camella—†	1545	housewife	45	"
H	Rago Antoinetta—†	1545	"	44	
K	Rago John	1545	mechanic	43	"

Page.	Letter.	FULL NAME.	Residence, Jan. 1, 1941.	Occupation.	Supposed Age.	Reported Residence, Jan. 1, 1940. Street and Number.

Columbus Avenue—Continued

L	Zepfler Frank	1551	laborer	56	here
M	*Zepfler Josephine—†	1551	housewife	57	"
N	Ferrera Ellen—†	1551	"	82	"
O	*Ferrera Joseph	1551	retired	79	"
R	Dacey Michael	1551	laborer	51	48 Arklow
P	Dacey Theresa—†	1551	housewife	47	48 "
T	Poli Bessie—†	1575	"	40	here
U	Poli Samuel	1575	salesman	42	"
V	McFarland Francis J	1575	laborer	53	Medford
W	Gilmartin Dorothy A—†	1575	housekeeper	28	here
X	Gilmartin Edward S	1575	clerk	21	"
Y	Gilmartin James	1575	brewer	54	"
Z	Gilmartin James	1575	entertainer	31	" \

226

A	Gilmartin Margaret T—†	1575	housewife	52	"
B	Gallant Agnes T—†	1577	housewife	48	"
C	Gallant Frederick J	1577	painter	51	
D	Gallant Frederick J, jr	1577	clerk	22	
E	Spellman Arthur F	1577	chauffeur	34	"
F	Spellman Domenic	1577	retired	89	
G	Spellman Domenic, jr	1577	clerk	58	
H	Crowley Agnes—†	1577	housekeeper	42	"
K	Ganey Helen C—†	1577	clerk	45	"
L	Ganey Jennie E—†	1577	housewife	44	"
M	Ganey Mary G—†	1577	clerk	39	"
N	Ganey Nora A—†	1577	maid	42	
O	Ganey Theresa N—†	1577	factoryhand	36	"

Echo Street

X	*De Rosa Antoinetta—†	2	housewife	54	here
Y	De Rosa Joseph	2	laborer	25	"
Z	De Rosa Liberato	2	shoeworker	20	"

227

A	*De Rosa Luigi	2	laborer	60	
B	De Rosa Paul	2	machinist	22	"
C	De Rosa James	2	shoeworker	32	"
D	De Rosa Nina—†	2	factoryhand	36	"
E	De Rosa Lillian—†	2	housewife	25	"
F	De Rosa Romeo	2	laundryman	27	"

Fort Avenue

G	*MacDonald Anna—†	66	housewife	38	20 Lawn
H	*MacDonald Maylo	66	millwright	50	20 "
L	*Hepp Louis	66A	baker	53	here
M	*Hepp Theresa—†	66A	housewife	83	"
N	Poulos Mary—†	66A	housekeeper	48	"

Heath Street

S	*Gismonde Alfredo	6A	merchant	55	here
T	Gismonde Americo	6A	shipper	34	"
U	Gismonde Florence—†	6A	beautician	25	"
V	*Gismonde Olga—†	6A	housewife	40	"
W	*McDonald Mary J—†	8	"	36	"
X	Rudnitsky Stanley Z	8	machinist	34	Connecticut
Y	*Wright Ann—†	8	housewife	22	here
Z	Wright Francis H	8	mechanic	23	"
	228				
B	Doherty George	10	laborer	27	11 Bickford
C	Doherty Margaret—†	10	housewife	23	11 "
D	Gilmore Francis	10	laborer	55	222 Amory
E	Gilmore Mary—†	10	housewife	29	222 "

Highland Street

G	Harper Cora—†	177	housewife	62	here
H	Harper Isaac	177	retired	72	"
K	McCormack Dorothy—†	177	teacher	27	"
L	McCormack Ruth—†	177	bookkeeper	22	"
M	Lynch Patrick J	177	laborer	36	"
N	Tighe Margaret—†	177	housewife	42	"
O	Tighe Michael F	177	laborer	52	
P	Gronberg Evald	177	mechanic	48	"
R	*Gronberg Helga—†	177	housewife	48	"
S	Gronberg Walter	177	chauffeur	21	"
T	Cutler Alfred	179	metalworker	47	"
U	Cutler Elizabeth—†	179	housewife	37	"
V	Burgess David G	179	watchman	47	81 Thornton
W	Burgess Sarah—†	179	housewife	45	81 "
X	Reed George A	179	chauffeur	32	here
Y	Reed Hazel I—†	179	housewife	30	"
Z	Seibel Alice—†	181	"	28	"

Page.	Letter.	Full Name.	Residence, Jan. 1, 1941.	Occupation.	Supposed Age.	Reported Residence, Jan. 1, 1940. Street and Number.

229
Highland Street—Continued

	Letter.	Full Name.	Res.	Occupation.	Age	Reported Residence
	A	Seibel Karl	181	chef	35	here
	B	Murray Bertha—†	181	housewife	30	13 Bartlett
	C	Murray Douglas W	181	clerk	28	13 "
	D	Burns Alice—†	181	housewife	46	83 Fort
	E	Fuller Josephine R—†	187	clerk	52	here
	F	Fuller Leo W	187	collector	42	"
	G	Fuller Mary T—†	187	clerk	54	"
	H	Poninski Julia A—†	187	saleswoman	41	"
	K	Poninski Theresa E—†	187	forewoman	47	"
	L	Lang Elinor L—†	189	housewife	23	"
	M	Lang Frank J	189	letter carrier	29	"
	N	Lang George	189	baker	66	
	O	Lang Veronica—†	189	housewife	60	"
	P	Mann Paul	191	clerk	41	
	R	Donnelly Catherine—†	191	housekeeper	72	"
	S	Kelley James	191	seaman	35	2809 Wash'n
	T	Kelley Jeanette—†	191	housewife	25	2809 "
	U	Brienza Frances—†	219	examiner	24	here
	V	Brienza John	219	laborer	29	"
	W	Brienza Philip	219	cabinetmaker	27	"
	X	Brienza Rose—†	219	housekeeper	25	"
	Y	Mazziotti Mary—†	219	housewife	54	"
	Z	Mazziotti Philip	219	shoeworker	49	"

230

	Letter.	Full Name.	Res.	Occupation.	Age	Reported Residence
	A	Mazziotti Victoria—†	219	bookkeeper	21	"
	B	Lynch Bartholomew J	219	printer	65	
	C	Lynch Catherine J—†	219	housewife	58	"
	D	Lynch Gerard F	219	manager	26	"
	E	Lynch Katherine—†	219	bookkeeper	28	"
	F	Lynch Mary G—†	219	stenographer	24	"
	G	Lynch Rita E—†	219	"	21	"
	H	Lynch Robert A	219	clerk	22	
	K	*Theodore Cleopatra—†	219	housewife	29	"
	L	Theodore Paskal	219	salesman	37	"
	M	McCloskey Laurence J	227	mechanic	33	"
	N	McCloskey Madeline—†	227	housewife	33	"
	O	Allen May—†	227	"	37	
	P	Allen Mobrey	227	finisher	44	
	S	McCann Christine—†	229	housewife	33	"
	T	McCann Theodore	229	laborer	35	"

11—2   17

Highland Street—Continued

u	Brown Catherine M—†	229	housewife	42	here
v	Brown George M	229	attendant	48	"
w	Kennedy Myrtle—†	229	housewife	24	78 Fulda
x	Kennedy Thomas	229	chauffeur	30	78 "
y	Fasano Alfonse	231	laborer	27	43 Bickford
z	Fasano Michelina—†	231	housewife	27	43 "

231

a	Josefowicz Leokadia—†	231	housekeeper	47	here
b	*Amyouny Joseph	231	cleaner	40	10A New Heath
c	Gallagher John J	233	porter	42	here
d	Gallagher Mary E—†	233	housewife	41	"
e	Johnson George	233	plumber	58	"
f	Johnson Harold	233	"	23	
g	Johnson Lydia—†	233	housewife	50	"
h	Mills Helen—†	233	"	24	"
k	Mills Roy	233	chef	32	Medfield
l	Rogers Estelle—†	233	housewife	28	here
m	Rogers William T	233	masseur	29	"
n	*Ferrante Antoinette—†	235	housewife	50	"
o	Ferrante Michael	235	laborer	20	
p	Ferrante Dominic	235	merchant	30	"
r	Ferrante Mary—†	235	housewife	29	"
s	Milani Albert	235	counterman	27	84 E Cottage
t	Milani Sabina—†	235	housewife	28	here
u	Boyd Barbara—†	237	"	42	53 Woodbine
v	Boyd James	237	mechanic	40	53 "
w	Valiquette Albert	237	dairyman	47	here
x	Valiquette Emily—†	237	housewife	44	"
y	Valiquette Henry	237	clerk	20	"
z	Driscoll John E	237	chauffeur	42	"

232

a	Driscoll Margaret—†	237	housewife	41	"
b	Glynn Frank A	237	laborer	24	
c	Glynn John J	237	"	34	"
d	Brady Edward J	251	machinist	42	3 Elmore pk
e	Shargabian Krikor	251	retired	43	here
f	Redler John	253	chauffeur	30	3 Regent ct
g	Redler Margaret—†	253	housewife	21	3 "
h	Nee Flore—†	253	"	42	here
k	Klein Helen—†	253	"	39	"
l	Klein Julius C	253	chauffeur	29	"

Page.	Letter.	FULL NAME.	Residence, Jan. 1. 1941.	Occupation.	Supposed Age.	Reported Residence, Jan. 1. 1940. Street and Number.

Highland Street—Continued

	M	Mullen Nora—†	255	housekeeper	52	45 Blue Hill av
	N	Peppard Elizabeth—†	255	housewife	58	here
	O	Peppard Helen—†	255	clerk	32	"
	P	Crane Patrick	255	laborer	50	"
	R	Morong Etta—†	257	housekeeper	76	"
	S	Kilroy Francis W	257	laborer	21	17 Dalkeith
	T	Kilroy Mildred K—†	257	housewife	45	Salem
	U	Kilroy William H	257	retired	48	17 Dalkeith
	V	Gallagher Laurence J	257	electrician	36	here
	W	Gallagher Mary—†	257	housewife	68	"
	X	Walizer Helen—†	259	housekeeper	67	"
	Y	Harrington Catherine—†	259	"	68	
	Z	Rockwell George E	259	chauffeur	41	"
233						
	A	Rockwell Lillian P—†	259	nurse	43	
	C	O'Toole Patrick F	260	custodian	40	"
	D	Sorenti Barbara—†	261	housewife	20	27 Swallow
	E	Bean Mary—†	261	housekeeper	44	65 Lamartine
	F	Rockwell Annie J—†	261	housewife	72	here
	G	Rockwell William H	261	retired	70	"
	H	Kelley Catherine—†	263	housewife	47	92 Heath
	K	Kelley Eileen—†	263	laundress	26	92 "
	L	Kelley Joseph	263	salesman	25	92 "
	M	McDonald Hannah—†	263	housewife	66	here
	N	McDonald John	263	chauffeur	44	"
	O	Botulinski Maria—† .rear	263	housekeeper	66	"
	P	McManamy Elizabeth J—†	269	housewife	62	"
	R	McManamy Mary A—†	269	housekeeper	32	"
	S	McManamy Robert C	269	student	22	"
	Y	Calderwood Alberta—†	277	housewife	44	1421 Col av
	Z	Cotillo Michael A	277	laborer	57	1421 "
234						
	A	Tibbits Simon J	277	painter	47	1421 "
	B	Collins Nellie J—†	277	cook	62	here
	D	Reiss Carrie—†	279	housekeeper	74	"
	E	Burns Catherine—†	279	"	70	"
	F	Jordan Geraldine—†	279	housewife	21	"
	G	Jordan Gerard	279	painter	24	
	H	Rowan Catherine A—†	281	housewife	68	"
	K	Rowan Edward P	281	laborer	29	
	L	Rock Thomas L	281	roofer	52	

Page.	Letter.	FULL NAME.	Residence, Jan. 1, 1941.	Occupation.	Supposed Age.	Reported Residence, Jan. 1, 1940. Street and Number.

Highland Street—Continued

	M	Rock Winifred K—†	281	housewife	37	here
	N	Murphy Bridget—†	281	"	42	163 Calumet
	O	Murphy Michael R	281	manager	49	163 "
	P	Murphy Richard J	281	clerk	22	163 "
	R	Cook Albert G	283	laborer	56	10 Amory ter
	S	Cook Anna M—†	283	housewife	58	10 "
	T	Laflin Jane—†	283	"	62	here
	U	Laflin Warren D	283	chauffeur	33	"
	V	Longell Ada—†	283	housewife	71	16 Adams
	W	Longell Thomas H	283	retired	71	16 "
	X	Harrington Mary—†	283	housewife	41	here
	Y	Harrington Timothy	283	laborer	50	"
	Z	Devaney Josephine—†	286	housewife	21	290 Highland

235

	A	Devaney William	286	laborer	24	290 "
	B	McLean Clara—†	286	housewife	42	here
	C	McLean Frank	286	laborer	44	"
	D	Lyka John	286	retired	64	"
	E	Downey Helen—†	287	housewife	39	"
	F	Downey Leo	287	laborer	43	"
	G	O'Reilly Charles L	288	shipper	24	14 Dana pl
	H	O'Reilly Rita—†	288	housewife	21	14 "
	L	Grant George	288	electrician	44	here
	M	Grant Louise—†	288	housewife	43	"
	N	Anctil Clarence	290	chef	38	78 Heath
	O	Anctil Lillian—†	290	housewife	35	78 "
	P	Reilly Agnes—†	290	"	46	98 Sheridan
	R	Milliken Elliott	290	U S N	36	here
	S	Milliken Nellie—†	290	housewife	33	"
	T	Newton Anna M—†	291	at home	74	"
	U	Newton Mary C—†	291	janitress	44	
	V	Newton William C	291	clerk	36	
	W	Puorro Catherine M—†	292	housewife	28	"
	X	Puorro James	292	plumber	28	
	Y	*Klimoski Victor	292	laborer	63	
	Z	Szerameta Betty—†	292	packer	23	

236

	A	*Szocik Joseph	292	butcher	45	
	B	Szocik Joseph	292	clerk	23	

Highland Street—Continued

c	*Szocik Louise—†	292	housewife	50	here	
d	Szocik Mary A—†	292	bookkeeper	22	"	
e	Bodge Anna—†	292	housekeeper	55	"	
f	Johnson Erhard J	292	laborer	57	"	
g	Newton Henry	293	letter carrier	31	"	
h	Newton Loretta—†	293	housewife	23	"	
k	Newton James H	293	laborer	48		
l	Newton Josephine—†	293	housewife	44	"	
m	*McLean Elizabeth—†	293½	housekeeper	65	"	
p	McDonald Catherine—†	294	housewife	68	742 Parker	
r	McDonald John J	294	cook	27	742 "	
s	Dooley Isabel—†	294	housekeeper	59	1183 Tremont	
t	Quattralli Anthony	294	laborer	41	here	
u	Quattralli Isabel—†	294	housewife	31	"	
v	Gorman Mary A—†	294	housekeeper	63	55 Centre	
w	Trainor Laura—†	294	housewife	30	here	
x	Trainor William	294	laborer	32	"	
z	Gorman Edward J	296	metalworker	25	"	
	237					
a	Marsoline Fannie—†	296	housewife	40	"	
b	Marsoline Louis	296	ropemaker	41	"	
c	McDonald Doris—†	296	housewife	39	"	
d	Marenghi Emilio	301	retired	66	"	
e	Marenghi Emilio	301	shoeworker	33	"	
f	Marenghi Ettore	301	"	26		
g	Marenghi Italia—†	301	boxmaker	22	"	
h	Marenghi John	301	shoeworker	36	"	
k	Marenghi Mary—†	301	housewife	26	"	
l	Marenghi Rafaela—†	301	"	67	"	
m	Garrison Florence—†	303	housekeeper	39	5 Park rd	
n	Dodge Elizabeth M—†	303	"	69	5 "	
o	Kordis Alice—†	303	operator	37	here	
p	Lindner Anton	303	carpenter	56	"	
r	Lindner Anton	303	printer	21	"	
s	Lindner Teresa—†	303	housewife	49	"	
t	Downey John	305	carpenter	26	"	
u	Downey Mildred—†	305	housewife	23	"	
v	Karavas Dorothea—†	305	"	24	71 Bromley	
w	Karavas Henry	305	busboy	24	71 "	

Marcella Street

	x	Kelly Annie J—†	75	housewife	50	here
	y	Kelly Kathleen B—†	75	operator	25	"
	z	Kelly Michael	75	oiler	54	"
238						
	a	Kelly Richard F	75	clerk	24	
	b	*Cahill Margaret—†	75	housewife	55	"
	c	Cahill Michael F	75	U S A	24	
	d	Cahill Peter J	75	printer	26	"
	e	O'Rourke Edward F	75	timekeeper	31	218 Highland
	f	O'Rourke Elizabeth—†	75	housewife	31	218 "
	g	Grace Catherine—†	75	"	50	here
	h	Grace William F	75	gasfitter	50	"
	k	Hennessey Joseph	75	painter	30	"
	l	Day Catherine E—†	77	clerk	35	
	m	Day George A	77	"	28	
	n	Day Nora—†	77	housewife	65	"
	o	Day Patrick W	77	roofer	38	
	p	Byrnes Marion—†	77	waitress	25	
	r	Morelli Mary—†	77	housewife	40	"
	s	*Morelli William	77	machinist	45	"
	t	Fox Anna T—†	77	housewife	34	"
	u	Fox Frederick C	77	finisher	44	
	v	Gabryelewski Josephine—†	79	housewife	47	"
	w	Gabryelewski Paul	79	shoeworker	47	"
	x	Arsenault Albert	79	assembler	28	174 Centre
	y	Arsenault Ethel—†	79	housewife	29	174 "
	z	Brennan Dennis	79	clerk	53	here
239						
	a	Brennan Ignatius	79	"	58	"
	b	Mulvey Catherine—†	79	housewife	54	"
	d	Sheldon Mary J—†	84	"	78	108 Conant
	e	*McKenzie Mary—†	84	"	44	here
	f	Waldon Julia—†	84	housekeeper	42	Brookline
	g	Murphy Edward	84	manager	32	here
	h	Bugantino Marian—†	86	stitcher	24	"
	k	*Bugantino Mary—†	86	housewife	46	"
	l	Glennon Ellen—†	86	"	76	
	m	Glennon William	86	machinist	40	"
	n	Tagliaferro Pauline—†	86	housewife	24	"
	o	Tagliaferro Salvatore	86	laborer	30	
	p	Singerella Frank	88	"	47	

Marcella Street—Continued

R	*Singarella Josephine—†	88	housewife	34	here
S	Falcone Lucy—†	88	"	26	"
T	Falcone Salvatore	88	salesman	26	"
U	*Rock Margaret—†	88	housekeeper	40	"
V	Mathis Eleanor—†	90	housewife	29	"
W	Elbery Mary—†	90	seamstress	33	"
X	Tucker Anna B—†	90	housekeeper	71	103 Marcella
Y	McKay Catherine—†	91	"	68	here
Z	Murray James	91	carpenter	28	"

240

A	Solomon Arthur	91	clerk	43	
B	Solomon Rose—†	91	housewife	40	"
C	Cantillo William	91	clerk	30	
D	Roth Anna—†	91	housewife	31	"
E	Roth Frederick	91	boilermaker	40	"
F	Roth Ralph	91	laborer	32	
H	Phelan Herbert	rear 91	"	23	
K	*Phelan Stella—†	" 91	housewife	21	"
L	Cabozzi Alexander	" 91	clerk	40	
M	Cabozzi Elizabeth—†	" 91	housewife	37	"
N	Mulvey Helen—†	" 91	"	67	
O	Mulvey Joseph T	" 91	painter	61	"
P	Coady Jennie—†	92	housekeeper	68	"
R	Coady Patrick	92	shipper	58	"
S	Donahue Florence—†	92	housewife	29	"
T	Donahue Harry	92	packer	39	
U	Spencer Luzerne—†	92	saleswoman	55	"
Y	Buckman Theresa E—†	94	housewife	40	14 Minden
Z	Egersheim Edward	94	welder	26	here

241

A	Poytras Marie—†	94	factoryhand	25	"
B	Ferrick Aloysius	94	laborer	36	
C	Ferrick Anne—†	94	housewife	33	"
G	Gauthier Mary—†	96	"	25	
H	Szadaj Catherine—†	96	housekeeper	51	"
K	Szadaj Frank	96	cook	28	"
L	Szadaj Michael	96	cleaner	53	
M	Schmitt Charles	96	laborer	32	
N	Schmitt Edna—†	96	housewife	29	"
O	Szadaj Joseph	96	chauffeur	23	"
P	*Elin John	97	merchant	56	"

Marcella Street—Continued

R	*Elin Milda—†	97	housewife	46	here	
S	Eastman Gertrude—†	97	"	36	"	
T	Eastman William	97	manager	30	"	
U	*McDonnell Anna—†	97	housewife	32	"	
V	McDonnell John	97	laborer	40		

242

C	Angello Alice—†	101	housewife	33	"	
D	Angello George	101	tester	37		
E	Dolan Joseph	101	laborer	39		
F	Dolan Rose—†	101	housewife	30	"	
G	Nauss Clarence	101	baker	35		
H	Nauss Mildred—†	101	housewife	37	"	
K	Dooley Stephania—†	102	housekeeper	39	21 School	
L	Muller Katherina—†	102	"	66	here	
M	Neal Julia L—†	102	"	46	"	
P	*Davidson Clarence	105	laborer	42	"	
R	*Davidson Margaret—†	105	housewife	37	"	
S	Cheney Ann—†	105	"	22		
T	Cheney James	105	laborer	24		
U	Danforth Henry J	105	"	23		
V	Danforth Sarah—†	105	housewife	43	"	
W	Halfkenney Ariel	106	laborer	42		
X	Lowe Mary A—†	106	housekeeper	62	"	
Y	Wainwright Mildred—†	106	"	38		

243

A	Burke James M	106	laborer	56		
B	Caffrey Emily—†	108	housewife	25	"	
C	Caffrey William	108	mechanic	29	"	
D	Petroff Catherine—†	108	housewife	46	"	
E	Petroff Helen—†	108	steamstress	21	"	
F	Fall Delia—†	108	housekeeper	60	"	
K	Barletto Florence—†	109	stenographer	22	"	
L	Barletto Helen—†	109	bookkeeper	26	"	
M	Barletto Margaret—†	109	teacher	30	..	
N	*Barletto Mary—†	109	housewife	49	"	
O	Barletto Theresa—†	109	bookkeeper	29	"	
P	De Voe Lawrence	109	mechanic	30	"	
R	De Voe Susan—†	109	housewife	67	"	
T	Dorney Dorothy—†	110	"	24	111 Park Drive	
U	Dorney George J	110	toolmaker	30	94 Alexander	
V	O'Brien John	110	factoryhand	24	here	

Page.	Letter.	FULL NAME.	Residence, Jan. 1, 1941.	Occupation.	Supposed Age.	Reported Residence, Jan. 1, 1940. Street and Number.

Marcella Street—Continued

	w	O'Brien Timothy	110	laborer	68	here
244						
	A	*DuWors Julia—†	113	housekeeper	31	"
	B	*Neary Irene—†	113	housewife	47	39 Codman pk
	c	*Neary Leo	113	tailor	47	39 "
	D	De Simone Mary—†	113	housewife	33	here
	E	De Simone Virgil	113	laborer	27	121 Marcella
	G	*Conrad Ernest	114	retired	62	here
	H	Garceau Frederick D	114	clerk	37	"
	K	Garceau Lillian—†	114	housewife	36	"
	L	Stenstrom Anna—†	114	housekeeper	66	"
	M	Libby Estelle—†	115	housewife	46	"
	N	Libby Kenneth	115	laborer	46	
	o	Libby Neville	115	painter	24	
	P	Turner Catherine—†	115	hairdresser	26	"
	R	Del Grosso Angelina—†	115	housewife	73	"
	s	Del Grosso Anna—†	115	stenographer	30	"
	T	Del Grosso Anthony	115	retired	73	
	U	Del Grosso Celia—†	115	forewoman	36	"
	v	Del Grosso Josephine—†	115	bookkeeper	38	"
	w	Del Grosso Laura—†	115	forewoman	34	"
	X	Del Grosso Mary—†	115	stenographer	27	"
	Y	Del Grosso Louis	115	plumber	42	..
	z	Del Grosso Mary—†	115	housewife	36	"
245						
	A	Carroll Nellie E—†	116	housekeeper	60	"
	B	Wheaton Frederick	116	salesman	43	"
	c	Wheaton Ruth M—†	116	housewife	37	"
	E	Craffey Margaret—†	118	"	25	
	F	Craffey Thomas	118	laborer	30	..
	G	O'Brien William	118	plasterer	60	"
	H	Bewsher Raymond	120	inspector	43	"
	K	Hare Helen—†	120	housewife	58	"
	L	Hare Ralph	120	engineer	58	
	M	Gray Elizabeth—†	120	housewife	23	"
	N	Gray John	120	chauffeur	24	"
	o	Woods John	120	"	25	
	P	Woods Margaret—†	120	housewife	25	"
	R	Johnson Leonard	121	laborer	38	
	s	Johnson Mary—†	121	housewife	38	"
	U	Cataldo Louis	121	janitor	45	

Page.	Letter.	FULL NAME.	Residence, Jan. 1, 1941.	Occupation.	Supposed Age.	Reported Residence, Jan. 1, 1940. Street and Number.

Marcella Street—Continued

v	Cataldo Rose—†	121	housewife	33	here
w	Von Kahle Beatrice—†	123	"	30	"
x	Von Kahle Kermit	123	mechanic	30	"
y	Von Kahle Beulah—†	123	housewife	54	"
z	Von Kahle Beulah—†	123	clerk	24	
	246					
a	Von Kahle Henry	123	mechanic	57	"
b	Von Kahle Herman	123	"	36	
c	Von Kahle Marie—†	123	housewife	33	"
d	Ryder Edmund	124	laborer	55	Quincy
e	Ryder John	124	chauffeur	24	here
f	Ryder John F	124	butcher	54	"
g	Sullivan Catherine—†	124	housewife	78	"
h	Sullivan Thomas	124	plumber	39	82 Jamaica
k	Sullivan William	124	painter	37	here
l	Fetler Carl A	125	policeman	34	"
m	Fetler Helen—†	125	housewife	31	"
n	Simboli Alex	125	painter	37	
o	*Simboli Helen—†	125	housewife	30	"
p	Simboli James	125	carpenter	59	"
r	Palma James	125	laborer	49	"
s	Palma Rose—†	125	housewife	40	"
t	Fall Maybelle E—†	126	housekeeper	30	"
u	Grauman Arvid R	126	carpenter	28	"
v	Grauman Irene N—†	126	housewife	26	"
w	Sherman Forest E	126	engineer	52	"
x	Sullivan Bridget—†	127	housekeeper	59	"
y	McClelland James	127	shipper	48	"
z	*McClelland Margaret—†	127	housewife	48	"
	247					
a	Sullivan Dorothy—†	127	"	27	
b	*Sullivan John	127	laborer	29	
c	Scanlon Edward	130	assembler	25	"
d	Scanlon Frank	130	chauffeur	29	"
e	Scanlon Mary E—†	130	housewife	63	"
f	Keefe James—†	130	clerk	53	6 Beech Glen
g	Little Carman—†	131	housewife	26	here
h	Little Ronald	131	clerk	29	"
k	Riel Mary—†	131	housekeeper	37	"
·l	Waldron Catherine—†	131	housewife	72	"

Marcella Street—Continued

M	Waldron James	131	salesman	38	here
N	Waldron John	131	chauffeur	36	"
O	Waldron Josephine—†	131	housewife	37	"
P	Cannon Mary—†	132	housekeeper	67	"
R	Heath Agnes—†	132	factoryhand	60	"
S	Cavicchi Frank	132	breweryworker	40	"
T	Cavicchi Margaret—†	132	"	32	"
V	Turowski Helen—†	133	housewife	22	147 Marcella
W	Turowski John	133	laborer	25	147 "
X	Marenghi Ettore	133	shoeworker	54	here
Y	Marenghi Jennie—†	133	housewife	52	"
Z	Marenghi John	133	clerk	21	"
	248				
A	Marenghi Rita—†	133	cashier	24	"
B	Aldred Anna—†	133	housewife	25	38 Green
C	Aldred John	133	fireman	24	38 "
D	O'Donnell Charles A	134	clerk	26	here
E	O'Donnell Ethel C—†	134	housekeeper	24	"
F	O'Donnell Hugh	134	fireman	69	"
G	O'Donnell Isabella—†	134	housewife	62	"
H	O'Donnell Isabella M—†	134	operator	35	"
K	Paige Charles W	135	clerk	25	
L	Paige Mary C—†	135	housewife	24	"
M	Tobin John F	135	operator	42	"
N	Tobin Margaret—†	135	housewife	26	"
O	Theireault Irene G—†	135	"	30	
P	Theireault Joseph	135	chauffeur	29	"
R	*Paley Lena—†	136	housekeeper	68	"
S	Smith Sarah A—†	136	housewife	85	"
T	Sherman Bertha V—†	136	"	61	
U	Bersin Marguerite—†	136	housekeeper	65	"
V	Cabot Beatrice—†	137	housewife	47	"
W	Cabot Louis	137	carpenter	55	"
X	Gaffey Francis C	137	retired	47	
Y	Gaffey John H	137	laborer	53	
Z	Gaffey Rose M—†	137	stenographer	20	"
	249				
A	Duffy Ellen—†	137	housekeeper	75	"
B	Ward Rose M—†	137	clerk	38	
C	Streeter Mary—†	138	housekeeper	70	"

Page.	Letter.	FULL NAME.	Residence, Jan. 1, 1941.	Occupation.	Supposed Age.	Reported Residence, Jan. 1, 1940. Street and Number.

Marcella Street—Continued

	D	O'Brien Edith A—†	138	housewife	46	here
	E	O'Brien John J	138	trainman	22	"
	F	O'Brien Joseph	138	fireman	54	"
	G	Berzin Emily—†	138	housekeeper	50	"
	H	Hamrock Helen—†	139	housewife	52	"
	K	Hamrock James	139	machinist	47	"
	L	Donnelly Winifred C—†	139	housekeeper	43	"
	M	Fitzgerald Catherine—†	139	"	32	
	N	Blasi Eda—†	140	hairdresser	24	"
	O	*Blasi Elvira—†	140	housewife	60	"
	P	Blasi Thomas	140	chauffeur	24	"
	R	*Blasi Vincent	140	barber	56	"
	S	De Lucca Anthony	140	manager	26	937 Albany
	T	De Lucca Margaret—†	140	housewife	23	1437 Col av
	U	Stewart Bernard	140	foreman	34	227 Highland
	V	Stewart Rita—†	140	housewife	25	227 "
	W	Donelan Charles A	141	fingerprinter	23	here
	X	Donelan Elizabeth—†	141	housewife	58	"
	Y	Donelan Genevieve M—†	141	operator	25	"
	Z	Donelan James E	141	engineer	27	
250						
	B	Donelan Matthias F	141	shipper	29	
	A	Donelan Matthias P	141	butcher	59	
	C	Donelan Paul G	141	messenger	21	"
	D	Noone Louise H—†	141	teacher	33	
	E	Campbell Jane A—†	143	housewife	48	"
	G	Powers Emily J—†	143	housekeeper	60	"
	H	Powers Ida M—†	143	"	65	"
	K	Russell Julia M—†	145	housewife	37	"
	L	Russell Thomas T	145	letter carrier	47	"
	M	Falcone Jeanne—†	145	housewife	23	"
	N	Falcone John	145	laborer	23	
	O	Treiman Alida K—†	145	stitcher	22	
	P	Treiman Alida M—†	145	housekeeper	50	"
	R	Treiman John A	145	clerk	21	"
	S	Needham Jessie—†	147	housekeeper	55	"
	T	Strother Charles A	147	mechanic	40	"
	U	Strother Gertrude A—†	147	housewife	29	"
	V	D'Amore Claire—†	147	"	24	270 W Third
	W	D'Amore Joseph	147	shoeworker	26	252 Dudley

New Heath Street

y	Coughlin Albert F	6	mechanic	24	here
z	Coughlin Catherine T—†	6	housewife	25	"
	251				
a	*Puorro Angelina—†	6	"	68	
b	Puorro Nicholas	6	retired	67	
c	Puorro Nicholas, jr	6	laborer	25	
d	Puorro Ida—†	6	housewife	31	"
e	Puorro Thomas	6	shoeworker	36	"
f	Reardon Frances—†	8	housewife	25	140A Cedar
g	Reardon John	8	bellboy	27	140A "
h	Anderson Albert	8	machinist	44	31 Lambert
k	Derow Ada—†	8	housekeeper	45	31 "
l	Fitzpatrick Margaret—†	8	housewife	31	here
m	Lenza Epifanio	10	laborer	30	"
n	Lenza Josephine—†	10	housewife	26	"
o	Davis Marion F—†	10	"	26	
p	Davis Stephen F	10	rubberworker	32	"
r	*De Marino Elizabeth—†	10	housewife	53	"
s	Rendal Antonio B	10A	houseman	41	36 Heath av
t	Rendal Grace E—†	10A	housewife	33	36 "
u	Lanza Joseph	10A	laborer	62	here
v	*Lanza Marie—†	10A	housewife	57	"
w	Raffaeli Christina—†	10A	housekeeper	22	1 Minden
x	*Raffaeli Michael	10A	laborer	58	1 "
y	*Raffaeli Rose—†	10A	housewife	56	1 "
z	Russo Alice—†	12	secretary	30	here
	252				
a	Russo Jean—†	12	tailor	30	
b	Lymneos Helen—†	12A	housewife	48	"
c	Lymneos Nicholas	12A	retired	58	"
d	*Russo Anthony	12A	tailor	63	"
e	*Russo Lena—†	12A	housewife	63	"
f	Moloney Charles	14	furrier	33	21 Marcella
g	Moloney Geraldine J—†	14	housewife	28	33 Beech Glen
h	Sumner Mary—†	14	"	47	here
k	Knight Henry W	14	seaman	32	"
l	Knight Josephine E—†	14	housewife	32	"
m	Gilmartin Mary A—†	18	housekeeper	45	"
n	Kelly Anna O—†	18	secretary	50	"
o	Kelly Mary T—†	18	housekeeper	55	"
p	Quinn Mary A—†	18	at home	70	"

29

New Heath Street—Continued

R	Reynolds Martin J	18	laborer	33	here
S	Reynolds Mary M—†	18	stenographer	30	"
T	Myers Anastasia L—†	18	housewife	34	"
U	Myers Thomas J	18	plumber	38	
V	Myers Margaret—†	18	housewife	60	"
W	Myers Patrick F	18	clerk	33	
X	White Mary—†	18	stitcher	38	
Y	Traniello Antonio	20	retired	76	"
Z	Gilman Irene—†	20	housewife	60	New York

253

A	Gilman Paul F	20	serviceman	57	"
B	Clayton Charles T	26	laborer	25	25 Alexander
C	Clayton Florence—†	26	housewife	23	25 "
D	Jacques Alfred	26	attendant	21	25 "

Oakview Avenue

H	McCallion Phillip	1	laborer	48	here
K	McCallion Rose—†	1	housewife	32	"
L	Schlaich Catherine A—†	2	clerk	26	"
M	Schlaich Gallus	2	"	62	
N	Schlaich Theresa—†	2	housewife	64	"
O	Gormley Joseph	4	chauffeur	36	25 Garfield av
P	Gormley Muriel—†	4	housewife	29	25 "
R	*Fabio Antoinetta—†	4	"	48	here
S	Fabio Antonio	4	laborer	51	"

Penryth Street

T	Ciresi Joseph	1	salesman	24	76 Eustis
U	Ciresi Josephine—†	1	housewife	22	1436 Col av
V	Ferrari Carmella—†	1	"	25	165 Marcella
W	Ferrari James	1	shoeworker	24	165 "
X	Incardone Sadie—†	4	housewife	35	here
Y	Incardone Salvatore	4	shoeworker	36	"
Z	*Belfiore Carmela—†	4	housewife	71	"

254

A	Belfiore John	4	chef	32	
B	*Belfiore Michael	4	retired	78	
C	*Iantosca Angelina—†	4	housewife	39	"
D	Iantosca Anthony	4	collector	40	"

Page.	Letter.	Full Name.	Residence, Jan. 1, 1941.	Occupation.	Supposed Age.	Reported Residence, Jan. 1, 1940. Street and Number.

Penryth Street—Continued

	E	Casey Catherine—†	5	housewife	78	here
	F	Casey Mary C—†	5	secretary	36	"
	G	Casey Timothy J	5	retired	79	"
	H	Starkey James	5	longshoreman	27	42 Lambert av
	K	Kirby Catherine—†	5	housewife	59	1865 Col av
	L	Kirby John	5	porter	59	1865 "
	M	Donelan John	6	student	24	here
	N	Donelan Sarah—†	6	housewife	48	"
	O	Donelan William J	6	janitor	52	"

Ritchie Street

	P	Nielsen Albert	10	carpenter	48	here
	R	Nielsen Myra—†	10	housewife	49	"
	S	Sullivan Eva—†	10	"	45	"
	T	Sullivan Timothy J	10	laborer	44	
	U	Boudreau Francis	10	chauffeur	39	"
	V	Boudreau Lillian—†	10	housewife	35	"
	W	*Cerullo Eugene	12	laborer	51	
	X	*Cerullo Rose—†	12	housewife	36	"
	Y	Giles Edward	12	laborer	32	
	Z	Giles Irene—†	12	housewife	32	"

255

	A	D'Agostino Dominic	12	factoryhand	48	"
	B	D'Agostino Mary—†	12	housewife	35	"
	C	Alexander Frederick P	15	chauffeur	26	"
	D	Denault Abigail—†	15	housewife	48	"
	E	Denault Edward F	15	chauffeur	24	"
	F	Denault Henry J	15	"	50	
	G	Denault Lawrence J	15	"	40	"

Thwing Street

	H	Shea Margaret—†	2	clerk	36	here
	K	McKenzie Edward	4	"	47	"
	L	McKenzie James	4	merchant	36	"
	M	McKenzie Teresa—†	4	housekeeper	72	"
	N	Byrnes Katherine—†	5	"	73	"
	O	Hunter Elizabeth M—†	5	operator	45	"
	P	Hunter Henry J	5	lather	42	
	R	Hunter Mary—†	5	housewife	83	"

Page	Letter	Full Name.	Residence, Jan. 1, 1941.	Occupation.	Supposed Age.	Reported Residence, Jan. 1, 1940. Street and Number.

Thwing Street—Continued

	s	Krim Anna E—†	6	housewife	72	here
	t	Krim Anna M—†	6	stenographer	33	"
	u	Krim Elizabeth M—†	6	"	31	"
	v	Krim Joseph A	6	houseman	78	"
	w	Krim Marie E—†	6	housekeeper	48	"
	x	Carr James V	7	chauffeur	40	"
	y	Carr Mary L—†	7	saleswoman	50	"
	z	Carr Michael X	7	lineman	38	
256						
	a	Keane John J	8	gardener	36	"
	b	*Keane Margaret—†	8	housewife	35	"
	c	Curley Mary A—†	8	"	40	
	d	Curley Peter J	8	foreman	47	"
	e	*Friedenberg Alma—†	10	housekeeper	48	"
	f	Friedenberg Edward	10	driller	46	"
	g	Shaw Ann—†	10	housewife	36	"
	h	Shaw Joseph	10	foreman	40	
	k	Walsh Dudley	10	driller	31	
	l	Bates Benjamin G	12	salesman	50	"
	m	Bates Benjamin G, jr	12	laborer	22	
	n	Bates Mary M—†	12	housewife	50	"
	o	Bates Peter J	12	salesman	25	"
	p	Bates Regis J	12	usher	21	
	r	Kenney Joseph F	12	painter	32	
	s	Kenney Margaret M—†	12	housewife	29	"
	t	Bukow John	14	carpenter	59	"
	u	Bukow Mary—†	14	housewife	58	"
	v	Ellsworth Gertrude—†	14	housekeeper	54	102 E Brookline
	w	Peddell Alice—†	14	housewife	28	19 Roach
	x	Peddell John	14	clerk	30	19 "
	y	Sandri Andrew	14	chauffeur	28	12 Wigglesworth
	z	Sandri Joseph	14	molder	48	4 Oneida
257						
	a	Sandri Reno	14	clerk	23	4 "
	b	Berrenberg Alfred	16	machinist	37	here
	c	Berrenberg Mary—†	16	housewife	72	"
	d	*Berrenberg Rita—†	16	"	32	"
	e	Miller Bertha T—†	18	"	48	
	f	Miller Eleanor M—†	18	student	20	"
	g	Miller John A	18	chemist	50	
	h	Rickmeyer Fredericka—†	20	housewife	66	"

Thwing Street—Continued

K	Rickmeyer William F	20	brewer	52	here
L	Ward Helen—†	20	wrapper	35	Georgia
M	Willoth Frederick	20	optician	39	here
N	Pare Albert C	22	fireman	46	"
O	Pare Gilbert	22	stenographer	21	"
P	Pare Imelda—†	22	housewife	42	"
R	Broderick Cecelia—†	22	"	48	
S	Broderick Joseph P	22	clerk	20	
T	Broderick Loretta M—†	22	stenographer	36	"
U	Broderick Martin J	22	clerk	22	,,
V	Broderick Martin S	22	shoeworker	55	"
W	Broderick Mary C—†	22	bookkeeper	28	"
X	Granger Helen G—†	24	secretary	28	"
Y	Motley Helen—†	24	housewife	59	"
Z	Motley Leo V	24	teacher	32	

Ward 11–Precinct 3

CITY OF BOSTON

LIST OF RESIDENTS
20 YEARS OF AGE AND OVER

(NON-CITIZENS INDICATED BY ASTERISK)
(FEMALES INDICATED BY DAGGER)

AS OF

JANUARY 1, 1941

JOSEPH F. TIMILTY, *Chairman*
FREDERIC E. DOWLING, *Secretary*
WILLIAM A. MOTLEY, JR.
FRANCIS B. McKINNEY
HILDA HEDSTROM QUIRK

Listing Board.

CITY OF BOSTON PRINTING DEPARTMENT

Page.	Letter.	FULL NAME.	Residence, Jan. 1, 1941.	Occupation.	Supposed Age.	Reported Residence, Jan. 1, 1940. Street and Number.

300

Bainbridge Street

A	Gaul Frances L—†	1	stenographer	26	here
B	*Gaul Mary—†	1	housewife	48	"
C	Patrician Charlotte—†	1	"	29	1 Vine av
D	Patrician Howard	1	chauffeur	31	5 "
E	*Sachnovitz Ida—†	1	housewife	56	here
F	Sachnovitz Jack	1	grader	29	"
G	Sachnovitz Max	1	inspector	22	"
H	Finn Anna—†	3	housewife	24	"
K	Finn George	3	laborer	26	
L	Taite Alice E—†	3	housewife	28	"
M	*Nickerson Eldridge	3	laundryworker	48	"
N	*Nickerson Gertrude—†	3	housewife	48	"
O	Richards Allen	5	painter	35	
P	Richards Beatrice—†	5	housewife	29	"
R	*Gavin Jennie—†	5	"	38	"
S	Colleran Margaret—†	5	"	29	24 Fenwick
T	Colleran William J	5	painter	32	24 "
U	Steen Elizabeth—†	7	housewife	23	here
V	Steen George	7	laborer	26	"
W	Whiteway Madeline—†	7	housewife	36	11 Rocky Nook ter
X	Wallace Margaret J—†	7	"	62	here

301

A	Pridham Edwin	11	laundryworker	61	"
B	Pridham Nina—†	11	housewife	55	"
C	Pridham Ruth—†	11	housekeeper	28	"
D	*MacLeod Angus	11	tailor	40	"
E	MacLeod Gertrude—†	11	housewife	34	"
F	Pridham Arthur	11	laundryworker	29	Swampscott
G	Pridham Violet—†	11	housewife	28	"
H	Pridham Carolyn—†	13	"	39	here
K	Pridham John E	13	laundryworker	38	"
L	Kelley George H	15	clerk	33	"
M	Kelley Margaret P—†	15	housekeeper	28	"
N	Kelley Mary M—†	15	housewife	62	"
O	Kelley Thomas	15	operator	26	"
P	Aleo Agnes—†	15	housewife	24	"
R	Aleo Alphonse	15	barber	24	"
S	Rooney Alice H—†	17	secretary	33	"
T	Rooney Frederick M	17	retired	68	
U	Rooney Walter P	17	U S A	24	

2

Page.	Letter.	FULL NAME.	Residence, Jan. 1, 1941.	Occupation.	Supposed Age.	Reported Residence, Jan. 1, 1940. Street and Number.

Bainbridge Street—Continued

v	Gauthier Delphine M—†	19	at home	68	here
w	Gauthier Lydia—†	19	seamstress	63	"
x	Gauthier Mary L—†	19	housekeeper	65	"
y	Gauthier Wilfred	19	painter	55	"
z	Hines Anna T—†	19	housewife	59	"
	302				
a	Hines Joseph M	19	clerk	28	
b	Hines Michael J	19	agent	61	
c	Hines Theresa L—†	19	student	21	"
d	Hurley David	19	retired	88	"
e	Hurley Mary—†	19	housewife	80	"
f	Hurley Mary V—†	19	superintendent	48	"
g	Anderson Ada—†	23	housewife	43	"
h	Anderson Walter K	23	porter	51	"
k	Babcock Ruth M—†	23	cook	45	Rhode Island
l	Gordan Fred	23	laborer	34	26 Catawba
m	McSweeney Joseph	23	waiter	57	26 "
n	Soars Louis	23	laborer	43	26 "
o	Soars Pearl—†	23	housewife	42	26 "
p	Williams Lesley—†	23	waitress	31	26 "
r	Jackson Dorothy—†	23	housewife	37	here
s	Jackson James	23	barber	42	"
u	Edmonds George W	25	porter	32	"
v	Edmonds LaBlanche—†	25	housewife	28	"
w	Booker Florence—†	25	"	50	82 Bower
x	Booker Louis	25	laborer	52	82 "
y	Booker Robert	25	"	25	82 "
z	Roberts Bertha L—†	27	housewife	44	here
	303				
a	Roberts Harold F	27	laborer	44	
b	Wyche Mercedes—†	27	housewife	31	"
c	Wyche Nathaniel	27	porter	35	
d	Haggie Carlton	27	painter	23	
e	Haggie Leonard	27	porter	27	"
f	Haggie Mildred—†	27	housewife	48	"
g	Haggie Virginia—†	27	"	24	
h	*MacDonald Daniel	29	retired	77	
k	MacDonald Jeanette—†	29	clerk	30	
l	*MacDonald Katherine—†	29	housewife	65	"
m	MacDonald Mary—†	29	bookkeeper	30	"
n	MacDonald Ronald	29	clerk	36	"

Page.	Letter.	FULL NAME.	Residence, Jan. 1, 1941.	Occupation.	Supposed Age.	Reported Residence, Jan. 1, 1940. Street and Number.

Bainbridge Street—Continued

o	MacPherson Mary A—†	29	housekeeper	60	here
p	Elliott John	29	chauffeur	56	"
r	Hayes Daniel F	29	toolmaker	54	"
s	Hayes James J	29	machinist	22	"
t	Hayes Nora S—†	29	housewife	47	"
u	Hayes Robert L	29	chauffeur	20	"
v	McHugh Edward W	29	inspector	47	"
w	McHugh Joseph R	29	"	26	
x	McHugh Mary F—†	29	housewife	47	"
y	McHugh Thomas P	29	U S A	20	"
z	Gilman Carl	31	B F D	42	

304

a	Gilman Mabel—†	31	housewife	48	"
b	Gilman Ralph	31	laborer	20	
d	Craven Albert T	31	clerk	21	
e	Craven Catherine A—†	31	housewife	44	"
f	Craven John A	31	clerk	52	
g	Craven John L	31	oiler	26	
h	McDermott Mary—†	33	dressmaker	63	"
k	Murphy Anna—†	33	housewife	56	11 Ingleside
l	Murphy John T	33	laborer	64	11 "
m	Gately Edward J	33	chauffeur	23	here
n	Gately Eleanor—†	33	operator	21	"
o	Gately Helen A—†	33	housewife	59	"
p	Gately William J	33	engineer	58	
r	O'Brien John T	33	custodian	42	"
s	O'Brien Margaret—†	33	housewife	38	"
t	Muir Dorothy B—†	35	hostess	28	
u	Muir Ellen T—†	35	housewife	55	"
v	Muir Francis C	35	salesman	30	"
w	Muir John S	35	bookkeeper	34	"
x	Muir Marion L—†	35	domestic	26	"
y	Ahearn Catherine E—†	35	clerk	60	
z	Ryan Margaret—†	35	nurse	40	

305

a	Kelle Dora B—†	35	housewife	72	"
b	Kelle Louis J	35	papercutter	76	"
c	DeNisco Carmine	37	storekeeper	40	"
d	DeNisco Rose—†	37	housewife	40	"
f	DiAngelo Edna—†	37	"	27	
g	DiAngelo Patrick	37	salesman	28	"

Bainbridge Street—Continued

H	Sullivan Catherine J—†	39	teacher	63	here
K	Sullivan Mary L—†	39	"	65	"
L	Crawford Bertha—†	43	housewife	63	"
M	McCorrison Cleveland J	43	steamfitter	56	"
N	McCorrison Gladys—†	43	housewife	44	"
O	McCorrison Sears	43	metalworker	21	"
P	Anderson Charles	43	clerk	33	117 Zeigler
R	Anderson Clara—†	43	housewife	31	here
S	Landers Alice M—†	43	factoryhand	21	35 Taber
T	Landers Douglas L	43	checker	27	35 "
U	Landers James W	43	chauffeur	62	35 "
V	Landers Mary F—†	43	housewife	60	35 "
W	Corboy Carrie—†	45	"	30	here
X	Corboy Phillip	45	laborer	32	"
Y	Driscoll Dorothy F—†	45	model	21	"
Z	Driscoll Esther—†	45	housewife	43	"

306

A	Driscoll John F	45	carpenter	47	"
B	*Anton Nicholetta—†	45	housewife	53	"
C	*Anton Peter	45	retired	63	
D	Anton Sophie—†	45	waitress	36	
E	Daly Elizabeth A—†	47	at home	75	
F	Flanagan Anne L—†	47	clerk	35	
G	Ryan Catherine T—†	47	housewife	58	"
H	Sullivan Stella B—†	47	at home	70	

Beech Glen Street

K	Carson Charles R	60	retired	67	here
L	Carson Evelyn—†	60	packer	22	"
M	Carson Jemilla—†	60	housewife	49	"
N	Carson Marjorie A—†	60	clerk	24	
O	Faulstich Charles M	60	"	22	
P	Faulstich Dorothy—†	60	operator	21	
R	Faulstich Emma—†	60	instructor	55	"
S	Faulstich Marie—†	60	housewife	45	"

Cedar Street

T	Carroll Lorenzo	28	janitor	65	here
U	Darben William M	28	clerk	62	34 St Germain

Cedar Street—Continued

	Letter	FULL NAME	Res.	Occupation	Age	Reported Residence
	v	Gray Marie—†	28	housewife	32	here
	w	Gray Walter G	28	laborer	39	"
	x	Franklin Blanche—†	30	housekeeper	66	"
	y	Galloway Mildred—†	30	housewife	41	"
	z	Galloway W	30	retired	47	

307liam

	Letter	FULL NAME	Res.	Occupation	Age	Reported Residence
	A	Kennedy Mildred—†	30	entertainer	21	"
	B	Payton Blanche—†	30	operator	38	"
	C	Johnson Charles S	32	machinist	33	"
	D	Johnson Inez E—†	32	housewife	31	"
	E	Hargraves Nancy—†	32	housekeeper	78	"
	F	Gray Arthur L	32	operator	22	"
	G	Jackson Eudora—†	32	housekeeper	40	"
	H	Terrelonge Anita—†	34	housewife	42	"
	K	Terrelonge Arnold R	34	porter	46	
	L	Lytle Laura—†	34	housewife	20	"
	M	Lytle William	34	waiter	26	
	N	Branker Eliza—†	34	housekeeper	69	"
	O	Stewart Mary—†	36	housewife	69	"
	P	*Martin Beatrice—†	36	"	23	
	R	Martin John	36	porter	25	
	S	Fleming Louise—†	36	housewife	49	"
	T	Fleming Scipio	36	laborer	52	
	U	Garrett Anderson	38	cook	33	
	V	Garrett Lucinda—†	38	domestic	32	"
	W	Gunderway Viola—†	38	nurse	37	"
	X	Watts Claudia—†	38	housewife	37	88 Munroe
	Y	Watts Richard	38	barber	38	88 "

308

	Letter	FULL NAME	Res.	Occupation	Age	Reported Residence
	B	Bruce Charles S	40	artist	48	here
	C	Bruce Elaine C—†	40	clerk	21	"
	D	Washington Addie—†	42	housekeeper	65	"
	E	Butler Ruth—†	42	"	42	
	F	Goslin Jellie—†	42	"	85	
	G	McNair Harlee	44	porter	25	
	H	McNair Marion—†	44	housewife	58	"
	K	McNair Parker	44	painter	22	"
	N	McLaughlin Gladys—†	46	housewife	23	226 Cabot
	O	*McLaughlin John	46	serviceman	26	226 "
	P	*Palazola Myrtle—†	46	waitress	41	2 Stanton pl
	R	Doherty James	46	laborer	30	28 King

Cedar Street—Continued

s	Doherty Nancy—†	46	housewife	28	28 King
t	Giangrande Pasquale	46	laborer	28	29 Kent
u	Giangrande Sadie—†	46	housewife	24	29 "
v	Reynolds Catherine—†	46½	"	39	59 Rutland sq
x	Kingsbury Dorothy—†	54	"	26	48 Minden
y	Kingsbury Paul V	54	painter	27	48 "
z	Mazmanian Beatrice—†	54	housekeeper	47	here

309

a	Groux Catherine—†	56	housewife	43	26 Rockford
b	Groux Joseph	56	laborer	21	26 "
c	Groux Louis	56	painter	50	26 "
d	Hunkiar Mildred—†	56	housewife	38	118 Cedar
e	Hunkiar Richard	56	photographer	41	118 "
f	Sattur Frank J	56	electrician	38	Pennsylvania
g	Sattur Kathryn—†	56	housewife	29	"
h	McDermott Gregory J	58	clerk	21	here
k	McDermott James A	58	supervisor	60	"
l	McDermott Margaret—†	58	housewife	50	"
m	Donahue Delia—†	60	"	75	
n	Donahue Thomas J	60	retired	73	
o	Fay Frances—†	60	housewife	40	"
p	Emery George E	71	manager	47	"
e	Emery Sarah E—†	71	at home	79	"
s	Dawber Helen S—†	73	housewife	23	64 Lambert av
t	Dawber John J	73	chauffeur	34	64 "
u	Serrichia Donato—†	73	seamstress	28	108 Heath
v	Serrichia Patrick	73	tailor	32	108 "
w	Howlett John R	75	B F D	40	here
x	Howlett Wanda M—†	75	housewife	30	"
y	Connelly Alice G—†	75	"	52	"
z	Connelly Peter J	75	B F D	51	

310

a	Dibblee Emily E—†	75	housewife	36	Maine
b	Dibblee Frederick W	75	salesman	38	368 Dudley
c	*Jones Arthur J	77	sailmaker	59	here
d	*Jones Christine E—†	77	housewife	55	"
e	*Jones Donald O	77	clerk	26	"
f	*Esson Allen M	77	"	32	
g	*Esson Isaac B	77	checker	39	
h	Sceles Morley M	77	chauffeur	32	"
k	*Sceles Muriel E—†	77	housewife	29	"

Page.	Letter.	Full Name.	Residence, Jan. 1, 1941.	Occupation.	Supposed Age.	Reported Residence, Jan. 1, 1940. Street and Number.

Cedar Street—Continued

L	Matthews Charles F	77	salesman	48	here
M	Matthews Charles F, jr	77	chauffeur	23	"
N	Matthews Marion R—†	77	housewife	43	"
O	Papasodero Joseph	79	shoemaker	42	65 Linden Park
P	Papasodero Julia—†	79	housewife	35	65 "
R	Rania Anthony	79	retired	74	1252 Tremont
S	Rania Anthony, jr	79	shoemaker	30	Somerville
T	Rania Clara—†	79	housewife	29	"
U	Rania Elizabeth—†	79	at home	64	1252 Tremont
V	Rania Joseph	79	laborer	38	1252 "
W	Kingston Elizabeth D—†	81	probat'n officer	37	here
X	Kingston Evelyn R—†	81	secretary .	49	"
Y	Laiweneek Emily—†	82	stitcher	54	10 Gardner
Z	Laiweneek Jacob	82	machinist	29	10 "

311

A	Proctor Roger	82	operator	35	33 Rosemary
B	Proctor Ruth—†	82	housewife	28	33 "
C	*Kreslin John	82	retired	55	16 Linwood sq
D	Weichel Mary—†	82	housekeeper	60	16 "
E	*Abalon John	82	baker	58	here
F	Kalnin Mary—†	82	housewife	55	"
G	Osis Frederick	82	cutter	38	"
H	Dunn Anna M—†	85	stenographer	25	"
K	Dunn Annie E—†	85	housewife	64	"
L	Dunn Bernard J	85	engineer	32	
M	Dunn Gordon F	85	manager	31	"
N	Dunn James F	85	social worker	28	"
O	Fewore Frank O	85	retired	62	
P	Fewore Frank W	85	loftsman	20	"
R	Fewore Marie B—†	85	stenographer	30	"
S	Hale Margaret S—†	85	housekeeper	68	"
T	McGovern Mary A—†	85	"	78	..
U	Shannon Margaret M—†	85	"	62	
V	Calvin John	88	painter	60	
W	Calvin Minna—†	88	housewife	61	"
X	Sonberg John	88	painter	50	
Y	Hurley John	88	doorman	36	"
Z	Hurley Margaret—†	88	operator	38	

312

A	Hurley Mary J—†	88	housewife	58	"
B	Doherty Daniel	88	guard	52	

8

Cedar Street—Continued

c	Sullivan Bella M—†	89	housewife	67	here
d	Sullivan Daniel A	89	retired	71	"
e	Gaughran Anthony J	89	painter	60	"
f	Gaughran Francis X	89	packer	22	"
g	Gaughran Kenneth J	89	clerk	26	
h	Gaughran Madeline M—†	89	stenographer	20	"
k	Gaughran Nora M—†	89	housewife	54	"
l	*Mogue Amy—†	91	"	61	Belmont
m	*Mogue James C	91	waiter	65	"
n	Calney Elizabeth—†	91	housewife	44	here
o	Calney Martin	91	bartender	45	"
p	Lindholm Helding	91	manager	40	"
r	Lindholm Matilda M—†	91	housewife	62	"
s	Olson Julius	91	shipper	50	
v	Scott Anna—†	98	housewife	37	"
w	Scott Eric	98	painter	38	"
x	Abbott Mary—†	98	housekeeper	70	18 Highland
y	Capuzzo Frederick P	98	laborer	20	here
z	*Capuzzo Laura—†	98	housewife	51	"
	313				
a	Capuzzo Paul	98	laborer	49	
b	Hermes Alfred	102	"	25	
c	Hermes Maude—†	102	housewife	60	"
d	Hermes Thelma—†	102	housekeeper	24	N Hampshire
e	Hermes Walter	102	student	21	here
f	Milligan Dorothy—†	102	housewife	37	"
g	Nelson Lorna—†	102	"	35	"
h	Nelson Percy	102	draftsman	40	"

Dale Street

k	Sheehan Elizabeth M—†	128	housewife	78	here
l	Sheehan Frederick A	128	retired	69	"
m	Gallagher Margaret A—†	130	housewife	68	"
n	Gallagher William A	130	chauffeur	42	"
o	Sullivan John F	130	clerk	63	
p	Sullivan William C	130	"	60	
r	Countie John T	132	policeman	52	"
s	Countie Katherine—†	132	clerk	45	
t	Countie Mary—†	132	housewife	48	"
u	Galvin Edward C	132	retired	60	

9

Page.	Letter.	FULL NAME.	Residence, Jan. 1, 1941.	Occupation.	Supposed Age.	Reported Residence, Jan. 1, 1940. Street and Number.

Dale Street—Continued

w	Galvin Helen M—†	132	stenographer	23	here
v	Galvin Helena M—†	132	housewife	54	"

Dorr Street

x	Farrell Peter	15	checker	55	here
y	Farrell Winifred—†	15	housewife	45	"
z	Schrader Carl	15	engraver	44	"

314

A	Schrader Rose—†	15	housewife	39	"
B	Winterstein Fredericka—†	15	housekeeper	75	"
c	*Johansen Hedwig—†	17	housewife	32	"
D	Johansen Johan	17	finisher	33	
E	*Johnson Alvhild—†	17	housewife	47	"
F	Johnson Gunnar	17	painter	40	
G	*Pederson Martin	17	"	62	
H	Muise Charles	17	blacksmith	55	"
K	Muise Margaret—†	17	stenographer	20	"
L	Muise Virginia—†	17	housewife	44	"
M	Dunn Dennis G	21	splicer	42	
N	Dunn James E	21	attendant	40	"
o	Dunn Sarah—†	21	housewife	60	"
P	Yeoman William	21	millwright	60	"
R	Yeoman William, jr	21	electrician	33	"
T	Cash Elizabeth—†	23	housewife	23	"
U	Cash Lee	23	mechanic	30	"
v	Kroleski Louise—†	23	housewife	25	4 Bower
w	Kroleski Walter	23	mechanic	29	4 "
x	Griswold Madeline—†	25	housewife	29	23 Dorr
y	Griswold Malvin	25	chef	29	23 "
z	Frazier Muriel—†	25	housewife	28	3 Pequot

315

A	Frazier Norman P	25	laborer	31	3 "
B	Belangel Eugene	25	chauffeur	29	158 W Brookline
c	Belangel Nora—†	25	housewife	30	158 "
F	Daley James C	29	investigator	29	here
H	*Langlois Alice—†	31	housewife	65	"
K	Langlois Frances—†	31	waitress	28	"
L	*Langlois Joseph	31	carpenter	62	"
M	Trainor Catherine—†	31	housewife	28	"

Page.	Letter.	FULL NAME.	Residence, Jan. 1, 1941.	Occupation.	Supposed Age.	Reported Residence, Jan. 1, 1940. Street and Number.

Dorr Street—Continued

	N	Trainor Charles J	31	chauffeur	30	here
	o	Raferty Charles	31	expressman	31	"
	P	Clarke Joseph	33	carpenter	65	"
	R	*Sullivan Mary—†	33	housewife	41	"
	s	Sullivan Patrick	33	laborer	41	
	T	Holland Gertrude—†	33	factoryhand	42	"
	U	McBride Dennis	35	painter	29	
	V	McBride Margaret—†	35	housewife	74	"
	W	McBride Michael J	35	retired	68	
	X	*Desmond Mary—†	35	domestic	35	"
	Y	Desmond Timothy	35	laborer	45	
	z	Wessling Frank X	37	retired	58	"
316						
	A	Wessling Herman	37	retired	88	
	B	Wessling Marguerite—†	37	secretary	43	"
	c	Wessling Mary D—†	37	"	45	"
	D	Cenedella Charles	37	molder	42	13 Fuller
	E	Cenedella Irene—†	37	housewife	24	13 "
	F	Jodrie Cecelia—†	37	"	58	Brookline
	G	*Jodrie Charles	37	watchman	62	41 Rockland
	H	Hiltz Marion T—†	39	teacher	41	here
	K	Champney Edward E	39	retired	77	"
	L	Champney Mary E—†	39	housewife	79	"
	M	Jackman Elida—†	39	"	63	255 Warren
	N	Jackman Vivian A—†	39	nurse	41	255 "
	o	Daly Eileen—†	41	housewife	58	here
	P	Daly Mary F—†	41	"	60	"
	R	Daly Patrick J	41	manager	65	"
	s	Holmes Alice—†	41	housewife	56	"
	T	Battiti Madelin—†	41	"	28	
	U	Battiti Nichols	41	chauffeur	30	"
	V	McNally Bertha A—†	41	stenographer	24	"
	W	McNally Bertha M—†	41	housewife	54	"
	X	McNally Hugh J	41	shipper	54	
	Y	McNally Marguerite—†	41	clerk	22	
	z	Dillon Mary—†	41	domestic	64	"
317						
	c	Gordon Isabel—†	41	clerk	22	
	A	Gordon Margaret—†	41	housewife	58	"
	B	Gordon Mary—†	41	clerk	20	

11

Page.	Letter.	Full Name.	Residence, Jan. 1, 1941.	Occupation.	Supposed Age.	Reported Residence, Jan. 1, 1940. Street and Number.

Ellis Street

	D	Fowler Evelyn—†	1	housewife	22	74 Fulda
	E	Fowler Oscar	1	machinist	22	74 "
	F	Grabowski Edmund	1	chauffeur	23	27 Oakburn av
	G	Nugent Esther M—†	1	teacher	21	here
	H	Nugent Florenz J	1	usher	23	"
	K	Nugent Mary V—†	1	housewife	56	"
	L	Nugent Ruth E—†	1	shoeworker	31	"
	M	Nugent William B	1	custodian	57	"
	N	Nash Frederick	9	chauffeur	26	195 Vermont
	O	Savage Elizabeth A—†	9	housewife	24	51 Beech Glen
	P	Savage Joseph F	9	welder	26	51 "
	R	Shillady Elizabeth—†	9	bookkeeper	55	here
	S	Shillady Grace—†	9	housekeeper	43	"
	T	Shillady Joseph	9	janitor	53	"
	U	Shillady Mabel—†	9	bookkeeper	48	"

Elmore Street

	V	Cadigan Ella A—†	12	housewife	42	here
	W	Cadigan James	12	salesman	36	"
	X	Leahy Alice I—†	12	operator	29	"
	Y	Murphy Donald	12	machinist	22	"
	Z	Brennan James J	12	painter	65	

318

	A	Brennan James J	12	salesman	32	"
	B	Brennan Margaret—†	12	housewife	61	"
	C	Hogan Madeline—†	12	"	26	
	D	Hogan Richard	12	longshoreman	26	"
	E	McDonnough John	12	"	44	
	F	McDonnough Lucy—†	12	housewife	78	"
	H	Gillis Agnes—†	14	silk winder	20	2 Circuit sq
	K	Gillis Alexander	14	laborer	55	2 "
	L	Gillis Alexander, jr	14	clerk	22	2 "
	M	Gillis James	14	operator	24	2 '
	N	Gillis Joseph	14	laborer	27	2 "
	O	Gillis William	14	porter	26	2 "
	P	Giordano Anthony	14	woodworker	42	19 Oakland
	R	Giordano Lena—†	14	housewife	38	19 "
	S	Visconti Ursula—†	14	factoryhand	20	19 "
	T	Looney Anna—†	16	clerk	26	here
	U	Looney Helen T—†	16	teacher	21	"

12

Elmore Street—Continued

v	Looney Joseph P	16	clerk	28	here
w	Looney Nora T—†	16	housewife	55	"
x	Young Edward	16	clerk	29	"
y	Young Florence—†	16	housewife	29	"
z	Keohane Jeremiah J	16	laborer	53	
	319				
a	Keohane Mary M—†	16	housewife	53	"
b	Mitchell Anna T—†	18	"	48	
c	Mitchell Martin J	18	repairman	52	"
e	Salisbury Leo	18	factoryhand	24	"
f	Salisbury Loretta—†	18	"	22	
g	Daley Catherine A—†	20	housewife	52	"
h	Reddish Margaret—†	20	"	23	
k	Archilles Anna—†	20	laundryworker	34	"
m	Archilles Francis	20	teamster	46	"
l	*Archilles Priscilla—†	20	housewife	80	"
n	Archilles William	20	metalworker	40	"
o	Reid Bessie—†	20	saleswoman	55	"
p	Kilroy Mary A—†	20	housewife	39	"
r	Kilroy Thomas	20	electrician	42	"
t	Cunneen John	22	clerk	42	
u	McHale Edward	22	"	50	
v	McHale Edward T	22	"	27	
w	McHale Marion—†	22	housewife	49	"
x	McHale Paul	22	clerk	23	

Fort Avenue

y	Philbin Anna M—†	4	housekeeper	71	here
z	Wilson Charles H	4	retired	61	"
	320				
a	Wilson Ernest	4	clerk	22	
b	Wilson George C	4	"	27	
c	Wilson Marion E—†	4	saleswoman	29	"
d	Lass Richard	4	watchman	62	"
e	Lass Sinaida—†	4	housewife	40	"
f	Manley Mary L—†	6	"	24	3 Thornton
g	Manley Raymond F	6	merchant	25	3 "
h	Roe Marion—†	6	housewife	40	here
k	Roe William	6	engineer	41	"
l	Larkin Joseph C	6	guard	41	"

M	Larkin Mary G—†	6	housewife	36	here
N	Arnott Emily—†	8	"	40	"
O	Arnott Howard	8	shipper	37	"
P	Ellsworth Josephine—†	8	housewife	29	"
R	Ellsworth Stephen	8	chauffeur	33	"
S	Genereux Harrison E	8	laborer	47	
T	Genereux Marguerite—†	8	housewife	40	"
U	Whelen Irene—†	10	"	21	12 Kingsbury
V	Whelen William	10	splicer	22	12 "
W	Finnell Alfreda—†	10	housewife	47	48 Ottawa
X	Finnell James	10	laborer	20	48 "
Y	McPhee Annie M—†	10	housewife	52	here
Z	McPhee James A	10	electrician	52	"
	321				
A	McPhee William J	10	cook	24	

Galena Street

C	*Kirkell Anthony	2	oiler	49	26 Bower
D	*Kirkell Nellie—†	2	housewife	49	26 "
E	Noyes Benjamin	2	clerk	23	26 "
F	Shaknites Adele—†	2	secretary	26	here
G	Shaknites Amelia—†	2	inspector	21	"
H	Shaknites Charles	2	foreman	53	"
K	Shaknites Sophie—†	2	forewoman	29	"
L	Shaknites Veronica—†	2	housewife	53	"
M	Vaughan Emily—†	4	housekeeper	28	4 Prentiss pl
N	Carney Helen—†	4	housewife	29	here
O	Carney Joseph	4	ironworker	29	"
P	Moran Mary—†	4	housekeeper	55	"
S	*Grant Rose—†	6	housewife	44	18 Elmore
T	McManus Anna M—†	6	"	26	here
U	McManus Robert D	6	waiter	28	"
V	Work Ellen L—†	6	housewife	44	"
W	Work Robert	6	attendant	48	"
X	Campbell Clarice—†	8	housewife	37	"
Y	Campbell Roy	8	leatherworker	39	"
Z	Foye Charles	8	machinist	44	"
	322				
A	Foye Marie—†	8	housewife	35	"
B	Davis Charles	8	foreman	46	

Galena Street—Continued

c	Davis Jessie—†	8	housewife	43	here
d	Davis Marjorie—†	8	clerk	20	"
e	Champagne Arthur	10	carpenter	47	"
f	Champagne Gladys—†	10	housewife	34	"
h	Gayton Lillian—†	10	housekeeper	36	"
k	Gayton Thomas	10	boilermaker	41	"
l	White Annie—†	12	housewife	56	14 Elmore
m	White Leslie	12	rigger	50	14 "
n	White William	12	U S A	20	14 "
o	Kelly Margaret—†	12	housewife	48	here
p	Kelly Richard	12	laborer	48	"
r	O'Brien Bernard A	12	"	45	"
s	O'Brien Marie—†	12	housewife	42	"
t	Corrigan Helen V—†	14	operator	38	
u	Corrigan Margaret A—†	14	housewife	60	"
v	Corrigan Phillip H	14	roofer .	62	
w	Meade Patrick E	14	retired	83	
x	Callahan Mabel—†	14	housewife	32	"
y	Callahan William	14	chauffeur	34	"
z	Myers Mary A—†	14	housewife	42	"
	323				
a	Myers Mary E—†	14	secretary	20	"
b	Myers William P	14	caretaker	48	"
c	Cassidy John	16	laborer	26	
d	Cassidy Ruth—†	16	housewife	22	"
e	Eriksen Alfred	16	packer	70	
f	Tower Mary—†	16	housekeeper	59	"
g	Curley Catherine R—†	16	cook	35	"
h	Curley Thomas J	16	shipper	32	

Hawthorne Street

m	Kenney John	12	plasterer	33	here
n	Kenney Laura—†	12	housewife	34	"
o	Duffey Annie—†	16	"	75	"
p	Wilson Percy ·	16	engraver	47	"
r	Hynes Francis	16	laborer	23	
s	Hynes Margaret—†	16	clerk	27	
t	Hynes Mary—†	16	"	25	
u	Hynes Michael	16	laborer	60	
v	Kenney Peter F	16	"	62	

15

Hawthorne Street—Continued

w	Tint Jacob	16	retired	70	here
x	Tint Regina—†	16	clerk	31	"
y	Whittaker Eileen G—†	18	bookkeeper	35	"
z	Whittaker Geraldine T—†	18	typist	27	"..

324

a	Whittaker Ida C—†	18	buyer	29	
b	Whittaker James	18	retired	71	
c	Whittaker Kevin D	18	manager	38	"
d	Whittaker Mary J—†	18	housewife	66	"
e	Whittaker Una P—†	18	secretary	40	"
f	Ruggles Hazel W--†	20	teacher	49	"
g	*Elliot Sadie—†	24	inspector	39	26 Hawthorne
h	Stammer Ralph	24	engraver	48	26 "
k	*Kerkell Anna—†	24	housewife	44	here
l	White Charlena—†	24	"	20	45 Linwood
m	White James	24	electrician	21	45 "
n	Defino Anthony	25	clerk	32	here
o	Defino Camilla—†	25	"	22	"
p	Defino George	25	carpenter	66	"
r	Defino Immaculata—†	25	dressmaker	20	"
s	McManus Thomas J	25	laborer	28	6 Waverly
t	McManus Yolanda—†	25	housewife	27	6 "
u	*Julius Irene—†	26	"	38	237 Highland
v	Julius Joseph C	26	painter	44	237 "
w	Cahill Viola—†	26	housewife	31	here
x	*Cahill William	26	painter	34	"
y	*Rice Jane—†	26	housewife	37	5 Codman pk
z	*Rice John	26	fisherman	43	5 "

325

a	Merten Agnes—†	28	housewife	31	here
b	*Merten Anna—†	28	"	65	"
c	Merten John W	28	clerk	37	"
d	Kirby Charles J	28	foreman	66	"
e	Kirby Delia C—†	28	housewife	68	"
f	Hayes James	29	fisherman	38	"
g	Hayes Marguerita—†	29	housewife	33	"
h	Londergan Pauline A—†	29	"	34	
k	Londergan Thomas F	29	policeman	38	"
l	Amoling Louise—†	30	laundress	52	"
m	*Stabers John	30	steelworker	29	"
n	Stabers Wallia--†	30	housewife	22	"

Page.	Letter.	FULL NAME.	Residence, Jan. 1, 1941.	Occupation.	Supposed Age.	Reported Residence, Jan. 1, 1940. Street and Number.

Hawthorne Street—Continued

o	Adams John J	30	constable	33	12 Kensington
p	Adams Mary T—†	30	housewife	33	12 "
r	Anderson Ella—†	30	"	32	here
s	Anderson Nils	30	engineer	43	"
t	Geidan Mary L—†	30	housekeeper	62	"
u	McLean George	rear 31	chauffeur	31	"
v	McLean Lillian—†	" 31	housewife	31	"
w	Fioretti Armando	32	rubberworker	39	"
x	Fioretti Lena—†	32	housewife	37	"
y	*Yark Abbie—†	32	"	33	
z	Yark Cristoff	32	brewer	62	

326

a	Long Agnes E—†	32	shoeworker	52	"
b	Long Alice—†	32	"	50	"
c	Murray James	33	clerk	21	19 Centre
d	Murray Mary—†	33	housekeeper	49	19 "
e	Burns Alice—†	33	at home	76	here
f	McPhee Josephine—†	33	housekeeper	79	"
g	Tirrell A Gertrude—†	33	clerk	37	"
h	Tirrell Mary E—†	33	seamstress	41	"
k	Connors Edward	35	steamfitter	35	"
l	Connors Irene—†	35	housewife	33	"
m	*Larkin Clara—†	35	clerk	37	Canada
n	*Murphy Catherine—†	35	housewife	43	here
o	Murphy John	35	fireman	43	"
p	*Avedisian Avedis	35	barber	47	64 Circuit
r	Avedisian Edna—†	35	stitcher	44	64 "
s	Montgomery Edna—†	36	housewife	44	here
t	Montgomery John J	36	carpenter	54	"
u	*McDonald Irene—†	36	clerk	39	"
v	*Moroney Georgianna—†	36	housewife	34	"
w	Moroney James D	36	letter carrier	36	"
x	Lally Ethel M—†	36	housewife	33	"
y	Lally Thomas	36	salesman	38	"
z	Bertoli Joseph	41	fireman	41	

327

a	Murray Catherine—†	41	housewife	78	"
b	Murray Catherine C—†	41	clerk	40	
c	Murray Eugene	41	laborer	35	"
d	Hucksam Emma R—†	51	housewife	65	"
e	Hucksam Francis W	51	retired	61	

11—3

17

Hawthorne Street—Continued

	F	McIntyre Peter	51	retired	69	here
	G	McIntyre Rose—†	51	manager	56	"
	H	Zengraft Bella—†	51	housekeeper	38	"

Highland Park

	K	Clarke Albert B	1	electrician	34	here
	L	Clarke Eldora—†	1	housekeeper	29	"
	M	Clarke Helen F—†	1	teacher	29	"
	N	Clarke Mary E—†	1	"	34	"
	O	Clarke Sarah M—†	1	at home	68	"
	P	Mulloney Arthur W	2	librarian	26	"
	R	Mulloney Catherine—†	2	housewife	58	"
	S	Mulloney Kathryn G—†	2	clerk	24	
	T	Mulloney William J	2	librarian	67	
	U	Mulloney William J, jr	2	clerk	23	
	V	Concannon Catherine—†	3	housewife	43	"
	W	Concannon John	3	mechanic	53	"
	X	Concannon John, jr	3	clerk	21	
	Z	Potter Herbert M	3	retired	71	"
	Y	Potter Mary A—†	3	housewife	74	"

328

	A	*Bigot Louis	4	retired	65	"
	B	Walsh David	4	porter	36	76 Chandler
	C	*Walsh Mary—†	4	housewife	33	188 Beacon
	D	Wardzala Amelia—†	4½	waitress	24	here
	E	Wardzala Mary—†	4½	housewife	47	"
	F	Wardzala William	4½	cook	48	"
	G	Baier Aloyse	5	wool sorter	38	"
	H	Baier Paulette—†	5	housewife	38	"
	K	McNulty Joseph	5	clerk	31	
	L	McNulty Valerie—†	5	waitress	28	
	M	Methison John	6	weaver	49	..
	N	Moran Ethel—†	6	clerk	22	
	O	Moran John	6	stonecutter	50	"
	P	Moran Minnie—†	6	housewife	46	"

Highland Street

	R	Kaskiw Anna—†	74	housewife	56	here
	S	Kaskiw Maria—†	74	student	23	"

Highland Street—Continued

Page.	Letter.	Full Name.	Residence, Jan. 1, 1941.	Occupation.	Supposed Age.	Reported Residence, Jan. 1, 1940. Street and Number.
	T	Kaskiw Vladimir A	74	clergyman	60	here
	U	Dolan Annie—†	74	housewife	57	"
	V	Dolan Charlotte—†	74	stenographer	23	"
	W	Dolan John	74	letter carrier	53	"
	X	Craffey Bridget—†	76	housewife	70	"
	Y	Craffey John	76	clerk	38	
	Z	Craffey Lawrence	76	"	27	
329						
	A	Craffey Martin	76	shipper	25	
	B	Craffey Thomas	76	retired	72	
	C	Craffey William	76	salesman	20	"
	D	Hughes Catherine—†	76	housewife	36	"
	E	Hughes Edward	76	chauffeur	36	"
	F	Hayes Dennis R	82	"	24	
	G	Hayes Jane V—†	82	saleswoman	22	"
	H	Hayes John J	82	laborer	50	
	K	Hayes John J, jr	82	clerk	26	
	L	Hayes Joseph L	82	"	21	
	M	Hayes Mary J—†	82	housewife	48	"
	N	Kane Charles	82	repairman	30	"
	O	Armata Mary—†	84	housewife	29	92 Everett
	P	Armata William B	84	shoeworker	35	92 "
	R	DelSette Frances—†	84	housewife	27	99 "
	S	DelSette Talimico	84	shoeworker	33	99 "
	T	Shargabian Garabed	86	merchant	55	here
	U	*Shargabian Isabelle—†	86	housewife	44	"
	V	Campbell Mary—†	86	"	28	48 Minden
	W	Lauer William	86	laborer	39	6 Weston
	X	Yanulis Adam	86	chauffeur	25	48 Minden
330						
	A	Hanley Ida—†	108	housekeeper	41	14 Fenwick
	B	Marshman Martha J—†	108	"	48	here
	C	Michaels James A	108	policeman	45	"
	D	Marston Margaret—†	118	housewife	52	206 Highland
	E	Savioli Guy	118	laborer	50	here
	F	Savioli Nora—†	118	housewife	44	"
	G	Crosby Ann R—†	120	clerk	25	"
	H	Crosby Anna T—†	120	housewife	62	"
	K	Crosby Catherine M—†	120	secretary	30	"
	L	Crosby Eileen F—†	120	clerk	27	
	M	Crosby Michael J	120	meatcutter	65	"

Highland Street—Continued

N	Crosby Thomas	120	salesman	26	here
O	Walsh John	120	retired	64	"
P	Stewart Albert W	140	agent	64	"
R	Stewart Sadie L—†	140	housewife	54	"
S	Fornaro Anthony	140	barber	32	
T	Fornaro Josephine—†	140	housewife	50	"
U	Fornaro Marguerite—†	140	secretary	29	"
V	Buckley Margaret—†	140	housewife	71	193 Grampian way
W	Buckley William F	140	clerk	28	193 "
X	Bogosian Ardash J	140	chauffeur	31	here
Y	Bogosian Katherine L—†	140	housekeeper	31	"

331

B	Feran Mary E—†	151	housewife	54	"
C	Feran William C	151	machinist	55	"
D	Greene Henry J	151	retired	74	
E	Greene Mary—†	151	housewife	62	"
F	Remmes Ann—†	153	"	40	
G	Fitzgerald Edward	153	laborer	51	
H	Fitzgerald Gladys—†	153	housewife	39	"
K	*Aronson Harold	153	carpenter	52	"
L	*Aronson Lena—†	153	housewife	54	"
O	*McGowen John	158	laborer	62	
P	McGowen Samuel	158	operator	22	"
R	*McGowen Sarah—†	158	housewife	60	"
S	Martineau Aimee—†	158	"	31	
T	Martineau Ulderic	158	metalworker	35	"
U	Connors Charles G	158	laborer	44	
V	Connors Helen F—†	158	housewife	40	"
W	Brennan Mary M—†	160	waitress	28	89 Mountfort
X	Pompeo Ellen—†	160	housewife	28	89 "
Y	Pompeo Giovanni	160	musician	49	89 "
Z	Boehner M Hedwig—†	162	housewife	55	here

332

A	Boehner Mary M—†	162	clerk	25	
B	Boehner Roberta P—†	162	librarian	23	
C	Boehner Walter R	162	clerk	25	
D	Boehner William J	162	manager	55	
E	Boehner William J	162	teacher	27	
F	Boyle Helen F—†	165	housewife	47	"
G	Boyle Joseph M	165	salesman	50	
H	Boyle Rita L—†	165	nurse	21	

Highland Street—Continued

K	O'Neil Helen M—†	165	stenographer	23	here
L	O'Neil Martin	165	salesman	28	"
M	Allen Amy—†	165	housewife	44	"
N	Allen Bernard	165	laborer	21	"
O	Allen Harold	165	salesman	46	"
P	Reiss Anna C—†	174	housewife	41	"
R	Reiss Joseph P	174	accountant	52	"
S	Zentgraf Isabel—†	174	housewife	60	Milton

Kensington Street

T	*Haight Jessie—†	1	housewife	40	here
U	*Haight Julius	1	laborer	35	"
V	Cherry Margaret E—†	1	housewife	34	8 Ray
W	Cherry Michael	1	lineman	37	8 "
X	Connolly James J	1	plumber	47	here
Y	Connolly Mary—†	1	housewife	43	"
Z	Kent Mary—†	3	"	40	"

333

A	Kent Thomas	3	letter carrier	42	"
B	Sheehan Brendon	3	stenographer	20	29 Juniper
C	Sheehan Julia—†	3	housewife	47	29 "
D	Sheehan Michael J	3	laborer	50	29 "
E	*Price Dora—†	3	housewife	66	here
F	Price Esther—†	3	saleswoman	31	"
G	Price Louis	3	shipper	33	"
H	Price Meyer	3	clerk	25	
K	Carroll Bridie—†	5	housewife	48	"
L	Carroll John	5	carpenter	52	"
M	Applin Charles	5	inspector	44	7 Crestwood pk
N	Applin Charles	5	clerk	22	7 "
O	Applin Frank E	5	retired	69	7 "
P	Applin Grace A—†	5	housewife	70	7 "
R	Applin Harold	5	nurse	21	7 "
S	Allen Elizabeth—†	5	at home	60	Foxboro
T	Merritt Frederick	5	janitor	66	here
U	Merritt Margaret—†	5	housewife	58	"
V	Dubin Benjamin	7	clerk	40	"
W	Dubin Dorothy—†	7	housewife	38	"
X	Needleman Anna—†	7	"	66	
Y	McGonagle Frances—†	7	"	45	

Page.	Letter.	FULL NAME.	Residence, Jan. 1, 1941.	Occupation.	Supposed Age.	Reported Residence, Jan. 1, 1940. Street and Number.

Kensington Street—Continued

	z	McGonagle Frank	7	clerk	48	here
334						
	A	McGonagle James	7	laborer	22	
	B	McGonagle William L	7	operator	24	
	c	Schwartz Benjamin	7	cutter	39	
	D	Schwartz Charles	7	clerk	22	
	E	Schwartz Rebecca—†	7	housewife	39	"
	F	*Baker Celia—†	9	domestic	36	"
	G	Baker Leonard	9	agent	40	
	H	*McPhee Henry	9	laborer	39	
	K	*McPhee Sadie—†	9	housewife	40	"
	L	Casavant Clarence	9	laborer	39	
	M	Casavant Grace—†	9	housewife	38	"
	N	Thompson Jennie—†	9	housekeeper	42	"
	O	Hartnett Alice—†	11	housewife	44	"
	P	Hartnett James	11	superintendent	41	"
	R	*Eramian Daniel	11	tailor	55	
	s	Eramian Harry	11	cook	29	
	T	Eramian Michael	11	tailor	24	
	U	Eramian Souran	11	attendant	26	"
	V	*Eramian Susan—†	11	housewife	52	"
	W	Abelson Doris—†	11	bookkeeper	29	"
	X	Abelson Max	11	merchant	50	"
	Y	Abelson Ralph	11	"	25	
	z	Abelson Sarah—†	11	housewife	51	"
335						
	A	Fitzgerald Helen—†	13	domestic	43	"
	B	Fraser Roderick A	13	laborer	48	
	c	*Fraser Theresa—†	13	housewife	41	"
	D	Murphy Daniel J	13	manager	44	"
	E	Murphy Julia—†	13	housewife	35	"
	F	O'Connor Lillian—†	13	clerk	28	
	G	Walker Edward C	13	laborer	21	
	H	Walker Medea—†	13	housewife	51	"
	K	Walker William	13	chauffeur	52	"
	L	Walker William	13	laborer	22	
	M	Fay Agnes E—†	15	housewife	75	"
	N	Fay Bernard A	15	retired	72	
	P	Fay Bernard F	15	operator	32	
	R	Fay Esther G—†	15	housewife	51	"
	s	Fay Joseph J	15	bartender	57	"

Page.	Letter.	Full Name.	Residence, Jan. 1, 1941.	Occupation.	Supposed Age.	Reported Residence, Jan. 1, 1940. Street and Number.

Kensington Street—Continued

	T	Fay Mildred A—†	15	stenographer	24	here
	U	Cole Cyril	17	laborer	45	17 Circuit
	V	Cole Mary—†	17	housewife	43	17 "
	W	Brennan Alice T—†	17	"	62	here
	X	Brennan Michael	17	laborer	63	"
	Y	Coyle Patrick J	17	B F D	63	"
	Z	Glynn Eugene P	17	clerk	30	
336						
	A	Glynn Mary E—†	17	housewife	25	"

Kingsbury Street

	B	Clark James	4	laborer	50	here
	C	Clark Signe—†	4	housewife	47	"
	D	*McPhee Mary L—†	4	"	38	"
	E	*McPhee Peter A	4	operator	40	
	F	Davis Emma—†	4	housewife	40	"
	G	Lihzis Anna—†	4	"	72	"
	K	Petrie John	6	laborer	34	6 Linwood rd
	L	Petrie Margaret—†	6	housewife	31	6 "
	M	Cucinotto George	6	barber	44	here
	N	Cucinotto Stella—†	6	housewife	47	"
	O	Perry Rose—†	8	"	70	"
	P	Perry William	8	retired	71	
	R	Goddard Ivan	8	welder	27	
	S	Goddard Margaret—†	8	clerk	24	"
	T	Matheson Gertrude—†	8	housewife	44	2 Nawn
	U	Matheson John	8	freighthandler	43	2 "
	V	Harrington Daniel	10	barber	33	here
	W	Harrington Effie—†	10	housewife	29	"
	X	Sheehan Daniel	10	carpenter	61	"
	Y	Sheehan Helen—†	10	housewife	60	"
	Z	Corr Frank	10	shipfitter	22	"
337						
	A	Corr Margaret—†	10	housewife	56	"
	B	Corr Peter	10	carpenter	64	"
	C	Greenlaw Mildred—†	12	housewife	23	2930 Wash'n
	D	Greenlaw Percy	12	rigger	32	2930 "
	E	Manning Delia—†	12	housewife	42	here
	F	Manning William J	12	laborer	40	"
	G	Flagg Frank	12	"	54	16½ Lakeside av

Kingsbury Street—Continued

H	Flagg Mary—†	12	housewife	51	16½ Lakeside av
K	Carpluk Mary—†	14	housekeeper	38	here
L	Zaiatz John	14	laborer	21	"
M	Fleming Mary—†	14	housewife	34	"
N	Fleming William	14	laborer	44	"
O	Kemp Mary—†	14	housewife	43	26 Maywood
P	Kemp William	14	watchman	43	26 "
S	Morrison Edna—†	16	housewife	28	Somerville
T	Morrison John	16	salesman	34	"
U	McInnis Isabel—†	16	housewife	42	13 Rockville pl
V	Marquis Anne—†	16	"	22	here
W	Marquis Edward	16	shipper	28	"
X	Davis Bessie—†	17	housewife	25	"
Y	Davis Myer	17	merchant	30	"
Z	Hirshberg Esther—†	17	housekeeper	28	"

338

A	Hirshberg Gertrude—†	17	housewife	59	"
B	Brown Kenneth	17	clerk	24	50A Sherman
C	McPhee Catherine—†	17	housewife	46	here
D	McPhee Joseph	17	carpenter	46	50A Sherman
E	Hughes John	18	operator	33	here
F	Hughes Olive—†	18	housewife	37	"
G	Phillips Barbara L—†	18	nurse	26	"
H	Phillips Herbert J	18	porter	59	
K	Phillips Minnie—†	18	housewife	57	"
L	Phillips Sylvia B—†	18	nurse	22	
M	Lapsley Gladys—†	18	housewife	31	"
N	Lapsley John	18	porter	35	
O	Crowell Charles F	21	laborer	67	
P	Peters Mary—†	21	housewife	72	"
R	Petraitis Albert	21	clerk	22	
S	Petraitis John	21	machinist	49	"
T	Petraitis Rose—†	21	housewife	48	"
U	Costello John F	21	retired	69	
V	Costello Margaret—†	21	housewife	63	"
W	Costello Mary—†	21	clerk	24	
X	Costello Peter	21	chauffeur	21	"
Y	Cunningham Edward	25	laborer	21	
Z	Cunningham Harriett—†	25	housewife	22	"

339

A	Cunningham James	25	projectionist	26	"

Kingsbury Street—Continued

B	*Gerus Adella—†	25	housewife	48	here
c	*Gerus Ignatius	25	laborer	53	"
D	Wegeler Adelle—†	25	housewife	52	"
E	Wegeler George	25	steamfitter	48	"
F	Wegeler Geraldine—†	25	inspector	21	"
G	Devlin Mary—†	29	housewife	66	"
H	Devlin Richard	29	chef	68	
K	Dillon Charles	29	clerk	26	
L	Dillon John	29	printer	24	
M	Dillon Mary—†	29	housewife	59	"
N	Dillon Mary—†.	29	operator	21	
O	Dillon William	29	janitor	70	
P	Leonard Catherine—†	29	housewife	57	"
R	Leonard James E	29	shipper	28	
S	Leonard Joseph	29	printer	23	
T	Leonard Mary H—†	29	saleswoman	27	"
U	Lynn Mary—†	29	domestic	56	"
V	Auerbach Helen—†	33	stenographer	30	"
W	Searle Maurice—†	33	manager	26	..
X	Selipsky Albert	33	agent	55	
Y	Selipsky Ann—†	33	housekeeper	21	"
Z	Selipsky Deborah—†	33	housewife	55	"

340

A	Selipsky Sophie—†	33	bookkeeper	28	"
B	Duffy Nellie—†	33	housekeeper	64	"
C	Theide Edna—†	33	housewife	36	"
D	Theide Francis	33	chauffeur	32	"

Lambert Avenue

F	Ahlgren Augustus J	63	retired	71	here
G	Ahlgren Charles A	63	shipper	35	"
H	Flannery Mary A—†	63	housewife	69	"
K	Kelly Catherine—†	63	at home	65	
L	Kelly Julia—†	63	housekeeper	68	"
N	Bobbin Mary—†	65	"	64	
O	Wasieluski Josephine—†	65	"	33	
P	Wasieluski Julia—†	65	at home	70	
R	Wasieluski Matthew J	65	mechanic	49	"
S	King Albert	65	shipper	45	"
T	King Helen—†	65	housewife	42	"

Lambert Avenue—Continued

u	King Josephine—†	65	clerk	20	here
v	Townsend Frank G	65	leatherworker	54	"
w	Townsend Genevieve—†	65	housewife	52	"
x	Townsend Ralph	65	student	24	
y	Townsend Robert G	65	leatherworker	22	"
z	Anderson Frank	67	machinist	63	"

341

a	Anderson Jane B—†	67	housewife	54	"
b	Root Barbara B—†	67	student	23	
c	Root Ida B—†	67	housewife	64	"
d	Root Marcia E—†	67	clerk	27	

Oakland Street

k	DiMarino Leo	4	laborer	47	here
l	*DiMarino Tranquilla—†	4	housewife	50	"
m	Runci Gertrude—†	6	"	35	"
n	Runci Nunzio	6	roofer	33	"
p	Parsons Elizabeth B—†	8	clerk	20	46 Guild
r	Parson Elizabeth E—†	8	housewife	44	46 "
s	Parson John C	8	mechanic	41	46 "
t	Forte Charles	10	barber	46	here
u	Forte Dorina—†	10	housewife	40	"
v	Crowley Catherine—†	10	housekeeper	69	1 Juniper
w	Drury Annie—†	10	"	54	1 "
x	Guitard Marie—†	10	housewife	25	1 "
y	Guitard Roland	10	painter	30	1 "
z	Jackson Catherine—†	12	laundress	23	here

342

a	Jackson Margaret—†	12	housewife	44	"
b	Jackson Victor	12	janitor	46	
c	Joyce Mary K—†	12	housewife	45	"
d	Joyce Patrick J	12	paver	47	"
e	Lavoie Charles	14	carpenter	26	Lawrence
f	*Lavoie Lucille—†	14	housewife	21	"
g	McPherson John	16	salesman	38	47 Rutland sq
h	McPherson Sadie—†	16	housewife	31	47 "
k	Souther Helen—†	18	clerk	32	7 Codman Hill
l	Souther William	18	laborer	40	7 "

Oakland Street—Continued

M	Fasulo Giovanni	18	finisher	55	here
N	*Fasulo Mary—†	18	housewife	32	"
O	Simms Alexander	20	shipper	34	181 Highland
P	Simms Elizabeth M—†	20	housewife	27	181 "
R	Simms John C	20	laborer	56	181 "
S	Wade Gertrude —†	20	housewife	44	here
T	Wade Roland R	20	machinist	44	"
U	Powers Herbert J	22	laborer	23	312 Dudley
V	Powers Nora T—†	22	housewife	50	312 "

Thornton Street

W	Newman Elsie H—†	75	secretary	59	here
X	Slocum Clara N—†	75	housewife	64	"
Y	McCorkle Beulah—†	81	"	40	700 Tremont
Z	McCorkle Charles	81	welder	42	700 "
	343				
A	McCorkle Mildred—†	81	domestic	37	Ohio
B	Stanley Arthur	81	polisher	60	here
C	Vaughn Louise—†	81	housekeeper	44	"
D	*Vaughn Margaret—†	81	at home	85	"
F	Eckman Elsie—†	rear 83	supervisor	41	"
G	Eckman Julia—†	" 83	housewife	71	"
H	Berchowski Alexander	85	baker	28	
K	Cheswick Frank	85	salesman	32	"
L	Filipowicz Anna—†	85	housewife	42	"
M	Filipowicz Peter	85	carpenter	55	"
N	Griffin Charles F	85	shipper	20	"
O	Griffin Esther—†	85	housewife	26	"
P	Gwaia Adam	85	butcher	36	
R	Dooley Edward F	91	clerk	20	
S	Dooley Grace E—†	91	housewife	42	"
T	Dooley James L	91	policeman	46	"
U	Jumpre Agnes L—†	rear 93	stenographer	24	"
V	Jumpre Charles S	" 93	steamfitter	44	"
W	Jumpre Devina M—†	" 93	housewife	45	"
X	Lynch Marie—†	96	"	38	12 School
Y	*Carroll Mildred—†	96	"	42	here
Z	Annis Ethel—†	98		40	65 Marcella

27

344
Thornton Street—Continued

A	Annis George	98	welder	42	65 Marcella
B	Hobbs Alice—†	102	at home	64	here
C	Hobbs Edith—†	102	"	·69	"
D	Malenfort Alice G—†	108	housewife	52	"
E	Malenfort Joseph E	108	counterman	47	"
F	Range Hans	108	cook	24	2 Putnam pl
G	Bennett Ermada—†	110	housewife	23	644 Hyde Park av
H	Bennett Raymond	110	musician	27	644 "
K	Carrazza Nicholas	110	cobbler	48	here
L	Carrazza Theresa—†	110	housewife	37	"
M	Silvey Annie—†	112	"	46	"
N	Silvey Robert	112	shipper	20	
O	Silvey Thomas	112	laborer	23	
P	Campbell Cora H—†	112	housekeeper	49	"
S	McGovern Mary A—†	114	at home	69	"
T	Pender Mary E—†	114	housewife	47	"
U	Pender William	114	laborer	46	
V	Brunetto Harriett—†	116	housewife	36	"
W	Brunetto Joseph	116	boilermaker	45	"
X	Grogan Elizabeth—†	116	laundress	21	74 Marcella
Y	Grogan William J	116	laborer	21	252 Dudley
Z	Lazott Helen—†	116	housewife	41	74 Marcella

345

A	Lazott Ralph	116	roofer	49	74 "
B	Colveas Mildred—†	120	clerk	20	307 Lamartine
C*| Kanes Catina—†	120	housewife	47	307 "
D	Kanes Charles	120	chef	50	307 "
G	Bondell Ellen—†	120	housewife	30	3 Walnut av
H	Bondell John	120	clerk	30	3 "
E	Cody Augustine	120	assembler	26	here
F	Cody Catherine—†	120	housewife	30	"
K	Lippi Angelo	126	manager	54	"
L	Lippi Elizabeth—†	126	housewife	59	"
M	Lippi Lola L—†	126	stenographer	27	"
N	Piotrowski Eva—†	126	housewife	29	"
O	Piotrowski Paul	126	baker	30	"
P	Smith Arthur T	132	chauffeur	40	"
R	Smith Jane E—†	132	housewife	31	"
U	Nestor Edward J	140	salesman	37	
V	Nestor Edwin	140	repairman	66	"

28

Page.	Letter.	FULL NAME.	Residence, Jan. 1, 1941.	Occupation.	Supposed Age.	Reported Residence, Jan. 1, 1940. Street and Number.

Thornton Street—Continued

	w	Nestor Ellen T—†	140	student	20	here
	x	Nestor Margaret A—†	140	housewife	63	"
	y	Nestor Margaret—†	142	"	23	Somerville
	z	Nestor Stephen	142	clerk	24	"
346						
	b	Durgin Jeannette—†	152	housewife	24	7 Rollins ct
	c	Durgin Robert	152	mechanic	30	7 "
	d	Shaughnessy Harry	152	laborer.	50	here
	e	Shaughnessy Josephine—†	152	housewife	45	"
	f	Haley David A	154	painter	45	"
	g	Haley Eva—†	154	housewife	40	"
	h	Rush John J	154	plasterer	49	"
	k	Rush Lillian—†	154	waitress	21	
	l	Rush Martin	154	laborer	20	
	m	Rush Mary—†	154	housewife	46	"
	n	Rush Mary T—†	154	clerk	25	
	o	*Cummings Bridget—†	154	housewife	47	"
	p	Cummings Lawrence	154	operator	23	"
	r	Cummings Leo	154	longshoreman	48	"
	t	Moschos George	156	cook	44	276 Ruggles
	s	Moschos Velma—†	156	housewife	39	276 "
	u	Woods Ellen E—†	156	"	56	here
	v	Woods George A	156	clerk	20	"

Valentine Street

	x	Driscoll Catherine F—†	4	housewife	53	here
	y	Driscoll James D	4	B F D	48	"
	z	McGloin Cecelia—†	6	housewife	30	"
347						
	a	McGloin John J	6	chauffeur	34	"
	b	*MacFarlane Donald	6	roofer	36	
	c	*MacFarlane Mary—†	6	housewife	40	"
	d	Lynch Catherine—†	6	"	31	
	e	Lynch James	6	chauffeur	34	"
	f	*Black Fannie—†	8	housewife	40	46 Minden
	g	*Black Samuel	8	painter	36	46 "
	h	Monaghan Madeline—†	8	housewife	29	7 McBride
	k	Monaghan Maurice	8	laborer	34	7 "
	l	Fortin Bella—†	8	housewife	30	here
	m	Fortin George	8	ropemaker	41	"

Page	Letter	Full Name.	Residence, Jan. 1, 1941.	Occupation.	Supposed Age.	Reported Residence, Jan. 1, 1940. Street and Number.

Washington Street

	P	Haley Edward F	2717	laborer	58	2 Putnam pl
	R	Haley Mary J—†	2717	housewife	48	2 "
	S	Murphy Agnes M—†	2717	"	39	here
	T	Murphy William H	2717	salesman	38	"
	W	Capuzzo Evelyn—†	2727	housewife	33	6 Oakland
	X	Capuzzo George	2727	mechanic	26	here
	Y*	Capuzzo Jennie—†	2727	housewife	65	"
	Z	Capuzzo Luigi	2727	retired	67	"

348

	A	Capuzzo Peter	2727	finisher	43	6 Oakland
	B	Capuzzo William	2727	machinist	25	here
	C	Morris David H	2727	laborer	33	"
	D	Morris Edith—†	2727	bookkeeper	29	"
	E	Rez Rupert	2727	laborer	33	"
	F	VonEtte Agnes—†	2729	housewife	35	Salisbury
	G	VonEtte Robert C	2729	chauffeur	44	"
	H	Gabree Joseph	2729	laborer	31	here
	K	Gabrce Mildred—†	2929	housewife	31	"
	M	Burke Julia—†	2732	waitress	30	"
	N	Oliver James	2732	clerk	22	
	O	Oliver Madeline R—†	2732	"	32	
	P*	Oliver Mary—†	2732	housewife	58	"
	S	Tarquini Arthur	2737	baker	32	
	T	Tarquini Dorothy—†	2737	housewife	24	"
	U	Tarquini Inez—†	2737	factoryhand	26	"
	V	Tarquini Theresa—†	2737	clerk	24	
	W	Bryan Gertrude—†	2741	domestic	22	"
	X	Bryan Mildred—†	2741	housewife	40	"
	Y	Bryan William	2741	laborer	24	"
	Z	Mills Henry	2741	"	36	New York

349

	A	Register Ivy—†	2741	clerk	38	here
	B	Thompson Sarah—†	2741	domestic	52	30 Townsend
	D	Mitchell George	2742A	clerk	38	here
	E	Mitchell Veleda—†	2742A	housewife	34	"
	F*	Leonard Annie—†	2742A	"	53	"
	G	Leonard Stephen	2742A	laborer	28	
	H	Lynch Martin	2742A	carpenter	53	"
	K	Jones Alice E—†	2747	housewife	37	"
	L	Jones James H	2747	clerk	37	
	M	Turnage Alexander	2747	porter	52	

Washington Street—Continued

	N	Turnage Margaret—†	2747	housewife	53	here
	O	King Catherine—†	2751	"	44	5 Malbon pl
	P	King Russell T	2751	molder	49	5 "
	R	O'Rourke Edward	2751	laborer	42	here
	S	O'Rourke Francis	2751	"	39	"
	T	O'Rourke James P	2751	"	45	"
	U	Battalia Rosina—†	2754	housewife	46	"
	V	Spinellia Josephine—†	2754	"	40	
	W	Chancholo Alice—†	2754	"	52	
	X	Chancholo Anthony J	2754	painter	43	
	Y	Chancholo Edward	2754	candymaker	54	"
	Z	Chancholo Thomas J	2754	shipper	29	

350

		Chancholo William J	2754	weaver	23	
	A	Davis Alice—†	2754	operator	20	
	C	Foster Helen R—†	2754	housewife	67	"
	D	Mason Daniel F	2754	U S N	34	
	E	Mason Lawrence P	2754	laborer	26	
	F	Burke Charles	2756	clerk	27	
	G	Burke Edna—†	2756	secretary	33	"
	N	Burke Elizabeth—†	2746	housewife	60	"
	K	Burke James	2756	clerk	22	
	L	Burke William J	2756	"	62	
	M	Burke William J	2756	student	25	
	N	Buonagurio Frances—†	2756	"	20	"
	O	Kallas Arthur	2756	painter	27	16 Albion
	P	Kallas Dennis	2756	merchant	64	16 "
	R	Kondos Eva—†	2756	housewife	22	here
	T	Calloway Edward	2757	operator	42	"
	U	Calloway Jennie—†	2757	housewife	76	"
	V	Calloway John	2757	clerk	48	"
	W	Peay Douglas	2757	"	20	"
	X	Peay Moses	2757	cook	56	"
	Y	Peay Ophelia—†	2757	clerk	23	
	Z	Peay Rosa—†	2757	housewife	53	"

351

	B	Pomeroy Margaret—†	2761	"	23	
		Pomeroy Robert	2761	tree surgeon	27	"
	D	Zellner Alice—†	2761	housewife	44	"
	E	Zellner Dorothy—†	2761	factoryhand	23	"
	E	Zellner Harry	2761	chef	46	

Page	Letter	Full Name.	Residence, Jan. 1, 1941.	Occupation.	Supposed Age.	Reported Residence, Jan. 1, 1940. Street and Number.

Washington Street—Continued

	G	Hanson Agnes—†	2761	housewife	40	here
	H	Hanson John	2761	janitor	40	"
	K	Johnson Mary E—†	2761	housekeeper	80	"
	S	Cahill Johanna M—†	2773	housewife	43	13 Elmore
	T	*Messina Anne—†	2773	"	46	here
	U	Messina Oradio	2773	laborer	47	"
	V	*Gianelis Argro—†	2773	housewife	50	519Harris'nav
	W	Gianelis George	2773	carpenter	52	519 "
	Y	Coyle Mary J—†	2775	housewife	49	here
	Z	Coyle Robert	2775	riveter	45	"
352						
	A	Doyle Charles P	2775	longshoreman	48	"
	B	Doyle Grace A—†	2775	housewife	48	"
	E	Dee Joseph	2777	retired	55	Washington
	F	Dillon Francis	2777	clerk	23	here
	G	Dillon John	2777	carpenter	28	"
	H	Dillon Sarah—†	2777	housewife	53	"
	K	Carley Edith—†	2779	"	64	
	L	Kendall William	2779	chauffeur	32	"
	M	MacNeil Lawrence	2779	"	24	
	N	Moriarty William	2779	clerk	28	
	O	Santoro Frank	2779	merchant	30	"
	P	Santoro Melda—†	2779	housewife	30	"
	R	Smith John	2779	laborer	34	
	S	Werner John	2779	"	43	
	T	Drinkwater Elma—†	2781	housewife	38	"
	U	Drinkwater John	2781	carpenter	41	"
	V	Drinkwater William	2781	retired	89	"
	W	Philbrick Beulah—†	2787	housekeeper	72	35½ Taber
	X	Mahoney Jeremiah	2787	salesman	55	here
	Y	Mahoney Julia—†	2787	housewife	51	"
	Z	Mahoney Timothy	2787	laborer	24	"
353						
	A	Selby Frank C	2787	chauffeur	34	"
	B	Selby Margaret—†	2787	housewife	25	"
	C	Peterson Alma—†	2789	"	43	
	D	Peterson Arthur O	2789	painter	44	
	E	Peterson Ernest F	2789	laborer	23	
	F	Sharp Ada S—†	2789	housekeeper	63	"

Page.	Letter.	Full Name.	Residence, Jan. 1, 1941.	Occupation.	Supposed Age.	Reported Residence, Jan. 1, 1940. Street and Number.

Washington Street—Continued

	G	Fitzgerald William J	2789	carpenter	61	here
	H	O'Laughlin Alice—†	2789	housewife	47	"
	K	O'Laughlin John T	2789	timekeeper	46	"
	L	O'Laughlin Michael	2789	merchant	48	"
	M	Long Margaret D—†	2789	housewife	51	"
	N	Long Samuel R	2789	machinist	49	"

Ward 11–Precinct 4

CITY OF BOSTON

LIST OF RESIDENTS
20 YEARS OF AGE AND OVER

(NON-CITIZENS INDICATED BY ASTERISK)
(FEMALES INDICATED BY DAGGER)

AS OF

JANUARY 1, 1941

JOSEPH F. TIMILTY, *Chairman*
FREDERIC E. DOWLING, *Secretary*
WILLIAM A. MOTLEY, Jr.
FRANCIS B. McKINNEY
HILDA HEDSTROM QUIRK

Listing Board.

CITY OF BOSTON PRINTING DEPARTMENT

400

Ellis Street

	A	Ross Gordon	2	operator	43	here
	B	Ross Greta—†	2	housewife	40	"
	C	Bowers Bernard A	2	welder	47	"
	D	Bowers Marcella—†	2	housewife	42	"
	E	Lee Bridget T—†	2	"	66	
	F	Lee Mary A—†	2	boxmaker	40	"
	G	McDougall Arthur	2	laborer	40	
	H	Sprague Charles	2	painter	48	
	K	Sprague Margaret—†	2	housekeeper	55	"
	L	McNamara Annie V—†	4	housewife	69	"
	M	McNamara Joseph	4	adjuster	43	
	N	Kamp Alphonse	4	salesman	40	
	O	Kamp Margaret—†	4	teacher	40	
	P	Kamp Theresa—†	4	at home	87	
	R	Cullinane Edward J	4	fireman	37	"
	S	Cullinane Julia M—†	4	housewife	38	"
	T	DeViller Arthur L		watchman	66	"
	U	Germain Mildred—†		housewife	68	"
	V	Germain Thomas R		retired	68	
	W	Murphy Georgine A—†		housewife	44	"
	X	Murphy William F		inspector	46	"
	Y	Germain Clarence R		mechanic	42	"
	Z	Germain Lauretta—†	6	clerk	40	

401

	A	Albrecht Amelia—†	10	at home	74	
	B	Alger Catherine J—†	10	matron	35	
	C	Berlo Catherine M—†	10	teacher	50	"
	D	Bernhardt Catherine M—†	10	sacristan	56	"
	E	Cameron Mary A—†	10	portress	40	"
	F	Christ Laura C—†	10	teacher	56	
	G	*Fischhaber Magdaline—†	10	"	36	
	H	Forrester Grace M—†	10	"	26	
	K	Hogan Anna M—†	10	"	29	
	L	Jerolymack Catherine—†	10	"	67	
	M	Jerolymack Margaret—†	10	"	29	
	N	*Lindenmayer Walburga—†	10	cook	40	
	O	Quinn Bridget M—†	10	laundress	62	"
	P	Schoenwald Catherine M—†	10	teacher	49	
	R	Voelker Mary—†	10	"	49	
	S	Weisser Gertrude—†	10	"	31	

Page	Letter	FULL NAME.	Residence, Jan. 1, 1941.	Occupation.	Supposed Age.	Reported Residence, Jan. 1, 1940. Street and Number.

Elmore Street

	Letter	FULL NAME.	Res.	Occupation.	Age	Residence
	T	McCarthy Francis	4	laborer	39	here
	U	McCarthy Frederick J	4	"	31	"
	V	McCarthy Justin	4	retired	67	"
	W	McCarthy Justin	4	clerk	35	
	X	*Hannigan Daniel	4	shoeworker	42	"
	Y	O'Brion Agnes—†	4	housewife	25	"
	Z	O'Brion John J	4	clerk	28	
402						
	A	Cotter Mary—†	6	housewife	70	"
	B	Cotter Patrick	6	retired	80	
	D	Nichols Edith M—†	8	housewife	28	"
	E	Nichols William J	8	chauffeur	28	"
	F	Bopp Charles W	8	U S A	24	
	G	Bopp Elizabeth G—†	8	housewife	54	"
	H	Bopp Emil J	8	foreman	54	
	K	Bopp Geraldine E—†	8	clerk	31	
	L	Bopp Helen—†	8	operator	23	"
	M	Bopp Jeanette G—†	8	clerk	32	
	N	Bopp Joseph E	8	"	26	
	O	Bopp Victoria—†	8	at home	87	
	P	Collins Fred B	10	chauffeur	52	"
	R	Collins John F	10	salesman	21	"
	S	Collins Margaret M—†	10	housewife	42	"
	T	Mellyn John	10	retired	70	"
	U	Mellyn Mary—†	10	housewife	50	"
	V	Mellyn Thomas	10	fireman	44	

Fulda Street

	Letter	FULL NAME.	Res.	Occupation.	Age	Residence
	W	Kimmel Frank A	12	painter	55	here
	X	Kimmel George	12	"	24	"
	Y	Kimmel Mary F—†	12	housekeeper	21	"
	Z	Kimmel Rose—†	12	housewife	47	"
403						
	A	Kimmel Rose M—†	12	clerk	22	
	B	*Blacksted Erling	16	laborer	37	
	C	*Blacksted Nancy—†	16	housewife	37	"
	D	Zengraft Joseph	16	laborer	53	
	E	Fitzgerald Mary E—†	16	stenographer	26	"
	F	Fitzgerald Mary M—†	16	housewife	55	"
	G	Fitzgerald Michael J	16	accountant	23	"

3

Page.	Letter.	FULL NAME.	Residence, Jan. 1, 1941.	Occupation.	Supposed Age.	Reported Residence, Jan. 1, 1940. Street and Number.

Fulda Street—Continued

	H	Krim George F	17	clerk	46	here
	K	Krim Mary—†	17	housewife	40	"
	L	Kranefuss Lena—†	17	housekeeper	75	"
	M	Swendeman Nat	17	mechanic	63	"
	N	Carey Anna M—†	18	housewife	36	"
	O	Carey John J	18	chauffeur	38	"
	P	Lohnes George A	18	clerk	42	
	R	Lohnes Theresa A—†	18	housewife	48	"
	S	Dhimos Arthur	18	merchant	40	"
	T	*Dhimos Eva—†	18	housewife	37	"
	U	Canisius Anna J—†	19	"	33	
	V	Canisius Joseph	19	baker	33	
	W	McLaughlin Charles H	19	salesman	55	
	X	McLaughlin Charles J	19	chauffeur	25	"
	Y	McLaughlin Francis C	19	machinist	23	"
	Z	McLaughlin Mary E—†	19	housewife	52	"

404

	A	Kohler Gertrude—†	19	"	52	
	B	Kohler Joseph	19	janitor	55	
	C	Keegan Ellen—†	20	housewife	21	"
	D	Keegan Ernest J	20	chauffeur	25	"
	E	Flanigan Mabel—†	20	housewife	37	"
	F	*Flanigan William E	20	brushworker	40	"
	G	Becker Joseph P	20	shoecutter	52	"
	H	Becker Nellie E—†	20	housewife	52	"
	K	Evelly John	23	watchman	42	52 Humphreys
	L	*Pitcher Eunice—†	23	housewife	30	here
	M	Pitcher Robert	23	painter	46	"
	N	Mullen James J	23	carpenter	29	"
	O	Mullen Margaret—†	23	housewife	60	"
	P	Mullen Patrick J	23	watchman	63	"
	R	Mullen Peter A	23	laborer	34	
	S	Kuhner Helen—†	23	bookbinder	36	"
	T	Kuhner John W	23	machinist	35	"
	V	Wehner Charles F	25	accountant	44	"
	X	Wehner Ann—†	25	secretary	36	"
	Y	Wehner Florian	25	retired	78	
	Z	Wehner Mary—†	25	housekeeper	36	"

405

	A	Connelly Mary B—†	26	"	59	121 Centre
	B	Lee Gerald F	26	laborer	23	121 "

Fulda Street—Continued

c	Lee Joseph	26	laborer	31	121 Centre
d	Kast Elizabeth—†	26	housewife	40	here
e	Kast John	26	machinist	55	"
f	Whelan Grace T—†	26	housewife	44	"
g	Whelan Thomas F	26	electrician	47	"
h	Troy Catherine—†	33	cook	40	
k	Kolf Marie—†	33	clerk	38	..
l	Kolf Peter	33	retired	73	
m	Pink Helen E—†	33	housewife	44	"
n	Pink John H	33	welder	21	
o	Pink John L	33	clerk	45	
p	Hohman Anna—†	35	stenographer	29	"
r	Hohman Gertrude M—†	35	"	23	..
s	Hohman Joseph	35	retired	67	
t	Mueller Victor	35	clerk	41	
u	Corkery Margaret—†	35	housewife	25	"
v	Corkery William	35	machinist	30	"
x	Laval Richard	41	laborer	25	38 Kent
y	Gately Ellen—†	41	housewife	32	here
z	Gately Richard	41	laborer	34	"
	406				
a	Plunkett Ethel—†	41	housewife	25	196 Green
b	Plunkett Leo M	41	clerk	30	196 "
c	Gavin Mary B—†	43	domestic	66	here
d	Ryan Joseph M	43	clerk	60	"
e	Ryan Mary C—†	43	housekeeper	68	"
f	Kraiggesman Hattie—†	43	"	68	63 Vale
g	Race Ernest C	43	chauffeur	54	63 "
h	Malloy Mary—†	43	housekeeper	48	here
k	McColgan Virginia—†	45	waitress	32	"
l	McColgan William	45	salesman	32	"
m	Burke Cornelius	45	clerk	45	
n	Smith Arline—†	45	housekeeper	25	"
o	*Hughes Dorothy—†	45	housewife	29	"
p	Hughes James E	45	laborer	39	
r	Hawley Charles	47	clerk	39	
s	Hawley Sophie—†	47	housewife	34	"
t	Sullivan James	47	laborer	35	
u	Sullivan Margaret—†	47	housewife	33	"
v	O'Brien James	47	laborer	54	
w	O'Brien Mary—†	47	housewife	54	"

Page.	Letter.	FULL NAME.	Residence, Jan. 1, 1941.	Occupation.	Supposed Age.	Reported Residence, Jan. 1, 1940. Street and Number.

Fulda Street—Continued

	x	Benner Margaret—†	49	housewife	26	67 Chadwick
	y	Benner William	49	clerk	27	67 "
	z	*Kirrane Margaret—†	49	housewife	34	here
407						
	a	Kirrane Peter	49	laborer	36	"
	b	Nunn Evelyn—†	49	housewife	24	568 Col av
	c	Nunn Lawrence	49	chauffeur	30	568 "
	f	Fowler Johanna—†	74	housekeeper	48	here
	g	Lavezzo Albert	76	cook	29	"
	h	Lavezzo Thelma—†	76	housewife	32	"
	k	*Leddy Joseph A	76	bricklayer	60	"
	l	Ryan Francis J	76	electrician	32	"
	m	Ryan Helena M—†	76	housewife	31	"
	n	Dolan Margaret F—†	78	laundress	21	96 Thornton
	o	Dolan Peter J	78	laborer	44	96 "
	p	Olsen Annie—†	78	housewife	59	here
	r	Olsen Martin	78	clerk	26	"
	s	Olsen Olaf	78	retired	71	"
	t	*Kingston Annie—†	78	housewife	49	"
	u	*Kingston Donald	78	chauffeur	20	"
	v	Dunbar Francis J	80	plumber	33	
	w	Dunbar Gertrude J—†	80	housewife	34	"
	y	Baier Elizabeth—†	80	housekeeper	40	"
	z	Baier Francis	80	packer	31	"
408						
	a	Baier Helen—†	80	clerk	27	
	b	Baier Valentine	80	retired	84	
	c	Doucette Mary—†	82	housekeeper	30	"
	d	Willis Caroline F—†	82	housewife	35	"
	e	Willis Henry	82	millwright	41	"
	f	Tobin Mary E—†	82	clerk	40	
	g	Tobin Mary T—†	82	housewife	70	"
	h	Tobin Richard M	82	machinist	38	"
	k	Paris Louise—†	83	housekeeper	47	"
	l	McGary Bernard P	83	chauffeur	42	"
	m	McGary Mary—†	83	housewife	39	"
	n	O'Connell Daniel E	83	chauffeur	40	"
	o	O'Connell Mary T—†	83	housewife	35	"
	p	Hennessey Elizabeth—†	85	"	21	
	r	Hennessey Thomas	85	bookbinder	25	"

Fulda Street—Continued

s	Dolan Joseph	85	clerk	25	here
T	Turner Thomas	85	laborer	45	"

Galena Street

v	Beal Frank	1	machinist	26	9 Chadwick
w	Beal Katherine—†	1	housewife	22	Brookline
Y	Horrigan John	3	clerk	50	here
x	Horrigan Mary—†	3	housewife	40	"
z	Dantas Edmund	3	baker	25	39 Blue Hill av
	409				
A	Dantas Marion—†	3	housewife	21	39 "
B	Collins Dorothy—†	5	"	24	62 Lambert av
c	Collins Thomas	5	laborer	25	62 "
D	Brooks Francis W	5	butcher	29	here
E	Brooks Mary—†	5	housewife	30	"
F	Brooks Michael	5	painter	60	"
G	Coffran Florence—†	7	housekeeper	62	"
H	Lake Mae—†	7	housewife	43	"
K	Lake Scholley	7	policeman	49	"
L	Carr Charles F	13	machinist	41	"
M	Crimmins Paul	13	clerk	44	
N	Lamprey Alfreda—†	13	housewife	40	"
o	Lamprey Arthur	13	pipefitter	43	"
P	*Chetwynd Catherine—†	13	housewife	64	"
R	Chetwynd Edith—†	13	saleswoman	29	"
s	Chetwynd James	13	laborer	21	
T	*Chetwynd Mitchell	13	janitor	72	"
U	Kinlin Edward J	15	clerk	50	
v	Kinlin Grace V—†	15	stenographer	21	"
w	Kinlin Stella—†	15	housewife	40	"
x	Hurley Anna—†	17	housekeeper	40	"
Y	Casey Fred W	17	seaman	39	..
z	Casey Margaret—†	17	housewife	29	"
	410				
A	Healey Catherine—†	17	housekeeper	37	"
B	Healey John J	17	retired	72	
c	Harley James W	17	porter	36	
D	Harley Rose—†	17	housewife	64	"
E	Cunningham Jane—†	19	"	39	
F	Cunningham Patrick	19	chauffeur	40	"

Galena Street—Continued

G	White George	19	clerk	43	here
H	Draper Anne M—†	19	housewife	54	"
K	Draper Christine M—†	19	saleswoman	24	"
L	Draper Evelyn—†	19	clerk	22	
M	Draper Frank E	19	retired	79	
N	Draper Frank W	19	attendant	21	"
O	Lucey Jessie—†	19	housewife	45	"
P	Lucey Michael	19	fireman	65	"
R	Baldasare Nicholas	21	salesman	25	"
S	Baldasare Rita—†	21	housewife	23	"
T	Austin Catherine—†	21	laundress	21	17 Elmore
U	Austin Grace—†	21	"	24	17 "
V	Connelly Anna—†	21	housewife	48	17 "
W	Connelly Henry F	21	ironworker	45	17 "
X	Megel John	21	student	21	here
Y	Megel Peter	21	baker	56	"
Z	Megel Theresa—†	21	housewife	57	"

411

A	Crosby Nina—†	23	"	58	6 Ripley rd
B	Crosby Samuel	23	painter	62	6 "
C	Kelley Henry	23	laborer	44	here
D	Kane Henry	23	fireman	55	"
E	Kane Mary R—†	23	saleswoman	21	"
F	Kane Rose—†	23	housewife	49	"
G	Chamberlain Jennie—†	25	"	60	
H	Chamberlain Millicent—†	25	clerk	25	"
K	Hall Arathusa—†	25	housewife	60	2837 Wash'n
L	Hall Charles	25	policeman	30	2837 "
M	Hall Harold	25	cleaner	28	2837 "
N	Miller Harriet E—†	25	saleswoman	50	2837 "
O	Sexton Delia—†	25	housewife	45	here
P	Sexton John	25	mechanic	50	"

Hawthorne Street

S	Keller Joseph A	46	clergyman	63	here

Highland Street

T	*Ingram Olive—†	188	housewife	39	here
U	Ingram Ralph	188	carpenter	39	"

Page.	Letter.	Full Name.	Residence, Jan. 1, 1941.	Occupation.	Supposed Age.	Reported Residence, Jan. 1, 1940. Street and Number.

Highland Street—Continued

	v	Scully George E	188	laborer	43	here
	w	Tagen Rose—†	188	housewife	68	"
	x	Donovan Catherine J—†	188	"	57	"
	y	Donovan Mary C—†	188	teacher	22	
	z	Donovan Michael F	188	letter carrier	61	"
412						
	a	Higgins Mary L—†	188	housekeeper	47	"
	b	Roche James M	190	engineer	30	68 Alpine
	c	Roche Phyllis—†	190	housewife	21	68 "
	d	Rettman Bertha E—†	190	"	33	here
	e	Rettman Henry C	190	mechanic	36	"
	f	Crowley Albert F	190	operator	42	23 Galena
	g	Crowley Caroline E—†	190	housewife	41	23 "
	h	Bernard Ann—†	192	"	54	here
	k	Bernard Ann J—†	192	clerk	21	"
	l	Bernard Joseph	192	carpenter	58	"
	m	Bernard Joseph	192	mechanic	27	"
	n	Sullivan Mary T—†	192	stenographer	20	"
	o	Sullivan Theresa C—†	192	housewife	54	..
	p	Becker Dorothy—†	192	student	21	
	r	Becker Emma—†	192	housewife	55	"
	s	Becker Godfrey	192	shoeworker	54	"
	t	Schmidt Henry	194	retired	85	
	u	Schmidt Mary E—†	194	housekeeper	52	"
	v	Vollmar Amelia H—†	194	housewife	56	"
	w	Vollmar Charles W	194	glasscutter	56	"
	x	Vollmar Paul F	194	mechanic	29	"
	y	Mitchell Catherine—†	194	waitress	50	
	z	Mitchell John	194	porter	42	
413						
	a	Mitchell Margaret—†	194	housewife	29	"
	b	Bischof Joseph	196	retired	72	"
	c	Bischof Justina H—†	196	housewife	70	"
	d	Gilman Eunice H—†	196	operator	26	
	e	Gilman Martha E—†	196	housewife	51	"
	f	Krebbs Marie—†	196	costumer	64	"
	g	MacFarlane Anna M—†	196	housewife	27	Braintree
	h	MacFarlane John	196	butcher	27	"
	k	Hession Delia—†	196	housewife	63	here
	l	Hession Henry J	196	clerk	23	"

9

Page	Letter	FULL NAME.	Residence, Jan. 1, 1941.	Occupation.	Supposed Age.	Reported Residence, Jan. 1, 1940. Street and Number.

Highland Street—Continued

M	Hession Thomas A	196	laborer	28	here
N	Hession William V	196	printer	28	"
o	*McHowell Anna—†	198	housewife	39	7 Fessenden
P	McHowell Charles	198	toolmaker	38	7 "
R	Yanulys Adam	198	laborer	24	48 Minden
s	Yanulys George	198	"	22	48 "
T	Yanulys Richard	198	mechanic	26	48 "
U	*Yanulys Victoria—†	198	housewife	50	48 "
v	Mueller John A	198	realtor	47	here
w	Mueller Marie A—†	198	housewife	46	"
x	Halpin Ann—†	200	housekeeper	68	"
Y	Halpin Arthur J	200	machinist	59	"
z	Winters Dorothy—†	200	housewife	32	"
	414				
A	Winters George	200	dyesetter	37	"
B	Dominick Rosa—†	200	housewife	20	10 Brinton
c	Dominick Vincent	200	mechanic	25	58 Codman pk
D	Sullivan Blanche—†	202	housewife	29	here
E	Sullivan Gordon	202	chauffeur	33	"
F	Fisher Beatrice—†	202	housewife	43	"
G	Fisher Richard	202	laborer	21	
H	Fisher William	202	machinist	43	"
K	Carr Margaret E—†	202	housekeeper	59	"
L	Wooding Lillian F—†	202	housewife	28	"
M	Wooding Royal W	202	mason	40	
N	Wooding Sadie I—†	202	housewife	58	"
o	McGillicuddy Jeremiah	204	porter	36	
P	McGillicuddy Mary—†	204	housewife	37	"
R	Kerr John A	204	polisher	27	
s	Kerr Mary A—†	204	housewife	52	"
T	Kerr William J	204	chauffeur	26	"
U	Archambeault Florida—†	204	housewife	45	112 W Concord
v	Perkins Abner	204	porter	21	112 "
w	Gocobbi Andrew J	206	mechanic	20	here
x	Gocobbi Dominic	206	doorman	49	"
Y	*Gocobbi Phillipa—†	206	housewife	46	"
z	Mahoney James	206	laborer	23	35 Marcella
	417				
A	Mahoney John	206	"	24	15 '
B	Mahoney Ruby—†	206	housewife	23	35 "

10

Highland Street—Continued

c	Horrigan Florence—†	206	housewife	29	30 Van Winkle
d	Horrigan Robert	206	artist	31	30 "
e	Pray Bessie—†	206	housewife	44	here
f	Pray Ralph	206	mechanic	40	"
g	*Conrod Earl	208	clerk	24	13 Highland av
h	*Conrod Lloyd	208	laborer	22	13 "
k	*Conrod Samuel	208	"	65	13 "
l	Kadlick James	208	clerk	22	here
m	Kadlick Mary—†	208	housewife	46	"
n	Kadlick Rita—†	208	cashier	20	"
o	Kadlick Stephen J	208	foreman	45	
p	Piaskowski Mildred—†	208	housewife	29	"
r	Sullivan Mary—†	208	housekeeper	52	"
s	O'Keefe Viola—†	210	housewife	30	"
t	*Murphy Anna—†	210	"	37	"
u	Murphy John	210	laborer	39	
v	McCafferty Catherine—†	210	housewife	45	"
w	McCafferty John J	210	steamfitter	45	"
y	Driscoll Alta—†	212	housewife	31	"
z	Driscoll Joseph	212	chauffeur	39	"
	416				
a	Kelley Sarah—†	212	housewife	40	"
b	McKenzie Francis	214	laborer	21	127 Millett
c	McKenzie Lela—†	214	housewife	40	127 "
d	McKenzie Stanley	214	electrician	42	127 "
e	McKenzie Vivian—†	214	clerk	20	127 "
f	Hogan Florence G—†	214	shipper	34	here
g	Hogan Muriel C—†	214	housewife	28	"
h	Lawler Ann—†	214	"	46	" ,
k	Lawler Walter G	214	manufacturer	53	"
l	Waidner Rita—†	214	waitress	35	
p	*Sweark Catherine—†	218	housewife	55	"
r	*Sweark Jacob	218	laborer	57	"
s	Woods Ruth—†	218	housewife	21	77 Marcella
t	Woods William J	218	teamster	22	156 Thornton
u	Benner Ellen—†	218	housewife	51	67 Chadwick
v	Estella Evelyn—†	226	"	38	here
w	Estella Robert	226	painter	43	"
x	Barr John I	226	bookkeeper	41	"
y	Barr Theresa M—†	226	housewife	41	"

Highland Street—Continued

z	Bray Ethel—†	226	housewife	38	here
417					
A	Bray John M	226	painter	34	
B	Bray Joseph	226	laborer	38	
C	Knapp Theresa—†	228	housewife	39	"
E	*Quinn Mary—†	228	"	43	8 Ulmer
F	Quinn Michael	228	watchman	49	8 "

Kingsbury Street

G	Keenan Charles	3	laborer	42	here
H	Keenan Susan—†	3	housewife	37	"
K	Whitney George	3	retired	54	"
L	Whitney Louise—†	3	housewife	39	"
M	Whitney Louise—†	3	clerk	21	
N	Casey James M	3	laborer	34	
O	Casey John	3	retired	75	
P	Casey Mary E—†	3	clerk	45	
R	Casey Nora—†	3	housewife	76	"
S	Chancholo Helen—†	5	"	24	
T	Chancholo James	5	attendant	26	"
U	Allen Lillian L—†	5	housekeeper	67	9 Fairfax
V	Magrath Elizabeth M—†	5	housewife	44	1024 Canterbury
W	Magrath James	5	clerk	40	1024 "
X	*Gilmartin Mary—†	7	housewife	34	here
Y	Sekula Basil	7	laborer	33	"
Z	*Sekula Julia—†	7	housewife	29	"
418					
A	Moynihan Joseph E	7	plumber	47	
B	*Moynihan Mary B—†	7	housewife	46	"
C	*Healey Margaret—†	9	"	28	
D	Healey Patrick	9	porter	32	"
E	Foley Anna—†	9	housewife	38	"
F	Tracey Gladys R—†	9	"	42	"
G	Goddard Russell	11	electrician	37	"
H	Goddard Susannah—†	11	housewife	76	"
K	Evitts Arthur	11	manager	31	
L	Evitts Cora—†	11	housewife	63	"
M	Robicheau Alys—†	11	"	26	
N	Robicheau William	11	gardener	36	

Page.	Letter.	Full Name.	Residence, Jan. 1, 1941.	Occupation.	Supposed Age.	Reported Residence, Jan. 1, 1940. Street and Number.

Kingsbury Street—Continued

	o	Leerr John	11	chauffeur	29	53 Bainbridge
	p	Leerr Rose—†	11	housewife	26	53 "

Marcella Street

	s	Leverone Helen—†	3	housewife	36	here
	t	Leverone John	3	retired	74	"
	u	Leverone John	3	painter	43	"
	v	Andrews Dorothy—†	4	housewife	28	470 Brookline av
	w*	Andrews Paul	4	laborer	31	537 Medford
	x	McKinnon Annie—†	4	stitcher	58	here
	y	McKinnon Mary—†	4	at home	65	"

419

	a	Kranklis Alson	5	collector	32	"
	b	Kranklis Mary—†	5	housewife	30	"
	c*	Kranklis Bertha—†.	5	"	59	
	d	Kranklis John	5	carpenter	59	"
	e	Kranklis Leone—†	5	countergirl	25	"
	f	Anderson Evelyn—†	6	housewife	24	3 Glen rd
	g	Anderson Lowell	6	clerk	25	8 Sylvia
	h	Walker Jennie—†	6	housekeeper	30	here
	m	Marenghi Bertha—†	8	hairdresser	40	"
	n	White Elizabeth—†	8	housekeeper	72	"
	p	Coughlin Delia—†	10	housewife	54	"
	r	Coughlin Edward	10	laborer	51	
	s	Coughlin Edward	10	"	20	
	t	Coughlin Harold	10	clerk	27	
	u	Kelly John	10	painter	52	
	v*	Mulkay Mary—†	11	housewife	33	"
	w	Mulkay Patrick	11	laborer	32	
	x	Owens Elizabeth A—†	12	student	21	
	y	Owens Graham L	12	machinist	26	"
	z	Owens John A	12	retired	75	

420

	a	Owens Margaret L—†	12	housewife	64	"
	b	Owens Paul T	12	shipper	31	
	c	Blackman Charles J	13	painter	56	
	d	Blackman Mary—†	13	housewife	52	"
	e	Farley Mary—†	13	housekeeper	63	521 Northampton
	f	McDonald Angus	13	retired	87	here

Page.	Letter.	Full Name.	Residence, Jan. 1, 1941.	Occupation.	Supposed Age.	Reported Residence, Jan. 1, 1940. Street and Number.

Marcella Street—Continued

G	McGinnis John A	13	retired	74	here
H	McGinnis Margaret—†	13	housewife	80	"
K	Bethune Mabel P—†	14	housekeeper	38	"
L	Bigelow Francis O	14	superintendent	72	"
M	Bigelow Mildred E—†	14	clerk	32	"
N	Archibald Annie E—†	15	housewife ·	66	13 Heath
O	Archibald George N	15	retired	71	13 "
P	Pratt Sidney C	15	machinist	22	72 Waverly
R	Palmer Margaret—†	16	housekeeper.	37	here
S	Palmer Melvin	16	messenger	45	"
T	Atkins David	16	laborer	58	"
U	Atkins Frances—†	16	teacher	26	
V	*Atkins Mary—†	16	housewife	60	"
W	Atkins William	16	plumber	24	
X	Johnson Anna—†	17	housewife	26	"
Y	Johnson Walter	17	carpenter	33	"
Z	Wade Alberta F—†	17	housewife	37	"

421

A	Wade Ira S	17	laborer	38	
B	Farrenkopf Anna B—†	18	housewife	53	"
C	Farrenkopf John C	18	salesman	53	"
D	Calhoun Charles	20	operator	23	
E	Calhoun Mary—†	20	housewife	54	"
F	Calhoun Walter	20	bookkeeper	55	"
G	Fay Julia—†	20	at home	82	"
H	Varley John	20	clerk	57	"
K	Moloney Charles P	21	plumber	67	
L	Moloney Paul V	21	teacher	28	
M	Reichert Helen M—†	21	housewife	35	"
N	Reichert Joseph D	21	furrier	37	
O	Murphy Nora—†	22	housewife	53	"
P	Murphy Timothy	22	laborer	55	
R	Shay Rebecca—†	22	at home	75	
S	Mons Marie A—†	22	waitress	48	
T	Thomas Horace L	22	clerk	26	
U	Thomas Margaret—†	22	housewife	50	"
V	Thomas Margaret—†	22	clerk	24	
W	Thomas Robert	22	salesman	21	"
X	D'Eon Anna—†	23	inspector	42	"
Y	D'Eon Maximin J	23	cutter	32	
Z	Gilmore John	23	retired	79	

14

Page.	Letter.	FULL NAME.	Residence, Jan. 1, 1941.	Occupation.	Supposed Age.	Reported Residence, Jan. 1, 1940. Street and Number.

Marcella Street—Continued

A	Gilmore Leo	23	floorman	47	here
B	Gilmore Marie M—†	23	clerk	42	"
C	Ochs Emily L—†	24	"	48	"
D	Rasch Florence H—†	24	housewife	41	"
E	Rasch Frederick V	24	fireman	47	"
F	Dion Albert	25	laborer	32	3 Fremont av
G	Dion Albertina—†	25	housewife	31	3 "
H	Huston Anna A—†	25	"	50	8 Seymour
K	Huston Charles V	25	retired	59	8 "
L	Sullivan Mary E—†	25	"	75	here
M	Hoehle Elizabeth—†	27	at home	91	"
N	Hoehle Marie L—†	27	secretary	57	"
O	Yetter Emilie H—†	27	housewife	65	"
P	Yetter Otto	27	retired	64	
R	Copatch Felicia—†	28	housewife	50	"
S	Copatch John M	28	mechanic	54	"
T	Moloney Edith—†	29	housewife	35	66 Tremont
U	Moloney James	29	operator	30	66 "
V	Gadman Arlene—†	29	housewife	24	226 Amory
W	Cole Mary—†	30	housekeeper	61	here
X	Hopkins Lionel	30	laborer	43	"
Y	Hopkins Nellie—†	30	housekeeper	41	"
Z	Chandler Rose M—†	30	clerk	29	"

A	Chandler Thomas V	30	salesman	29	1043 Dor av
B	Runci Angelina—†	30	housewife	66	here
C	Runci Edward E	30	salesman	25	"
D	Runci John	30	chauffeur	38	"
E	Runci Virginia—†	30	clerk	23	..
F	Runci William	30	U S A	31	"
K	Fernandes Ethel—†	32	housewife	39	65 Wensley
L	Fernandes Manuel	32	mechanic	44	65 "
M	Will Emily F—†	34	housewife	50	here
N	Will Leo F	34	machinist	52	"
O	Lasman Anna—†	34	housekeeper	57	93 Centre
P	Mueller Francis	34	retired	80	here
R	Mueller Henry	34	clerk	43	"
S	Mueller Louise—†	34	housekeeper	50	"
T	Brophy Helen L—†	rear 34	housewife	26	21 Centre
U	Brophy Walter	" 34	painter	28	21 "

Marcella Street—Continued

v	Gallier Lewis E	35	painter	60	41 Bickford
w	Gallier Nora E—†	35	housewife	56	41 "
x	Rollins Alfred	35	painter	50	here
y	Rollins Carmen	35	U S A	21	"
z	Rollins Edith—†	35	housewife	48	"

424

A	Caddle Emily—†	35	"	56	25 Ellingwood
B	Caddle George	35	clerk	26	25 "
C	Caddle John	35	polisher	56	25 "
D	Flynn Frank H	36	clerk	53	here
E	Flynn Mary F—†	36	housekeeper	59	"
F	Vickerson Florence—†	37	artist	45	"
G	Arnott George R	37	laborer	26	
H	Arnott Ida—†	37	housewife	53	"
N	Gallagher Arthur	42	laborer	50	
O	Ward Alpheus	42	"	45	
P	Ward Mary—†	42	at home	80	"
R	Huckle Albert	43	clerk	35	74 Fulda
S	Huckle Ann—†	43	housewife	20	74 "
T	Ware John E	43	engineer	71	here
U	Ware Minnie A—†	43	housewife	64	"
V	Casey Edward	43	U S A	20	"
W	Casey Joseph P	43	constable	61	"
X	Casey Julia—†	43	housewife	53	"
Y	Friel Walter	43	steamfitter	35	"
Z	Keane Annie S—†	47	cashier	26	

425

A	Keane Annie M—†	47	housewife	60	"
B	Keane Margaret—†	47	bookkeeper	20	"
C	Keane Richard	47	chauffeur	61	"
D	Keane Rose—†	47	maid	23	
E	McDonald Anna—†	51	housewife	48	"
F	McDonald Thomas	51	seaman	20	"
G	Rideout Claire H—†	51	housekeeper	21	12 Herman
H	Rideout Frederick J	51	laborer	22	12 "
K	Rideout George W	51	"	62	12 "
L	Rideout Howard O	51	"	26	12 '
M	Rideout Lois F—†	51	housekeeper	25	12 "
N	Rideout Marion I—†	51	housewife	55	12 "
O	Doyle Helen—†	51	matron	39	here
P	Gately Mary E—†	51	housewife	48	"

Page.	Letter.	Full Name.	Residence, Jan. 1, 1941.	Occupation.	Supposed Age.	Reported Residence, Jan. 1, 1940. Street and Number.

Marcella Street—Continued

	R	Gately Patrick J	51	retired	48	here
	S	Corbett Lillian—†	53	housewife	27	63 Fort av
	T	Corbett Roy W	53	chauffeur	29	63 "
	U	*Serrecchia Maria—†	53	housewife	53	here
	V	Serrecchia Salvatore	53	laborer	53	"
	W	*Hardy Julia—†	53	housewife	33	156 Thornton
	X	*O'Neil Mary—†	55	domestic	54	here
	Z	Nicholas Henry E	57	painter	60	"
		426				
	A	*Nicholas Hilda—†	57	housewife	46	"
	B	Nicholas Ina—†	57	stenographer	24	"
	C	Gibbons Olivia—†	rear 57	housekeeper	38	1110 Harrison av
	D	Dailey Andrew T	59	laborer	29	here
	E	Dailey Celia E—†	59	stenographer	21	"
	F	Dailey Michael	59	retired	69	"
	G	DePaoli Anthony	59	tilesetter	47	"
	H	DePaoli Celestina—†	59	housewife	44	"
	K	Hooley James F	61	salesman	36	"
	L	Hooley John J	61	"	41	
	M	Hooley Nora—†	61	housewife	65	"
	N	McIlvene Charles	65	laborer	44	33 Glenwood
	O	Levesque Claire—†	65	housewife	34	here
	P	Levesque Joseph E	65	chauffeur	37	"
	S	Bartol Margaret—†	67	at home	67	65 Marcella
	T	Nee George	67	guard	46	65 "
	U	Nee Margaret—†	67	housewife	41	65 "
	V	Curran Catherine—†	67	"	79	here
	W	Curran John	67	chauffeur	34	"
	X	Curran Patrick jr	67	laborer	48	"

Merriam Place

	Z	Mulhern Barbara—†	1	housewife	46	here
		427				
	A	Mulhern Patrick		checker	44	

Thornton Place

	B	Kilcoyne Ann—†	1	housewife	54	here
	C	Kilcoyne John J	1	laborer	25	"
	D	Kilcoyne Mary E—†	1	clerk	23	"

Page.	Letter.	Full Name.	Residence, Jan. 1, 1941.	Occupation.	Supposed Age.	Reported Residence, Jan. 1, 1940. Street and Number.

Thornton Place—Continued

E	Kilcoyne Patrick J	1	instructor	54	here
F	Hohmann Angela P—†	3	secretary	27	"
G	Hohmann Anna R—†	3	stenographer	35	"
H	Hohmann Edmund F	3	clerk	28	"
K	Hohmann John W	3	"	25	
L	Hohmann Josephine M–†	3	at home	30	
M	Hohmann Karl E	3	floorlayer	74	"
N	Hohmann Loretta C—†	3	bookkeeper	32	"
O	Hohmann Mary A—†	3	stenographer	36	"
P	McNally Mary—†	4	housewife	27	"
R	McNally Robert	4	mechanic	26	"
S	Levitsky Fanny—†	4	housewife	54	"
T	Levitsky Joseph	4	plumber	54	
U	Levitsky Ruth—†	4	shoeworker	23	"
V	Pedersen Frederick L	5	operator	44	"
W	Pedersen Maria—†	5	housewife	76	"
X	Kilcoyne John J	7	laborer	45	
Y	Kilcoyne Mary—†	7	housewife	42	"

Thornton Street

Z	Bennett Merton	133	accountant	24	21 Wakullah
	428					
A	Bennett Millicent—†	133	housewife	24	21 "
B	Linden Vida—†	133	houseworker	23	21 "
C	Flynn George V	133	installer	44	here
D	Flynn Joseph A	133	examiner	42	"
E	Flynn Katherine L—†	133	housewife	44	"
F	Locke John	133	clerk	30	
G	Locke Joseph	133	chauffeur	23	"
H	Locke Julia—†	133	housewife	54	"
K	Locke William	133	mechanic	52	"
L	Cronin John	135	porter	23	"
M	White Mary—†	135	housewife	34	"
N	Parks Lillian P—†	135	"	33	1 Danforth pl
O	Parks Robert	135	salesman	30	1 "
P	Townsend Frank G	137	shipper	26	here
R	Townsend Paula A—†	137	housewife	27	"
S	Schuerkamp Clara—†	137	examiner	58	"
T	Wright Anna J—†	137	housewife	45	"

Thornton Street—Continued

u	Wright George H	137	expressman	53	here
v	Finnigan James J	137	metalworker	56	"
w	Finnigan James M	137	chauffeur	27	"
x	Finnigan Margaret—†	137	housewife	55	"
y	Nehily Walter	139	metalworker	36	"
z	*Hanlon Anna—†	139	housewife	36	"
	429				
a	*Hanlon Walter	139	longshoreman	38	"
b	Doyle John	139	bricklayer	40	"
c	Doyle Margaret—†	139	housewife	36	"
d	Seufert Albert	143	chauffeur	38	"
e	Seufert Anna—†	143	housewife	36	"
f	Bross Rosina—†	143	"	69	"
g	Bross William J	143	salesman	46	"
h	*Foote Mary J—†	143	housewife	45	"
k	Foote Michael J	143	machinist	44	"
m	Sampson Bert	151	attendant	40	425 Harvard
n	Sampson Marion E—†	151	hairdresser	26	97 Perkins
o	Robinson Fred W	151	painter	48	here
p	Duffy Beatrice—†	151	housewife	32	"
r	Duffy John V	151	timekeeper	29	"
s	Glancy Jane—†	153	housewife	82	"
t	Glancy Peter	153	retired	83	
u	McLean Doris—†	153	housewife	26	"
v	Gray Ida—†	153	"	41	
w	Gray Maynard M	153	chef	31	
x	Hayner Stanley	153	counterman	21	"
y	Byrne Mary—†	155	housewife	29	128 Chelsea
z	Byrne Thomas	155	longshoreman	39	128 "
	430				
a	McCoy Alma—†	155	housewife	25	18 Rochdale
b	McCoy Predore	155	mechanic	37	18 "
c	Becker Fred	155	bookkeeper	28	here
d	Becker Irene—†	155	factoryworker	29	"
f	Patterson Sarah—†	163	housewife	65	26 Valentine
g	Reynolds Ethel L—†	163	"	48	here
h	Reynolds William H	163	laborer	52	"
k	Myers Annie—†	163	housewife	48	"
l	Myers Charles	163	laborer	47	
m	Keating Daniel B	178	boilermaker	25	"

Page.	Letter.	FULL NAME.	Residence, Jan. 1, 1941.	Occupation.	Supposed Age.	Reported Residence, Jan. 1, 1940. Street and Number.

Thornton Street—Continued

	N	Keating Edna—†	178	saleswoman	23	here
	O	Keating Ellen—†	178	housewife	50	"
	P	Keating Ellen A—†	178	clerk	20	"
	R	Keating Timothy	178	fireman	67	
	S	Keating Constance—†	178	housewife	24	"
	T	Keating Timothy D	178	clerk	26	
	U	McCarthy John J	180	retired	71	
	V	Keaveney Edward F	180	clerk	20	
	W	Keaveney Joseph	180	mechanic	23	"
	X	Keaveney Mary E—†	180	housewife	50	"
	Y	Keaveney Michael	180	shoecutter	54	"
	Z	Keaveney Rita—†	180	stenographer	24	"
431						
	A	Kraby Dorothy—†	182	checker	22	
	B	Kraby Elizabeth J—†	182	housewife	45	"
	C	Kraby Robert C	182	packer	20	"
	D	Kraby Thurston C	182	policeman	52	"
	E	Kraby Warren J	182	salesman	24	"
	F	Garrett Edward	184	fireman	62	Amesbury
	G	Rogers Clayton	184	merchant	35	here
	H	Rogers Ruth—†	184	housewife	32	"
	K	Barrett Catherine—†	184	"	66	"
	L	Barrett Mary E—†	184	clerk	37	"
	M	Beltchoff Robert M	185	U S A	31	15 Marcella
	N	Gibney Edna M—†	185	buyer	46	here
	O	Gibney Fred J	185	student	25	"
	P	Lysaght Elizabeth—†	188	attendant	23	"
	R	Lysaght James	188	laborer	50	
	S	*Lysaght Nellie—†	188	housewife	54	"
	T	Evangelista Anthony	188	baker	30	
	U	Evangelista Helen—†	188	housewife	23	"
	W	Carew Charles	192	bookkeeper	42	"
	X	Carew Gertrude—†	192	housewife	46	"
	Y	Sargent Rose—†	192	"	32	
	Z	*Matthews Afrondita—†	194	"	34	
432						
	A	*Matthews Athena—†	194	"	57	
	B	Matthews Christo	194	retired	68	
	C	Matthews Nicholas	194	merchant	36	"
	D	Schnabel Harold J	194	laborer	22	

Page.	Letter.	FULL NAME.	Residence, Jan. 1, 1941.	Occupation.	Supposed Age.	Reported Residence, Jan. 1, 1940. Street and Number.

Thornton Street—Continued

| | E | Schnabel Mary M—† | 194 | housewife | 56 | here |
| | F | Schnabel Oscar A | 194 | shoelaster | 54 | " |

Vale Street

	G	Martin Charles	9	watchman	53	2 Hulbert
	H	Patriquin George	9	clerk	27	2 "
	K	Patriquin Helen—†	9	housewife	23	2 "
	L	Souther William	9	clerk	26	2 "
	M	Winston Blanche—†	9	housewife	27	2 "
	N	Winston Robert	9	laborer	34	2 "
	O	Goessl Florence M—†	12	housewife	56	here
	P	Goessl John A	12	roofer	55	"
	R	McClay Gertrude S—†	12	housewife	46	"
	S	McClay John	12	roofer	55	
	T	Finneran Anne—†	16	housewife	51	"
	U	Finneran Joseph	16	merchant	54	"
	V	Finneran Rita—†	16	typist	24	
	W	Timmons Joseph	16	laborer	22	
	X	Timmons Margaret—†	16	housewife	21	"
	Y	Carey Mary—†	18	"	27	8 Ashley
	Z	Carey Peter	18	laborer	29	8 "

433

	A	Mitchell Christine—†	18	housewife	24	24 Vale
	B	Mitchell Edmund	18	tree surgeon	31	6 Conrad
	C	Alexander Albert	20	laborer	31	16 Albert
	D	Alexander Catherine—†	20	housewife	29	16 "
	E	Bowers Mary—†	20	domestic	30	32 Newark
	F	McClellan Joseph	20	painter	36	here
	G	McClellan Mary—†	20	housewife	36	"
	K	Flanders Ann—†	22	"	38	"
	L	Flanders John	22	laborer	54	"
	M	Bolger Victoria—†	22	housewife	24	2996 Wash'n
	N	Bolger William	22	entertainer	41	2996 "
	O	Green George L	22	carpenter	33	277 Centre
	P	Green Marion—†	22	housewife	30	277 "
	S	Nicholson James	24	carpenter	74	here
	T	Nicholson Marion—†	24	laundress	30	"
	U	Nicholson Mary—†	24	housewife	64	"
	V	McDonald Evelyn—†	24	"	34	

Page.	Letter.	FULL NAME	Residence, Jan. 1, 1941.	Occupation.	Supposed Age.	Reported Residence, Jan. 1, 1940. Street and Number.

Vale Street—Continued

	w	McDonald Murdoch	24	carpenter	40	here
	x	*McKay Catherine—†	24	housewife	35	"
	y	*McKay Frederick E	24	laborer	36	"
	z	McMann William	26	"	43	
434						
	F	Fisher Anna—†	32	housewife	30	"
	G	Fisher Joseph	32	laborer	34	"
	H	McLaughlin Edith—†	32	housewife	30	985 Col av
	K	McLaughlin Peter J	32	laborer	38	985 "
	L	Catarius Frank	34	retired	58	here
	M	Catarius George	34	clerk	29	"
	N	Catarius Helen—†	34	saleswoman	20	"
	O	Catarius Mary—†	34	housewife	53	"
	P	Catarius Peter	34	clerk	27	
	R	Dabrowsky Ann—†	38	housewife	29	"
	S	Dabrowsky Walter	38	bricklayer	31	"
	T	Plunkett Edward	40	chauffeur	32	"
	U	Plunkett George	40	laborer	35	
	V	Plunkett John	40	"	34	
	x	MacDonnell Angus J	44	carpenter	57	"
	Y	*MacDonnell Jeanette—†	44	housewife	48	"
	z	Moloney Alice G—†	46	"	36	25 Fulda
435						
	A	Moloney Phillip C	46	steamfitter	39	25 "
	B	Ross James	48	electrician	41	here
	C	Ross Mildred—†	48	housewife	37	"
	D	Ross Margaret—†	50	clerk	35	"
	E	Ross Rachael—†	50	housekeeper	33	"
	F	Ross Walter	50	carpenter	80	"
	G	Ross Walter, jr	50	"	45	
	H	McNally Ella—†	51	housewife	38	"
	K	McNally Joseph	51	chauffeur	30	"
	L	Stallings Evelyn—†	51	housewife	33	132 Terrace
	M	Stallings James	51	gardener	36	132 "
	N	Finn Ethel J—†	51	housewife	37	2767 Wash'n
	O	Finn George	51	laborer	44	2767 "
	P	O'Keefe Catherine J—†	53	housewife	68	here
	R	O'Keefe Edward C	53	retired	67	"
	S	O'Keefe Francis P	53	metalworker	34	"
	T	Ford Frances C—†	57	housewife	28	61 Robinson
	U	Ford James P	57	chauffeur	32	61 "

22

Vale Street—Continued

v	Kennedy John J	57	steamfitter	62	here
w	Elliott Caroline J—†	61	housekeeper	45	"
x	Elliott Hazen B	61	collector	44	"
z	Wilfert Edward A	61	retired	71	
y	Wilfert Edwin J	61	lineman	31	

436

a	Wilfert James A	61	clerk	27	··
b	Wilfert Martha S—†	61	housewife	68	"
c	Bagley Anna—†	63	"	34	
d	Bagley Joseph	63	laborer	35	"
e	Bannon Bernard	63	"	30	3 Whittier
f	Bannon Victoria—†	63	housewife	29	3 "
g	Yeaton Harry	63	metalworker	60	Somerville

Valentine Street

h	*McDonald Agnes—†	3	at home	54	here
k	*McDonald Catherine J—†	3	housewife	58	"
l	McDonald James A	3	mechanic	26	"
m	Caswell Warren	3	machinist	48	Pennsylvania
n	*Dorrian Stephen	3	painter	47	2984 Wash'n
o	O'Neil Frank	3	retired	57	here
p	Stott Annette—†	5	housewife	29	27 Valentine
r	Stott John W	5	welder	40	27 "
s	Calevro Della—†	5	housewife	45	here
t	Calevro John	5	butcher	41	"
u	Derosia Thomas	5	retired	69	N Hampshire
v	James Mary—†	5	waitress	28	here
w	Mahoney Dennis	5	retired	66	"
x	Mahoney James	5	clerk	31	"
y	Mahoney Margaret—†	5	"	26	
z	McGary Claire—†	7	housewife	38	"

437

a	McGary Mathias	7	laborer	34	
b	Coletta Emma—†	7	housewife	30	"
c	*Paul Mathilda—†	7	housekeeper	57	"
d	McCarthy Mary A—†	7	housewife	40	"
e	Leach Charles	9	laborer	29	
f	Leach Ralph	9	retired	78	
g	Leach William	9	"	72	
h	Long Jessie—†	9	housewife	32	"

Valentine Street—Continued

K	Long William	9	operator	34	here
L	O'Brien Everett	9	salesman	39	"
M	O'Brien Mary—†	9	housewife	37	"
O	Black Winifred—†	11	operator	41	
P	Burns Anna—†	11	boxmaker	43	"
R	Burns Dorothy—†	11	operator	33	
S	Burns Frances—†	11	secretary	39	"
N	Gunn Anna—†	11	housekeeper	65	"
T	*Dube Celina—†	13	housewife	42	"
U	Dube Ernest	13	U S A	22	"
V	*Dube Phillip	13	silversmith	44	"
W	*Manna Anthony W	15	laborer	39	
X	Manna Victoria—†	15	housewife	35	"
Y	*Dayron Aubin	15	counterman	31	"
Z	Dayron Mary—†	15	housewife	27	"

438

B	Deassacos Edith—†	19	"	30	53 Heath
C	Deassacos Michael J	19	restaurantman	30	53 "
E	Cadillic Catherine—†	19	housewife	40	here
F	Cadillic Joseph	19	mechanic	41	"
G	Foley Cyril	20	salesman	26	"
H	Foley Eileen—†	20	housewife	25	"
K	Sline Annie—†	20	"	65	
L	Sline John	20	retired	67	
M	Methot Florence—†	20	housewife	25	"
N	Methot William	20	chauffeur	25	"
O	McAneny Cecelia—†	21	housekeeper	80	"
P	Weniger Mabel—†	21	nurse	50	7 Bartlett ter
R	Carlton Cora—†	21	housekeeper	61	here
S	Gove Caroline—†	21	"	82	"
T	Cameron Robert	22	boilermaker	28	Somerville
U	Steele Margaret—†	22	housekeeper	35	287 Highland
V	Keating Ellen T—†	22	housewife	66	here
W	Keating Michael J	22	laborer	65	"
X	Gill Alena—†	23	saleswoman	38	New York
Y	Michaud Frank	23	ironworker	67	here
Z	Waters Marion—†	23	housewife	41	"

439

A	*Waters Patrick	23	hostler	48	
B	Barry Annie J—†	24	housewife	56	"
C	*Barry James F	24	laborer	58	

Page.	Letter.	Full Name.	Residence, Jan. 1, 1941.	Occupation.	Supposed Age.	Reported Residence, Jan. 1, 1940. Street and Number.

Valentine Street—Continued

	D	Burroughs Albert	24	metalworker	28	here
	E	Burroughs Johanna—†	24	housewife	58	"
	F	Manning Ida—†	24	"	32	"
	G	Manning Michael	24	laborer	36	
	H	Tucker Marion—†	25	housewife	31	"
	K	Sline Elizabeth—†	25	"	29	
	L	Sline John	25	laborer	30	
	M	Bunnell Agnes M—†	25	housewife	53	"
	N	Bunnell Frederick	25	painter	54	
	O	Bunnell Theodore J	25	attendant	21	"
	P	Kerwin Charles F	26	chauffeur	28	"
	R	*Starratt Ann—†	26	maid	40	
	S	*Starratt Jessie—†	26	operator	49	"
	T	Purtell James	26	chef	58	2776 Wash'n
	U	Wynne Martina—†	27	cook	35	here
	V	Pritchard Catherine—†	27	housekeeper	73	"
	W	*Powers Ella—†	27	"	58	Brookline
	X	Sellon Henry	28	chauffeur	33	here
	Y	*Sellon Nora—†	28	housewife	23	"
	Z	McDonald Catherine—†	28	"	34	"
		440				
	A	McDonald Joseph	28	laborer	33	
	B	Curley Catherine—†	28	housewife	68	"
	C	Curley Peter	28	retired	66	
	D	Bliss Ida B—†	29	housewife	68	"
	E	Bliss Joseph F	29	retired	72	"
	F	Mansfield Catherine—†	29	housewife	48	170 Winthrop
	G	Mansfield Rita—†	29	cashier	23	170 "
	H	Vandenberg John	29	retired	70	here
	K	Surette John	30	janitor	26	7 Haynes
	L	*Kight Elizabeth—†	30	housewife	27	here
	M	Kight Joseph	30	ironworker	27	"
	N	Hicks Eleanor—†	30	housewife	28	"
	O	Hicks Frank	30	machinist	29	"
	P	Brown Mona—†	31	housewife	26	"
	R	Brown William	31	tinsmith	25	"
	S	Belyea Everett	31	welder	21	191 Eustis
	T	*McNamara Bridget M—†	31	housewife	52	here
	U	*McNamara John	31	laborer	50	"
	V	McNamara Thomas	31	U S A	21	"
	W	Uhrig Francis	32	mechanic	21	"

Valentine Street—Continued

	x	Uhrig Rita—†	32	housewife	21	here
	y	Martin Eileen—†	32	"	26	"
	z	Martin John	32	chauffeur	33	"
441						
	b	Wilkes George	33	laborer	29	
	c	Wilkes Gerene—†	33	housewife	27	"
	d	Kerwin Margaret—†	33	"	40	
	e	Kerwin Marjorie—†	33	clerk	20	
	f	Carney John	33	laborer	28	
	g	Carney Mary—†	33	housewife	31	"
	h	Foulis George	35	machinist	25	53 Dudley
	k	Foulis Talitha—†	35	housewife	26	53 "
	l	Brown Arthur	35	painter	57	here
	m	Brown Helen—†	35	housewife	20	"
	n	Brown Wilbert L	35	operator	25	"
	o	Robertson Forest	35	baker	33	11 Norfolk
	p	Robertson Minnie—†	35	factoryhand	23	105 W Dedham

Washington Street

	s	Doherty Bernard	2774	grocer	35	4 Marcella
	t	Doherty Margaret M—†	2774	housewife	31	4 "
	u	Marquis Rose—†	2774	"	50	here
	v	Marquis Stella—†	2774	clerk	26	"
	w	Marquis William	2774	"	60	"
442						
	c	Turner George	2782	chauffeur	42	"
	d	Turner Gladys—†	2782	clerk	36	"
	e	Gilbert Della—†	2784	housewife	53	26 Hawthorne
	f	Gilbert Earl	2784	student	22	26 "
	g	Gilbert Leon	2784	mason	54	26 "
	h	Gallant Columbia—†	2784	housewife	48	here
	k	Gallant Joseph	2784	clerk	51	"
	l	Gallant Marguerite—†	2784	"	27	"
	p	O'Brien John	2788A	"	57	
	r	Fallon John F	2788A	carpenter	53	"
	s	McCambly John H	2788A	"	67	
	t	McCambly Mary F—†	2788A	housewife	66	"
	u	McCambly Richard	2788A	clerk	25	
443						
	a	Hahir Ellen E—†	2794	housewife	41	"

Washington Street—Continued

B	Hahir John	2794	ironworker	44	here
c	Bragel George	2794	mechanic	47	132A Main
D	Bragel Margaret—†	2794	housewife	41	132A "
E	Witham Catherine—†	2794	maid	31	here
F	Witham Phillip H	2794	painter	28	"
G	Irving Charles	2796	"	40	"
H	Irving Ida—†	2796	housewife	36	"
K	McLean Minnie—†	2796	"	48	
L	Elwin Albion	2796	carpenter	49	"
M	Elwin Carl	2796	butcher	25	
N	*Elwin Ellen—†	2796	housewife	58	"
o	*Elwin Gustaf	2796	clerk	23	
R	*Carr Elizabeth—†	2800½	housewife	37	"
s	*Carr John	2800½	baker	37	212 Highland
T	Gamer Ada—†	2800½	bookkeeper	33	here
U	Gamer Anita R—†	2800½	housewife	30	"
v	*Gamer Elizabeth—†	2800½	"	65	"
w	*Gamer George	2800½	retired	66	
x	*Gamer Jacob	2800½	fireman	43	
Y	Rosenfield Mitchell	2800½	attorney	42	..

444

B	Masse Helen—†	2806	clerk	44	
D	*Cresto Alexandria—†	2806	housewife	63	"
E	Cresto Elizabeth—†	2806	student	20	
F	Cresto Paul	2806	clerk	38	"
N	Gordon Bernard L	2809	painter	42	2817 Wash'n
o	Gordon Mary—†	2809	housewife	33	2817
P	Jackson Lucille—†	2809	"	33	here
R	Jackson Raymond	2809	operator	35	"
U	Shortell Johanna—†	2812	housewife	38	"
v	Shortell Peter J	2812	molder	40	"
x	*Wong George	2815	laundryman	38	"
Y	*Wong Florence—†	2815	housewife	35	"

445

A	Ritchie George	2817	machinist	29	128 Minden
B	*Ritchie Jane—†	2817	housewife	25	128 "
c	Young Isabel—†	2817	"	35	31 "
D	Young James	2817	freighthandler	36	31 "
F	Chartrand Lillian—†	2821½	saleswoman	43	1 Leyland
G	Kelley Gladys—†	2821½	"	43	here
M	McMahon Michael J	2831A	merchant	65	"

Washington Street—Continued

N	McMahon Nora—†	2831A	housewife	67	here
O	Young Mary—†	2831A	housekeeper	65	"
S	*Campo Florence—†	2837	operator	20	2888 Wash'n
T	Campo George	2837	janitor	25	2888 "
U	*Dorion Christine—†	2837	housewife	45	2888 "
V	*Dorion Emmanuel	2837	mechanic	50	2888 "
W	*Dorion Emmanuel C	2837	chauffeur	22	2888 "
X	Kilroy John	2839	laborer	49	53 Forest Hills
Y	Kilroy Lena—†	2839	housewife	70	53 "
446						
A	Gillogley George E	2843	laborer	46	here
B	*Gillogley Hugh F	2843	lumberjack	45	"
C	Gillogley Marie R—†	2843	housewife	46	"
G	O'Dwyer Elizabeth C–†	2855	"	67	
H	O'Dwyer Myles	2855	retired	70	
K	Mellen Jeffrey	2855	manager	41	"
L	Wilson Isabel M—†	2855	clerk	29	
M	Young Florence L—†	2855	nurse	61	"
N	Young Joseph M	2855	retired	73	
O	Long Edna—†	2855	teacher	46	"
P	Mahoney John	2855	laborer	52	42 W Newton
R	McCall Frances—†	2855	housewife	32	here
S	McCall Thomas F	2855	clerk	36	"
T	Bloomfield Mary—†	2855	waitress	45	"
U	Bloomfield Michael	2855	gardener	73	"
V	Blair Albert	2855	supervisor	31	"
W	Blair Sally—†	2855	housewife	28	"
X	McDonald Mildred—†	2857	stitcher	27	"
Y	Morris Marjorie—†	2857	housewife	29	5 St James ter
Z	Green Michael	2859	laborer	67	here
447						
A	Slusze Ronald	2859	butcher	20	51 Montebello rd
B	Foley Cornelius	2859	letter carrier	36	here
C	*Lind Mabel—†	2859	nurse	30	"
D	Brennan Helen B—†	2893	at home	76	"
E	Brogan Anna M—†	2893	domestic	31	"
F	Brogan Cecilia M—†	2893	teacher	43	
G	Burke Catherine—†	2893	at home	77	
H	*Burke Mary E—†	2893	"	73	
K	Callahan Grace A—†	2893	teacher	29	
L	Carle Theresa—†	2893	domestic	35	"

Page.	Letter.	FULL NAME.	Residence, Jan. 1, 1941.	Occupation.	Supposed Age.	Reported Residence, Jan. 1, 1940. Street and Number.

Washington Street—Continued

M	Carroll Clare C—†	2893	teacher	42	Tyngsboro
N	Collins Anna L—†	2893	"	24	here
O	Cullen M Irene—†	2893	"	34	"
P	Cullinane Anna F—†	2893	"	64	"
R	Cunningham Nan—†	2893	housekeeper	47	"
S	Curran Anna M—†	2893	teacher	21	Somerville
T	Day Margaret M—†	2893	housekeeper	62	here
U	DeFlo Jeanette—†	2893	teacher	30	"
V	Dennehy Evangeline K–†	2893	"	29	"
W	Donovan Mary E—†	2893	"	65	
X	*Dorsey Bridget—†	2893	housekeeper	72	"
Y	Dorsey Gertrude M—†	2893	teacher	41	..
Z	Dwight Sarah C—†	2893	"	55	
	448				
A	Fallon Clara M—†	2893	"	53	
B	Feeney Elizabeth J—†	2893	domestic	49	"
C	Fitzmaurice Elizabeth–†	2893	housekeeper	52	"
D	Flynn Catherine E—†	2893	teacher	28	"
E	Galvin Kathleen E—†	2893	"	35	
F	Gorham Anna—†	2893	"	31	
G	Grady Mary D—†	2893	"	34	
H	Graney Mary C—†	2893	"	30	"
K	Gutowski Helen A—†	2893	domestic	22	"
L	Hussey Mary J—†	2893	at home	78	
M	Kearney Winifred—†	2893	domestic	57	"
N	Kennedy Mary—†	2893	housekeeper	64	"
O	Kenney Mary F—†	2893	teacher	24	..
P	Kilroy Mary E—†	2893	seamstress	60	"
R	Kingston Mary E—†	2893	teacher	37	
S	Larkin Helena—†	2893	"	43	"
T	Lynch Mary A—†	2893	"	39	"
U	Mahoney Margaret L–†	2893	"	43	..
V	McBride Evelyn E—†	2893	"	56	
W	McCann Teresa L—†	2893	"	38	"
X	McCarthy Helen A—†	2893	"	33	Worcester
Y	McCarthy Mary C—†	2893	"	34	here
Z	McClosky Regina—†	2893	"	61	"
	449				
A	*McDonough Bridget—†	2893	housekeeper	58	"
B	Mohan Anna R—†	2893	teacher	47	..
C	Mullen Mary A—†	2893	"	33	

29

Page	Letter	FULL NAME.	Residence, Jan. 1. 1941.	Occupation.	Supposed Age.	Reported Residence, Jan. 1, 1940. Street and Number.

Washington Street—Continued

D	Mulvaney Kate T—†	2893	housekeeper	39	here
E	Murphy A Gertrude—†	2893	teacher	25	Waltham
F	Murphy Margaret—†	2893	housekeeper	47	here
G	Murphy Margaret B—†	2893	teacher	32	"
H	Murphy Mary V—†	2893	"	28	"
K	O'Brien Catherine F—†	2893	"	32	
L	O'Connell Rebecca—†	2893	"	67	
M	O'Connor Alice—†	2893	housekeeper	71	"
N	Palenkas Julia M—†	2893	"	40	"
O	Phelps Agnes G—†	2893	teacher	48	
P	Piela Jane C—†	2893	"	25	
R	Quinn Grace V—†	2893	"	51	"
S	Quinn Nora M—†	2893	"	25	Lawrence
T	Reilly Mary R—†	2893	"	31	here
U	Roberts Mary E—†	2893	domestic	75	"
V	Smith Ellen M—†	2893	teacher	68	"
W	Steinmeyer Mary A—†	2893	"	20	Tyngsboro
X	Sullivan Mary V—†	2893	"	33	here
Y	Symonds Lila—†	2893	"	28	"
Z	Ward Sarah E—†	2893	"	77	"
	450				
A	Watson Margaret M—†	2893	"	36	
B	Wessling Mary—†	2893	"	64	
C	Zalla Louise M—†	2893	seamstress	56	"

Ward 11—Precinct 5

CITY OF BOSTON

LIST OF RESIDENTS
20 YEARS OF AGE AND OVER

(NON-CITIZENS INDICATED BY ASTERISK)
(FEMALES INDICATED BY DAGGER)

AS OF

JANUARY 1, 1941

JOSEPH F. TIMILTY, *Chairman*
FREDERIC E. DOWLING, *Secretary*
WILLIAM A. MOTLEY, JR.
FRANCIS B. McKINNEY
HILDA HEDSTROM QUIRK

Listing Board.

CITY OF BOSTON PRINTING DEPARTMENT

Page.	Letter.	FULL NAME.	Residence, Jan. 1, 1941.	Occupation.	Supposed Age.	Reported Residence, Jan. 1, 1940. Street and Number.

500

Brinton Street

A	Leach Theresa—†	9	housewife	26	21 Whipple
B	Leach William	9	machinist	31	21 "
C	Cormier Joseph	9	printer	25	Waltham
D	*Daly Catherine—†	9	housewife	36	here
E	*Daly Lawrence	9	fisherman	40	"
F	Paquette Mary—†	9	at home	42	3 Hazel pk
H	O'Donnell Mary—†	9	housewife	32	here
K	O'Donnell Michael	9	mason	40	"
M	Deitchman Anna—†	10A	housewife	64	"
N	Deitchman Louis	10A	retired	74	
O	Deitchman Samuel	10A	attendant	39	"
P	*Shumilla Adam	11	laborer	56	
R	*Shumilla Anna—†	11	housewife	48	"
S	O'Leary Jeremiah F	11	laborer	61	
T	O'Leary Mary—†	11	trimmer	64	
U	O'Leary Nellie—†	11	housewife	48	"
V	King Earl V	11	bartender	49	"
W	King Mary H—†	11	housewife	50	"
X	Shumilla Edward	11	chauffeur	30	"
Y	Shumilla Mabel—†	11	housewife	29	"
Z	Venetskas Beatrice—†	11	"	38	

501

A	Venetskas William	11	barber	49	
B	Russo Frank	11	clerk	25	
C	Russo Stella—†	11	housewife	23	"
D	Harris Mabel—†	14	"	52	8 Townsend
E	Harris William	14	clerk	52	8 "
F	Cameron Margaret—†	14A	housewife	29	here
G	Raleigh Mary—†	14A	"	57	"
H	Raleigh Michael	14A	attendant	58	"

Cardington Street

K	Punchard Catherine M—†	1	clerk	22	2994 Wash'n
L	Punchard Jane E—†	1	housewife	49	2994 "
M	*Punchard William T	1	chauffeur	65	2995 "
N	MacKay Emma L—†	2	housewife	77	here
O	MacKay Mary M—†	2	"	49	"
P	MacKay William R	2	clerk	21	"
R	Flaherty Charles C	2	policeman	44	"
S	Flaherty Minnie A—†	2	housewife	42	"

2

Cardington Street—Continued

T	Rourke Margaret J—†		housewife	55	here
U	Rourke Margaret T—†		stenographer	30	"
V	Clarke James M	½	brakeman	50	Watertown
W	Crosby Anna C—†	½	housewife	25	"
X	Crosby Walter T	½	mechanic	28	"
Y	Kimbrell Mildred I—†	2	housewife	33	here
Z	Kimbrell Philip E	4	operator	32	"

502

A	Foley Anna—†	4	stenographer	34	"
B	Foley Arthur	4	timekeeper	30	"
C	Foley John	4	laborer	38	
D	Foley Joseph	4	"	32	
E	Foley Katherine—†	4	clerk	36	
F	Foley Mary—†	4	operator	37	"
G	Muttart Frank J	5	painter	50	25 Gartland
H	Muttart Phyllis A—†	5	housewife	48	25 "
K	Burkhardt Anna K—†	5	"	66	here
L	Burkhardt Charles J	5	accountant	36	"
M	O'Connell Ellen—†	6	housewife	51	"
N	O'Connell Thomas J	6	laborer	49	
O	Sullivan Mary A—†	6	inspector	48	"
P	Farmer George T	6	printer	41	
R	Farmer Helen L—†	6	housewife	41	"
S	Varley Walter F	6	laborer	44	"
T	Wiehe Albert L	7	shipper	33	91 Bragdon
U	Wiehe Emma—†	7	housewife	56	91 "
V	Wiehe George A	7	musician	65	91 "
W	Hurney Evelyn T—†	7	operator	28	here
X	Hurney Michael F	7	freighthandler	64	"
Y	Hurney Winifred T—†	7	housewife	46	"
Z	McFarland James F	9	clerk	46	

503

A	McFarland Pauline G—†	9	housewife	42	"
B	Polo Carmen	9	mechanic	21	"
C	Polo Ciro	9	shoemaker	56	"
D	*Polo Lena—†	9	housewife	49	"
E	Polo Vincent	9	musician	25	"

Cobden Street

F	Wolff Albert G	1	lawyer	56	here
G	Wolff Nellie B—†	1	housewife	49	"

3

Cobden Street—Continued

	Letter	FULL NAME	Residence Jan. 1, 1941	Occupation	Supposed Age	Reported Residence Street and Number
	H	Baker Arline—†	1	domestic	45	223A Walnut av
	K	Baker Dayton	1	clerk	31	223A "
	L	Baker Julia—†	1	housewife	71	223A "
	M	Baker Thomas	1	janitor	73	223A "
	N	Baker Virgil	1	musician	37	223A "
	O	Frazier Lawrence	1	porter	40	here
	P	Smith Callie M	1	teacher	25	"
	R	Alexis Mabel—†	3	housewife	47	"
	S	Alexis Milton	3	student	20	
	T	Alexis Spiro	3	hairdresser	50	"
	U	Alexis Walter W	3	truckman	21	"
	V	Turcotte Catherine A—†	3	housewife	49	"
	W	Turcotte Charles D	3	clerk	49	
	X	Turcotte Marie E—†	3	student	20	
	Z	Klett Anna—†	15	housewife	48	"
504						
	A	Klett Gertrude—†	15	clerk	21	
	B	Klett Henry	15	custodian	58	"
	C	Coughlin Dennis J	15	shoeworker	53	"
	D	Coughlin Helen E—†	15	instructor	44	"
	E	Ruck Francis M	15	shoeworker	53	"
	F	Ruck Hanorah T—†	15	housewife	52	"
	G	Imbrogna James	17	barber	50	
	H	Imbrogna Livia—†	17	clerk	25	
	K	Imbrogna Stella—†	17	housewife	41	"
	L	Friese Gustaf	19	meatcutter	45	179 Heath
	M	Friese Heinz	19	operator	21	179 "
	N	Friese Martha—†	19	housewife	44	179 "
	O	*Kennealy Betty—†	21	domestic	22	36 Castle
	P	Wallace Charles	21	policeman	61	here
	R	Wallace Charles J	21	clerk	30	"
	S	Wallace Madelyn—†	21	student	23	"
	T	Golden George F	25	chauffeur	40	"
	U	Golden Harriet E—†	25	housewife	33	"
	V	Tausey Catherine—†	25	clerk	26	
	W	Tausey Helen—†	25	"	28	
	X	Tausey Patrick	25	laborer	73	
	Y	Comeau Ethel F—†	25	housewife	34	"
	Z	Comeau John W	25	mechanic	34	"
505						
	A	Nolan Ellen F—†	25	housewife	59	"

Page.	Letter.	FULL NAME.	Residence, Jan. 1, 1941.	Occupation.	Supposed Age.	Reported Residence, Jan. 1, 1940. Street and Number.

Cobden Street—Continued

	B	Nolan Valentine B	25	fireman	59	here
	c	Nolan William R	25	clerk	35	"
	D	Swanson Arnold	27	machinist	32	"
	E	Swanson Esther—†	27	housewife	32	"
	G	David Agnes—†	27	"	20	1 Dunford
	H	David Aram G	27	clerk	23	1 "
	K	MacDonald Allan J	29	laborer	40	8 Rochdale
	L	MacDonald Mary G—†	29	housewife	36	8 "
	M	Regan Charles J	29	waiter	66	here
	N	Regan Charles J, jr	29	clerk	34	"
	o	Regan Margaret M—†	29	housewife	33	"
	P	Regan William F	29	laborer	33	"
	R	Curtis Ruth H—†	33	housewife	24	23 Byron ct
	s	Curtis William J	33	operator	27	23 "
	T	Bray James	33	laborer	31	23 Danforth
	U	Bray Mary J—†	33	housewife	30	22 "
	v	Goodrich Edward P	33	laborer	61	80 Vernon
	w	Goodrich Elizabeth—†	33	housewife	49	80 "
	X	Waugh Lillian—†	33	"	29	80 "
	Y	Albee James H	35	chauffeur	45	here
	z	McManus Philip F	35	longshoreman	41	"
		506				
	A	McManus Rita—†	35	clerk	20	
	B	Cronan Agnes L—†	35	matron	39	
	c	King Mary—†	35	housewife	52	"
	D	Sullivan James	37	porter	23	574 Canterbury
	E	Sullivan Winifred—†	37	housewife	59	here
	F	Seymourian Edward	37	salesman	32	"
	G	Seymourian Ellen—†	37	housewife	28	"
	H	Maxfield Stacey	37	shipper	38	
	K	Gannon William	39	clerk	31	"
	L	*Long Alfred	39	carpenter	54	"
	M	*Long Catherine—†	39	housewife	59	"
	N	Foley Catherine—†	39	"	63	
	o	Foley Timothy D	39	laborer	63	

Codman Park

	R	Marks George	5	chef	40	Malden
	s	*Marks Pauline—†	5	housewife	34	"
	T	Wagner Jason	5	machinist	27	5 Glen rd

Codman Park—Continued

U	Doyle Annie—†	5	housewife	43	here
V	Doyle Joseph	5	painter	21	"
W	Doyle Louis	5	"	44	"
X	Doyle Thomas	5	orderly	21	
Y	Golden Mabel I—†	5	housewife	39	"
Z	Golden Patrick P	5	machinist	43	"
	507					
A	Ladd Florence—†	5	housewife	32	35 Hawthorne
B	Ladd John	5	teamster	35	35 "
C	*Miller Henry	5	mechanic	35	here
D	Miller Winifred—†	5	housewife	26	"
E	Murphy Thomas	5	clerk	20	"
F	Whipple Katherine—†	5	housewife	36	"
G	Whipple Thomas	5	mechanic	40	"
H	Gass Francis L	6	engineer	45	
K	Gass Mary A—†	6	housewife	48	"
L	*Dalton Katherine A—†	6	"	30	
M	Dalton Oswald F	6	paymaster	32	"
N	Donovan Elizabeth—†	6	housewife	57	5 Valentine
O	Donovan Jeremiah	6	retired	78	5 "
P	McCall Elizabeth—†	6	hostess	29	5 "
R	Rosen Harry P	6	salesman	50	here
S	Rosen Lena—†	6	housewife	40	"
T	Eskerstrom Fritz	6	retired	76	"
U	Houghton Florence—†	6	clerk	37	
V	DeMarino Helen—†	6	housewife	31	"
W	DeMarino John	6	chauffeur	29	"
X	*Bakunas Anna—†	9	housewife	63	"
Y	Bakunas Francis	9	waiter	28	
Z	*Bakunas Joseph	9	pressman	73	"
	508					
A	Fales Lester T	9	sailmaker	67	"
B	Fales Mabel E—†	9	housewife	69	"
C	Fales Russell L	9	clerk	43	
D	McAuliffe Elizabeth—†	9	housewife	35	"
E	McAuliffe Jeremiah	9	porter	44	
F	Fougere Albert J	9	steward	32	
G	Fougere Dorothy—†	9	housewife	28	"
H	Haddad Adele—†	9	cook	30	73 E Brooklin
K	Haddad Assad	9	"	27	73 "
L	Haddad James	9	"	26	73 "

Page.	Letter.	Full Name.	Residence, Jan. 1, 1941.	Occupation.	Supposed Age.	Reported Residence, Jan. 1, 1940. Street and Number.

Codman Park—Continued

	M	Collins Arline D—†	9	housewife	24	5 Albemarle
	N	Collins James M	9	packer	23	5 "
	o	*D'Entremont Beatrice—†	10	housewife	36	here
	P	*D'Entremont Robert	10	machinist	38	"
	R	D'Eon Isaie	10	waiter	35	"
	s	*D'Eon Redina—†	10	housewife	31	"
	T	*Boyle Beatrice—†	10	"	40	
	U	Boyle Hugh	10	machinist	47	"
	v	Wile Henry A	10	contractor	34	"
	w	*Wile Jean A—†	10	nurse	34	
	x	*Andrews Lillian—†	10	housewife	65	"
	Y	Andrews William R	10	ironworker	63	"
	z	Mulcahy Alice I—†	10	housewife	54	10 Marie
		509				
	A	Mulcahy Michael B	10	laborer	56	10 "
	B	*Walentas Ona—†	15	housewife	65	here
	c	*Walentas Peter	15	retired	70	"
	D	*Wallace Alfred	15	tailor	43	"
	E	Wallace Peter	15	chauffeur	27	"
	F	*O'Brien Patrick	15	fisherman	30	"
	G	*Stack Alexander	15	"	44	
	H	*Stack Theresa—†	15	housewife	43	"
	K	Kral Ferdinand L	15	manager	25	"
	L	Kral Rita M—†	15	housewife	25	"
	M	Nielsen Hans C	15	finisher	56	
	N	Nielsen Petra M—†	15	housewife	54	"
	o	Wojciechowski Anna—†	15	"	38	"
	P	Ward Margaret A—†	15	"	66	Quincy
	R	Ward Stephen J	15	operator	73	"
	s	Witcofsky Helen—†	30	housewife	39	137 Crawford
	T	Micelotti Frank	30	machinist	60	here
	U	White Rachel S—†	30	waitress	24	"
	v	*Dillon Edna—†	32	housewife	24	39 Codman pk
	w	Dillon William	32	presser	25	39 "
	x	Katsianes Christos	32	bookkeeper	40	here
	Y	Katsianes Louise—†	32	housewife	30	"
	z	Manion John J	32	chauffeur	37	8 Magnolia
		510				
	A	Mohan Charles L	32	shipper	50	61 Bainbridge
	B	Mohan Nora E—†	32	housewife	39	61 "
	c	Mellon Agnes—†	34	operator	20	here

Codman Park—Continued

D	*Mellon Agnes F—†	34	housewife	42	here
E	Mellon Alexander A	34	machinist	45	"
F	Feeley Anna—†	35	bookkeeper	33	"
G	*Feeley James	35	gardener	68	"
H	*Nehiley Dorothy—†	35	housewife	27	"
K	*Nehiley Gordon	35	clerk	.34	"
L	Brown John	36	porter	55	14 Calumet
M	*Doherty Anthony	36	laborer	55	here
N	Pearson Iver	36	gardener	45	"
O	Pearson Margaret—†	36	housewife	45	"
P	Vuilleumier Arthur	37	chemist	22	2 Marine rd
R	Vuilleumier Marie—†	37	housewife	21	17 Oakland
S	Jameson Katherine—†	37	"	42	here
T	Moritz Albert	38	mechanic	28	"
U	Moritz Helen—†	38	housewife	24	"
V	Champlain Olive—†	38	seamstress	50	248 Spring
W	Bedington Louis	39	forester	24	2530 Wash'n
X	Bedington Martha—†	39	clerk	53	2530 "
Y	Pike Agnes M—†	39	housewife	42	67 Codman pk
Z	*Pike Joseph	39	machinist	43	67 "

511

A	Salpi Catherine—†	40	housewife	29	here
B	McGough Ruth—†	40	"	27	Melrose
C	McGough William	40	packer	34	"
D	Cotter Helen L—†	41	housewife	45	here
E	Cotter Patricia—†	41	clerk	21	"
F	Shaughnessy Edna—†	42	housewife	30	"
G	Shaughnessy John	42	clerk	32	
H	Madden Margaret—†	42	housewife	33	"
K	Madden Thomas	42	compositor	35	"
L	Finer Eliot	43	student	21	
M	Finer Harry	43	storekeeper	55	"
N	Simon Morris	43	shipper	25	"
O	Simon Rosalie—†	43	housewife	24	"
P	Bowman Albert C	44	mechanic	41	"
R	Bowman Dorothy C—†	44	housewife	41	"
S	Ritchie Lena—†	44	"	26	"
T	Ritchie William	44	clerk	32	"
U	*Anderson Harriet—†	45	housewife	40	"
V	Anderson Jens	45	machinist	45	"
W	Anderson Ralph	45	"	20	

Page.	Letter.	FULL NAME.	Residence, Jan. 1, 1941.	Occupation.	Supposed Age.	Reported Residence, Jan. 1, 1940. Street and Number.

Codman Park—Continued

x	Philbin Phyllis M—†	46	housewife	25	Winchendon
y	Philbin Thomas J	46	ironworker	34	4 Fort av
z	McCarthy Anna—†	46	housewife	26	here
	512				
a	McCarthy Charles	46	laborer	24	..
b	Riley John	47	retired	80	
c	Riley Margaret—†	47	housewife	70	"
d	Toomey Emma—†	48	"	24	
e	Toomey Michael J	48	laborer	31	
f	Good Abina—†	48	housewife	51	"
g	Good James	48	cutter	24	"
h	Cullinane Jeremiah	48	laborer	48	69 Maywood
k	*Cullinane Mary—†	48	housewife	42	69 "
l	McCarthy Catherine E—†	49	"	63	here
m	McCarthy Charles	49	retired	56	"
n	Greenfield Frank	51	collector	47	"
o	*Greenfield Ida—†	51	housewife	37	"
p	*Greenfield Lillian—†	51	clerk	39	"
r	Frith Elizabeth—†	51	housewife	32	Winthrop
s	*Frith Harry C	51	painter	35	"
t	Mulvey Catherine E—†	52	at home	47	here
u	Mulvey Elizabeth E—†	52	"	72	"
v	*D'Eon Norbert	53	painter	54	"
w	*D'Eon Theresa—†	53	housewife	44	"
x	Little Everett	53A	laborer	35	1812 Col av
y	Little Mary—†	53A	housewife	20	1812 "
z	Cameron Clifford	53A	laborer	40	here
	513				
a	Cameron Helen—†	53A	housewife	35	"
b	*Waters John J	54	clerk	68	"
c	Devalle Lida—†	55	housewife	36	133 I
d	Devalle Rufino	55	steward	53	133 "
e	Brehaut Gertrude—†	56	at home	70	here
f	*McPhee Katherine—†	57	housewife	30	133 Highland
g	*McPhee Michael	57	houseman	37	133 "
h	Fitzpatrick Helen A—†	57	housewife	53	here
k	Cullen James F	57	chauffeur	43	"
l	Cullen Margaret A—†	57	housewife	38	"
m	*Deon Abel	58	operator	40	10 Codman pk
n	Luride Richard	58	painter	60	here
o	Lunde Selma—†	58	housewife	59	"

9

Page.	Letter.	FULL NAME.	Residence, Jan. 1, 1941.	Occupation.	Supposed Age.	Reported Residence, Jan. 1, 1940. Street and Number.

Codman Park—Continued

	P	Salfarro Thomas	58	operator	56	here
	R	Jenkins Alfred	59	student	23	Texas
	S	Jenkins Martin	59	laborer	64	here
	T	Thibeault Felix	59	die setter	63	"
	U	Thibeault Leona—†	59	housewife	57	"
	V	Thibeault Mary L—†	59	assembler	23	"
	W	Bulger Francis G	59	attendant	25	"
	X	O'Connor Louise—†	59	housewife	23	"
	Y	O'Connor Thomas J	59	chauffeur	26	"
	Z	Mullally Bridget—†	60	housewife	70	"
		514				
	A	Mullally Francis	60	shipper	22	
	B	Mullally Patrick	60	retired	67	
	C	Smith Daniel	60	physician	75	"
	D	Blouin Irene—†	61	housewife	45	"
	E	*O'Connor Esther—†	61	"	52	
	F	O'Connor Thomas	61	ironworker	64	"
	G	Kimtis Hilda—†	61	housewife	26	"
	H	Kimtis Joseph	61	carpenter	29	"
	K	Wilfert Andrew	62	clerk	27	
	L	Wilfert Mary—†	62	housewife	53	"
	M	Geno Delore A	64	chef	43	6 Crestwood pk
	N	Geno Doris—†	64	housewife	34	6 "
	O	Franzi Leo	65	chauffeur	45	here
	P	Franzi Margaret—†	65	housewife	47	"
	R	Corrigan Margaret J—†	65	"	29	"
	S	Corrigan Philip	65	steamfitter	33	"
	T	Hernandez Frederick	65	painter	26	
	U	Hernandez Mildred—†	65	housewife	26	"
	V	Fitzgerald James	66	locksmith	23	143 Cedar
	W	Fitzgerald Mary—†	66	housewife	50	143 "
	X	Regan Richard	66	laborer	60	143 "
	Y	Jennings Margaret—†	66	housewife	28	Somerville
	Z	*Jennings Martin	66	machinist	31	"
		515				
	A	*Cottreau Genevieve—†	67	housewife	28	here
	B	Cottreau Mark E	67	cook	29	"
	C	D'Entremont Lucien	67	decorator	38	"
	D	*Bylander Anna—†	67	housewife	40	"
	E	Bylander Carl	67	painter	42	"
	F	Benjaminsen Marion—†	67	housewife	30	82 Codman pk

10

Page.	Letter.	FULL NAME.	Residence, Jan. 1, 1941.	Occupation.	Supposed Age.	Reported Residence, Jan. 1, 1940. Street and Number.

Codman Park—Continued

	G	Benjaminsen Oscar	67	painter	39	82 Codman pk
	H	Williams Ralph	68	laborer	34	here
	K	*Woodburn Agnes—†	68	housewife	32	"
	L	Woodburn Chester	68	tree surgeon	34	"
	M	Perry George	69	truckman	40	11 Atherton
	N	Perry Mary R—†	69	housewife	31	11 "
	O	Della Russo Gertrude—†	69	clerk	23	2436 Wash'n
	P	Zitoli Margaret H—†	69	housewife	23	here
	R	Zitoli Robert	69	oil dealer	23	"
	S	Armington Clara J—†	69	housewife	38	"
	T	Armington George C	69	chauffeur	45	"
	U	Armington George F	69	printer	20	
	V	Conlon Helen—†	70	domestic	39	"
	W	Rabita Ella—†	70	housewife	44	"
	X	Rabita Liborio	70	tinsmith	52	
	Y	Johnson Anna—†	71	housewife	53	"
	Z	Johnson Fritz	71	carpenter	64	"

516

	A	DeBury Cora—†	71	housewife	48	"
	B	DeBury Cyril	71	salesman	52	"
	C	Dacey Claire M—†	71	housewife	28	97½ Brookside av
	D	Dacey Daniel A	71	laborer	31	97½ "
	E	McDonough Barabra—†	72	housewife	46	here
	F	McDonough Michael	72	caretaker	48	"
	G	Jordan George	73	draftsman	42	"
	H	Jordan Irene—†	73	housewife	40	"
	K	*Murphy Mary—†	73	"	65	
	L	*Murphy William	73	laborer	69	"
	M	Hendrickson Clarence A	73	painter	43	2454 Wash'n
	N	Hendrickson Florence E-†	73	housewife	35	2454 "
	O	Hughes Bernard T	74	blacksmith	66	here
	P	Hughes Gertrude—†	74	inspector	24	"
	R	Hughes James J	74	oil dealer	22	"
	S	Hughes Mary D—†	74	housewife	59	"
	T	Hughes Thomas M	74	chauffeur	21	"
	U	Sears Matilda J—†	76	housewife	50	"
	V	Sears Otto	76	typist	22	
	W	Spillane Anna F—†	78	housewife	50	"
	X	Spillane Joseph P	78	clerk	24	"
	Y	Spillane Anna F—†	78	"	20	"
	Z	Spillane John F	78	foreman	22	

11

517

Codman Park—Continued

A	Hachey Joseph C	80	entertainer	36	27 Sydney
B	Hanlon John	80	salesman	50	here
C	Harris Harry J	80	retired	63	"
D	*Harris Josephine—†	80	housewife	61	"
F	*Grishaber Beulah—†	82	"	34	
G	Grishaber John G	82	baker	34	
H	Supitkowsky Anna—†	84	housewife	36	"
K	*Webb Hilda—†	84	"	40	
L	Webb Owen	84	carpenter	42	"
M	Holden Fred J	85	electrician	64	"
N	Holden Frederick H	85	glazier	36	
O	Holden Mary C—†	85	housewife	59	"
P	Walsh Martin F	85	carpenter	45	"
R	Walsh Mary—†	85	housewife	45	"

Codman Place

S	Mortenson Anna—†	1	housewife	75	10 Alvan ter
T	Mortenson George	1	mechanic	29	10 "
U	Nickerson George	1	shipper	40	10 "
V	Murray Alice—†	2	housewife	32	here
W	Murray Walter	2	rigger	32	41 W Walnut pk
X	Manning Joseph	3	pedler	23	here
Y	Downey James M	3	"	54	"
Z	Downey James M, jr	3	chauffeur	30	"

518

A	Mason Frank C	5	"	33	
B	Mason Freeman	5	pedler	64	
C	Mason Sarah M—†	5	housewife	63	"

Corliss Street

D	Finnegan Thomas J	2	foreman	59	here
E	Hassett Arthur J	2	"	65	"
F	Hassett Walter T	2	hostler	64	"
G	Boyd Alexander	3	lineman	51	
H	Boyd Mary—†	3	housewife	41	"
K	Chigas Jacob	3	stitcher	50	
L	*Chigas Mary—†	3	housewife	44	"
M	DiMuzio Concetta—†	3	"	27	10 Wiget

12

Corliss Street—Continued

N	DiMuzio Frank	3	laborer	44	10 Wiget
O	Wailgum Isabelle—†	4	housewife	49	here
P	Wailgum Louis	4	electrician	55	"
R	Damato Gussie—†	4	waitress	27	104 Bickford
S	Denning Bertha—†	4	housewife	29	58 Northampton
T	Denning Edward J	4	laborer	63	5 Minden
U	Denning Edward J	4	chauffeur	29	58 Northampton
V	Berube Felix F	4	clerk	52	here
W	Berube Felix F, jr	4	attendant	21	"
X	Berube Mary A—†	4	housewife	48	"
Y	Berube Ruth E—†	4	clerk	20	
Z	Jackson Lillian F—†	5	housewife	53	"

519

A	Jackson Owen J	5	clerk	20	
B	Kaunelis Anthony	5	weaver	48	
C	Kaunelis Emily—†	5	housewife	47	"
D	*Schutzer Martha—†	5	"	46	
E	Schutzer Rudolph	5	finisher	56	
F	Grealy Katherine J—†	6	housewife	48	"
G	Grealy Thomas	6	operator	49	
H	*Markussen Erling	6	butcher	38	..
K	*Markussen Gertrude—†	6	housewife	32	"
L	*Rosswagner Frederick	6	butcher	53	
M	Lundberg Francis	7	painter	37	
N	Lundberg Harriet—†	7	housewife	25	"
O	Lundberg John	7	janitor	72	577 Blue Hill av
R	Turner Anna V—†	7	housewife	58	here
S	Turner Frank H	7	U S A	25	"
T	Turner Frank W	7	retired	71	"
U	Vachon Fernand	9	cleaner	20	
V	*Vachon Melanie—†	9	housewife	40	.."
W	Vachon Norbert	9	janitor	47	
X	O'Leary Eva—†	9	housewife	53	"
Y	O'Leary Thomas J	9	laborer	42	"
Z	Kickham Nora—†	9	housewife	34	"

520

A	Kickham Richard	9	chauffeur	45	"
B	Gately Joseph	11	laborer	28	2828 Wash'n
C	Hulse Florence—†	11	housewife	30	here
D	Hulse Franklin	11	operator	35	"
E	Sherman Margaret—†	11	housewife	39	"

13

Corliss Street—Continued

	Letter	Full Name	Res.	Occupation	Age	Reported Residence
	F	Sherman Paul	11	chauffeur	40	here
	G	Kickham Hilda—†	11	operator	32	28 Marcella
	H	Kickham Ralph	11	mechanic	34	34 Codman pk

Dennison Street

	Letter	Full Name	Res.	Occupation	Age	Reported Residence
	K	Hurwitz Pauline—†	4	housewife	52	here
	L	Hurwitz Ruth E—†	4	chemist	26	"
	M	Hurwitz Sidney W	4	merchant	24	"
	N	Alpert Harry	4	clerk	31	
	O	Rubinstein Elizabeth—†	4	housewife	48	"
	P	Rubinstein Louis	4	merchant	52	"
	R	Rubinstein Pearl—†	4	chemist	23	
	S	Mooney Muriel P—†	5	housewife	26	"
	T	Mooney William E	5	attorney	34	"
	U	Denisuk Peter	6	storekeeper	50	"
	V	Goldberg Esther—†	6	housewife	32	"
	W	Goldberg Jacob	6	pharmacist	27	"
	X	Merelis David	6	retired	61	"
	Y	Merelis Mildred—†	6	housewife	58	"
	Z	Merelis Rebecca—†	6	dressmaker	30	"
521						
	A	Rubin Lillian—†	6	secretary	32	"
	B	Golnick Minnie—†	6	factoryhand	35	"
	C	Lichtman Anna—†	6	housewife	40	"
	D	Lichtman Israel	6	operator	43	
	E	Graglia Angelo	7	barber	20	
	F	Graglia Elinor—†	7	waitress	26	
	G	Graglia Felix	7	laborer	63	
	H	Graglia Mary—†	7	bookkeeper	22	"
	K	Graglia Melania—†	7	housewife	58	"
	L	White Charles	7	musician	34	"
	M	White Irene—†	7	housewife	29	"
	N	Yarckin Frances—†	8	"	35	
	O	Yarckin Isadore	8	electrician	40	"
	P	Cohen Frances—†	8	housewife	30	87 Lawrence av
	R	Cohen Morris	8	chauffeur	32	87 "
	S	Mahler Robert	8	salesman	27	87 "
	T	Mahler Samuel	8	tailor	58	87 "
	U	Marenburg Hyman	8	meatcutter	26	15 Gaston
	V	Marenburg Phyllis—†	8	housewife	25	15 "

Page.	Letter.	Full Name.	Residence, Jan. 1, 1941.	Occupation.	Supposed Age.	Reported Residence, Jan. 1, 1940. Street and Number.

Dennison Street—Continued

w	Smith Hyman	9	storekeeper	46	here
x	Smith Mary—†	9	housewife	47	"
y	Bloom Edith—†	9	"	29	"
z	Bloom Morris	9	operator	40	1 Franklin Garden
	522				
b	*Goldman Edith—†	10	housewife	40	here
c	*Goldman Samuel	10	painter	50	"
d	Berman Max	10	junk dealer	62	"
e	Gruber Ethel—†	10	housewife	24	"
f	Lefkowith Freda—†	10	"	26	
g	Lefkowith Max	10	pedler	29	
h	Rosenthal Abraham	10	dispatcher	27	"
k	Rosenthal Albert	10	teacher	28	10 Homestead
l	Rosenthal Ruth—†	10	housewife	23	10 "
m	Greenberg Henry	27	operator	35	11 Carmen
n	Greenberg Mary—†	27	housewife	33	11 "
p	Buzak Albert	28	mechanic	31	here
o	Buzak Joseph	28	painter	35	"
r	Buzak Tekla—†	28	housewife	70	"
s	Smith John C	28	social worker	33	Cambridge
t	Smith Lee W—†	28	housewife	32	"
u	Resnick Abraham J	28	painter	37	here
v	Resnick Theresa—†	28	housewife	24	"
w	Banks Catherine—†	29	"	28	"
x	Banks Charles	29	welder	34	"
y	Portnoy Ann—†	29	housewife	26	98 Nightingale
z	Portnoy Louis	29	salesman	30	98 "
	523				
a	Sheiber Benjamin	32	grocer	40	here
b	Sheiber Frances—†	32	housewife	37	"
c	Gerstein Lillian—†	32	"	27	199 Townsend
d	Gerstein Manuel	32	salesman	29	199 "
e	Solov Benjamin	32	welder	57	199 "
f	Solov Harry	32	technician	25	199 "
g	Solov Pauline—†	32	housewife	54	199 "
h	D'Entremont Admanta—†	32	"	33	here
k	D'Entremont Ethel—†	32	"	31	"
l	D'Entremont Lester	32	fisherman	36	"
m	D'Entremont Theodore	32	"	38	"
n	Bergman Frances—†	32	housewife	34	"
o	Bergman Jacob	32	storekeeper	40	"

15

Dennison Street—Continued

P	Halpern Clara—†	32	housewife	53	here
R	Halpern Gilda—†	32	student	20	"
S	Halpern Louis	32	storekeeper	54	"
T	Brown Celia—†	32	housewife	45	138 Crawford
U	Brown James	32	salesman	45	138 "
V	Hyman Henry	32	mechanic	52	138 "
W	Thompson Elizabeth—†	35	cashier	57	here
X	Thompson Margaret—†	35	at home	55	"
Y	Thompson Mary—†	35	housewife	52	"
Z	Thompson Anna M—†	35	"	54	

524

A	Thompson Arthur W	35	grocer	60	
B	Wagner Emma—†	36	housewife	70	"
C	Wagner Isaac E	36	realtor	75	
D	Asmous Eugenie—†	38	housewife	40	"
E	Asmous Vladimir	38	mechanic	49	"

Dunford Street

F	David Julia—†	1	housewife	62	here
G	David Oscar	1	meatcutter	66	"
H	David Satanig—†	1	cashier	31	"
K	Carey Andrew	2	contractor	64	"
L	Carey Andrew J	2	painter	35	
M	Carey Anne B—†	2	secretary	30	"
N	Carey James L	2	manager	26	"
O	Carey Mary J—†	2	housewife	66	"
P	Carey Mary J—†	2	clerk	36	
R	Carey William M	2	salesman	24	"
S	*Keenan Rose—†	3	housewife	58	83 Rossmore rd
T	*Keenan Thomas	3	shipper	55	83 "
U	Russell Andrew J	3	mechanic	50	here
V	Russell Catherine M—†	3	housewife	48	"
W	Russell Lilliam M—†	3	secretary	20	"
X	Hartnett Francis T	4	clerk	44	
Y	Hartnett Mary E—†	4	housewife	44	"
Z	Connolly Ellen—†	4	"	56	

525

A	Fisher Henry	6	engineer	48	"
B	*Fisher Margaret—†	6	housewife	43	"

16

Dunford Street—Continued

	c	Egan William M	6	foreman	60	here
	d	Queeney Catherine—†	6	housekeeper	49	"

Elmore Park

	e	Powers Elsie—†	1	housewife	38	here
	f	Powers John	1	clerk	34	"
	g	Sweeney Catherine—†	1	housewife	53	9 Liberty
	h	Sweeney Dorothy—†	1	"	26	here
	k	Sweeney John	1	machinist	30	"
	l	Jordan John	1	laborer	32	"
	m	Jordan Mary—†	1	housewife	31	"
	n	Cadlick Andrew	2	pressman	36	"
	o	Cadlick Margaret—†	2	housewife	36	"
	p	Maxwell Annie K—†	2	"	56	
	r	Maxwell Thomas L	2	superintendent	63	"
	s	Maxwell Wallace R	2	clerk	24	
	t	Fichtner Louis M	2	"	47	
	u	Fichtner Mary—†	2	housewife	80	"
	v	Fichtner Sarah—†	2	"	37	
	w	Choukas Christos	3	cook	40	
	x	Choukas Rachael—†	3	housewife	33	"
	y	Mitchell Catherine—†	3	"	35	71 Townsend
	z	McCormack Robert	3	mechanic	24	13 Bainbridge
526						
	a	McCormack Ruth—†	3	housewife	21	13 "
	b	Clement Catherine—†	3	"	22	2989 Wash'n
	c	Clement Chester	3	watchmaker	29	2989 "

Elmore Street

	d	Smith Frederick A	3	draftsman	40	here
	e	Smith Mary—†	3	housewife	39	"
	f	Moroney Elsie—†	3	"	57	83 Clifton
	g	Moroney William	3	laborer	65	83 "
	h	Sosna Helen M—†	3	clerk	22	here
	k	Sosna Joseph J	3	pipefitter	27	"
	l	Sosna Mary M—†	3	clerk	30	"
	m	Sosna Pauline—†	3	housewife	55	"
	n	*Foley Margaret—†	5	"	30	

Page.	Letter.	FULL NAME.	Residence, Jan. 1, 1941.	Occupation.	Supposed Age.	Reported Residence, Jan. 1, 1940. Street and Number.

Elmore Street—Continued

o	*Foley Patrick J	5	porter	34	here
p	Downing Harry H	5	engineer	48	15 Kensington
r	Downing Josephine—†	5	housewife	30	15 "
s	*Sheffield Mary—†	5	housekeeper	74	15 "
t	*Bihl Alfred	5	chauffeur	54	here
u	*Bihl Wilhelmina—†	5	housewife	59	"
v	MacFarland Mary M—†	9	housekeeper	39	225 Dudley
w	Ryan Ellen A—†	9	housewife	52	26 Alpine
x	Ryan Ruth—†	9	clerk	24	26 "
y	*Janczunski Annie—†	9	housewife	42	here
z	Janczunski Joseph	9	manager	23	"

527

a	Janczunski Roman	9	longshoreman	46	"
b	*Kremke Adolph	9	gardener	47	"
c	Sedlin Charles	11	carpenter	54	"
d	*Sedlin Elizabeth—†	11	housewife	41	"
e	Lekas Eva—†	11	"	53	
f	Lekas Jacob	11	carpenter	57	"
g	Pinkul Adela N—†	11	housewife	26	"
h	Pinkul Gustav A	11	engineer	32	"
k	Kelly Annie M—†	13	housekeeper	44	"
l	Doherty Catherine—†	13	clerk	20	30 Sherman
m	Foley Eileen M—†	13	housewife	27	30 "
n	Foley Joseph D	13	painter	30	30 "
o	Jordan Edward	13	attendant	28	here
p	Jordan Laurence	13	porter	23	"
r	Jordan Margaret—†	13	housewife	48	"
s	Searle Lily R—†	15	clerk	38	
t	Searle Rosella M—†	15	housewife	63	"
u	Buey Esther F—†	15	saleswoman	48	Cambridge
v	Cushing Walter H	15	bartender	58	here
w	MacEwan Gretta—†	15	nurse	25	Cambridge
x	Downey Jeanette—†	15	stenographer	24	here
y	Hogan Eileen—†	15	housewife	29	"
z	Hogan James	15	salesman	30	"

528

a	McCarthy Daniel	17	clerk	25	Weymouth
b	McCarthy Doris—†	17	housewife	21	53 Parker Hill av
c	Sweeney Grace V—†	17	"	41	208 Shawmut av
d	Sweeney Jeremiah	17	mechanic	58	208 "
e	Carey Bridget—†	17	housewife	71	here

Elmore Street—Continued

F	Carey John J	17	laborer	42	here
G	Carey Patrick	17	"	70	"
H	Carey Terrence	17	painter	36	"
K	Lewis Margaret C—†	17	waitress	35	"
M	Anello Andrew	21	tailor	45	Malden
N	Anello Josephine—†	21	housewife	37	"
O	Blackwood Clarence	21	chauffeur	28	3 Fountain sq
P	Blackwood Muriel—†	21	waitress	22	3 "
R	Blackwood Pauline—†	21	operator	21	3 "
S	Blackwood Wallace I	21	retired	71	3 "
T	Gates John H	21	clerk	57	23 Burard
U	Rumrill Lawrence G	21	shipper	33	384 Amory
V	Rumrill Phyllis—†	21	housewife	25	384 "
W	*Asker Ingeborg—†	23	housekeeper	85	here
X	Kalland Gerda—†	23	saleswoman	22	"
Y	Kalland John B	23	printer	45	"
Z	Kalland Lily—†	23	housewife	43	"

529

A	Skrzyszowski Bernard	23	postal clerk	29	"
B	*Skrzyszowski Nellie—†	23	housewife	49	"
C	Skrzyszowski Stanley	23	shoeworker	50	"
D	Finn Mary A—†	29	housekeeper	76	"
E	Dunn Emily K—†	29	at home	59	"
F	*Graham Ann B—†	29	dressmaker	36	"
G	*McIntyre George E	29	clerk	50	
H	*McIntyre Mary E—†	29	housewife	53	"
K	Russo Alice C—†	29	"	48	
L	Russo Frank	29	chauffeur	50	"
M	Gilman Mary F—†	31	stenographer	28	"
N	Gilman Mary K—†	31	housewife	59	"
O	Gilman Thomas S	31	meatcutter	59	"
P	Craffey Catherine M—†	31	housewife	68	"
R	Craffey Helen M—†	31	teacher	30	
S	Craffey James T	31	retired	71	
T	McElroy Joseph E	31	accountant	26	"
U	McElroy Joseph H	31	chef	68	
V	Whittaker Margaret T—†	31	housekeeper	44	"
W	Glynn Josephine M—†	33	housewife	42	"
X	Glynn Thomas P	33	laborer	52	
Y	Wagner Charles R	33	clerk	29	
Z	Wagner Edward	33	laborer	21	

530
Elmore Street—Continued

A	Wagner Frederick W	33	watchman	63	here
B	Wagner James	33	clerk	30	"
C	Wagner Mary E—†	33	housewife	59	"
D	Birszianowski Mary—†	33	packer	24	
E	Piotrowicz Alexander	33	baker	30	
F	Piotrowicz Helena—†	33	housewife	28	"
G	Samardak Lucy—†	33	packer	24	..
H	*Samardak Mary—†	33	housewife	55	"
K	McCarthy Catherine—†	35	clerk	21	151 Centre
L	*McCarthy Mary—†	35	housewife	57	151 "
M	*McCarthy Michael	35	laborer	62	151 "
N	O'Brien Beatrice M—†	35	housewife	40	Revere
O	O'Brien Harold B	35	policeman	44	610 Dudley
P	Forsyth Mary—†	35	housewife	22	16 Dresden
R	Forsyth William	35	shipper	26	16 "
S	Jarvis Arthur	35	clerk	29	9 Elmore
T	Jarvis Margaret—†	35	housewife	50	9 "
U	Wiencus Elinore—†	35	"	25	9 "
V	Stevenson Josephine D—†	39	housekeeper	61	here
W	Connor Elizabeth B—†	41	housewife	63	"
X	Connor George H	41	manager	62	"
Y	Connor Thomas F	41	court officer	36	"
Z	Connor Walter T	41	clerk	28	

531

A	Gildea Catherine—†	43	at home	73	"
B	Gildea Charles F	43	salesman	41	"
C	Gildea J Henry	43	collector	33	..
D	Gildea Josephine—†	43	teacher	· 34	
E	Gildea Winifred—†	43	secretary	36	"
F	*Gardiner Bertha—†	45	housekeeper	66	65 Monadnock
G	Gunther Catherine—†	45	chemist	30	Malden
H	Hanson John S	45	retired	76	here
L	Carriere Alfonse	47	salesman	29	"
M	Carriere Mafalda—†	47	housewife	28	"
N	*Cusato Crescenzo	47	tailor	54	
O	Cusato Hugh	47	printer	21	
P	Cox Gerald C	49	clerk	31	
R	Cox Henrietta T—†	49	housewife	23	"
S	Cardozo Antonio	49	attorney	36	

Page.	Letter.	FULL NAME.	Residence, Jan. 1, 1941.	Occupation.	Supposed Age.	Reported Residence, Jan. 1, 1940. Street and Number.

Elmore Street—Continued

	T	Cardozo Evelyn—†	49	housewife	33	here
	U	Jones Grace—†	49	"	34	"
	V	Jones Walter	49	laborer	36	"
	W	Burke Anna—†	51	clerk	43	"
	X	Burke Margaret—†	51	housewife	48	"
	Y	Carney Anna A—†	51	"	56	"
	Z	Hawes Mary C—†	51	housekeeper	55	Revere
532						
	A	Matthei Bernhard	51	engineer	34	here
	B	Matthei Evelyn R—†	51	housewife	29	"

Fenner Street

	C	Reiser George	1	chauffeur	32	208 Highland
	D	Reiser Mary H—†	1	housewife	28	208 "
	E	Brady Catherine—†	1	"	79	here
	F	Brady James H	1	weaver	46	"
	G	Brady John T	1	foreman	50	"
	H	Brady Martha—†	1	housewife	43	"
	K	*Collins Mary—†	7	"	36	
	L	*Collins Michael	7	laborer	40	
	M	Garvey Bridget—†	7	housewife	43	"
	N	Garvey Patrick J	7	upholsterer	44	"
	O	Keegan Alice—†	7	housewife	54	"
	P	Keegan William	7	bartender	56	"
	R	Keegan William, jr	7	operator	25	"
	S	*Pentz Arthur	16	clerk	20	
	T	*Pentz Bertha—†	16	housewife	46	"
	U	Pentz Frank L	16	mechanic	47	"
	V	Winkler Edna L—†	16	clerk	29	
	W	Winkler Gertrude C—†	16	housewife	62	"
	X	Chamberlain Elizabeth—†	18	"	27	25 Galena
	Y	Chamberlain William H	18	salesman	27	25 "

Haley Street

	Z	Golden Louis	1	laundryman	44	here
533						
	A	Golden Sadie—†	1	housewife	40	"

Page.	Letter.	Full Name.	Residence, Jan. 1, 1941.	Occupation.	Supposed Age.	Reported Residence, Jan. 1, 1940. Street and Number.

Haley Street—Continued

B	Gordon Anne—†	1	housewife	33	here
C	Gordon Joshua	1	cashier	36	"
D	Imbrogna Lillian—†	5	housewife	32	"
E	Imbrogna Pasquale	5	barber	37	
F	Mason Leonard	6	mason	36	
G	Mason Luoneal	6	"	31	
H	Mason Martha—†	6	housewife	34	"
K	Mason Mildred—†	6	"	33	
L	Quarles Lorenzo	6	waiter	38	
M	Quarles Margaret—†	6	housewife	34	"
N	McKinney Aubrey	6	retired	65	
O	McKinney Aubrey R	6	electrician	29	"
P	McKinney Charles B	6	porter	26	
R	McKinney Eva—†	6	housewife	55	"
S	McKinney George	6	messenger	21	"
T	McKinney Warda—†	6	secretary	23	"
U	Van Alfred	7	wrecker	44	
V	Van Edward	7	salesman	22	"
W	Van May—†	7	housewife	42	"
X	Miller Abraham	7	operator	42	"
Y	Miller Lillian—†	7	clerk	41	"
Z	Miller Sarah—†	7	housewife	37	"
	534				
A	Pollack Arnold	7	manager	31	"
B	Pollack Lillian—†	7	housewife	22	"
C	Cort Boris	8	salesman	47	"
D	Cort Eva—†	8	housewife	45	"
E	Naiman Bertha—†	8	"	54	
F	Naiman Isadore	8	pharmacist	27	"
G	Naiman Miriam—†	8	housewife	23	"
H	Naiman Raphael	8	storekeeper	57	"
K	Naiman Robert	8	student	20	"
L	Lindsey Archibald	9	decorator	46	"
M	Lindsey Ruth D—†	9	housewife	38	"
N	Anderson Axel	9	retired	64	
O	Anderson Christine—†	9	housewife	65	"
P	Anderson Evelyn—†	9	bookkeeper	28	"
R	Anderson Gertrude—†	9	"	25	"
S	Anderson O Regina—†	9	"	39	
T	Johnson Swan	9	retired	77	

22

Page.	Letter.	Full Name.	Residence, Jan. 1, 1941.	Occupation.	Supposed Age.	Reported Residence, Jan. 1, 1940. Street and Number.

Harrishof Street

u	Levy Sarah T—†	167	housewife	42	here	
v	Moody Albert	167	janitor	55	"	

Rochdale Street

w	Burns Alfred M	2	salesman	49	here	
x	Burns Mary G—†	2	housewife	40	"	
y	Burns Thomas P	2	salesman	51	"	
z	Murphy Christine M—†	2	housewife	32	"	
	535					
a	Murphy Peter R	2	chauffeur	36	"	
b	Harris Allan A	2	salesman	54	"	
c	Harris Helen F—†	2	housewife	50	"	
d	*Lynch Margaret—†	2A	"	32	"	
e	*McIsaac Catherine—†	2A	"	46	14 Gartland	
f	McIsaac Roderick J	2A	chauffeur	49	14 "	
g	*McPherson Mary—†	2A	housekeeper	80	14 "	
h	Charney Amelia—†	4	"	36	3544 Wash'n	
k	Carson James H	4	painter	44	41 Morton	
l	Mossman Edward	4	clerk	26	here	
m	Mossman Margaret—†	4	housewife	52	"	
n	Lawrence Marguerite—†	6	"	27	"	
o	Lawrence Raymond V	6	laborer	28	"	
p	Lyon Dorothy—†	6	housewife	21	22 Valentine	
r	Lyon Joseph	6	counterman	24	22 "	
s	Hogkvist Anna C—†	6	housewife	71	here	
t	Hogkvist Emil N	6	painter	70	"	
u	Durant David	8	carpenter	58	"	
v	Durant George R	8	clerk	25		
w	Durant Mary—†	8	housewife	57	"	
x	Durant Mary L—†	8	stenographer	31	"	
y	Durant Mildred—†	8	"	21	"	
z	Cutter George	8	clerk	51		
	536					
a	Cutter Sarah—†	8	waitress	56	"	
b	Molloy Agnes—†	8	housewife	27	218 Wash'n	
c	Malloy William	8	boilermaker	28	218 "	
d	Powers Nora A—†	12	housewife	58	287 Bellevue	
e	Powers William B	12	wool sorter	59	287 "	
f	McKinnon Joseph	14	laborer	35	4 Erie pl	

Rochdale Street—Continued

	G	McKinnon Margaret—†	14	housewife	32	4 Erie pl
	H	Kelliher Cornelius J	16	clerk	34	here
	K	*Kelliher Mary F—†	16	housewife	34	"
	L	Brown Stephen M	18	mechanic	48	"
	M	Holmes Marjorie—†	18	housekeeper	53	New York

Townsend Street

	N	Burroughs Edith M—†	8	housewife	47	56 Clifford
	O	Burroughs George L	8	caretaker	60	56 "
	P	Day Dorothy—†	8	clerk	29	56 "
	R	Burns Edwin	8	salesman	62	here
	S	Burns Maude M—†	8	housewife	52	"
	T	Berman Frank E	8	attorney	40	"
	U	Berman Rose—†	8	housewife	34	"
	V	Rosenberg Morris	8	pedler	64	
	W	Rosenberg Rebecca—†	8	housewife	58	"
	X	McKenna James	8	marbleworker	51	"
	Y	McKenna James E	8	clerk	22	"
	Z	McKenna Margaret—†	8	housewife	25	"

537

	A	Riley Fergus	8	operator	47	"
	B	Riley John B	8	mechanic	26	"
	C	Riley Mary D—†	8	waitress	20	
	D	Riley Mary R—†	8	housewife	42	"
	E	Riley Mildred—†	8	housekeeper	22	"
	G	Partello Dorothy—†	11	housewife	28	12 Warren pl
	H	Partello Harry	11	chauffeur	26	12 "
	K	Andrey Charles	14	iceman	53	here
	L	Markus Anna—†	14	housewife	49	"
	M	Markus Frank	14	salesman	53	"
	N	*Connolly James	14	laborer	33	
	O	Cowley Johanna—†	14	housewife	31	"
	P	Cowley Patrick	14	fisherman	36	"
	R	Dunphy Flora E—†	14	housewife	35	"
	S	Dunphy Raymond	14	counterman	37	"
	T	French Josephine R—†	14	clerk	63	
	U	Grigar Selma—†	14	at home	60	
	V	Parker Selma—†	14	housewife	38	"
	W	Parker Weston	14	chauffeur	40	"
	X	Whitley Dorothy F—†	14	seamstress	55	"

24

Page.	Letter.	FULL NAME.	Residence, Jan. 1, 1941.	Occupation.	Supposed Age.	Reported Residence, Jan. 1, 1940. Street and Number.

Townsend Street—Continued

	y	Whitley Virginia M—†	14	bookkeeper	23	22 Dunreath
	z	Cullen Mary C—†	14	at home	85	21 Galena
538						
	a	Keane John L, jr	14	clerk	40	21
	b	Keane Nell C—†	14	housewife	44	21 "
	c	*Boath Alice—†	15	"	63	here
	d	*Boath Anna—†	15	cook	43	"
	e	Nash John H	15	retired	66	"
	f	Gross Dora—†	19	housewife	45	"
	g	Gross Matthew	19	salesman	47	"
	h	Gross Robert	19	student	20	"
	k	Kelley Christina—†	19	operator	25	381 Centre
	l	Kelley James	19	painter	67	381 "
	m	Kelley James	19	messenger	30	381 "
	n	Kelley Joseph	19	clerk	28	381 '
	o	Kelley Mary—†	19	housewife	61	381 "
	p	Kelley Veronica—†	19	clerk	23	381 "
	r	Varnerin Frank	23	manager	33	here
	s	Varnerin Helen—†	23	housewife	28	"
	t	Moccia Angelo	23	laborer	51	"
	u	Moccia Ella—†	23	housewife	51	"
	v	Moccia Florence—†	23	clerk	26	
	w	Moccia George	23	"	20	
	x	Moccia Marie—†	23	houseworker	23	"
	y	Tracy Annie—†	27	housewife	49	"
	z	Tracy Bernard	27	clerk	21	"
539						
	a	Tracy John	27		22	
	b	Tracy Thomas	27	"	20	
	c	Dacey Theresa A—†	27	teacher	62	
	d	McCann Cecelia M—†	27	at home	70	
	e	Dunn Margaret A—†	28	"	60	
	f	Marshall Florence A—†	28	teacher	60	
	h	McMorrow John	31	retired	68	
	k	Millett Mildred—†	31	waitress	32	
	l	Sweeney Gertrude—†	31	housewife	34	"
	m	Sweeney Lawrence	31	clerk	34	
	n	Gour Kathleen—†	31	housewife	30	"
	o	Gour William	31	manager	30	"
	p	Gray Ora—†	31	waitress	36	
	r	Herron George	35	garagenan	48	"

Page.	Letter.	Full Name.	Residence, Jan. 1, 1941.	Occupation.	Supposed Age.	Reported Residence, Jan. 1, 1940. Street and Number.
	s	Herron George, jr	35	clerk	20	here
	T	Herron Isabel—†	35	housewife	40	"
	U	Thebado Charles E	35	rubberworker	30	"
	v	Thebado Charles H	35	carpenter	63	"
	w	Thebado Ernest R	35	clerk	28	"
	x	Thebado Genevieve—†	35	housewife	56	"
	Y	Thebado Mary—†	35	"	28	"
	z	Freeman A Maude—†	44	"	50	2654 Wash'n
540						
	A	Freeman George M	44	chauffeur	52	2654 "
	B	*Irving Henry	44	laborer	22	56 W Eagle
	c	Irving Margaret—†	44	housewife	41	56 "
	D	Matlin Elizabeth—†	44	"	47	58 Erie
	E	Matlin Harold	44	laborer	22	58 "
	F	Matlin Phineas	44	"	53	58 "
	G	Cook Oliver P	45	janitor	42	here
	H	McCarthy Anna—†	45	nurse	42	"
	K	McLaughlin Catherine R—†	45	"	30	740 Benningt'n
	L	*Morton Paula S—†	45	"	21	here
	M	*Port Marian—†	45		24	"
	N	Scott Margaret M—†	45	"	35	N Bedford
	o	Slomovitch Esther—†	46	housewife	30	15 Norwell
	P	Slomovitch Harry	46	salesman	33	15 "
	R	Varnerin Aida—†	47	clerk	38	here
	s	Varnerin Henry P	47	garageman	40	"
	T	Varnerin Emma M—†	47	student	34	"
	U	Varnerin William J	47	foreman	29	
	v	*Himelfarb Dora—†	50	housewife	48	"
	w	*Himelfarb Israel	50	gasfitter	51	
	x	Himelfarb Joseph	50	clerk	23	
	Y	Leppo Ruth—†	50	"	27	
	z	Weiner David	50	bartender	28	"
541						
	A	Weiner Marcia—†	50	housewife	28	"
	B	Pugatch Gertrude—†	50	"	27	
	c	Pugatch Henry	50	salesman	30	"
	D	Rabinovitz Joseph	52	storekeeper	48	"
	E	*Rabinovitz Rebecca—†	52	housewife	41	"
	F	Feldman Isaac	52	clerk	52	227 Harold
	G	*Feldman Rose—†	52	"	24	227 "
	H	Feldman Sidney	52	"	22	227 "

Townsend Street—Continued

	K	Winer Gertrude—†	52	nurse	25	227 Harold
	L	Baker David	52	tailor	43	here
	M	Baker Ida—†	52	housewife	45	"
	N	*Walter Elizabeth—†	54	"	39	"
	O	*Walter Henry A	54	sculptor	44	
	P	*Epstein Rose—†	58	housewife	60	"
	R	*Epstein Samuel	58	meatcutter	60	"
	S	Horowitz Celia—†	58	housewife	46	"
	T	Horowitz Louis	58	laborer	46	"
	W	Randolph Effie—†	67	housewife	40	609 Col av
	X	Randolph Marion—†	67	waitress	21	609 "
	Y	Randolph Ralph	67	longshoreman	40	609 "
	Z	Lane James	67	student	21	here
542						
	A	Lane John	67	attorney	40	"
	B	Lane Ruth—†	67	housewife	37	"
	D	*Goldberg Aaron	71	metalworker	44	"
	E	*Goldberg Fannie—†	71	housewife	42	"
	F	Goldberg Natalie H—†	71	saleswoman	21	"

Walnut Avenue

	G	Hosten Mabel—†	221	housewife	53	here
	H	Hosten Steadford	221	steward	52	"
	K	Phillibert Cuthbert	221	physician	40	"
	L	Phillibert Marjorie—†	221	housewife	28	"
	M	Freeman George W	221A	court officer	49	"
	N	Freeman Josephine—†	221A	houseswife	52	"
	O	Williams Conover	221A	clerk	52	
	P	Williams Louise—†	221A	housewife	52	"
	R	Council Daniel H	223	retired	68	
	S	Council Essie—†	223	housewife	52	"
	T	Greene Leon	223A	fireman	54	38 Cedar
	U	Greene Mildred—†	223A	housewife	48	38 "
	V	Avery Blanche—†	223A	"	30	here
	W	Avery George	223A	clerk	35	"
	X	Hughes Henry	225	"	47	"
	Y	Hughes Rosalie—†	225	housewife	39	"
	Z	Roberts Erskine C	225A	retired	65	
543						
	A	Roberts Lillian M—†	225A	clerk	31	

Walnut Avenue—Continued

B	Roberts Ruth M—†	225A	housewife	52	here
C	Whiting Ella—†	225A	"	65	"
D	Whiting Frank I	225A	retired	67	"
E	Corey George	227	attendant	23	"
F	*Corey Sadie—†	227	housewife	46	"
G	Groosman Ida—†	227A	"	57	
H	Groosman Jacob	227A	retired	59	
K	*Gordon Etta—†	227A	housewife	43	"
L	Gordon Samuel	227A	woodworker	48	"
M	Croake Thomas	231	retired	72	22 Chambers
N	Bellew James	237	"	70	here
O	*Donahue Patrick	237	"	84	"
P	Fennelly James	237	"	71	"
R	Griffin Hyland	237	custodian	50	"
S	Hallorano Jeremiah	237	architect	50	
T	Keane Daniel	237	retired	78	"
U	Leishman John	237	"	62	62 Hecla
V	Nagle David	237	"	59	here
W	*Olsen Peter	237		81	"
X	Sullivan Jeremiah	237	"	84	"
Y	Breen Mary—†	241	at home	62	25 Templeton
Z	Brett John	241	retired	77	here

544

A	Brine Louise—†	241	nurse	24	
B	*Burgess Elizabeth—†	241	at home	76	"
C	Cunningham Elizabeth–†	241	"	67	10 Chapman
D	Darling Ada—†	241	nurse	55	here
E	Dolan Mary—†	241	housewife	32	"
F	Donnigan Fred	241	retired	62	"
G	Dwyer Margaret—†	241	at home	81	
H	*Fitzpatrick Julia—†	241	"	53	
K	Flynn Judith—†	241	"	77	
L	Halloran Rose—†	241	nurse	55	"
M	Horne Mary—†	241	housewife	56	94 Marcella
O	*Jackson Mary—†	241	at home	80	here
P	Johnson Jacobine—†	241	"	77	"
R	Jones Alice—†	241	"	81	11 Chapman
N	Kenney John	241	retired	84	here
S	Leonard Elizabeth—†	241	at home	74	"
T	Lindberg Della—†	241	"	80	"
U	*MacDonald Christine—†	241	"	70	

Page.	Letter.	FULL NAME.	Residence, Jan. 1, 1941.	Occupation.	Supposed Age.	Reported Residence, Jan. 1, 1940. Street and Number.

Walnut Avenue—Continued

	v	Mack Lillian—†	241	clerk	43	230 Hemenw'y
	w	Madden Mary—†	241	at home	62	here
	x	*Maskell Mary—†	241	"	55	"
	y	Miskelly Prudence—†	241	"	78	"
	z	O'Leary Patrick	241	retired	80	
545						
	a	Parnell Agnes—†	241	housewife	56	"
	b	Poch Charles	241	retired	67	
	c	Price Albert E	241	"	81	
	d	Slate Mary—†	241	nurse	45	
	e	Smith Annie—†	241	at home	79	
	f	Stromback Selma—†	241	"	83	
	g	Ward George	241	retired	61	"
	h	Webster Elizabeth—†	241	at home	80	80 Sullivan
	k	Whalen Ellen—†	241	"	80	Long Island
	l	Lamont Joseph J	247	cook	37	here
	m	Lamont Margaret R—†	247	housewife	31	"
	n	Sperling Edward	247	merchant	36	"
	o	Sperling Fay—†	247	housewife	30	"
	p	Miller Ralph	247	breweryworker	42	39 Hampstead rd
	r	Wilgoren Samuel	247	salesman	28	here
	s	Wilgoren Zelda—†	247	housewife	29	"
	t	Ulitsky Isaiah	247	salesman	25	40 Woolson
	u	Ulitsky Mollie—†	247	housewife	24	40 "
	v	Rabinovitz Max	247	salesman	50	here
	w	Rabinovitz Thelma A—†	247	housewife	41	"
	x	*Cohen Israel	247	storekeeper	50	"
	y	*Cohen Lillian—†	247	housewife	40	"
	z	*Sacks Celia—†	247	"	49	
546						
	a	Sacks Jacob	247	storekeeper	42	"
	b	Galles Nathan	247	baker	48	"
	c	Galles Sarah—†	247	housewife	53	"
	d	O'Leary Gertrude—†	247	operator	37	"
	e	O'Leary James	247	bartender	40	"
	f	*Ziskind Esther—†	247	housewife	65	"
	g	*Ziskind Hyman	247	shoemaker	67	"
	h	Fox Celia—†	247	housewife	23	"
	k	Fox Sidney H	247	pharmacist	26	"
	l	Golub Eva—†	247	housewife	43	"
	m	Kushner Anna—†	247	"	37	

Walnut Avenue—Continued

N	Kushner Joseph	247	salesman	42	here
o	Cohen Charles	247	retired	60	"
P	Cohen Jennie—†	247	housewife	48	"
R	Sawyer Beatrice—†	255	saleswoman	28	"
S	Sawyer Evelyn—†	255	"	25	
T	Sawyer Fannie—†	255	housewife	60	"
U	Sawyer James	255	salesman	65	"
V	Wald Jennie—†	255	housewife	58	"
W	Wald Louis	255	tailor	63	
X	Polin David	255	attorney	35	"
Y	Polin Mary—†	255	housewife	30	"
Z	Schwartz Anne—†	255	"	31	Chelsea

547

A	Schwartz Jacob	255	chauffeur	37	"
B	Block Bernard	273	newspaperman	32	here
C	Block Louis O	273	"	51	"
D	Levine Jennie—†	275	at home	68	"
E	Rosenberg Albert	275	retired	65	
F	Rosenberg Celia—†	275	housewife	63	"
G	Rosenberg Charles	275	clerk	36	"
H	Chernack Benjamin	275	manufacturer	30	71 Rossmore rd
K	Chernack Margaret—†	275	housewife	24	71 "
L	Berenberg Joseph	275A	merchant	55	here
M	Berenberg Leah—†	275A	housewife	52	"
N	Greenwald Dorothy—†	275A	"	34	"
o	Greenwald Joel	275A	social worker	36	"
P	Stroup Katherine A—†	277	housewife	66	"
R	Stroup Katherine M—†	277	teacher	41	
S	Stroup Mary H—†	277	"	44	
T	Stroup Millicent S—†	277	"	38	
U	Nyen Annie—†	277A	housewife	72	"
V	Nyen Donald E	277A	clerk	38	"
W	Nyen Gerald E	277A	chauffeur	28	"
X	Goldman Augusta—†	279	stenographer	22	"
Y	Goldman Isadore	279	salesman	50	"
Z	Goldman Sadie—†	279	housewife	48	"

548

A	Goldman Sarah—†	279	clerk	25	
B	Berkman Gertrude—†	279	secretary	37	"
C	Berkman Sophie—†	279	housewife	59	"
D	Fritz Herbert	279	tailor	26	

Walnut Avenue—Continued

	E	Fritz Vivian—†	279	housewife	24	here
	F	Metcalf Charles	279	buyer	61	"
	G	Metcalf Jennie—†	279	housewife	57	"
	H	Mult Samuel	279	salesman	47	"
	K	Cuzzens Lorena M—†	283	milliner	35	"
	L	Shaw Anna F—†	283	housewife	47	"
	M	Shaw Clarence F	283	embalmer	41	"
	N	Yates Everett C	283	teacher	47	
	O	Yates Thelma M—†	283	housewife	35	"
	P	Finkle Fannie—†	285	"	45	
	R	Finkle Morris	285	newsdealer	54	"
	S	Bloom James	285	pharmacist	28	"
	T	Bloom Sadie—†	285	housewife	28	"
	U	Tynes Alfred C	287	realtor	41	25 Gaston
	V	Tynes Dorothy E—†	287	housewife	38	108 Harrishof
	W	Tynes Timothy G	287	letter carrier	43	108 "
	X	Tynes Virginia—†	287	housewife	40	25 Gaston
	Y	Hudson Joseph N	289	superintendent	51	93 Howland
	Z	Hudson Rachel—†	289	housewife	52	93 "
549						
	A	Lindsey Edna—†	289	"	31	121 Harrishof
	B	Lindsey Lionel	289	shipper	37	121 "
	C	Holt George	291	waiter	41	here
	D	Holt Mary—†	291	housewife	35	"
	E	McAdoo Gladys—†	291	"	35	"
	F	Woods Ethel—†	291	cook	40	

Washington Street

		Methot Joseph	2818A	machinist	52	here
		Methot Levina—†	2818A	housewife	50	"
	H	Methot Elsie—†	2818A	"	24	"
		Methot Omar	2818A	watchmaker	27	"
	M	Carter Maurice	2818A	cook	28	Maine
	R	*Pavone Mary—†	2820A	housewife	69	here
	S	Pavone Pasquale	2820A	clerk	29	"
	T	Connell Florence—†	2822	"	39	"
	U	Crisp Susan E—†	2822	housewife	38	"
	V	McRae Joseph P	2822	grocer	39	
	W	McRae Margaret M—†	2822	operator	40	"
	X	Cole Annie—†	2822	housewife	40	"

Washington Street—Continued

z	Gaulrapp Elsie—†	2826	housekeeper	38	5 Arklow
550						
A	Graul William	2826	baker	61	5 "
B	Doyle Edward	2826	laborer	37	here
c	*Doyle Elizabeth—†	2826	housewife	32	"
D	Smith George	2826	laborer	71	"
E	Smith Laura M—†	2826	housewife	61	"
F	Ochs Florence—†	2828	"	40	
G	Ochs William A	2828	laborer	44	
H	Gately George T	2828	shipper	26	
K	Kennedy Mildred—†	2828	clerk	22	
L	Reinhardt Geraldine—†	2828	housewife	56	"
M	*Reinhardt Julius F	2828	watchman	60	"
N	Hayes Evelyn—†	2828	waitress	23	
o	Hayes Flora—†	2828	housewife	40	"
s	Cotton Barbara—†	2842	"	28	
T	Cotton Laura—†	2842	"	60	
U	Cotton Robert T	2842	clerk	30	
V	Young Eleanor—†	2842	housewife	42	"
551						
A	Ouellette Alice—†	2888	"	33	1370 Dor av
B	Ouellette Joseph	2888	painter	37	1370 "
c	Larsen Anders	2888	finisher	65	11 Corliss
D	Larsen Henry	2888	laborer	35	11 "
E	Larsen Signe—†	2888	housewife	58	11 "
F	Feeney Anna—†	2888	"	38	here
G	Feeney Daniel	2888	fireman	48	"
H	Lynch Emily M—†	2890	housewife	32	"
K	Lynch Peter J	2890	painter	27	"
L	Fountain Doris—†	2890	housewife	28	3 Corliss
M	Fountain Harold	2890	chauffeur	39	3 "
N	Natorp Herman	2890	laborer	52	here
o	Natorp Mary—†	2890	housewife	47	"
P	Grant Florence—†	2892	"	48	"
R	Grant John	2892	plater	50	
s	Twohig Bridie—†	2892	housewife	50	"
T	Twohig John A	2892	clerk	24	
U	Donovan Alice—†	2892	housewife	42	"
V	Donovan Alice—†	2892	clerk	21	
w	Donovan Francis	2892	laborer	28	
x	Donovan Samuel	2892	"	66	

Washington Street—Continued

Y	Donovan Vincent	2892	clerk	26	here
z	Poole John	2894	laborer	44	"
	552				
A	*Poole Muriel—†	2894	housewife	29	"
B	*Jamieson Mary A—†	2894	"	54	
c	Jamieson Mary E—†	2894	operator	22	"
D	*Jamieson Sidney J	2894	ironworker	54	"
E	*Tobin Richard	2894	proprietor	55	"
F	*Hickey Alexander	2894	laborer	56	..
G	*Hickey Ida—†	2894	housewife	49	"
H	Hickey John L	2894	U S A	21	
K	Hickey Lawrence J	2894	chauffeur	46	"
L	Hickey Rita—†	2894	operator	22	
N	Foley Alphonsus	2898	meatcutter	41	"
O	Foley Rose—†	2898	housewife	51	"
P	Memos James J	2898	waiter	42	
R	Memos Mary M—†	2898	housewife	40	"
U	Carroll Helen J—†	2928	saleswoman	21	"
V	Carroll Josephine M—†	2928	housewife	51	"
W	Carroll Josephine M—†	2928	laundress	25	"
X	Carroll Marion V—†	2928	waitress	22	
Y	Carroll William F	2928	U S A	23	
z	Feeley Annie—†	2928	housewife	50	"
	553				
A	Feeley Thomas	2928	laborer	54	
B	King Anna E—†	2930	housewife	72	"
c	King John J	2930	laborer	37	
E	Buchanan Leland	2930	"	41	
F	*Buchanan Violet—†	2930	housewife	47	"
G	McDonald Russell	2932	chauffeur	26	147 O
H	Montgomery Cyril	2932	laborer	45	25 Valentine
K	Montgomery Mary—†	2932	housewife	40	25 "
L	*Brady Delia—†	2932	"	40	here
M	*Brady James F	2932	laborer	36	"
T	Frawley Charles	2942	"	74	"
U	Donovan Mary—†	2944	housewife	72	Brookline
V	Keller Andrew	2944	retired	65	Wash'n D C
W	*Bennett Charles A	2944	blacksmith	62	here
X	*Bennett Mary C—†	2944	housewife	67	"
	554				
A	Roach Francis A	2946	janitor	44	2794 Wash'n

11—5

Washington Street—Continued

B	Roach Louisa M—†	2946	housewife	46	2794 Wash'n
c*	Gray Ella—†	2946	"	37	here
D	Gray Ernest H	2946	chauffeur	36	"
E	Dantos Alfred M	2946	chef	34	"
F	Dantos Mae—†	2946	housewife	31	"
G	Mason Richard	2948	laborer	46	29 Lamartine
H	Vierkant Francis	2948	foreman	27	29 "
K	Vierkant Marion—†	2948	housewife	26	29 "
L	Vierkant Sarah—†	2948	"	69	29 "
M	Reis Benvinda—†	2948	"	32	55 Codman pk
N	Reis Caesar	2948	steward	45	55 "
o	Cunningham Thomas	2948	laborer	45	45 Bickford
P	Davis Dorothy—†	2948	housewife	27	45 "
R	Davis Lewis	2948	chauffeur	29	45 "
T	Tebeau Joseph R	2956	decorator	39	here
U	Tebeau Mary B—†	2956	housewife	40	"
v	Walsh Frank C	2956	laborer	68	"
w	Hamilton Sarah—†	2958	housewife	52	"
x	Randall Mildred—†	2958	"	29	"
y	Turner George	2958	clerk	20	"
z	Quatromini Alphonse	2958	painter	23	41 Highland av
	555				
A	Quatromini Delia—†	2958	housewife	24	41 "
B	McCarthy Ruth—†	2958	"	29	here
c	McCarthy William	2958	laborer	31	"
D	Nicholson Eugenia—†	2960	housewife	35	48 Woodlawn
E	Nicholson Hugh	2960	printer	31	48 "
G	Kelley Allan	2960	chauffeur	31	here
H	Kelley Frances—†	2960	housewife	27	"
K	Jones Clarence	2962	chauffeur	31	"
L	Jones Dorothy—†	2962	housewife	40	"
M	Silverman Gilbert D	2962	laborer	28	"
N	Silverman Martina—†	2962	housewife	22	"
o	Cheney Clifton D	2962	laborer	49	77 Call
R	Shepherd Albert	2964	roofer	29	2996 Wash'n
s	Shepherd Juanita—†	2964	housewife	21	2996 "
T	Shepherd Catherine—†	2964	"	27	2993 "
U	Shepherd Ernest	2964	roofer	31	2993 "
v	Kenyon Elgie—†	2964	housewife	35	2960 "
w	Kenyon Robert	2964	laborer	44	2960 "
y	McLay Helen—†	2966	housewife	58	here

Page.	Letter.	FULL NAME.	Residence, Jan. 1, 1941.	Occupation.	Supposed Age.	Reported Residence, Jan. 1, 1940. Street and Number.

Washington Street—Continued

	z	McLay James	2966	painter	65	here
556						
	A	Larkin Annette—†	2966	housewife	30	"
	B	Larkin Henry	2966	clerk	42	
	c	Engeian Margaret--†	2974	housewife	27	"
	D	Engeian Peter	2974	barber	31	
	E*	Richardson Annie—†	2974A	housewife	49	"
	F	Richardson Harold	2974A	clerk	27	
	G	Conrad Florence—†	2974A	housewife	36	"
	H	Conrad Frederick	2974A	chef	42	"
	K	Quinn Louise—†	2976	housewife	36	57 Worcester
	L	James Albert	2976A	bartender	26	24 Springfield
	M	James Lillian—†	2976A	housewife	24	24 "
	N	Karavas Georgia---†	2976A	"	32	here
	O	Karavas Nicholas	2976A	waiter	54	"
	P	Karavas Spiros	2976A	bartender	48	"
	R	Gatley Ada E—†	2978	housewife	26	"
	s	Gatley Herbert F	2978	clerk	37	
	T	McMahon Harold	2978	steamfitter	41	"
	U	McMahon Margaret--†	2978	housewife	39	"
	v	Ryan Patrick	2978	clerk	36	
	w	McGowan Delia A—†	2978	housewife	53	"
	x	McGowan Helen J—†	2978	saleswoman	25	"
	Y	McGowan Mary E—†	2978	maid	30	
	z	McGowan Owen	2978	laborer	67	..
557						
	A	McGowan William J	2978	printer	20	
	D	Cocoyzeallo Rose—†	2980A	housewife	33	"
	E	DeGloria Albert	2982	shoeworker	28	332 Amory
	F	DeGloria Frances—†	2982	housewife	26	332 "
	G	Burnie Avis—†	2982	"	55	here
	H	Burnie Douglas	2982	cook	50	"
	M	Simmons William	2984A	laborer	73	"
	N*	Giltinan Louise—†	2984A	housekeeper	64	"
	O	Hyslop Kenneth	2984A	clerk	31	"
	P	Hyslop Lillian—†	2984A	housewife	32	"
	R*	Jelalian Catherine—†	2986	"	37	
	s*	Jelalian Hapet	2986	grocer	46	

Ward 11–Precinct 6

CITY OF BOSTON

LIST OF RESIDENTS
20 YEARS OF AGE AND OVER

(NON-CITIZENS INDICATED BY ASTERISK)
(FEMALES INDICATED BY DAGGER)

AS OF

JANUARY 1, 1941

JOSEPH F. TIMILTY, *Chairman*
FREDERIC E. DOWLING, *Secretary*
WILLIAM A. MOTLEY, JR.
FRANCIS B. McKINNEY
HILDA HEDSTROM QUIRK

Listing Board.

CITY OF BOSTON PRINTING DEPARTMENT

Page.	Letter.	FULL NAME.	Residence, Jan. 1, 1941.	Occupation.	Supposed Age.	Reported Residence, Jan. 1, 1940. Street and Number.

600

Amory Avenue

A	Miller Mary—†	2	housewife	44	here
B	Verrochi Delores—†	2	"	25	"
C	Verrochi Ralph	2	chauffeur	29	"
D	Rochon Helen—†	2	housewife	33	103 Lamartine
E	Rochon Joseph	2	mechanic	33	103 "
F	*Worrall Perley	4	contractor	47	here
H	Slavinsky Jennie—†	4	clerk	29	102 Heath
K	Slavinsky John	4	retired	72	102 "
L	Slavinsky John O	4	instructor	24	102 "
M	Slavinsky Minnie—†	4	housewife	67	102 "
N	Squire Edith C—†	20	"	38	here
O	Borrelli Francis	20	operator	28	Somerville
P	Borrelli Rena—†	20	housewife	23	"
R	Wolfgang Marion—†	20	"	26	68 Weld Hill
S	*Fehrenbacher Elizabeth–†	24	"	42	here
T	Fehrenbacher Joseph	24	steward	46	"

Amory Street

Y	Azzariti Ella—†	81	housewife	21	80 Hyde Park av
Z	Ceci Sandro A	81	clerk	27	109 Marcella

601

A	Millett Eugene L	81	"	30	109 '
B	Millett Mary L—†	81	housewife	29	109 "
C	Snyder Flora M—†	81	inspector	42	here
D	Snyder Fred M	81	operator	41	"
E	Boehner Elsie M—†	83	housewife	49	"
F	Boehner Fred J	83	musician	52	"
G	O'Connell Julia—†	83	housekeeper	54	"
H	O'Connell Nora—†	83	inspector	35	"
K	O'Connell Thomas	83	roofer	47	
M	McGuire William B	89	storekeeper	54	"
N	Curley Anna—†	91	housewife	29	"
O	Curley James M	91	chauffeur	34	"
P	Silva John W	91	machinist	38	120 Heath
R	Silva Loretta—†	91	housewife	36	120 "
S	Silva William	91	painter	30	136 "
T	Cook John	93	chauffeur	31	here
U	Cook Mary—†	93	housewife	31	"
V	Welsh Edward P	93	machinist	65	"

2

Amory Street--Continued

w	Welsh Mary—†	93	housekeeper	65	here
x	Dana Frank W	95	tinsmith	47	"
y	Dana Gertrude E—†	95	housewife	40	"
z	Lamond John L	112	repairman	24	7 Jackson pl

602

a	Lamond Mary E—†	112	housewife	22	7 "
b	*Moran Annie F—†	112	"	48	2 Montrose
c	*Moran Peter	112	carpenter	48	2 "
d	Leonard James H	112	timekeeper	25	74 Montebello rd
e	Leonard Mary—†	112	housewife	24	Newton
f	Wickman John G	112	laborer	59	2859 Wash'n
g	Wickman Julia—†	112	housewife	54	2859 "
h	Havey John E	112	shipfitter	29	174 Chestnut av
k	Havey Josephine R—†	112	housewife	26	174 "
l	Mosher Daniel C	112	foreman	32	Florida
m	Mosher Ruby—†	112	housewife	26	"
n	Daniels Harry	114	salesman	56	20 Royce rd
o	Woodbridge Natalie—†	114	clerk	28	Brookline
r	McCreadie Anna—†	114	secretary	29	22 Green
s	McCreadie Gordon	114	counterman	29	162 W Concord
v	Hopfgarden Marie E—†	153	housewife	67	here
w	Burkart Emily M—†	153	"	43	"
x	Burkart Joseph R	153	superintendent	45	"
y	Cutcliffe Eleanor—†	153	housewife	21	16 Wolfe
z	Cutcliffe Paul	153	serviceman	22	16 "

603

a	Finn Arthur B	155	rigger	23	here
b	Finn James	155	"	50	"
c	Sheehan Franklin F	155	presser	23	"
d	Sheehan Isabel—†	155	housewife	21	"
e	Anderson Dorothy—†	155	"	35	
f	Anderson Gustave	155	brewer	41	
g	Mitchell Katherine F—†	155	packer	53	
h	Shepler Ethel G—†	171	housewife	31	"
k	Shepler John R	171	clergyman	39	"
l	Canney Daniel	173	fireman	41	
m	Richards Elizabeth—†	173	factoryhand	20	"
n	*Richards Margaret—†	173	at home	56	
o	Duerr Michael	173	retired	76	
p	McEleney Josephine—†	173	housekeeper	50	"
r	McLaughlin Bernard	173	clerk	23	"

3

Amory Street—Continued

s	McLaughlin Edward	173	laborer	49	here	
T	McLaughlin Elizabeth—†	173	stenographer	21	"	
U	Bertsch Joseph L	175	retired	74	"	
v	*Nicol Ernestine—†	175	housekeeper	54	"	
w	Haussler Francis	175	salesman	32	83 Paul Gore	
x	Hosenfeld August	175	machinist	57	here	
y	Hosenfeld Lena—†	175	housewife	51	"	
z	Glennon Edward L	181	cableman	37	"	

604

A	Glennon Timothy F	181	retired	72		
B	Glennon Timothy F, jr	181	mechanic	45	"	
C	MacMillan Ruth—†	181	hairdresser	37	"	
D	Southwick Eugene H	181	guard	56		
E	Southwick Eugene H, jr	181	meatcutter	23	"	
F	Southwick Laura—†	181	housewife	49	"	
G	English Philip F	183	steamfitter	52	"	
H	English Rose E—†	183	housewife	52	"	
K	Trull Elizabeth P—†	183A	"	25	181 Amory	
L	Trull Harry E	183A	mechanic	29	181 "	
N	Belfield Sylvia—†	187	polisher	25	here	
O	Dwyer Alvin	187	counterman	22	"	
P	Prentis James E	187	retired	66	"	
R	Prentis James E	187	counterman	23	"	
S	Prentis Myrtle E—†	187	housewife	43	"	
T	Richards Mabel—†	187	housekeeper	23	"	

Amory Terrace

w	Roukey Arthur	1	laborer	38	41 Minden	
x	Roukey Corrinne—†	1	housewife	39	41 "	
y	*Cheromche Helen—†	1	"	40	here	
z	Letwin Leo	1	shipper	55	"	

605

A	Leonard Mary—†	3	housekeeper	75	"	
B	Sweetland Nancy—†	3	"	81	"	
c	*Walsh Elizabeth—†	3	housewife	57	"	
D	*Walsh Mary—†	3	clerk	22		
E	*Walsh Phillip F	3	rigger	64		
F	Sajowich Anna—†	3	stitcher	25		
G	*Sajowich Constance—†	3	housewife	51	"	

4

Page	Letter	Full Name	Residence, Jan. 1, 1941.	Occupation.	Supposed Age.	Reported Residence, Jan. 1, 1940. Street and Number.

Amory Terrace—Continued

	Letter	Full Name	Res.	Occupation	Age	Reported Residence
	H	Sajowcih Helen—†	3	waitress	20	here
	K	Sajowcih John	3	chauffeur	27	"
	L	*Sajowcih Joseph	3	packer	55	"
	M	Sajowcih Mary—†	3	stitcher	23	"
	N	*Kurapotkin Martha—†	10	"	56	48 Elmwood
	O	Alward Daniel	10	laborer	27	91 Amory
	P	Brown Christina—†	10	housekeeper	70	91 "
	R	Brown Wanda—†	10	"	23	91 "
	S	Brown William H	10	plumber	35	91

Atherton Place

	Letter	Full Name	Res.	Occupation	Age	Reported Residence
	T	Doherty Evelyn K—†	1	housekeeper	57	109 Peterboro
	U	Fagen Mary C—†	1	nurse	48	109 "
	V	Sellman George F	1	laborer	69	109 "
	W	Sellman Grace E—†	1	housewife	47	109 "
	X	Cosindas Angil	1	shipfitter	29	here
	Y	Cosindas Mary—†	1	housewife	22	"
	Z	*Koster Ella—†	2	"	61	"
606						
	A	Koster Helen—†	2	clerk	25	"
	B	Morella Dorothy—†	3	housewife	26	"
	C	Morella Frank	3	laborer	31	
	D	Neary Fred	3	"	26	
	E	Neary Grace—†	3	housewife	24	"
	F	Apoldo Salvatore	4	florist	34	
	G	Sauro Anna—†	4	stenographer	25	"
	H	Sauro Carmela—†	4	teacher	27	"
	K	Sauro Frances—†	4	clerk	25	"
	L	Sauro Givacchimo	4	barber	58	"
	M	Sauro Marie—†	4	housewife	55	"
	N	Hasenfuss Agnes—†		clerk	55	
	O	Hasenfuss Clara—†		"	47	
	P	Hasenfuss Mary—†		"	42	
	R	Vincent Cornelius		waiter	70	
	S	Vincent Cornelius, jr		student	21	
	T	Vincent Elizabeth—†		teacher	24	
	U	Vincent Mattie—†		housewife	53	"
	V	Vincent Ruth—†	6	teacher	23	

Atherton Street

w	Grinnell Catherine—†	2	housewife	23	48 Dacia
x	Grinnell Otto	2	factoryhand	24	46 W Walnut pk
y	Boggier Dolores—†	2	bookbinder	34	here
z	Boggier Jennie—†	2	housewife	65	"

607

A	Ford Catherine G—†	2	"	60	
B	Ford Herbert E	2	electrician	35	"
c	Ford Mary A—†	2	clerk	28	
D	Ford Ruth G—†	2	teacher	26	
E	Nilson Anna—†	2	at home	78	
F	Duffily Cecelia M—†	3	waitress	30	
G	Kenny Edward T	3	clerk	32	
H	Kenny John F	3	inspector	36	"
K	Kenny John H	3	retired	65	
L	Kenny Mary A—†	3	housewife	63	"
M	Kenny Paul W	3	repairman	30	"
N	Kenny Walter	3	chauffeur	24	"
o	Doyle Dominic	4	foreman	36	20 Tower
P*	Doyle Mary—†	4	housewife	34	20 "
R	Atsales Arthur	4	salesman	49	here
s	Atsales Pauline—†	4	housewife	36	"
T	Flood Stephen E	5	laborer	49	"
U	McDonald Stephen M	5	retired	65	"
v	McNamara James C	5	bartender	53	77 Montebello rd
w	Dowhanczuk Agnes—†	5	housewife	24	40 Lambert
x	Dowhanczuk Jeremiah	5	clerk	29	40 "
z	Mills John J	7	shipper	30	8 Emsella ter

608

A	Mills Mary—†	7	housewife	29	8 "
B	Haasis Helen—†	7	"	47	4 Amory av
c	Haasis William	7	carpenter	43	4 "
D	Connolly Delia—†	8	at home	68	28 Forest Hill av
E	Davey Elizabeth—†	8	housewife	39	here
F	Davey John J	8	laundryman	45	"
G	Gasner Barbara—†	8	at home	60	"
L	Lannon Rose—†	8	operator	37	"
H	Sullivan Frank	8	laborer	43	"
K*	Wildgoose Harold	8	molder	67	Rhode Island
M	Brown Chester A	9	carpenter	45	here
N	Hamilton Eliza—†	9	housewife	63	"
o	Hamilton John J	9	carpenter	72	"

Page.	Letter.	FULL NAME.	Residence, Jan. 1, 1941.	Occupation.	Supposed Age.	Reported Residence, Jan. 1, 1940. Street and Number.

Atherton Street—Continued

	P	Keefe Gregory	9	chauffeur	33	here
	R	Czuk Anna—†	10	housewife	36	"
	S	Czuk Philip	10	clerk	42	"
	T	Morrow Florence—†	10	housekeeper	53	"
	U	Pettigrew Archibald	11	laborer	53	"
	V	Pettigrew Leah—†	11	housewife	52	"
	W	Legrow Clyde	11	foreman	36	6 Crestwood pk
	X	Legrow Mary—†	11	nurse	26	6 "
	Y	Noonan Nora M—†	11	housewife	57	here
	Z	Noonan Patrick H	11	retired	66	"
609						
	B	Wilkins Gladys—†	11	nurse	40	6 Crestwood pk
	C	Cadarette Antonio J	12	plumber	50	5 Atherton
	D	Cadarette Theresa—†	12	housewife	46	5 "
	E	Pettigrew Archibald, jr	13	machinist	32	here
	F	Pettigrew Evelyn—†	13	housewife	28	"
	G	*Garrity Mary—†	14	at home	70	"
	H	O'Donnell Margaret—†	14	housewife	53	"
	K	O'Donnell Mary—†	14	student	20	
	L	O'Donnell Thomas	14	operator	53	"
	M	Buckley Jeannette—†	15	housewife	20	92 Mozart
	N	Buckley Vincent	15	chauffeur	20	16 Gay Head
	O	Crowley Michael	15	laborer	48	3289 Wash'n
	P	Mangone Hazel—†	15	housewife	46	30 Dalrymple
	R	Mangone Joseph	15	inspector	48	here
	S	Hannaford Anna—†	16	at home	66	"
	T	Lipshultz Mary E—†	16	"	76	"
	U	Lipshultz Nellie—†	16	"	73	
	V	Brown Delia A—†	17	housewife	50	"
	W	Brown John	17	inspector	53	"
	X	Harrington Arthur	17	chauffeur	28	"
	Y	Levesque Michael	17	carpenter	43	Maine
	Z	Stencer Bernard	17	laborer	33	17 Williams
610						
	A	MacBirney Joseph L	18	clerk	36	here
	B	MacBirney Laura—†	18	housewife	34	"
	C	Fallon Bernard	18	chauffeur	40	"
	D	MacBirney Anna—†	18	manager	31	
	E	MacBirney Eleanor—†	18	housekeeper	61	"
	F	MacBirney Peter	18	painter	39	"
	G	Connor Bernard	19	clerk	52	"

Page.	Letter.	FULL NAME.	Residence, Jan. 1, 1941.	Occupation.	Supposed Age.	Reported Residence, Jan. 1, 1940. Street and Number.

Atherton Street—Continued

H	Connor Bernard B	19	proprietor	23	here
K	Connor Edmund G	19	student	20	"
L	Connor Rebecca M—†	19	housewife	48	"
M	Ganley Mary A—†	19	housekeeper	50	7 Atherton
¹M	Cass William C	20	realtor	57	here
N	Abel Mary E—†	20	housewife	60	"
O	Abel William S	20	guard	61	"
P	Perkins Allen L	21	laborer	23	32 Clarence
R	Perkins William H	21	machinist	58	32 "
S	Rumrill Arthur	21	laborer	35	Everett
T	Rumrill Ida—†	21	housewife	26	"
U	Mullen James P	37	salesman	65	here
V	Mullen Mary—†	37	housewife	53	"
W	Colburn Ellen—†	39	"	66	"
X	Colburn Eugene J	39	carpenter	67	"
Y	Colburn Eugene J, jr	39	clerk	33	
Z	Colburn Henry W	39	"	27	

611

A	Colburn Mary K—†	39	housewife	32	"
B	Biewend Elizabeth—†	41	at home	74	
C	Kraesse Agnes—†	41	housekeeper	69	"
E	Biewend Adolf	41	attorney	41	"
D	Biewend Ruth—†	41	housewife	36	"
F	Arbuckle Margaret—†	45	"	26	"
G	Arbuckle William	45	electrician	29	"
H	Fox Josephine A—†	45	housewife	50	"
K	Fox William W	45	printer	64	"
L	Seitz Irene—†	45	waitress	35	Dedham
M	Tracy Catherine P—†	49	clerk	49	here
O	Tracy Mary C—†	49	housewife	50	"
P	Tracy Mary J—†	49	teacher	28	"
N	Tracy Philip	49	attorney	27	"
S	Mayr Cecelia D—†	51	secretary	36	"
R	Mayr John A	51	registrar	46	"
T	Mayr Matilda—†	51	at home	75	
U	Kelly Cecelia—†	55	stenographer	35	"
V	Kelly James	55	retired	76	"
W	Kelly Susan—†	55	housewife	75	"
X	Coughlin Helen—†	59	bookkeeper	38	"
Y	Coughlin Rita—†	59	supervisor	36	"
Z	Cobe Marion—†	61	stenographer	34	33 Taft

8

Page.	Letter.	FULL NAME.	Residence, Jan. 1, 1941.	Occupation.	Supposed Age.	Reported Residence, Jan. 1, 1940. Street and Number.

612
Atherton Street—Continued

	A	Hart George	61	chauffeur	60	here
	B	Hart Myrtis C—†	61	housewife	45	"
	C	O'Toole Carrie—†	75	"	49	"
	D	O'Toole Joseph	75	trainman	56	"
	E	O'Toole Joseph P	75	chauffeur	45	"
	F	O'Toole Margaret L—†	75	teacher	60	
	G	O'Toole Mary—†	75	at home	95	
	H	O'Toole Mary A—†	75	housekeeper	62	"
	K	O'Toole Mary A—†	75	"	38	"
	L	Leonard Delia F—†	75	"	70	
	M	Leonard Marguerite L—†	75	teacher	40	"
	N	Corby Earl F	79	mechanic	26	"
	O	Corby Edward	79	carpenter	52	"
	P	Corby Frederick F	79	dyer	33	
	R	Corby Mary—†	79	housewife	51	"
	S	Corby Russell J	79	watchman	20	"
	T	Gagnon Alyce—†	79	nurse	37	4467 Wash'n
	U	Gagnon Edward	79	wireman	48	4467 "
	V	Tracy Emma F—†	83	housewife	76	here
	W	Tracy William J	83	retired	79	"
	X	*Diner Lena—†	83	housekeeper	60	"
	Y	Keeble Dorothy W—†	83	housewife	47	"
	Z	Keeble Herbert L	83	bank examiner	49	"

613

	A	Getz Harriet F—†	87	housewife	48	"
	B	Getz Henry J	87	laborer	54	"
	C	Getz James W	87	"	28	"
	D	Epps Alice—†	87	domestic	45	"
	E	Conlon Charles M	87	inspector	52	"
	F	Parker Geraldine—†	87	housekeeper	27	"

Bancroft Street

	G	Sullivan Dorothy—†	1	housewife	31	here
	H	Sullivan John J	1	shipper	31	"
	K	*McNulty John	1	plasterer	50	"
	L	McNulty Margaret—†	1	clerk	21	
	M	*McNulty Mary—†	1	housewife	50	"
	N	Green John	1	laborer	37	82 Bragdon
	O	Walsh James J	3	shoecutter	55	here

P	Walsh James J	3	mechanic	28	here
R	Walsh Katherine—†	3	teacher	26	"
S	Walsh Mary—†	3	packer	23	"
T	Burns Beatrice—†	3	laundress	23	"
U	Burns Ethel—-†	3	"	26	
V	Burns Margaret—†	3	"	49	"
W	Norton Elizabeth—†	3	clerk	40	1 Miles
X	Norton John W	3	salesman	38	1 "
Y	Norton Josephine—†	3	housewife	34	1 "
Z	Gear James	5	painter	57	here

614

A	Gear Emily—†	5	housewife	56	"
B	Gear Thomas	5	painter	30	"
C	Gear Wilfred	5	clerk	26	"
D	Ciasullo Alfred	5	shoemaker	35	"
E	Ciasullo Gabriel	5	"	47	
F	Ciasullo Mary—†	5	housewife	35	"
G	Allen Mary—†	5	"	46	
H	Allen Stanley C	5	machinist	21	"
K	Allen Stanley E	5	retired	47	
L	Mulcahy Agnes—†	7	dressmaker	63	"
M	Mulcahy John	7	retired	68	"
N	Conlon Joseph	7	laborer	26	9 Leniston
O	Conlon Julia—†	7	housewife	28	9 "
P	Rosemark Helen—†	7	housekeeper	58	53 Bainbridge
R	Finley Katherine E—†	7	at home	63	here
S	Finley Mary F—†	7	operator	59	"
T	Flanders Charles	9	foreman	51	15 Wensley
U	Polk Ruth—†	9	housekeeper	21	95 Alexander
V	Gibbord Florence—†	9	housewife	46	here
W	Gibbord Kenneth	9	laborer	49	"
X	McNally Helen—†.	9	clerk	20	"
Y	Parfenchook Gertrude M—†	9	housekeeper	52	63 Centre
Z	Steele Hugh F	11	inspector	61	here

615

A	Steele John	11	polisher	35	
B	Steele Mary—†	11	housewife	57	"
C	Ward Mary A—†	11	housekeeper	49	"
D	Ward Thomas B	11	laborer	52	"
E	Brown Mary—†	11	housekeeper	56	"
F	Dern Joseph	11	sorter	31	"

Page.	Letter.	FULL NAME.	Residence, Jan. 1, 1941.	Occupation.	Supposed Age.	Reported Residence, Jan. 1. 1940. Street and Number.

Bancroft Street—Continued

	G	Dern Marion—†	11	operator	33	here
	H	Finch Edgar	11	clerk	32	"
	K	Brennan John	15	laborer	58	"
	L	Brennan Maria A—†	15	housewife	65	"
	M	Brennan Patrick J	15	retired	65	
	N	Coleman Mary A—†	15	saleswoman	26	"
	O	Dwelley Alice—†	15	packer	28	
	P	Turnbull Mary J—†	15	housewife	47	"
	R	Turnbull William R	15	salesman	48	"
	S	Turnbull William R	15	messenger	26	"
	T	McAuley John J	18	clerk	40	28 Rugby rd
	U	Reidy Martha—†	18	housewife	36	101 Sidney
	V	Reidy William J	18	engineer	45	101 "
	W	Wakefield Anna—†	20	clerk	25	here
	X	Wakefield Dorothy—†	20	shoemaker	27	"
	Y	Wakefield Mary—†	20	housekeeper	23	"
	Z	Wakefield Matilda—†	20	"	21	"

616

| | A | Wakefield Walter | 20 | shipper | 49 | |

Beethoven Street

	C	Catenacci Anthony	6	custodian	54	here
	D	Catenacci Francis	6	student	23	"
	E	Catenacci Mary—†	6	teacher	26	"
	F	Catenacci Susan—·†	6	housewife	48	"
	G	Bravoco Lena—†	8	"	55	
	H	Bravoco Mary—†	8	"	24	
	K	Bravoco Raphael	8	bookkeeper	26	"
	L	Bravoco Rocco	8	watchman	49	"
	M	McGovern Helen—†	8½	clerk	37	"
	N	McGovern Mary—†	8½	at home	68	"
	O	Buckley Mary F—†	9	"	67	
	P	Carey Anna R—†	9	secretary	22	"
	R	Carey Eleanor B—†	9	"	24	
	S	Carey Frances G—†	9	stenographer	26	"
	T	Carey James M	9	lather	63	"
	U	Carey Mary J—†	9	housewife	57	"
	V	Carey Mary M—†	9	saleswoman	27	"
	W	Hatchman Henry F	10	retired	73	14 Union av
	X	Hatchman Winifred H—†	10	housewife	52	14 "

Page.	Letter.	Full Name.	Residence, Jan. 1, 1941.	Occupation.	Supposed Age.	Reported Residence, Jan. 1, 1940. Street and Number.

617
Beethoven Street—Continued

A	*Lucyk Anna—†	12	housewife	61	here	
B	Lucyk Michael	12	laborer	68	"	
C	Trabish Sophie—†	12	housewife	26	"	
D	Trabish William	12	shipper	28	"	
E	*Keko Mariantha—†	14	housewife	44	45 Middlesex	
F	Keko Peter	14	manager	42	45 "	
G	Drummond Jennie—†	14	at home	57	10 Ernest	
H	Keough John J	14	shipper	32	10 "	
K	Keough Ruth—†	14	housewife	29	10 "	
L	James Arthur	15	custodian	35	48 Buswell	
M	James Marion F—†	15	housewife	30	N Hampshire	
N	Botolinski George	15	mechanic	26	here	
O	Botolinski Joseph	15	"	29	"	
P	Botolinski Katherine—†	15	housewife	57	"	
R	Botolinski Michael	15	packer	32		
S	Botolinski Sophie—†	15	secretary	23	"	
T	Cummings John J	16	repairman	66	"	
U	Cummings Susan—†	16	housewife	56	"	
V	Keenan Anna—†	16	"	27		
W	Keenan John M	16	repairman	31	"	
X	Emery Harris C	17	operator	52		
Y	*MacDonald Felicia—†	17	housewife	56	"	
Z	Moore George	17	laborer	50	42 Warren	

618

A	Sears Catherine—†	17	housewife	27	here	
B	Sears Daniel	17	clerk	47	"	
C	Watkins Ralph G	17	salesman	43	"	
D	Watkins Theresa M—†	17	housewife	47	"	
E	Fay John H	18	operator	63	"	
F	Fay Sarah—†	18	housewife	63	"	
G	Donaruma George	18	clerk	36		
H	Donaruma Margaret—†	18	housewife	37	"	
K	Denney Matthew	19	blacksmith	55	14 Beethoven	
L	Fulton Jean—†	19	operator	34	here	
M	*Fulton Sarah—†	19	housekeeper	24	"	
N	*Hodge James	19	mechanic	37	14 Beethoven	
O	*Hodge Thomasina—†	19	housewife	32	14 "	
P	McGeoch Margaret—†	19	"	36	here	

Beethoven Street—Continued

	R	McGeoch Robert	19	carpenter	37	here
	S	McGougan Jean—†	19	cook	57	"
	T	Kloser Gertrude E—†	20	hairdresser	56	"
	U	Kloser Oswald	20	machinist	54	"
	V	Lamont George	20	shipper	60	
	W	Mulqueeney Celia—†	20	nurse	50	"
	X	Larson Holger	21	machinist	53	143 W Concord
	Y	Larson Victoria R—†	21	housewife	42	143 "
	Z	Monbouquett Joseph	21	retired	75	143 "
619						
	A	Butler Charles V	21	painter	49	here
	B	Butler Elizabeth A—†	21	housewife	52	"
	C	VanTassel Charles J	21	salesman	69	"
	D	MacDonald Alexander	22	manager	25	"
	E	MacDonald John E	22	mechanic	28	"
	F	*MacDonald Mary—†	22	housewife	63	"
	G	*Easter Dorothy L—†	24	"	37	
	H	*Easter George R	24	carpenter	35	"
	K	Albertson Hans	25	cooper	56	Sharon
	L	Gibbs Isadora—†	25	housewife	68	here
	M	Gibbs Matthias	25	retired	76	"
	N	Joyce Thomas	25	laborer	39	139 Lamartine
	O	Mills Arthur H	25	chef	48	81 School
	P	Perry Marion L—†	25	nurse	23	10 Dimock
	S	Weidlach Fred E	26	painter	27	here
	R	Weidlach Frederick	26	"	61	"
	T	Weidlach Julia—†	26	housewife	59	"
	U	Gebhard Alice L—†	26	"	33	
	V	Gebhard Frederick S	26	clerk	42	

Boylston Street

	Y	Knopf Julius	128	brewer	44	here
	Z	*Knopf Olga—†	128	housewife	50	"
620						
	A	Young Fred D	128	fireman	64	"
	B	Young Fred D, jr	128	assembler	20	"
	C	Young Mary—†	128	housewife	51	"
	D	Young Mary P—†	128	seamstress	24	"

Page.	Letter.	FULL NAME.	Residence, Jan. 1, 1941.	Occupation.	Supposed Age.	Reported Residence, Jan. 1, 1940. Street and Number.

Bragdon Street

	F	Brigham Gladys—†	9	housewife	36	here
	G	Brigham James E	9	clerk	39	"
	H	Frizzell John	9	"	22	20 Delle av
	K	Frizzell Margaret—†	9	housewife	20	here
	L	*Schorr Edith R—†	15	designer	21	England
	M	*Schorr Gertrude—†	15	housekeeper	55	"
	N	Toomey Helen—†	15	housewife	45	here
	O	Toomey William	15	laborer	56	"
	P	Keating Ebba—†	25	domestic	54	"
	R	Peterson Ethel—†	25	presser	23	
	S	Reed Gertrude—†	25	housewife	43	"
	T	*Cowie Helen—†	56	"	36	
	U	*Cowie William	56	baker	38	
	V	Brown Kenneth L	56	porter	33	
	W	Brown Rita—†	56	housewife	26	"
	X	Lowder Charles	56	laborer	22	
	Y	Lowder Elizabeth—†	56	housewife	59	"
	Z	Lowder Mark T	56	laborer	59	
		621				
	A	Baird Eleanor—†	56	nurse	22	
	B	Baird Helen L—†	56	housewife	47	"
	C	Baird William J	56	cutter	47	
	D	Watt Annie—†	56	housewife	39	"
	E	Watt Lovering	56	painter	53	
	F	Fulton Jessie—†	56	housewife	25	"
	G	Fulton Robert	56	clerk	35	
	H	Murphy Edward	60	retired	66	
	K	Murphy Edward J	60	clerk	26	
	L	Murphy Mary—†	60	stenographer	24	"
	¹L	Murphy Winifred—†	60	housewife	50	"
	M	Mulkern Bernard	60	agent	37	
	N	Ward Ethel V—†	60	housekeeper	47	"
	O	Downes Francis J	60	mechanic	44	"
	P	Downes Margaret M—†	60	housewife	44	"
	R	Kearns Florence E—†	60	"	40	
	S	Kearns Harold J	60	mechanic	38	"
	T	DeBassio Hermina—†	60	housekeeper	34	"
	U	Kleuber Elizabeth—†	60	stitcher	64	"
	V	Kelly Cornelius J	70	manager	65	9 Codman pk
	W	Kelly Dora M—†	70	housewife	62	9 "
	X	Kimball Margaret T—†	70	"	55	here

Bragdon Street—Continued

Y	Kimball Thomas C	70	cutter	55	here
Z	Kimball Thomas W	70	carpenter	27	"
	622				
A	Burgess Anne—†	70	housewife	53	"
B	Burgess Donald	70	buyer	25	
C	Burgess Robert	70	clerk	23	
D	McBride Francis L	72	chauffeur	32	"
E	McBride Marie—†	72	housewife	30	"
F	Guinan Doris—†	72	"	27	
G	Guinan Francis J	72	chauffeur	33	"
H	Linn Jacob	72	cabinetmaker	39	"
K	*Linn Martha—†	72	housewife	28	"
L	Griffin Ellen—†	74	housekeeper	75	"
M	Westwood Lillian—†	74	housewife	44	"
N	Westwood Phoebe—†	74	waitress	22	
O	Callahan Daniel	74	compositor	30	"
P	Callahan Marjorie—†	74	housewife	31	"
R	DeStephano Agnes—†	74	"	34	3 Dunford
S	DeStephano Armand	74	cutter	34	3 "
T	Knight Harry	76	machinist	27	Randolph
U	Murphy Joseph H	76	clerk	27	here
V	Murphy Mary—†	76	housewife	65	"
W	Murphy William J	76	printer	28	"
X	Mahoney Catherine—†	76	housewife	20	488 Hyde Park av
Y	Mahoney Francis	76	mechanic	51	488 "
Z	Bouthillette Catherine—†	78	housewife	24	162 Lamartine
	623				
A	Bouthillette Patrick E	78	cutter	29	162 "
B	Nilson Arthur C	78	laborer	47	here
C	Nilson Arthur C	78	salesman	21	"
D	Nilson Ruby F—†	78	housewife	46	"
E	King Charles H	78	investigator	34	92 W Walnut pk
F	King Charlotte F—†	78	housewife	34	92 "
G	Richards Annie C—†	78	domestic	59	2 Ernest
H	Schaffer Jamesina—†	78	housekeeper	68	92 W Walnut pk
K	Linehan Frederick C	80	manager	28	here
L	Linehan Marie—†	80	housewife	26	"
M	Knighton Lloyd F	80	carpenter	59	"
N	Knighton Sarah A—†	80	housewife	44	"
O	Keiderling Freda—†	80	"	32	
P	Keiderling John H	80	manager	33	"

Page.	Letter.	FULL NAME.	Residence, Jan. 1, 1941.	Occupation.	Supposed Age.	Reported Residence, Jan. 1, 1940. Street and Number.

Bragdon Street—Continued

	R	Salie Alfred W	82	clerk	24	39 Millmont
	S	Salie Mary—†	82	housewife	20	48 Yeoman
	T	Santoro Agnes—†	82	"	33	here
	U	Santoro Charles	82	chauffeur	32	"
	V	Beissner Frederick	82	mechanic	46	92 Bragdon
	W	Beissner Stella—†	82	housewife	53	92 "
	X	Whiteside Catherine—†	91	"	32	here
	Y	Whiteside Joseph	91	clerk	32	"
	Z	Schwarz Louise—†	91	housekeeper	52	"
624						
	A	Schwarz William	91	salesman	21	"
	B	*Hood Margaret—†	91	domestic	51	3109 Wash'n
	C	Deittrich Caroline—†	92	housewife	44	here
	D	Deittrich Robert	92	chauffeur	44	"
	E	McLaughlin Thomas	92	"	28	126 Blue Hill av
	F	McLaughlin Winifred—†	92	housewife	26	126 "
	G	Johnson Thomas	92	salesman	49	here
	H	McRae Dorothy—†	93	housewife	26	"
	K	McRae George A	93	foreman	30	"
	L	Krikorian Mary—†	93	housewife	29	"
	M	Krikorian Walter	93	mechanic	28	"
	N	Andrews Margaret T—†	93	housewife	40	"
	O	Andrews William F	93	carpenter	42	"
	P	McCoy Jessie—†	94	housewife	44	"
	R	McCoy Raymond	94	mechanic	43	"
	S	McCoy Raymond J	94	clerk	20	
	T	Kearney Michael	94	fireman	35	
	U	*Kearney Rose—†	94	housewife	37	"
	V	Mulhern John	94	plumber	42	64 Day
	W	Mulhern Mae—†	94	housewife	40	64 "
	X	Doyle Joseph	95	laborer	30	here
	Y	Doyle Vera—†	95	housewife	29	"
	Z	Stimson Charlotte—†	95	housekeeper	33	"
625						
		McCauley Alice—†	95	"	65	18 Dixwell
		McCauley Chester R	95	plasterer	32	18 "
		McCauley Francis W	95	shoeworker	30	18 "
		Fortim Mary A—†	97	housekeeper	44	92 Bragdon
		Fisher James	97	retired	84	here
		Rice Ethel—†	97	housewife	48	377 Bunker Hill
	G	Rice Ethel M—†	97	waitress	22	377 "
	H	Rice Laurence	97	engineer	47	377 "

Page.	Letter.	Full Name.	Residence, Jan. 1, 1941.	Occupation.	Supposed Age.	Reported Residence, Jan. 1, 1940. Street and Number.

Columbus Avenue

K	DeGregorio Anna—†	1841	housewife	42	here
L	DeGregorio Marie—†	1841	stenographer	23	"
M	DeGregorio Michael	1841	shoeworker	48	"
N	Inserro Joseph	1841	hairdresser	42	"
O	Inserro Theresa—†	1841	housewife	40	"
P	DeGregorio Annie—†	1841	"	50	
R	DeGregorio James	1841	chauffeur	23	"
S	DeGregorio Rocco	1841	barber	52	
T	Marenghi Americo	1843	foreman	46	
U	Marenghi Henrietta—†	1843	housewife	38	"
V	Mongillo Emma—†	1843	inspector	30	"
W	Belton Theodore D	1843	chauffeur	46	"
X	Opederbecke Elizabeth—†	1843	housekeeper	65	"
Y	Opederbecke Hugo	1843	mechanic	59	"
Z	Arruda Phyllis—†	1843	presser	53	

626

A	Bush Gertrude E—†	1843	inspector	43	"
B	Bush Thomas J	1843	chef	32	
C	Quatrommi John	1843	porter	22	
D	Quatrommi Joseph	1843	painter	20	"
E	Pecoraro Grace F—†	1845	social worker	32	4365 Wash'n
F	Pecoraco Michael	1845	meatcutter	26	1030 Dor av
G	Regan Forrest L	1845	machinist	39	here
H	Regan Mary R—†	1845	housewife	35	"
K	Scanlon Catherine A—†	1845	at home	79	"
L	Scanlon Francis J	1845	inspector	44	"
M	Johnson Arthur G	1845	operator	44	"
N	Johnson Rachel—†	1845	housewife	36	"
O	Kelly Catherine—†	1845	housekeeper	63	"
P	Kelly Elizabeth—†	1845	bookkeeper	65	".
R	White Mary E—†	1845	housekeeper	74	"
S	Jackley Anna—†	1845	housewife	67	"
T	Jackley Theodore	1845	tinsmith	75	
U	Mullen Frederick J	1845	clerk	47	
V	Mullen Teresa L—†	1845	housewife	49	"
W	Golay Leon H	1845	realtor	25	Waltham
X	Golay Marion—†	1845	housewife	20	"
Y	Roche John B	1845	ironworker	43	here
Z	Roche Vera L—†	1845	housewife	33	"

627

A	Dale John	1845	plumber	29	
B	Dale Irene—†	1845	waitress	26	

11—6

1

Page.	Letter.	FULL NAME.	Residence, Jan. 1, 1941.	Occupation.	Supposed Age.	Reported Residence, Jan. 1, 1940. Street and Number.

Columbus Avenue—Continued

c	Hurley George N	1845	supervisor	31	53 Prince
D	Hurley Muriel I—†	1845	nurse	28	1853 Col av
E	Sharko Anne—†	1849	student	21	Maine
F	Sharko Louise—†	1849	nurse	27	Maryland
G	Johnson Charles	1849	machinist	26	Wellesley
H	Johnson Florence—†	1849	clerk	24	381 Broadway
K	Gaston Esther—†	1849	packer	63	here
L	Giuva Ernest	1849	chauffeur	40	"
M	Giuva Mary—†	1849	housewife	33	"
N	Burgess Clarence E	1849	salesman	44	"
P	Gregorie Blanche—†	1849	cashier	46	
O	Grenier Alexander J	1849	retired	66	
R	Scott Ida M—†	1849	stitcher	44	
S	Holland Arthur J	1849	operator	45	"
T	Holland Helen T—†	1849	housewife	44	"
U	Sunelbergh John	1849	salesman	26	Milton
V	Sunelbergh Josephine—†	1849	saleswoman	24	"
W	Gardner Jennie—†	1849	housewife	43	here
X	Gardner William E	1849	patternmaker	42	"
Y	Johnson Clinton	1849	laborer	30	"
Z	Johnson Hilma—†	1849	housewife	61	"

628

A	Johnson Hortense—†	1849	secretary	27	"
B	Johnson John B	1849	janitor	59	
C	Cameron Grace—†	1853	housekeeper	47	"
D	Griffiths James	1853	operator	53	57 Reed
E	Highet Andrew	1853	laborer	53	Peabody
F	Highet Edith G—†	1853	housewife	50	"
G	Green Ida M—†	1853	"	60	69 Walden
H	Green William R	1853	printer	56	69 "
K	Conlon Mary T—†	1853	investigator	52	680 Parker
M	McBerney John F	1853	clerk	31	here
N	McBerney Madeline M-†	1853	"	30	"
L	Hapgood Helen—†	1853	housewife	29	2031 Col av
O	Dinsmore Mary—†	1855	waitress	45	here
P	Keefe Mary—†	1855	housekeeper	39	"
R	Murphy Charles J	1855	chauffeur	35	"
S	Bennett Marie—†	1855	housewife	37	"
T	Bennett Walter	1855	mechanic	40	"
U	Doyle Jane—†	1855	housewife	50	"
V	Doyle Leo	1855	janitor	50	

Columbus Avenue—Continued

w	Twigg Helen—†	1855	housekeeper	20	167 Faneuil
x	Twigg Kenneth	1855	laborer	27	here
y	Twigg Wesley	1855	"	22	"
z	Frank Alfred	1857	printer	34	1 Bancroft
	629				
a	Frank Rose C—†	1857	housewife	32	1 "
b	O'Reilly James P	1857	laborer	54	here
c	O'Reilly John	1857	retired	82	"
d	O'Reilly Michael P	1857	"	75	"
e	O'Reilly Theresa A—†	1857	teacher	27	
f	Nangerone Jeanette M-†	1857	housewife	42	"
g	Nangerone Joseph A	1857	technician	21	"
h	Nangerone Napoleon	1857	bartender	53	"
k	Logovich Peter	1859	laborer	23	
l	*Logovich Samuel	1859	painter	48	
m	*Logovich Victoria—†	1859	housewife	47	"
n	Mayeski Anna T—†	1859	"	36	
o	Mayeski William	1859	laborer	35	
p	Murphy Bartholomew	1859	policeman	52	"
r	Mulloney Dorothy M-†	1859	teacher	27	
s	Mulloney Frank H	1859	salesman	62	"
t	Mulloney Herbert F	1859	policeman	26	"
u	Mulloney Jennie F—†	1859	housewife	55	"
v	Mulloney Ruth M—†	1859	musician	21	
w	Donahue Annie—†	1861	housewife	64	"
x	Donahue David F	1861	engineer	59	
y	Bernstein Bertha—†	1861	housekeeper	70	"
z	Goodwin Grace—†	1861	nurse	30	"
	630				
a	Bryant Charles	1861	chauffeur	41	Holyoke
b	Bryant Josephine—†	1861	housewife	44	"
c	*McCarthy Catherine—†	1861	"	41	752 Tremont
d	McCarthy Thomas	1861	salesman	47	752 "
e	King Margaret—†	1861	housewife	40	here
f	King Thomas	1861	engineer	47	"
g	Valliere Arthur	1861	clerk	27	"
h	Valliere Catherine F—†	1861	housekeeper	52	"
k	White Sarah—†	1861	nurse	37	"
l	Ashe Idah—†	1861	"	37	
m	O'Neil Madeline—†	1861	"	49	
n	Berkwald Pauline—†	1861	forewoman	57	"

Columbus Avenue—Continued

o	Littlefield Alice—†	1861	nurse	29	86 Mt Pleasant av
p	Littlefield Bertha—†	1861	hairdresser	25	86 "
r	Grossman Anna—†	1861	waitress	47	here
s	Grossman William	1861	laborer	51	"
t	*Binda Aldina S—†	1861	housekeeper	63	"
u	Binda Frederick	1861	technician	26	"
v	Binda Louis J	1861	starter	43	"
w	*Maitland Robert	1865	seaman	32	New York
x	Watt Ann—†	1865	housewife	51	here
y	Watt Catherine—†	1865	bookkeeper	26	"
z	Watt John	1865	laborer	57	"

631

A	Connell Doris—†	1865	housewife	28	"
B	Connell Leo M	1865	guard	40	
c	Snodgrass Ansel E	1865	manager	52	
D	Snodgrass Marion K—†	1865	housewife	48	"
E	Snodgrass Mary E—†	1865	clerk	20	
F	Snodgrass Robert	1865	laborer	26	..
G	Gallagher Catherine—†	1865	housewife	60	"
H	Gallagher Catherine—†	1865	bookkeeper	26	"
K	Gallagher Helen—†	1865	secretary	27	"
L	Webster Bettie M—†	1865	artist	22	282 Mass av
M	Webster Patricia H—†	1865	nurse	25	282 "
N	Robinson Donald	1865	packer	42	1871 Col av
o	Robinson Gladys—†	1865	nurse	37	1871 "
P	Lorenz Carl O	1865	brewer	60	here
R	*Lorenz Marie W—†	1865	housewife	84	"
s	Schaal John	1865	manager	43	"
T	Ferrandine Frances—†	1865	housewife	23	"
u	*Ferrandine Joseph	1865	laborer	21	126 K
v	Gelormini Charles	1865	"	20	here
w	Gelormini Gabriel	1865	shoeworker	22	"
x	Gelormini Josephine—†	1865	clerk	21	"
y	Gelormini Otto	1865	shoeworker	49	"
z	Gelormini Palmina—†	1865	housewife	43	"

632

A	Remick Clarence A	1865	mechanic	56	"
B	Remick Florence—†	1865	waitress	43	
c	Dowd Bernard L	1865	operator	57	
D	Dowd Bernard L, jr	1865	laborer	24	"
E	Dowd George T	1865	chef	28	

Page	Letter	FULL NAME	Residence, Jan. 1, 1941.	Occupation.	Supposed Age.	Reported Residence, Jan. 1, 1940. Street and Number.

Columbus Avenue—Continued

	F	Dowd John J	1865	chauffeur	29	here
	G	Dowd Mary A—†	1865	housewife	55	"
	H	Dowd William J.	1865	laborer	21	"
	K	McDermott William E	1865	collector	34	..
	O	McDonald Grant	1871	optician	53	
	P	McDonald Lorraine—†	1871	secretary	25	"
	R	McDonald Vera—†	1871	housewife	43	"
	S	Gassian Eva—†	1871	housekeeper	25	"
	T	Grunts Barney	1871	storekeeper	49	"
	U	Murphy Edward D	1871	manager	46	Taunton
	V	Murphy Helen A—†	1871	housewife	43	"
	W	Fay Florence M—†	1873	"	38	Dedham
	X	Fay Henry G	1873	operator	53	"
	Y	Burt Margaret—†	1873	housewife	52	here
	Z	Burt Walter	1873	engineer	51	"

633

	D	Gibson Cora J—†	1899	housewife	41	"
	E	Gibson Henry H	1899	musician	43	"
	F	Yancey Chester P	1899	clerk	42	
	G	*Roberto Antonio	1899	laborer	39	
	H	*Roderick Julia—†	1899	seamstress	21	"
	K	*Santos Mary—†	1899	housekeeper	65	"
	L	*Tinel Ernestine—†	1899	housewife	45	"
	M	Tinel Manuel	1899	laborer	53	
	N	Coles Arthur	1899	storekeeper	49	"
	O	Coles Mabel—†	1899	housewife	37	"
	P	Coles Charles J	1901	retired	74	
	R	Coles Sarah—†	1901	housewife	67	"
	S	Washington Mary—†	1901	domestic	31	Newton
	T	Silvera Barbara—†	1901	housewife	22	59 St Germain
	U	Silvera Kenneth F	1901	presser	31	59 "
	V	Gray Helen—†	1901	domestic	45	here
	W	Hall Florence—†	1901	"	49	"
	X	Hill Minnie—†	1901	"	47	"
	Y	Logan Gladys—†	1901	"	40	
	Z	Lambert James A	1903	musician	49	"

634

	A	Lambert Mary A—†	1903	housewife	50	"
	B	Papastavros George	1903	storekeeper	54	20 Dixwell
	C	Papastavros Helen—†	1903	housewife	49	20 "
	D	Bell Frank W	1903	repairman	21	here

21

Columbus Avenue—Continued

E	Bell Lillian G—†	1903	housewife	54	here
F	Bell Thomas J	1903	porter	54	"
G	Lambert George H	1905	musician	48	"
H	Lambert Mary—†	1905	retired	73	
K	Lambert Virginia I—†	1905	housewife	24	"
L	McCormick Thomas E	1905	engineer	45	..
M	Driscoll Lorretta—†	1905	housewife	54	"
N	Cuseck Edward A	1905	laborer	25	"
O	Jennings John J	1905	"	49	158 School
P	Powers Albert J	1905	"	46	here
R	Powers Anna—†	1905	housewife	44	"
S	Seaverns Arthur L	1907	retired	68	"
T	Seaverns Nellie T—†	1907	housewife	59	"
U	*Dodds Anna K—†	1907	housekeeper	76	"
V	Brennan George T	1907	mason	63	235 W Newton
W	Brennan Thomas J	1907	clerk	29	235 "
X	Slepian Ida—†	1909	housewife	64	19 Townsend
Y	Slepian Louis	1909	storekeeper	66	19 "
Z	Egan Mary—†	1909	domestic	46	here
	635				
B	Orr Clara—†	1922	"	59	Dedham
C	*Glynn Martin	1922	retired	75	here
D	*Glynn Mary—†	1922	housewife	65	"
E	Glynn Winifred E—†	1922	stenographer	40	"
K	Berndt August	1937	retired	77	"
L	Berndt Bertha—†	1937	housewife	69	"
M	Berndt Charles H	1937	machinist	46	"
N	Cliffe John	1937	glazier	48	
O	Williams Emily—†	1937	housewife	52	"
P	Williams Mathias	1937	garageman	52	"
R	Williams Mathias, jr	1937	laborer	20	
S	Drabentowicz Emma—†	1937	housekeeper	20	"
T	*Drabentowicz Ignaz	1937	shipper	46	"
U	*Drabentowicz Louise—†	1937	housewife	48	"
X	Chin Sam	1951	laundryman	36	"
Y	McCabe Edward	1953	laborer	29	
Z	McCabe Helen—†	1953	housewife	28	"
	636				
C	Cassons Florence B—†	1955	"	52	
D	Cassons Llewellyn	1955	fireman	61	

22

Columbus Avenue—Continued

E	Zenick George	1955	dyer	27	here
F	Zenick Marion—†	1955	bookkeeper	26	"
G	Harzbecker Frank C	1955	salesman	48	"
H	Harzbecker Grace J—†	1955	housewife	34	"
K	Pickett Thomas	1957	molder	71	
L	Handren Martha—†	1957	housewife	37	"
M	Handren Patrick	1957	laborer	39	
N	*Genes Lefcula—†	1957	housewife	33	"
O	Genes Nicholas	1957	storekeeper	44	"
S	*Zinck Delphine—†	1963	housewife	27	"
T	Zinck William	1963	cutter	29	"
U	Pasek Frank	1963	laborer	56	
V	Pasek Laura—†	1963	housewife	51	"

Copley Street

W	Cokinos Spiros	16	salesman	50	here
X	Eck Beatrice C—†	16	nurse	45	"
Y	Fallon Elizabeth C—†	16	housekeeper	80	"
Z	Christopher George	17	chauffeur	34	"
	637				
A	Christopher Mary—†	17	housewife	29	"
B	Nuzzelo James	17	student	21	"
C	Weber Jane M—†	17	housewife	30	21 Beethoven
D	Weber John D	17	foreman	29	21 "
E	Dolan Frances—†	18	student	21	here
F	Dolan Margaret—†	18	teacher	42	"
G	Dolan Virginia M—†	18	student	22	"
H	Killian Grace E—†	18	inspector	36	"
K	Killian James F	18	retired	79	"
L	Lillian Mary A—†	18	housewife	72	"
M	Killian Ruth—†	18	secretary	34	"
N	Hemmer George M	19	salesman	40	"
O	Hemmer Marguerite A—†	19	housewife	39	"
P	Devine Anastasia—†	20	"	56	
R	Devine Simon P	20	dentist	22	
S	Devine Walter J	20	printer	35	"
T	Devine Walter S	20	bartender	58	"
U	Devine Catherine M—†	22	secretary	42	"
V	Devine Hugh S	22	clerk	45	

Dimock Street

	Letter	Full Name	Res.	Occupation	Age	Reported Residence
w	McMahon Elizabeth—†	1	housewife	36	here
x	McMahon James	1	bartender	39	"
y	Sobasco Annie—†	1	housekeeper	58	"
z	Sobasco Edward	1	laborer	26	"

638

	Full Name	Res.	Occupation	Age	Reported Residence
A	Ingerson Ava—†	1	housewife	63	"
B	Ingerson Hiram	1	watchman	68	"
C	Bowman Catherine—†	2	housewife	22	29 Marcella
D	Bowman Christopher	2	laborer	25	29 "
E	Poodiack Frank	2	mechanic	32	Connecticut
F	Poodiack Julia—†	2	housewife	22	"
G	Keenan Joseph	3	clerk	30	27 Cobden
H	Keenan Theresa—†	3	housewife	25	27 "
K	Silva Catherine—†	3	"	43	here
L	Silva Constance—†	3	housekeeper	23	"
M	Silva Gabrilla—†	3	maid	20	"
N	Silva Helen—†	3	domestic	25	Brookline
o	Silva Julius	3	chef	53	here
P	*Chandler Marjorie T—† N E Hosp	dietitian	26	"
R	Martin Jean F—† "	superintendent	55	"
S	Mulville Josephine A—† "	"	50	
T	*Zaudy Eleanor—† "	physician	31	"
U	Doherty Alfred J	4	watchman	27	"
V	Doherty Evelyn J—†	4	housewife	24	"
W	Glynn Phillip	4	bricklayer	64	"
X	Glynn Mary J—†	4	housewife	71	"
Y	McNeil Hugh	8	painter	39	
Z	*McNeil Rose—†	8	housewife	40	"

639

	Full Name	Res.	Occupation	Age	Reported Residence
A	*Brain Effie M—†	14	nurse	43	"
B	Chancholo Rose M—†	14	operator	28	9 Copeland pl
C	Cleland Gertrude V—†	14	nurse	28	221 Longwood av
D	Coletti Marie—†	14	waitress	32	here
E	*Cote Marie—†	14	maid	35	"
F	Cross Marjorie J—†	14	nurse	28	"
G	Dawes Dorothy E—†	14	director	47	"
H	De Entremont Mary L—†	14	laundress	39	"
K	Dillon Marion S—†	14	cook	47	108 Myrtle
L	Drummey Kathleen M—†	14	maid	29	19A Asticou
M	*Kelly Mary—†	14	laundress	44	here
N	*Laflin Mabel—†	14	waitress	30	"

Page.	Letter.	FULL NAME.	Residence, Jan. 1, 1941.	Occupation.	Supposed Age.	Reported Residence, Jan. 1, 1940. Street and Number.

Dimock Street—Continued

	o	Lehan Helen C—†	14	maid	34	here
	p	Marotta Jean J—†	14	nurse	24	"
	r	McGrath Nora—†	14	maid	36	"
	s*	McKay Margaret K—†	14	"	37	
	t	McLaughlin Susan P—†	14	laundress	42	"
	u	Shaw Marjorie E—†	14	nurse	30	
	v	Smith Esther M—†	14	"	44	
	w	Traine Katherine M—†	14	maid	39	
	x	Wendell Rose C—†	14	laundress	31	"
	y	Wilkie Kathleen R —†	14	nurse	37	
	z	Yeo Catherine—†	14	"	41	
640						
	a	McGillicuddy James F	84	chauffeur	53	"
	b	McGillicuddy Mary E—†	84	housewife	48	"
	c	Zinck Catherine—†	84	"	59	"
	d	Zinck William	84	watchman	59	"
	e	Solomonides Emily—†	84	housewife	40	"
	f	Solomonides Kemon D	84	butler	43	
	g*	McCarthy Alice—†	86	housekeeper	65	"
	h*	McCarthy Anna—†	86	"	67	
	k	Thorson George	86	painter	40	
	l	Thorson Viola—†	86	housewife	35	"
	m	McCauley Madeline—†	86	housekeeper	32	3232A Wash'n

Ernst Street

	n	Coombs Frances—†	1	housewife	34	11 Havey
	o	Hickey Alice F—†	1	"	42	4 Rockdale
	p	Hickey James J	1	editor	43	4 "
	r	King Emma F—†	1	housewife	44	here
	s	King Francis J	1	attendant	21	"
	t	King Joseph	1	electrician	48	"
	u*	Graham Blanche—†	2	housewife	44	120 Heath
	v	Graham William	2	painter	45	120 "
	w	McAlduff Chester	2	chauffeur	35	here
	x	McAlduff Margaret—†	2	housewife	33	"
	y	White Leonard	2	mechanic	33	"
	z	Gatturna William J	2	salesman	45	2971 Wash'n
641						
	a	Gerry Della M—†	2	housewife	39	2971 "
	b	Magee Margaret M—†	4	"	30	16 Greenley pl

Ernst Street—Continued

c	Magee Thomas A	4	custodian	31	16 Greenley pl
d	Kelley Louis	4	mechanic	40	here
e	Kelley Mary N—†	4	housewife	35	"
f	Armstrong John E	4	boilermaker	28	"
g	Armstrong Manda—†	4	housewife	22	"
h	Gallagher Daniel F	6	chauffeur	34	"
k	Gallagher Mary T—†	6	housewife	37	"
l	Rhodes Fotika—†	6	"	48	
m	Rhodes George P	6	merchant	57	"
n	Buhl Cecile—†	6	housewife	24	3 W Canton
o	Buhl Ernest	6	bartender	29	3 "
p	Farnaris Charles	8	shoeworker	39	here
r	Farnaris Mary B—†	8	housewife	26	"
s	DeFilippo Anthony	8	clerk	39	"
t	DeFilippo Elizabeth—†	8	housewife	34	"
u	Davis Catherine—†	8	"	58	
v	Davis Francis	8	machinist	30	"
w	Davis William	8	mechanic	25	"
x	D'Entremont David	10	shoeworker	31	"
y	D'Entremont Edgar	10	engineer	31	6 Galena
z	D'Entremont Redina—†	10	housewife	31	here

642

a	*Sjoquist Axel	10	ironworker	49	"
b	*Sjoquist Tekla—†	10	housewife	52	"
c	Jordan Wilfred	10	metalworker	39	15 Royce rd
d	Withers Rupert	10	salesman	46	15 "
e	Withers Rupert, jr	10	clerk	24	15 "
f	Withers Sarah—†	10	housewife	43	15 "
g	Greenhow Joseph	12	janitor	40	here
h	*Greenhow Mary—†	12	housewife	38	"
k	Niedzwiecki Felix	12	painter	46	"
l	Niedzwiecki Malvina—†	12	housewife	47	"
m	Fallon Daniel E	12	operator	52	
n	Fallon Helen—†	12	housewife	48	"
o	Sideleau Julia—†	14-16	housekeeper	75	"
p	Stella James	14-16	musician	35	"
r	Stella Leona—†	14-16	housewife	31	"
s	Weeman Anna—†	14-16	"	47	
t	Weeman Edward	14-16	chauffeur	47	"
u	Weeman Edward	14-16	clerk	24	
v	Weeman Walter	14-16	machinist	21	"

Page.	Letter.	FULL NAME.	Residence, Jan. 1, 1941.	Occupation.	Supposed Age.	Reported Residence, Jan. 1. 1940. Street and Number.

Ernst Street—Continued

	w	Picariello Antonio	15-17	investigator	31	here
	x	Picariello Rose—†	15-17	housewife	30	"
	y	Picariello Salvatore	15-17	agent	63	"
	z	Bartlett Eva—†	15-17	housewife	47	"
643						
	A	Bartlett Everett N	15-17	inspector	53	"
	B	James Arthur B	15-17	clerk	23	

Mahn's Terrace

	D	Cutter Jennie L—†	1	housewife	46	here
	E	Carlson Charlotte—·†	1	"	35	"
	F	Carlson Robert A	1	laborer	43	"
	G	Walsh John J	2	"	53	
	H	Walsh Kathleen—†	2	houseworker	20	"
	K	Gerstel Charles H	2	painter	50	
	L	Gerstel Dorothy A—†	2	laundress	22	"
	M	Gerstel Gladys L—†	2	housewife	43	"
	N	Gerstel James A	2	mechanic	20	"

Marbury Terrace

	P	McKay Mary E—†	2	housewife	55	here
	R	McKay William W	2	machinist	55	"
	S	Moylan Annie J—†	2	housewife	54	"
	T	Moylan James J	2	chauffeur	60	"
	U	Moylan James J, jr	2	"	20	
	V	Hiltz Anne M—†	2	housewife	25	"
	W	Hiltz Phillip G	2	mechanic	29	"
	X	Fowles Priscilla A—†	4	housewife	51	"
	Y	Fowles Ruth L—·†	4	domestic	20	"
	z	Fowles Wilbur	4	clerk	55	
644						
	A	Kleinberg Lillian—·†	4	teacher	35	
	B	Lasensky Fred	4	electrician	31	"
	C	Gogan Thomas D	4	clerk	29	"
	D	Hogan Winifred A—·†	4	housewife	25	"
	E	Deminger Anna—†	8	"	62	
	F	Deminger Frederick E	8	shoecutter	36	"
	H	Deminger Otto C	8	gardener	63	"
	G	Deminger Ruth C—·†	8	stenographer	23	"

Page.	Letter.	FULL NAME.	Residence, Jan. 1, 1941.	Occupation.	Supposed Age.	Reported Residence, Jan. 1, 1940. Street and Number.

Marbury Terrace—Continued

K	Kelley Alma B—†	8	operator	34	here
L	Callahan Alice M—†	8	housewife	50	"
M	Callahan Joseph E	8	laborer	25	"
N	Callahan Joseph P	8	carpenter	50	"
O	Callahan Virginia H—†	8	clerk	22	
P	DeLang Ferdinand J	8	merchant	40	"
R	DeLang Margaret A—†	8	housewife	40	"
S	MacKinnon Colin F	10	policeman	44	43 Gartland
T	*MacKinnon Martha—†	10	housewife	35	43 "
U	Graham Hannah M—†	10	"	66	here
V	Graham John L	10	clerk	37	"
W	Graham Rita V—†	10	stenographer	25	"
X	Kirk Esme A—†	10	nurse	56	2 Arcadia
Y	*Paquette Octave J	10	retired	82	36 "
Z	*Kilduff Celia—†	18	housewife	35	here
	645				
A	Kilduff John	18	builder	43	"
B	*McKay Mary—†	18	housewife	26	Medford
C	McKay William H	18	carpenter	31	20 Marbury ter
D	Mercer Mary V—†	18	housewife	42	here
E	Mercer Sidney	18	carpenter	50	"
F	Dempsey Edwin P	20	chef	52	"
G	Dempsey Ida L—†	20	housewife	43	"
H	Dempsey Ross M	20	clerk	23	
K	Dempsey Wellman H	20	machinist	21	"
L	Morrison Helen—†	20	housewife	29	"
M	Morrison Woodbury W	20	paint mixer	29	"
N	Sash Elizabeth—†	20	housewife	63	"
O	Sash Jacob	20	machinist	60	"

Miles Street

P	Burgess Lillian R—†	1	housewife	22	188 Durnell av
R	Burgess Michael H	1	ropemaker	27	188 "
S	Robbins Beatrice—†	1	housewife	24	53 Marcella
T	Robbins William C	1	serviceman	24	53 "
U	Burns Albert E	1	millwright	31	here
V	Burns Florence—†	1	housewife	32	"
W	Linehan Katherine—†	2	"	32	"
X	Linehan William J	2	clerk	32	
Y	Lemieux Charles	2	machinist	22	"

Page.	Letter.	FULL NAME.	Residence, Jan. 1, 1941.	Occupation.	Supposed Age.	Reported Residence, Jan. 1, 1940. Street and Number.

Miles Street—Continued

	z	Lemieux Lillian—†	2	clerk	24	here
646						
	A	Lemieux Peter	2	machinist	48	"
	B	Lemieux Rose—†	2	housewife	45	"
	C	Sargent Catherine E—†	2	saleswoman	39	61 Beechcroft
	D	Sargent Murray A	2	engineer	41	61 "
	E	Pizza Lillian—†	14–16	housewife	27	61 Brookley rd
	F	Pizza Ralph	14–16	pressman	34	61 "
	G	Smeade Lewis	14–16	laborer	28	61 "
	H	Ponn Alice—†	14–16	housewife	26	here
	K	Poun Julius	14–16	steamfitter	32	"

Notre Dame Street

	R	Merritt Delia—†	8	housewife	52	here
	S	Merritt Robert L	8	janitor	73	"
	T	Butler Gerald	10	laborer	28	"
	U	Butler Mildred—†	10	housewife	28	"
	V	Pearson Bertha—†	10	"	30	2 Marble
	W	Pearson George	10	janitor	29	2 "
	X	Dickerson Grace—†	10	domestic	38	Cambridge
	Y	Dickerson Walter	10	chauffeur	20	"
	Z	Janey Benetta—†	12	housewife	24	29 Humboldt av
647						
	A	Janey Charles E	12	bracer	25	29 "
	B	Iniss Joseph	12	seaman	55	here
	C	Iniss Viola—†	12	housewife	55	"
	D	Tebeau Bernard	12	chauffeur	37	"
	E	Tebeau Dorothy—†	12	housewife	26	"
	F	Janey Clara M—†	20	"	48	
	G	Janey Daniel B	20	shipper	50	
	H	Janey Kenneth L	20	upholsterer	20	"
	K	Janey William H	20	"	22	
	L	Jackson Elizabeth—†	22	housewife	26	"
	M	Jackson James	22	laborer	25	"
	N	Fonseca Fred	22	pedler	43	66 Westminster
	O	Fonseca Gladys—†	22	housewife	30	66 "
	P	Driscoll Catherine—†	24	"	51	here
	R	Driscoll Isaac	24	laborer	27	"
	S	Driscoll Monroe	24	clerk	21	"
	T	Blanchard Ellen—†	26	domestic	53	"

29

Notre Dame Street—Continued

u	Darden Davis	26	longshoreman	51	here
v	Darden Harriet B—†	26	housewife	51	"
w	Broadus Mabel—†	28	"	35	"
x	Broadus Raymond	28	wrestler	29	"
y	Stith Andrew B	28	U S N	21	20 Notre Dame
z	Miller Louella—†	29	housewife	30	here

648

A	Murray Leila—†	29	housekeeper	60	"
B	White Carrie L—†	31	housewife	55	"
c	White John A	31	clerk	55	
D	White John A, jr	31	student	23	
E	McKnight John	35	laborer	43	
F	McKnight William	35	"	22	
G	Thomas Edward	35	retired	78	
H	Thomas Nellie—†	35	housewife	55	"
K	Butler Bertha—†	37	laundress	28	"
L	Butler Mary—†	37	housewife	67	"
M	Butler Viola—†	37	housekeeper	23	"
N	Butler William	37	laborer	70	"
o	Blanchard Oscar	43	"	55	1086 Tremont
P	Charles Ethel—†	43	housekeeper	42	1086 "
R	Muncey Henry	45	retired	68	here
s	Muncey Susan—†	45	housewife	73	Lynn
T	Thornton Josephine—†	45	housekeeper	59	here
U	Thornton Martha—†	45	"	64	"
v	Erasmi Albina—†	47	housewife	44	"
w	Erasmi Mario	47	mason	44	
x	Dioz Catherine M—†	47	housewife	45	"
Y	Dioz Walter N	47	laborer	50	
z	Dioz Walter N	47	chauffeur	29	"

649

A	Holland Frank	47	retired	76	

School Street

B	Coulton Gordon S	101	chemist	28	here
c	Coulton Josephine L—†	101	housekeeper	65	"
D	Coulton Lillian I—†	101	clerk	25	"
E	Kennedy John T	101	launderer	72	"
F	Ryder Donald D	101	usher	21	
G	Ryder Eva M—†	101	housewife	41	"

30

Page	Letter	Full Name	Residence, Jan. 1, 1941.	Occupation.	Supposed Age.	Reported Residence, Jan. 1, 1940. Street and Number.

School Street—Continued

H	Ryder Owen A	101	meter reader	46	here
K	Whitney Walter C	103	clerk	69	"
M	Fallon Mary E—†	105	at home	75	"
N	Scott Catherine—†	105	"	65	
O	Harzbecker Frank H	105	salesman	75	"
P	Hughes Elizabeth L—†	105	saleswoman	31	"
R	Roche Marie—†	105	housewife	38	"
S	Bastable Dagmar—†	105	"	55	
T	Bastable Mildred—†	105	nurse	33	
U	Bastable Thomas	105	operator	59	
V	Bastable Thomas A	105	salesman	35	"
W	Hillen Catherine E—†	107	housewife	38	2973 Wash'n
X	Hillen Charles	107	manager	43	2973 "
Y	*Martell Rose M—†	107	housewife	56	20 Greenwood
Z	McInnes John	107	carpenter	71	Malden

650

A	Roslund Maria—†	107	at home	74	14 Beethoven
B	Hughes Kathleen—†	107	"	20	here
C	*Hunter George A	107	salesman	43	"
D	*Hunter Mary A—†	107	housewife	42	"
F	Moreau Annette—†	107	dietitian	21	
E	Moreau Antoinette—†	107	supervisor	44	"
G	Moreau Olive—†	107	at home	20	
H	Seward Charles	107	retired	76	"
K	Menz George J	111	inspector	31	34 Goldsmith
L	Mens Marion F—†	111	housewife	24	34 "
M	Fiore Alphonse	111	clerk	22	here
N	Fiore Amelia—†	111	"	25	"
O	Fiore Edith—†	111	stenographer	23	"
P	Fiore Gerard	111	U S N	20	"
R	Fiore Helen—†	111	clerk	27	
S	Fiore Lucy—†	111	housewife	49	"
T	Fiore Salvatore	111	barber	58	
U	*Schurest Augusta—†	115	nurse	32	
V	*Schurest Robert	115	inspector	45	"
W	Donnelly Alice—†	115	at home	30	
X	Donnelly Harold H	115	shoecutter	36	"
Y	McCormack George A	117	clerk	22	
Z	McCormack Gertrude E-†	117	housewife	49	"

651

A	McCormack John R	117	foreman	49	

School Street—Continued

	B	Cockshaw Catherine—†	117	housewife	29	here
	c	Cockshaw Clifford W	117	pressman	28	"
	D	Reams Anna B—†	119	housewife	35	"
	E	Reams George M	119	machinist	21	"
	F	Reams William H	119	"	38	"
	G	Banz Susanna—†	119	at home	76	
	H	Gimpel Frieda—†	119	"	66	
	K	Glassett Dennis	121	shipper	66	"
	L	Glassett Rebecca—†	121	at home	74	"
	M	McLaughlin Rose—†	121	"	72	473 La Grange
	N	Sandelind Alma M—†	121	instructor	45	17 Woodlawn
	O	Sandelind Axel	121	painter	62	17 "
	P	Conroy Anna G—†	125	broker	50	here
	R	Conroy Jennie L—†	125	at home	65	"
	S	McLaughlin Henry T	125	painter	29	"
	T	McLaughlin John F	125	student	21	"
	U	McLaughlin John G	125	custodian	59	"
	V	McLaughlin Mary H—†	125	at home	60	
	W	McLaughlin Mary K—†	125	teacher	31	"
	X	Farrington Alice—†	127	housewife	40	Quincy
	Y	Farrington Wendel	127	painter	46	"
	Z	Gately Margaret—†	127	housekeeper	65	here
652						
	A	Morse William W	127	retired	75	
	B	Roche James	131	ironworker	25	"
	E	Roche Lawrence	131	manager	35	108 Chestnut av
	C	Roche Mary F—†	131	housewife	67	here
	D	Roche Mary J—†	131	nurse	25	"
	F	Roche Nicholas	131	retired	70	"
	G	Roche Raymond I	131	bricklayer	37	"
	H	French Joseph H	135	physician	45	"
	K	French Katherine—†	135	supervisor	51	"
	L	Maxwell Clement	135	teacher	40	
	M	McEntee Ellen—†	135	housekeeper	50	"
	N	Brickley Edith C—†	137	at home	41	"
	O	Morris Florence—†	137	housewife	24	"

Washington Street

	R	Prior Alice—†	2937	housewife	38	19 Walnut pk
	S	Prior Moses	2937	janitor	45	19 "

Page.	Letter.	FULL NAME.	Residence, Jan. 1, 1941.	Occupation.	Supposed Age.	Reported Residence, Jan. 1, 1940. Street and Number.

Washington Street—Continued

v	O'Hare William A	2941	plumber	44	here
w	Mason Arabell—†	2941	domestic	64	"
x	Thomas Sarah—†	2947A	housekeeper	59	"
y	Murphy Mary A—†	2947A	housewife	50	"
z	Murphy Mary M—†	2947A	housekeeper	26	"

653

a	Walsh Albert F	2947A	mechanic	30	72 Boylston
b	Walsh Helen C—†	2947A	housewife	26	72 "
c	Daley Elizabeth—†	2949	"	21	22 Valentine
d	Daley John	2949	porter	22	22 "
f	Sears Elizabeth—†	2949	housewife	36	here
g	Sears Joseph	2949	laborer	35	"
k	Gallagher Catherine—†	2963	housewife	61	"
l	Noonan Ina—†	2963	"	37	9 Mohawk
m	Noonan John	2963	painter	20	9 "
n	Euscher Emily F—†	2963	housewife	46	95 Regent
o	Euscher Marat C	2963	shoeworker	58	95 "
p	Andrews Delia B—†	2965	housewife	47	C Derby pl
t	*Andrews Catherine—†	2969	waitress	38	here
u	*Burns Florence—†	2969	housekeeper	52	"
v	*Evaninger Paul	2969	steamfitter	35	"
w	Cahill John	2969	laborer	27	219 Amory
x	DiPaolo Alfred	2969	serviceman	30	988 Parker
y	DiPaolo Marie—†	2969	housewife	25	988 "
z	Davies George T	2971	ironworker	48	3001 Wash'n

654

a	Hait Mary—†	2971	housewife	38	here
b	Hait Patrick	2971	laborer	39	"
c	Kennedy Clara—†	2971	housewife	32	12 Arklow
d	Kennedy Joseph	2971	factoryhand	33	12 "
e	Riordan Charles V	2971	extractor	25	25 Magazine
f	Riordan Mary B—†	2971	housewife	24	25 "
g	Swaydowich Daisy—†	2973	"	44	here
h	Swaydowich Michael	2973	painter	48	"
k	Baxter Florence M—†	2973	waitress	54	"
l	Marston William A	2973	bartender	52	"
m	Giancola Louis	2973	factoryhand	25	173 Boylston
n	Giancola Theresa—†	2973	housewife	24	173 "
o	Henry Edward	2973	houseman	46	here
p	Henry Evelyn—†	2973	housewife	34	"
s	*Antonucci John	2975	retired	73	"

11—6

Washington Street—Continued

T	Benedetto Daniel	2975	laborer	37	here
U	Falso Fred	2975	"	32	"
V	Falso Nicoletta—†	2975	housewife	35	"
X	DeFrancisco Angelina–†	2975	"	30	2948 Wash'n
W	DeFrancisco Ettore	2975	chauffeur	32	2948 "
Y	Krohmer Robert	2975	laborer	20	2948 "
Z	Runzo Ernest	2975	chauffeur	25	2948 "

655

B	Craven Caroline E—†	2983	bookbinder	62	3 Johnson pk
C	Murphy Mary—†	2983	housewife	35	3 "
D	Sweeney Catherine M–†	2983	domestic	59	Saxonville
E	*Boghosian Agnes—†	2983	housewife	40	here
F	Boghosian Thomas	2983	carpenter	50	"
G	Arnold Joseph	2985	roofer	71	"
H	Smith Harry	2985	"	65	
K	Smith Harry	2985	houseman	20	"
L	Smith Laura—†	2985	waitress	42	
M	*Nigohosian Hagop	2985	retired	71	
N	*Nigohosian Isabel—†	2985	factoryhand	25	"
O	*Nigohosian Virginia—†	2985	housekeeper	26	"
P	Sarky Albazetian	2985	laborer	46	"
R	*Sarky Nartonke—†	2985	housewife	41	"
T	Carr Margaret A—†	2989	"	56	2991 Wash'n
U	McKay Mary L—†	2989	"	66	here
V	*Gourzoia Kirkor	2989	retired	64	"
W	Yenikonsan Margaret–†	2989	housewife	67	"
X	Nigohosian Alice—†	2989	"	27	Lowell
Y	Nigohosian Nicholas	2989	clerk	31	2985 Wash'n
Z	*Hanson Margaret—†	2991	housewife	37	2995 "

656

A	Litchman Maurice	2991	shipfitter	28	128 Ellington
B	*West Christine—†	2991	housewife	29	332 Amory
C	West Willard C	2991	chef	29	332 "
F	McWilliams Florence—†	2991	nurse	30	New York
D	*Platt Irene—†	2991	housewife	32	here
E	Platt William	2991	serviceman	34	"
H	Mosher Mabel—†	2993	saleswoman	64	16 Symmes
K	Joris Margaret—†	2993	housewife	23	New York
L	Winn Catherine—†	2993	"	45	109 Warren av
M	Winn Harry	2993	chauffeur	58	109 "
N	Winn Helen—†	2993	housewife	23	126 Blue Hill av

Page.	Letter.	Full Name.	Residence, Jan. 1, 1941.	Occupation.	Supposed Age.	Reported Residence, Jan. 1, 1940. Street and Number.

Washington Street—Continued

	o	Winn James	2993	chauffeur	20	126 Blue Hill av
	p	Boucher Frances—†	2995	housewife	31	23 Clarence
	r	Chamberlain Mary—†	2995	bookbinder	35	here
	s	Butterfield Albert	2995	salesman	47	23 Dorr
	t	Butterfield Louise—†	2995	housewife	43	23 "
	u	Killion Agnes—†	2995	"	29	11 Bartlett
	v	Killion Louis	2995	rigger	36	11 "
	w	Brown William	2997	carpenter	53	here
	x	Morris Havlin	2997	boilermaker	59	"
	y	Morris Isabelle—†	2997	housewife	50	"
	z	*Hodgson Eric	2997	clerk	23	

657

	a	*Hodgson Janet—†	2997	domestic	54	"
	b	St George Anna J—†	2997	housewife	49	"
	c	St George Wilfred	2997	laborer	49	"
	d	Knapp Ivory	2999	retired	68	2948 Wash'n
	e	Riley Joseph	2999	laborer	63	here
	f	Riley Mary—†	2999	housewife	65	"
	g	DiPaolo Guido	2999	laborer	30	"
	h	DiPaolo Lena—†	2999	housewife	29	"
	k	Eaton Frederick	2999	chauffeur	38	"
	l	*Eaton Jessie—†	2999	housewife	31	"
	m	Walsh Emma E—†	3001	"	45	61 Montebello rd
	o	Panico Dorothy—†	3001	"	26	here
	p	Panico Phillip	3001	chauffeur	30	"
	r	Bruton Mattie—†	3003	housekeeper	59	"
	s	McCraw Cobble G	3003	electrician	45	"
	t	McCraw Frances—†	3003	nurse	22	
	u	McCraw Howard	3003	machinist	42	"
	v	Morton Edward	3003	painter	32	"
	w	Myers Philip	3003	waiter	42	"
	x	Williams Ellen—†	3003	at home	70	"
	y	Snowden Jennie—†	3003	domestic	32	"

658

	c	Williams Nora—†	3069	housewife	52	"
	d	Williams Robert H	3069	repairman	55	"
	e	Cheney Mary—†	3069	housekeeper	52	"
	f	Ippolito Henry	3069	chauffeur	32	39 W Walnut pk
	g	Wilkinson Henry	3069	laborer	39	here
	h	Hannon Delia A—†	3069	housewife	57	"
	k	Poulos Bessie—†	3069	"	24	Middleboro

Washington Street—Continued

L	*Poulos Evelyn—†	3069	housewife	64	here
M	*Poulos George	3069	clerk	29	"

659

B	Atwood Beatrice—†	3103	housewife	58	"
C	Atwood Harry	3103	seaman	25	"
D	Hutchins Edith C—†	3103	housewife	58	2033 Col av
E	Hutchins Joseph	3103	chef	48	2033 "
K	*Flynn Kathleen F—†	3109	at home	24	2618 Wash'n
L	Flynn Nina—†	3109	housewife	46	2618 "
M	Sundin Mary E—†	3111	"	37	here
N	Sundin Thure J	3111	mechanic	38	"
O	Murphy Evelyn C—†	3111	waitress	29	2976 Wash'n
P	Pearson Ebba V—†	3111	"	20	2976 "
R	Pearson Emil L	3111	painter	55	2976 "
U	Reynolds Albert J	3117	chauffeur	42	here
V	Reynolds Julia M—†	3117	housewife	40	"
W	Scully Thomas P	3117	chauffeur	37	"
X	Haigh Joseph W	3117	laborer	38	3123 Wash'n
Y	Hicks Gertrude E—†	3117	housewife	40	here
Z	McFadden Francis T	3117	shipper	34	"

660

A	*McFadden Mary E—†	3117	housewife	30	"
B	*Banks Charlotte—†	3117	"	51	
C	Banks Enoc E	3117	repairman	46	"
D	*Darrah William T	3117	laborer	23	"
E	Lowder Alice M—†	3117	housewife	34	56 Bragdon
F	Lowder James F	3117	chauffeur	32	56 "
G	Horgan Catherine H—†	3117	housewife	28	73 School
H	Horgan John J	3117	chauffeur	35	73 "
K	Quinlan Helen G—†	3117	inspector	27	73 "
L	Quinlan Nellie—†	3117	housewife	57	73 "
O	Haines Joseph E	3123	social worker	43	here
P	Haines Margaret V—†	3123	housewife	63	"
R	*McGloin Bridget—†	3123	at home	67	"
S	George Celia M—†	3123	housewife	28	"
T	George Edward	3123	chauffeur	35	"
U	George Julia E—†	3123	housewife	69	3117 Wash'n
V	George William S	3123	retired	66	3117 "
W	Dakesian Alice—†	3123	at home	27	here
X	Dakesian Kerop	3123	merchant	44	"
Y	Reynolds Gertrude P—†	3123	packer	49	"

Page.	Letter.	Full Name.	Residence, Jan. 1, 1941.	Occupation.	Supposed Age.	Reported Residence, Jan. 1, 1940. Street and Number.

Washington Street—Continued

	z	Reynolds Louisa R—†	3123	housewife	72	here
661						
	A	Reynolds Thomas F	3123	retired	70	"
	B	Dodge Lucy A—†	3123	operator	58	7 Bancroft
	C	Lienemann Edward	3123	retired	68	7 "
	E	Connell Ruth E—†	3123	clerk	30	6 Helena
	F	Cunniff Catherine A—†	3123	housewife	28	6 "
	G	Cunniff Patrick J	3123	instructor	30	6 "
	D	Grant Dorothy L—†	3123	collector	53	6 '

West Walnut Park

	H	*McLaughlin James	20	laborer	59	3320 Wash'n
	K	McLaughlin Mary A—†	20	housewife	54	3320 "
	L	Cahill Catherine—†	20	"	61	here
	M	Cahill James F	20	painter	70	"
	N	Cahill Lillian—†	20	clerk	23	"
	O	Cahill Mary—†	20	"	25	
	P	Heffernan Louise—†	20	shoeworker	35	"
	R	Reximes Athena—†	20	housewife	40	12 Kingsbury
	S	Reximes Efstradios	20	laborer	54	12 "
	T	*Edminston Edna—†	22	housewife	49	here
	U	Edminston Edna—†	22	nurse	22	"
	V	Edminston William	22	laborer	49	"
	W	Edminston Annie—†	22	housewife	53	"
	X	Edminston James	22	carpenter	53	"
	Y	Lindsey John	22	shipfitter	43	"
	z	*Lindsey Mary—†	22	housewife	40	"
662						
	A	Barker Daniel	24	porter	61	
	B	Field Sara E—†	24	housekeeper	52	"
	C	Richardson Agnes A—†	24	clerk	49	
	D	Stewart Robert J	24	retired	74	
	E	*Lloyd Freda—†	28	housewife	26	"
	F	Lloyd William	28	operator	33	
	G	Peacock Cora—†	30	laundress	31	"
	H	Peacock Norman	30	clerk	49	
	K	Noonan Dennis	32	retired	67	"
	L	Noonan Nellie J—†	32	at home	77	"
	M	Foster Charles	33	chauffeur	55	"
	N	Slade Lydia—†	33	housewife	42	"

West Walnut Park—Continued

o	Slade William	33	manager	45	here
p	O'Brien Edward	34	clerk	60	"
r	Wesley Ernest	34	laborer	65	"
s	Wesley Mary—†	34	housekeeper	36	"
t	Donlan Mary E—†	35	dietitian	45	"
u	St Ongi Florence—†	35	housekeeper	50	"
v	Perino Catherine—†	37	clerk	32	"
w	Perino Mary—†	37	"	30	
x	Eichner Agnes—†	38	housewife	33	"
y	Eichner John	38	ironworker	39	"
z*	McPherson Hugh	38	painter	53	

663

a	McPherson Martha—†	38	housewife	53	"
b	McInnis Agnes—†	39	singer	23	
c	McInnis Mary—†	39	housewife	63	"
d	O'Brien Maude—†	39	domestic	53	"
e	Broderick Josephine A—†	39	operator	46	"
f	Aristides Angela—†	39	housekeeper	32	71 W Walnut pk
g	Bell Gertrude—†	40	"	32	here
h	Bell Mary—†	40	housewife	66	"
k	Bell Walter	40	agent	38	"
l	Bell William	40	clerk	40	"
m	Haddock Hazen E	41	foreman	48	
n	Fesler Dean	41	bookkeeper	45	"
o	Fesler Helen—†	41	housewife	43	"
p	Cunniffe Catherine—†	41	"	58	128 Williams
r	Cunniffe Joseph P	41	clerk	24	128 "
s	Cunniffe Patrick J	41	laborer	57	128 "
t	Ferris Claire P—†	43	packer	20	50 Austin
u	Ferris Harvey N	43	clerk	26	Randolph
v	Stuteville Olive—†	43	housewife	29	Maine
w	Stuteville Overton	43	manager	37	874 South
x	Cronin Mildred—†	44	clerk	29	here
y	Sacco Elizabeth—†	44	housewife	37	"
z	Sacco Joseph	44	foreman	36	"

664

a	Grinnell Charles	46–48	salesman	48	"
b	Locher Mark A	46–48	"	44	
c	Locher Mary E—†	46–48	housewife	44	"
d	Kearns Edward F	47–49	salesman	38	"
e	Kearns Margaret—†	47–49	housewife	36	"

Page.	Letter.	Full Name.	Residence. Jan. 1. 1941.	Occupation.	Supposed Age.	Reported Residence, Jan. 1. 1940. Street and Number.
	F	O'Brien Annie M—†	47–49	housekeeper	68	here
	G	Henneberry Elizabeth—†47–49		housewife	41	"
	H	Henneberry James	47–49	clerk	43	"
	K	Mulhern George I	50–52	"	46	..
	L	Mulhern Mary A—†	50–52	housewife	41	"
	M	Edwards Alexander W	50–52	clerk	37	5 Glenvale ter
	N	Edwards Elizabeth—†	50–52	housewife	26	5 "
	O	Hardiman George	51	chauffeur	31	here
	P	Hardiman Mary—†	51	housewife	31	"
	R	Gounis Angelo	51	manager	42	186 Amory
	S	Gounis Demetrius—†	51	housewife	42	186 "
	T	Parsons Louise E—†	54–56	"	37	11½ Spring Park av
	U	Parsons Walter M	54–56	clerk	43	11½ "
	V	Bellows Albert M	54–56	salesman	39	here
	W	Bellows Ebba—†	54–56	housewife	36	"
	X	McCullough Jennie—†	54–56	storekeeper	67	"
	Y	Nelson Hilda—†	54–56	housekeeper	67	"
	z	*Coutoulakis Irene—†	55	housewife	47	505 Mass av
665						
	A	Coutoulakis John	55	chef	50	505 "
	B	Salis Helen—†	55	housewife	28	here
	C	Salis Peter	55	chauffeur	40	"
	D	Oberlander Mary T—†	58–60	housewife	36	"
	E	Oberlander Warren	58–60	fireman	40	
	F	Rohanna Florence—†	58–60	stitcher	41	
	G	Cutler Herbert	58–60	student	21	
	H	Cutler Isabelle—†	58–60	housewife	53	"
	K	Cutler Laurence M	58–60	carpenter	25	"
	L	Cutler Mildred—†	58–60	clerk	27	
	M	Cutler Samuel	58–60	carpenter	54	"
	N	Ross Genevieve—†	59	housewife	43	"
	O	Ross John	59	chef	54	
	P	Falcone Dominic	59	clerk	40	
	R	Falcone Minnie—†	59	housekeeper	28	"
	S	Stone Catherine—†	62–64	cashier	33	27 Forest
	T	Stone Catherine A—†	62–64	housewife	54	27 "
	U	Stone Irene—†	62–64	housekeeper	31	27 "
	V	Stone Samuel	62–64	engineer	59	27 "
	W	Cavallaro Camella—†	62–64	housewife	26	76 Sumner
	X	Cavallaro Raymond	62–64	barber	28	76 "
	Y	Donabedian Ashod	66–68	clerk	37	here

Page.	Letter.	Full Name.	Residence, Jan. 1, 1941.	Occupation.	Supposed Age.	Reported Residence, Jan. 1, 1940. Street and Number.

West Walnut Park—Continued

	z	Donabedian Florence-†	66–68	housewife	37	here
666						
	A	*Margosian Almas—†	66–68	"	74	
	B	*Margosian Onan	66–68	retired	72	"
	c	Koutrouba Gertrude–†	66–68	housewife	39	1871 Col av
	D	Koutrouba Michael	66–68	carpenter	41	1871 "
	E	Anagnos Anna—†	70–72	housewife	30	here
	F	*Anagnos Bessie—†	70–72	at home	75	"
	G	Anagnos William	70–72	storekeeper	36	"
	H	*Barnett Alfreda—†	70–72	housewife	65	"
	K	Barnett Alice—†	70–72	clerk	32	
	L	*Barnett Mary M—†	70–72	"	36	"
	M	Clooney Catherine—†	71–73	housewife	44	7 Atherton
	N	Clooney Catherine D–†	71–73	housekeeper	24	7 "
	o	Clooney James	71–73	manager	53	7 "
	P	Clooney James L	71–73	attendant	22	7 "
	R	Clooney John F	71–73	machinist	21	7 "
	s	Lolos Aphrodite—†	71–73	housekeeper	29	51 W Walnut pk
	T	Lolos Charles	71–73	chef	43	51 "
	U	Tapper Gertrude—†	74–76	nurse	35	here
	v	Vorbeau Melvin	74–76	shipper	34	"
	w	Vorbeau Ruby J—†	74–76	housewife	30	"
	x	Jung Gertrude—†	74–76	clerk	27	
	Y	Jung Karl	74–76	salesman	54	"
	z	Jung Sophia—†	74–76	housewife	49	"
667						
	A	Papadinis George	75–77	chauffeur	46	"
	B	*Papadinis Mary—†	75–77	housewife	41	"
	c	*Triantos Bessie—†	75–77	"	47	
	D	Triantos Harry	75–77	pedler	22	
	E	Triantos Nicholas	75–77	"	50	
	F	McLeod Alex	78–80	chauffeur	54	"
	G	McLeod Margaret—†	78–80	housewife	47	"
	H	Sullivan Catherine F–†	78–80	clerk	29	
	K	Sullivan Florance	78–80	retired	63	"
	L	Toivo Ethel—†	79–81	housekeeper	28	82 W Walnut pk
	M	Wright Etta—†	79–81	"	64	82 "
	N	Murray Donald	79–81	chauffeur	28	here
	o	Murray Helen—†	79–81	housewife	54	"
	P	Murray James	79–81	retired	68	"
	R	Murray Mary—†	79–81	housekeeper	21	"

Page.	Letter.	FULL NAME.	Residence, Jan. 1, 1941.	Occupation.	Supposed Age.	Reported Residence, Jan. 1, 1940. Street and Number.

West Walnut Park—Continued

	s	Murray Raymond	79-81	receiver	24	here
	T	Murray Veronica—†	79-81	clerk	26	"
	U	DiNicola Barney	82-84	laborer	27	635 Cummins H'way
	V	DiNicola Dominic	82-84	"	60	9 Bickford
	w*	DiNicola Mary—†	82-84	housewife	47	9 "
	x	Simon Nicholas	82-84	waiter	48	71 W Walnut pk
	Y*	Simon Olympia—†	82-84	housewife	35	71 "
	z	Greene Elmer T	83-85	tailor	35	1847 Col av
668						
	A	Stern Dorothy A—†	83-85	housewife	37	here
	B	Stern Morris	83-85	bookbinder	42	"
	D	Daley Margaret G—†	83-85	operator	31	"
	C	Daley Mary E—†	83-85	housekeeper	58	"
	E	Blue Helen G—†	83-85	housewife	48	"
	F	Blue John D	83-85	ironworker	47	"
	G	Waters Abbie—†	86-88	housewife	34	"
	H	Waters Nicholas J	86-88	policeman	41	"
	K	Costa Frank	86-88	laborer	45	43 Bickford
	L	Costa Ida—†	86-88	housewife	40	43 "
	O	Mahoney Dennis	90-92	policeman	50	here
	P	Mahoney Ella—†	90-92	housewife	43	"
	R	Sloan Catherine—†	90-92	clerk	43	"
	T	Stockman Karl E	94-96	"	22	
	U	Tumashais Emma—†	94-96	housewife	50	"
	V	Tumashais Karl	94-96	carpenter	51	"
	w	Minehan John A	94-96	salesman	47	"
	x	Minehan Mary J—†	94-96	housewife	47	"
	Y	Minehan Rita—†	94-96	clerk	22	"
	z*	Menechios Catherine-†	95-97	housewife	40	89 W Walnut pk
669						
	A	Menechios Thomas	95-97	grocer	50	89 "
	B	Zervas Effie—†	95-97	housewife	41	here
	C	Zervas William	95-97	chef	49	"
	D	McKinnon Helen—†	99-101	housewife	47	"
	E	McKinnon Philip	99-101	mechanic	46	"
	F	Harris Ernest L	99-101	salesman	45	5 Rollins ct
	G	Harris Ernest L	99-101	baker	28	5 "
	H	Howard Eugene	103-105	repairman	53	here
	K	Howard Nancy—†	103-105	shoemaker	54	"
	L	O'Donnell Bernard A	103-105	clerk	20	1 Ernst
	M	O'Donnell John J	103-105	"	45	1 "

Page.	Letter.	Full Name.	Residence, Jan. 1, 1941.	Occupation.	Supposed Age.	Reported Residence, Jan. 1, 1940. Street and Number.

West Walnut Park—Continued

N	O'Donnell Rose G—†103–105		housewife	45	1 Ernst
o	Jago Frank S	109	chauffeur	24	here
P	Jago Jeanne—†	109	housewife	23	"
R	Williams John C	109	plumber	29	"
s	Williams Mary—†	109	housewife	24	"
T	Elmowitz Abraham	109	superintendent	41	"
U	Elmowitz Evelyn—†	109	housewife	43	"
V	Elmowitz Leonard	109	student	20	..
W	O'Donnell Catherine M—†	109	housewife	35	"
X	O'Donnell William F	109	manager	38	"
Y	Tucker Eleanor M—†	109	secretary	21	8 Isabella
Z	Tucker Elmer E	109	fireman	63	8 "

670

A	Tucker Mary—†	109	housewife	58	8 "
B	Pursley Jeanette—†	109	"	36	here
C	Pursley Thomas	109	shoeworker	42	"
D	Pursley Thomas A	109	student	20	"
E	Kenney Daniel	109	mechanic	52	156 Lamartine
F	Kenney Lillian—†	109	housewife	31	156 "
G	Lucas Beatrice—†	109	"	30	here
H	Lucas Charles	109	clerk	35	"
K	Gerber Myer	109	operator	37	"
L	Gerber Stella—†	109	housewife	21	"
M	Hite Arnold	109	storekeeper	28	"
N	Hite Sylvia—†	109	housewife	25	"
o	Burnham Ann—†	109	operator	44	"
P	Card Rose—†	109	housewife	39	"
R	Card William	109	carpenter	39	"
s	*Epstein Fannie—†	109	housekeeper	62	"
T	Gerson Edward	109	manager	32	"
U	Gerson Gertrude—†	109	housewife	27	"

Ward 11–Precinct 7

CITY OF BOSTON

LIST OF RESIDENTS
20 YEARS OF AGE AND OVER

(NON-CITIZENS INDICATED BY ASTERISK)
(FEMALES INDICATED BY DAGGER)

AS OF

JANUARY 1, 1941

JOSEPH F. TIMILTY, *Chairman*
FREDERIC E. DOWLING, *Secretary*
WILLIAM A. MOTLEY, Jr.
FRANCIS B. McKINNEY
HILDA HEDSTROM QUIRK

Listing Board.

700

Ashworth Park

A	Lamond Annie L—†	6	housewife	46	35 Marcella
B	Lamond John	6	boilermaker	46	35 "
C	Lamond William F	6	U S N	22	35 "
D	Rockwell Anna—†	8	housewife	32	here
E	Rockwell William H	8	merchant	33	"
F	Donohue Eleanor R—†	10	stenographer	33	"
G	Donohue John J	10	retired	64	"
H	Donohue Mary C—†	10	housekeeper	70	"
K	Donohue Nellie F—†	10	housewife	65	"
L	Horan Mary F—†	10	stenographer	36	"

Cleaves Street

M	Ruddy Anna—†	5	accountant	70	here
N	Lazerborg Ruth—†	5	clerk	40	226 Fuller
O	Proctor Laura E—†	5	housewife	59	26 Iffley rd
P	Rawitz Jacob	5	clerk	50	here
R	Rawitz Rebecca—†	5	housewife	45	"
S	Leavitt Mollie—†	6	"	27	"
T	Leavitt Morris	6	jobber	26	
U	Singer Adelaide—†	6	housewife	33	"
V	Singer Barney	6	salesman	37	"
W	Facktoroff Augusta—†	6	housewife	40	"
X	Facktoroff Henry	6	salesman	43	"
Y	Cohen Emma—†	7	housewife	35	1420 Blue Hill av
Z	Cohen Morris	7	salesman	34	1420 "

701

A	Dosick John	7	"	31	here
B	Dosick Martha—†	7	housewife	32	"
C	Graham Margaret—†	7	clerk	25	"
D	Hochberg Mary—†	7	housewife	39	559 Ashmont
E	Solomon Charlotte—†	8	"	29	here
F	Solomon Leo J	8	manager	29	"
G	Helman Dora—†	8	housewife	32	"
H	Helman Philip	8	accountant	34	"
K	Levison Bessie—†	8	at home	75	
L	Levison Manuel	8	salesman	36	"
M	Savransky Idelle—†	9	housewife	32	"
N	Savransky Louis	9	salesman	37	"
O	Albert Bessie—†	9	housewife	53	"

Cleaves Street—Continued

	Letter	Full Name	Residence	Occupation	Age	Reported Residence
	P	Albert Samuel	9	tailor	57	here
	R	Joseph Frances—†	9	housewife	38	Revere
	s*	Joseph Louis	9	laborer	45	"
	T	Kravitz Evelyn—†	10	housewife	32	here
	U	Kravitz Harry	10	salesman	37	"
	V	Golner Mildred—†	10	housewife	37	"
	W	Golner Nathan	10	clerk	38	
	X	Goldman Bertha—†	10	housewife	28	"
	Y	Goldman Robert	10	manager	31	"
	Z	Ross Evelyn—†	11	housewife	30	44 Highland
702						
	A	Blondin Catherine—†	11	housekeeper	62	here
	B	Blondin Ellen V—†	11	"	64	"
	C	Blondin Margaret M—†	11	saleswoman	56	"
	D	Moran Catherine—†	11	clerk	56	
	E	Beloin Sarah A—†	11	housewife	68	"
	F	Flood Dorothy J—†	11	librarian	27	"
	G	Flood Florence D—†	11	saleswoman	46	"
	H	Gurazdonik Katherine—†	12	housewife	54	"
	K	Gurazdonik Louis	12	janitor	55	
	L*	Goldberg Helen—†	12	housewife	64	"
	M	Goldberg Joel M	12	manager	38	
	N	Goldberg Ruth—†	12	saleswoman	24	"
	O	Spiro Edmund	12	shipper	20	
	P	Cutbill Beatrice—†	12	housewife	36	"
	R	Cutbill Harold C	12	instructor	43	"
	S	Nadler Edwin B	14	agent	42	
	T	Nadler Gertrude—†	14	housewife	36	"
	U	Rothwell Anne—†	14	"	33	
	V	Rothwell George F	14	foreman	33	"
	W	Davidson Burgal—†	14	housewife	39	"
	X	Davidson Joel	14	dentist	50	"
	Y	Fritz Bernard	15	clerk	33	
	Z	Fritz Jean—†	15	housewife	33	"
703						
	A	Chyet Ella—†	15	"	28	188 Woodrow av
	B	Chyet Hyman B	15	cutter	29	188 "
	C	Frost Asa R	15	clerk	29	36 Reyem Circle
	D	Frost Dorothy—†	15	housewife	23	36 "
	E	Oakman Lillian—†	16	"	29	here
	F	Oakman Victor	16	agent	32	"

Page.	Letter.	FULL NAME.	Residence, Jan. 1, 1941.	Occupation.	Supposed Age.	Reported Residence, Jan. 1, 1940. Street and Number.

Cleaves Street—Continued

	G	Rasnick Bessie—†	16	housewife	31	8 Irwin av
	H	Rasnick Hyman	16	engineer	32	8 "
	K	Brickman John	16	barber	58	here
	L	Brickman Mildred—†	16	housewife	57	"
	M	Bornstein Herman	16	manager	45	"
	N	Bornstein Melvin	16	"	21	"
	O	*Bornstein Mildred—†	16	housewife	42	"
	P	Lofchie Fred	17	letter carrier	31	"
	R	Lofchie Pearl—†	17	housewife	30	"
	S	Harris Barney J	17	carpenter	52	"
	T	Harris Mary—†	17	housewife	43	"
	U	Lavin Catherine—†	17	"	46	
	V	Lavin William H	17	repairman	52	"

Cobden Street

	W	Archer Carrie E—†	4	housewife	47	here
	X	Archer James A	4	clerk	51	"
	Y	Strom Elias	8	caretaker	67	"
	Z	Strom Esther E—†	8	housewife	66	"
		704				
	A	Garrity Dennis	16	motorman	84	"
	B	Garrity Francis	16	mechanic	32	"
	C	Garrity John	16	waiter	47	
	D	Garrity Margaret—†	16	matron	37	
	E	Molloy Henry	18	plumber	64	
	F	Molloy Thomas	18	metalworker	57	"
	G	*Hoene Henry	20	woodcarver	59	"
	H	Martin Agnes C—†	20	housewife	54	"
	K	Martin Benjamin	20	clerk	54	
	L	Alexander Orca—†	22	"	35	
	M	Kelliher Georgianna—†	22	housewife	25	"
	N	Kelliher Vincent P	22	clerk	26	
	O	McCraith Elizabeth—†	24	housewife	77	"
	P	McCraith James F	24	retired	82	
	R	Kelleher Frances C—†	26	housewife	52	"
	S	Kelleher Patrick J	26	leatherworker	55	"
	T	Rooney Eugenia M—†	28	housewife	37	"
	U	Rooney Walter J	28	accountant	46	"
	V	Gebfert Carl H	rear 28A	artist	78	
	W	Kahlmeyer Mary C—†	" 28A	housewife	75	"

Cobden Street—Continued

Letter	Full Name	Residence	Occupation	Age	Reported Residence
x	Livingston Lillian—†	rear 28A	housewife	71	here
z	McIntyre Hugh	30	attorney	43	"
y	McIntyre Jeannette R—†	30	housewife	75	"
	705				
A	Zriegin Helen—†	rear 30	"	36	
B	Zriegin Louis	" 30	merchant	42	"
C	Coleman Mary H—†	32	housewife	41	"
D	Coleman Mary J—†	32	clerk	21	
E	Coleman Ralph J	32	"	42	
F	Coleman Ralph J, jr	32	"	22	
G	Rivers George A	32	druggist	53	
H	Rivers Theresa A—†	32	housewife	52	"
K	Rivers Virginia—†	32	stitcher	29	
L	Cavarnos Constantine	32	student	22	
M	Cavarnos Irene—†	32	housewife	55	"
N	Cavarnos John	32	student	24	
O	Cavarnos Peter	32	manager	59	
P	Koutsaftis Frances—†	32	housewife	25	"
R	*Koutsaftis James	32	mechanic	26	Greece
S	Leet Robert H	34	chauffeur	50	here
T	Leet Sarah K—†	34	baker	48	"
U	Hatzimanolis George	34	laborer	22	"
V	Hatzimanolis Marie—†	34	housewife	56	"
W	Hatzimanolis Millicent—†	34	clerk	30	
X	Khachadoin David	34	baker	40	
Y	Watson Dorothy—†	36	clerk	25	
Z	Watson Esther—†	36	housewife	50	"
	706				
A	Watson Leonard	36	laborer	21	
B	Watson Peter J	36	chauffeur	54	"
C	Watson Peter J, jr	36	U S A	22	"
D	Blanchard Prudence—†	36	housewife	38	"
E	Blanchard Rudolph	36	painter	43	
F	Connolly Mary—†	36	housewife	55	"
G	Hillen John	38	laborer	52	
H	Hillen Marie—†	38	housewife	39	"
K	Panopoulos George	38	chef	52	
L	Panopoulos Masina—†	38	housewife	50	"
M	Scaltsas Patricia—†	38	"	43	"
N	*Richardi Florence—†	40	"	64	
O	Richardi Frank	40	laborer	64	"

5

Cobden Street—Continued

P	Richardi Nicholas	40	clerk	24	here	
R	Benjamin John F	40	"	22	70 Bragdon	
S	Benjamin Mildred—†	40	housewife	21	70 "	
T	Ferrara Louise—†	40	"	31	here	
U	Ferrara Rocco	40	repairer	34	"	
V	McKenna Anna—†	44	clerk	38	"	
W	Young Albert D	44	chauffeur	27	"	
X	Young Mary D—†	44	housewife	55	"	
Y	Drew Emma—†	44	milliner	64		
Z	Drew Richard	44	machinist	74	"	

707

A	Herder Arthur	44	laborer	22		
B	Herder Celia—†	44	operator	26		
C	Herder Frank	44	lather	60		
D	Herder Mary—†	44	housewife	60	"	
E	Herder Mary—†	44	operator	30		
F	Walsh James J	46	custodian	58	"	
G	Speero Christopher	46	laborer	45		
H	Speero Margaret—†	46	housewife	44	"	
K	Walsh Alice L—†	46	"	58		
L	Walsh Edward J	46	clerk	21		
M	Walsh George A	46	custodian	28	"	
N	McNeil Vernon	48	laborer	40		

Columbus Avenue

T	*Lew George	1975	laundryman	34	here	
Z	Norton Helen—†	1990	housewife	21	5 Weld av	

708

A	Norton William	1990	roofer	22	5 "	
B	Costa Virginia—†	1990	housekeeper	67	749 W Roxbury Pkwy	
C	Pimental Alice B—†	1990	housewife	33	749 "	
D	Pimental John	1990	policeman	43	749 "	
E	Aramian Mary—†	1991	housewife	33	here	
F	Aramian Sarkis	1991	tailor	44	"	
G	Christopher Urban	1991	dentist	63	"	
H	Kakatsakis George	1991	merchant	44	"	
K	*Kakatsakis Maria—†	1991	at home	76		
L	*Kakatsakis Thalia—†	1991	housewife	34	"	
M	Yiannacopoulos Anna-†	1991	waitress	21		
N	Yiannacopoulos Helen-†	1991	"	20	"	

Page.	Letter.	FULL NAME.	Residence, Jan. 1, 1941.	Occupation.	Supposed Age.	Reported Residence, Jan. 1, 1940. Street and Number.

Columbus Avenue—Continued

o	Yiannacopoulos Peter	1991	salesman	52	here
P	*Yiannacopoulos Theodora—†	1991	housewife	39	"
R	*Tingus Constantine—†	1991	"	50	"
s	Tingus Stephen	1991	merchant	60	"
T	*Grattan Grace—†	1991	housekeeper	45	"
u	Harkins Joseph	1991	chef	46	"
v	Larvey John	1991	butcher	48	
w	Shaughnessy John P	1991	plumber	56	
x	Flanders Alden L	1996	physician	76	"
y	Gullickson Jennie—†	1996	housekeeper	71	"

709

D	McMasters Donald S	2012	salesman	25	5 Atherton
E	McMasters Ida M—†	2012	housewife	54	6 "
F	McMasters Stanley E	2012	shipper	59	6 "
G	McMasters Thelma D–†	2012	clerk	20	5 "
L	Mulhern Anna E—†	2029	housewife	62	here
M	Mulhern Louise M—†	2029	teacher	40	"
N	Bell Frank W	2029	collector	48	"
o	Bell Mary—†	2029	housewife	47	"
P	Haskell Jeannette A—†	2029	"	69	"
R	Haskell Warren B	2029	manager	68	"
s	Sacks Agnes B—†	2031	housewife	24	7 Cleaves
T	Sacks Harold B	2031	laborer	23	60 Callender
u	Starobin Morris	2031	painter	46	18 Dixwell
v	*Starobin Sarah I—†	2031	housewife	39	18 "
W	Catherwood Catherine A—†	2031	"	40	here
x	Catherwood William J	2031	superintendent	44	"
y	Kurth Elizabeth D—†	2032	housekeeper	35	"
z	Kurth Katherine D—†	2032	housewife	67	"

710

A	Kurth William J	2032	attorney	70	"
B	Porter Effie E—†	2033	housewife	58	"
c	Porter Victor H	2033	manager	68	"
D	Flaherty Bernard A	2033	inspector	54	49 Stoughton
E	Flaherty Dora—†	2033	housewife	44	87 School
F	Flaherty William C	2033	transitman	48	49 Stoughton
G	Nelson Clara—†	2033	housewife	56	here
H	Nelson Peter W	2033	engineer	59	"
K	Nelson Robert E	2033	laborer	23	"
L	*Malloy Margaret A—†	2035	housewife	71	"
M	Totman Annie A—†	2035	"	58	"

Page.	Letter.	FULL NAME.	Residence, Jan. 1, 1941.	Occupation.	Supposed Age.	Reported Residence, Jan. 1, 1940. Street and Number.

Columbus Avenue—Continued

N	Totman Ariel F—†	2035	boxmaker	38	here
O	Totman Hazel I—†	2035	stenographer	29	"
P	Totman Levi D	2035	salesman	64	"
R	Nelson Clara—†	2035	housewife	56	"
S	Nelson Peter W	2035	engineer	59	
T	Nelson Robert E	2035	clerk	23	
U	Inman James J	2037	painter	52	
V	Inman James J, jr	2037	repairman	21	"
W	Inman Margaret M—†	2037	housewife	45	"
X	Donahue Richard	2037	waiter	29	
Y	Gannon Catherine A—†	2037	housewife	55	"
Z	Hart Edward	2037	operator	58	Arlington
	711				
A	Merlin Edward J	2037	cashier	23	here
B	Merlin Mary L—†	2037	housewife	52	"
C	Merlin Rita M—†	2037	laboratory	20	"
D	Gettis Arthur J	2041	laborer	37	3144A Wash'n
E	Gettis Lily S—†	2041	housewife	40	3144A "
F	Gettis Mary—†	2041	"	64	3144A "
G	Flynn Marie C—†	2041	"	50	14 Dixwell
H	Flynn William J	2041	salesman	52	14 "
K	Aikins George E	2041	manager	27	Medford
L	*Aikins Jennie M—†	2041	housewife	62	"
M	Magee May K—†	2043	clerk	45	here
N	Malloy Andrew P	2043	laborer	64	"
O	Malloy Bridget—†	2043	housewife	67	"
P	Prindeville Helen G—†	2043	"	67	
R	Prindeville William F	2043	laborer	64	
S	Dahl Elizabeth—†	2044	housewife	73	"
T	Dahl Rosina—†	2044	"	72	"
U	O'Brien Eleanor M—†	2045	"	29	34 Moreland
V	O'Brien John J	2045	mason	30	34 "
W	Ryan Mary W—†	2045	housewife	65	here
X	Ryan Natalie C—†	2045	stenographer	40	"
Y	Quinn Frank F	2045	painter	36	17 Weld av
Z	Quinn Mabel H—†	2045	nurse	34	17 "
	712				
A	Carey Mary A—†	2047	housewife	75	here
B	Collins Bernard E	2047	retired	85	"
C	Collins Sarah A—†	2047	housewife	79	"
D	Lydon Mary V—†	2047	"	40	

Page.	Letter.	FULL NAME.	Residence, Jan. 1, 1941.	Occupation.	Supposed Age.	Reported Residence, Jan. 1, 1940. Street and Number.

Columbus Avenue—Continued

E	Lydon Stephen A	2047	cable splicer	41	here
F	Roundburg John	2049	foreman	67	"
G	Roundburg Richard L	2049	assembler	25	"
H	Gilman Fred F	2049	baggagemaster	53	"
K	Gilman Mary A—†	2049	housewife	53	"
L	Knapp Herbert R	2049	executive	60	"
M	Knapp Mary A—†	2049	housewife	61	"
N	Adams Elizabeth M—†	2055	at home	81	
O	Adams Ella L—†	2055	"	86	
P	Adams Fred H	2055	retired	86	
R	Allen Minnie M—†	2055	superintendent	58	"
S	Andrews Walter H	2055	retired	80	
T	Annikov Alexander S	2055	"	87	
U	Annikov Sophie S—†	2055	at home	70	
V	Arnold William E	2055	retired	83	
W	Ashton Ellen H—†	2055	at home	74	
X	Ashton James W	2055	retired	77	
Y	Baggs Helen M—†	2055	operator	22	"
Z	Bateman Carrie T—†	2055	at home	76	"
	713				
A	Bowen Theresa—†	2055	cook	35	
B	Brackett Charlotte U–†	2055	at home	77	
C	Brackett George R	2055	retired	80	
D	Briggs Ada L—†	2055	at home	67	"
E	Briggs Benjamin F	2055	retired	67	"
F	*Brown Edith—†	2055	domestic	55	"
G	Brown Fannie W—†	2055	at home	68	
H	Brown John F	2055	retired	87	"
K	Bullard Carrie J—†	2055	at home	78	
L	Bullard George A	2055	retired	74	
M	Burgstahler Elsie—†	2055	at home	69	"
N	Butler Herbert W	2055	retired	85	
O	Butler Minnie B—†	2055	at home	77	
P	*Butterfield Susan Y—†	2055	"	80	
R	*Butterfield William	2055	retired	78	"
S	Cameron Winfield	2055	watchman	35	68 Meridian
T	Carlson Ludwig F	2055	retired	90	here
U	Carlson Martha A—†	2055	at home	88	"
V	Carson Idella—†	2055	"	74	"
W	Chambers Johanna—†	2055	"	74	
X	Chambers John T	2055	retired	72	

Page.	Letter.	FULL NAME.	Residence, Jan. 1, 1941.	Occupation.	Supposed Age.	Reported Residence, Jan. 1, 1940. Street and Number.

Columbus Avenue—Continued

Y	Cheever Clarence I	2055	retired	81	here	
Z	Cheever Nellie R—†	2055	at home	78	"	
	714					
A	Clough Ellen—†	2055	"	89		
B	Collins Louise—†	2055	housekeeper	62	"	
C	Comstock Edna E—†	2055	at home	75	..	
D	Comstock Otho H	2055	retired	76		
E	Cranbrock Annabelle–†	2055	at home	85		
F	Crawford Charles	2055	retired	80	"	
G	Crawford Grace L—†	2055	at home	80		
H	Dickson Rose A—†	2055	"	71		
K	Drade Albert R	2055	retired	78		
L	Drade Ellen W—†	2055	at home	80		
M	Dyer Hattie H—†	2055	"	79	"	
N	Dyer Wendell T	2055	retired	83		
O	Erb Edna H—†	2055	attendant	45	"	
P	Evans Elizabeth A—†	2055	at home	62	Newtonville	
R	Evans Frederick E	2055	retired	74	"	
S	Farren Etta—†	2055	at home	78	here	
T	Fay Mae I—†	2055	"	72	"	
U	Fernald Carroll T	2055	retired	81	"	
V	Fernald Mellie A—†	2055	at home	77	"	
W	Fulton Alice—†	2055	domestic	23	1857 Hyde Park av	
X	Greenwood Frank W	2055	retired	80	here	
Y	Guild Anna J—†	2055	at home	77	"	
Z	Guillet Estelle—†	2055	"	82	"	
	715					
A	Hager Clifford J	2055	retired	78		
B	Hager Ella A—†	2055	at home	78		
C	Henderson Grace—†	2055	"	68		
D	Henderson Henry F	2055	retired	71		
E	Hewitt Chauncy D	2055	"	76		
F	Hewitt Eliza A—†	2055	at home	80		
G	Hill Helen C—†	2055	"	79	"	
H	Hill Johanna E—†	2055	"	74	Malden	
K	Hill Walter F	2055	retired	85	"	
L	Hinckley Edna—†	2055	at home	77	here	
M	Hinckley Edward C	2055	retired	82	"	
N	Hodgson Benjamin	2055	"	76	"	
O	Hodgson Mary L—†	2055	at home	74		

Page.	Letter.	FULL NAME.	Residence, Jan. 1, 1941.	Occupation.	Supposed Age.	Reported Residence, Jan. 1, 1940. Street and Number.

Columbus Avenue—Continued

P	Hogg John	2055	engineer	62	here
R	Holmes Caroline—†	2055	at home	62	"
S	Hubbard Edith G—†	2055	"	70	"
T	Hubbard Henry E	2055	retired	71	
U	Hyde Ida—†	2055	at home	76	
V	Hyde William	2055	retired	78	
W	*Jaycock Bessie E—†	2055	at home	74	
X	*Jaycock William	2055	retired	86	
Y	Jenkins Addie M—†	2055	at home	81	
Z	Jones Clifford A	2055	retired	68	

716

A	Jones Louise M—†	2055	at home	69	
B	Lord Charles F	2055	retired	84	
C	Lord Emily E—†	2055	at home	86	
D	*MacAskill Anna—†	2055	waitress	32	"
E	MacAskill Katherine—†	2055	cook	30	"
F	MacAskill Rebecca—†	2055	at home	80	
G	MacAskill Roderick	2055	retired	77	
H	MacDonald Katherine—†	2055	cook	56	
K	MacLean Margaret—†	2055	at home	80	
L	*MacLeod Agnes—†	2055	domestic	48	"
M	*MacLeod Johanna—†	2055	"	43	
N	*MacLeod Sadie—†	2055	"	38	
O	MacNear Robert	2055	porter	21	
P	Macomber Amanda—†	2055	at home	80	
R	Macomber George	2055	retired	80	
S	MacQueen Flora—†	2055	attendant	62	"
T	Marina Elsa—†	2055	domestic	20	"
U	Mayo Carrie—†	2055	at home	71	
V	Mayo Charles	2055	retired	80	
W	McInnis Elizabeth C—†	2055	at home	73	"
X	McInnis Neil	2055	retired	76	"
Y	Morse Mary C—†	2055	at home	70	
Z	Morse William	2055	retired	71	

717

A	Morrison Mary—†	2055	at home	77	
B	Moulton Elizabeth—†	2055	"	70	
C	Moulton Frederick	2055	retired	71	
D	Naughton Florence—†	2055	domestic	22	"
E	Newton Isabelle—†	2055	at home	88	

11

Page.	Letter.	FULL NAME.	Residence, Jan. 1, 1941.	Occupation.	Supposed Age.	Reported Residence, Jan. 1, 1940. Street and Number.

Columbus Avenue—Continued

	F	Nolan Edith—†	2055	at home	63	Cambridge
	G	Owens Anna M—†	2055	"	75	N Hampshire
	H	Owens John	2055	retired	74	"
	K	Palmer Marshall	2055	engineer	37	here
	L	Parker Dora—†	2055	at home	74	"
	M	Parker Harris	2055	retired	80	"
	N	Powers Charles	2055	"	77	
	O	Powers Gertrude—†	2055	at home	72	"
	P	Schiertz Frederick	2055	retired	69	Milton
	R	Schiertz Hedwig—†	2055	at home	68	"
	S	Severence George	2055	retired	81	here
	T	Severence Marietta—†	2055	at home	72	"
	U	Shorey Blanche—†	2055	"	70	"
	V	Shorey Leonard	2055	retired	71	
	W	Sidebottom John	2055	"	80	
	X	Silver Marie—†	2055	at home	78	
	Y	Silver William	2055	retired	83	
	Z	Smith William	2055	"	80	
		718				
	A	Southerland Blanche—†	2055	attendant	55	Lynn
	B	Speakman Amanda—†	2055	at home	69	here
	C	Speakman Frederick	2055	retired	84	"
	D	Stafford David	2055	"	79	"
	E	Stearns Alice W—†	2055	at home	69	"
	F	Stearns George F	2055	retired	76	"
	G	Stone Luella J—†	2055	at home	83	N Hampshire
	H	Stone Mary—†	2055	"	72	here
	K	Stone Otwell	2055	retired	73	N Hampshire
	L	Strout Emma—†	2055	at home	88	here
	M	Swaffer Geraldine F—†	2055	nurse	37	"
	N	Thoms Annie—†	2055	at home	82	"
	O	Tuells Eva—†	2055	"	76	
	P	Tuells Francis	2055	retired	72	"
	R	Walsh Albert	2055	"	68	Medford
	S	Walsh Alice—†	2055	"	62	"
	T	Washburn Frances—†	2055	at home	68	here
	U	Washburn William	2055	retired	73	"
	V	Weston Annie—†	2055	housekeeper	60	"
	W	Wilder Elizabeth—†	2055	at home	75	
	X	Wilder George	2055	retired	75	
	Y	Williams Emily—†	2055	at home	79	

Columbus Avenue—Continued

z	Wilmot George	2055	retired	77	here
	719				
A	Wilmot Theresa—†	2055	at home	79	"

Dixwell Street

B	Tingus Andrew	4	student	21	here
c	Tingus George	4	manager	63	"
D	Tingus Helen—†	4	housewife	52	"
E	Kevorkian John D	4	barber	49	235 Highland
F	Kevorkian Mary—†	4	housewife	38	235 "
G	MacDonald Helen—†	6	"	40	here
H	MacDonald Stewart	6	manager	44	"
K	Peppin Arthur J	6	"	56	Weymouth
L	Higgins Elizabeth—†	6	housewife	52	here
M	Higgins Frederick	6	mechanic	58	"
N	Malin Benjamin	6	clerk	43	82 Holworthy
O	Malin Frances—†	6	housewife	39	82 "
P	McKay Alice—†	7	inspector	50	here
R	McKay John W	7	retired	60	"
S	Bakalar Gertrude—†	7	housewife	59	"
T	Bakalar William	7	tailor	60	"
U	Lindsay May—†	7	housewife	38	302 W Walnut pk
V	*Lindsay Thomas	7	mechanic	45	302 "
w	Berg Theodore	9	salesman	34	New York
X	Gazzam Goldie—†	9	housewife	52	here
Y	Gazzam Robert A	9	retired	65	"
z	White Evelyn—†	9	housewife	33	"
	720				
A	White Julius	9	salesman	37	"
B	Kanserstein Celia—†	9	housewife	30	" "
c	Kanserstein Samuel	9	pharmacist	33	"
D	Leavitt Frances—†	11	housewife	37	"
E	Leavitt Hyman	11	salesman	41	"
F	Goldstein Harry	11	"	38	19 Flint
G	Goldstein Ida—†	11	housewife	45	20 Ruthven
H	*Yahnis Helen—†	11	"	42	here
K	Yahnis James	11	florist	48	"
L	Banta Anna—†	12	housewife	45	Saugus
M	*Banta Gustav	12	glassblower	53	"
N	Radiches Alexander	12	shipper	20	here

13

Page.	Letter.	FULL NAME.	Residence, Jan. 1, 1941.	Occupation.	Supposed Age.	Reported Residence, Jan. 1, 1940. Street and Number.

Dixwell Street—Continued

o	Radiches James	12	barber	30	here
p	*Radiches Nazira—†	12	housewife	47	"
R	Brown Louise—†	12	stenographer	21	"
s	Brown Medina—†	12	nurse	23	"
T	Brown William F	12	inspector	56	"
U	Leavitt Jeanette—†	13	housewife	40	"
v	Leavitt Leon	13	salesman	36	"
w	*Portman Abraham	13	tailor	53	
x	*Portman Edith—†	13	housewife	42	"
Y	Portman Jacob	13	pharmacist	25	"
z	Zwirn Louis	13	barber	29	18 Warner

721

A	Zwirn Renee—†	13	housewife	29	18 "
B	Stewart Julia E—†	14	"	44	here
c	Kavanagh Michael P	14	fitter	50	"
D	Kavanagh Nellie—†	14	housewife	65	"
E	Lawrence Josephine—†	14	"	23	8 Valentine
F	Lawrence Margaret—†	14	beautician	33	102 Paul Gore
G	Lawrence Robert	14	machinist	24	102 "
H	Cameron Jefferson D	17	retired	78	here
K	MacDonald John M	17	"	75	"
L	*Fabiano Bella—†	17	housewife	36	"
M	*Fabiano James	17	machinist	38	"
N	Newmark Bertha—†	17	clerk	20	
o	Newmark Samuel	17	operator	43	"
R	Daly Ada—†	18	housewife	47	121 George
s	Daly Joseph	18	chauffeur	40	121 "
T	Yankowsky Joseph	18	"	44	36 Winthrop
U	Emanuel John A	19	printer	31	here
v	Emanuel Louise—†	19	housewife	25	"
w	*Smigliani Eva—†	19	"	41	"
x	Smigliani Massimino	19	contractor	42	"
Y	Lombardini Costante	19	porter	49	
z	Lombardini Theresa—†	19	housewife	43	"

722

A	Ludwig Clarence L	20	policeman	44	"
B	Ludwig Lillian C—†	20	saleswoman	22	"
c	Ludwig Margaret T—†	20	housewife	43	"
D	Chessman Arthur S	20	carpenter	37	11 Jackson pl
E	Chessman Marguerite H—†	20	housewife	27	11 "
F	Hurd Harry	20	rubberworker	55	here

14

Dixwell Street—Continued

G	Hurd Robert	20	operator	58	here
H	Pengroth Andrew	21	welder	53	"
K	Pengroth Irving	21	painter	26	"
L	Pengroth Maxine—†	21	stenographer	22	"
M	Pengroth Rose—†	21	housewife	52	"
N	McElman Edna P—†	21	secretary	22	"
O	McElman Thomas A	21	operator	50	
P	McElman Thomas A, jr	21	secretary	24	"
R	Webb Evelyn—†	21	housewife	29	"
S	Webb John A	21	guard	30	
T	Chatelain Ernest	23	lineman	56	
U	Chatelain Harriet—†	23	housewife	55	"
V	Chatelain Lorraine—†	23	secretary	21	"
W	Chatelain Robert	23	draftsman	22	"
X	Welsh Estelle—†	23	housewife	35	"
Y	Welsh James F	23	letter carrier	54	"
Z	Rose Anna M—†	23	housewife	52	"

723

A	Rose Harold A	23	die sinker	51	"

School Street

B	Lennon Catherine—†	27	at home	55	here
C	Lennon Elizabeth—†	27	clerk	57	"
D	Lennon Margaret—†	27	at home	59	"
E	Blackadar Charles C	29	machinist	22	385 Warren
F	Blackadar Frances E—†	29	housewife	21	55 King
H	Gummeson Christina—†	31	at home	68	here
K	Thompson Bertha M—†	31	housewife	53	"
L	Thompson Edward S	31	retired	68	"
M	Mullen Helen L—†	33	secretary	39	" "
N	Mullen Mary F—†	33	at home	68	
O	Walsh Blanche W—†	33	"	60	
P	Walsh Catherine R—†	33	housewife	62	"
R	Walsh Richard T	33	retired	56	
S	Walsh Richard P	33	"	75	"
T	Kaplan Bernard	35	laborer	41	6 School
U	Kaplan Gertrude—†	35	saleswoman	40	6 "
W	DeCarl Catherine M—†	35	clerk	20	here
X	DeCarl Catherine V—†	35	housewife	41	"
Y	Rantz Rose J—†	35	"	50	"

School Street—Continued

z	Rantz Samuel H	35	salesman	53	here
	724				
A	Priola Barbara—†	35	domestic	22	"
B	Priola Catherine—†	35	stitcher	20	
C	Priola Helen—†	35	housewife	44	"
D	Terelak John J	35	operator	25	"
E	Terelak Stephanie—†	35	housewife	23	"
F	O'Connell John J	37	machinist	35	"
G	*O'Connell Margaret—†	37	housewife	35	"
H	Cull Freeman	37	painter	40	
K	*Rafuse Evelina—†	37	at home	74	
L	Rafuse Nina—†	37	corsetiere	40	"
M	Rafuse Rose—†	37	stitcher	44	"
N	*Zoes Della—†	37	housewife	45	1280A Tremont
O	Zoes Efstatheos	37	chef	46	1280A "
P	Daly Edith B—†	41	housewife	30	here
R	Daly James R	41	salesman	42	"
S	Williams Edna M—†	41	saleswoman	28	"
T	Brooks Rose—†	41	housewife	32	"
U	Brooks Thomas E	41	salesman	35	"
V	*Machakos Leonora—†	43	housewife	42	"
W	Machakos Trifon	43	barber	53	"
X	Hoyt Clara—†	43	housewife	38	Maine
Y	Hoyt Ralph W	43	barber	41	72 Wadsworth
Z	*Cook Amy—†	43	housewife	23	here
	725				
A	Cook Francis A	43	draftsman	31	"
B	Ingram Norman	45	instructor	30	"
C	*Siokas Frances—†	45	housewife	55	"
D	Siokas Nicholas	45	chef	52	"
E	Brennan Frances M—†	45	housewife	43	22 Wenham
F	Brennan Raymond P	45	manager	38	22 "
G	*Boulter Edward	45	janitor	47	here
H	*Boulter Laura—†	45	housewife	47	"
L	*Milne Jean—†	47	"	39	"
M	Milne William	47	butcher	42	
N	Hall Helen M—†	47	beautician	20	"
O	Hall Jacob	47	custodian	48	"
P	Hall Johanna—†	47	housewife	43	"
S	Crowe Anna H—†	69	"	49	30 Hawthorne
T	Oliver George F	69	retired	45	30 "

Page.	Letter.	FULL NAME.	Residence, Jan. 1, 1941.	Occupation.	Supposed Age.	Reported Residence, Jan. 1, 1940. Street and Number.

School Street—Continued

	U	Skwarek Anna—†	69	housewife	46	here
	V	Skwarek Frank	69	student	22	"
	W	Skwarek Michael	69	bartender	52	"
	X	Skwarek Victoria—†	69	bookkeeper	25	"
	Y	Bourke Joseph T	71	clerk	61	..
	Z	Bourke Martha A—†	71	housewife	58	"
726						
	A	Kelleher Hannah—†	71	"	59	
	B	Kelleher Timothy J	71	foreman	58	"
	C	Nathan Andrew I	71A	agent	54	71 Rossmore rd
	D	Nathan Elizabeth—†	71A	housewife	53	71 "
	E	Nathan Louise—†	71A	waitress	20	71 "
	F	Nathan Mark A	71A	shipper	26	71 "
	G	*Vlachos Minnie—†	73	housewife	37	here
	H	Vlachos Theodore	73	waiter	44	"
	K	Gessner Albert	73A	welder	27	308 Chestnut av
	L	Gessner Beatrice—†	73A	housewife	29	308 "
	M	Shea Patrick T	73A	retired	76	72 Brighton av
	N	Shea Thomas	73A	laborer	32	72 "
	O	Boue Jean	73A	mechanic	56	here
	P	*Boue Louise—†	73A	housewife	54	"
	R	Cook Charles E	81	clerk	26	"
	S	Cook Florence C—†	81	supervisor	53	"
	T	Herron Annie—†	83	at home	63	
	U	Herron Arthur	83	molder	62	"
	V	Hollo Ruth—†	83	housewife	26	31 Fort av
	W	Rumrill Grace—†	83	at home	66	31 "
	X	Dolan Agnes T—†	85	checker	29	here
	Y	Dolan Alice V—†	85	matron	55	"
	Z	Dolan Frances M—†	85	checker	26	"
727						
	A	Dolan John J	85	laborer	32	
	B	Dolan Sara F—†	87	housewife	56	"
	C	McElhinney Rose A—†	87	seamstress	44	"
	D	Wildberger Charles	87	watchman	65	"
	E	Wildberger Emma—†	87	housewife	39	"
	F	Wildberger Ethel N—†	87	"	41	
	G	Wildberger May L—†	87	bookkeeper	44	"
	H	Wildberger William C	87	physician	26	"
	K	Buckley Dorothy A—†	87	waitress	31	
	L	Carr Emery P	87	machinist	29	"

11—7   17

School Street—Continued

M	Carr Sarah W—†	87	housewife	55	here	
N	Lowe Catherine—†	87	seamstress	49	"	
O	Shea Eugene N	87	painter	59	"	
P	Gallivan Mary—†	87	at home	64		
R	Gallivan Patrick	87	engineer	59	"	
S	Morrill Horace	87	electrician	53	5 Glines av	
T	O'Brien John J	87	painter	42	here	
U	Schwartz Mark	87	retired	69	15 Maynard	
V	Bella John J	87	chauffeur	44	here	
W	Bella Josephine—†	87	at home	65	"	
X	Bella Ruth—†	87	housewife	22	"	
Y	Clarke Charles	87	retired	67		
Z	Shea Ellen—†	87	at home	59		

728

A	Gardner Emma—†	87	housewife	51	"	
B	Gardner Robert F	87	garageman	61	"	
C	Keefe Patrick	87	retired	70	"	
D	Murphy John T	87	engineer	56	75 Weld Hill	
E	Severence Frank B	87	retired	81	here	

School Street Place

F	Kohl Mary A—†	2	housewife	86	here	
G	Kohl Otto	2	retired	63	"	
H	Kohl William C	2	carpenter	49	"	
K	Parker Etta J—†	4	housewife	50	"	
M	Parker Harold B	4	fireman	54		
L	Parker Harriet B—†	4	at home	81	"	
N	Burns Evelyn—†	4	housewife	26	2 Miles	
O	Kutz Frank A	4	laborer	53	here	
P	Kutz Mary A—†	4	housewife	54	"	
R	Olsen Maude—†	4	at home	50	2 Miles	
S	Sweeney Nellie J—†	7	housewife	47	60 School	
T	Sweeney Robert S	7	chef	47	60 "	
U	Anderson Caroline—†	7	clerk	33	here	
V	Anderson Ottila—†	7	housewife	61	"	
W	Anderson Ralph	7	retired	36	"	
X	Donohue Catherine—†	8	housewife	46	"	
Y	Donohue William L	8	printer	48		
Z	Lamb Bernard	8	"	40		

Page.	Letter.	FULL NAME.	Residence, Jan. 1, 1941.	Occupation.	Supposed Age.	Reported Residence, Jan. 1, 1940. Street and Number.

729
School Street Place—Continued

A	Hadley Edward A	9	starter	53	here
B	Hadley Emma L—†	9	housewife	43	"
C	Gaffey Bridget—†	11	"	80	"
D	Gaffey Helen M—†	11	bookkeeper	36	"
E	Gaffey Henry P	11	retired	33	"
F	Schueler Louise W—†	27	housewife	68	"
G	Trainor Bridget—†	27	at home	74	
H	Carlson Helen—†	27A	housewife	39	"
K	Carlson Walter	27A	foreman	42	

Waldren Road

L	Weinfeld Charles W	7	engineer	24	here
M	Weinfeld Matilda—†	7	housewife	48	"
N	Weinfeld Morris	7	chemist	51	"
O	Butler Anna—†	7	housewife	36	"
P	Butler Samuel	7	retired	42	
R	Herman Albert	7	instructor	30	"
S	Grodsky David	7	registrar	28	
T	Grodsky Jennie—†	7	computer	30	"
U	Grodsky Lillian—†	7	bookkeeper	26	"
V	Tannenbaum Jacob	7	tailor	55	"
W	Tannenbaum Shirley—†	7	bookkeeper	21	"
X	Tannenbaum Tillie—†	7	housewife	52	"
Y	Klemens Gertrude—†	7	"	45	
Z	Klemens Jacob	7	realtor	45	

730

A	Bender Anna—†	7	bookkeeper	30	"
B	Bender Hilda—†	7	housewife	60	"
C	Bender Joseph	7	paperhanger	61	"
D	Gateman Max	11	attendant	38	"
E	Gateman May—†	11	housewife	37	"
F	Sahl David	11	upholsterer	39	109 Waumbeck
G	Sahl Mae—†	11	housewife	34	here
H	*Marcalle Lifsha—†	11	dressmaker	46	"
K	*Shapiro Dora—†	11	housewife	44	"
L	*Shapiro Morris	11	operator	54	"
M	Zunder Esther—†	11	housewife	49	360 Walnut av
N	Zunder Maurice	11	physician	28	360 "

19

Waldren Road—Continued

o	Mintz Beatrice—†	11	housewife	34	here
p	Mintz Morton	11	salesman	36	"
r	Kaufman Beatrice—†	11	housewife	25	"
s	Kaufman Samuel	11	painter	30	
t	Clare Rose R—†	15	housekeeper	37	"
u	Ratner Molly—†	15	housewife	38	"
v	Ratner Samuel	15	watchmaker	45	"
w	Barg Henry	15	florist	47	"
x	Barg Ida—†	15	housewife	39	"
y	Cohen David	15	salesman	44	"
z	Fishman Phillip	15	mechanic	32	"

731

a	Fishman Winifred—†	15	housewife	31	"
b	Ganick Irwin	15	attorney	25	"
c	Ganick William	15	artist	23	"
d	Arkin Julia—†	15	housewife	70	"
e	Arkin Sarah—†	15	bookkeeper	36	"
f	Winner Isadore	15	tailor	42	"
g	Salvin Dorothy S—†	15	bookkeeper	22	"
h	Salvin James S	15	realtor	50	"
k	Salvin Minnie—†	15	housewife	50	"
l	Salvin Samuel C	15	salesman	28	"

Walnut Avenue

m	Rosenberg Aaron	297	manager	29	here
n	Rosenberg Charlotte—†	297	student	20	"
o	Rosenberg Hannah—†	297	housewife	55	"
p	Rosenberg Leonard	297	manager	25	"
r	Rosenberg Phillip	297	merchant	60	"
s	Brown Leonard	297A	broker	34	
t	Brown Samuel	297A	merchant	65	"
u	Israelson Evelyn—†	297A	housewife	36	"
v	Israelson Jacob	297A	manager	38	"
w	Robbins Ida—†	297A	housewife	38	"
x	Robbins Israel	297A	printer	45	
y	Stamler Morris	297A	pedler	34	
z	Stamler Sara—†	297A	housewife	34	"

732

a	*Rotefsky Ida—†	297A	"	65	"
b	Gallagher Margaret—†	315	domestic	51	Brookline

Page.	Letter.	Full Name.	Residence, Jan. 1, 1941.	Occupation.	Supposed Age.	Reported Residence, Jan. 1, 1940. Street and Number.

Walnut Avenue—Continued

	c	Hersey Ada H—†	315	at home	82	here
	d	Smith Anna J—†	315	waitress	44	"
	e	Pearse Alice W—†	317	housewife	60	"
	f	Richardson Elizabeth M—†	331	"	70	
	g	Richardson Laura E—-†	331	at home	72	
	h	Shute Mary C—†	331	housewife	69	"
	l	Brien Alice—†	361	"	31	Cambridge
	m	Brien Frank	361	janitor	44	"
	n	Epstein Regina—†	361	housewife	69	here
	o	Michaelson Jacob	361	manager	34	"
	p	Michaelson Rose—†	361	housewife	34	"
	r	Beeman Abraham	361	broker	34	
	s	Beeman Annette—†	361	housewife	31	"
	t	Rose Esther—†	361	"	60	
	u	Rose Max	361	bookbinder	65	"
	v	Miller Bess—†	361	housewife	36	"
	w	Miller George	361	dentist	38	"
	x	Brickel Elsie—†	361	housewife	22	547 Blue Hill av
	y	Brickel Manuel	361	clerk	23	547 "
	z	Needle Hyman	361	manager	29	here

733

	a	Needle Sophie—†	361	housewife	27	"
	c	*Heshoff Pesha—†	361	"	70	
	b	Sampler Benjamin	361	tailor	58	
	d	*Sampler Gertrude—†	361	housewife	53	"
	e	Sampler Max	361	shipper	33	
	f	Rommell Beatrice—†	361	housewife	28	"
	g	Rommell Julius	361	attorney	32	"
	h	Spack Allen	361	" .	22	
	k	*Spack Samuel	361	tailor	58	
	l	Natelson Joseph	361	buyer	25	
	m	Natelson Rena—†	361	bookkeeper	24	"
	n	Miseph Anna—†	361	housewife	42	"
	o	Miseph Joseph	361	presser	45	
	p	Miseph Lillian—†	361	saleswoman	22	"
	r	Miseph Samuel	361	student	20	
	s	Perlmutter Anita—†	361	housewife	23	"
	u	Perlmutter Benjamin	361	clerk	25	
		Ladin Blanche—†	361	housewife	36	"
	v	Ladin Charles	361	salesman	40	"
	x	Superior Abraham	363	"	67	

21

Walnut Avenue—Continued

Y	Superior Anna—†	363	housewife	68	here	
Z	Simmons Jacob	363	retired	68	"	
	734					
A	Simmons Sadie—†	363	housewife	60	"	
B	Ephross Bessie—†	363	"	49		
C	Ephross Israel W	363	accountant	53	"	
D	Gediman Anna—†	363	housewife	46	77 Savin	
E	Gediman Samuel	363	clerk	53	77 "	
F	*Yaffe Max	363	tailor	57	Cambridge	
G	*Yaffe Sophie—†	363	housewife	54	"	
H	Sherman Dora—†	363	"	49	here	
K	Sherman George	363	clerk	29	"	
L	Sherman Hyman	363	merchant	56	"	
M	Sherman Norman	363	student	21		
N	Rubbins Bernard	363	shipper	21		
O	Rubbins Charles	363	salesman	49	"	
P	Rubbins Lillian—†	363	housewife	41	"	
R	Sawyer Arthur	363	clerk	56	Brookline	
S	Sawyer Esther—†	363	housewife	56	"	
T	Gilman Dora—†	363	"	44	here	
U	Gilman Samuel	363	merchant	48	"	
V	Warshaw Ralph	363	clerk	22	"	
W	Warshaw Sylvia—†	363	housewife	27	"	
X	*Oven Joseph	363	merchant	31	"	
Y	Oven Ruth—†	363	housewife	25	"	
Z	Shapiro Rose—†	363	bookkeeper	29	"	
	735					
A	Shapiro Simon	363	salesman	30	"	
B	Broderick Ann V—†	367	student	23		
C	Broderick Anna G—†	367	housewife	50	"	
D	Broderick John H	367	contractor	60	"	
E	Broderick Paul D	367	student	21		
F	Finnegan Charles F	377	clergyman	70	"	
G	Murphy Francis J	377	"	45		
H	Norton Arthur J	377	"	27		

Walnut Park

K	Neckes Beatrice—†	8	bookkeeper	30	here	
L	*Neckes Jennie—†	8	housewife	65	"	
M	Neckes Lena—†	8	social worker	43	"	

Walnut Park—Continued

N	Wolf Elliott	8	salesman	21	New York
O	Ricardo Eva—†	8	housewife	24	here
P	Ricardo John	8	salesman	22	"
R	Adwin David	10	"	39	"
S	Adwin Ida—†	10	housewife	34	"
T	Lerner Israel	10	merchant	56	"
U	Lerner Sara—†	10	housewife	56	"
V	*Voutselas Angelina—†	12	"	78	
W	Voutselas Gerald	12	merchant	41	"
X	Voutselas Katherine—†	12	housewife	36	"
Y	Swift Elizabeth—†	12	agent	47	
Z	Swift John H	12	salesman	66	"

736

A	Swift Pauline E.—†	12	clerk	28	"
B	*Karimbakas Anastasia—†	14	housewife	27	3096 Wash'n
C	Karimbakas Charles	14	merchant	40	3096 "
D	Visvis Andromachi—†	15	housewife	37	here
E	Visvis Arthur	15	manager	50	"
F	Basquil Catherine—†	15½	messenger	26	28 Grovenor rd
G	Basquil Elizabeth—†	15½	housewife	62	here
H	Basquil Elizabeth—†	15½	bookkeeper	32	"
K	Basquil Mary—†	15½	clerk	26	"
L	Basquil William	15½	laundryman	27	28 Grovenor rd
N	Johnson Ernest	17	singer	45	here
O	Johnson Ernestine—†	17	stitcher	21	"
P	Johnson Ethel—†	17	housewife	43	"
M	Johnson John	17	waiter	55	
R	Lewis Mary—†	17	housekeeper	47	"
S	Rideout Thomas	17	porter	52	"
T	Booker Frances—†	19	housewife	22	5 Chesterton
U	Booker Manuel	19	waiter	31	5 "
V	Marchioni Elbino	20	shoeworker	52	here
W	Marchioni Rose—†	20	"	40	"
X	Bressler Esther—†	20	housewife	65	22 Abbotsford
Y	Bressler Phillip	20	window cleaner	70	22 "
Z	Mendick John	20	laborer	32	22 "

737

A	Mendick Molly—†	20	housewife	29	22 "
B	Hanbury Catherine—†	24	domestic	46	here
C	Hanbury Cory	24	clerk	21	"
D	Hanbury Thomas	24	"	25	"

Page.	Letter.	FULL NAME.	Residence, Jan. 1. 1941.	Occupation.	Supposed Age.	Reported Residence, Jan. 1. 1940. Street and Number.

Walnut Park—Continued

	E	Foye Jodie	24	custodian	45	here
	F	Foye Rose M—†	24	housewife	42	"
	G	Brown Bertha—†	24	clerk	33	"
	H	*Singer Goldie—†	24	"	21	
	K	Clayman Benjamin	24	pharmacist	32	"
	L	Clayman Ida—†	24	housewife	31	"
	M	Gates Lillian—†	24	stenographer	28	"
	N	Gates Mary—†	24	leatherworker	48	"
	O	Robner Hannah—†	24	housewife	34	"
	P	Robner William	24	merchant	37	"
	R	Brown Dora—†	24	housewife	27	1451 Blue Hill av
	S	Brown Eugene	24	manager	28	1451 "
	T	Nathan Carl	24	salesman	42	here
	U	Nathan Dora—†	24	housewife	41	"
	V	Slafsky Sylvia—†	24	teacher	21	Gloucester
	W	Wolk David	24	retired	70	here
	X	Strumph Leonard	24	florist	35	247 Clay
	Y	Strumph Rose—†	24	clerk	32	247 "
	Z	Lowenstein Benjamin	24	salesman	34	here
		738				
	A	Lowenstein Ruth—†	24	housewife	30	"
	B	Darcey Catherine—†	24	operator	38	
	C	Mosher Mary—†	24	clerk	36	
	D	Goldberg Albert	24	"	30	
	E	Goldberg Ruth—†	24	housewife	28	"
	F	Carrey Albert	24	jeweler	32	
	G	Carrey Leah—†	24	housewife	29	"
	H	Hooley Mary—†	24	"	25	
	K	Hooley Paul J	24	merchant	34	"
	L	Dahl Edward	25	instructor	63	"
	M	Dahl George J	25	attorney	64	"
	N	Dahl Lorenz	25	clerk	67	
	O	Metten Harriet D—†	25	housewife	53	"
	P	Metten William H	25	engineer	29	
	R	Furey Janet—†	30	housewife	30	"
	S	Furey Robert	30	salesman	29	"
	T	Greene Bernard	30	"	42	
	U	Greene Dora—†	30	housewife	35	"
	V	Goldberg Bertha—†	30	"	38	
	W	Goldberg Harry	30	operator	46	"
	X	Slobins Anna—†	30	furrier	37	

Page.	Letter.	FULL NAME.	Residence, Jan. 1, 1941.	Occupation.	Supposed Age.	Reported Residence, Jan. 1, 1940. Street and Number.

Walnut Park—Continued

	Y	Slobins Bella—†	30	furrier	39	here
	z	Yuron Joseph	30	pedler	48	"
739						
	A	Yuron Mary—†	30	housewife	45	"
	B	Federman Myer	30	merchant	45	"
	c	Federman Rose—†	30	housewife	42	"
	D	Ostrofsky Esther—†	30	clerk	36	75 Ruthven
	E	Cohen Julia M—†	30	housewife	25	here
	F	Cohen Louis S	30	salesman	26	"
	G	Bernstein Julius	30	student	21	"
	H	Bernstein Rose—†	30	housewife	45	"
	K	Bernstein Solomon	30	merchant	46	"
	L	Karlin Ida—†	30	housewife	64	"
	M	Karlin Louis	30	merchant	70	"
	N	Berman Ann—†	30	housewife	30	"
	o	Berman Sydney	30	electrician	33	"
	P	Cohen Hannah—†	30	housewife	55	71 Westminster av
	R	Cohen Hyman	30	manager	59	71 "
	s	Cohen Victor	30	salesman	32	71 "
	U	Glutman Goldie—†	30	housewife	47	here
	v	*Glutman Joseph	30	egg selector	49	"
	w	Moshcovitz Ethel—†	30	housewife	28	"
	x	Moshcovitz Samuel J	30	accountant	33	"
	Y	Levine Bessie—†	30	housewife	30	"
	z	Levine Leo	30	merchant	30	"
740						
	A	Hyman Jack	30	agent	32	
	B	Hyman Sylvia—†	30	housewife	27	"
	c	*Chofnas Ida E—†	30	"	50	
	D	Chofnas Jacob W	30	foreman	52	"
	F	Solberg Carl	30	cutter	25	16 Standish
	G	Solberg Gertrude—†	30	bookkeeper	23	Winthrop
	H	Erickson Eileen—†	30	masseuse	25	Gloucester
	K	Thomas Alice—†	30	housewife	43	here
	L	Thomas John	30	painter	46	"
	M	Segel Bernard	30	paperhanger	53	"
	N	*Segel Molly—†	30	housewife	49	"
	R	Grosenstein Mary—†	37	clerk	21	"
	s	Snider Abraham	37	salesman	35	1133 Com av
	T	Snider Alice—†	37	clerk	25	here
	u	Snider Harry	37	pedler	68	"

25

Page.	Letter.	FULL NAME.	Residence, Jan. 1, 1941.	Occupation.	Supposed Age.	Reported Residence, Jan. 1, 1940. Street and Number.

Walnut Park—Continued

	v	Snider Rebecca—†	37	housewife	66	here
	w	Snider Samuel	37	salesman	39	"
	x	Snider Sarah—†	37	bookkeeper	30	"
	z	Cohen Hyman	38	chauffeur	45	"
741						
	A	*Cohen Rebecca—†	38	housewife	75	"
	B	*Cohen Samuel	38	tailor	74	"
	E	Glazer Hyman	38	machinist	25	53 Stanwood
	F	Glazer Mollie—†	38	housewife	22	54 Hollander
	G	Leavitt Ruth R—†	38	"	40	here
	H	Leavitt William	38	shipper	42	"
	K	Praise Anna—†	38	stenographer	32	"
	L	Frankel Adele—†	38	housekeeper	33	"
	M	Frankel Irving	38	musician	43	"
	N	*Frankel Sadie—†	38	housewife	70	"
	O	Miller Charles	38	merchant	31	"
	P	Miller Dorothy—†	38	housewife	27	"
	R	Nesson Ada—†	38	"	32	36 Deering rd
	S	Nesson Harold	38	decorator	35	36 "
	U	Goldberg Frank J	38	accountant	34	here
	V	Goldberg Naomi—†	38	housewife	25	"
	W	Goldman Albert B	38	attorney	41	"
	X	Goldman Tessie—†	38	clerk	29	
	Y	Rosen Celia—†	38	housewife	26	"
	Z	Rosen Ruben	38	teacher	28	
742						
	A	Goldberg Gertrude—†	39	saleswoman	38	"
	B	Goldberg Lena—†	39	attorney	36	"
	C	Ladoulis Nicoletta—†	39	housewife	40	"
	D	Ladoulis Theodore	39	merchant	43	"
	E	*Ladoulis William	39	retired	72	
	F	Krock Nathan R	41	printer	51	
	G	Krock Rebecca R—†	41	housewife	46	"
	H	Krock Ruth—†	41	teacher	22	"
	K	*Rosen Bessie—†	41	housewife	51	"
	L	Rosen Samuel	41	plumber	51	
	M	Rosen Sidney	41	"	22	
	P	Daley Honora—†	46	clerk	65	
	S	Ferry Charlotte—†	46	teacher	29	
	R	Ferry Mary A—†	46	housewife	68	"
	T	Miller Jacob	50	salesman	44	New York

26

Page.	Letter.	Full Name.	Residence, Jan. 1, 1941.	Occupation.	Supposed Age.	Reported Residence, Jan. 1, 1940. Street and Number.

	U	Miller Katherine—†	50	housewife	40	New York
	V	Gale Harry	50	foreman	51	40 Tennis rd
	W	Gale Pearl—†	50	saleswoman	21	40 "
	X	Gale Ruth—†	50	clerk	26	40 "
	Y	Gale Sadie—†	50	saleswoman	46	40 "
	Z	Isenberg Lillian—†	50	clerk	23	here
743						
	A	Isenberg Manuel	50	salesman	52	"
	B	Isenberg Rose—†	50	housewife	48	"
	C	Barsky Freda—†	50	"	51	61 Walnut pk
	D	Barsky Samuel	50	merchant	58	61 "
	E	Lakin Charles	50	chauffeur	44	16 Copeland
	F	Levy Barbara—†	50	housekeeper	22	16 "
	G	Levy Louis	50	merchant	56	16 "
	H	Levy Sarah—†	50	housewife	52	16 "
	K	Rottenberg Alice—†	50	"	45	here
	L	Rottenberg Charlotte—†	50	stenographer	25	"
	M	Rottenberg Hyman	50	beautician	45	"
	N	Rottenberg Marvin	50	accountant	20	"
	O	Schneiderman Jacob	51	salesman	42	"
	P	Schneiderman Rhoda—†	51	housewife	33	"
	R	Seligman Edward	51	machinist	22	21 Arbutus
	S	Seligman Isadore	51	retired	55	21 "
	T	Seligman Sadie—†	51	housewife	50	21 "
	U	Zoll Annie—†	51	"	60	here
	V	Zoll Jessie—†	51	stenographer	21	"
	W	Clarke Mary T—†	57	secretary	60	"
	X	Scudney Gertrude—†	57	clerk	38	
	Y	Scudney Hannah—†	57	housekeeper	32	"
	Z	Scudney Jacob	57	salesman	62	"
744						
	C	Rottenberg Eva—†	60	housewife	52	"
	D	Rottenberg Mildred—†	60	clerk	22	
	E	Rottenberg Victor	60	porter	61	"
	F	Gries Sophie—†	60	housewife	60	"
	G	*Harkins Clara—†	60	"	60	
	H	*Harkins Joseph	60	retired	62	
	K	Anderson Margaret—†	60	nurse	50	
	L	Aptaker Alexander	60	tailor	55	
	M	Aptaker May—†	60	housewife	50	"
	N	*Bruell Marianne—†	60	at home	56	Austria

Page.	Letter.	FULL NAME.	Residence, Jan. 1, 1941.	Occupation.	Supposed Age.	Reported Residence, Jan. 1, 1940. Street and Number.

Walnut Park—Continued

o	*Bruell Paul	60	accountant	30		59 Mountfort
p	*Stern Levy	60	retired	62		here
r	*Stern Ludwig	60	clerk	34		Brookline
s	*Stern Rose—†	60	housewife	58		here
t	*Wolff Harry	60	clerk	34		"
u	*Wolff Henrietta—†	60	housewife	32		"
v	*Schwartz Annie—†	60	"	68		
w	Schwartz Ida D—†	60	bookkeeper	41		"
x	*Berlin Arthur	60	merchant	42		"
y	*Berlin Goldie—†	60	housewife	43		"
z	Horlick Lena—†	60	cashier	34		

745

A	*Sawyer Rose—†	60	at home	82		
B	Finkelstein Charles	61	stitcher	48		
c	Finkelstein David	61	tailor	73		
D	Finkelstein Rhea—†	61	housewife	45		"
E	Lach Anna—†	61	waitress	21		81 Ruthven
F	Lach Catherine—†	61	housewife	51		81 "
G	Lach Charles	61	chauffeur	26		81 "
H	Lach Matthew	61	"	28		81 "
K	*Lach Walter	61	janitor	51		81 "
N	Cohen Anna R—†	67	housewife	30		here
o	Cohen George	67	salesman	32		"
P	*Foilb Helen—†	67	housewife	48		"
R	Foilb Morris	67	butcher	48		
s	Foilb Robert	67	"	24		
T	Foilb Selma—†	67	clerk	21		"
U	Katz Bernard	67	"	29		Connecticut
V	Katz Joseph L	67	merchant	53		here
w	Katz Sarah—†	67	housewife	53		"
x	Yaffe Aaron	67	manager	59		"
Y	Yaffe Eva—†	67	housewife	57		"

746

A	Lachapelle Mary—†	71	"	75		
B	Lachapelle William	71	retired	72		
c	Mennard Edgar	71	janitor	42		
D	Mennard Florida—†	71	housewife	39		"
E	Steiner Ruth—†	71	"	22		
F	Steiner Walter W	71	auditor	30		
G	Wolbarst Beatrice—†	71	teacher	26		
H	Wolbarst Fannie—†	71	housewife	56		"

Page.	Letter.	Full Name.	Residence, Jan. 1, 1941.	Occupation.	Supposed Age.	Reported Residence, Jan. 1, 1940. Street and Number.

Walnut Park—Continued

	K	Wolbarst Sidney A	71	salesman	33	here
	L	Wolbarst Tobias	71	"	58	"
	M	Spiegel Mary—†	71	housewife	40	"
	N	Spiegel Meyer	71	clerk	23	
	O	Spiegel Samuel	71	counterman	49	"
	P	Korowitz Edward	72	salesman	28	4 Fernboro
	R	Korowitz Lillian—†	72	housewife	28	4 "
	S	Sheff Frank	72	merchant	55	4 "
	T	Sheff Hyman	72	shipper	20	4 "
	U	Brock Rose—†	72	housewife	32	here
	V	Brock Samuel	72	buyer	38	"
	W	Brown Calvin	72	salesman	27	164 Seaver
	X	Brown Evelyn—†	72	housewife	22	164 "
	Y	*Korsun Ethel—†	72	"	38	here
	Z	Korsun Joseph	72	capmaker	44	"

747

	A	Rosenberg Israel	72	salesman	40	"
	B	Rosenberg Lillian—†	72	housewife	37	"
	C	Giller Fannie—†	72	"	59	
	D	Giller Harry	72	merchant	60	"
	E	Giller Lillian—†	72	clerk	23	
	F	Bloomberg Rose—†	72	stenographer	23	"
	G	Grodensky David	72	roofer	39	"
	H	Grodensky Lena—†	72	housewife	36	"
	K	Brock Esther—†	72	clerk	46	
	L	Brock Leah—†	72	housewife	69	"
	M	Brock Maxwell	72	salesman	51	"
	N	Brock William	72	tailor	73	"
	O	*Aronson Dora—†	72	housewife	53	"
	P	Aronson Lillian—†	72	clerk	34	Palmer
	R	*Aronson Maurice	72	painter	58	here
	S	Brown Lena—†	72	housewife	38	"
	T	Brown Samuel	72	butcher	39	"
	U	Challant Clara—†	73	housewife	50	"
	V	Challant Max	73	butcher	55	
	W	Clayman David	73	clerk	37	
	X	Segel Charles	73	presser	58	
	Y	*Segel Fannie—†	73	housewife	58	"
	Z	Segel Gladys—†	73	clerk	20	

748

	A	Spivac Ralph	73	merchant	44	298 Chestnut av

29

Walnut Park—Continued

B	Spivac Rose—†	73	housewife	39	298 Chestnut av
C	Hymoff Bella—†	73	"	26	32 Crawford
D	Hymoff Nathan	73	operator	27	32 "
E	Roseman Julia—†	73	housewife	49	32 "
F	Roseman Morris	73	salesman	53	32 "
G	*Solomon Goldie—†	76	housewife	68	137 Hutchings
H	Sooper Nettie—†	76	"	27	here
K	Sooper Samuel	76	salesman	29	"
L	Goralnick Benjamin	76	merchant	30	"
M	*Goralnick Rose—†	76	housewife	29	"
N	Gorenstein Bella—†	76	"	31	
O	Gorenstein Harry	76	attorney	27	"
P	Reed Jack	76	tailor	45	
R	Reed Rae—†	76	housewife	34	"
S	Bromfield Ethel—†	76	"	34	
T	Bromfield Samuel	76	salesman	35	"
U	Herson Gladys—†	76	housewife	24	"
V	Herson Harold	76	clerk	26	
W	Esner Bessie—†	76	secretary	39	"
X	Esner Herbert	76	chauffeur	34	"
Y	Esner Ida—†	76	housewife	34	"
Z	Cantor Bessie—†	76	"	40	
	749				
A	Cantor Joseph	76	chauffeur	50	"
B	Schneider Barnett	77	custodian	45	"
C	Schneider Winifred—†	77	housewife	42	"
D	Stone Lena—†	77	saleswoman	39	"
E	Stone William	77	bartender	40	"
F	Hill Emma—†	77	shoeworker	42	"
G	Fine Charlotte—†	77	clerk	31	
H	Fine Henry	77	attorney	29	"
K	Fine Max	77	painter	56	
L	Fine Tillie—†	77	housewife	54	"
M	Michelman John H	77	salesman	71	"
N	Michelman Kate E—†	77	housewife	65	"
O	Michelman Tessie—†	77	housekeeper	39	"
P	Sherman Max	77	pharmacist	30	"
R	Sherman Shirley—†	77	housewife	28	"
S	Meltzer Edward	77	mortician	42	"
T	Meltzer Ida S—†	77	housewife	39	"
U	Glick Abraham A	77	salesman	49	"

Walnut Park—Continued

Page.	Letter.	Full Name.	Residence, Jan. 1, 1941.	Occupation.	Supposed Age.	Reported Residence, Jan. 1, 1940. Street and Number.
	v	Glick Dorothy—†	77	housewife	42	here
	w	Smokler Bernard	77	salesman	37	"
	x	Smokler Sophie—†	77	housewife	37	"
	y	Cohen Abraham	77	contractor	53	"
	z	*Cohen Elsie—†	77	housewife	45	"
750						
	A	Cohen Hilda—†	77	clerk	20	
	B	Cohen Lillian—†	77	"	21	
	D	Neckes Edith—†	77	secretary	28	"
	E	Neckes Eva—†	77	clerk	26	
	F	Neckes Sarah—†	77	housewife	60	"
	G	Lazarus Betty—†	79	"	41	
	H	Lazarus John	79	merchant	43	"
	K	Rosen Jacob	79	clerk	46	
	L	Rosen Rebecca—†	79	housewife	44	"
	M	Cohen Sadie—†	79	saleswoman	35	70 Ruthven
	N	Kahn Jeannette—†	79	housewife	48	here
	O	Ratkowsky Charles	79	salesman	53	"
	P	Drucker Betty—† .	79	housewife	39	"
	R	Drucker Murray	79	salesman	43	"
	S	Harrison Lewis P	79	clerk	35	
	T	Harrison Lottie—†	79	housewife	34	"
	U	Simes Ann—†	79	clerk	46	
	V	Simes Ethel—†	79	stenographer	32	"
	W	Simes Florence—†	79	"	30	,,
	X	Simes Grace—†	79	clerk	36	
	Y	Morrison Helen—†	79	housewife	46	"
	Z	Morrison Marion—†	79	clerk	21	
751						
	A	Morrison Morris	79	agent	47	
	B	Weinstein Dora—†	79	housewife	45	"
	C	Weinstein Herbert	79	student	22	
	D	Olansky Louis	79	salesman	40	"
	E	Olansky Rose—†	79	housewife	37	"
	G	Lazarus Abraham	79	baker	43	"
	H	Lazarus Anne S—†	79	clerk	20	
	K	*Lazarus Minnie—†	79	housewife	41	"
	L	Segal Lillian—†	79	"	45	
	M	Segal Mandell J	79	salesman	55	"
	N	Burtman Charles	80	merchant	50	"
	O	*Burtman Esther—†	80	housewife	70	"

31

Page.	Letter.	FULL NAME.	Residence, Jan. 1, 1941.	Occupation.	Supposed Age.	Reported Residence, Jan. 1, 1940. Street and Number.

Walnut Park—Continued

	P	Burtman Jennie—†	80	housewife	50	here
	R	Weiner Nathan	80	retired	80	"
	T	Matross Eva—†	81	housewife	60	71 Wellington Hill
	U	Matross Irving	81	clerk	23	71 "
	S	Matross Israel	81	operator	60	71 "
	V	Kaplan Ephrain	81	clerk	65	63 Walnut av
	W	Kaplan Fannie—†	81	housewife	65	63 "
	X	Berger Esther—†	81	"	29	here
	Y	Berger Louis	81	manager	34	"
	Z	*Caplan Rae—†	81	housewife	38	"

752

	A	*Caplan Richard L	81	manager	40	"
	B	Osobow Rose—†	81	housewife	33	126 Hutchings
	C	Osobow Samuel	81	salesman	36	126 "
	E	Selya Abraham S	81	clerk	55	here
	F	Selya Minnie M—†	81	housewife	54	"
	G	Selya Zelda B—†	81	nurse	27	"
	H	Green Harry	81	salesman	56	"
	K	Green Rebecca—†	81	housewife	50	"
	L	Epstein Boris	81	retired	64	
	M	Epstein Celia—†.	81	housewife	57	"
	N	Stults Dorothy—†	81	"	29	
	O	Stults Harry H	81	janitor	41	
	P	Finkelstein Frances—†	81	housewife	37	"
	R	Finkelstein Max	81	accountant	33	"

Wardman Road

	S	Sidman Elizabeth—†	3	operator	27	here
	T	*Sidman Fannie—†	3	housewife	54	"
	U	Sidman Max	3	musician	29	"
	V	Sidman Samuel	3	mechanic	31	"
	X	Williams Louis	3	chauffeur	47	"
	Y	Williams May—†	3	housewife	42	"
	Z	Jacobs Bedonna—†	3	nurse	22	

753

	A	Jacobs Florence—†	3	"	24	
	B	Jacobs Irving	3	salesman	52	"
	C	*Jacobs May—†	3	housewife	48	"
	D	Robinson Esther—†	3	"	37	106 Waumbeck
	E	Robinson Robert I	3	chauffeur	33	106 "

Wardman Road—Continued

F	Rubin Bernard	3	shipper	60	here
G	Rubin Evelyn—†	3	bookkeeper	21	"
H	Rubin Rose—†	3	housewife	56	"
K	Brown Esther—†	3	bookkeeper	45	"
L	Brown Irving	3	operator	43	"
M	Brown Rose—†	3	housewife	66	"
O	Zonis Oscar	7	cutter	49	Leominster
P	*Zonis Reva—†	7	housewife	37	"
R	Haffer Herbert	7	neckwear	36	here
S	Haffer Zelma—†	7	housewife	31	"
T	Glynn John	7	clerk	53	17 Morse
U	Glynn Mildred—†	7	"	22	17 "
V	Glynn Nettie—†	7	housewife	41	17 "
W	Glynn Ruth—†	7	clerk	21	17 "
X	Bornstein Louis	7	merchant	46	9 Wolcott
Y	Bornstein Rose—†	7	housewife	40	9 "
Z	Shepett Harry	7	tailor	50	here
	754				
A	*Shepett Lena—†	7	housewife	44	"
B	Shepett Samuel	7	student	22	"
C	Fearer Benjamin	7	merchant	49	"
D	Sharfman Freda—†	8	housewife	40	"
E	Sharfman Maurice	8	printer	42	
F	Block Ada—†	8	housewife	37	"
G	Block Herman L	8	physician	29	"
H	Block Julius	8	realtor	64	
K	Block Max	8	mechanic	39	"
L	Bennett Ida—†	8	bookkeeper	26	"
M	Bennett Louis	8	attorney	35	"
N	Bennett Rose—†	8	housewife	65	"
O	Goldstein Harry	9	pedler	29	
P	*Goldstein Ida—†	9	housewife	58	"
R	*Codish Adolph	9	tailor	60	
S	Codish Esther—†	9	bookkeeper	26	"
T	*Codish Ida—†	9	housewife	58	"
U	Codish Sarah—†	9	bookkeeper	24	"
V	Barskey Celia—†	9	housewife	41	"
W	Barskey Louis	9	salesman	41	"
X	Burtman Esther—†	9	housewife	75	"
Y	Hoffman Abraham	9	salesman	48	"
Z	Hoffman Rose—†	9	housewife	43	"

11—7

755
Wardman Road—Continued

A	Wolff Jennie—†	9	housewife	43	here
B	Wolff Simon	9	furrier	48	"
C	Heller Leo	9	merchant	46	125 Ormond
D	Heller Rose—·†	9	housewife	33	2 Michigan av
E	Pearlstein Abraham	10	broker	41	here
F	Pearlstein Esther—†	10	housewife	36	"
G	Fisher Gertrude—·†	10	"	40	"
H	Fisher Walter	10	shipper	48	
K	Kaufman Harry	10	merchant	54	"
L	Kaufman Mary L—·†	10	housewife	49	"
M	Rosenberg Paul	11	salesman	33	28 Seaver
N	Rosenberg Shirley—†	11	housewife	28	28 "
O	Freidman Celia—†	11	"	55	37 Kingsdale
P	Freidman Emmaneul H	11	pharmacist	25	37 "
R	Freidman Joseph	11	tailor	58	37 "
S	Bennett Katie—†	11	housewife	46	here
T	Bennett Martin	11	student	24	"
U	Bennett Robert	11	shipper	21	"
V	Laskey Evelyn—†	11	bookkeeper	22	"
W	Laskey Joseph	11	chauffeur	26	"
X	Zides Charlotte—†	11	bookkeeper	22	"
Y	Zides Rebecca—†	11	housewife	55	"
Z	Zides Rita—†	11	bookkeeper	20	"

756

A	Lerner Abraham	11	florist	51	
B	Lerner Hattie—·†	11	housewife	46	"
C	Antick Ida—†	11	"	44	
D	Antick Sydney	11	accountant	44	"
E	Alpert Israel	12	tailor	59	41 Hollander
F	Alpert Molly—†	12	housewife	42	41 "
G	*Grunthalt Max	12	chef	62	here
H	*Grunthalt Rose—†	12	housewife	61	"
K	*Frank Lena—†	12	"	44	"
L	*Frank Louis	12	merchant	48	"
M	Frank Pearl—†	12	bookkeeper	21	"
N	Frank Samuel	12	merchant	23	"
O	Simon Etta—†	15	housewife	42	"
P	Simon Irving	15	carpenter	42	"
R	*Gunders Herta—†	15	housewife	41	"
S	*Gunders Paul	15	bookkeeper	43	"

Page	Letter	FULL NAME.	Residence, Jan. 1, 1941.	Occupation.	Supposed Age.	Reported Residence, Jan. 1, 1940. Street and Number.

Wardman Road—Continued

	T	Becker Joseph.	15	printer	46	here
	U	Becker Rudolph	15	shoemaker	43	"
	V	Clayman Sadie—†	15	housekeeper	35	"
	W	Silverman Bessie—†	15	housewife	65	"
	X	Silverman Irving	15	physician	28	"
	Y	Weiner Israel	15	cutter	48	
	Z	Weiner Rena—†	15	housewife	40	"

757

	A	Neidle Harry	15	merchant	44	1052 Tremont
	B	Neidle Rose—†	15	housewife	45	1052 "
	C	Kopel Julius	16	pedler	29	54 Jones av
	D	Kopel Matilda—†	16	housewife	28	54 "
	E	Wheeler Anna—†	16	saleswoman	24	here
	F	Wheeler Ida—†	16	housewife	47	26 Harvard av
	G	Wheeler Joseph	16	pharmacist	25	26 "
	H	Wheeler Maurice	16	salesman	58	26 "
	K	Reiser Israel	16	"	35	Connecticut
	L	Reiser Minnie—†	16	housewife	41	"
	M	Landa Harry	17	watchman	64	9 Wardman rd
	N	Landa Lena—†	17	housewife	53	9 "
	O	Sacks Israel	17	agent	36	9 "
	P	Miskin Abraham	17	clerk	39	New York
	R	Miskin Mary—†	17	housewife	38	"
	S	Lemack Bessie—†	17	"	31	here
	T	Lemack David	17	cutter	35	" .
	U	Lerner Jacob	17	clerk	38	"
	V	Lerner Sonia—†	17	housewife	37	"
	W	Miller Abraham	17	salesman	41	"
	X	Miller Hannah—†	17	housewife	41	"
	Y	Kenigsberg Esther—†	17	boxmaker	34	"
	Z	Kenigsberg Jacob	17	clergyman	70	. ",

758

	A	Kenigsberg Olga—†	17	stitcher	39	
	B	Kenigsberg Shirley—†	17	bookkeeper	30	"
	C	Sidman James	17	cutter	32	"
	D	Sidman Sally—†	17	housewife	33	"
	E	Slanger David	17	pedler	55	17 Oneida
	F	Slanger Evelyn—†	17	housewife	56	17 "
	G	Slanger Frances—†	17	nurse	27	17 "
	H	Glass Anna—†	18	housewife	51	here
	K	*Glass Harry	18	salesman	56	"

35

Page.	Letter.	Full Name.	Residence, Jan. 1, 1941.	Occupation.	Supposed Age.	Reported Residence, Jan. 1, 1940. Street and Number.

Wardman Road—Continued

	L	Levine Ida—†	18	housewife	65	here
	M	Levine Jean—†	18	bookkeeper	30	"
	N	Gould Betty—†	18	housewife	30	"
	o	Gould Lewis	18	pharmacist	35	"
	P	Leitowitz Harry	18	mechanic	58	"
	R	*Stein Celia—†	18	housewife	70	"
	s	Stein David	18	retired	72	
	T	Block Nancy—†	19	housewife	48	"
	U	Block Samuel	19	watchman	50	"
	V	Leventhal Julius	19	jeweler	55	
	W	Leventhal Leo	19	attorney	28	"
	X	Leventhal Sarah—†	19	housewife	53	"
	Y	Cohen Bertha—†	19	"	45	
	Z	Cohen Joseph	19	metalworker	52	"

759

	A	Cohen Lillian—†	19	bookkeeper	23	"
	B	Cohen Sylvia—†	19	"	21	"
	C	Karger Rose—†	19	"	28	
	D	Glick Bernard H	19	salesman	28	"
	E	Glick Bessie—†	19	housewife	48	"
	F	Glick Maurice	19	accountant	24	"
	G	Glick Phillip	19	foreman	54	
	H	Cohen Julius	19	pharmacist	32	"
	K	Cohen Pauline—†	19	housewife	30	"
	L	Goldstein Maurice	19	merchant	34	17 Norfolk ter
	M	Goldstein Minnie—†	19	housewife	31	17 "
	N	Simanofsky Lillian—†	20	bookkeeper	26	here
	o	Simanofsky Rose—†	20	"	29	"
	P	Simanofsky Sarah—†	20	housewife	68	"
	R	Gilman George	20	beautician	30	"
	s	Gilman Julius	20	shoecutter	41	"
	T	Gilman Nettie—†	20	housewife	40	"
	U	Glazer Harry	20	merchant	45	"
	V	Glazer Minnie—†	20	housewife	40	"

Washington Street

	W	Queen Mary—†	2990	housewife	21	40 W Walnut pk
	X	Queen William	2990	clerk	29	40 "
	Y	Reveliotis Alexander N	2990	"	25	here
	Z	Reveliotis Elizabeth—†	2990	housewife	22	"

36

760
Washington Street—Continued

Page.	Letter.	FULL NAME.	Residence, Jan. 1, 1941.	Occupation.	Supposed Age.	Reported Residence, Jan. 1, 1940. Street and Number.
	A	Rankin Helen—†	2990	housewife	21	here
	B	Rankin Margaret—†	2990	"	56	"
	C	Rankin Thomas	2990	clerk	26	"
	D	Williams Louise J—†	2992	housewife	86	"
	E	Hill Albert F	2992	chemist	28	
	F	Hill Catherine—†	2992	housewife	50	"
	G	Hill Joseph	2992	houseman	57	"
	H	Lasman Albert	2992	carpenter	28	"
	K	Lasman Lily—†	2992	housewife	29	"
	L	Ely Eleanor—†	2994	"	78	
	N	*Canning Elizabeth—†	2994	"	58	
	O	Canning James J	2994	laborer	32	
	S	Greene Catherine E—†	2996	housewife	40	"
	T	Greene Elizabeth—†	2996	clerk	22	
	U	Greene John	2996	machinist	48	"
	V	Murch Mary E—†	2998	housewife	38	"
	W	Gibbons Anna F—†	2998	"	35	
	X	Gibbons Anthony M	2998	clerk	39	
	Z	Nelson Margaret—†	3000	housewife	80	"

761

Page.	Letter.	FULL NAME.	Residence, Jan. 1, 1941.	Occupation.	Supposed Age.	Reported Residence, Jan. 1, 1940. Street and Number.
	A	Carton Della—†	3000	"	44	
	B	Carton Leo	3000	inspector	44	"
	D	Williams Florence R-†	3028	dressmaker	50	"
	E	Williams Martha—†	3028	housewife	80	"
	P	Cushing Edna B—†	3088	"	31	
	R	Cushing Sherman J	3088	salesman	35	"
	S	Brennan Beatrice M—†	3088	nurse	20	
	T	Brennan Cecelia M—†	3088	housewife	45	"
	U	Brennan Edward F	3088	salesman	45	"
	V	Brennan Marion E—†	3088	nurse	22	
	W	Brennan Raymond F	3088	salesman	24	"
	Y	Gartland Estelle N—†	3090	housewife	46	"
	Z	Gartland George L	3090	clerk	50	

762

Page.	Letter.	FULL NAME.	Residence, Jan. 1, 1941.	Occupation.	Supposed Age.	Reported Residence, Jan. 1, 1940. Street and Number.
	A	Grueter Anna M—†	3090	inspector	22	82 Bragdon
	B	Grueter Annie V—†	3090	housewife	59	82 "
	D	Grueter Edward J	3090	printer	24	82 "
	C	Grueter George E	3090	chef	20	82 "
	L	Lee Raymond	3104	laundryman	30	here
	P	MacDonald George J	3110	retired	65	"

Page.	Letter.	FULL NAME.	Residence, Jan. 1, 1941.	Occupation.	Supposed Age.	Reported Residence, Jan. 1, 1940. Street and Number.

Washington Street—Continued

	R	MacDonald John F	3110	laborer	20	here
	S	MacDonald Mildred A—†	3110	housewife	46	"
	T	Wall Gertrude A—†	3110	"	59	"
	U	Wall Walter F	3110	retired	58	"
	V	Wall Walter F, jr	3110	chauffeur	21	"

763

	A	Silver Clarence H	3114	laborer	54	
	B	Silver Marian E—†	3114	housewife	51	"
	C	Cable Charles H	3114	laborer	52	
	D	Turell Frederick H	3114	retired	69	
	E	Turell Ida M—†	3114	housewife	54	"
	H	Turell Florence W—†	3114	dressmaker	56	147 Whitfield
	L	O'Connell Annie—†	3118	housewife	50	here
	M	O'Connell Daniel F	3118	fireman	55	"
	N	O'Connell Daniel F, jr	3118	clerk	21	"
	O	Bartols Louis	3118	retired	68	
	R	Donovan Charles E	3118	laborer	32	
	P	Imbescheid Otto	3118	clerk	49	
	S	McIntire Esther E—†	3118	"	39	"
	T	Sullivan James H	3118	laborer	61	254 Amory
	U	Byron Martha W—†	3118	operator	51	here
	V	Schultz Veronica—†	3118	housewife	78	"
	W	Merriam Annie L—†	3118	at home	73	Dedham
	X	Check Thomas	3118	metalworker	45	Medford
	Y	Fraser Matilda C—†	3118	housewife	53	here
	Z	O'Brien James F	3118	chauffeur	33	"

764

	A	O'Brien William	3118	laborer	47	8 Atherton pl
	B	Burke James H	3118	painter	35	8 Fairbury
	C	Dolan Walter L	3118	salesman	45	36 Geneva av
	D	Garrow Ralph	3118	chef	27	219 Amory
	E	Porter Helen M—†	3118	housekeeper	42	17 Weld av
	F	Gaskill Frank S	3118	janitor	47	here
	G	Gaskill Hilda M—†	3118	housewife	44	"

Weld Avenue

	L	Doherty John	1	retired	74	23 Byron ct
	M	Doherty Mary J—†	1	housewife	79	23 "
	N	Noonan Annabelle F—†	1	at home	33	23 "
	O	Hastings Charles M	2	laborer	52	6 Dixwell

Weld Avenue—Continued

	P	Hastings Helen H—†	2	at home	22	6 Dixwell
	R	Hastings Lillian L—†	2	housewife	53	6 "
	S	Hastings Walter C	2	laborer	24	6 "
	T	Colcord Ada J—†	3	at home	88	here
	U	McAuley Doris—†	4	housewife	24	15 Weld av
	V	McAuley Kenneth A	4	laborer	24	15 "
	W	Brady Belle—†	4	housewife	36	here
	X	Brady William	4	painter	45	"
	Y	Blair Raymond E	4A	nurse	35	"
	Z	Blair Ruth M—†	4A	housewife	31	"
		765				
	A	Lynch Bernard	4A	ironworker	55	"
	B	*Lynch Rose A—†	4A	housewife	40	"
	C	Smith Elizabeth W—†	4A	at home	75	
	D	Ayer Catherine J—†	4A	housewife	65	"
	E	Ayer Frederick N	4A	engineer	30	
	F	Ayer James W	4A	retired	65	
	G	Lane Alice A—†	5	matron	49	
	H	O'Handley Daniel	5	laborer	47	
	K	O'Handley Joseph P	5	policeman	45	"
	L	O'Handley Mary M—†	5	housewife	43	"
	M	Rafter Elizabeth A—†	6	"	73	
	N	MacDonald Alice M—†	6	"	56	"
	O	MacDonald Hugh	6	carpenter	65	"
	P	Reardon Ellen M—†	7	housewife	23	368 Quincy
	R	Reardon Jeremiah J	7	salesman	31	368 "
	S	Embree Fredonia E—†	7	housewife	65	here
	T	Embree George N	7	retired	80	"
	U	Walker Dorothea E—†	7	designer	42	"
	V	Crossman Carl H	8	janitor	44	
	W	Crossman Violet—†	8	housewife	46	"
	X	McClarity George R	8	chauffeur	35	"
	Y	McClarity Hazel D—†	8	housewife	30	"
	Z	Horrigan Annie F—†	9	"	41	
		766				
	A	Horrigan John J	9	manager	46	"
	B	Quigley Francis W	10	clerk	27	
	C	Quigley Mary F—†.	10	housewife	54	"
	D	Quigley William F	10	fireman	57	
	E	Bickford Agnes M—†	11	housewife	43	"
	F	Bickford Jacqueline M—†	11	stitcher	21	"

Weld Avenue—Continued

G	Bickford Leslie B	11	policeman	46	here
H	Bickford Lorraine M—†	11	stenographer	20	"
K	Campbell Mabel—†	11	"	26	"
L	Cassidy James P	11	salesman	25	29 Orchard
M	Cassidy Ruth M—†	11	housewife	21	29 "
N	Demmon Arlene E—†	11	technician	31	Fitchburg
O	Campbell Jean—†	13	waitress	24	here
P	Huffnagle Charles	13	laborer	45	"
R	McGuinness Joseph W	13	chauffeur	24	"
S	McGuinness Theresa C—†	13	housewife	39	"
T	Maloley Alice M—†	14	saleswoman	24	"
U	Maloley Lillian E—†	14	at home	21	
V	*Maloley Mary—†	14	housewife	43	"
W	Maloley Nora M—†	14	at home	28	
X	Stanley Audley H	16	pipefitter	23	"
Y	Stanley Susan F—†	16	housewife	65	"
Z	Stringe Beulah M—†	17	"	46	212 Boylston
	767				
A	Stringe Edward I	17	steamfitter	46	212 "
B	Lydon Helena M—†	18	housewife	41	here
C	Lydon Thomas F	18	fireman	46	"
D	Mackintosh Mary—†	18	at home	47	"
E	McLeod Margaret D—†	18	"	68	
F	McLeod Roderick D	18	shipper	28	
G	*DeStefano Camella—†	22	housewife	59	"
H	DeStefano Mary—†	22	clerk	32	"
K	*DeStefano Salvatore	22	retired	71	
L	DeStefano Vitorio	22	U S A	22	
M	DeStefano Dominic J	22	timekeeper	31	"
N	*DeStefano Lucienne A—†	22	housewife	32	29 Green

Westminster Avenue

O	Brown Mary—†	4	clerk	25	Hyannis
P	Carlos James	4	retired	70	here
R	Carlos Mary E—†	4	housewife	62	"
S	Mann Clifford E	4	porter	45	"
T	Mann Daniel E	4	"	22	
U	*Halloran Ellen—†	6	housekeeper	57	"
V	Johnson Margaret—†	6	housewife	58	"
W	Johnson William	6	messenger	65	"

Westminster Avenue—Continued

x	Murphy Michael	6	laborer	32	here	
y	Nesley Alexander L	6	waiter	63	14 Glenburne	
z	Roche Joseph R	6	machinist	53	4 Hollander	
	768					
a	Roche Odie L—†	6	housewife	41	4 "	
b	Walker Jessie—†	6	clerk	50	here	
c	*Lotto Charles	8	cleaner	48	"	
d	*Lotto Gertrude—†	8	housewife	47	"	
e	Lotto Irving	8	cleaner	21		
f	Fleigelman George	8	plumber	42	"	
g	Fleigelman Sadie—†	8	housewife	33	"	
h	*Arsenault Leo	10	carpenter	38	116 School	
k	O'Brien Joseph	10	chauffeur	37	here	
l	Powell Clifford	10	timekeeper	68	"	
m	Wynott Charles	10	motorman	48	"	
n	Wynott Herbert	10	chauffeur	23	"	
o	Wynott Myrtle—†	10	housewife	45	"	
p	Young Alec	10	janitor	40		
r	*Young Christina—†	10	housewife	38	"	
s	Ginn Sarah A—†	12	teacher	45		
t	Ginn Susan J—†	12	clerk	50	"	
u	Ginn William	12	secretary	60	"	
v	Hoye Mary J—†	12	housewife	77	"	
x	Henderson Huldah A—†	18	"	66	91 Munroe	
y	Henderson Lawrence H	18	clerk	42	91 "	
z	Henderson Myrtle—†	18	housewife	35	91 "	
	769					
a	Dinsmore Dorothy—†	19	waitress	33	here	
b	Dinsmore Eva—†	19	housewife	53	"	
c	Kelley Catherine—†	19	saleswoman	36	"	
d	Kelley Rita—†	19	factoryhand	25	"	
e	Winters Constance—†	19	housewife	60	"	
f	Winters Donald	19	attendant	26	"	
g	Dow Charles	19	cutter	40		
h	Dow Mary—†	19	housewife	36	"	
k	Prodan Frank	19	laborer	30		
l	Prodan Marie—†	19	housewife	28	"	
m	*Schafheimer Emma—†	19	"	42	Germany	
n	*Schafheimer Herman	19	factoryhand	42	"	
o	Freiwald Mary—†	19	housewife	26	here	
p	Freiwald Robert	19	painter	28	"	

Westminster Avenue—Continued

R McElroy Frank J	19	operator	27	here
s McElroy Mary J—†	19	housewife	27	"
T *Lippman Eva—†	22	"	39	"
u Lippman Samuel	22	clerk	48	
v Pasco Bertha—†	22	housewife	62	"
w Pasco Louis E	22	guard	62	
x Pasco Louis E, jr	22	vocalist	30	
y Pasco Ruth—†	22	housewife	28	"
z Pasco Wendell M	22	student	23	
770				
A Gross Ethel—†	24	housekeeper	45	"
D Dolan Agnes—†	65	stitcher	43	162 Lamartine
E Adelman Frances—†	65	teacher	42	here
F Goldberg Milton	65	repairman	25	"
G Korinow Freida—†	65	housewife	23	32 Waumbeck
H Korinow Maurice	65	teacher	29	13 Schuyler
K Bernstein Anna—†	65	housewife	31	here
L Bernstein Daniel	65	salesman	42	"
M Wittenberg Morris	65	"	25	Framingham
N Jackson Betty—†	65	housewife	44	220 Harold
o Jackson Myer	65	factoryhand	55	Chelsea
R Abramowitz Abraham	65	salesman	33	Milton
s *Biller Clara—†	65	housewife	49	1314 Blue Hill av
T *Biller Nathan	65	stitcher	58	1314 "
u Lieberman Alma E—†	65	housewife	42	38 Moreland
v Lieberman Maurice	65	inspector	45	38 "
w Madoff Isadore	65	jeweler	53	here
x Lightman Bernice—†	65	housewife	21	6 Fabyan
y Lightman Gabriel A	65	manager	26	40 Kingsdale
771				
A Hyatt Charles F	65	painter	36	11 Royce rd
B Wood Ann—†	65	laundress	30	1 Ernst
c Miller Lillian—†	71	secretary	36	here
D Paradis Blanche—†	71	housewife	30	"
E Paradis Ovila	71	janitor	42	"
F VanDernoot Anna—†	71	housewife	47	3 Wardman rd
G VanDernoot Morris	71	salesman	44	3 "
H Moffitt Celia G—†	71	housewife	32	here
K Moffitt George J	71	manager	33	"
L *Rosenberg Abraham	71	tailor	63	"
M *Rosenberg Fannie—†	71	housewife	64	"

Westminster Avenue—Continued

	Letter	Name	Res	Occupation	Age	Residence
	N	Rosenberg Maurice S	71	student	25	here
	O	Resnick Rae—†	71	housewife	38	"
	P	Resnick Reuben	71	clerk	38	"
	R	Rubin Edith—†	71	housewife	38	"
	S	Rubin Harold	71	salesman	41	"
	T	Feldman Marcia—†	71	housewife	49	"
	U	Feldman Milton	71	buyer	27	"
	V	Monopole Frances—†	71	bookkeeper	33	Rutland
	W	Levinson Gertrude—†	77	housewife	48	here
	X	Levinson Julius	77	merchant	52	"
	Y	Levinson Melvin	77	student	20	"
	Z	Levinson Selma—†	77	stenographer	22	"

772

	Letter	Name	Res	Occupation	Age	Residence
	A	*Levin Anna—†	77	housewife	74	"
	B	*Prager Israel	77	printer	35	
	C	Prager Minnie—†	77	housewife	38	"

Westminster Terrace

	Letter	Name	Res	Occupation	Age	Residence
	D	Schneider Mary—†	3	housekeeper	40	here
	E	*Warshawsky Annie F—†	3	housewife	70	"
		Gateman Ida—†	3	"	35	"
		Gateman Jacob	3	bookbinder	37	"
		Silverman Albert	3	chauffeur	24	"
		Silverman Alice—†	3	milliner	38	
		Silverman Harold	3	clerk	21	
	M	Silverman Lillian—†	3	"	29	"
	N	Silverman Minnie—†	3	housewife	60	"
	O	Silverman Zelda—†	3	dressmaker	34	"
	P	Golden Lillian—†	5	housewife	32	"
	R	Golden Louis	5	chauffeur	34	"
	S	Baker Celia—†	5	housewife	54	"
	T	Baker Marshall	5	salesman	54	"
	U	Baker Walter	5	clerk	27	
	V	Rubinowitz Esther—†	5	housewife	50	"
	W	Rubinowitz Myer	5	merchant	54	"
	X	Stern Jennie—†	7	secretary	45	"
	Y	Bailey Beatrice—†	7	housewife	40	"
	Z	Bailey George	7	upholsterer	41	"

773

	Letter	Name	Res	Occupation	Age	Residence
	A	Fishbein Evelyn—†	7	housewife	34	5 Norfolk ter

Page.	Letter.	FULL NAME.	Residence, Jan. 1, 1941.	Occupation.	Supposed Age.	Reported Residence, Jan. 1, 1940. Street and Number.

Westminster Terrace—Continued

B	Fishbein Nathan	7	retailer	36	5 Norfolk ter
c	*Nimkoff Eva F—†	9	housewife	39	here
D	Nimkoff Louis	9	salesman	44	"
E	*Segal David	9	merchant	55	"
F	*Segal Mary—†.	9	housewife	60	"
G	Hotze Edward	9	salesman	45	20 Seaver
H	Levitan Nettie—†	9	operator	43	20 "
K	*Nuhlig Frances—†	9	housekeeper	50	20 "
L	Bayer Max	9	merchant	43	here
M	Lennack Edward	9	chauffeur	23	"
N	Lennack Hannah—†	9	housewife	42	"
O	Opochinsky Carl	9	retired	90	
P	Opochinsky Pauline—†	9	housewife	80	"

8

13

Ward 11—Precinct 8

CITY OF BOSTON

LIST OF RESIDENTS
20 YEARS OF AGE AND OVER

(NON-CITIZENS INDICATED BY ASTERISK)
(FEMALES INDICATED BY DAGGER)

AS OF

JANUARY 1, 1941

JOSEPH F. TIMILTY, *Chairman*
FREDERIC E. DOWLING, *Secretary*
WILLIAM A. MOTLEY, Jr.
FRANCIS B. McKINNEY
HILDA HEDSTROM QUIRK
Listing Board.

CITY OF BOSTON PRINTING DEPARTMENT

800

Boylston Street

A	McIsaac Hector A	209	longshoreman	53	here
B	McIsaac Margaret—†	209	housewife	48	"
C	Quinn Antoinette H—†	209	"	27	"
D	Quinn William A	209	policeman	30	"
E	Curran Mary B—†	209	housewife	52	"
F	Curran Thomas F	209	waiter	51	"
G	Powers Mary M—†	211	housewife	28	89 Henley
H	Powers Thomas J	211	laborer	31	89 "
K	Simpson Bertha A—†	211	housewife	51	12 Holden pl
L	Simpson Edward.T	211	clerk	65	12 "
M	Gilson Ellen B—†	211	housewife	60	here
N	Gilson Naomi C—†	211	teacher	31	"
O	Gilson Richard A	211	bookkeeper	61	"
P	*MacPherson Margaret—†	213	housewife	34	"
R	Meade William J	213	baker	43	
S	Smith Elizabeth—†	213	housekeeper	55	"
U	Gately Winifred—†	215	housewife	79	"
V	Gately Winifred M—†	215	clerk	26	
W	Gately Nellie A—†	215	housewife	60	"
X	Gately Thomas F	215	laborer	57	
Y	Fallon John	215	mason	36	"
Z	Kelley Nora E—†	217	housewife	75	"

801

A	Kelley Patrick J	217	retired	76	
B	Emerson Donald G	217	laborer	39	
C	*Emerson Gertrude D—†	217	housewife	30	"
D	O'Toole Ruth O—†	217	"	23	214 Boylston
E	Philbin Sarah—†	217	milliner	46	here
F	Bell Herbert C	219	laborer	22	6 Gordon
G	Bell Lola G—†	219	housewife	20	6 "
H	Smith Herbert	219	laborer	45	here
K	Smith Marion N—†	219	housewife	40	"
L	Alajian Florence—†	219	"	30	"

Byron Court

M	Cannata Anna—†	7	housewife	53	here
N	Cannata Joseph	7	barber	64	"
O	Harkins Margaret A—†	7	secretary	26	"
P	Harkins Thomas J	7	salesman	27	"

Page.	Letter.	FULL NAME.	Residence, Jan. 1, 1941.	Occupation.	Supposed Age.	Reported Residence, Jan. 1, 1940. Street and Number.

Byron Court—Continued

	R	Caruso Domenic	9	barber	42	here
	S	Caruso Mary—†	9	housewife	37	"
	T	*McNeil Angeline—†	9	"	40	"
	U	*McNeil William M	9	packer	52	
	V	Hohleen Alice—†	10	housewife	29	"
	W	Hohleen Eric	10	mechanic	37	"
	X	Boghossian Krikar	10	pedler	47	"
	Y	*Boghossian Ramala—†	10	housewife	38	"
	Z	Marotta Joseph	11	machinist	21	94 Heath
802						
	A	*Marotta Margaret—†	11	housewife	40	94 "
	B	Marotta Phillip	11	laborer	53	94 "
	C	Busa Alfred	11	foreman	23	here
	D	Busa Charles	11	operator	21	"
	E	*Busa John	11	shoemaker	38	"
	F	Busa Joseph	11	"	64	
	G	*Busa Pasqua—†	11	housewife	59	"
	H	Busa Robert	11	printer	21	
	K	Blatchford Henry	14	salesman	39	"
	L	*Fox Catherine—†	14	at home	84	
	M	Hennrikus Ellen—†	14	"	68	
	N	Kelly Catherine T—†	14	dressmaker	68	"
	O	Crowley John	15	operator	54	
	P	*Buckley Anna M—†	16	domestic	40	"
	R	Buckley Nellie—†	16	at home	57	"
	S	Cannatta Jeannette—†	16	bookkeeper	36	"
	T	Riley James F	18	B F D	43	"
	U	Sproul Anna G—†	18	at home	51	
	V	Sproul Edward B	18	operator	22	"
	W	Sproul Mary E—†	18	housewife	57	"
	X	*Balliro Isabella—†	19	"	34	"
	Y	Balliro Salvatore	19	foreman	39	
	Z	Dunn Herbert	19	chauffeur	29	"
803						
	A	Dunn Marjorie—†	19	housewife	27	"
	B	Dee Doris—†	19	"	20	41 Rossmore rd
	C	Dee Joseph	19	counterman	30	41 "
	D	Berti Dorothy—†	20	housewife	25	23 Byron ct
	E	Berti Victor	20	salesman	29	23 "
	F	Hayes Daniel	20	packer	26	29 Bainbridge
	G	Hayes Marjorie—†	20	housewife	20	54 Jewett

Page.	Letter.	FULL NAME.	Residence, Jan. 1, 1941.	Occupation.	Supposed Age.	Reported Residence, Jan. 1, 1940. Street and Number.

Byron Court—Continued

H	Hernon Thomas	20	retired	72	here
K	Penning Bridget—†	20	housewife	74	"
L	Penning Ruth—†	20	"	37	"
M	Penning William F	20	clerk	40	
N	Manfredi Joseph	22	retired	60	
O	Manfredi Louis	22	clerk	20	
P	Manfredi Philomena—†	22	packer	24	
R	*Manfredi Philomena—†	22	at home	85	
S	Manfredi Frank	22	contractor	58	"
T	*Manfredi Theresa—†	22	housewife	57	"
U	Christopher Ellen—†	23	"	29	Middleton
V	Rich Richard L	23	laborer	23	here
W	Stanley Fannie—†	23	at home	78	"
X	*DiCarlo Antonio	23	laborer	63	"
Y	Gouvia Constance—†	23	housewife	25	49 Bickford
Z	Gouvia Frank	23	laborer	27	49 "

804

B	DeSimone Giovannina—†	23	stitcher	48	55 '
A	DeSimone Matteo	23	retired	67	55 "
C	Lamberti Celia—†	23	at home	23	55 '
D	Lamberti Lucy—†	23	stitcher	21	55 '

Chilcott Place

E	Wheeler Nellie—†	3	housewife	47	here
F	Wheeler Ralph A	3	mechanic	47	"
G	Wheeler Ralph L	3	clerk	23	"
H	Wheeler Raymond J	3	"	22	
K	Moore Esther—†	3	operator	42	"
L	Moore John	3	retired	81	"
M	Scher Gertrude—†	3	operator	42	"
N	Hillen Frank K	5	plumber	47	
O	Magee Ellen—†	5	housewife	52	"
P	Magee Joseph F	5	janitor	55	
R	Sheil Mary—†	5	at home	66	"
S	Connors Annie—·†	5	"	71	35 Cobden
T	Connors Michael	5	machinist	66	35 "
U	Connors Thomas	5	"	54	35 "
V	Leeds Katherine—†	5	at home	64	35 "
W	Driscoll Cornelius	5	attorney	45	7 Regent ct
X	Driscoll Dorothy M—†	5	housewife	36	7 "

Page.	Letter.	FULL NAME.	Residence, Jan. 1, 1941.	Occupation.	Supposed Age.	Reported Residence, Jan. 1, 1940. Street and Number.

Chilcott Place—Continued

Y	Driscoll Margaret—†	5	saleswoman	48	7 Regent ct
Z	Reardon Anne—†	5	"	48	421 Old Colony av
805						
A	McIsaac Dorothy—†	6	housewife	31	19 Gordon
B	McIsaac Roland	6	guard	33	19 "
C	Saunders Hugh	6	engineer	52	here
D	Saunders Hugh N	6	student	22	"
E	Saunders Mary—†	6	housewife	49	"
F	Sanderson Helen E—†	6	"	27	
G	Sanderson John	6	teacher	28	
H	Jacobson Adolph	7	confectioner	60	"
K	Jacobson Ella—†	7	clerk	21	
L	Jacobson Ida—†	7	housewife	54	"
M	Jacobson William	7	counterman	24	"
N	Carr Elizabeth—†	7	at home	83	
O	Murray Joseph L	7	secretary	47	"
P	Murray Mary A—†	7	saleswoman	57	"
R	Booth Simpson	7	retired	75	"
S	Prescott Arthur T	7	policeman	45	"
T	Prescott Gladys B—†	7	housewife	45	"
U	Tedeschi Albino	9	chef	48	
V	*Tedeschi Providenza—†	9	housewife	43	"
W	Dors Anne—†	9	factoryhand	26	11 Brookside av
X	Forsyth Annie—†	9	housewife	65	11 "
Y	Forsyth William	9	molder	69	11 "
Z	Lavers Lily W—†	9	at home	73	Southbridge
806						
A	Margeson Eltha M—†	9	housewife	50	3123 Wash'n
B	Margeson Wilner J	9	chauffeur	55	3123 "
C	Sullivan Harold	9	clerk	21	60 Brookside av
D	Zager John A	10	"	39	here
E	Zager Ruth M—†	10	housewife	37	"
F	Faubert Martha C—†	10	"	32	"
G	Faubert Raymond L	10	watchman	26	"
H	MacDonald Tryphena—†	11	at home	67	
K	Mahoney Tryphena—†	11	saleswoman	41	"
M	McEldowney Agnes—†	11	housewife	58	"
N	McEldowney Ernest W	11	inspector	59	"
O	McEldowney Ernest W, jr	11	laborer	23	
P	McEldowney Robert W	11	"	21	
R	Bell Fritz	12	"	73	

Chilcott Place—Continued

s	Larson Hans P	12	laborer	49	here
T	Lieber Ernest	12	"	49	"
U	Lieber Wanda—†	12	housewife	45	"
V	Schell Gladys—†	15	"	31	
W	*Schell John	15	painter	29	
X	Stewart Dorothy T—†	15	secretary	20	"
Y	Stewart Horace G	15	mechanic	43	"
Z	Stewart Lillian A—†	15	housewife	42	"
	807				
A	*Lynds Annie—†	15	"	46	
B	*Lynds Louis	15	janitor	47	"
C	Newell Lillian—†	15	clerk	25	"
D	Newell Mary—†	15	"	21	
E	Smith Martha D—†	16	housewife	64	"
F	Smith Warren E	16	retired	65	"
G	Roemer Alice E—†	16	housewife	37	"
H	Roemer William J	16	contractor	44	"
K	Johnstone James, jr	16	mechanic	37	"
L	Johnstone Josephine—†	16	housewife	31	"
M	Rose Edward A	17	salesman	38	"
N	Rose Eleanor R—†	17	housewife	36	"
O	Griffin Delia J—†	17	"	55	
P	Griffin Mary—†	17	at home	67	"
R	Joyce Elizabeth F—†	17	housewife	28	Nantasket
S	Norstrom Carl W	17	machinist	33	here
T	Norstrom Dorothy—†	17	stenographer	34	"
U	*Norstrom Maria—†	17	housewife	58	"
V	Dobson Ann M—†	19	"	48	
W	Dobson John A	19	supervisor	48	"
X	Doody D Ernest	19	clerk	52	
Y	Murray Eleanor—†	19	at home	26	
Z	Maguire Catherine E—†	19	housewife	47	"
	808				
A	Maguire Catherine E—†	19	artist	26	
B	Maguire Peter J	19	laborer	52	
C	Magee Bernard	19	retired	69	
D	Magee Bernard J	19	clerk	35	
E	Magee George A	19	retired	65	
F	Magee Mary E—†	19	matron	64	
G	Magee Thomas A	19	plumber	59	
H	Layton George	20	machinist	56	"

Page.	Letter.	FULL NAME.	Residence, Jan. 1, 1941.	Occupation.	Supposed Age.	Reported Residence, Jan. 1, 1940. Street and Number.

Chilcott Place—Continued

K	Layton Nellie—†	20	housewife	55	here
L	Horgan Ethel M—†	20	"	28	"
M	Horgan James J	20	manager	29	"
N	Mills Mary E—†	20	housewife	68	"
O	Mills Thomas J	20	retired	81	
P	Mills Thomas J, jr	20	painter	31	
R	Short Alice W—†	20	housewife	33	"
S	Short John F	20	chauffeur	37	"
T	Fox Margaret—†	21	at home	65	
V	Miller Stella—†	21	operator	21	"
U	O'Hare Mary—†	21	at home	48	
W	Kelley Alice T—†	21	proprietress	61	"
X	Kelley Eileen A—†	21	student	22	
Y	Kelley Ferdinand F	21	accountant	28	"
Z	White Albert	23	clerk	41	

809

A	*White Harriet E—†	23	housewife	35	"
B	Tringali Antoinette—†	24	operator	28	"
C	Tringali Domenic	24	chauffeur	24	"
D	*Tringali Gaetano	24	fisherman	60	"
E	Tringali Gaetano, jr	24	"	22	
F	*Tringali Maria—†	24	housewife	56	"
G	Tringali Mary—†	24	operator	20	
H	Tringali Salvatore	24	chauffeur	26	"
K	Tringali Rosaria—†	24	housewife	32	"
L	*Tringali Sebastiano	24	fisherman	36	"
M	Welsh Catherine—†	25	housewife	35	"
N	Welsh John	25	retired	46	
O	Baker J Murray	25	"	66	
P	*Cherrett Florence—†	25	housewife	46	"
R	Cherrett William A	25	motorman	46	"
S	Bowen Gertrude C—†	26	saleswoman	38	"
T	Buckley Grace R—†	26	operator	33	
U	Quinn Ellen J—†	26	at home	69	
V	Totten Esther—†	26	waitress	40	
W	Waldron Irene H—†	26	"	40	
X	*Cutillo Maria—†	26	housewife	42	"
Y	Cutillo Sabino	26	shoemaker	42	"
Z	Redden Walter L	26	guard	46	

810

A	Zager Aurelia—†	27	housewife	60	"

Chilcott Place—Continued

B	Zager Harold	27	teacher	44	here
C	Zager Louis	27	retired	69	"

Ellsworth Street

D	Bradley Alberta—†	5	housewife	24	11 Byron ct
E	Bradley Robert	5	machinist	27	11 "
F	Hennessy Olive—†	5	housekeeper	52	11 "
G	Elias Assad J	7	laborer	53	18 Dixwell
H	Elias Martha—†.	7	housewife	36	18 "
K	Bullock Janie T—†	9	waitress	20	107 Sheridan
L	Bullock Jennie C—†	9	housewife	55	107 "
M	Bullock William	9	mechanic	55	107 "
N	Foran John	14	laborer	67	here
O	Foran Mary—†	14	housewife	65	"
P	McLain Martha—†	18	"	67	"
R	McLain Odessa—†	18	"	22	
S	McLain Russell	18	laborer	26	"
T	Scott Charles E	18	janitor	64	14 Market
U	McLain Alonzo W	18	mechanic	42	here
V	McLain Cora—†	18	domestic	20	"
W	McLain Gertrude—†	18	housewife	38	"
X	McLain Theodore	18	machinist	21	"
Y	Brauner Elizabeth—†	22	housewife	24	"
Z	Brauner Frederick	22	clerk	26	

811

A	Kenny Catherine—†	22	housewife	35	"
B	Kenny Charles	22	clerk	25	
C	Kenny John	22	laborer	38	
D	Kenny Robert	22	U S N	31	
E	Kenny Thomas J	22	retired	68	..
G	Pearson Eric	26	"	63	
H	Peterson Freda—†	26	housekeeper	52	"

Erie Place

K	Sanderson Charles	4	meter reader	32	here
L	Sanderson Helen—†	4	housewife	31	"
M	Pevorunas Alex	4	machinist	49	"
N	Pevorunas Monica—†	4	housewife	45	"
O	MacDonald Loughlin	9	carpenter	68	"

Page.	Letter.	Full Name.	Residence, Jan. 1, 1941.	Occupation.	Supposed Age.	Reported Residence, Jan. 1, 1940. Street and Number.

Erie Place—Continued

p	MacDonald Loughlin C	9	engineer	31	here
r	MacDonald Thomas H	9	accountant	29	"
s	Sullivan Dennis	9	manager	27	55 Hillside
t	Sullivan Rita—†	9	housewife	26	here
u	Wilson Anne—†	10	"	32	"
v	Wilson Horace	10	salesman	33	"
w	Wilson Rebecca—†	10	housewife	60	"
x	DiCarlo Edna—†	15	"	20	15 Dana pl
y	DiCarlo Emilio	15	chauffeur	26	15 "
z	DeIorio Joseph	15	laborer	37	here
	812				
a	*DeIorio Phyllis—†	15	housewife	27	"

Forest Hills Street

b	Nolan Anne—†	10	stenographer	29	here
c	Nolan John S	10	manager	28	"
d	Nolan Mary—†	10	housewife	55	"
e	McCarthy Angela—†	10	"	43	
f	McCarthy Fred	10	laborer	49	
g	Welby Martin	10	mechanic	48	"
k	Hogarty John	12	musician	39	"
l	Hogarty Mary—†	12	housewife	29	"
	Reynolds Patrick	12	engineer	56	
	Alexander Marguerite—†	14	saleswoman	23	"
n	Schwarz Carleton N	14	salesman	47	"
p	Schwarz Helen—†	14	housewife	47	"
r	*Doyle Margaret—†	14	"	44	
s	Mills John F	14	shipper	36	
t	Mills Mary M—†	14	housewife	36	"
u	Lennon P Joseph	19	laundryworker	31	24 Haslet
v	Murray Anne—†	19	housewife	27	11 Dell av
w	Murray Ralph C	19	foreman	31	11 "
x	McLaughlin Mary E—†	20	operator	26	here
y	McLaughlin Mary H—†	20	housewife	64	"
z	McLaughlin William	20	retired	73	"
	813				
a	McGreehan James	20	operator	47	
b	McGreehan Ruth—†	20	housewife	42	"
c	Leehan Ellen—†	20	"	50	46 Forest Hills
d	Leehan William E	20	repairman	49	46 "

9

Forest Hills Street—Continued

F	Kelly John	21	steamfitter	45	here
G	Kelly Mary—†	21	housewife	40	"
H	Egan Mary J—†	21	housekeeper	42	"
K	Tripp Edith E—†	22	housewife	46	306 Amory
L	Tripp Edward R	22	tinsmith	50	306 "
M	Tippo Anna—†	22	housewife	57	here
N	Tippo Edward	22	porter	23	"
O	Tippo John	22	cabinetmaker	57	"
P	Ford Catherine—†	22	housewife	40	"
R	Ford Joseph	22	shipper	41	
S	Applebaum Abraham	23	retired	65	
T	*Farquharson Anna—†	23	housewife	64	"
U	Samble William	23	laborer	58	
V	*Therrien Ruth—†	23	operator	40	"
W	*Boyd James	23	retired	72	
X	Boyd Mary—†	23	housewife	64	"
Y	Morrow Thomas A	23	chef	67	
Z	Clark Francis	24	electrician	40	"

814

A	Clark Margaret—†	24	housewife	36	"
B	Schillemat Edward	24	molder	29	23 Iffley rd
C	Schillemat Marie—†	24	housewife	29	Pennsylvania
D	Klan Louise—†	24	housekeeper	58	here
E	Ramm Peter	24	carpenter	65	"
G	Leonard Anne—†	25	nurse	34	"
H	Leonard Catherine—†	25	clerk	36	
K	Leonard James M	25	"	32	
L	Leonard Susan—†	25	housewife	64	"
M	Sullivan Eileen—†	25	stenographer	36	"
N	Sullivan John J	25	mechanic	74	"
P	*Benson Arne	26	operator	44	"
R	*Benson Margaret—†	26	housewife	40	"
S	Kenney Elizabeth T—†	26	"	60	
T	Kenney John F	26	attorney	32	"
U	Kenney Mary C—†	26	secretary	35	"

Glines Avenue

V	Grundy Fred	1	merchant	36	here
W	Grundy Marie—†	1	housewife	32	"
X	*McGowan Charles	rear 2	chauffeur	36	"

Page.	Letter.	FULL NAME.	Residence, Jan. 1, 1941.	Occupation.	Supposed Age.	Reported Residence, Jan. 1, 1940. Street and Number.

Glines Avenue—Continued

y	*McGowan Hanora—†	rear 2	housewife	38	here
z	McDonough Evelyn—†	" 2	clerk	21	"
	815				
A	McDonough Mary—†	" 2	stenographer	25	"
B	McDonough Sarah—†	" 2	clerk	23	''
C	McDonough Walter	" 2	chauffeur	65	"
D	McDonough Walter, jr	" 2	student	24	
E	Tirrell Mary—†	" 2	housewife	50	"
F	Tirrell Robert J	" 2	glazier	61	"
G	Spellman Emily—† ·	3	housewife	29	"
H	Spellman Harold	3	laborer	29	
K	Bonner Alice I—†	3	housewife	55	"
L	Bonner John .	3	operator	48	"
M	Burke Mary L—†	4	"	35	
N	Dunn Agnes—†	· 4	housewife	29	"
O	Dunn John F	4	laborer	31	
P	Dunn John	4	watchman	64	"
R	Dunn Mary—†	4	housewife	59	"
S	Dunn William C	4	machinist	24	"
T	McDermott Henry T	5	mechanic	33	"
U	McDermott Mary M—†	5	housewife	31	"
V	Hickey James J	5	longshoreman	27	45 Soley
W	Hickey Mary T—†	5	housewife	23	45 "
X	Oppelaar Jennie—†	6	" ·	42	105 Boylston
Y	*Schmidt Emil	6	ironworker	39	here
Z	*Schmidt Hilda—†	6	housewife	29	"
	816				
A	Humphrey Helen—†	7	housekeeper	38	"
B	Maslanka Basil	7	carpenter	55	"
C	*Maslanka Mary—†	7	housewife	45	"
D	Maslanka Michael	7	laborer	23	

Haverford Street

E	Keating Gertrude S—†	35	housewife	26	here
F	Keating Joseph T	35	chauffeur	30	"
G	Keating Mary C—†	35	housewife	68	"
H	Duzan James C	37	laborer	47	
K	Duzan Jennie C—†	37	housewife	47	"
L	Merrill William F	37	retired	78	
M	Murphy John J	41	mechanic	46	"

11

Page.	Letter.	Full Name.	Residence, Jan. 1, 1941.	Occupation.	Supposed Age.	Reported Residence, Jan. 1, 1940. Street and Number.

Haverford Street—Continued

	N	Murphy Margaret—†	41	artist	21	here
	o	Murphy Mary—†	41	housewife	44	"
	P	Downey Katherine—†	43	housekeeper	45	"
	R	*Campanella Blanche—†	45	housewife	30	"
	s	Campanella Joseph	45	clerk	33	
	T	Campanella Frank	47	barber	57	
	u	Campanella John A	47	printer	23	
	v	Campanella Mary A—†	47	housewife	56	"
	w	Campanella Matthew	47	mechanic	25	"
	x	Campanella Rose F—†	47	stenographer	30	"

817   Iffley Road

	A	Englert Edward L	18	clerk	42	here
	B	Englert Mabel E—†	18	housewife	31	"
	c	Kirchgassner Joseph	18	watchman	62	"
	D	Grant Bertha S—†	18	housewife	28	"
	E	Grant Charles L	18	clerk	28	
	F	Grant Florence—†	18	typist	32	
	G	Mathews Frederick H	18	shoemaker	63	"
	H	Sweeney Blanche E—†	18	housewife	40	"
	K	Sweeney Edward J	18	instructor	44	"
	L	Jacomin Isadore	19	retired	74	
	M	Jacomin Stephen F	19	machinist	44	"
	N	O'Connor Charles A	19	inspector	53	65 Glen rd
	o	Mathony Amelia—†	19	restaurateur	62	here
	P	Bassett Earle S	19	chef	52	"
	R	Bassett Fremont S	19	manager	24	"
	s	Bassett Lillian J—†	19	housewife	53	"
	T	Barrett John F	22	teacher	34	
	u	O'Brien Catherine E—†	22	packer	22	
	v	O'Brien John E	22	machinist	60	"
	w	O'Brien Margaret A—†	22	housewife	58	"
	x	O'Brien Mary T—†	22	clerk	27	
	Y	Edmands Minnie E—†	22	at home	60	
	z	Swansburg Frank L	22	machinist	57	"

818

	A	Swansburg Louise S—†	22	housewife	54	"
	B	Warecki Alphonse P	22	baker	22	
	c	Warecki Julius J	22	"	50	
	D	Warecki Olga P—†	22	housewife	43	"

12

Page.	Letter.	Full Name.	Residence, Jan. 1, 1941.	Occupation.	Supposed Age.	Reported Residence, Jan. 1, 1940. Street and Number.

Iffley Road—Continued

	E	Warecki Phyllis J—†	22	clerk	25	here
	F	Gerlacher Edward B	23	foreman	66	"
	G	Gerlacher Flora—†	23	housewife	55	"
	H	Moore Joseph L	23	laborer	61	
	K	Moore Mary A—†	23	housewife	66	"
	L	Moore Thomas F	23	operator	62	"
	M	Sheedy Catherine—†	23	housewife	68	"
	N	Sheedy John J	23	salesman	35	"
	O	Sheedy Marion K—†	23	secretary	41	"
	P	Sheedy Patrick J	23	fireman	68	"
	R	Canney Margaret A—†	26	housewife	35	18 Haverford
	S	Canney William J	26	engineer	38	18 "
	T	Bruce Ada B—†	26	housewife	63	here
	U	Bruce Fred E	26	retired	62	"
	V	Hoare James J	26	clerk	37	"
	W	Hoare Mary T—†	26	beautician	33	"
	x*	Walsh Elizabeth—†	26	"	24	"
	Y	Coffey Daniel J	27	retired	65	17 Perrin
	Z	Coffey Eleanor M—†	27	clerk	23	17 "

819

	A	Coffey Joseph L	27	operator	25	17 "
	B	Coffey Lorraine D—†	27	clerk	22	17 '
	C	Coffey Rose E—†	27	housewife	55	17 "
	D	Doherty Mary E—†	27	at home	57	17 "
	E	Garrity Margaret M—†	27	housewife	39	here
	F	Garrity Patrick J	27	policeman	45	"
	G	Sundberg John V	27	chauffeur	52	"
	H	Sundberg Mary—†	27	housewife	49	"
	K*	Sundberg Matilda—†	27	at home	81	
	L	Morse Augusta E—†	30	housewife	58	"
	M	Morse Charles F	30	retired	60	
	N	Hassett Anna—†	31	housewife	49	"
	O	Hassett George H	31	fireman	53	
	P	Fitzpatrick Alice M—†	31	clerk	28	
	R	Fitzpatrick Lawrence H	31	salesman	36	"
	S	Fitzpatrick William H	31	retired	69	
	T	Fitzpatrick William J	31	agent	26	"
	U	Finneran Katherine M—†	31	housewife	26	"
	V	Finneran Thomas F	31	salesman	24	"
	W	Chronopoulos George E	32	restaurateur	49	"
	X*	Chronopoulos Theodora G—†	32	housewife	38	"

13

Iffley Road—Continued

Y	Fleming Catherine A—†	32	housewife	68	here
z	Fleming Catherine V—†	32	secretary	30	"
820						
A	Fleming Francis P	32	shipper	27	
B	Fleming Patrick J	32	retired	71	
c	Savini Jennie—†	32	housewife	53	"
D	Savini Salvatore	32	butcher	53	
E	Cullen Matthew J	35	chauffeur	48	"
F	Cullen Sarah C—†	35	housewife	45	"
G	Mastrine Anna F—†	35	"	53	
H	Mastrine Louis F	35	chef	54	"
K	Nolan Theresa—†	35	at home	56	179 Marlboro
L	Cahill Mary C—†	36	domestic	41	here
M	Fay Daniel J	36	chauffeur	53	"
N	Fay Marie C—†	36	stenographer	29	"
o	Fay Rita M—†	36	"	25	
P	Thyne Josephine A—†	36	housewife	39	"
R	Thyne Martin A	36	gateman	41	"
s	Green Catherine E—†	36	clerk	28	
T	Green Francis J	36	laborer	25	
U	Green Margaret J—†	36	housewife	58	"
v	Green Mary M—†	36	clerk	26	
w	Green Michael J	36	guard	60	
x	Hopkins Errol G	39	operator	37	
Y	Hopkins Lulie K—†	39	housewife	34	"
z	Lane Louise B—†	39	at home	63	
821						
A	O'Neil Charles C	39	guard	54	
B	O'Neil Frances M—†	39	secretary	24	"
c	O'Neil Mary A—†	39	housewife	52	"
E	Carlson Florence B—†	40	"	33	N Hampshire
F	Carlson Reidar I.	40	salesman	31	"
G	Tuohey Catherine S—†	40	typist	30	here
H	Tuohey John	40	retired	65	"
K	Tuohey Margaret M—†	40	domestic	32	"
L	*Tuohey Mary A—†	40	housewife	65	"
M	Tuohey Mary F—†	40	stenographer	26	"
N	Tuohey Michael J	40	manager	33	"
o	Hurley Bernard F	40	mechanic	64	"
P	Hurley Mary L—†	40	housewife	50	"
R	Turley Rose G—†	40	clerk	55	

Iffley Road—Continued

	Letter	Full Name	Residence	Occupation	Age	Reported Residence
	s	Kelly Francis J	41	clerk	23	203 Boylston
	t	Kelly Marion E—†	41	housewife	42	203 "
	u	Kelly Thomas F	41	steamfitter	43	203 "
	v	Moore Francis L	41	realtor	34	here
	w	Moore Genevieve M—†	41	housewife	28	"
	x	Moore Lawrence F	41	retired	70	"
	y	Dinkelberg Margaretha M—†	41	housewife	66	"
	z	Dinkelberg Marguerite M-†41		clerk	30	
822						
	a	Quinn Alice—†	43	stenographer	22	"
	b	Quinn Margaret—†	43	"	25	"
	c	*Quinn Mary E—†	43	housewife	60	"
	d	Quinn Ruth—†	43	bookkeeper	20	"
	e	MacDonald Alexander	43	merchant	57	24 Edgewood
	f	MacDonald Charlotte M-†43		housewife	52	24 "
	g	MacDonald Katherine D-†43		nurse	31	24 "
	h	*MacDonald Leonard W	43	machinist	29	24 "
	k	Chakarian Mabel—†	43	clerk	28	here
	l	Chakarian Warren	43	butcher	38	"
	m	Clifford Jeremiah J	44	laborer	42	35 Peter Parley rd
	n	Clifford Mary A—†	44	housewife	37	35 "
	o	*McCarthy Anna—†	44	"	68	35 "
	p	McCarthy Catherine—†	44	waitress	39	35 "
	r	Yanus Ann G—†	44	housewife	33	here
	s	Yanus Bronislaw J	44	foreman	28	"
	u	Alasevicius Joseph S	45	bartender	50	"
	v	*Alasevicius Veronica A—†	45	housewife	30	"
	w	Calliontzis Huranea—†	45	"	40	
	x	Calliontzis Peter	45	manager	50	
	y	*Buckland Cleve B	45	chef	38	
	z	*Hayes Carlton H	45	packer	23	
823						
	a	*Hayes Mae P—†	45	housewife	42	"
	b	Kolka Alvina M—†	47	"	48	
	c	Kolka George H	47	signmaker	22	"
	d	Kolka John F	47	shipfitter	21	"
	e	*Kolka John M	47	signmaker	56	"
	f	Scally Elizabeth M—†	47	housewife	28	"
	g	Scally Joseph W	47	social worker	29	"
	h	Scally Josephine A—†	47	cook	51	
	k	Quinn James F	47	retired	70	

Iffley Road—Continued

L	Quinn Margaret A—†	47	secretary	30	here
M	Quinn Margaret E—†	47	housewife	68	"
N	Ricker Anna V—†	48	"	50	"
O	Ricker Elizabeth A—†	48	student	20	
P	Ricker George V	48	salesman	50	"
S	Igoe Thomas	48	laborer	22	
T	Igoe Thomas M	48	operator	50	"
U	Hester John J	50	bartender	44	"
V	Hester Mary M—†	50	housewife	35	"
W	Doherty Catherine E—†	50	"	64	
X	Doherty Jeremiah L	50	attorney	26	"
Y	Doherty Kathleen L—†	50	teacher	31	"
Z	Doherty Timothy C	50	attorney	30	"

824

A	McElhinney Winifred E-†	50	domestic	29	989 Parker
B	Cronin Dorothea A—†	50	stenographer	22	here
C	Cronin Katherine E—†	50	housewife	54	"
D	Cronin Ruth J—†	50	stenographer	27	"
E	Graham Eliza D—†	55	at home	65	
F	Devlin Bernard F	55	teacher	32	
G	Devlin Margaret G—†	55	housewife	31	"
H	Matthews Mary A—†	55	"	49	
K	Matthews Michael J	55	operator	49	"
L	Rayner Mary A—†	55	seamstress	50	Quincy
M	Zevitas George A	60	merchant	63	here
N	Zevitas Louis G	60	laborer	26	"
O	Zevitas Mary G—†	60	housewife	51	"
P	Zevitas Polly G—†	60	clerk	24	
R	Pappas John N	60	"	40	
S	Pappas Nafsika J—†	60	housewife	28	"
T	Kennedy Emeline K—†	60	"	21	20 Nottingham
U	Kennedy Joseph E	60	meatcutter	22	520 Park
V	Skier Norman M	64	salesman	22	451 Walnut av
W	Skier Sarah—†	64	housewife	55	451 "
X	Diamond Edward	64	merchant	38	5 Glenburne
Y	Diamond Sarah—†	64	housewife	34	72 Iffley rd
Z	Jacobson Elizabeth R—†	64	"	31	here

825

A	*Jacobson Max D	64	contractor	46	"

Iffley Road—Continued

B	Tobey Esther R—†	64	housewife	40	here
C	Tobey Mitchell	64	merchant	42	"
D	*Krips Esther—†	64	dressmaker	40	"
E	*Levenson Anna—†	64	housewife	43	"
F	*Levenson Arthur	64	operator	51	..
G	*Kasloff Benjamin	64	merchant	48	"
H	*Kasloff Sophie—†	64	housewife	40	"
K	*Feldman Dorothy—†	68	"	29	
L	Feldman Ellis	68	photographer	29	"
M	Jacobs Jacob	68	merchant	43	"
N	Jacobs Lena C—†	68	housewife	42	"
O	Lubot Charles	68	tailor	50	
P	Lubot Ethel—†	68	housewife	48	"
R	Cohen Irving D	68	merchant	54	"
S	Cohen Leonard A	68	manager	22	"
T	*Cohen Sadie E—†	68	housewife	44	"
U	*Feingold Bessie—†	68	"	44	
V	Feingold George	68	merchant	46	"
W	Curwin Ann—†	68	housewife	32	"
X	Curwin Louis J	68	merchant	38	"
Y	Gorodetzky Rose—†	72	housewife	34	65 Homestead
Z	Gorodetzky Saul	72	musician	37	65 "
	826				
A	Litsky Ethel—†	72	housewife	27	10 Grove
B	Litsky Isadore	72	cutter	35	10 Homestead
C	Litsky Jacob A	72	merchant	28	10 "
D	Abelsky Roslyn—†	72	saleswoman	25	168 Ruthven
E	Svetkey David	72	printer	34	168 "
F	Svetkey Shirley—†	72	housewife	32	168 "
G	Ruddman Mary—†	72	"	49	here
H	Ruddman Norma—†	72	saleswoman	24	"
K	Scholnick Julia—†	72	housewife	28	"
L	Scholnick Theodore	72	agent	31	
M	Karp Beatrice—†	72	stenographer	21	"
N	Karp Dorothy—†	72	"	26	"
O	Karp Jacob	72	junk dealer	52	"
P	*Karp Rose—†	72	housewife	49	"
R	Castaline Harry	72	merchant	32	"
S	Castaline Vida—†	72	housewife	32	"

Page.	Letter.	Full Name.	Residence, Jan. 1, 1941.	Occupation.	Supposed Age.	Reported Residence, Jan. 1, 1940. Street and Number.

Montebello Road

	Letter	Full Name	Residence	Occupation	Age	Reported Residence
	T	Loth Eric C	28	physician	28	New Jersey
	U	Walcott Gloria J—†	28	housekeeper	54	"
	V	Callahan Anna T—†	28	housewife	60	here
	W	Callahan Dennis J	28	foreman	64	"
	X	Devine Rose—†	28	operator	24	"
	Y	Devine Rose H—†	28	housewife	57	"
	Z	Devine Thomas F	28	watchman	62	"

827

	Letter	Full Name	Residence	Occupation	Age	Reported Residence
	A	Devine William F	28	student	20	
	B	McDermott Bridget A—†	30	housewife	63	"
	C	McDermott Mary R—†	30	"	33	
	D	McDermott Peter J	30	manager	38	
	E	Flynn John J, jr	30	gardener	60	•"
	F	Flynn Josephine—†	30	housewife	55	"
	G	Flynn Mary A—†	30	"	62	
	H	McDermott Evelyn C—†	30	"	32	
	K	McDermott Thomas L	30	electrician	33	"
	L	Rossi Josephine—†	47	housekeeper	47	"
	M	Ventri Carmella—†	47	housewife	66	"
	N	Ventri Sebastian	47	foreman	56	
	O	Hall Herbert J	47	painter	34	
	P	Hall Willard J	47	attendant	36	"
	R	Phelan John J	47	policeman	42	"
	S	Phelan Marion G—†	47	housewife	42	"
	T	Taxier Albert	47	manager	42	"
	U	Taxier Theresa—†	47	housewife	49	"
	V	O'Neil Edward	51	laborer	40	
	W	O'Neil Frank A	51	chauffeur	46	"
	X	O'Neil Johanna—†	51	housewife	62	"
	Y	Sheils Alice—†	51	housekeeper	35	"
	Z	*Bowman Adeline E—†	51	housewife	39	"

828

	Letter	Full Name	Residence	Occupation	Age	Reported Residence
	A	*Bowman Alexander	51	printer	43	
	B	*Cover Augusta—†	51	housekeeper	70	"
	C	*Malina Anna—†	51	housewife	33	"
	D	Malina Reuben	51	manager	35	"
	E	Kohl Bertram	51	pressman	37	79 Call
	F	Kohl Sally—†	51	housewife	32	79 "
	G	McDermott Esther L—†	51	"	35	here
	H	McDermott John J	51	shipper	41	"
	K	Slusze Helen—†	51	inspector	24	"

18

Montebello Road—Continued

	L	Slusze Laura—†	51	housekeeper	28	here
	M	*Slusze Michael	51	meatcutter	67	"
	N	Burns Esther—†	52	housewife	32	"
	O	Burns James W	52	engineer	39	"
	P	Glavin Harold F	52	laborer	36	
	R	*Glavin Victoria—†	52	housewife	32	"
	S	Cully Arthur J	52	retired	68	
	T	Cully Margaret J—†	52	housewife	48	"
	V	Benjamin Phyllis—†	52	"	35	
	W	Benjamin Wilfred	52	foreman	30	
	X	Marcianna Dominic	52	painter	27	
	Y	Marcianna Thomasina—†	52	beautician	26	"
	Z	Cairnes Daniel J	55	bottler	61	

829

	A	Cairnes Thomas G	55	janitor	56	
	B	Linden Alice E—†	55	housewife	52	"
	C	Linden Patrick J	55	chauffeur	56	"
	D	*Armakaucis Elizabeth—†	55	housewife	46	"
	E	Armakaucis Peter	55	rugmaker	55	"
	F	Laucke Alice—†	55	saleswoman	22	"
	G	Laucke John	55	meatcutter	26	393 E Fifth
	H	Cunningham Arthur	61	agent	38	211 Wachusett
	K	Cunningham Catherine—†	61	housewife	37	211 "
	L	Turley Albert A	61	clerk	51	here
	M	Turley Rose R—†	61	housewife	51	"
	N	Fleischer Maria—†	61	"	36	"
	O	Fleischer Max A	61	broker	40	"
	P	Crowley John J	61	clerk	33	161 H
	R	Crowley Rose M—†	61	"	26	here
	S	Davis Rosamond—†	61	seamstress	38	"
	T	Malouf Agabia M—†	62	housewife	47	"
	U	Malouf Allia S—†	62	housekeeper	49	"
	V	Malouf Elias S	62	manufacturer	50	"
	W	Malouf Faris S	62	attorney	48	"
	X	*Malouf George N	62	laborer	20	
	Y	Malouf Heney F—†	62	housewife	54	"
	Z	*Malouf Rachedi N—†	62	stitcher	22	

830

	A	*Malouf Salemi N—†	62	housekeeper	47	Brazil
	B	McTernan Bernard J	69	manager	26	875 Hunt'n av
	C	McTernan Mary A—†	69	housewife	25	875 "

19

D	Leonard Charles	69	clerk	23	307 Lamartine
E	Leonard Delia—†	69	housewife	64	307 "
F	Leonard Mary—†	69	secretary	27	307 "
G	Luby Elizabeth M—†	69	housewife	45	here
H	Luby James J	69	salesman	38	"
K	Luby Thomas F	69	retired	95	"
L	Luby Thomas F, jr	69	teacher	42	
M	Cotter John J	70	laborer	45	
N	Cotter Miriam—†	70	housewife	55	"
O	Galvin Agnes—†	70	"	49	
P	Galvin John	70	clerk	26	
R	Galvin Mary—†	70	housekeeper	20	"
S	Galvin Thomas	70	fireman	51	
T	Horgan Joseph D	70	clerk	29	
U	Horgan Mary—†	70	housewife	31	"
V	Caffey Bridget—†	73	"	53	
W	Caffey Matthew J	73	plasterer	55	"
X	Cushing Nora M—†	73	nurse	48	
Y	Sullivan Margaret M	73	housewife	58	"
Z	Sullivan Timothy F	73	inspector	57	"
	831				
A	McCabe Anna—†	73	housewife	68	"
B	McCabe John	73	retired	67	
C	McCabe Mary V—†	73	stenographer	33	"
D	McDonald Kathleen—†	74	housewife	45	"
E	McDonald Mona J—†	74	clerk	23	
F	Tarvizian Annie—†	74	housewife	58	"
G	Tarvizian Bartov	74	polisher	28	
H	Tarvizian Charles	74	salesman	33	"
K	Tarvizian Vahan	74	polisher	30	
L	Leonard Helen E—†	74	housewife	37	"
M	Leonard James H	74	retired	63	
N	Northway Joseph F	77	accountant	26	"
O	Northway Mary A—†	77	housewife	66	"
P	Northway William J	77	retired	78	
R	Peaslee Leland	77	chauffeur	56	"
S	Peaslee Margaret—†	77	housewife	55	"
T	Mathony Ida C—†	77	secretary	46	"
U	Mathony Mary E—†	77	housewife	66	"
V	Feeley Catherine—†	78	"	65	
W	Henry Charles	78	chauffeur	34	"

Page.	Letter.	FULL NAME.	Residence, Jan. 1, 1941.	Occupation.	Supposed Age.	Reported Residence, Jan. 1, 1940. Street and Number.

Montebello Road—Continued

	x	Henry James	78	laborer	26	here
	y	Henry John J	78	"	61	"
	z	Power John	78	"	36	"
832						
	a	Power Joseph	78	supervisor	61	"
	b	Power Laura—†	78	housekeeper	34	"
	c	Power Mary—†	78	housewife	33	"
	d	Conlon Patrick	78	fireman	43	11 Dalrymple
	e	Conlon Theresa—†	78	housewife	44	11 "
	f	Tighe Patrick J	81	policeman	41	here
	g	Tighe Sadie J—†	81	housewife	40	"
	h	Wagner Clara—†	81	"	68	"
	k	Wagner Henry J	81	retired	69	
	l	Craddock James	81	clerk	36	
	m	Craddock Nora—†	81	housewife	33	"
	n	Thornton Margaret—†	82	"	40	200 Boylston
	o	Thornton Michael	82	janitor	42	200 "
	p	Hathaway Edward W	82	salesman	38	here
	r	Hathaway Mary L—†	82	housewife	38	"
	s	Days Annie—†	82	"	70	"
	t	Days Charles E	82	salesman	46	"
	u	Days Olive—†	82	housewife	44	"
	v	Keyes Mildred—†	82	demonstrator	21	"
	y	Chaisson Arthur	86	cutter	53	
	z	Chaisson Dolores—†	86	saleswoman	27	"
833						
	a	Chaisson Susan—†	86	housewife	51	"
	b	Lemieux Violet—†	86	stitcher	22	
	c	Lemieux Wilrod	86	carpenter	23	"
	d	*Langevin Amelia—†	86	housewife	54	"
	e	Langevin Edmund	86	carpenter	45	"
	f	Wolfe Celia—†	86	housewife	50	"
	g	Wolfe Esther H—†	86	stenographer	23	"
	h	Wolfe Max	86	printer	54	"
	k	Rasmussen Clara P—†	89	teacher	34	
	l	Rasmussen Eleanor G—†	89	stenographer	25	"
	m	Rasmussen Nicolina—†	89	housewife	61	"
	n	Rasmussen Rasmus C	89	broker	60	
	o	Pettiti Dominic	89	manager	54	"
	p	Pettiti Josephine—†	89	housewife	52	"
	r	Rogers Margaret—†	89	secretary	40	"

Page.	Letter.	FULL NAME.	Residence, Jan. 1, 1941.	Occupation.	Supposed Age.	Reported Residence, Jan. 1, 1940. Street and Number.

Montebello Road--Continued

s	Walsh Adela—†	89	housewife	49	here
T	Walsh Helen L—†	89	clerk	21	"
U	Walsh William P	89	policeman	49	"
v	Bornstein Augusta—†	90	stenographer	35	"
w	Bornstein Esther—†	90	housewife	63	"
x	Bornstein Harry	90	retired	65	
Y	Bornstein Ruth J—†	90	housekeeper	33	"
z	Spack Abraham A	90	teacher	31	"

834

A	Spack Phyllis G—†	90	housewife	26	"
B	Kussmaul Martha C—†	90	"	48	
C	Kussmaul Rudolph J	90	artist	48	"
D	Stearns Frances—†	93	housewife	28	65 Homestead
E	Stearns Jack	93	manager	28	65 "
F	Conviser Benjamin	93	engineer	33	here
G	*Conviser Sophie—†	93	housewife	33	"
H	*Feldman Esther—†	93	"	54	"
K	Feldman Joseph	93	tailor	56	
L	Miller Harry	93	salesman	35	"
M	Miller Tillie—†	93	housewife	35	"
N	Sullivan Agnes C—†	94	"	43	193 Boylston
O	Sullivan John J	94	clerk	47	193 "
P	Thurber Gertrude E—†	94	housewife	32	here
R	Thurber Susan G—†	94	"	60	"
S	Thurber Wallace N	94	repairman	40	"
T	Burns Daniel P	94	retired	75	..
U	Carty Hermina W—†	97	housewife	33	"
v	Carty William L	97	clerk	34	..
w	Morgan Frances T—†	97	"	32	
x	Carty Daniel P	97	"	32	
Y	Carty Norma M—†	97	housewife	29	"
z	Creighton Annie C—†	97	"	63	

835

A	Creighton Arthur	97	chauffeur	66	"
B	Diettrich Bernard F	97	machinist	49	"
C	Diettrich Margaret L—†	97	housewife	49	"
D	Perry Mary—†	97	"	51	
E	Perry Robert H	97	machinist	52	"
F	Laffey Helen M—†	98	housewife	45	"
G	Laffey John	98	student	23	"
H	Laffey Patrick	98	steamfitter	58	"

Montebello Road—Continued

K	Pow A Florence—†	98	teacher	49	here
L	Pow C Flora—†	98	housewife	73	"
M	Nelson Alexander G	98	machinist	50	"
N	Nelson Charlotte R—†	98	housewife	48	"
O	Nelson James A	98	clerk	22	
P	Wallace Dorothea M—†	100	operator	25	"
R	Wallace Joseph F	100	fireman	56	
S	Wallace Mary F—†	100	housewife	49	"
T	Kussmaul Ernest F	100	retired	80	
U	Kussmaul Marguerita—†	100	housewife	72	"
V	Collatos Bessie—†	100	"	45	63 Emerald
W	Collatos Charles	100	student	23	63 "
X	Collatos Eva—†	100	saleswoman	21	63 "
Y	Collatos Nicholas	100	printer	50	63 "
Z	Connaughton James R	101	agent	35	here

836

A	Connaughton Theresa—†	101	housewife	35	"
B	Gavin Bridget—†	101	"	71	
C	Gavin Helen—†	101	operator	42	"
D	Gavin Martin	101	salesman	27	"
E	Gavin Thomas J	101	laborer	36	
G	Barry Louis	104	manager	60	"
H	Barry Rose—†	104	housewife	52	"
K	Barry Samuel	104	clerk	31	
L	Goldstein Benjamin	104	manager	40	"
M	Goldstein Clara—†	104	housewife	42	"
N	Wells Charles G	105	retired	77	
O	Wells Emily F—†	105	housewife	82	"
T	*Domey Johanna—†	109	housekeeper	74	"
U	*Emblum Arthur	109	laborer	40	"
V	*Emblum Margaret—†	109	housewife	40	"
W	Ward John H	109	teacher	42	"
X	Ward Mae L—†	109	housewife	40	"
Y	Sateriale Albert M	109	teacher	44	
Z	Sateriale Mary E—†	109	housewife	40	"

837   Olmstead Street

A	Moller Astrid A—†	8	clerk	25	here
B	Moller Elva S—†	8	housewife	50	"
C	Moller Maurice	8	metalworker	50	"

23

Page.	Letter.	FULL NAME.	Residence, Jan. 1, 1941.	Occupation.	Supposed Age.	Reported Residence, Jan. 1, 1940. Street and Number.

Olmstead Street—Continued

D	Ornstedt Gustaf A	8	metalworker	56	here
E	Ornstedt Laura K—†	8	student	23	"
F	Ornstedt Signe K—†	8	housewife	51	"
G	McVean Allen	8	engineer	33	"
H	McVean Jeanette—†	8	housewife	30	"
K	Koehler Doris M—†	10	"	36	
L	Koehler Harold O	10	inspector	39	"
M	Teichman Emil	10	manufacturer	59	7 Arcola
N	Teichman Selina—†	10	housewife	57	7 "
O	Rudolph Felix	10	operator	30	here
P*	Rudolph Freida—†	10	housewife	25	"
R	Cate Charlotte A—†	11	"	61	"
S	Cate Walter A	11	molder	66	
T	Gabrielson Gustaf A	11	machinist	62	"
U	Gabrielson Sophie C—†	11	housewife	64	"
V	Bergquist Fritz J	11	toolmaker	65	"
W	Bergquist Olga E—†	11	housewife	58	"
X	Pearson Emil	12	metalworker	63	"
Y	Pearson Zelma—†	12	housewife	57	"
Z	O'Donnell Catherine—†	12	nurse	43	10 Puritan rd
	838				
A	O'Donnell Dorothy—†	12	at home	20	10 "
B	Ekholm Carl D	12	machinist	57	here
C	Ekholm Valborg E—†	12	housewife	54	"
D	Donovan Catherine—†	14	at home	66	12 Olmstead
E	Goode Eileen—†	14	teacher	28	12 "
F	Goode Mary E—†	14	housewife	65	12 "
G	Cunningham Lila—†	15	at home	40	here
H	Doyle Francis J	15	restaurateur	51	"
K	Doyle Mary L—†	15	at home	61	"
L	Sullivan Catherine J—†	16	housewife	48	"
M	Sullivan Julia M—†	16	beautician	28	"
N	Sullivan Mary M—†	16	at home	22	
O	Sullivan Michael J	16	steamfitter	23	"
P	Sullivan Patrick J	16	tavernkeeper	58	"
R	Sullivan Thomas F	16	bartender	26	"
S	Cunningham Elizabeth—†	18	at home	82	
T	Cunningham Margaret—†	18	"	80	
U	Ulrich Anna—†	18	housewife	63	"
V	Ulrich James	18	U S A	22	
W	Ulrich John F	18	attendant	24	"

24

Olmstead Street—Continued

x	Ulrich Joseph H	18	lithographer	30	here
y	Ulrich Louise—†	18	hairdresser	25	"
z	Ulrich Martha A—†	18	bookkeeper	28	"
	839				
a	Ulrich Mary E—†	18	secretary	32	"
b	DerHohannesian Agavnie—†	19	at home	58	"
c	DerHohannesian Anna—†	19	clerk	22	
d	DerHohannesian Harry	19	salesman	32	"
e	DerHohannesian Levon	19	clerk	34	
f	Read Edwin S	19	chauffeur	37	"
g	Kelly Mary K—†	20	domestic	26	63 Moore
h	Murray Agnes G—†	20	clerk	46	here
k	Murray John T	20	retired	64	"
l	Murray Margaret E—†	20	auditor	58	"
m	Wall Michael	20	retired	95	
n	Moriarty Ellen F—†	23	stenographer	31	"
o	Moriarty Hannah M—†	23	housewife	66	"
p	Moriarty John E	23	clerk	27	
r	Moriarty Katherine M—†	23	"	29	
s	Moriarty Margaret C—†	23	stenographer	33	"
t	Moriarty Timothy J	23	student	26	..
u	*O'Brien Mary—†	23	at home	75	
v	McLaughlin Eileen B—†	24	decorator	32	"
w	McLaughlin William T	24	retired	72	
x	Carey Gertrude M—†	28	teacher	37	
y	Plunkett Agnes G—†	28	"	63	
z	Flynn Dorothea L—†	34	secretary	22	"
	840				
a	Flynn Edward J	34	manager	42	"
b	Flynn Marguerite L—†	34	housewife	42	"
c	Foley Mary F—†	38	"	58	"
d	Lyons Florence R—†	38	"	38	"
e	Lyons John J	38	engineer	43	"
f	Sullivan James F	38	mechanic	45	"

Park Lane

g	Deveney Martin F	4	manager	48	here
h	Devaney Minnie R—†	4	housewife	44	"
l	Bellamy Arthur	7	engineer	51	"

Page.	Letter.	FULL NAME.	Residence, Jan. 1, 1941.	Occupation.	Supposed Age.	Reported Residence, Jan. 1, 1940. Street and Number.

Park Lane—Continued

M	Bellamy Gladys H—†	7	housewife	39	here
N	Hale Carolyn—†	7	writer	60	"
O	Ormsby Daisy—†	8	housekeeper	55	"
P	Wight Evelyn—†	8	at home	74	"
R	Cooke Margaret—†	9	domestic	28	"
S	Crosby Alice B—†	9	at home	86	
T	Finklestein Helen—†	10	dietitian	31	
U	Finklestein Sarah—†	10	housewife	65	"
V	Nitz Anna F—†	12	"	67	
W	Nitz William H	12	inspector	67	"
X	Schuerer Anna C—†	12	bookkeeper	42	"
Y	Baker Anna V—†	14	secretary	54	"
Z	Baker Eleanor—†	14	clerk	25	

841

A	Lyons Joseph T	14	appraiser	63	"
B	Lyons Mary A—†	14	housewife	58	"
C	Lyons Robert J	14	engineer	56	
D	Sullivan Charles L	15	salesman	62	"
E	Sullivan James P	15	student	23	
F	Sullivan Mary H—†	15	housewife	60	"
G	Howe Joseph	18	laborer	62	
H	Keane Helga—†	18	at home	45	
K	Breen Ruth C—†	19	secretary	41	"
L	Ring Evelyn—†	19	housewife	28	69 Robeson
M	Ring Samuel	19	agent	37	69 "
N	Davidmeyer Frank H	28	electrician	65	here
O	Davidmeyer Mary A—†	28	housewife	52	"
P	Davidmeyer Mary G—†	28	secretary	32	"

Peter Parley Road

R	McLaughlin Catherine I—†	2	housewife	40	here
S	McLaughlin Charles P	2	clerk	42	"
T	Turner Arthur E	2	bookkeeper	35	"
U	Turner Frank S	2	attendant	67	"
V	Turner Mabel F—†	2	musician	26	"
W	Turner Nellie T—†	2	housewife	66	"
X	Creegan Catherine M—†	4	"	70	
Y	Creegan Margaret E—†	4	clerk	37	
Z	Creegan Veronica E—†	4	"	34	

842
Peter Parley Road—Continued

		FULL NAME.	Residence, Jan. 1, 1941.	Occupation.	Supposed Age.	Reported Residence Jan. 1, 1940
A	*Minehan Catherine—†	6	at home	74	here
B	Sheehan Annie J—†	6	housewife	55	"
C	Sheehan John J	6	guard	55	"
D	McCarthy Dorothy A—†	22	at home	33	
E	McCarthy Thomas V	22	merchant	33	"
F	McCready Frederick J	22	student	23	
G	McCready Genevieve—†	22	teacher	21	
H	McCready Leo T	22	physician	60	"
K	McCready Margaret J—†	22	housewife	56	"
L	Sheridan Marguerite—†	22	at home	25	
M	Sweeney Annie L—†	30	housewife	38	"
N	Sweeney Peter P	30	supervisor	51	"
O	Parlon Frank	32	retired	34	
P	Parlon Grace—†	32	teacher	32	
R	Parlou Thomas	32	agent	53	
S	Hoffman Edward W	34	teller	38	
T	Hoffman Hazel N—†	34	housewife	38	"
U	Coleman George S	42	engineer	56	
V	Coleman Mary A—†	42	housewife	50	"
W	Coleman Mary C—†	42	teacher	23	
X	Coleman Paul S	42	student	20	
Y	Coleman Winifred B—†	42	waitress	26	
Z	Cummings Agnes L—†	44	at home	60	

843

A	McLaughlin Joseph D	48	retired	69	
B	McLaughlin Mary A—†	48	housewife	62	"
C	*Marsh Hazel G—†	56	"	46	
D	Marsh John A	56	teacher	61	
E	Kelley Ellen E—†	64	housewife	63	"
F	Kelley Mary A—†	64	teacher	32	"
G	McCarthy Mary—†	64	"	50	
H	Sullivan Mary V—†	70	"	48	
K	Welch Grace S—†	70	housewife	43	"
L	Welch John F	70	banker	44	

School Street

N	Stone Anne—†	4	housewife	36	here
O	Stone Myer B	4	proprietor	36	"
R	Irving Dorothy F—†	6	housewife	36	"

School Street—Continued

s	*Irving John P	6	chauffeur	36	here
T	Parsons Charles G	6	laborer	31	Dedham
U	*Shine Jeremiah	6	chauffeur	60	here
V	Shine Margaret —†	6	housewife	65	"
W	Shine William	6	seaman	25	"
X	Reardon Mary—†	6	housewife	63	81 Coleman
Y	Reardon Michael	6	engineer	65	81 "
Z	Stanley Levi	8	basketmaker	28	33 St Francis de Sales

844

A	Stanley Martha H—†	8	housewife	29	33 "
B	White Forrest E	8	chauffeur	26	184 Centre
C	White Georgia E—†	8	housewife	26	184 "
D	Grimm Frederick	8	foreman	56	here
E	Grimm Marie—†	8	housewife	44	"
F	Frazer Catherine—†	10	operator	48	"
G	Cooper Bessie—†	10	at home	40	"
H	Murphy Catherine—†	10	housewife	35	"
K	Murphy Charles	10	tree surgeon	36	"
L	Ford Catherine F—†	12	at home	46	"
M	Coffin Marguerite—†	12	"	32	39 Bickford
O	Scipione Anna—†	18	housewife	58	here
P	Scipione Guerino F	18	welder	25	"
R	Scipione Josephine—†	18	cashier	20	"
S	Scipione Nickolo	18	retired	67	"
T	Ginkus John	18	laborer	35	
U	*Ginkus Mary—†	18	dressmaker	41	"
V	Riley Eva M—†	22	secretary	40	"
W	Donnelly Andrew R	22	clerk	23	
X	Donnelly Ellen V—†	22	housewife	56	"
Y	Donnelly Frank A	22	retired	57	
Z	Snyder Frank J	22	foreman	61	

845

A	Snyder Helen F—†	22	housewife	52	"
B	Hollinger Otto	22	painter	43	110 School
C	Hollinger Willa—†	22	housewife	32	110 "
E	Gilfeather Grace E—†	22	"	29	here
F	Gilfeather James D, jr	22	clerk	23	"
G	*McGrath Harold S	22	bottler	21	Somerville
H	McGrath Lorraine—†	22	housewife	20	"
K	Kelley Jennie—†	26	"	44	here
L	Kelley Martin	26	policeman	41	"

School Street—Continued

m	Fitzgerald Rebecca—†	26	housewife	32	here
n	Fitzgerald Walter E	26	technician	38	"
o	DeCoste Elizabeth—†	26	seamstress	46	"
p	Minden Frances—†	26	saleswoman	35	"
r	Minden Joseph	26	chauffeur	44	"
s	White Frieda—†	26	housewife	39	"
t	White Maurice—†	26	clerk	44	
u	Conkey Herbert F	26	"	53	
v	Conkey Lillian G—†	26	housewife	52	"
w	Dolan John	36	barber	25	64 School
x	Dolan Marjorie—†	36	housewife	23	64 "
y	McQueen Charles	36	foreman	45	Malden
z	McGrath Helen E—†	36	decorator	27	9 Harold
	846					
a	McGrath Herbert E	36	electrician	33	9 "
b	*McGrath Ida M—†	36	at home	38	9 '
c	McGrath Pearl—†	36	manager	36	9 "
d	Cunniff Frank	38	chauffeur	49	here
e	Cunniff Helen—†	38	housewife	44	"
f	Robertson James	38	laborer	56	"
g	Regan Ida—†	42	housewife	70	"
h	Regan Muriel—†	42	clerk	44	"
k	*Shire Edward	46	chauffeur	35	79 Waltham
l	*Shire Ruth—†	46	housewife	31	79 "
m	Davy Delia—†	46	"	62	here
n	Goldberg Natalie—†	46	"	30	"
o	Kayikjian Sarkis	48	painter	53	"
p	Kayikjian Vartouhy—†	48	housewife	44	"
r	McKeever Daniel L	48	student	20	"
s	McKeever James L	48	clerk	46	
t	McKeever Mary R—†	48	housewife	40	"
v	Lombardo Angelo	50	clerk	29	50 Spencer
w	Lombardo Trenta—†	50	housewife	22	34 Oakdale
x	Gore Catherine A—†	50	bookkeeper	56	here
y	Gore Joseph R	50	cutter	22	"
z	*Mallik Helen—†	50	waitress	46	"
	847					
a	Slattery Delia M—†	50	housewife	48	"
b	Slattery John J	50	salesman	52	"
c	Slattery Maria F—†	50	at home	83	
d	Malloy Emma G—†	52	housewife	37	"

School Street—Continued

E	Malloy William H	52	retired	50	here
F	Pepper Louis S	52	"	72	"
G	Pepper Mary J—†	52	housewife	58	"
H	Pepper Norman D	52	clerk	25	
K	Pepper Robert A	52	stenographer	20	"
L	Seabaugh Albert C	52	molder	59	"
M	Seabaugh Minnie E—†	52	housewife	52	"
N	Drew Frank J	54	clerk	66	
O	Drew Sarah G—†	54	housewife	43	"
P	McGowen Isabelle—†	54	"	50	"
R	McGowen Lloyd R	54	mechanic	43	"
S	Buckley Timothy	54	laborer	38	"
T	Redmond Arthur P	56	electrician	53	"
U	Redmond Mary E—†	56	housewife	46	"
V	Maniatis Demetrios	56	baker	70	
W	Maniatis Xanthippe—†	56	dressmaker	52	"
X	Hachadoorian Balsam	56	guard	63	"
Y	Hachadoorian Helen Y—†	56	housewife	61	"

848

A	Bryant Evelyn M—†	60	stenographer	31	"
B	Carrol Elizabeth—†	60	at home	62	"
C	Morabito Camella—†	60	"	56	
D	Morabito Paul	60	clerk	29	"
E	McCool Catherine—†	60	housewife	37	35 School
F	McCool Floyd	60	painter	38	35 "
G	Crawford Astrid E—†	60	housewife	29	here
H	Crawford Robert G	60	clerk	32	"
K	Cummings Gertrude—†	64	housewife	30	"
L	Cummings James	64	operator	38	"
M	Carroll John H	64	baker	24	Waltham
N	Carroll Pauline—†	64	housewife	25	88 Wyman
O	Visnorovitz Elba—†	64	"	24	here
P	Visnorovitz Walter	64	presser	29	"
R	Rice Annie E—†	66	at home	63	"
S	Rice Ethel M—†	66	stenographer	28	"
T	Rice George M	68	engineer	34	"
U	Rice Jean—†	68	housewife	26	"
V	*Backman Adolph	70	molder	56	2949 Wash'n
W	Backman Edwin H	70	shipper	20	2949 "
X	*Backman Ellen—†	70	housewife	46	2949 "

Page.	Letter.	FULL NAME.	Residence, Jan. 1, 1941.	Occupation.	Supposed Age.	Reported Residence, Jan. 1, 1940. Street and Number.

School Street—Continued

| | Y | Backman Helen—† | 70 | bookkeeper | 22 | 2949 Wash'n |
| | z | Levis Lucy P—† | 70 | housewife | 49 | here |

849   Walnut Avenue

	D	Stone Dora M—†	427	housewife	69	here
	E	Stone Samuel	427	storekeeper	71	"
	F	Donlan John	429	laborer	25	"
	G	*Donlan Margaret—†	429	housewife	48	"
	H	Donlan Michael	429	plasterer	48	"
	K	Keefe Mary—†	rear 429	seamstress	31	"
	M	Wellman Charles D	431	salesman	31	"
	N	Wellman Julia F—†	431	housewife	65	"
	R	Sinabian Genevieve—†	433	housekeeper	37	"
	S	*Shapiro Bessie—†	433	housewife	72	"
	T	*Shapiro Nathan	433	laborer	74	
	U	Harris Aaron	435	tailor	72	
	V	*Harris Bertha—†	435	housewife	67	"
	W	Ludwig Deborah H—†	435	secretary	27	"
	X	Ludwig Melvin S	435	clerk	29	
	Y	Abrams Bessie—†	435	housewife	66	"
	Z	Abrams Richard	435	clerk	31	

850

	A	Abrams Thomas	435	proprietor	66	"
	B	Nesman Fay—†	435	housewife	30	"
	C	Nesman Jack	435	salesman	33	"
	D	Rich Bertha—†	435	housewife	61	"
	E	Rich Maurice	435	engineer	35	
	F	Rich Saul A	435	salesman	62	"
	G	Weener Joseph	435	dentist	48	
	H	Weener Minnie M—†	435	housewife	47	"
	K	Gordon Emma—†	435	"	30	"
	L	Gordon Irving	435	salesman	35	"
	M	Bronkhorst Julia—†	435	housewife	50	"
	N	Bronkhorst Nathan	435	porter	55	
	O	*Supranas Beatrice R—†	435	operator	25	
	P	*Supranas Mary—†	435	hosewife	55	··
	R	Litvan Robert	435	U S A	22	
	S	*Meshon Fannie—†	435	housekeeper	58	"
	T	Phillips Anne—†	435	housewife	27	"

Page.	Letter.	FULL NAME.	Residence, Jan. 1, 1941.	Occupation.	Supposed Age.	Reported Residence, Jan. 1, 1940. Street and Number.

Walnut Avenue—Continued

	U	Phillips George J	435	tailor	37	here
	V	Starr Florence—†	435	housewife	25	Medford
	W	Starr Milton	435	salesman	28	"
	X	Allen Albert	435	painter	32	Milton
	Y	Allen Mollie W—†	435	housewife	30	44 Pasadena rd
	Z	Slade Celia—†	435	cashier	26	35 Lawrence av
851						
		Slade Samuel	435	manager	34	35 "
		Singer Dora—†	439	housewife	40	here
		Singer Paul	439	salesman	43	"
		McGonagle Helen—†	439	operator	36	"
		McGonagle Phillip	439	salesman	44	"
	A B	McGonagle William	439	clerk	20	
	G	McGee Alexander	441	retired	71	
	H	McGee Eleanor J—†	441	housewife	59	"
	K	Tierney Alvina V—†	445	"	31	
	L	*Tierney Joseph E	445	shipper	36	
	M	Cosgrove Joseph P	445	laborer	40	
	N	Cosgrove Rose—†	445	housewife	33	"
	O	French Elsa A—†	447	"	32	90 Marcella
	P	French Mark	447	operator	31	90 "
	R	Sessler Aagot—†	447	housewife	58	here
	S	Sessler Jacob	447	baker	63	"
	T	Shepard Bertha L—†	449	housewife	36	"
	U	Shepard Charles E, jr	449	janitor	34	
	V	*Raymond Maurice	449	clerk	34	"
	W	Raymond Rita—†	449	housewife	30	"
	X	*Siegal Max	449	retired	75	
	Y	*Siegal Sarah—†	449	housewife	73	"
	Z	Coppelman Isaac P	449	manufacturer	68	"
852						
	A	Coppelman Rose—†	449	housewife	67	"
	B	Galben Sarah—†	449	stenographer	41	Newton
	D	Leeder Annie—†	449	clerk	40	here
	E	*Leeder Celia—†	449	housewife	65	"
	F	Leeder Harold	449	salesman	26	"
	G	Leeder Louis	449	bookkeeper	36	"
	H	Leeder Simon	449	manufacturer	66	"
	K	Gass Fannie—†	449	housewife	48	"
	L	Gass Louis	449	proprietor	50	"
	M	Gass Marcia—†	449	clerk	22	"
	N	Remer Carl	449	"	42	Springfield

Walnut Avenue—Continued

o	Remer Sara—†	449	housewife	39	Springfield
p	Reitman Bella—†	449	bookkeeper	37	20 Deckard
r	Reitman Mary—†	449	stenographer	36	20 "
s	Reitman Rixie—†	449	bookkeeper	25	20 "
t	Reitman Samuel	449	newsboy	36	20 "
u	Hoffman Rebecca—†	451	at home	66	here
v	Lewis Jeanne H—†	451	housewife	41	"
w	Lewis Maurice H	451	salesman	43	"
x	Kanter Mae—†	451	housewife	45	"
y	Kanter Nathan	451	tailor	46	
z	Kanter Selma—†	451	stenographer	20	"

853

a	Krapur Jeannette T—†	451	clerk	36	
b	Vernick Elizabeth—†	451	housewife	34	"
c	Vernick Victor	451	manager	35	"
d	Brooker Anne—†	451	stenographer	27	31 Lawrence av
e	Brooker Etta—†	451	housewife	51	31 "
f	Brooker Ida—†	451	bookkeeper	20	31 "
g	Brooker Pearl—†	451	secretary	21	31 "
h	Brooker Rose—†	451	stenographer	24	31 "
m	*Berman Ethel—†	461	at home	67	here
n	Weiner Lee—†	461	housewife	32	"
o	Weiner Samuel J	461	attorney	38	"
p	Neustadt Bessie—†	461	housewife	70	"
r	Neustadt Joseph	461	realtor	75	
s	Karp John	461	agent	46	
t	Karp Mary—†	461	housewife	46	"
u	*Finklestein Ida—†	461	at home	72	20 Seaver
v	Finklestein Ruth—†	461	saleswoman	45	20 "
w	Finland Sarah—†	461	housewife	42	20 "
x	*Rosen Lena—†	461	"	48	here
y	*Rosen Morris	461	merchant	48	"
z	Kisloff Esther—†	461	bookkeeper	39	"

854

a	Kisloff Louis	461	salesman	45	"
b	Lynn Isabella—†	489	domestic	42	"
c	Scannell David D	489	physician	65	"
d	Scannell David D, jr	489	attorney	27	
e	Scannell Elizabeth A—†	489	housewife	64	"
g	Baker John W	495	retired	80	New Jersey
h	Bradley Eleanor R—†	495	nurse	24	here
k	Bradley Frederick E	495	teacher	29	"

Walnut Avenue—Continued

L	Bradley Gerald W	495	proprietor	20	here
M	Bradley Kathleen L—†	495	nurse	26	"
N	Bradley Marjorie M—†	495	bookkeeper	22	"
O	Bradley Mary F—†	495	at home	52	"
P	Bradley Warren F	495	shipfitter	23	"
R	Donovan Ellen—†	495	at home	79	65 School
S	Martin Mary—†	495	"	72	here
T	Seward Benjamin E	495	retired	49	"
U	White Albert	495	"	67	"

Washington Street

V	McDonough Mark	3140	clerk	31	here
W	McDonough Mary E—†	3140	housewife	66	"
X	Ryan Kathryn L—†	3140½	clerk	24	Canada
Y	Saunders Douglas L	3140½	manager	21	116 School
Z	Saunders Ellsworth L	3140½	superintendent	42	116 "
	855				
A	Saunders Lilah B—†	3140½	housewife	44	Canada
D	McLaren Agnes R—†	3142B	operator	32	here
E	McLaren John C	3142B	laborer	22	"
F	McLaren Lillian R—†	3142B	operator	27	"
G	*McLaren Sarah—†	3142B	domestic	55	"
H	*McLaren Thomas	3142B	machinist	58	"
K	McLaren Thomas	3142B	laborer	25	"
L	Munier Margaret J—†	3144A	at home	65	109 W Sixth
M	Munier Paul J	3144A	printer	27	109 "
N	Johnson Thomas E	3144A	attendant	22	33 Blakeville
O	Levingston Annie—†	3144A	housewife	47	here
P	Levingston Louis	3144A	salesman	53	"
R	Fitzgerald Helen K—†	3144A	housewife	39	3 Beale
S	*Fitzgerald Walter J	3144A	counterman	35	3 "
T	Dolan Arthur T	3144A	shipper	43	here
U	Dolan Sadie J—†	3144A	at home	51	"
V	*Logan Beatrice T—†	3144A	housewife	35	253 Highland
W	*Logan John J	3144A	laborer	37	253 "
X	Villari Joseph S	3144A	barber	24	here
Y	Villari Ruth E—†	3144A	housewife	24	"
Z	Hollis Charles	3144A	foreman	75	"
	856				
A	White Marjorie L—†	3144A	cashier	31	3451 Wash'n

Page	Letter	FULL NAME.	Residence, Jan. 1, 1941.	Occupation.	Supposed Age.	Reported Residence, Jan. 1, 1940. Street and Number.

Washington Street—Continued

c	MacKay Isabelle—†	3144C	housewife	65	here
d	MacKay Kenneth M	3144C	retired	71	"
f	Holden Catherine C—†	3146	housewife	64	"
g	Holden James J	3146	chauffeur	35	"
h	Holden Katherine M-†	3146	operator	26	"
k	Holden William M	3146	laborer	33	
l	Fleming Margaret E—†	3146	stitcher	46	
m	Arsenault Alyre	3148	carpenter	42	"
n	*Arsenault Marion—†	3148	housewife	38	"
o	Nickerson Bernard I	3148	laborer	36	
p	Nickerson Violetta M-†	3148	housewife	38	"
r	Nee Mary K—†	3148	"	48	52 Thomas pk
s	Nee Patrick V	3148	laborer	52	52 "
t	Broderick Edith F—†	3150	housewife	31	Rhode Island
u	Broderick James L	3150	mechanic	30	"
v	*MacAulay Ann—†	3150	nurse	31	here
w	*MacAulay John W	3150	ironworker	34	"
x	Waters Elmer F	3150	laborer	22	"
y	Waters Mary E—†	3150	housewife	55	"
z	Waters Myrtle M—†	3150	seamstress	28	"
	857				
d	Hing Wong Ark	3158	laundryman	44	"
f	Argyris Markus P	3161	tailor	42	
h	Scriven Helen J—†	3163	housewife	20	"
k	Scriven Lawrence C	3163	laborer	24	
l	Bosonac Nellie E—†	3163	housewife	34	"
m	Bosonac Robert L	3163	laborer	40	
x	LeBlanc Edward E	3171	mechanic	38	"
y	LeBlanc John B	3171	painter	64	"
z	Sheehan Clifford C	3171	U S A	21	143 Cabot
	858				
a	Sheehan Mina M—†	3171	housewife	51	143 "
l	*McGonagle Anna—†	3189	"	40	12 Haverford
m	McGonagle Hugh	3189	laborer	40	12 "
n	*Kelly Helen T—†	3189	housewife	31	3274 Wash'n
o	Kelly Phillip	3189	gardener	34	3274 "
x	Phee Henry F	3224	retired	77	here
y	Cheever Annie F—†	3224	housewife	42	"
z	Cheever John C	3224	painter	44	"
	859				
a	Briscoe John J	3226	chauffeur	43	"

35

Washington Street—Continued

B	Briscoe Margaret T—†	3226	housewife	43	here
C	Briscoe Mary L—†	3226	packer	20	"
D	Callahan Joseph D	3226	clerk	23	"
E	Mitchell Daniel F	3226	salesman	44	"
F	Mitchell Gladys E—†	3226	housewife	41	"
G	Vaughn Everett S	3226A	salesman	40	"
H	Vaughn Mary R—†	3226A	housewife	32	"
K	Sanger Calvin O	3228	painter	71	
L	Sanger Joseph H	3228	clerk	41	
M	Sanger Nora F—†	3228	housewife	71	"
N	Burton Bernard	3228A	cutter	45	
O	Norman Herbert L	3228A	laborer	25	
P	Norman Margaret J—†	3228A	housewife	44	"
R	Callahan Cornelius J	3228A	laborer	39	
S	Callahan Gladys M—†	3228A	housewife	36	"
T	Ryan Helen A—†	3230	"	40	
U	Ryan Herbert J	3230	cutter	40	
V	Blair Josephine G—†	3230	housewife	39	"
W	McHassell John L	3230A	machinist	53	"
X	McHassell Margaret—†	3230A	housewife	52	"
Y	Curran Francis J	3232	laborer	23	
Z	Talbot Catherine A—†	3232	housekeeper	74	"

860

A	Wallace Catherine L—†	3232A	housewife	33	3274 Wash'n
B	Thompson Anna R—†	3232A	"	38	here
C	Thompson Walter J	3232A	chauffeur	31	"
D	Koenig Edwin P	3234	instructor	37	"
E	Koenig Leila J—†	3234	housewife	47	"
F	*Martin Sarah A—†	3234	"	30	
G	Martin William E	3234	laborer	32	
H	*Kent Agnes A—†	3234A	housewife	40	"
K	Kent James A	3234A	laborer	38	"
L	Sullivan Anna T—†	3236	bookkeeper	26	2679 Wash'n
M	Sullivan James J	3236	laborer	60	2679 "
N	Sullivan James V	3236	chauffeur	23	2679 "
O	Golding Joseph H	3236	laborer	38	here
P	Golding Mary C—†	3236	housewife	39	"
R	Cairnes Amathy A—†	3236	"	26	Needham
S	Cairnes Arthur	3236	bottler	53	here
T	Cairnes Bertha M—†	3236	housewife	55	"
U	Cairnes Robert L	3236	carpenter	28	"

Page.	Letter.	FULL NAME.	Residence, Jan. 1, 1941.	Occupation.	Supposed Age.	Reported Residence, Jan. 1, 1940. Street and Number.

Washington Street—Continued

	v	Cairnes Walter T	3236	chauffeur	25	Needham
	w	Partridge Dorothy L—†	3238	housewife	30	here
	x	Partridge Horace E	3238	instructor	34	"
	y	Bowden Arthur L	3238	shoemaker	36	"
	z	Bowden Mae F—†	3238	housewife	36	"
861						
	a	*Perry Catherine A—†	3238	"	49	
	b	*Perry John J	3238	steelworker	50	"
	c	Johnston Eleanor A—†	3240	housewife	37	"
	d	Johnston John G	3240	instructor	50	"
	e	Murphy Andrew F	3240	bartender	39	201 Boylston
	f	Murphy Marie F—†	3240	housewife	41	201 "
	g	Healy Helen L—†	3240	"	49	here
	h	Healy John J	3240	attendant	22	"

Ward 11—Precinct 9

CITY OF BOSTON

LIST OF RESIDENTS
20 YEARS OF AGE AND OVER

(NON-CITIZENS INDICATED BY ASTERISK)
(FEMALES INDICATED BY DAGGER)

AS OF

JANUARY 1, 1941

JOSEPH F. TIMILTY, *Chairman*
FREDERIC E. DOWLING, *Secretary*
WILLIAM A. MOTLEY, JR.
FRANCIS B. McKINNEY
HILDA HEDSTROM QUIRK

Listing Board.

CITY OF BOSTON PRINTING DEPARTMENT

900

Adams Circle

A	Lohrer Elizabeth L—†	3	housewife	50	here
B	Lohrer Leo	3	engineer	51	"
C	Lohrer Martin R	3	student	23	"
D	Connolly Charles	5	shipfitter	22	706 Adams
E	Connolly Theresa—†	5	housewife	20	25 Sheridan
F	Lyons Emily—†	5	"	27	23 Ferrin
G	Lyons Joseph	5	strawcutter	34	22 "
H	Sheridan Louise L—†	5	at home	29	2261 Dor av
K	*Trabish Mary—†	7	housewife	46	5 Weldon
L	*Trabish William	7	salesman	47	5 "
M	Sullivan Edna M—†	7	housewife	26	7 Cline
N	Sullivan Roy B	7	operator	32	7 "

Amory Street

O	Droid Helen—†	170	domestic	36	here
P	Kinch Marion—†	170	"	54	9 Chilcott pl
R	Zalis Lena—†	170	clerk	33	here
S	Felton James F	170	roofer	52	"
T	Felton Prudence—†	170	housewife	58	"
U	Harvey Roy	170	salesman	45	"
V	Johnson Maude—†	170	housewife	59	"
W	Kelley Timothy	170	decorator	41	"
X	Shea Susan E—†	170	housekeeper	53	"
Y	Talanian Sarah—†	186	housewife	32	79 Atherton
Z	Talanian Sumpad	186	merchant	35	79 "

901

A	*Talanian Yeghsa—†	186	at home	56	79 "
B	Meier Alice M—†	186	housewife	50	126 Centre
C	Meier Robert	186	baker	47	126 "
D	McEleaney Alexander	186	clerk	22	here
E	McEleaney Eleanor—†	186	teacher	24	"
F	McEleaney Neil	186	janitor	50	"
G	Griffin Daniel	188	gardener	45	"
H	Griffin Elizabeth—†	188	housewife	42	"
K	Nanian Arthur H	190	merchant	36	"
L	Nanian Roxie—†	190	housewife	34	"
M	Cummings Irene—†	190	clerk	29	
N	Cummings John J	190	shipper	57	
O	Cummings Mary—†	190	housewife	58	"

2

Page.	Letter.	Full Name.	Residence, Jan. 1, 1941.	Occupation.	Supposed Age.	Reported Residence, Jan. 1, 1940. Street and Number.

Amory Street—Continued

	P	Cummings Veronica—†	190	operator	31	here
	R	Cummings William	190	factoryhand	28	"
	S	Bates Albert H	192	tailor	47	269 Lamartine
	T	Bates Bella S—†	192	housewife	48	269 "
	U	Butler Thomas J	192	laborer	32	here
	V	*Kileen Delia—†	192	housewife	45	"
	W	Kileen Francis	192	attendant	21	"
	X	Kileen Mary—†	192	factoryhand	22	"
	Y	Kileen Patrick	192	laborer	47	..
	Z	Myers Anna—†	194	waitress	28	
902						
	A	Myers Helen—†	194	clerk	24	
	B	Myers Nellie—†	194	housewife	62	"
	C	Rivard Emile J	196	fireman	42	
	D	Rivard Hermine—†	196	housewife	45	"
	E	Blood Arthur J	196	mechanic	25	"
	F	Blood Bertha—†	196	housewife	47	"
	G	Blood James E	196	printer	51	
	H	Blood Norma H—†	196	clerk	20	
	K	McCoy Edward	198	salesman	26	"
	L	McCoy Helen—†	198	saleswoman	20	"
	M	McCoy Loretta—†	198	operator	24	"
	N	McCoy Margaret—†	198	domestic	27	"
	O	*McCoy Mary—†	198	housewife	57	"
	P	McCoy Mary—†	198	operator	28	
	R	McCoy Walter	198	laborer	22	
	S	Connolly Mary A—†	200	teacher	47	
	T	Fitzpatrick Edmund S	200	clerk	29	
	U	Fitzpatrick Mary C—†	200	housewife	23	"
	V	Gallagher James	200	carpenter	60	"
	W	Gallagher Margaret A—†	200	housewife	52	"
	X	Doherty Eileen M—†	200	clerk	27	
	Y	Doherty Margaret A—†	200	matron	60	
	Z	Cowen Lillian—†	210	housekeeper	32	"
903						
	A	Sullivan John J	210	salesman	35	"
	B	Sullivan Mildred—†	210	housewife	35	"
	C	Glazebrooke John	210	clerk	30	Medford
	D	Glazebrooke Mildred—†	210	housewife	28	here
	E	Anderson Gertrude—†	210	factoryhand	41	"
	F	Anderson Jeanette—†	210	"	32	"

3

Amory Street—Continued

G	Fitzpatrick Gertrude—†	210	housewife	34	here
H	Fitzpatrick James	210	chauffeur	35	"
K	Lamond Freida—†	210	housewife	37	"
L	Lamond George	210	clerk	41	"
N	Evans Hugh	213	molder	25	85 Fort av
O	Gerstel William C	213	janitor	56	here
P	Gerstel Freda—†	213	housewife	55	"
R	Gerstel Walter	213	clerk	31	"
S	O'Donnell Hugh	215	tree surgeon	27	"
T	O'Donnell Philip	215	chauffeur	29	"
U	Whitman Harry	215	laborer	33	
V	*Hackey Katherine M—†	215	maid	34	
W	*McLean Jennie—†	215	"	60	
X	*McLean Mary J—†	215	housekeeper	38	"
Y	*Schwollman Eliza—†	215	housewife	60	"
Z	*Schwollman William	215	machinist	67	"

904

A	Fallon Rita—†	217	housewife	23	Rhode Island
B	Fallon Stephen	217	foundryman	26	"
D	*Donlon Clementine—†	217	housewife	30	here
E	Donlon James	217	doorman	30	"
F	Manley Isabelle—†	217	housekeeper	35	"
G	Brinkert Alice—†	219	housewife	37	"
H	Brinkert Frederick	219	shipper	39	"
K	Perrello Evelyn—†	219	housewife	21	6 Alfred
L	Perrello Ralph	219	chauffeur	26	6 "
M	Burns John	219	shipper	32	7 Rollins ct
N	Burns Maria—†	219	housewife	28	7 "
O	Treeler Esther—†	221	housekeeper	51	15 Dresden
R	Walker Emily G—†	221	housewife	42	here
S	Negri Frank	222	contractor	46	34 Bushnell
T	*Negri Ida—†	222	housewife	49	34 "
U	Murray Francis	223	shipworker	29	here
V	Murray John T	223	painter	60	"
W	Murray Joseph	223	factoryhand	21	"
X	Murray Rose E—†	223	housewife	48	"
Y	Murray Thomas F	223	bartender	51	"
Z	Paul Anna—†	223	operator	30	6 Porter

905

A	Harcbacker Edwin	225	painter	32	here
B	Harcbacker Martha—†	225	housewife	71	"

Amory Street—Continued

c	Harcbacker William	225	laborer	34	here
E	Taylor Hannah—†	226	at home	80	39 Bickford
F	Sheehan Madeline F—†	226	housekeeper	46	here
G	DeCoste Albert	227	bookkeeper	22	"
H	DeCoste Augusta	227	ironworker	54	"
K	DeCoste Elizabeth B—†	227	housewife	43	"
L	Saunders Augusta—†	229	"	50	
M	Saunders William G, jr	229	laborer	26	
N	Esterbrook Lena—†	230	housewife	37	"
O	Esterbrook Leon	230	chauffeur	38	"
P	Weigold Arthur C	230	shipper	31	
R	Weigold Clara—†	230	housekeeper	65	"
S	Madden James	230	messenger	21	"
T	Madden Paul	230	compositor	23	"
U	Madden Thomas C	230	shipper	26	
V	Madden Thomas J	230	breweryworker	46	"
W	Madden Viola H—†	230	housewife	45	"
X	Roberts Irma—†	231	"	39	"
Y	Hankins Clair—†	233	"	39	
Z	Hankins Joseph	233	painter	47	
	906				
A	*Seagel August	234	porter	35	24 Marcella
B	Seagel Augusta M—†	234	housewife	38	24 "
D	Griffin Bertha—†	234	clerk	41	here
E	Stegmaier Mary—†	234	housewife	71	"
F	Perrotto Biagio	235	bricklayer	43	"
G	*Perrotto Secondina—†	235	housewife	33	"
H	Powers Marie—†	236	"	40	
K	Powers Michael	236	shipper	44	"
L	Cronin Florence—†	236	housewife	23	20 Walden
M	Steinberg Henry	236	chauffeur	25	20 "
N	*Steinberg Lydia—†	236	domestic	55	20 "
O	Stegerman Anna—†	236	housewife	80	here
P	Stegerman Herman	236	factoryhand	40	"
R	Breen David	237	laborer	68	"
S	Breen Harold E	237	"	30	
T	Breen Marie Y—†	237	housewife	28	"
U	Breen Selina M—†	237	"	53	
V	Cossette Marion—†	237	laundress	27	"
W	Holmes Dorothy—†	239	housewife	29	32 Newark
X	Holmes Joseph D	239	carpenter	30	32 "

Amory Street—Continued

Y	*Lavoie Oliver	241	longshoreman	54	here
z	Lavoie Rose—†	241	housewife	52	"

907

A	O'Rourke Dennis	243	laborer	45	
B	*O'Rourke Susan—†	243	housewife	41	"
C	*Lucier Ellen—†	245	"	40	
D	Lucier Walter	245	laborer	41	
E	Wiklund Oscar	247	watchman	55	"

Arcadia Street

H	Sullivan Catherine—†	1	clerk	26	26 Codman
K	Sullivan Thomas J	1	chauffeur	26	73 Montebello rd
L	Sawyer Harold I	1	salesman	35	here
M	Sawyer Ida M—†	1	housewife	36	"
N	Arnold Ethel—†	2	at home	52	4 Dalrymple
O	Arnold Marjorie—†	2	musician	22	4 "
P	Davis Frank A	2	builder	53	Somerville
R	Davis Roland A	2	manager	30	"
S	Davis Wilhelmina H—†	2	housewife	56	"
T	Hill Julia B—†	3	at home	89	here
U	Simpson Ella B—†	3	nurse	61	"
V	Simpson George E	3	"	61	"
W	Spendler Catherine—†	3	retired	90	178 Boylston
X	Roulston Amos C	4	blacksmith	61	here
Y	Roulston Bertha—†	4	housewife	58	"
Z	Roulston Eleanor—†	4	saleswoman	23	"

908

A	Roulston Lillian—†	4	clerk	21	
B	Senf Emma—†	4	housewife	58	"
C	Senf Richard W	4	broker	59	
D	Bourque Joseph	5	manager	46	"
E	Bourque Olive—†	5	clerk	41	
F	Coghlan Josephine—†	5	housekeeper	50	"
G	Murray Alice E—†	5	housewife	36	53 Mozart
H	Murray Joseph W	5	clerk	50	53 "
K	Cushing Dorothy G—†	6	teacher	32	here
L	Cushing Helen E—†	6	secretary	27	"
M	Cushing Sarah A—†	6	housewife	59	"
N	Fitzgerald Thomas D	6	retired	70	
O	Hogarty Frank M	6	salesman	57	"

Page.	Letter.	FULL NAME.	Residence, Jan. 1, 1941.	Occupation.	Supposed Age.	Reported Residence, Jan. 1, 1940. Street and Number.

Arcadia Street—Continued

P	Day Charles L	7	electrician	20	here
R	*Day Margaret C—†	7	housewife	48	"
S	Day Margaret H—†	7	housekeeper	25	"
T	Day Walter E	7	salesman	54	"
U	Day Walter J	7	electrician	23	"
V	MacDonald Lillian G—†	7	housewife	28	"
W	MacDonald Robert	7	manager	29	"

Atherton Street

X	Quinn Alexander	28	laundryman	62	here
Y	Quinn Josephine—†	28	housewife	61	"
Z	Quinn Theresa H—†	28	presser	23	"
	909				
A	Conway Katherine C—†	30	nurse	21	Gloucester
B	Koehler Emma L—†	30	housewife	60	here
C	Feeley Gertrude—†	36	"	50	"
D	Feeley Mary T—†	36	student	21	"
E	Doucette Anna—†	36	housewife	60	Florida
F	Fettig Emma—†	36		46	here
G	Fettig Joseph	36	waiter	47	"
H	Clark Dorothy—†	38	nurse	21	"
K	Hayner Joseph	38	retired	53	"
L	Hayner Marie M—†	38	housewife	51	"
M	Mullen Ada F—†	42	"	53	
N	Mullen James E	42	pharmacist	58	"
O	Fotch Gisela—†	46	at home	78	"
P	Schmitz Henry J	46	foreman	58	
R	Schmitz Henry T	46	student	21	
S	Schmitz Olga—†	46	housewife	58	"
U	Haffenreffer Christine M–†	48	"	77	
T	Sessler Anna L—†	48	housekeeper	50	"
V	Crockett George R	50	manager	59	"
W	Crockett Helen R—†	50	at home	28	
X	Crockett Jennie E—†	50	housewife	59	"
Y	Moras Anna—†	52	at home	64	
Z	Parker Anita—†	52	winder	20	"
	910				
A	Parker August J	52	machinist	45	"
B	Parker Gertrude—†	52	housewife	40	"
C	Schaaf Ernest R	52	carpenter	44	N Hampshire

Page.	Letter.	FULL NAME.	Residence, Jan. 1. 1941.	Occupation.	Supposed Age.	Reported Residence, Jan. 1, 1940. Street and Number.

Atherton Street—Continued

| | D | Schaaf Mabel E—† | 52 | housewife | 41 | N Hampshire |
| | E | Schmidt Lena—† | 52 | at home | 86 | here |

Bismarck Street

	G	Murphy Mary—†	5	stitcher	46	here
	H	Mills Harvey	5	U S N	20	"
	K	Wallace Patrick	5	steamfitter	50	"
	M	Krause August	11	retired	85	
	N	Evans James	13	laborer	32	
	O	Evans Lillian—†	13	housewife	37	"
	P	Connell Margaret—†	13	"	36	
	R	Connell Thomas F	13	chauffeur	48	"
	S	Cappel Karl	13	breweryworker	52	"
	T	Cappel Laura R—†	13	housewife	43	"
	U	Golding Emma R—†	13	assembler	22	"

Boylston Place

	V	Dillion Burton J	1	manager	30	here
	W	Dillion Ruth G—†	1	housewife	30	"
	X	Meikle Harold W	1	clerk	31	"
	Y	Speierman Alma A—†	1	housewife	64	"
	Z	Speierman Arthur C	1	bookkeeper	33	"
911						
	A	*Speierman Elizabeth—†	1	packer	34	"
	B	Taylor Dorothy—†	1	housewife	33	22 Forest Hills
	C	Taylor Sidney	1	chauffeur	35	22 "
	D	Tennihan Anna H—†	3	housewife	64	here
	E	Tennihan Joseph H	3	retired	70	"
	F	Mahoney-Eva B—†	3	housewife	66	"
	G	McCarthy Mary B—†	3	at home	70	
	H	Woodside Alfred	4	clerk	32	
	K	Woodside Helen C—†	4	housewife	25	"
	M	Sharpe Caroline A—†	4	packer	22	
	L	Sharpe Clara L—†	4	housewife	53	"
	N	Sharpe Percy	4	operator	53	"
	O	Burton James	4	machinist	68	"
	P	Thornton Mary E—†	8	housewife	23	15 Oakview ter
	R	Thornton Michael J	8	shipper	36	15 "
	S	McLellan Gordon	8	carpenter	57	here

8

Boylston Place—Continued

T	McLellan Gordon, jr	8	electrician	20	here
U	McLellan Magdalene—†	8	housewife	57	"
V	Frey Dorothy—†	rear 8	bookkeeper	29	"
W	Frey Marie B—†	" 8	housewife	56	"

Boylston Street

X	Marshman Mildred—†	123	housewife	62	Brookline
Y	*Marshman William	123	painter	64	85 Lamartine
Z	*Doyle Michael	123	operator	66	here
	912				
A	Reardon Leonard	123	chauffeur	32	"
B	Reardon Mary—†	123	housewife	33	"
C	Moore Francis A	123	chauffeur	24	"
D	*Moore Joseph	123	butcher	52	
E	*Moore Mary—†	123	housewife	50	"
F	MacLeod John	125	floorlayer	67	"
G	*MacLeod Julia—†	125	housewife	68	"
H	Dustin James E	125	laborer	55	
K	Dustin Mary E—†	125	housewife	39	"
L	Moore Bernice H—†	125	"	24	"
M	Moore William A	125	painter	24	
V	Limmer Mary—†	135	housewife	42	"
W	Limmer Peter	135	shoeworker	45	"
X	Limmer Peter, jr	135	"	20	"
Y	Drinkman Harriet—†	135	housewife	48	"
Z	Drinkman Julius	135	supervisor	48	"
	913				
C	Cameron Angela—†	145	housewife	22	"
D	Cameron Malcolm	145	entertainer	36	"
E	Schofield Anna—†	145	housewife	44	"
F	Schofield Joseph L	145	repairman	37	"
G	Berry Catherine F—†	146	housewife	31	"
H	Berry James C	146	painter	31	
K	Boates Howard F	146	machinist	32	"
L	*Boates Norine S—†	146	housewife	35	"
M	Cryan Helen A—†	146	"	50	29 Cobden
N	Cryan Michael F	146	laborer	49	29 "
O	Lindblad Aile H—†	146	housewife	36	here
P	Lindblad Otto	146	salesman	37	"
R	Quirk Bridget M—†	146	housewife	48	"

Boylston Street—Continued

s	Quirk John J	146	sexton	24	here
t	Hulbert George A	146	mechanic	30	15 Beethoven
u	Hulbert Mary H—†	146	housewife	22	15 "
v	Hartwig Elise—†	147	"	33	here
w	Hartwig Kurt P	147	paperhanger	35	"
y	*Small Annie—†	150	at home	61	"
z	*White Charles	150	retired	85	

914

a	*White Melina—†	150	housewife	76	"
b	*Apolon Adolph	150	painter	43	
c	*Apolon Jennie—†	150	at home	68	"
d	Tector Alfred J	151	plumber	33	"
e	Tector James J	151	retired	72	
f	*Tector Nora—†	151	housewife	36	"
g	*Connors Catherine—†	152	at home	70	7 Brookside av
h	Shedrick Hannah E—†	152	housewife	50	here
k	Shedrick Ivan B—†	152	laborer	55	"
l	Burton Alice—†	152	housewife	55	"
m	Linden Michael F	153	laborer	60	
n	Martin Guy M	153	conductor	61	"
o	Martin Susan M—†	153	housewife	53	"
p	Ihlefeldt Edmund G	153	breweryworker	45	"
r	Ihlefeldt Harold G	153	messenger	20	"
s	Ihlefeldt Madeline L—†	153	housewife	44	"
t	*Oxford Alma—†	153	at home	39	"
u	Henry John F	154	laborer	28	78 Montebello rd
v	Henry Sophie J—†	154	housewife	25	78 "
w	Cirino Sadie L—†	154	"	31	here
x	Cirino Samuel J	154	shoeworker	32	"
y	*Larson Ada—†	154	housewife	47	"
z	McGowan Gerald C	156	packer	28	732 E Eighth

915

a	McGowan Mary M—†	156	housewife	25	732 "
b	*Pomoranz Daniel	156	merchant	45	here
c	*Pomoranz Tillie—†	156	housewife	45	"
d	Sites Catherine E—†	156	"	52	314 Wood av
e	Sites George A	156	clerk	60	314 "
f	Roth Charles F	157	retired	71	here
g	Roth Charles F	157	draftsman	37	"
h	Ingram Alice G—†	158	housewife	30	"
k	Ingram Francis J	158	chauffeur	36	"

10

Page.	Letter.	Full Name.	Residence, Jan. 1, 1941.	Occupation.	Supposed Age.	Reported Residence, Jan. 1, 1940. Street and Number.

Boylston Street—Continued

	L	Dowd Christina B—†	158	housewife	54	here
	M	Dowd Daniel F, jr	158	chauffeur	55	"
	N	Dowd Ralph H	158	machinist	32	"
	O	Sullivan Eli	158	laborer	42	
	P	*Sullivan Elsie M—†	158	housewife	35	"
	R	Barrett Agnes J—†	159	saleswoman	40	"
	S	Barrett Mary E—†	159	clerk	44	
	T	Barrett Richard F	159	retired	37	
	U	Kelley Patrick	160	laborer	53	
	V	Mulrie Catherine G—†	160	housewife	48	"
	W	Craven Annie M—†	160	"	38	
	X	Craven William F	160	operator	44	"
	Y	Hall John J	160	janitor	22	3140½ Wash'n
	Z	Rist Bernard J	160	machinist	41	here
916						
	A	Rist Frances R—†	160	housewife	38	"
	B	Martin Florence R—†	162	"	43	"
	C	Martin Harold E	162	carpenter	47	"
	D	Ferguson Anna—†	162	housewife	70	"
	E	Ferguson Annie T—†	162	at home	32	
	F	Ferguson John W	162	laborer	37	
	G	Ferguson Peter H	162	repairman	38	"
	H	McGrath Florence M—†	162	housewife	23	"
	K	McGrath William	162	clerk	26	
	L	Stumpf Marie—†	163	typist	22	
	M	Stumpf Mary J—†	163	housewife	46	"
	N	Stumpf Bridget J—†	163	"	48	
	O	Stumpf John J	163	janitor	53	
	P	Smith Michael J	163	window washer	34	"
	R	Faust Addie—†	165	housewife	31	61 Minden
	S	Faust Rudolf	165	machinist	37	61 "
	T	Hamilton Aubrey	165	welder	53	48 Sheridan
	U	Hamilton Christine—†	165	housewife	43	48 "
	V	Thiele Emma—†	166	"	64	12 Round Hill
	W	Brower Anna—†	166	laundryworker	45	47 School
	X	O'Hara Alice—†	166	operator	48	3118 Wash'n
	Y	*Biggar Ira W	166	clerk	25	16 Heath av
	Z	*Everett Edward M	166	retired	53	16 "
917						
	A	*Everett Mary A—†	166	housewife	51	16 "
	B	O'Brien Edward J	167	laborer	42	here

11

Page.	Letter.	FULL NAME.	Residence, Jan. 1, 1941.	Occupation.	Supposed Age.	Reported Residence, Jan. 1, 1940. Street and Number.

Boylston Street—Continued

c	O'Brien Mary J—†	167	housewife	41	here
d	Lehan John F	167	laborer	47	"
e	Lehan Mary J—†	167	housewife	35	"
f	Richburg Albert	167	teamster	50	"
g	Richburg John	167	retired	70	
h	*Noseworthy Annie G—†	169	housewife	37	"
k	*Noseworthy James	169	salesman	38	"
l	Cohen Herbert J	169	"	41	17 Worcester sq
m	*Long Ernest	169	laborer	20	3296 Wash'n
n	*Long Rhoda—†	169	laundress	40	3296 "
o	Caraher Andrew	169	carpenter	21	here
p	Caraher Archie	169	"	22	"
r	Caraher Viola—†	169	merchant	47	"
s	Kotsalis Christos	169	cobbler	42	
u	Dunne Celia A—†	172	clerk	29	
v	Dunne William	172	laborer	29	
w	Moriarty Clarence W	172	chauffeur	32	"
x	Moriarty Theresa—†	172	housewife	34	"
y	O'Neill Margaret—†	172	clerk	35	
z	O'Neill Margaret—†	172	housewife	65	"
	918				
a	O'Neill Owen	172	laborer	70	
b	Burke Ellen E—†	172	at home	70	
c	Carey Helen C—†	172	stenographer	37	"
d	Carey Mildred G—†	172	packer	38	"
e	Jefferson Emma—†	173	at home	45	159 Arlington
f	*Long Arthur F	173	chauffeur	21	19 Byron ct
g	Long Ethel—†	173	housewife	21	19 "
h	Morrison Ethel I—†	173	at home	50	47 Dalrymple
k	*Kelly Elizabeth A—†	173	housewife	33	here
l	Kelly William J	173	laborer	34	"
m	*Milot Bella A—†	173	housewife	21	"
n	Milot George A	173	chef	25	
p	Scollins Mary E—† rear	173	housewife	36	"
r	Scollins Roland A "	173	laborer	40	
s	Salisbury Charles D "	173	chauffeur	43	"
t	*Salisbury Margaret—† "	173	housewife	40	"
u	Engstrom Elizabeth—†	174	"	54	
v	Patch Henry	174	shipper	27	
w	Patch Rose—†	174	shoeworker	55	"
x	Wieland Henry	174	bottler	57	

Page.	Letter.	FULL NAME.	Residence, Jan. 1, 1941.	Occupation.	Supposed Age.	Reported Residence, Jan. 1. 1940. Street and Number.

Boylston Street—Continued

	Y	*McGonigle John	175	signmaker	34	here
	Z	*McGonigle Katherine—†	175	housewife	40	"
919						
	B	Mills Henry B	175	porter	28	285 Chestnut av
	A	Mills Lillian C—†	175	housewife	26	285 "
	C	Pforte Elizabeth H—†	175	secretary	21	here
	D	Pforte Helen E—†	175	housewife	56	"
	E	Pforte Robert J	175	coffee grinder	57	"
	F	Sweeney Delia A—†	176	merchant	43	"
	G	Sweeney James J	176	retired	42	
	H	Davis Francis R	178	porter	22	
	K	Davis Katherine G—†	178	at home	56	
	L	Johnstone James	178	porter	64	
	M	Johnstone Mary H—†	178	housewife	65	"
	N	*Sullivan Hilda—†	178	"	32	7 Haverford
	O	Sullivan Richard J	178	janitor	37	7 "
	P	Dooley John	180	chauffeur	41	here
	R	Homer Charles C	180	porter	67	"
	S	Springer Rudolph C	180	egg candler	56	"
	T	Long Charles W	180	printer	37	
	U	Long Vera R—†	180	housewife	37	"
	W	West Catherine—†	180	"	60	
	X	West Henry F	180	realtor	65	
	Y	West Warren	180	factoryhand	21	"
	Z	Gormley Marie F—†	182	nurse	35	
920						
	A	Weed Francis A	182	repairman	30	"
	B	Weed Mildred L—†	182	housewife	38	"
	C	Collins Margaret C—†	182	"	30	
	D	Collins Michael J	182	bartender	29	"
	E	McGrath Madge—†	182	housewife	41	"
	F	McGrath Maurice	182	operator	42	"
	G	Satory Hubert	183	printer	74	"
	H	*Wortmann Maria—†	183	operator	32	"
	K	Wortmann Mary—†	183	housewife	60	"
	L	Fickers Caroline—†	183	maid	48	
	M	Fickers Eva—†	183	stitcher	43	
	N	Fickers Louise—†	183	housewife	50	"
	O	Goode Celia—†	183	"	50	
	P	Goode Dorothy—†	183	typist	24	
	R	Goode Thomas E	183	printer	52	

13

Page.	Letter.	FULL NAME.	Residence, Jan. 1, 1941.	Occupation.	Supposed Age.	Reported Residence, Jan. 1, 1940. Street and Number.

Boylston Street—Continued

	s	Goode Thomas N	183	probat'n officer	23	here
	t	McCarthy Jeremiah F	184	roofer	38	"
	u	McCarthy Sarah—†	184	housewife	30	"
	v	Henning Lillian—†	184	at home	77	
	w	Baxter Sarah B—†	184	housewife	41	"
	x	Baxter William M	184	carpenter	46	"
	y	*Dempsey Agnes—†	185	housewife	37	"
	z	*Dempsey George	185	waiter	43	

921

	b	Corchenny Frederick	185	carpenter	62	88 W Cedar
	a	*Corchenny Julia—†	185	housewife	63	88 "
	c	Carter John J	185	machinist	43	here
	d	Carter Joseph F	185	"	20	"
	e	Carter Margaret M—†	185	housewife	38	"
	f	Becker Joseph F	186	inspector	55	"
	h	Goode Helen J—†	186	housewife	33	"
	g	Goode Thomas M	186	buffer	32	
	k	Blair Allen	186	salesman	62	"
	l	Blair Isabella—†	186	housewife	60	"
	m	Blair Thomas W	186	salesman	39	"
	n	*Hart Ira F	186	manager	34	7 Adams circle
	o	*Hart Mary V—†	186	housewife	33	7 "
	p	Marks Loretta—†	187	"	34	Revere
	r	Lyons James E	187	clerk	32	here
	s	Lyons Margaret L—†	187	housewife	32	"
	t	Hall Margaret—†	187	seamstress	42	"
	u	*Neuman Mary—†	187	housewife	77	"
	v	Yanarella Louisa—†	188	"	33	
	w	Yanarella Warren M	188	attendant	33	"
	x	DiCarlo Angelo	188	carpenter	35	"
	y	DiCarlo Annie L—†	188	at home	61	"
	z	*DiCarlo Caroline—†	188	housewife	29	"

922

	a	DiCarlo John	188	laborer	37	
	b	*DiCarlo Bridget—†	188	housewife	31	"
	c	DiCarlo Samuel	188	contractor	29	"
	d	Doherty Bernard	189	laborer	37	
	e	*Doherty Winifred—†	189	housewife	35	"
	f	Rehm Anna L—†	189	seamstress	23	9 Mark
	g	Rehm George F	189	laborer	55	9 "
	h	Rehm George H	189	bookkeeper	26	9 "

14

Boylston Street—Continued

K	Rehm Louella—†	189	housewife	46	9 Mark
L	Rehm Mary J—†	189	student	21	9 "
M	Bettencourt Joseph	189	mechanic	37	here
N	Bettencourt Louise—†	189	housewife	32	"
O	Tennihan Dorothy L—†	191	clerk	20	"
P	Tennihan Mary A—†	191	saleswoman	22	"
R	Tennihan Mary E—†	191	housewife	43	"
S	Tennihan Ralph E	191	shipper	46	
T	Rogers Dorothy—†	191	attendant	20	"
U	Rogers Frank	191	foreman	52	"
V	Rogers Gertrude—†	191	maid	22	
W	Rogers Lillian—†	191	clerk	25	
X	Rogers Yvonne—†	191	housewife	49	"
Y	Fahey Barbara—†	191	packer	20	189 Boylston
Z	Fahey Ellen V—†	191	housewife	51	189 "

923

A	Fahey John	191	clerk	22	189 '
B	Fahey Martin J	191	painter	55	189 "
C	Krug Florence J—†	192	housewife	37	here
D	Krug Henry J	192	inspector	41	"
E	O'Leary Bridget J—†	192	housewife	64	"
F	O'Leary Cornelius F	192	investigator	26	"
G	O'Leary Ellen J—†	192	secretary	32	"
H	O'Leary James J	192	fireman	69	"
K	O'Leary James J	192	physician	30	"
L	O'Leary Marguerite A—†	192	stenographer	27	"
M	O'Leary Timothy J	192	foreman	35	"
N	Baldwin John C	192	painter	41	
O	Baldwin Sarah E—†	192	housewife	36	"
P	*Lynch Mary—†	193	"	28	44 Amory
R	Lynch Matthew	193	engineer	36	44 "
S	Dempsey Joseph	193	retired	86	here
T	Dempsey Katherine—†	193	housewife	41	"
U	Dempsey Mabel—†	193	maid	55	"
V	Dempsey Nellie—†	193	"	56	
W	Dempsey Thomas	193	printer	47	"
X	Albrecht Alberta G—†	193	housewife	41	96 Jamaica
Y	Albrecht Constant	193	fireman	45	96 "
Z	Crawford —†	193	waitress	41	96 "

924 Charlotte

A	*MacPherson Minnie—†	193	at home	78	96 '

Boylston Street—Continued

B	Mueller Frieda—†	194	at home	64	here
c	Mueller Marie J—†	194	clerk	33	"
D	Walther George W	194	retired	60	"
E	Landry Charles H	194	machinist	39	"
F	Landry Elizabeth M—†	194	at home	74	
G	Landry Thomas S	194	welder	30	..
H	Carlson Jennie C—†	194	bookkeeper	67	"
K	Jellis Arthur	194	manager	58	∴
L	Jellis Elizabeth C—†	194	housewife	55	"
M	Gudjons Julius	195	clerk	67	..
N	Schmore Olive E—†	195	at home	87	
O	Schumann Barbara—†	195	clerk	22	
P	Schumann Beatrice—†	195	housewife	48	"
R	Schumann Philip E	195	policeman	52	"
S	Doherty James	196	laborer	46	
T	Doherty Margaret—†	196	housewife	43	"
U	Glennon John J	196	chauffeur	20	"
V	Glennon Madeline S—†	196	housewife	42	3215 Wash'n
W	Glennon William E	196	chauffeur	46	3215 "
X	Glennon William E, jr	196	printer	23	here
Y	Doherty Margaret—†	196	housewife	43	"
Z	Freymann Elsie M—†	196	at home	59	1 Cardington
	925				
A	Matthei Eva—†	198	housewife	65	here
B	Matthei Herman	198	manager	27	"
C	McGregor Elizabeth D-†	198	housewife	68	"
D	McGregor James P	198	factoryhand	27	"
E	McGregor Janet—†	198	at home	37	
F	McGregor Margaret M-†	198	clerk	39	
G	McGregor Marion M—†	198	seamstress	33	"
H	Stephansky Helen M—†	200	factoryhand	21	"
K	Stephansky Lillian B—†	200	clerk	31	
L	Stephansky Marie M—†	200	at home	28	
M	Stephansky Otto C	200	painter	64	
N	Hargraves Agnes—†	201	at home	78	
O	Hargraves George	201	printer	48	
P	Hargraves Loretta—†	201	housewife	45	"
R	O'Leary Clara—†	201	"	40	3109 Wash'n
S	O'Leary Eugene J	201	shipfitter	44	3109 "
T	Twitchell Alfa—†	201	at home	76	Rhode Island
U	Diggins Christine—†	201	housewife	48	here

Boylston Street—Continued

v	Diggins Christine C—†	201	clerk	22	here
w	Diggins Dennis E	201	laborer	49	"
x	Hill David	203	sign writer	32	"
y	Hill Ellen—†	203	at home	24	
z	Hill George, jr	203	clerk	38	
	926				
a	Hill Walter	203	mechanic	21	"
b	Sullivan Margaret B—†	203	clerk	23	
c	Welch James J	203	salesman	46	"
d	Welch Jeanette—†	203	housewife	43	"
e	Welch Katherine—†	203	at home	70	"
f	Maguire Doris—†	203	housekeeper	43	89 Amory
g	Richburg Elizabeth C—†	205	housewife	55	here
h	Richburg Elizabeth P—†	205	typist	22	"
k	Richburg Frank	205	operator	67	"
l	Koelsch Catherine-†	205A	housewife	33	"
m	Koelsch Edgar	205A	operator	42	"
n	Koelsch Frank	205A	laborer	73	
o	Koelsch Frank X	205A	"	33	
r	Bennett John C	212	chauffeur	42	"
s	Bennett Mary B—†	212	housewife	39	"
t	Bowen Cornelius J—†	212	laborer	58	
u	Bowen Mary E—†	212	housewife	55	"
v	Crawford Albert B	212	at home	60	1954 Centre
w	*Crawford Valerie J—†	212	housewife	40	1954 "
x	Cream Elizabeth E—†	214	"	52	177½ Green
y	*Cream William	214	cabinetmaker	66	177½ "

Brookside Avenue

z	Walraven Cornelius	2	retired	81	here
	927				
a	Walraven Cornelius, jr	2	carpenter	42	"
b	Walraven Tena—†	2	housewife	78	"
c	Bausch George C	2	breweryworker	59	"
d	Bausch Helen M—†	2	housewife	37	"
e	Stabin Fred	2	painter	50	
f	Stabin Martha—†	2	housewife	43	
g	Cronie Elizabeth—†	5	"	68	3144A Wash'n
h	Cronie William	5	retired	71	Pennsylvania
k	Carroll Margaret G—†	5	cashier	25	here

11—9   17

Brookside Avenue—Continued

L	Carroll Mary A—†	5	housewife	73	here	
M	Carroll Owen G	5	glazier	40	"	
N	Carroll Rhea L—†	5	typist	29	"	
O	Smith Ernest P	5	clerk	21		
P	*Smith Margaret—†	5	housewife	55	"	
R	Smith Robert E	5	clerk	24		
S	*Smith Thomas	5	retired	68		
T	McEachern Margaret—†	7	housewife	40	"	
U	*McEachern Roderick	7	carpenter	43	"	
V	McInnes Annie—†	7	housewife	66	120 Heath	
W	McInnes Margaret—†	7	waitress	26	120 "	
X	McInnes Robert	7	usher	25	120 "	
Y	Londergan Geraldine—†	7	stitcher	23	35 Barry pl	
Z	*Murphy Lillian A—†	7	housewife	48	35 "	

928

A	Murphy William H	7	ironmolder	63	35 "	
B	Connor Helen L—†	8	housewife	38	187 Boylston	
C	Connor Morton J	8	clerk	40	187 "	
D	Dugal Anna—†	8	at home	63	here	
E	Dugal Frank G	8	clerk	26	"	
F	Dugal Victor G	8	merchant	32	"	
G	Dauberschmidt George J	8	breweryworker	62	"	
H	Dauberschmidt Philipena—†	8	housewife	58	"	
K	Foley Margaret—†	9	"	35	"	
L	Foley Timothy	9	laborer	35	"	
M	Moulton George W	9	salesman	52	"	
N	Moulton Helen—†	9	housewife	51	"	
O	Rowe William C	9	retired	74		
P	Greenough Clifford	9	machinist	46	"	
R	Hood Edmund M	10	attendant	27	5 Brookside av	
S	Hood Eleanor S—†	10	nurse	27	5 "	
T	Sexton Lawrence	10	clerk	22	5 "	
U	Dauberschmidt Bertha—†	10	housewife	33	here	
V	Dauberschmidt George	10	serviceman	35	"	
W	O'Hear Charles	10	chauffeur	39	"	
X	*O'Hear Margaret—†	10	housewife	44	"	
Y	*Maguire Bridget—†	11	"	68		
Z	Maguire Thomas	11	retired	76		

929

B	Fitzemeyer Frederick M	11	engineer	47		
C	Fitzemeyer Ida F—†	11	stenographer	21	"	

Page.	Letter.	FULL NAME.	Residence, Jan. 1, 1941.	Occupation.	Supposed Age.	Reported Residence, Jan. 1, 1940. Street and Number.

Brookside Avenue—Continued

D	Kane Catherine—†	11	at home	68	here
E	Kelly Clara E—·†	22	housewife	40	"
F	Kelly Thomas	22	laborer	40	"
G	Foster Katherine—†	22	factoryhand	32	"
H	Foster Leon	22	foreman	33	
K	Rodd Anna—†	22	housewife	54	"
L	*Murphy Catherine—†	22	"	33	
M	Murphy Eugene	22	waiter	39	
N	Albach Amelie—†	24	at home	80	"
O	Albach Anna—†	24	housewife	42	"
P	Albach Harry	24	mechanic	44	"
R	*DeMinico Angelo	24	chauffeur	41	"
S	DeMinico Julia—†	24	housewife	38	"
T	Reusch Katherine—†	28	"	77	
U	Reusch Louis	28	retired	65	
V	Nash John	28	laborer	61	
W	Nash Nora—†	28	fitter	51	
X	Goode John W	28	gardener	57	..
Y	Goode Mary E—†	28	housewife	51	"
Z	Goode William F	28	attendant	23	"
	930				
A	Burwell Alfred	32	barber	62	
B	Burwell Mary E—†	32	housewife	64	"
C	Haley Francis E	32	mechanic	29	"
D	Haley Winnetta—†	32	housewife	64	"
E	Plaeinitz Charles	32	cabinetmaker	73	"
F	*Plaeinitz Meta—†	32	housewife	50	"
G	Laffey Ellen A—†	34	"	29	
H	Laffey James J	34	polisher	29	
K	Roemer Carl R	34	breweryworker	50	"
L	Roemer Frieda—†	34	housewife	45	"
M	*Petersen Florentine—†	34	"	62	"
N	*Petersen Fred	34	musician	28	"
O	Petersen John	34	cabinetmaker	59	"
P	Cullen Bertha—†	36	housewife	49	117 Paul Gore
R	Cullen James P	36	steelworker	53	117 "
S	Perry Mary—†	36	housewife	42	here
T	Perry Peter	36	operator	46	"
U	Cosgrove Martin	38	retired	70	"
V	Cosgrove Mary—†	38	housewife	68	"
W	Finch Katherine—†	40	waitress	49	

Page.	Letter.	Full Name.	Residence, Jan. 1, 1941.	Occupation.	Supposed Age.	Reported Residence, Jan. 1, 1940. Street and Number.

Brookside Avenue—Continued

	x	Jones Alice M—†	40	housewife	28	here
	y	Jones Thomas J	40	salesman	29	"
	z	Carey Catherine—†	40	at home	70	"
		931				
	A	*Spiegelhalter Joseph H	40	machinist	42	"
	B	Spiegelhalter Josephine—†	40	housewife	35	"
	c	Bertrand Ernest	42	mechanic	37	"
	D	Bertrand Mildred—†	42	housewife	39	"
	E	Burke Thomas J	46	clergyman	52	"
	G	Dowling James P	46	"	47	
	F	Fahey Margaret—†	46	maid	58	
	H	Kelly James F	46	clergyman	68	"
	K	McCarthy Mary H—†	46	housekeeper	66	"
	L	McCarthy Mary J—†	46	cook	68	"
	M	O'Connor William R	46	clergyman	47	"

Copley Street

	o	Blockman Bessie—†	2	housekeeper	42	here
	P	Gerofski Jennie—†	2	"	54	"
	R	*Bishop Elsie—†	5	"	55	"
	s	Weis Julius A	5	secretary	71	"
	T	Weis Louise B—†	5	housewife	70	"
	U	Beal Frederick W	6	laborer	58	
	v	Beal Vera M—†	6	housewife	58	"
	w	Beal William H	6	broker	35	
	x	Cox Charles B	7	contractor	34	"
	Y	Cox J Frederick	7	"	68	
	z	Cox Louise M—†	7	housewife	65	"
		932				
	A	Hantz Beatrice G—†	8	teacher	38	
	B	Hantz Helen M—†		housewife	50	"
	c	Hantz John J		tailor	80	
	D	Hantz John J		agent	40	
	E	Beck Alice L—†	8	housekeeper	50	"
	F	O'Hearn Katherine E—†	11	technician	44	"
	G	O'Hearn Katherine T—†	11	housewife	81	"
	H	O'Hearn Mary M—†	11	teacher	46	
	K	Wall William J	11	attorney	37	"
	L	Tucker Harold B	12	printer	42	
	M	Tucker Winifred C—†	12	housewife	39	"

20

Copley Street—Continued

N	Cottle Clara V—†	15	housekeeper	60	here
O	Cottle Louise M—†	15	teacher	62	"
P	Cottle Phoebe C—†	15	housekeeper	57	"

Dalrymple Street

R	Hessian Charlotte M—†	4	housewife	68	here
S	Hessian Henry M	4	retired	66	"
T	Schmuck Erwin	4	clerk	59	18 Dalrymple
U	Schmuck Johanna B—†	4	housewife	54	18 "
V	Festel Arthur P	4	clerk	27	here
W	Festel Gertrude H—†	4	housewife	30	"
X	Franz Sabina E—†	5	clerk	55	"
Y	Franz Sebastian	5	retired	79	
Z	Kelley Helen C—†	5	housewife	30	"
	933					
A	Kelley John L	5	inspector	30	"
B	Gonser Christine M—†	6	clerk	26	
C	Gonser Herman F	6	shoecutter	42	"
D	Gonser Marie T—†	6	housewife	68	"
E	Brenn Anne A—†	6	stitcher	59	
F	Egershein Carl G	6	decorator	50	"
G	Egershein Catherine A—†	6	housewife	52	"
H	Murphy Francis G	6	clerk	26	
K	Murphy Paul E	6	laborer	31	
L	Anderson Arthur O	6	chauffeur	40	"
M	Anderson Dorothy C—†	6	secretary	31	"
N	Blye Mary—†	7	stitcher	55	
O	Gartland Sabina—†	7	saleswoman	35	"
P	Kasper Herman P	7	clerk	48	
R	Kasper Margaret E—†	7	housewife	51	"
S	Wolfrum Alice C—†	10	"	36	"
T	Wolfrum Carl A	10	engineer	35	
U	Condon Catherine C—†	10	wrapper	27	"
V	Condon Christine—†	10	housewife	53	"
W	Condon Dorothy A—†	10	timekeeper	23	"
X	Condon William H	10	shipper	51	
Y	Condon William J	10	inspector	21	"
Z	McDonough Mary A—†	10	hostess	25	163 South
	934					
A	Harting Cornelius	10	manager	26	here

Dalrymple Street—Continued

B	Harting Jane J—†	10	bookbinder	20	here
c	Harting Jennie G—†	10	shipper	22	"
D	Harting John	10	photographer	22	"
E	Harting Nellie—†	10	housewife	53	"
F	Harting Tena—†	10	at home	30	
G	Harting William	10	builder	54	
H	Starr Bernard J	11	clerk	37	
K	Starr Wilma J—†	11	housewife	32	"
L	Bulger Bernice C—†	11	nurse	24	"
M	Gillis Sophia—†	11	"	46	"
N	Ring Albert K	11	operator	30	101 School
o	Ring Anna C—†	11	nurse	27	43 Melrose
P	Finnegan George E	12	boilermaker	43	here
R	Finnegan Hannah—†	12	housewife	43	"
s	Finnegan Rita C—†	12	nurse	21	"
T	Walsh James M	12	merchant	53	"
U	Walsh Kathleen H—†	12	stenographer	21	"
v	*Walsh Mary M—†	12	housewife	49	"
w	Dorney Caroline J—†	12	secretary	22	"
x	Dorney Caroline W—†	12	waitress	49	
Y	Dorney John J	12	laborer	28	
z	Neumann Edith M—†	14	housewife	44	"

935

A	Neumann Harry L	14	policeman	49	"
B	Hauns Adolph C	14	ironworker	55	"
c	Hauns Ella V—†	14	at home	23	
D	Hauns Herbert A	14	laborer	22	
E	*Hauns Valentina—†	14	housewife	50	"
F	Caskie John	14	retired	78	
G	Jordan Elise M—†	14	at home	77	
H	Moriarty Daniel F	15	bricklayer	37	"
K	Moriarty Mary R—†	15	housewife	37	"
L	*Foley Mabel B—†	15	"	47	
M	Foley Peter A	15	laborer	53	
N	*Ring Pauline G—†	15	housewife	29	"
o	*Ring Selwyn E	15	supervisor	31	"
P	Allgaier John A	16	laborer	49	
R	Allgaier Mary A—†	16	housewife	44	"
s	*Collins Mary—†	16	"	75	
T	*Collins Timothy	16	retired	77	
U	Wolfrum Adam	16	loom fixer	61	"

Page.	Letter.	FULL NAME.	Residence, Jan. 1, 1941.	Occupation.	Supposed Age.	Reported Residence, Jan. 1, 1940. Street and Number.

Dalrymple Street—Continued

	v	Wolfrum Sophie—†	16	housewife	66	here
	w	Wolfrum Walter F	16	engineer	28	"
	y	Starr Anna M—†	17	housewife	40	"
	z	Starr James H	17	chauffeur	40	"
936						
	a	Perkins Edward R	17	printer	45	
	b	Perkins Margaret M—†	17	housewife	33	"
	c	Tingus Constantine G	17	manager	29	"
	d	Tingus Mimi T—†	17	housewife	28	"
	e	Lally John J	18	chauffeur	43	4 Glade av
	f	Lally Margaret—†	18	housewife	34	4 "
	g	Blaney Daniel J	18	custodian	55	here
	h	Blaney Daniel J, jr	18	porter	20	"
	k	Blaney John F	18	machinist	25	"
	l	*Blaney Matilda—†	18	housewife	55	"
	m	Rooney John H	18	printer	49	
	n	Rooney Lillian T—†	18	housewife	35	"
	o	Brennan Alice P—†	20	auditor	24	
	p	Brennan Mary—†	20	housewife	69	"
	r	Brennan Walter J	20	clerk	33	
	s	Shea Margaret A—†	20	inspector	37	"
	t	Shea Thomas A	20	porter	39	
	u	Mills Daniel A	20	clerk	23	
	v	Mills Francis J	20	foreman	53	..
	w	Mills Katherine V—†	20	housewife	58	"
	x	Owen Louisa W—†	20	"	41	
	y	Rau Joseph F	20	retired	73	
	z	Rau Wilhelmine—†	20	housewife	65	"
937						
	a	Carty John	22	mechanic	55	"
	b	Carty John J	22	engineer	24	
	c	Carty Mary E—†	22	housewife	45	"
	d	Carty Mary T—†	22	auditor	21	
	e	Carty Thomas F	22	mechanic	23	"
	f	Schueler Emil F	22	technician	36	"
	g	Schueler Florence A—†	22	housewife	34	"
	h	Connolly Delia—†	22	"	55	
	k	Connolly James J	22	laborer	25	
	l	Connolly John J	22	boilermaker	60	"
	m	Connolly Margaret R—†	22	at home	22	
	n	Connolly Michael	22	laborer	23	

Dalrymple Street—Continued

	o	Rosen Fannie—†	23	at home	50	here
	p	Forsythe Dwight B	23	engineer	64	"
	r	Forsythe Lillian M—†	23	housewife	46	"
	s	McHugh Charles J	23	bookkeeper	33	"
	t	McHugh Elizabeth—†	23	housewife	60	"
	u	McHugh James E	23	timekeeper	27	"
	v	McHugh John T	23	clerk	29	
	w	Starr Anna M—†	24	housewife	43	"
	x	Starr Thomas A	24	letter carrier	47	"
	y	Schumann Frederick A	24	clerk	66	
	z	Schumann Ida M—†	24	housewife	66	"
938						
	a	Stone Lydia M—†	24	companion	69	"
	b	Enders Marie M—†	24	housewife	70	"
	c	O'Rourke Lena—†	24	saleswoman	43	"
	d	MacInnis Catherine—†	25	houseworker	60	Malden
	f	Mehegan Katherine—†	25	housewife	35	"
	e	Mehegan William J	25	retired	43	"
	g	Engleman Lillian—†	25	housewife	30	here
	h	Engleman Robert	25	electrician	36	"
	k	Fetter Annie—†	25	laundress	55	27 Dalrymple
	l	Cronin Alice M—†	25	housewife	31	here
	m	Cronin Philip J	25	manager	33	"
	n	Campbell Hannah E—†	26	secretary	36	"
	o	*Campbell Mary C—†	26	saleswoman	38	"
	p	*Campbell Mary J—†	26	housewife	62	"
	r	*Campbell Ralph J	26	laborer	21	"
	s	Quigley Catherine—†	26	housewife	64	213 Boylston
	t	Quigley Francis A	26	repairman	42	213 "
	u	Vail Mary J—†	26	clerk	43	213 "
	v	Vail Maurice F	26	"	49	18 Bulfinch
	w	Clarke Annie M—†	26	housewife	58	here
	x	Clarke Francis X	26	manager	24	"
	y	Clarke James P	26	accountant	26	"
	z	Clarke John M	26	manager	34	"
939						
	a	Clarke Joseph A	26	social worker	30	"
	b	Clarke Owen	26	watchman	59	"
	c	Clarke Owen L	26	clerk	28	
	d	Strick Margaret G—†	28	housewife	37	"
	e	Strick Rudolph P	28	machinist	41	"

Dalrymple Street—Continued

F	Matthews Arthur R	28	accountant	37	17 Woodside av
G	Matthews Margaret E—†	28	housewife	31	17 "
H	Benkart Frank C	28	machinist	54	here
K	Benkart Isabella—†	28	housewife	52	"
L	Benkart Raymond A	28	dyesetter	24	"
M	*Keenan Margaret M—†	29	housewife	32	"
N	*Keenan Michael M	29	manager	33	"
O	Jackson Carl J	29	mechanic	43	"
P	Jackson Selma M—†	29	housewife	35	"
R	McViney Howard A	29	policeman	36	"
S	McViney Mary F—†	29	housewife	32	"
T	McCarthy Virginia H—†	30	"	23	
U	McCarthy William A	30	painter	27	
V	Yanaro Robert	30	metalworker	25	"
W	Clark Walter E	30	U S N	24	N Hampshire
X	Mouritsen Lillian M—†	30	at home	68	Randolph
Y	Tower Harold W	30	clerk	45	"
Z	Tower Ruth E—†	30	housewife	43	"
	940				
A	Olson Gustav E	30	mechanic	70	here
B	Olson Hilda A—†	30	housewife	58	"
C	Olson June M—†	30	typist	22	"
D	Haddigan Phoebe—†	31	housewife	81	"
E	Johnson Julia E—†	31	waitress	49	..
F	North Mazie—†	31	at home	47	
G	Toye Florence E—†	31	housewife	60	"
H	Haddigan Josephine R—†	33	"	25	
K	Haddigan Raymond L	33	letter carrier	37	"
L	Barnes Alice A—†	35	housewife	52	28 Dalrymple
M	Barnes Samuel A	35	coppersmith	21	28 "
N	Barnes Samuel H	35	shipwright	52	28 "
O	Kenney Lillian F—†	35	housewife	30	28 "
P	Mangan Margaret W—†	36	"	70	39 Forest Hills
R	Mangan William A	36	chauffeur	63	39 "
S	Pecci Artilio	36	laborer	25	here
T	Pecci Margaret M—†	36	assembler	23	"
U	Johnson Carl W	36	laborer	32	"
V	Johnson Margaret W—†	36	stenographer	28	"
W	Olson Rita M—†	36	housewife	24	"
X	Olson William B	36	machinist	27	"
Y	Gennerazzo Francis	36	shoeworker	36	"

Dalrymple Street--Continued

z	Gennerazzo Gertrude—†	36	housewife	30	here	
941						
a	Kincannon Grace M—†	36	student	23		
b	Kincannon Mary—†	36	examiner	40	"	
c	Lynch Rita—†	37	housewife	30	"	
d	Lynch William H	37	draftsman	40	"	
e	*Foley Theresa A---†	39	clerk	26	Canada	
f	Harrington Mary A—†	39	housewife	30	15 Germania	
g	Harrington William A	39	chauffeur	31	15 "	
h	Sullivan Emma—†	39	housewife	33	here	
k	Sullivan William A	39	painter	44	"	
l	Calella Angelo J	39	roofer	34	"	
m	Calella Elmer	39	upholsterer	31	"	
n	Calella John	39	laborer	25		
o	*Calella Mary C—†	39	housewife	60	"	
p	Calella Philomena M—†	39	factoryhand	29	"	
r	Murray Andrew J	40	porter	37		
s	*Murray Catherine T—†	40	housewife	35	"	
t	Murray Thomas J	40	porter	35		
u	Kudryk Eugene B	40	chauffeur	27	"	
v	Kudryk Sonia E—†	40	housewife	26	"	
w	Ostapchuk Catherine D---†	40	"	48		
x	Ostapchuk Feodose M	40	retired	45	"	
y	Ferguson Charles	40	engineer	41	18 Egleston	
z	*Ferguson Mary—†	40	housewife	41	18 "	
942						
a	Wood Calvin S	43	machinist	34	here	
b	Wood Georgina B---†	43	housewife	29	"	
c	Tipping Clara—†	43	"	48	"	
d	Tipping John E	43	laborer	26		
e	Tipping Leonard	43	mason	50		
f	Tipping Leonard, jr	43	engraver	21	"	
g	*Adkin Hilda M—†	43	nurse	29		
h	Tipping Ethel—†	43	housewife	50	"	
k	Tipping John S	43	polisher	56		
l	Moran James A	47	chauffeur	28	"	
m	Moran Mary E—†	47	housewife	25	"	
n	Marshall Emily—†	47	"	56	47 Reyem Circle	
o	Marshall Ephraim	47	carpenter	62	47 "	
p	Mulvee Francis X	47	clerk	22	here	
r	Mulvee Jennie T—†	47	housewife	45	"	

Page.	Letter.	FULL NAME.	Residence, Jan. 1, 1941.	Occupation.	Supposed Age.	Reported Residence, Jan. 1, 1940. Street and Number.

Dalrymple Street—Continued

| | s | Mulvee John F | 47 | clerk | 50 | here |
| | т | Mulvee John J | 47 | bookkeeper | 20 | " |

Egleston Street

	u	Grant Abbie T—†	10	housewife	63	here
	v	Grant Nathan A	10	retired	63	"
	w	Levreault Catherine—†	10	housewife	38	"
	x	Levreault William	10	repairman	36	"
	y	Rasmussen Agnes—†	10	housewife	44	"
	z	Rasmussen Francis	10	salesman	22	"

943

	A	Nixon Annette J—†	11	operator	25	
	B	Nixon Blanche M—†	11	clerk	21	
	c	Nixon Diana M—†	11	housewife	48	"
	D	Nixon John W	11	laundryman	48	"
	E	Costello Anne M—†	11	cashier	22	
	F	Costello Dorothy A—†	11	waitress	27	
	G	Costello John J	11	sorter	29	
	H	Costello Lena M—†	11	housewife	51	"
	K	Coy William F	11	laborer	55	
	L	Nevins Joseph A	11	chef	36	
	N	Gilson Christina—†	14	housewife	48	"
	O	Gilson Horace M	14	manager	46	"
	P	Schneider Christina—†	14	at home	85	
	R	Kirstein Frederick E	14	painter	56	
	s	Kirstein Martha C—†	14	housewife	52	"
	T	McElhill Frank B	15	manager	46	"
	U	McElhill Gertrude C—†	15	housewife	42	"
	V	McElhill Margaret—†	15	student	20	"
	w	Walsh Beatrice M—†	16	housewife	69	196 Boylston
	x	Walsh Edward	16	mason	71	196 "
	Y	Walsh Patrick E	16	operator	28	196 "
	z	Cella Gino J	16	machinist	49	here

944

	A	Cella Mary—†	16	housewife	43	"
	B	Marsolini Henry A	16	hat finisher	38	"
	c	Brophy Frank H	17	retired	73	
	D	MacGowan Mary E—†	17	housekeeper	58	"
	E	Murphy Catherine—†	18	housewife	43	Somerville
	F	Murphy John	18	porter	45	"

Egleston Street—Continued

G	Gavin Alice—†	18	clerk	21	here
H	Gavin Anna—†	18	packer	22	"
K	Gavin Catherine—†	18	clerk	23	"
L	Gavin Edward J	18	operator	52	
M	Gavin Marie J—†	18	housewife	48	"
N	Gavin Mary—†	18	packer	24	"
o	*Foles Devina—†	18	housewife	42	"
P	Foles Edward	18	repairman	20	"
R	Raymond Henry W	20	glassblower	64	"
s	Raymond Mary A—†	20	housewife	39	"
T	Hanley John J	20	steamfitter	48	"
U	Hanley Mary E—†	20	housewife	52	"
v	Hanley William J	20	electrician	53	"
w	May Mary A—†	20	housewife	64	"
x	May Nicholas P	20	metalworker	66	"
Y	Donavan Helen M—·†	23	secretary	23	"
z	Donavan John A	23	salesman	48	"

945

A	Donavan Mary T—†	23	saleswoman	20	"
B	Donavan Theresa M—†	23	housewife	46	"
c	Anderson Anna—†	24	"	62	169 Boylston
D	Ferreira Madaline—·†	24	"	39	169 "
E	Ferreira Vincent J	24	painter	42	169 "
F	Kelley Helen—†	24	housewife	28	31 Palmer
G	Carpenter Arthur	26	laborer	30	here
H	Carpenter Louise—†	26	housewife	28	"
K	*Nagle Mary—†	26	at home	74	"
L	Nagle Mary E—·†	26	clerk	29	
M	Cunningham Alfred	26	machinist	22	"
N	Cunningham Cecilia—†	26	housewife	55	"
o	Cunningham Isabel—†	26	clerk	26	"
P	Broderick Helena—†	27	winder	55	5 Acadia
R	Giancola John	27	fireman	52	here
s	House Horatio E	27	machinist	58	"
T	Kelliher Anna A—·†	27	housewife	42	"
U	Kelliher Francis M	27	salesman	41	"
v	Murphy Bridget—†	27	housewife	53	"
w	Murphy Hannah—†	27	"	61	"
x	Woods Lucy—†	30	"	63	14 Wenham
Y	Woods William	30	inspector	51	14 "
z	Backer Elizabeth—†	30	housekeeper	68	here

Page.	Letter.	FULL NAME.	Residence, Jan. 1, 1941.	Occupation.	Supposed Age.	Reported Residence, Jan. 1, 1940. Street and Number.

946

Egleston Street—Continued

A	Schlaich Charles	30	clerk	42	here
B	Jefferds Susan B—†	30	housewife	67	"
C	Troiano Amadio	34	bartender	34	"
D	Troiano Helen R—†	34	housewife	29	"
E	Palmer Theresa M—†	34	housekeeper	43	"
F	Welsh Catherine T—†	34	seamstress	58	"
G	Welsh Mary A—†	34	housewife	69	"
H	Welsh Peter A	34	clerk	62	
K	Tardiff Arthur A	34	machinist	49	"
L	Tardiff Edna M—†	34	clerk	20	
M	Tardiff Eva M—†	34	housewife	51	"
N	Tardiff Rita L—†	34	clerk	22	

Germania Street

O	Kilroy John J	4	electrician	32	here
P	Kilroy Vera G—†	4	housewife	33	"
R	Longley Catherine J—†	4	at home	60	New York
S	Moore Sarah A—†	4	housewife	42	78 Montebello rd
T	*Lynch Jean—†	4	"	52	here
U	Lynch William	4	laborer	50	"
V	Breen John	6	"	56	"
W	Breen Mary—†	6	housewife	54	"
X	*Barrett Margaret—†	6	"	42	
Y	Barrett Patrick J	6	butcher	44	"
Z	*Donahue Ellen A—†	6	housewife	47	"

947

A	Donahue Mary E—†	6	bookkeeper	21	"
B	Roy Janet—†	7	housewife	45	"
C	*Brogg Ann—†	7	at home	75	Groton
D	*Kisby Ernest	7	machinist	47	here
E	*Kisby Ethel—†	7	housewife	43	"
F	Canavan Annie J—†	8	waitress	54	"
G	Canavan Mary—†	8	housewife	43	"
H	Canavan Mary F—†	8	at home	21	
K	Canavan Thomas	8	clerk	56	"
L	*Spellman Annie J—†	8	housewife	38	12 Galena
M	Spellman Francis J	8	clerk	42	12 "
N	MacDonald Alexander W	8	paver	43	here
O	*MacDonald Catherine—†	8	at home	68	"

29

Page.	Letter.	FULL NAME.	Residence, Jan. 1, 1941.	Occupation.	Supposed Age.	Reported Residence, Jan. 1, 1940. Street and Number.

Germania Street—Continued

P	MacDonald Gertrude—†	8	housewife	40	here
R	Byrnes Eben F	9	engineer	57	"
S	Byrnes Eben F, jr	9	chauffeur	26	"
T	Byrnes Gladys L—†	9	cutter	21	
U	Byrnes Lulu A—†	9	housewife	53	"
V	Somes Caroline W—†	9	at home	80	
W	Burns Susan A—†	12	"	65	
X	O'Neill Clarence T	12	chauffeur	39	"
Y	O'Neill Mary K—†	12	housewife	34	"
Z	*Lynch Ann—†	12	factoryhand	60	"

948

A	*Lynch Katherine—†	12	saleswoman	54	"
B	Breedis Anna—†	12	housewife	55	196 Boylston
C	Breedis John	12	breweryworker	56	196 "
D	Keller Eleanor—†	14	housewife	40	9 Jackson pl
E	Keller George W	14	serviceman	40	9 "
F	Erhard Albert J	14	laborer	61	here
G	Erhard Albert T	14	clerk	24	"
H	Erhard Mary E—†	14	at home	60	"
K	Erhard Virginia M—†	14	"	26	"
L	Johnston Catherine J—†	14	housewife	49	1 Boylston pl
M	Johnston John J	14	painter	44	1 "
N	Barnes John	15	laborer	58	here
O	Barnes Katherine—†	15	housewife	56	"
P	Burke William J	15	guard	28	"
R	Burke Mary A—†	15	housewife	31	"
S	Burke Thomas P	15	electrician	35	"
T	Kloth Herman	15	seaman	37	153 E Newton
U	Thompson Fred A	15	mechanic	44	82 Newburg
V	*Thompson Mary—†	15	housewife	46	82 "
W	Hufnagel Alice V—†	17	at home	39	here
X	Hufnagel Bridget C—†	17	housewife	66	"
Y	Young Frederick W	17	bookbinder	42	"
Z	Young Miriam E—†	17	housewife	32	"

949

A	Carney James G	17	clerk	53	
B	Mills Nellie—†	17	at home	67	
C	Hickey Annie J—†	21	clerk	53	
D	O'Brien Arthur	21	druggist	40	
E	O'Brien Lillian—†	21	housewife	38	"
F	Jacobs Emma J—†	21	"	35	
G	Jacobs John J	21	plumber	40	

2

Page.	Letter.	FULL NAME.	Residence, Jan. 1, 1941.	Occupation.	Supposed Age.	Reported Residence, Jan. 1, 1940. Street and Number.

Haverford Street

	H	Spellman Ann E—†	36	saleswoman	23	here
	K	Spellman Annie—†	36	housewife	53	"
	L	Spellman James F	36	clerk	21	"
	M	Spellman Michael	36	laborer	55	
	N	Spellman Catherine—†	38	housewife	49	"
	O	Spellman Edward F	38	operator	49	
	P	*Fatopoulas John	42	"	61	
	R	*Leffos Peter	42	pedler	61	
	S	*Catalforn Concetta—†	42	housewife	64	"
	T	Kirby Catherine—†	44	"	69	
	U	Goode Anna I—†	44	"	30	
	V	Goode Joseph M	44	operator	34	"
	W	Shea Evelyn—†	46	housewife	28	223 South
	X	Shea John J	46	counterman	26	223 "
	Y	Bastable Mary G—†	46	housewife	25	here
	Z	Bastable William E	46	laborer	27	"

950

| | A | Kelly Wilhelmina—† | 52 | at home | 82 | |

Marmion Street

	E	Fischer Herman J	44	chauffeur	32	here
	F	Fischer Mildred M—†	44	housewife	26	"
	G	Fischer Arthur H	44	machinist	45	"
	H	Fischer Thyra E—†	44	housewife	35	"
	K	Heavern John J	51	proprietor	39	"
	L	O'Connor Eileen—†	51	housewife	35	"
	M	O'Connor Timothy	51	bartender	40	"
	N	Kussmaul Albert	54	bookkeeper	50	"
	O	Kussmaul Charlotte—†	54	housewife	49	"
	P	Lawler John F	55	chauffeur	30	"
	R	Lawler Margaret A—†	55	supervisor	39	"
	S	Hufnagle Cecelia P—†	55	housewife	39	"
	T	Hufnagle John J	55	steamfitter	39	"
	U	Cady James A	55	clerk	30	
	V	Cady Mary A—†	55	housewife	26	"

Porter Street

	X	Anderson Helen T—†	6	housewife	22	49 Worthington
	Y	Anderson Ralph G	6	laborer	23	49 "
	Z	*Lundstron Carl G	6	"	31	here

951
Porter Street—Continued

A	*Lundstron Hilda—†	6	housewife	48	here
B	*Lundstron John	6	molder	52	"
C	*Allison Cora A—†	6	housewife	30	"
D	Allison Kenneth L	6	laborer	29	
E	Hicks Carrie A—†	8	housewife	50	"
F	Hicks Willard B	8	carpenter	42	"
G	Nelson Albertina G—†	8	at home	56	
H	Nelson Hugo R	8	patternmaker	30	"
K	Mullis George J	8	accountant	24	"
L	Mullis Harry	8	rubberworker	58	"
M	Mullis Lillian—†	8	housewife	52	"
N	Chatterton Clifton	10	painter	76	
O	Chatterton Lillian—†	10	housewife	55	"
P	Acker Rose—†	12	at home	64	
R	Williams Mary—†	12	"	66	
T	Mrosk Christina—†	14	"	67	
U	Mrosk William F	14	retired	47	"
V	Himmel Bertha E—†	18	at home	58	6 Union av
W	Himmel John A	18	machinist	22	6 "
X	Himmel Joseph C	18	clerk	25	6 "
Y	Aspacher Clara M—†	18	nurse	21	here
Z	Aspacher Martha M—†	18	housewife	46	"

952

A	Aspacher William C	18	chauffeur	52	"
B	Aspacher William J	18	electrician	20	"
D	Rist Adolph F	20	foreman	38	
E	Rist Dorothea K—†	20	housewife	35	"
F	Neukam Annie—†	20	"	67	
G	Schlotter Dorothea C—†	20	at home	59	

School Street

K	Frank Allura J—†	104	housewife	47	here
L	Frank John C	104	seaman	49	"
M	Frank Mildred C—†	104	stenographer	22	"
N	Frank William T	104	electrician	49	"
O	Curtis Annie J—†	104	housewife	73	"
P	Curtis William H	104	retired	73	"
R	Coleman John	106	supervisor	40	116 School
S	Fleming Florence L—†	106	nurse	34	here

Page.	Letter.	FULL NAME.	Residence, Jan. 1. 1941.	Occupation.	Supposed Age.	Reported Residence, Jan. 1. 1940. Street and Number.

School Street—Continued

T	Fleming Kathleen P—†	106	nurse	32	here
U	Higgins Joseph	106	foreman	38	20 Beethoven
V	Reiling Heinrich	106	retired	60	here
W	Adams Robert	108	chauffeur	24	29 School
X	Gormley Frank J	108	supervisor	43	2 Atherton
Y	Mandell Alfred R	108	cook	30	Medford
Z	Moore Shirley A—†	108	nurse	23	Lowell
	953				
A	Wilbur Edna F—†	108	housewife	42	here
B	Wilbur Leonard V	108	mechanic	42	"
E	Hurley Joseph J	110	engineer	63	"
F	Hurley Margaret A—†	110	housewife	53	"
C	Maguire Aloysius	110	laborer	21	
D	Maguire Helen—†	110	typist	23	"
G	Freestone Lillian—†	110	nurse	40	Rhode Island
H	Hayes Mabel—†	110	"	35	2840 Wash'n
K	Parker Idell—†	110	"	27	Quincy
L	Rose Edith—†	110	"	32	30 Walnut pk
M	Bartlett Margaret R—†	110	housewife	24	here
N	Bartlett Roy O	110	chauffeur	29	"
O	Berglund Ruth—†	112	nurse	25	N Reading
P	Ranney Gerald	112	musician	29	here
R	Ranney Helen—†	112	housewife	29	"
S	Gillespie Dorothy H—†	112	"	31	120 Selden
T	Gillespie John J	112	operator	32	120 "
U	Gillespie Mary—†	112	bookkeeper	36	here
V	Gillespie Nora—†	112	housewife	63	"
W	*Aliberti Joseph	112	painter	31	"
X	*Aliberti Vincenta—†	112	examiner	30	"
Y	*Aliberti Vivian—†	112	housewife	26	"
Z	Gormley Henry L	114	merchant	47	"
	954				
A	Gormley Margaret F—†	114	housewife	43	"
B	Lorenzo Sue—†	116	waitress	25	Rhode Island
D	Quinlan Austin	116	chauffeur	36	3090 Wash'n
E	Quinlan Helen—†	116	housewife	33	3090 "
F	VanDitty Helen—†	116	waitress	34	1448 Park av
G	Wright Josephine E—†	120	housewife	72	here
C	Wright Susan—†	120	stitcher	38	Virginia
H	Bugbee Agnes—†	142	housewife	59	here
K	Bugbee Fred J	142	builder	22	"

11—9   33

School Street—Continued

L	Bugbee June A—†	142	clerk	20	here
M	Anderson Elizabeth—†	142	housewife	53	"
N	Anderson James W	142	hatter	55	"
O	Anderson Marie T—†	142	clerk	22	
P	Anderson Thomas F	142	brakeman	27	"
R	McCabe Annie—†	142	clerk	60	
S	Blair Mary—†	154	housekeeper	47	"
T	Gilmore William	154	fireman	47	"
U	Kelley Catherine—†	154	supervisor	47	"
V	Kelly Catherine—†	154	housewife	53	"
W	Kelly James	154	repairman	60	"
X	Kelly Mary A—†	154	stenographer	20	"
Y	Stier Christian A	157	ironworker	51	"
Z	Stier Christian J	157	clerk	27	

955

A	Stier Doris M—†	157	shoeworker	22	"
B	Stier Leo J	157	clerk	24	
C	Stier Mary E—†	157	housewife	51	"
D	Cusick James A	158	policeman	42	"
E	Cusick Sybil B—†	158	housewife	38	"
F	Chamberlin Berta M—†	158	at home	63	"
G	Sawyer Ella G—†	158	"	71	
H	Anselmo John	165	presser	34	
K	Anselmo Maybelle—†	165	clerk	37	"
L	Anselmo Tullio	165	presser	32	Everett
M	Forrest Eleanor C—†	165	clerk	26	here
N	Forrest John W	165	seaman	24	Pennsylvania
O	Reid David A	165	retired	71	here
P	Waterman Albert L	165	operator	62	"
R	Waterman Chester H	165	machinist	22	"
S	Waterman Mary J—†	165	housewife	56	"
T	Bennett Mary F—†	167	maid	24	
U	Bennett Mary J—†	167	housewife	50	"
V	Bennett William H	167	chauffeur	53	"
W	Brash Duncan	169	machinist	63	68 S Hunt'n a
X	Brickner Franklin	169	woodcarver	52	here
Y	Kenney Edith—†	169	waitress	34	49 Marcella
Z	Pauly Elise L—†	169	housewife	64	here

956

A	Pauly George	169	butcher	65	"
B	Winn Francis B	169	clerk	34	65 Westminster av

School Street—Continued

c	Winn Marie F—†	169	housewife	32	65 Westminster av
D	Humphrey Robert L	171	reporter	44	here
E	Malone Harriet—†	173	housekeeper	37	"
F	Burkhardt Augusta—†	173	at home	75	"
G	Caldwell Marie—†	173	"	64	"
H	Goddard Rae—†	175	housewife	31	Plymouth
K	Goddard Robert W	175	clerk	31	"
L	Hanbury Anna M—†	175	housewife	54	here
M	Hanbury Joseph	175	laborer	57	140 Minden
N	Hanbury Patrick B	175	machinist	55	here
o	*Thurber Viola—†	175	nurse	33	"
P	Puleo Carmello	176	manager	64	"
s	Puleo Concetta—†	176	housewife	65	"
T	Puleo Leo	176	carpenter	38	"
R	Puleo Stephena—†	176	student	21	"
U	Hoffmann Alfred	176	clerk	20	50 Forest Hills
v	*Hoffmann Emilie—†	176	housewife	48	50 "
w	Hoffmann Max	176	baker	52	50 "
x	Scalletta Anna—†	177	housewife	40	15 Gartland
Y	Scalletta John	177	marbleworker	50	15 "
z	*Buchta Anna—†	177	housewife	36	here
	957				
A	Buchta Max	177	breweryworker	35	"
B	Toal Florence M—†	177	housewife	28	"
c	Toal James	177	salesman	28	"
D	Hopkins Frederick E	178	retired	79	
E	Hopkins Frederick E, jr	178	stenographer	24	"
F	Hopkins Grace L—†	178	housewife	66	"
G	Hopkins Ruth C—†	178	decorator	26	"
H	Miley Ethel F—†	178	packer	29	
K	Morrill Lillian D—†	178	inspector	31	"
L	Schmidt Fred S	179	physician	67	"
M	Schmidt Jean—†	179	gardener	31	"
N	Schmidt Marie C—†	179	housewife	65	"
o	Bodman Norma—†	179	nurse	23	Lynn
P	Donnis Nellie—†	179	"	25	here
T	Hogan Minerva—†	179	housekeeper	66	"
R	Lane Marguerite—†	179	nurse	21	Lynn
s	Leary Louise—†	179	saleswoman	44	here
U	Nichols Lucille—†	179	nurse	28	Worcester
v	O'Neil Irene M—†	179	"	26	11 Weld av

School Street—Continued

	w	O'Brien Edward L	180	retired	71	here
	x	O'Brien Francis E	180	chauffeur	38	"
	y	O'Brien Helen G—†	180	housewife	35	"
	z	Mitchell Catherine—†	180	"	39	
958						
	A	Mitchell Roy	180	clerk	46	"
	B	Joyce Gertrude M—†	184	housewife	53	1122 River
	c	Joyce Herbert P	184	pharmacist	55	1122 "
	D	Joyce Wilfred H	184	salesman	25	1122 "
	E	Downey Anna—†	184	housewife	46	here
	F	Downey John	184	steamfitter	51	"
	G	Connolly Christopher	184	longshoreman	49	"
	H	Connolly John P	184	student	20	
	K	Connolly Margaret—†	184	housewife	48	"
	L	Connolly Mary—†	184	boxmaker	24	"
	M	Connolly Thomas J	184	student	22	
	P	Pickett Edna—†	188	housewife	60	"
	o	Pickett Frederick W	188	carpenter	66	"
	R	Pickett Helen—†	188	clerk	30	

959   Washington Street

	B	Vaughan Cora H—†	3135A	housekeeper	57	here
	c	Bruce John S	3135A	laborer	57	3000 Wash'n
	D	Fitzgerald Catherine M—†	3135A	housewife	53	here
	E	Fitzgerald John F	3135A	engineer	55	"
	F	Fitzgerald Mary B—†	3135A	at home	21	"
	H	*Elchuk Jennie—†	3135A	housewife	51	55 Coleman
	o	Martin Anna—†	3139	seamstress	40	here
	P	Tilton Gertrude E—†	3139	housewife	31	3 Oakdale
	R	Tilton Joseph H	3139	chauffeur	33	3 "
	U	Foster Ruth E—†	3141	housewife	40	here
	V	Diamon Lydia M—†	3141	"	40	"
	w	*Birnbaum Fannie—†	3141	"	52	"
	x	*Birnbaum Joseph	3141	cobbler	52	
960						
	A	Drews Grover C	3141C	plumber	48	"
	B	Grinnell Robert E	3145	salesman	23	46 W Walnut pk
	c	Grinnell Ruth F—†	3145	housewife	20	18 Dixwell
	D	Callanan Joan E—†	3145	"	43	here
	E	Callanan Lawrence J	3145	chauffeur	43	"

Page.	Letter.	FULL NAME.	Residence, Jan. 1, 1941.	Occupation.	Suppresed Age.	Reported Residence, Jan. 1. 1940. Street and Number.

Washington Street—Continued

	K	Kizeuk Mary—†	3147	at home	70	here
	L	*Kotipski Olga—†	3147	housewife	32	"
	M	Kotipski Theodore A	3147	porter	32	"
	N	*Rowicki Anthony	3147	barber	53	
	O	Alexander Alice M—†	3149	housewife	64	"
	P	Alexander Leo P	3149	laborer	24	
	R	Alexander William B	3149	musician	68	"
	S	Alexander William R	3149	bartender	35	"
	T	Costa Joseph A	3149	musician	35	"
	U	Costa Olive A—†	3149	"	37	"
	W	*Cammack Albert G	3149	electrician	24	15 Arcola
	V	Cammack Albert L	3149	carpenter	59	15 "
	X	Cammack Mabel H—†	3149	housewife	46	15 "
	Y	Cammack Philip E	3149	painter	22	15 "
	Z	Carty Edwina S—†	3151	housewife	26	here
		961				
	A	Carty Paul L	3151	clerk	30	
	C	*Grudznski Johanna D—†	3151	at home	78	
	D	Naruszewicz Anna M—†	3151	housewife	54	"
	E	Naruszewicz Stanley F	3151	baker	64	
	F	Palinkas Anna—†	3151	at home	21	
	G	Palinkas Elizabeth E—†	3151	operator	35	"
	H	Scheufele Irma R—†	3151	housewife	28	Illinois
	K	Cannata Bertha G—†	3155	"	25	here
	L	Cannata Sarino A	3155	barber	30	"
	M	Brophy Richard L	3155	clerk	36	"
	N	Brophy Thomas R	3155	pipefitter	65	"
	O	Cannata Charles J	3155	laborer	29	
	P	Cannata Mary L—†	3155	housewife	29	"
	R	Chase Minnie B—†	3157	at home	64	82 Forest Hills
	S	Richmond Ethel M—†	3157	housewife	38	82 "
	T	Richmond Louis J	3157	chauffeur	40	82 "
	U	O'Donnell Katherine J—†	3157	housewife	39	here

Ward 11–Precinct 10

CITY OF BOSTON

LIST OF RESIDENTS
20 YEARS OF AGE AND OVER

(NON-CITIZENS INDICATED BY ASTERISK)
(FEMALES INDICATED BY DAGGER)

AS OF

JANUARY 1, 1941

CITY OF BOSTON PRINTING DEPARTMENT

Page.	Letter.	FULL NAME.	Residence, Jan. 1, 1941.	Occupation.	Supposed Age.	Reported Residence, Jan. 1, 1940. Street and Number.

1000

Amory Street

B	Hinter Frank	244	machinist	49	here
c	*Hinter Prula—†	244	housewife	48	"
D	Leitner Alfred	244	cabinetmaker	26	"
E	Leitner Bertha—†	244	clerk	25	
F	Doerr Anna—†	246	housewife	52	"
G	Doerr Frank W	246	plumber	23	"
H	Doerr John	246	laborer	54	
K	Doerr Otto E	246	"	25	
L	Norman Clementine—†	248	storekeeper	55	"
M	*Norman Harry A	248	retired	47	"
N	*Norman Helen—†	248	at home	49	
O	Murray Joseph J	248	chauffeur	29	"
P	Murray Mary E—†	248	housewife	30	"
R	Rist Agnes—†.	250	at home	77	
S	Alber Gustav	250	chauffeur	36	"
T	Alber Marguerite E—†	250	bookkeeper	33	"
U	Getz Charles A	252	laborer	52	"
V	Getz Freida C—†	252	housewife	50	"
W	Cahill Francis E	252	chauffeur	30	"
X	Cahill Ruth M—†	252	housewife	27	"
Y	Smith Mildred S—†	254	"	31	123 Boylston
Z	Smith Ralph E	254	mason	22	123 "

1001

A	Clark Frederick C	254	laborer	43	here
B	Clark Henry	254	painter	38	59 Boylston
C	Smith Howard A	256	bricklayer	29	here
D	Smith Marjorie—†	256	housewife	25	"
E	Cunningham Helen—†	256	"	22	"
F	Ming Edith—†	258	cook	60	"
G	Lisle Almeda—†	258	housewife	45	239 Amory
H	Lisle Andrew W	258	waiter	54	239 "
K	Bandlow Freida S—†	260	secretary	44	here
L	Lannon Leo N	260	carpenter	44	"
M	Lannon Mona—†	260	housewife	42	"
N	MacNeill Annie K—†	264	"	64	
O	MacNeill John	264	stockman	26	"
P	MacNeill Mary—†	264	typist	28	
R	*Goss Elizabeth—†	266	housewife	32	"
S	*Goss William J	266	fisherman	32	"
T	Carney Catherine—†	266	at home	50	

Amory Street—Continued

u	Carney John	266	bookbinder	22	here
v	Danforth Clifford	266	presser	49	"
w	Danforth Elizabeth—†	266	housewife	78	"
	1002				
A	Smith Harriet—†	280	"	33	
B	Smith W Everett	280	mason	35	
c	Manning John	280	"	37	
D	Manning Margaret—†	280	housewife	33	"
E	Ouellette Mary C—†	282	"	53	
F	Ouellette Omer A	282	teacher	57	"
G	Johnson Katherine E—†	282	housewife	22	176 Hyde Park av
H	McKee Elizabeth E—†	282	"	26	176 "
K	Rosen Estelle M—†	282	"	58	176 "
L	Ellis Ernest	284	painter	40	here
M	*Ellis Rose—†	284	housewife	31	"
N	Harding Bridie—†	286	"	46	"
o	Kimball Fred P	286	laborer	57	
P	Kimball Juliette--†	286	housewife	48	"
R	*Dunscomb Mae—†	286	waitress	27	Cambridge
s	Maloney Elizabeth—†	286	laundress	37	here
T	Thompson Dorothy M-†	286	housewife	22	"
u	Thompson Joseph F	288	shipfitter	26	"
v	Rosen Dorothy—†	288	housewife	23	"
w	Rosen Victor	288	tree surgeon	29	"
x	Smith Antoinette—†	288	housewife	54	"
y	Smith Frank J	288	grinder	55	
z	DeRosa Estelle—†	290	housewife	47	"
	1003				
A	DeRosa John	290	chef	24	"
B	DeRosa Joseph	290	"	48	
c	May Hubert A	292	clerk	35	
D	May Margaret—†	292	housewife	31	"
E	May Hubert W	292	retired	77	
F	May John	292	laborer	37	
G	Burkhardt Gottlieb W	296	retired	86	
H	Burkhardt John F	296	mover	44	
K	Alberg Alice C—†	300	housewife	46	"
L	Alberg Alice L—†	300	typist	20	
M	Alberg Frederick	300	mover	51	"
N	Hanley Joseph M	300	chauffeur	29	76 Bragdon
o	Hanley Virginia—†	300	housewife	25	76 "

3

Amory Street—Continued

P	DeAngelis Mary—†	304	inspector	23	Malden
R	Sabadini Louis	304	salesman	33	here
S	Sabadini Mary—†	304	housewife	35	"
T	Hanley Bridget—†	308	"	64	"
U	Hanley Malachi	308	retired	73	
V	Hanley Matthew F	308	tea blender	31	"
W	Walsh Mary J—†	312	housewife	40	"
X	Walsh Michael F	312	chauffeur	39	"
Y	Cunningham Catherine C—†	314	housewife	46	"
Z	Cunningham Christopher B	314	laundryworker	22	"

1004

A	Cunningham George J	314	carpenter	49	"
B	Cunningham John J	314	laborer	23	
C	Cunningham Marion—†	314	clerk	20	
D	Scriven Edwin A	314	toolmaker	31	"
E	Scriven Marie B—†	314	housewife	26	"
F	Burns Louvina—†	314	at home	64	
G	Joaquin Francis	314	chauffeur	37	"
H	Joaquin Katherine—†	314	housewife	31	"
K	Cummings Beatrice—†	320	"	23	57½ Marcella
L	Cummings Paul	320	chauffeur	26	57½ "
M	*Alman Frances—†	320	housewife	48	here
N	*MacDonald Bernard	320	operator	25	"
O	Mills Anna F—†	320	housewife	42	"
P	Mills Edward	320	laborer	54	
R	Mills Thomas	320	machinist	44	"
S	*Duggan Harold	322	carpenter	40	"
T	Duggan Mary—†	322	housewife	34	"
U	Hardcastle James T	322	mover	35	
V	Hardcastle John F	322	"	34	
W	Hardcastle Joseph M	322	"	31	
X	Hardcastle Margaret E—†	322	housewife	63	"
Y	Hardcastle Margaret F—†	322	benchworker	37	"

1005

A	Gallivan Elizabeth—†	332	attendant	41	"
B	Gallivan James W	332	mover	39	"
C	Smithers Annie—†	332	at home	68	6 Cable
D	Weymouth Rose—†	332	"	51	285 Chestnut av
E	Tierney Jeannette M—†	334	housewife	46	3239 Wash'n
F	Tierney William A	334	janitor	52	3239 "
G	*Kilday Anna—†	336	housewife	35	here

Page	Letter.	Full Name.	Residence. Jan. 1, 1941.	Occupation.	Supposed Age.	Reported Residence, Jan. 1, 1940. Street and Number.

Amory Street—Continued

	H	Kilday James	336	laborer	37	here
	K	Webb Eva M—†	336	housewife	31	"
	L	Webb Minas I	336	barber	30	"
	M	Webb Wylie W	336	welder	33	
	N	Powers George	342	laborer	45	"
	O	*Powers Nora—†	342	housewife	45	"
	P	Finley Catherine A—†	342	"	41	
	R	Finley Terence L	342	laborer	43	
	S	Arnold Herbert W	342	foreman	43	
	T	*Arnold Stella A—†	342	housewife	43	"
	U	*Foley Hester M—†	350	"	38	
	V	Foley Maurice J	350	engineer	39	"
	W	Arnott Adeline A—†	350	waitress	23	11 Manila av
	X	Arnott George E	350	U S N	22	3 Woolsey sq
	Y	Arnott Mary A—†	350	housewife	49	3 "
	Z	Keegan James J	350	carpenter	52	here

1006

	A	*Keegan Mary A—†	350	housewife	48	"
	C	Adams Mary—†	352	"	27	Maine
	D	Adams R Maurice	352	chauffeur	30	"
	E	Carey Helen M—†	352	housewife	31	here
	F	Carey John J	352	painter	32	"
	G	Goldsworthy Dorothy—†	366	housewife	26	"
	H	*Goldsworthy John H	366	chauffeur	27	"
	K	McGeggen Edna—†	366	housewife	31	"
	L	McGeggen Hugh	366	retired	35	"
	N	Lyons Hilda I—†	368	housewife	31	8 School
	O	Lyons William E	368	gardener	43	8 "
	P	*Holtzman Charlotte—†	368	at home	72	here
	R	Bebbington Elizabeth—†	370	seamstress	64	171 School
	S	Hamman Annie E—†	370	housewife	49	here
	T	Hamman Frank	370	laborer	57	"
	U	Hamman John A	370	"	26	"
	V	Hamman Madeline—†	370	typist	20	"
	W	McKay Bernard	372	timekeeper	26	"
	X	*McKay Catherine—†	372	housewife	54	"
	Y	McKay Sarah—†	372	laundress	21	"
	Z	Donovan Cornelius J	372	clerk	23	

1007

	A	Donovan John F	372	laborer	25	
	B	Donovan Mary—†	372	housewife	52	"

5

Page.	Letter.	Full Name.	Residence, Jan. 1, 1941.	Occupation.	Supposed Age.	Reported Residence, Jan. 1, 1940. Street and Number.

Amory Street—Continued

	c	Donovan Timothy J	372	rubberworker	29	here
	d	DeCoste Edward	372	ironworker	39	"
	e	*DeCoste Mary—†	372	housewife	37	"
	h	Brandt Mary J—†	384	"	37	"
	k	*Reardon Mary—†	384	"	36	156 Lamartine
	l	Paschal Archie	384	chauffeur	47	here
	m	Paschal Elizabeth—†	384	housewife	40	"
	n	*Joyce John	384	retired	53	"
	o	*Joyce Mary—†	384	housewife	54	"
	p	Joyce Mary A—†	384	clerk	20	"
	r	*Williams Mary—†	384	housewife	37	183 E
	t	Busconi Angelina—†	384	"	49	here
	u	Busconi Peter	384	upholsterer	46	"
	v	Cunniff Catherine—†	384	housewife	23	"
	w	Cunniff Peter	384	mover	29	10 Spring Park av
	z	Stewart Daniel	384	boilermaker	41	here

1008

	a	Stewart Lottie F—†	384	housewife	35	"
	b	Mathisen Helen—†	384	"	43	50 Bickford
	c	Quinn David	384	bookbinder	46	here
	d	Quinn Sarah A—†	384	housewife	40	"
	e	*Zeogas Charles	384	cook	48	"
	f	*Zeogas Pauline—†	384	housewife	36	"
	g	Skeffington Harry	384	attendant	28	23 Burard
	h	Skeffington Ruth—†	384	housewife	28	23 "
	k	*DeCostantino Angela—†	384	"	35	52 Chestnut
	l	McLeod Alice—†	384	"	32	1394 Col av
	m	McLeod John	384	mover	52	1394 "
	o	Prive Veda—†	392	housewife	37	here
	p	Prive Wallace	392	junkman	39	"
	r	Burton Harold	394	porter	24	"
	s	Burton John	394	grinder	21	
	t	Gately James	394	washer	39	
	u	Gately Josephine—†	394	housewife	35	"
	v	Gately Patrick	394	retired	80	
	w	Gately Thomas	394	laborer	49	
	x	Gately Bertha—†	394	housewife	39	"
	y	Gately John F	394	laborer	47	
	z	Meroth Louis A	394	retired	74	

1009

	a	*Doran Catherine—†	402	housewife	73	30 Oakdale

6

Page.	Letter.	Full Name.	Residence, Jan. 1, 1941.	Occupation.	Supposed Age.	Reported Residence, Jan. 1, 1940. Street and Number.

Amory Street—Continued

	B	*Doran Joseph	402	retired	81	30 Oakdale
	c	Colwill Earl	402	mason	23	here
	D	Colwill Ethel—†	402	housewife	53	"
	E	Colwill Robert	402	clerk	21	N Hampshire
	F	Mullins Evelyn—†	402	maid	33	here
	G	Efraimson Lydia—†	404	housewife	33	103A Lamartine
	H	Efraimson Thorsten	404	laborer	36	103A "
	K	*Buote Bertha—†	404	housewife	39	here
	L	*Buote George	404	painter	38	"
	M	*Cauldwell Basil	404	operator	22	"
	N	*Cauldwell Dora—†	404	housewife	43	"
	o	Cauldwell Dorothy—†	404	typist	20	"
	P	Love Edward	406	orderly	20	26 Ruggles
	R	Cantoni Attario	406	cook	60	here
	s	Cantoni Mary R—†	406	housewife	51	"
	T	Doncaster George W	408	mechanic	41	238 Lamartine
	U	Doncaster Mildred—†	408	housewife	31	238 "
	V	Licciardi Anne—†	408	"	26	here
	W	Licciardi Vincent	408	laborer	28	"
	X	Feeney Nora J—†	408	clerk	25	"
	Y	Feeney Thomas F	408	accountant	28	"
	Z	Feeney Thomas J	408	retired	63	

1010

	A	Wagner Lawrence J	412	painter	44	
	B	Wagner Mabel C—†	412	housewife	36	"
	E	Farrell Frank	440	U S N	41	
	F	Yoder Margaret—†	440	housewife	32	"
	G	Yoder Norman	440	guard	37	

Brookside Avenue

	H	Anderson Charles A	21	brewmaster	45	here
	K	Anderson Hazel—†	21	housewife	44	"
	L	Anderson Pearl—†	21	saleswoman	20	"
	M	Plouff Adaline J—†	21	at home	73	
	N	McCormick Catherine A-†	27	housewife	55	"
	o	McCormick John W	27	machinist	20	"
	P	O'Brien Margaret E—†	27	waitress	28	"
	R	Riordan Agnes C—†	27	clerk	38	48 Haverford
	s	Hinterleitner John J	27	"	23	59 Forest Hills
	T	Hinterleitner Nancy—†	27	housewife	22	59 "

Brookside Avenue—Continued

u	McCormick Michael	29	retired	65	here
v	Milliard Caroline—†	29	housewife	63	"
w	Milliard Joseph W	29	printer	54	"
x	Cronin Jeremiah	29	retired	58	
y	Delorey Frank	29	cook	57	
z	Delorey Frank E	29	shipper	21	

1011

a	Delorey Mary—†	29	housewife	55	"
b	Kerr Mary—†	29	housekeeper	26	"
c	Davin Elizabeth—†	29	housewife	68	"
d	Davin Rita M—†	29	saleswoman	26	"
e	Davin Thomas F	29	broker	33	"
f	McCarthy Dennis	33	superintendent	38	"
g	McCarthy Margaret—†	33	housewife	32	"
h	Sullivan Delia M—†	33	"	47	
k	Sullivan Harry A	33	steamfitter	47	"
l	Egan Mabel—†	33	housekeeper	40	"
m	*Bock Jeanne—†	53	housewife	45	"
n	Bock Robert C	53	chef	45	"
o	Mullen Frederick W	53	fireman	57	40 Union Park
p	Reynolds Robert J	53	clerk	23	here
r	Reynolds Rosa—†	53	housewife	38	"
s	*Doyle Dorothy A—†	56	"	33	"
t	Doyle Lawrence	56	garageman	33	"
u	Connolly Martin	56	watertender	55	"
v	Connolly Mary—†	56	operator	23	
w	Connolly Sarah T—†	56	housewife	59	"
x	MacGillivary John	56	waiter	35	
y	*MacGillivary Mary—†	56	housewife	25	"

1012

a	Alconada Dorothea—†	58	"	33	
b	Alconada Joseph J	58	machinist	37	"
c	Richard Agnes B—†	58	housewife	44	"
d	Richard Edmund	58	repairman	44	"
e	Richard Eleanor—†	58	inspector	20	"
f	Moore Gertrude—†	58	waitress	29	221 Florence
g	Paley Arthur J	58	guard	34	221 "
h	Paley Marjorie—†	58	housewife	30	221 "
k	O'Connor Bridget M—†	60	"	40	36 Forbes
l	O'Conner Michael J	60	janitor	38	36 "
m	Olsen Agnes—†	60	housewife	30	here

Page.	Letter.	FULL NAME.	Residence, Jan. 1, 1941.	Occupation.	Supposed Age.	Reported Residence, Jan. 1, 1940. Street and Number.

Brookside Avenue—Continued

	Letter	FULL NAME	Residence	Occupation	Age	Reported Residence
	N	Olsen Clifford	60	chauffeur	32	here
	o	Boomer James	60	mechanic	31	"
	P	Boomer Mildred—†	60	housewife	27	"
	R	Shea Mary—†	60	at home	58	
	T	Diggins Joan—†	62	housewife	39	"
	U	Diggins John	62	policeman	39	"
	v	*MacDonald Irene—†	62	housewife	36	"
	w	MacDonald Peter	62	shipper	37	
	x	Sweeney Dennis	62	oiler	32	
	Y	*Sweeney Helen—†	62	housewife	34	"
1013						
	A	Conners Lillian—†	64	"	40	
	B	Whitten Francis M	64	machinist	24	"
	c	Whitten Martin	64	salesman	58	"
	D	Whitten Sadie C—†	64	housewife	55	"
	E	Duffin Margaret C—†	64	clerk	20	"
	F	Duffin Mary—†	64	housewife	47	"
	G	Duffin Michael	64	molder	48	"
	K	Sargent Albert	66	welder	26	151 Lamartine
	L	Sargent Mary—†	66	housewife	58	151 "
	M	Willett Andrew	66	photographer	32	here
	N	Willett Marie—†	66	housewife	25	"
	o	Grant Henry L	66	laborer	56	"
	P	Grant James P	66	usher	20	"
	R	Grant Nora J—†	66	housewife	47	"
	s	*Canning Florence—†	68	"	41	299 Lamartine
	T	*Canning Walter	68	repairman	43	299 "
	U	Foley James D	68	waiter	53	here
	w	Boettcher Frances—†	70	housewife	24	"
	x	Boettcher Joseph	70	chauffeur	26	"
	Y	*Giannelli Carmelia—†	70	housewife	42	"
	z	Giannelli Ettore	70	cook	44	"
1014						
	A	Crawford Bridget—†	70	housewife	34	"
	B	Crawford Henry	70	chauffeur	35	"
	c	Reilly Bernard	79	"	43	
	D	Reilly Cecelia—†	79	housewife	45	"
	E	'Reilly Rose C—†	79	stenographer	33	"
	F	Murray Thomas E	81	instructor	51	62 Cornwall
	G	Stone Carl P	81	guard	44	62 "
	H	Stone Helen R—†	81	housewife	44	62 "

9

Page.	Letter.	FULL NAME.	Residence, Jan. 1, 1941.	Occupation.	Supposed Age.	Reported Residence, Jan. 1, 1940. Street and Number.

Brookside Avenue—Continued

	K	McLaughlin Alice—†	83	at home	70	here
	L	McLaughlin Edward	83	chemist	32	"
	N	McGrath Annie—†	87	housewife	51	"
	O	McGrath Dennis P	87	foreman	52	"
	P	Perkins Earl	89	laborer	30	25 Dorr
	R	Perkins Mary—†	89	housewife	30	25 "
	T	Kelley Anna—†	91	housekeeper	29	here
	U	Kelley Charles	91	salesman	23	"
	V	Kelley John E	91	retired	58	"
	W	Kelley John F	91	shipper	33	
	X	Kelley Joseph	91	foundryman	25	"
	Y	*Kelley Margaret—†	91	housewife	58	"
	Z	Kelley Marguerite—†	91	packer	21	
		1015				
	A	Morgan Anthony	91	operator	26	"
	B	Morgan Dominick	91	"	55	
	D	Morgan Frank	91	student	21	
	E	Morgan George	91	clerk	25	
	C	Morgan Henrietta—†	91	housewife	55	"
	F	Morgan Manuel	91	clerk	24	
	G	Doyle John	91	laborer	36	"
	H	Tobin Mary—†	91	housewife	40	"
	K	Tobin Thomas	91	engineer	47	"
	L	Coska Clara M—†	93	housewife	28	2 Lamartine ct
	M	Coska John	93	painter	30	2 "
	N	McLeod Anna—†	93	housewife	50	here
	O	McLeod Malcolm	93	mechanic	53	"
	P	Latendorf Frederick C	94	projectionist	46	"
	R	Latendorf Valentine J—†	94	housewife	46	"
	S	Huebner Alexander R	94	painter	77	
	T	Huebner Olga—†	94	housewife	72	"
	U	Nemet Henry	95	carpenter	43	"
	V	Nemet Mary—†	95	housewife	38	"
	W	Ahearn John	97	freighthandler	51	"
	X	Ahearn John J, jr	97	mechanic	23	"
	Y	Ahearn Margaret—†	97	housewife	47	"
	Z	Ahearn Mary—†	97	saleswoman	21	"
		1016				
	A	Mulvey Dorothy—†	rear 97	housewife	26	"
	B	Mulvey James	" 97	laborer	24	"
	C	Davis Robert E	" 97	counterman	21	37 Child

10

Brookside Avenue—Continued

D	Peterson Joseph E	98	diemaker	53	here
E	Peterson Leslie	98	machinist	22	"
F	Peterson Marie A—†	98	housewife	47	"
H	Barth Gertrude—†	99	saleswoman	22	"
K	Barth Martha—†	99	housewife	49	"
L	Barth Paul	99	painter	53	
M	Devlin Patrick	103	cook	48	
N	Devlin Sarah—†	103	housewife	42	"
O	Finnerty Gerald	103	laborer	42	
P	Finnerty Lena M—†	103	bookkeeper	52	"
R	Finnerty Margaret—†	103	housewife	73	"
S	Nielsen Emma—†	105	"	45	"
T	*Taglieri Eliza—†	105	"	32	155 Saratoga
U	Taglieri Gene	105	operator	30	24 Prince
V	Wille Olga—†	105	housewife	71	here
W	Whalen John J	108	retired	· 65	"
X	Freier Anton	108	electrician	69	154 Boylston
Y	Freier Emma—†	108	housekeeper	24	154 "
Z	Freier Regina—†	108	housewife	64	154 "

1017

A	*Halbert Alice—†	108		63	here
B	McNamee Ellen—†	112	"	35	519 St Theresa av
C	McNamee Henry	112	spreader	40	868 Hunt'n av
D	Curran Bernard	112	retired	74	here
E	Curran Francis	112	clerk	30	"
F	Curran Letitia—†	112	housewife	70	"
G	Curran Susan—†	112	housekeeper	42	"
H	McLean Mary—†	112	housewife	39	3310 Wash'n
K	Townsend Dorothy—†	112	"	45	here
L	Townsend Robert F	112	barber	55	"
O	Gillespie James A	121	ironworker	45	3326 Wash'n
P	Gillespie Margaret—†	121	housewife	30	3326 "
R	*Roffe Margaret—†	121	"	53	here
S	*Roffe William	121	painter	51	"
V	Morris Alonzo B	125	mechanic	33	"
W	Morris Virginia—†	125	housewife	30	"

1018   **Cable Street**

E	Sudbey Ellen W—†	2	housewife	58	120 Sycamore
F	Sudbey James J	2	repairman	30	120 "

Cable Street—Continued

G	Harrison Arthur	2	janitor	63	here
H	Harrison Arthur H	2	laborer	25	"
K	Harrison Hannah—†	2	housewife	62	"
L	O'Brien James	4	laborer	44	"
M	*Durkin Annie—†	4	housekeeper	80	384 Amory
N	Hagen John F	4	polisher	43	384 "
O	Jordan Dorothy—†	6	housewife	31	here
P	Jordan George	6	U S N	30	"
S	Dalton Nicholas	10	chimneysmith	31	"
T	Dugley Albert	10	laborer	61	
U	Dugley Elizabeth—†	10	housewife	53	"
V	Sabol Boleslaw	10	carpenter	24	122 Paul Gore
W	Sabol Olga J—†	10	housewife	25	180 Heath
X	*Hanley Michael	12	retired	65	here
Y	Russell Elizabeth—†	12	housekeeper	57	"
Z	Young Arthur W	14	laborer	41	"

1019

A	Young Mary J—†	14	housewife	39	"
B	*Sheppard Jean—†	14	"	36	
C	*Sheppard Stuart	14	machinist	40	"
D	Eshenwald Anna—†	14	housewife	56	"
E	Eshenwald Ernest	14	laborer	27	
F	Eshenwald Fred	14	"	56	
G	*Coy Beatrice—†	16	housewife	34	"
H	*Coy Frank L	16	lumberman	36	"
K	Haney Dennis	16	clerk	25	Maine
L	Haney Gertrude M—†	16	waitress	26	here
M	Woodward Almon	16	chauffeur	50	"
N	Woodward Winifred M—†	16	housewife	57	"
O	Feeney Catherine—†	16	"	58	
P	Feeney James	16	clerk	24	
R	Feeney John	16	laborer	20	

Cornwall Street

S	DePasquale Angelina—†	8	housewife	51	here
T	DePasquale Ralph	8	stonesetter	60	"
U	DePasquale Sebastian	8	laborer	22	"
V	Berube John B	9	watchman	37	"
W	Berube Ruth B—†	9	housewife	32	"
X	Gilchrist Edna—†	9	"	35	Dedham

Page	Letter	Full Name	Residence, Jan. 1, 1941.	Occupation.	Supposed Age.	Reported Residence, Jan. 1, 1940. Street and Number.

Cornwall Street—Continued

	Y	Gilchrist Kenneth	9	foreman	38	here
	Z	Deutsch Anthony	9	chauffeur	33	127 Lamartine
1020						
	A	Deutsch Blanche L—†	9	housewife	32	127 "
	B	Moore Anna M—†	10	stenographer	22	here
	C	Moore Bridget C—†	10	housewife	45	"
	D	Moore Martin T	10	laborer	20	"
	E	Coye Annie—†	11	maid	65	
	F	Coye Catherine—†	11	cook	67	
	H	White Dorothea C—†	11	clerk	21	
	G	White Edward J	11	electroplater	53	"
	K	White Frances M—†	11	housewife	56	"
	L	White Frances T—†	11	stenographer	26	"
	M	Eldridge Francis W	15	retired	41	7 Ellsworth
	N	Eldridge Loretta M—†	15	housewife	39	7 "
	O	Hughes Ann T—†	18	housekeeper	44	here
	P	Hughes Henry	18	retired	83	"
	R	Hughes Mary E—†	18	teacher	46	"
	S	*Victor Jessie M—†	21	housewife	35	"
	T	Victor John J	21	mechanic	34	"
	U	Van der Snoek Catharina—†	21	housewife	51	"
	V	Van der Snoek Paul	21	birdkeeper	49	"
	W	Graham Blanche G—†	21	housewife	29	"
	X	Graham Emery	21	repairman	29	"
	Y	Careless Francis D	25	chauffeur	45	"
	Z	Careless Mary C—†	25	housewife	40	"
1021						
	A	Albrink Mary—†	25	housekeeper	67	53 Boynton
	B	Watson Florence W—†	25	clerk	48	53 "
	C	Krusé Emil	28	drop forger	57	here
	D	Kruse Helena—†	28	housewife	54	"
	E	Kruse Hugo	28	breweryworker	42	"
	F	Kruse Otto	28	shoecutter	55	"
	G	Connolly Anna E—†	28	housewife	38	"
	H	Connolly Robert L	28	superintendent	37	"
	K	Lynch Henry C	28	operator	34	
	L	Lynch Mary D—†	28	housewife	28	"
	M	Mahoney Albina J—†	29	"	33	
	N	Mahoney John F	29	clerk	38	"
	O	Harrington Julia K—†	29	matron	42	
	P	Keegan Joseph A	29	porter	35	

Page.	Letter.	FULL NAME.	Residence, Jan. 1, 1941.	Occupation.	Supposed Age.	Reported Residence, Jan. 1, 1940. Street and Number.

Cornwall Street—Continued

R	*Keegan Nancy—†	29	housewife	34	here
s	*Ryan Mary F—†	29	"	30	"
T	Ryan Michael E	29	machinist	45	"
U	McGreevy Anne V—†	33	housewife	39	3304 Wash'n
V	McGreevy Thomas A	33	chauffeur	36	3304 "
W	Conroy Catherine V—†	33	housewife	26	here
X	Conroy James J	33	electrician	31	"
Y	Dubois Victoria—†	33	housewife	61	"
z	Willis Arthur E	41	florist	33	56 Green

1022

A	Willis Christine A—†	41	housewife	31	56 "
B	Hall Christine G—†	41	housekeeper	32	here
C	Hall Margaret M—†	41	housewife	58	"
D	Hall William T	41	manager	29	"
E	Cunningham James	45	retired	86	
F	Cunningham John J	45	electrician	45	"
G	Ivers Mary A—†	45	housewife	48	"
H	Ford Alice L—†	47	"	40	127 Paul Gore
K	Ford Thomas F	47	chauffeur	42	127 "
L	Keough Joseph	47	cook	22	127 "
M	Casey Hannah—†	47	housewife	45	here
N	Casey Michael	47	laborer	45	"
O	Brennan Mary—†	47	housewife	54	"
P	Brennan William J	47	plasterer	52	"
R	Sundin Andrew G	51	retired	68	70 School
S	Sundin Sophie—†	51	housewife	62	70 "
T	Dolan Hermina H—†	51	"	32	here
U	Dolan James A	51	laborer	31	"
V	Kenney Elizabeth M—†	51	housewife	52	"
W	Kenney John E	51	U S A	20	
X	McLaughlin Frank J	62	foreman	38	
Y	McLaughlin Valeria M—†	62	housewife	39	"
z	Craig Catherine M—†	62	"	39	

1023

A	Craig Edward H	62	machinist	39	"
C	List William	64	retired	68	
D	Killion John	64	chauffeur	39	"
E	Killion Mary C—†	64	housewife	36	"
F	*Bartlett Mary A—†	64	"	58	
G	*Bartlett Walter H	64	retired	66	
H	Daley Joseph T	64	laborer	33	

Cornwall Street—Continued

K	Reinhardt Frank J	66	inspector	38	here
L	Reinhardt Wilfred F	66	salesman	28	"

Dolan's Court

M	*Fuller Florence—†	2	housewife	26	here
N	Fuller Louis W	2	plumber	29	"
O	*MacDougal Mary—†	2	housekeeper	74	"
P	Galvin Eugene F	4	machinist	73	42 Woodlawn
R	Perry George D	4	chauffeur	29	42 "
S	Perry Mary A—†	4	housewife	28	here
T	Currie Addie V—†	6	"	36	"
U	Currie George	6	laborer	46	"
V	Fuller Everett P	8	plumber	64	
W	Fuller Everett P, jr	8	dyesetter	22	"
X	Fuller Mabel W—†	8	housewife	61	"
Y	Johanson Dorothy W—†	8	housekeeper	27	"

Forest Hills Street

Z	Pezzulo Albert	37	serviceman	41	34 Carolina av
	1024				
A	Pezzulo Concetta—†	37	housewife	33	34 "
B	Barca Michael	37	teacher	28	75 Rossmore rd
C	Barca Nora—†	37	housewife	27	75 "
D	*Nilsson Axel	39	mason	55	186 Boylston
E	Nilsson Robert E	39	roofer	31	186 "
F	*Nilsson Ruth—†	39	housewife	51	186 "
G	Feeney John N	39	clerk	31	here
H	Feeney Mary A—†	39	housewife	64	"
K	Anderson Thorsten S	39	laborer	57	"
L	Atton Augusta—†	39	housekeeper	66	"
M	Johnson Axel S	39	manager	45	"
N	Groves Charles	43	carpenter	34	"
O	Groves Lillian—†	43	housewife	33	"
P	McCormack Alice—†	43	"	52	
R	McCormack Daniel J	43	laborer	58	
S	Woelfel Edward	43	factoryhand	30	"
T	Woelfel Marguerite—†	43	"	29	"
U	Woelfel Theresa—†	43	nurse	23	Quincy
V	Grogan Alice A—†	45	operator	30	75 Howard av

15

Forest Hills Street—Continued

		Full Name	Res.	Occupation	Age	Reported Residence
	w	Grogan Julia M—†	45	clerk	32	75 Howard av
	x	McGann Andrew T	45	carpenter	22	here
	y	McGann Louise R—†	45	housewife	46	"
	z	McGann Patrick	45	clerk	51	"
1025						
	A	Crane Alice M—†	45	housekeeper	38	"
	B	Crane Catherine F—†	45	housewife	60	"
	c	Crane Dennis E	45	operator	62	"
	D	Haines Cecelia—†	47	housewife	41	112 H
	E	Rollins Eliot	51	painter	28	here
	F	Rollins Pearl—†	51	housewife	27	"
	G	Elfving Harry	51	blacksmith	33	"
	H	Elfving Theresa F—†	51	housewife	27	"
	K	*Flynn Mary—†	51	domestic	34	10 Brookside av
	L	Flynn Thomas	51	laborer	33	10 "
	M	Carter Marie—†	53	nurse	38	here
	N	Healy Francis J	53	clerk	28	"
	o	Healy Hilda—†	53	housewife	30	"
	P	Healy Thomas A	53	shipper	23	
	R	Allsop Esther M—†	53	housewife	40	"
	s	Allsop James	53	mechanic	55	"
	T	deLesdernier Bessie—†	55	housewife	61	"
	U	deLesdernier Frederick M	55	retired	65	
	V	Palmer Mary C—†	55	housewife	30	"
	w	Palmer Robert T	55	laborer	36	
	x	Felton Evelyn—†	55	housewife	35	"
	Y	Felton John	55	cigarmaker	40	"
	z	Hinterlietner Annie—†	59	housewife	49	"
1026						
	A	Hinterlietner Jacob	59	ironworker	52	"
	B	Swanborn Edwin	59	machinist	30	30 Lenoxdale av
	c	*Swanborn Jean—†	59	housewife	25	16 Cheshire
	D	Boyle Mary L—†	63	"	57	here
	E	Boyle Patrick J	63	agent	58	"
	F	Murphy Cornelius M	63	clerk	40	71 Forest Hills
	G	Murphy Joseph L	63	attorney	29	71 "
	H	Murphy Nora—†	63	housewife	60	71 "
	K	Murphy William F	63	shoeworker	37	71 "
	L	Frank Edna D—†	63	nurse	37	here
	M	*Frank Harold M	63	salesman	44	"

Forest Hills Street—Continued

N	Frank Hilda D—†	63	corsetiere	46	here
o	Frank Julius J	63	salesman	78	"
p	Frank Marion—†	63	housekeeper	39	"
R	Andrews James C	71	salesman	37	69 Montebello rd
s	Andrews Mary—†	71	housewife	29	69 "
T	Nordahl Carl E	71	pressman	32	Arlington
u	Nordahl Ruth L—†	71	housewife	32	"
v	Procum Alma M—†	71	"	32	here
w	Procum Francis W	71	attorney	33	"
x	Osol Eva—†	75	housewife	53	"
y	Osol Jacob A	75	machinist	54	"
z	McGurk Arthur J	75	U S A	20	35 Ainsworth

1027

A	McGurk Catherine G—†	75	housewife	50	35 "
B	McGurk Frederick L	75	clerk	28	35 '
c	McGurk George G	75	student	21	35 '
D	McGurk James F	75	clerk	30	35 "
E	Fitzgerald Ella G—†	75	housekeeper	69	here

Green Street

u	Flanagan Helen L—†	190	housewife	68	here
v	Flanagan Madeline G—†	190	"	28	"
w	Flanagan Thomas W	190	manager	38	"
x	Kelly Thomas F	190	retired	67	
y	MacDonald Frank H	194	bricklayer	44	"
z*	MacDonald Helen E—†	194	housewife	38	"

1028

A	Thompson Leroy	194	laborer	64	2 Hubbard
B	Devereau Ethel A—†	196	housewife	46	here
c	Devereau George E	196	clerk	21	"
D	Devereau William C	196	gateman	53	"
E	Devereau William J	196	shipper	25	
F	Barrio Hubert T	198	painter	60	
G	Barrio Joseph J	198	meter reader	55	"
H	Barrio Thomas F	198	laborer	58	
K	Galvin Almina F—†	198	housewife	32	"
L	Galvin Francis J	198	chauffeur	39	"
M	Merrill Margaret—†	198	cleaner	68	
N	Swanson Alice E—†	198	operator	32	"

Page	Letter	Full Name.	Residence, Jan. 1, 1941.	Occupation.	Supposed Age.	Reported Residence, Jan. 1, 1940. Street and Number.

Green Street—Continued

	o	Swanson Annie C—†	198	housewife	72	here
	p	Swanson Ernest M	198	retired	76	"
	r	Swanson Ernest T	198	mechanic	27	"

Greenley Place

	u	Stewart Donald	5	salesman	33	here
	v	Stewart Mary E—†	5	housewife	34	"
	w	Blest Bertha E—†	5	"	39	"
	x	Blest George	5	chauffeur	40	"
	y	Snow Cecelia E—†	5	housewife	52	"
	z	Snow Earl L	5	mechanic	61	"
1029						
	a	Snow John S	5	laborer	22	
	b	Snow Paul L	5	operator	21	"
	c	Peterson Nicholas	7	fireman	45	
	d	*Peterson Susan—†	7	housewife	48	"
	e	Goetze Christina—†	7	"	75	"
	f	Goetze Henry G	7	toolmaker	48	"
	g	Mitchell Clarence L	rear 7	clerk	22	
	h	Mitchell Nellie J—†	" 7	housewife	53	"
	k	Mitchell Wallace M	" 7	machinist	55	"
	l	Nye George P	8	"	24	New York
	m	*Nye Ruth—†	8	housewife	26	here
	n	Nye Walter R	8	contractor	28	"
	o	Smith Edward A	8	packer	45	"
	p	Smith Mary N—†	8	housewife	45	"
	r	Anderson Claire E—†	9	"	23	
	s	Anderson Harvey A	9	electroplater	20	"
	t	*Zabczuk Rose—†	9	housewife	43	"
	u	Zabczuk Vincent	9	cook	48	"
	v	Abberton Marguerite C—†	10	operator	20	7 Sylvia
	w	Abberton Rose A—†	10	housewife	41	7 "
	x	Brith Mary A—†	10½	clerk	26	here
	y	Brith Mary A—†	10½	housewife	47	"
	z	Brith Peter J	10½	driller	51	"
1030						
	a	Brith Peter J, jr	10½	clerk	24	"
	b	Gustafson Dorothy R—†	11	housewife	27	6 Alfred
	c	*Gustafson Jacob	11	factoryhand	30	6 "
	d	Lennon Mary E—†	11	housewife	43	here

18

Greenley Place—Continued

E	Lennon Thomas F	11	ironworker	50	here
F	*MacKenzie Maude—†	11	housekeeper	35	"
G	Atanasio Anna J—†	12	housewife	36	"
H	Atanasio Salvatore C	12	repairman	42	"
K	Crowell Hazel—†	12	housewife	39	"
L	Crowell Kenneth	12	estimator	46	"
M	Reardon Bridget—†	14	housewife	46	"
N	Reardon Michael	14	chauffeur	50	"
O	Grover Edgar	14	electrician	79	"
P	Grover Gertrude M—†	14	housewife	55	"
R	Hofmann Violet M—†	14	"	44	74 Forbes
S	Hofmann William F.	14	retired	70	74 "
U	O'Neill Eileen—†	14½	housekeeper	21	here
V	O'Neill Mae—†	14½	"	42	"
W	*Trulson Nils A	14½	longshoreman	42	"
X	*Trulson Vera A—†	14½	housewife	35	"
Y	Webster Virginia M—†	15	housekeeper	32	"
Z	Gilmore Anna V—†	15	housewife	37	"

1031

A	Gilmore Howard A	15	bricklayer	37	"
B	Leonard Mary T—†	15	stitcher	56	
D	Maher Katherine—†	18	housewife	45	"
E	Maher William J	18	chauffeur	48	"

Haverford Street

F	Kelly Arthur J	4	carpenter	42	here
G	Kelly Margaret F—†	4	housewife	40	"
H	Letteriello Isabella—†	4	"	27	"
K	Letteriello Ralph	4	laborer	32	
L	*Dykens Frances A—†	4	millworker	22	"
M	Vandersnoek Everett H	4	chauffeur	45	"
N	*Vandersnoek Gertrude A—†	4	housewife	46	"
O	McAuley Jane A—†	5	stenographer	24	"
P	McAuley Nellie A—†	5	housewife	64	"
R	Robinson Margaret M—†	5	waitress	20	"
S	Scipione Alfred D	5	shoeworker	33	"
T	Scipione Grace V—†	5	housewife	28	"
U	Degan Cecelia M—†	5	"	68	
V	Degan Charles H	5	clerk	45	
W	Degan Florence E—†	5	"	29	

Page.	Letter.	FULL NAME.	Residence, Jan. 1, 1941.	Occupation.	Supposed Age.	Reported Residence, Jan. 1, 1940. Street and Number.

Haverford Street—Continued

	x	Clancy Hannah M—†	6	housewife	54	here
	y	Hughes Mary G—†	6	"	39	3 Forbes
	z	Carr Herbert G	6	chauffeur	31	here
1032						
	A	Carr Lillian E—†	6	housewife	31	"
	B	Nordman Abraham	6	packer	55	8 Haverford
	C	Hoey Mary A—†	7	housewife	44	14 Greenley pl
	D	Hoey Patrick G	7	chauffeur	47	14 "
	E	Spears Frank M	'7	carpenter	36	here
	F	Spears Kathryn A—†	7	housewife	35	"
	G	Craig Mabel R—†	8	"	50	59 Glen rd
	H	Craig Milton T	8	architect	52	59 "
	K	Crowley Joseph F	8	bookkeeper	23	here
	L	Crowley Mary T—†	8	housewife	57	"
	M	Crowley Patrick	8	laborer	64	"
	N	Lawless James F	8	retired	69	
	O	Lawless John J	8	attorney	27	"
	P	Lawless Mary G—†	8	teacher	29	
	R	*Corcoran Isabelle R—†	9	housewife	32	"
	S	Corcoran John F	9	florist	33	
	T	Linse Francis X	9	clerk	30	
	U	Linse Hirlanda—†	9	housewife	63	"
	V	Linse Joseph F	9	collector	34	
	W	Linse Marie E—†	9	clerk	26	
	X	Linse William J	9	welder	22	
	Y	Linse Xavier	9	laborer	70	
	Z	Craven Thomas	10	bottler	58	..
1033						
	A	*Kilbride Elizabeth M—†	10	housekeeper	48	"
	B	Sauer Catherine I—†	10	housewife	38	"
	C	Sauer George J	10	woolworker	40	"
	D	*Horgan Anna M—†	10	housewife	33	"
	E	Horgan John	10	porter	36	
	F	Feeney Mary C—†	11	stenographer	40	"
	G	Cannon Frederick P	11	lineman	27	..
	H	Cannon Patrick F	11	laborer	55	
	K	Cannon Rose A—†	11	housewife	50	"
	L	Feeney James F	11	rubberworker	31	"
	M	Feeney Mary G—†	11	housewife	29	"
	O	Walsh Clement L	12	mover	39	
	P	Walsh Elizabeth A—†	12	housewife	38	"

Page.	Letter.	FULL NAME.	Residence, Jan. 1, 1941.	Occupation.	Supposed Age.	Reported Residence, Jan. 1, 1940. Street and Number.

Haverford Street—Continued

R	Foley Elizabeth F—†	12	housewife	59	here
s	Foley Gerard X	12	clerk	24	"
T	McCarthy Gerard	12	"	20	"
u	*Daley Edward	14	laborer	21	
v	*Daley Edward J	14	chauffeur	50	"
w	*Daley Mary—†	14	housewife	50	"
x	*Daley Mary C—†	14	waitress	24	
y	*Daley Patrick J	14	salesman	22	"
z	Gallagher Sarah A—†	14	housewife	44	"

1034

A	Gallagher William E	14	policeman	49	"
B	Gallagher William T	14	student	20	
C	O'Connell Francis J	14	clerk	55	
D	O'Connell Francis J, jr	14	"	20	
E	O'Connell Mary A—†	14	housewife	43	"
F	Carey Anna P—†	16	"	38	
G	Carey William T	16	electrician	35	"
H	Uhrle Matilda M—†	16	clerk	42	"
K	Dugan Cecilia—†	16	housewife	35	2 Decher av
L	Funcannon Edith M—†	16	"	36	here
M	Funcannon Ray	16	supervisor	38	"
N	Dullea Edward J	18	shipper	20	"
O	Dullea Julia J—†	18	housewife	54	"
P	McLaughlin Elizabeth—†	18	"	52	
R	McLaughlin Elizabeth R-†	18	examiner	23	"
s	McLaughlin John	18	machinist	52	"
T	McLaughlin Antoinette—†	18	housewife	23	259 Chestnut av
u	McLaughlin Cornelius V	18	fireman	25	here
v	Leary Cornelius M	19	chauffeur	62	"
w	Leary Delia L—†	19	housewife	61	"
x	Horgan Hanora—†	19	"	55	
y	Horgan Maurice	19	laborer	58	
z	Manning John T	19	clerk	33	

1035

A	Manning Margaret—†	19	housewife	63	"
B	Manning Mary M—†	19	teacher	29	
C	Barrett Martin J	21	laborer	38	
D	*Barrett Mary E—†	21	housewife	35	"
E	Dempsey Norah F—†	21	"	52	
F	Dempsey William J	21	machinist	56	"
G	Dempsey William J, jr	21	clerk	20	

Haverford Street—Continued

H	Casey John T	21	porter	40	here
K	Casey Margaret C—†	21	housewife	39	"

Jackson Place

L	Eastman Beatrice—†	7	housewife	26	here
M	Eastman Howard	7	porter	33	"
N	Cooper Mary—†	9	housewife	36	2 Akron
O	Cooper Roy	9	operator	42	2 "
P	*McCarthy Margaret—†	11	housewife	29	Brookline
R	McCarthy Michael	11	porter	38	70 Brookside av
T	Deatte Gerald	11	retired	67	here
S	Deatte Hannah—†	11	housewife	73	"
U	Burke Clare—†	16	cashier	27	"
V	Burke Joseph	16	clerk	26	
W	Burke Leo	16	laborer	30	
X	Burke Mary J—†	16	clerk	43	
Y	Burke Mary R—†	16	housekeeper	27	"
Z	Hayes James J	19	chauffeur	35	77 Neponset av

1036

A	Hayes Marie A—†	19	housewife	30	77 "
B	Barrows Thaddeus	19½	operator	52	here
C	Collicott Irene E—†	19½	teacher	33	"
D	Collicott Robert E	19½	accountant	29	"
E	Collicott Robert H	19½	electrician	59	"
F	Crowell Clifton	20	beltmaker	62	"
G	Crowell Esther—†	20	housewife	56	"
H	Paskell Muriel—†	22	"	36	3 Meehan pl
K	Paskell William	22	painter	39	3 "

Jess Street

L	Clancy Joseph F	1	mechanic	45	here
M	*Clancy Mary A—†	1	housewife	44	"
N	*McAdams Amelia—†	1	"	30	"
O	McAdams William J	1	chauffeur	32	"
P	McColgan Daniel	2	retired	73	3236 Wash'n
R	McColgan Theresa E—†	2	housewife	73	3236 "
S	Kimball Howard V	2	leatherworker	26	3240 "
T	Kimball Margaret G—†	2	housewife	24	3240 "
U	Conway Ann F—†	2	"	29	here
V	Conway John J	2	welder	30	"

Page.	Letter.	FULL NAME.	Residence, Jan. 1, 1941.	Occupation.	Supposed Age.	Reported Residence, Jan. 1, 1940. Street and Number.

Jess Street—Continued

w		Crawford Bertille G—†	3	housewife	46	here
x		*Crawford James J	3	carpenter	46	"
y		*Murphy John J	3	laborer	48	"
z		*Murphy Mary A—†	3	maid	48	
		1037				
A		Timlin Harold S	3	laborer	23	
c		Mulcahy George J	4	"	36	"
D		Mulcahy Lois M—†	4	housewife	27	"
E		Lundgren Carl E	4	machinist	46	142 Carolina av
F		Weston Carrie—†	4	housewife	41	142 "
G		Sullivan Bridget—†	5	"	70	here
K		Sullivan John D	5	retired	72	"
H		Sullivan Joseph F	5	laborer	30	"
L		Sullivan Mary E—†	5	housekeeper	38	"
N		Rafferty Margaret C—†	6	housewife	37	"
o		Rafferty William C	6	laundryworker	45	"
P		*MacEachen Catherine M-†	6	housewife	42	165 Boylston
R		Flynn Mary J—†	7	"	61	here
s		Flynn Michael J	7	retired	73	"
T		Murphy Marjorie A—†	7	housewife	30	176 School
U		Murphy Paul E	7	baker	31	176 "
v		Donovan Mary M—†	8	housewife	40	here
w		Donovan Thomas J	8	fireman	48	"
X		Baker Florence M—†	9	housewife	23	"
Y		Baker Robert H	9	machinist	23	"
z		Peterson John	9	retired	69	
		1038				
A		*Walsh Delia—†	10	housewife	39	"
B		Odabashian Barton	11	shoeworker	52	"
c		*Odabashian Mary—†	11	housewife	44	"
D		Kenney Mary A—†	11	"	36	"
E		Kenney William H	11	foreman	28	"
F		Chappell Hattie—†	15	cleaner	45	919 Hyde Park av
G		Chappell Margaret B—†	15	examiner	20	here
H		Connolly James D	15	laborer	59	"
K		Munzenmaier Olive A—†	15	housewife	55	"

Marmion Street

L		Jordan Joseph C	6	clerk	45	here
M		Jordan Mary J—†	6	housewife	33	"
N		Liddell Susan—†	8	"	60	"

Marmion Street—Continued

o	Keating John	8	fireman	52	here
p	Keating Sarah—†	8	housewife	43	"
r	Glennon Charles J	9	chauffeur	33	"
s	Glennon Clara J—†	9	housewife	57	"
t	Glennon Frank J	9	chauffeur	72	"
u	McDevitt Francis J	10	houseman	32	"
v	McDevitt John	10	gardener	59	"
w	McDevitt Marjorie T—†	10	housekeeper	21	"
x	Smith Edith M—†	11	stenographer	36	"
y	Smith Eleanor F—†	11	housewife	59	"
z	Smith George P	11	fireman	65	

1039

a	Thompson Catherine M—†	12	housekeeper	28	30 Montebello rd
b	Thompson Joseph F	12	painter	62	30 "
c	Martin Anna M—†	12	waitress	33	here
d	Schatz Catherine—†	12	housewife	68	"
e	Schatz Catherine M—†	12	factoryworker	28	"
f	Schatz Francis J	12	clerk	26	
g	Schatz John A	12	retired	68	"
h	Johnson Bertha O—†	13	housewife	67	"
k	Johnson Bertha W—†	13	teacher	35	
l	Johnson Ernest W	13	patternmaker	70	"
m	*Clarke Margaret—†	14	housewife	41	"
n	Clarke William S	14	laborer	43	
o	Earle Mary—†	14	at home	55	
p	Hesselschwerdt Carl A	14	watchman	55	"
r	Hesselschwerdt Carl A, jr	14	clerk	22	
s	Hesselschwerdt Catherine T—†	14	housewife	58	"
t	Hesselschwerdt John J	14	clerk	20	
u	DeBassio Alexander	15	cabinetmaker	64	"
v	DeBassio Alexander K	15	chauffeur	29	Florida
w	*DeBassio Christine—†	15	housewife	63	here
x	DeBassio John	15	laborer	31	"
y	DeBassio Joseph J	15	shipper	22	"
z	DeBassio Margaret—†	15	clerk	25	"

1040

a	DeBassio Theresa A—†	15	housewife	28	Florida
b	Spellman John J	15	chauffeur	21	here
c	*Harris George A	16	mover	35	"
d	Harris Gladys W—†	16	housewife	30	"
e	Johnson Charles F	16	chauffeur	33	"

24

Page.	Letter.	FULL NAME.	Residence, Jan. 1, 1941.	Occupation.	Supposed Age.	Reported Residence, Jan. 1, 1940. Street and Number.

Marmion Street—Continued

F	Johnson Emily C—†	16	housewife	35	here
G	Moriarty Clarence M	16	retired	74	"
H	Concannon Margaret G—†	20	housewife	44	"
K	Concannon Michael J	20	roofer	49	
L	Concannon Michael J, jr	20	student	21	

Merriam Street

M	Arsenault Avis J	1	carpenter	50	here
N	Arsenault Margaret A—†	1	housewife	53	"
O	Pettipaw Harold F	5	plumber	41	"
P	*Pettipaw Lucy C—†	5	housewife	40	"

Minton Street

S	Barnaby Frederick	1	milkman	26	384 Amory
T	Barnaby Katherine—†	1	inspector	20	384 "
U	Golden Francis	1	chauffeur	23	here
V	Golden Helen—†	1	housewife	23	"
W	Costello Elizabeth A—†	1A	"	64	"
X	Costello John J	1A	painter	55	
Y	Gilbert Doris—†	1A	housewife	45	"
Z	Gilbert Earl	1A	laborer	50	
	1041				
A	Woernle Marie—†	2	housekeeper	68	24 Cranston
B	*Rogers Helen—†	2	housewife	52	here
C	Rogers Janice—†	2	bookkeeper	22	"
D	Pearl Edward J	3	printer	30	"
E	Pearl Marion E—†	3	housewife	30	"
F	Howard Hazel—†	3	"	35	"
G	Howard Hugh	3	tailor	38	"
H	*Vander Spruit Cornelius	3	laborer	60	
K	*Bohane Agnes—†	4	housewife	30	"
L	Bohane Francis J	4	tree surgeon	36	"
M	Gebhard Josephine—†	4	housekeeper	74	2 Minton

Montebello Road

O	Crossette Dorothy K—†	15	teacher	23	here
P	Finneran Mary G—†	15	"	30	"
R	Grassie Mary G—†	15	"	44	"

25

Page.	Letter.	FULL NAME.	Residence, Jan. 1, 1941.	Occupation.	Supposed Age.	Reported Residence, Jan. 1, 1940. Street and Number.

Montebello Road—Continued

	s	Heagney Anne M—†	15	teacher	21	here
	T	Hurley Julia A—†	15	"	42	"
	U	LeSage Gladys—†	15	"	38	"
	V	MacDonald Katharine I-†	15	"	55	
	W	Maitorana Ellen—†	15	".	40	
	X	Mancini Christine—†	15	"	43	
	Y	McCarthy Mary E—†	15	"	29	
	Z	McCloskey Katherine C-†	15	"	52	

1042

	A	McKenzie Madeline—†	15	"	28	
	B	McSherry Theresa—†	15	"	31	
	c	O'Brien Mary T—†	15	".	21	
	D	Reddington Margaret M-†	15	"	52	
	E	Sullivan Margaret E—†	15	"	47	
	F	Tobin Lillian R—†	15	"	40	
	Ġ	Johnson Anna A—†	27	housekeeper	55	"
	H	Johnson John A	27	molder	57	".
	K	Johnson Lillian E—†	27	clerk	30	
	L	Kelley Esther—†	27	housewife	33.	"
	M	Kelley Francis L	27	bartender	41	"
	N	Drinan Gertrude—†	27	housewife	31	"
	o	Hiltz Philip G	27	drop forger	55	"
	P	Wilkinson Albert E	27	engineer	51	68 Brookside av
	R	Wilkinson Elizabeth M—†	27	housekeeper	21	68 "
	s	Wilkinson Mary—†	27	housewife	43	68 "
	T	Bates Evelyn—†	29	beautician	35	here
	U	Wythe Thomas J	29	laborer	58	"
	v	*Johnson Josephine—†	29	housekeeper	76	"
	w	Mulhane Alice—†	29	housewife	35	"
	x	Mulhane William	29	letter carrier	42	"
	Y	Murphy Arthur D	29	plumber	49	111 School
	z	Murphy John F	29	retired	77	79 St Marks

1043

	A	Murphy Margaret E—†	29	housewife	46	111 School

Ophir Street

	B	Exworthy John E	10	machinist	33	1 Rosslyn pl
	c	Sumpter George	10	retired	63	1 "
	D	Sumpter George J	10	machinist	27	1 "
	E	Sumpter John D	10	photographer	25	1 "

Page.	Letter.	Full Name.	Residence, Jan. 1. 1941.	Occupation.	Supposed Age.	Reported Residence, Jan. 1. 1940. Street and Number.

Ophir Street—Continued

F		Sumpter Lucena—†	10	housewife	56	1 Roslyn pl
G		Carr Helen E—†	12	"	44	7 Woodside av
H		Carr Ralph L, jr	12	foundryman	23	7 "
K		Stringe Dorothy—†	12	housewife	21	7 "
L		Stringe Edward W	12	checker	21	212 Boylston
M		Allen Carl R	16	U S A	28	here
N		Allen Clara G—†	16	operator	53	"
O		Allen Irene D—†	16	nurse	23	"
P		McNally Jeremiah	16	starter	46	
R		Murphy Alexander	16	retired	68	
S		Murphy Arthur D	16	clerk	27	
T		Murphy Bridget M—†	16	housewife	67	"
U		O'Donnell Mary R—†	18	"	34	
V		O'Donnell William F	18	chauffeur	35	"
W	*Corbett Anna—†	18	housewife	23	8 Sylvia
X		Corbett Elwood	18	operator	34	8 "
Y	*Lymeos Charles	30	chef	59	here
Z		Lymeos Charles, jr	30	cook	26	"

1044

A	*Lymeos Mary—†	30	housewife	49	"
B		Lymeos Paul	30	waiter	21	
C		Varkas Pelagia—†	30	housewife	38	"
D		Varkas George D	30	barber	52	
E		Varkas Irene—†	30	housewife	41	"
F		Varkas Michael	30	chef	40	
G	*Varkas Persephone—†	30	housewife	85	"
H		Hatch Mary—†	34	"	48	
K		Hatch Rita M—†	34	secretary	25	"
L		Hatch William	34	boilermaker	53	"
M		Ufheil Genevieve—†	34	housekeeper	80	"
N	*Gagnon Ernestine—†	36	seamstress	48	114 Newbury
O		King Frank	36	salesman	27	111 Heath
P		King Ruth—†	36	housewife	27	111 "
R		Schmier Elizabeth—†	36	housekeeper	48	here

Porter Street

S		McCone Mary J—†	9	housewife	61	here
T		Dow George O	9	chauffeur	37	44 W Eagle
U		Dow Jean—†	9	housewife	40	44 "

Sylvia Street

v	Tower Harold	2	roofer	44	660 Mass av
w	Tower Harriet—†	2	housewife	41	Middleboro
x	Howe Annie—†	2	housekeeper	54	here
y	Anderson Etta—†	2	housewife	63	2965 Wash'n
z	Anderson John W	2	laborer	46	2965 "

1045

A	Lynch Anne M—†	5	housewife	32	here
B	Lynch Thomas J	5	teacher	34	"
c	Lynch Catherine G—†	5	housewife	40	"
D	Lynch Joseph I	5	upholsterer	41	"
E	Klopf Elizabeth C—†	5	housekeeper	54	"
F	Frost Bridget E—†	7	"	55	"
G	Noonan Mary B—†	7	housewife	63	"
H	Noonan Patrick J	7	laborer	62	"
K	Schlosky Harold	7	"	37	183 Chestnut av
L	Schlosky Robert	7	clerk	20	here
M	Schlosky Sadie—†	7	housewife	52	"
N	Schlosky Theodore	7	electrician	52	"
o	Schlosky Theodore G	7	gardener	34	"
P	Mulcahy Frances—†	7	housewife	34	31 Conway
R	Mulcahy James	7	clerk	27	31 "
s	Chute Lenora J—†	8	housekeeper	46	24 Business
u	Watkins Ethel—†	8	housewife	31	here
v	Watkins Glenn	8	weigher	32	"
w	Anderson Alverne	8	draftsman	22	"
x	Anderson Grace—†	8	housewife	46	"
y	Campbell Edward	8	clerk	21	"
z	Mountain Henry	8	machinist	28	N Hampshire

1046

A	Oser Marie—†	8	housewife	26	21 Newark
B	Bailis Alice—†	8	"	46	here
c*	Bailis Anthony	8	finisher	50	"
D	Bailis Helen—†	8	housekeeper	25	"
E	Bailis Lucilla—†	8	saleswoman	21	"
F	Quinn Ruth—†	8	packer	27	

Washington Street

N	Leong Walter	3209	laundryman	57	here
R	Panigada Marie—†	3215	housewife	54	3546 Wash'n
s	Gallagher Joseph	3215	meatcutter	60	here

Washington Street—Continued

	Letter.	Full Name.	Residence, Jan. 1, 1941.	Occupation.	Supposed Age.	Reported Residence, Jan. 1, 1940. Street and Number.
	T	O'Brien John	3215	laborer	21	here
	U	O'Brien Margaret—†	3215	housewife	55	"
	V	O'Brien Mary—†	3215	packer	20	"
	W	O'Brien Thomas	3215	laborer	31	"
	X	Panigada Louise—†	3215	nurse	26	3546 Wash'n
	Y	*McCauley Catherine—†	3219	at home	69	here
	Z	O'Connor Elizabeth—†	3219	housewife	49	"
1047						
	A	O'Connor John	3219	shipper	50	"
	B	DeLang Frank H	3219	operator	29	24 Egleston
	C	*Finnernan Anne—†	3219	at home	84	here
	D	Molloy Prudence A—†	3219	housewife	48	24 Egleston
	E	Molloy Thomas A	3219	operator	52	24 "
	F	Campbell Helen—†	3223	corsetiere	69	here
	G	Nyhan Bridget—†	3223	housewife	61	"
	H	Nyhan James J	3223	retired	62	"
	K	Rossetti Mary—†	3223	housewife	32	"
	L	Nyhan Irène—†	3223	"	37	
	M	Nyhan Timothy	3223	accountant	35	"
	N	Grenham Anna—†	3227	bookkeeper	22	"
	O	Grenham Francis	3227	shipper	32	..
	P	Grenham John J	3227	carpenter	33	"
	R	*Grenham Mary—†	3227	housewife	63	"
	S	Grenham Michael	3227	foreman	64	
	T	Coffey Helen—†	3227	housewife	22	"
	U	Coffey Timothy	3227	chauffeur	28	"
	V	Carine Henry	3231	painter	31	
	W	*Carine Viola—†	3231	housewife	28	"
	X	O'Donnell Rose L—†	3231	"	58	
	Y	O'Donnell William P	3231	watchman	59	"
1048						
	A	Kerwin John J	3235	toolmaker	69	"
	B	Kerwin Rose—†	3235	housewife	46	"
	D	Kubler Joseph	3239	chauffeur	27	146 Boylston
	E	Kubler Rita—†	3239	housewife	23	146 "
	F	McGuire Mary—†	3239	"	49	here
	G	McGuire Patrick	3239	carpenter	62	"
	H	McLaughlin James	3239	inspector	21	"
	K	Leonard James P	3243	chauffeur	36	"
	L	Leonard Vera—†	3243	housewife	33	"
	M	Fay Arthur J	3243	salesman	28	"

Page.	Letter.	FULL NAME.	Residence, Jan. 1, 1941.	Occupation.	Supposed Age.	Reported Residence, Jan. 1, 1940. Street and Number.

Washington Street—Continued

N	Fay Catherine—†	3243	housewife	51	here
o	Fay John J	3243	shipper	58	"
P	Fay Ruth E—†	3243	manager	24	"
T	Hesselschwerdt Wilhelmina—†	3243	cook	58	
U	Hoff Lydia B—†	3252	housewife	51	"
V	Hoff William F	3252	engineer	52	
W	Reilly Edith—†.	3252	housewife	38	"
X	*Reilly James W	3252	printer	73	"
Y	Reilly Theresa—†	3252	clerk	21	"
Z	Goss Albert	3252	engraver	47	"

1049

A	Goss Anna—†	3252	housewife	37	"
E	Finn Alice—†	3266	waitress	23	3308 Wash'n
F	Finn Ronald	3266	roofer	25	3306 "
G	Finn Theodore	3266	chauffeur	21	3308 "
H	Finn Theresa G—†	3266	housewife	51	3306 "
K	Gleason Claire J—†	3266	stenographer	26	here
L	Gleason Dorothy M—†	3266	"	24	"
M	Gleason Francis J	3266	laborer	28	"
N	Gleason Mary C—†	3266	housewife	51	"
o	Cappucco Angela—†	3266	"	29	Cambridge
P	Cappucco Anthony	3266	shoeworker	31	"
R	Harzbecker Robert G	3270	clerk	45	here
S	*Hynds Bert	3270	machinist	23	"
T	Hynds Daniel K	3270	laborer	20	"
U	*Hynds David	3270	retired	54	
V	*Hynds Flora—†	3270	housewife	55	"
W	Hynds Jean—†	3270	saleswoman	21	"
X	Hynds Jessie—†	3270	operator	25	
Y	Murray Rose—†	3270	housekeeper	37	"
Z	Goode Catherine B—†	3273	housewife	26	"

1050

A	Goode Joseph T	3273	accountant	31	"
B	Morrill George	3273	shoeworker	42	"
C	Morrill Julia—†	3273	housewife	34	"
D	Morrill Madaline—†	3273	at home	50	Dedham
E	Visser Mary K—†	3273	housewife	36	here
F	*Visser Thomas W	3273	painter	37	"
G	Porter Joseph	3274	attendant	36	24 Harlow
H	Porter Lillian—†	3274	housewife	31	24 "
K	*Connolly Mary A—†	3274	"	48	here

Washington Street—Continued

L	*Connolly Michael J	3274	laborer	49	here
M	Connolly Michael J	3274	"	21	"
N	Connolly Catherine—†	3274	housewife	22	12 New Heath
O	Connolly James	3274	painter	26	1479 Col av
P	Crowley Patrick	3274	laundryworker	28	11 Cornwall
R	Flynn Catherine A—†	3275	waitress	52	here
S	Tuttle Erland	3275	machinist	24	30 Clarence
T	Tuttle Helen—†	3275	housewife	23	here
U	MacDonald George L	3275	foreman	41	7 Brookside av
V	MacDonald Margaret-†	3275	housewife	37	7 "
W	*Reynolds Alice—†	3275	"	30	here
X	Reynolds John P	3275	painter	52	Milton
Y	Reynolds William A	3275	"	29	here
Z	Holmes Marie L—†	3276	housewife	31	Dedham
	1051				
A	Holmes Thomas E	3276	laborer	38	"
B	Dennett George W	3276	"	44	here
C	Dennett Yvonne—†	3276	housewife	35	"
D	Mills Doris—†	3276	"	22	"
E	Mills William	3276	chauffeur	21	"
F	Bird Blanche—†	3278	domestic	56	3282 Wash'n
G	Watkins Arnold	3278	cook	44	53 Belvidere
H	Dorr John	3278	painter	59	here
K	Meredith Joseph	3278	porter	53	"
L	Meredith Margaret—†	3278	housewife	36	"
M	Fletcher Ella—†	3278	stitcher	55	"
N	Neff Eunice—†	3278	at home	68	Saugus
O	Cox May—†	3282	housewife	57	Dedham
P	Cox William L, jr	3282	buffer	36	"
R	Cobbett Charles E	3282	laborer	60	here
S	Cobbett Mary E—†	3282	housewife	48	"
T	Davis Arthur	3282	cook	43	97 Glendower rd
U	Davis Grace—†	3282	housewife	23	97 "
X	Robbs Albert	3286	serviceman	31	141 Lamartine
Y	Robbs Helena—†	3286	housewife	26	141 "
Z	Fox Charles	3286	porter	57	here
	1052				
A	Fox John	3286	clerk	20	
B	Fox Sarah—†	3286	housewife	59	"
C	Fox Sarah—†	3286	maid	22	"
D	Burke Paul	3286	chauffeur	31	10 Emsella ter

Page.	Letter.	FULL NAME.	Residence, Jan. 1, 1941.	Occupation.	Supposed Age.	Reported Residence, Jan. 1, 1940. Street and Number.

Washington Street—Continued

	E	Burke Yola—†	3286	housewife	30	10 Emsella ter
	G	Jacobs Dora—†	3294	housekeeper	44	6 Fairbury
	H	Harrington Catherine-†	3294	housewife	38	here
	K	Harrington Timothy	3294	laborer	44	"
	L	*Boyajian Mary—†	3294	housewife	45	"
	M	Boyajian Richard	3294	wireman	46	
	N	*Mouridian Havass—†	3294	housekeeper	65	"
	O	Fleury Gerard	3296	serviceman	22	N Hampshire
	P	Fleury Marie—†	3296	housewife	44	"
	S	Webber Bertha—†	3296	"	42	here
	T	Webber Edwin	3296	laborer	45	"
	U	Webber Edwin, jr	3296	salesman	22	"
	V	Webber Russell	3296	merchant	21	"
	W	McCartin Peter	3298	laborer	42	3571 Wash'n
	X	Shea Dorothy—†	3298	housewife	25	3304 "
	Y	Ufheil Catherine—†	3298	"	48	3304 "
	Z	Ufheil Joseph	3298	laborer	27	3304 "
1053						
	A	Travers Albert	3298	chauffeur	37	here
	B	Travers Laura—†	3298	housewife	37	"
	C	Heffernan Martin	3298	carpenter	62	"
	D	Morris John	3298	mechanic	22	"
	E	Morris Margaret—†	3298	housewife	45	"
	F	Morris Stanley J	3298	fireman	51	
	G	Horgan Michael J	3300	laborer	44	
	H	Horgan Sarah—†	3300	housewife	46	"
	K	Long Arthur	3300	rigger	45	
	L	*Long Charlotte—†	3300	housewife	41	"
	M	*Collins Evelyn—†	3300	"	34	
	N	Collins John	3300	welder	36	
	O	DeRoma Andrew J	3302	chauffeur	26	"
	P	DeRoma Mary—†	3302	housewife	21	"
	R	Tracy Catherine J—†	3302	factoryhand	20	"
	S	Tracy Helen C—†	3302	housewife	43	3385 Wash'n
	T	Coogan Ida—†	3302	"	51	here
	V	Gillis Charles E	3304	clerk	28	"
	W	Gillis James H	3304	salesman	41	26 Charles
	X	Gillis John C	3304	chauffeur	40	here
	Y	Gillis Ralph H	3304	merchant	34	"
	Z	Gillis Sarah H—†	3304	housewife	65	"

1054
Washington Street—Continued

B	Laing Anna H—†	3305	housewife	33	here
C	Laing George B	3305	agent	33	"
D	Thanisch Edith L—†	3305	housewife	63	"
E	Shenett Alfred R	3306	laborer	39	Wrentham
F	Shenett Anna H—	3306	housewife	35	"
G	Doherty Charles R	3306	engineer	45	here
H	Doherty Eleanor—†	3306	factoryhand	23	"
K	Doherty Roger	3306	mechanic	22	"
L	Doherty Sarah—†	3306	housewife	42	"
M	O'Brien Josephine—†	3306	"	39	"
N	O'Brien Patrick F	3306	painter	43	
O	Graham Mary—†	3307	housewife	41	"
P	Graham Maxwell	3307	machinist	42	"
S	Westburg Anna M—†	3309	housewife	68	"
T	Westburg John	3309	retired	69	"
U	Frasier Helen—†	3309	housewife	32	"
V	Frasier Joseph T	3309	serviceman	33	"
W	*Kennedy Hughena—†	3310	housekeeper	72	"
X	Kennedy John N	3310	operator	48	"
Y	Petrillo Frederick	3310	laborer	61	243 Beech
Z	*Petrillo Josephine—†	3310	housewife	55	243 "

1055

A	Salamy Abdou B	3312	clerk	30	here
B	Salamy Sherman	3312	merchant	63	"
C	*Salamy Virginia—†	3312	housewife	25	"
D	*Chiampa Caroline—†	3312	"	40	"
E	Chiampa Ralph	3312	barber	40	"
F	Anastos Joseph	3313	steelburner	53	"
G	Anastos Louise—†	3313	housewife	38	"
K	Hough Frederick W	3317	painter	44	
L	Hough Gertrude—†	3317	housewife	43	"
M	Sheehan Monica—†	3317	domestic	25	"
N	Sheehan Ralph	3317	chauffeur	26	"
O	Petrillo Albina—†	3319	factoryhand	21	"
P	Petrillo Carmen	3319	laborer	26	
R	*Petrillo Josephine—†	3319	housewife	54	"
S	Petrillo Salvatore	3319	chauffeur	23	"
T	Vitiello Adeline—†	3319	housewife	30	"
U	Vitiello Dominico	3319	laborer	44	

1056

Woodside Avenue

E	Cobbett Florence—†	4	housekeeper	54	18 Ophir
F	Defren Emily A—†	4	housewife	61	here
G	Defren Gertrude—†	4	stenographer	26	"
H	Defren Matthew W	4	waiter	30	"
K	*Cooney Patrick	4	baker	38	
L	*Thornton Julia—†	4	housewife	61	"
M	*Thornton Michael	4	laborer	59	..
N	Nolan John	6	retired	67	
O	Nolan Nellie B—†	6	housewife	67	"
P	Hopkins Bernard	6	salesman	30	384 Amory
R	Hopkins Gertrude—†	6	housewife	30	384 "
S	*Steele George	6	chauffeur	40	here
T	*Steele Jessie—†	6	housewife	41	"
U	Welby Margaret—†	8	"	42	"
V	Welby Matthew	8	chauffeur	43	"
W	Hanley Helen M—†	10	housewife	33	"
X	Hanley John P	10	chauffeur	35	"
Y	Walsh Martha—†	10	secretary	21	"
Z	Hoffman Charles	10	chauffeur	45	"

1057

A	Hoffman Edward C	10	porter	22	"
B	Hoffman Frances M—†	10	waitress	40	"
C	Charyna Joseph	16	painter	28	
D	Charyna Mildred—†	16	housewife	28	"
E	Koretzky Helen—†	16	cook	47	
F	*Koretzky John	16	"	49	
G	Wishnosky John	16	presser	27	
H	Wishnosky Kornel	16	painter	48	
K	Wishnosky Martin	16	operator	25	"
L	Wishnosky Mary—†	16	housewife	40	"

Ward 11–Precinct 11

CITY OF BOSTON

LIST OF RESIDENTS
20 YEARS OF AGE AND OVER

(NON-CITIZENS INDICATED BY ASTERISK)
(FEMALES INDICATED BY DAGGER)

AS OF

JANUARY 1, 1941

JOSEPH F. TIMILTY, *Chairman*
FREDERIC E. DOWLING, *Secretary*
WILLIAM A. MOTLEY, JR.
FRANCIS B. McKINNEY
HILDA HEDSTROM QUIRK

Listing Board.

CITY OF BOSTON PRINTING DEPARTMENT

1100
Forest Hills Street

D	Mitchell Margaret—†	46–48	housewife	39	here
E	Mitchell Patrick J	46–48	butcher	40	"
F	Donovan Robert E	46–48	gardener	59	"
G*	Donlon Catherine—†	46–48	housewife	28	14 Germania
H	Donlon John	46–48	toolmaker	42	Foxboro
K	Donlon Peter J	46–48	laborer	40	14 Germania
L	Shaughnessy Anne I—†	50–52	housewife	29	here
M	Shaughnessy Thomas J	50–52	manager	30	"
N	Morse Grace L—†	50–52	housewife	27	263 Chestnut av
O	Morse Ralph L	50–52	machinist	29	263 "
P	McGillicuddy Eliza—†	50–52	housewife	28	11 Granfield av
R	McGillicuddy James C	50–52	librarian	28	11 "
S	Goode Christopher A	54–56	manager	25	here
T	Goode Delia M—†	54–56	housewife	59	"
U	Goode James F	54–56	porter	21	"
V	Goode John B	54–56	shipper	26	
W*	Goode William J	54–56	retired	57	
X	Goode William J	54–56	engineer	28	"
Y	Ross Elsie J—†	54–56	clerk	28	
Z	Ross Mary A—†	54–56	housewife	59	"

1101

A	Ross Mary A—†	54–56	clerk	30	
B	Ross Waldo C	54–56	machinist	55	"
C*	Deveney Margaret A–†	54–56	at home	73	
D	Griffin Anna—†	54–56	"	48	
E	Griffin James P	54–56	watchman	52	"
F	Griffin Julia J—†	54–56	housewife	46	"
G	Griffin Roger G	54–56	U S A	22	
H	Griffin Thomas J	54–56	clerk	25	
K	Groswald A Wilma—†	58	housewife	26	"
L	Groswald Alma R—†	58	"	55	
M	Groswald Arvid J	58	brewer	27	"
N	Groswald Zenta E—†	58	bookkeeper	26	New York
O	Nicholson Bridget T—†	58	housewife	54	here
P	Nicholson Catherine R—†	58	typist	20	"
R	Nicholson John G	58	electrician	58	"
S	Nicholson Mary A—†	58	secretary	23	"
T	DerAvedisian Agnes—†	58	housewife	44	"
U	DerAvedisian Mugurditch	58	printer	44	
V	Timons James	70	chauffeur	34	"

Page.	Letter.	FULL NAME.	Residence, Jan. 1, 1941.	Occupation.	Supposed Age.	Reported Residence, Jan. 1, 1940. Street and Number.

Forest Hills Street—Continued

w	Timons Louise—†	70	housewife	33	here
x	Gorman Michael	76	retired	72	"
y	Gorman Mary—†	76	housewife	72	"
z	Madden Anna M—†	76	"	36	
	1102				
a	Madden William F	76	pharmacist	44	"
b	Sennott Mary T—†	78	housewife	54	"
c	Sennott Olivia—†	78	entertainer	29	"
d	Sennott Ruth J—†	78	"	31	
e	Sennott William J	78	custodian	55	"
f	Sennott William J	78	shipper	22	
g	Larson Robert T	78	student	20	"
h	*Larson Roberta W—†	78	housewife	41	Watertown
k	Larson Thure G	78	florist	46	"
m	Tahaney Eleanor J—†	82	teacher	23	here
n	Tahaney James	82	policeman	63	"
o	Tahaney Mary—†	82	housewife	55	"
p	Coates Blanche—†	82	clerk	44	25 Bardwell
r	Coates William	82	machinist	45	25 "
s	Bowes Helen—†	82	housewife	31	here
t	Bowes John H	82	surveyor	35	"
v	Durning A Ralph	86	merchant	38	"
w	Durning Lillian B—†	86	housewife	36	"
x	Brickett Frances H—†	86	"	33	24 Cheshire
y	Brickett John O	86	clerk	27	24 "
z	Gendrolius Constance—†	86	housewife	56	here
	1103				
a	Gendrolius Edward	86	clerk	27	
b	Gendrolius Nicodemus	86	machinist	59	"
c	Gendrolius William	86	compositor	24	"
d	Galvin James J	89	policeman	45	"
e	Galvin Mary A—†	89	housewife	37	"
f	McLaughlin Daniel P	89	laborer	36	
g	McLaughlin Hugh	89	retired	70	
h	Sullivan John J	89	policeman	43	"
k	Sullivan Mary E—†	89	housewife	38	"
l	Gross Eric N—†	89	breweryworker	30	"
m	Gross Wilma M—†	89	housewife	24	"
n	Rogers Esther M—†	90	nurse	29	85 Rockview
o	Rogers Rosalind G—†	90	housewife	53	85 "
p	Rogers Ruth E—†	90	secretary	25	85 "

3

Page.	Letter.	FULL NAME.	Residence, Jan. 1, 1941.	Occupation.	Supposed Age.	Reported Residence, Jan. 1, 1940. Street and Number.

Forest Hills Street—Continued

R	Brenz Anna P—†	90	housewife	51	here
S	Brenz Edgar J	90	clerk	25	"
T	Brenz Peter	90	printer	52	"
U	Landry Alma R—†	90	secretary	34	"
V	Landry Francis X	90	chef	25	
W	Landry Frank X	90	retired	76	
X	Landry Jean M—†	90	secretary	28	"
Y	*Landry Margaret R—†	90	housewife	69	"
Z	Landry Patrick V	90	chauffeur	24	"

1104

A	Geer Martha E—†	93	housewife	52	"
B	Geer Phillip W	93	writer	53	
C	Harrington Catherine M—†	94	housewife	38	"
D	Harrington James G	94	guard	42	
E	McDonald James W	94	contractor	56	"
F	McDonald Mary W—†	94	housewife	54	"
G	Flynn Helen E—†	94	"	37	
H	Flynn John J	94	clerk	42	
K	Shine George F	94	upholsterer	59	"
L	Flanagan Catherine—†	98	housewife	74	"
M	Flanagan James G	98	fireman	35	
N	Flanagan Thomas F	98	laborer	33	
O	McDermott Esther R—†	98	bookkeeper	44	"
P	*McDermott Jean—†	98	at home	66	"
R	McDermott Mary D—†	98	housewife	57	"
S	McDermott Raymond A	98	agent	42	
T	Grant Daniel	98	laborer	65	
U	Grant Margaret—†	98	housewife	60	"
V	Grant William J	98	operator	28	
W	Palmer James A	101	merchant	52	"
X	Palmer Lillian J—†	101	secretary	23	"
Y	Palmer Sadie—†	101	housewife	42	"
Z	Tibbetts John	101	laborer	31	N Hampshire

1105

A	Tibbetts Rosalind—†	101	housewife	22	"
B	Mullen Daniel, jr	101	accountant	34	here
C	Mullen Mary—†	101	secretary	34	"
E	Finn Katherine M—†	105	teacher	49	"
F	Finn Martin J	105	contractor	48	"
G	Kelly Arthur J	105	executive	51	"
H	Kelly Helen F—†	105	housewife	50	"

Page.	Letter.	FULL NAME.	Residence, Jan. 1, 1941.	Occupation.	Supposed Age.	Reported Residence, Jan. 1, 1940. Street and Number.

Forest Hills Street—Continued

	K	Kelly Sheila K—†	105	student	20	here
	L	Mason Etheline V—†	105	domestic	21	"
	M	Cox James	106	inspector	41	"
	N	Patz Clara H—†	106	housewife	62	"
	o	*Pede Reinhold	106	laborer	29	
	P	Voss Bruno F	106	pharmacist	35	"
	R	Cooney Mary—†	118	domestic	64	131 Moreland
	s	Dillard Peter	118	physician	26	246 Longwood av
	T	Mattatall Levi	118	caretaker	59	here
	U	Ross Myrtle B—†	118	nurse	54	"
	v	Austin August J	139	toolmaker	59	"
	w	Austin Matilda S—†	139	housewife	55	"
	x	Austin Wally Z—†	139	operator	24	
	Y	Farrell Katherine A—†	139	domestic	56	"
	z	Farrell Margaret M—†	139	saleswoman	37	"
1106						
	A	Leahan Frank E	139	telegrapher	42	124 Marlboro
	B	Leahan Margaret—†	139	housewife	37	124 "
	c	Claffey Francis J	143–145	accountant	39	here
	D	Claffey Margaret J–†	143–145	housewife	36	"
	E	Devine Bridget—†	143–145	"	80	"
	F	McLaughlin Genevieve G—†	143–145	"	34	
	G	McLaughlin John T	143–145	letter carrier	41	"
	H	McLaughlin Mary A—†	143–145	at home	78	
	K	Vuozzo Gaetano A	143–145	cutter	45	
	L	Vuozzo Louis G	143–145	leatherworker	20	"
	M	Vuozzo Teresa R—†	143–145	housewife	43	"
	N	Conroy Mary—†	146	laundress	35	"
	o	O'Brien Mary—†	146	cook	54	
	P	Ross Henry F	146	realtor	78	..
	R	Kenney Annie M—†	147–149	housewife	41	"
	s	Kenney Luke J	147–149	shipper	52	
	T	Curley Elizabeth—†	147–149	teacher	54	
	U	Flynn Mildred A—†	147–149	bookkeeper	32	"
	v	Wildermuth Louise-†	147–149	housewife	48	"
	W	Wildermuth Louise D—†	147–149	clerk	22	
	x	Wildermuth Max	147–149	coffee roaster	55	"
	Y	*Joyce Ann—-†	151	housewife	31	"
	z	Joyce Patrick J	151	engineer	33	
1107						
	A	Cusack Elizabeth M—†	151	housewife	37	"

5

Forest Hills Street—Continued

B	Cusack Thomas F	151	operator	48	here	
C	Lammers Albert T	151	mechanic	59	265 Belgrade av
D	Lammers Dorothy M—†	151	saleswoman	21	265 "
E	Lammers Mary—†	151	housewife	53	265 "
F	Galeota Catherine T—†	155	"	31	here
G	Galeota Joseph M	155	engineer	32	"
H	Hogarty George H	155	letter carrier	34	"
K	Hogarty Margaret C—†	155	housewife	34	"
L	Galeota Catherine T—†	155	cashier	21	
M	*Galeota Mary—†	155	housewife	49	"
N	*Galeota Raphael	155	merchant	58	
O	Carew Michael	156	fisherman	36	"
P	Redmond Chester I	156	salesman	37	"
R	*Redmond Ella M—†	156	housewife	39	"
S	Carty Frances—†	159	"	27	
T	Carty Stephen H	159	chauffeur	46	"
U	Harlow Elsa—†	159	housewife	57	"
V	Harlow Frederick G	159	foreman	63	
W	McCollum Joseph R	159	carpenter	63	"
X	O'Reilly John M	159	salesman	52	
Y	O'Reilly John W	159	chauffeur	29	"
Z	O'Reilly Mabel E—†	159	housewife	48	"

1108

A	O'Reilly Mary L—†	159	saleswoman	26	"
B	Kane James F	167	foreman	42	
C	Kane Winifred M—†	167	housewife	42	"
D	Stark Eleanor T—†	157	"	39	
E	Stark Herbert A	167	clerk	38	
F	Sullivan Frances C—†	167	housewife	35	"
G	Sullivan James J	167	salesman	47	26 Ridlon rd
H	Edmunds Belle—†	171	housewife	54	here
K	Edmunds Natt C	171	guard	59	"
L	Faurer Charles	171	retired	73	"
M	Faurer Ida—†	171	at home	66	
N	Faurer Martin	171	salesman	34	
O	Faurer Ruth E—†	171	housewife	33	"
P	Burton James	171	chauffeur	50	144 Williams
R	Burton Kathleen F—†	171	housewife	42	144 "
T	Dusik Julia—†	175	at home	39	204 Lamartin
U	Miller Mary E—†	175	housewife	60	5 Chilcott pl
R	Miller Paul H	175	pressworker	22	5 "

6

Forest Hills Street—Continued

	Letter	Full Name	Residence	Occupation	Age	Reported Residence
	w	Parlon Martin J	175	retired	65	40 Bowdoin
	x	Shamon Josephine—†	175	housewife	44	here
	y	Boyle Margaret M—†	191	teacher	20	"
	z	Boyle Rose M—†	191	housewife	47	"
1109						
	a	Boyle William E	191	manager	52	
	b	Norton Margaret—†	191	at home	87	
	c	Eatinger Mary—†	215	teacher	43	
	d	Ouren Kristine P—†	215	cook	62	"
	e	Sparks Susan C—†	215	secretary	74	"
	f	Donahue Isabel C—†	235	housewife	49	"
	g	Donahue Joseph J	235	attorney	53	"

Glade Avenue

	Letter	Full Name	Residence	Occupation	Age	Reported Residence
	k	Fennessy James	4	policeman	40	here
	l	Fennessy Elizabeth—†	4	housewife	77	"
	m	Fennessy Elizabeth L—†	4	"	40	"
	n	Kenney John J	4	watchman	44	"
	o	Kenney Mary G—†	4	housewife	38	"
	p	Kerrigan Mary—†	6	"	29	"
	r	Kerrigan Paul	6	carpenter	43	"
	u	Gardner Alice B—†	6	housewife	64	"
	t	Gardner James A	6	fireman	54	
	s	Gardner James F	6	clerk	21	"
	v	Akus Anne—†	6	housewife	51	19 Heath av
	w	Akus Carl	6	shoeworker	56	19 "
	x	Akus Carl	6	accountant	25	19 "
	y	Akus Henry S	6	U S A	23	19 "
	z	Ryan John G	7	operator	35	here
1110						
	a	Ryan Marion T—†	7	housewife	36	"
	b	Anderson Carl A	7	machinist	54	"
	c	Anderson Svea—†	7	housewife	50	"
	d	Waible Florence—†	7	"	41	21 Grovenor rd
	e	Waible Wendall	7	repairman	42	21 "
	f	Holmberg Herman W	8	mechanic	37	Chelsea
	g	Holmberg Janet A—†	8	housewife	42	660 Hunt'n av
	h	Donoghue Ellen—†	8	"	28	44 Elliot
	k	Donoghue John	8	engineer	33	Medford
	l	Nowell George W	8	collector	55	here

Glade Avenue—Continued

		FULL NAME	Res.	Occupation	Age	Reported Residence
M		Scollin Anne A—†	8	housekeeper	65	here
o		McDermott Amy—†	11	housewife	47	"
p		McDermott Arthur J	11	clerk	54	"
R		McDermott Arthur J, jr	11	laborer	24	
s		McDermott John P	11	clerk	21	
T		McDermott Madelyn—†	11	"	20	"
U		Devin John J	12	draftsman	36	49 Adams
V		Devin Margaret—†	12	housewife	31	N Hampshire
W		Grisdale J Howard	12	engineer	44	here
X		Grisdale Louise—†	12	housewife	69	"
Y		Grisdale Thomas I	12	clerk	45	"
z		Belliveau Joseph D	12	foreman	61	

1111

		FULL NAME	Res.	Occupation	Age	Reported Residence
A		Belliveau Margaret—†	12	housewife	52	"
B		Belliveau Marion C—†	12	clerk	26	"
c		Murphy Jeanett—†	16	housewife	22	"
D	*	Murphy Patrick J	16	chauffeur	25	"
E		Swanson Gothwill	16	mechanic	46	"
F		Swanson Karen—†	16	housewife	44	"
G		Pulster Edwin F	16	mechanic	52	"
H		Pulster Mary E—†	16	housewife	51	"
K		Tarr Benjamin W	17	operator	32	"
L		Tarr Ruth—†	17	housewife	33	"
M		Walsh Selma—†	17	"	57	
N		Walsh Susan—†	17	stenographer	34	"
o		Derzanski Mary—†	17	housewife	22	"
P	*	McInnis Catherine—†	17	"	43	
R		McInnis Neil	17	laborer	52	"
s		McInnis Thomas	17	chauffeur	20	
T		DeCosta Charles	17	factoryhand	32	1990 Col av
U		DeCosta Mary—†	17	housewife	28	1990 "
V		Cavanaugh Hannah—†	19	"	48	here
W		Cavanaugh Michael T	19	policeman	43	"
X		Conroy Bridget—†	19	housewife	60	"
Y		Conroy Thomas	19	merchant	62	"
z		Doherty Dennis	19	clerk	48	

1112

		FULL NAME	Res.	Occupation	Age	Reported Residence
A		Hart Catherine—†	19	housewife	45	"
B		Hart Martin J	19	manager	45	"
c		English Helen C—†	20	housewife	38	"
D		English Michael J	20	lather	48	

8

Glade Avenue—Continued

	Letter	Full Name	Residence	Occupation	Age	Reported Residence
	E	McNalley Madeline N—†	20	housekeeper	45	here
	F	*Smith William	20	merchant	46	"
	G	*Stewart Jean—†	20	housewife	43	"
	H	Stewart William	20	salesman	44	"
	K	Clevestrom Anna—†	20	housewife	62	"
	L	Clevestrom Evald	20	mechanic	65	"
	M	Clevestrom Harry	20	clerk	33	"
	N	Osh Howard	21	buyer	31	
	O	Osh Lena—†	21	housewife	61	"
	P	McCarthy Charles	21	U S N	20	
	R	McCarthy Eileen M—†	21	secretary	26	"
	S	McCarthy Ellen C—†	21	nurse	30	
	T	McCarthy Mary H—†	21	housewife	65	"
	U	Durkin James	21	policeman	50	"
	V	Durkin Lillian—†	21	housewife	45	"

Glen Road

	Letter	Full Name	Residence	Occupation	Age	Reported Residence
	W	DeDoming Mary C—†	3	housewife	36	here
	X	DeDoming Rose—†	3	"	35	"
	Y	DeDoming Russell C	3	retired	46	"
	Z	Webster Catherine—†	3	matron	40	
1113						
	A	Berry John	3	plumber	45	"
	B	Berry Paul	3	clerk	21	
	C	Jacobs Catherine—†	3	housewife	22	"
	D	Jacobs Joseph	3	laborer	24	
	E	Dutczak Henry	3	"	28	
	F	Dutczak Julia—†	3	housewife	50	"
	G	Dutczak Michael	3	machinist	57	"
	H	Dutczak Michael	3	metalworker	26	"
	K	Dutczak Robert	3	tester	23	
	L	Long Olive H—†	5	housewife	25	"
	M	Long Thomas F	5	printer	21	Belmont
	N	*MacLean Prudence—†	5	housekeeper	52	here
	O	Reilly William E	5	physician	46	"
	P	Zimmer Arthur S	5	mechanic	44	"
	R	Zimmer Helen—†	5	housewife	42	"
	T	Wells Edwin M	5	social worker	54	"
	U	Wells Helen F—†	5	housewife	50	"
	V	Wells Thomas G	5	plumber	21	

Glen Road—Continued

w	Wells Walter J	5	clerk	24	here
x	Ford Elizabeth—†	16–18	housewife	67	"
y	Ford Frank J	16–18	laborer	42	"
z	Ford Wilford	16–18	retired	71	

1114

A	McGuiness Daniel H	16–18	clerk	27	
B	Carroll Catherine—†	16–18	housewife	36	"
c	Carroll David	16–18	welder	38	"
D	Landry Alice C—†	16–18	clerk	29	
E	Landry Alice C—†	16–18	housewife	59	"
F	Landry Amelia A—†	16–18	clerk	25	
G	Landry Charles D	16–18	carpenter	62	"
H	Landry Julian B	16–18	engineer	27	
K	Hanley Anne—†	20–22	housewife	45	"
L	Hanley Grace—†	20–22	clerk	21	
M	Hanley James	20–22	merchant	48	"
N	Hanley James jr	20–22	manager	26	"
o	Linnehan Mary C—†	20–22	housewife	38	"
P	Linnehan William	20–22	fireman	40	"
R	McKay Catherine—†	20–22	housewife	49	86 Brookley rd
s	McKay William J	20–22	salesman	48	86 "
T	McKay William J	20–22	chauffeur	24	86 "
U	Galvin Catherine S—†	26	housewife	36	here
v	Galvin John J	26	painter	55	"
w	Sweeney Anne—†	26	domestic	52	"
x	Ward Margaret E—†	26	housekeeper	60	"
Y	Baumeister Catherine—†	26	housewife	35	"
z	Baumeister Edward	26	upholsterer	46	"

1115

A	Adams Alice A—†	28	secretary	36	"
B	Adams Anne F—†	28	housewife	60	"
c	Adams Helen D—†	28	secretary	21	"
D	Adams Marion M—†	28	"	24	"
E	Willis Eugene T	28	serviceman	24	5 Green
F	Willis Lucia—†	28	housewife	26	5 "
G	Young Elmer A	28	seaman	30	here
H	Young Marjorie—†	28	teacher	28	"
K	Young Nellie C—†	28	housewife	61	"
M	Conaghan Charles	29A	mechanic	36	"
N	*Conaghan Mary—†	29A	housewife	34	"
o	Koen Frances D—†	29A	"	43	

Glen Road—Continued

	P	Koen Francis X	29A	printer	57	here
	R	Huntington Elizabeth L–†	31	housekeeper	60	"
	S	Dudley Catherine F—†	39	"	68	"
	T	Girard Henry	39	musician	51	"
	U	Girard Rene—†	39	housewife	39	"
	V	Girard Rene—†	39	student	20	
	W	Magnett John F	39	clerk	37	
	X	Magnett Marguerite—†	39	housewife	37	"
	Y	Salles Andrew	42	electrician	24	107 Howland
	Z	Salles Bernard	42	cook	57	107 "
		1116				
	A	Salles Edna—†	42	housewife	25	107 "
	B	Salles Melanie—†	42	"	47	107 "
	C	Henning Edward	42	manager	49	here
	D	Henning Theresa—†	42	housewife	47	"
	E	Sterling Andrew	42	chauffeur	26	"
	F	Sterling Margaret M—†	42	housewife	58	"
	G	Sterling Richard J	42	machinist	57	"
	H	Sterling Richard J	42	clerk	21	
	K	Sterling Thomas	42	adjuster	25	
	L	Connaughton Delia—†	43	housewife	55	"
	M	Connaughton John J	43	chauffeur	34	"
	N	Connaughton Sarah L—†	43	housewife	34	"
	O	Higgins Catherine F—†	43	"	39	
	P	Higgins William E	43	executive	41	"
	R	Kelly Mary K—†	43	merchant	53	"
	S	Kelly Michael	43	chauffeur	61	"
	T	Woods Grace—†	46	housewife	30	"
	U	Woods Robert E	46	engineer	37	"
	V	Sullivan Emma—†	46	housekeeper	50	"
	W	Dulsky Sabina—-†	46	saleswoman	34	"
	X	Riedl Helen M—†	46	domestic	34	"
	Y	Riedl Robert	46	retired	73	
	Z	Riedl Robert F	46	clerk	31	
		1117				
	A	Riedl Veronica J	46	housewife	24	"
	C	McCarthy Annie E—†	50	at home	75	
	D	McCarthy Catherine R—†	50	housewife	45	"
	E	McCarthy Justin J	50	electrician	47	"
	F	Schilling Frances—†	50	operator	31	
	G	Schilling Henry P	50	molder	29	

Glen Road—Continued

H	Schilling Hugh J	50	clerk	48	here
K	Schilling Johanna—†	50	housewife	52	"
L	Schilling Philip	50	laborer	52	"
M	Schilling Veronica—†	50	housewife	36	"
N	Davis Helen—†	rear 53	nurse	26	"
O	Kirkby Elinore—†	" 53	"	33	
P	*Petro Gladys—†	" 53	"	21	"
R	Smith Martha—†	" 53	"	23	Vermont
S	Weiss Murial—†	" 53	housekeeper	40	Watertown
T	Hankey Charles W	54	policeman	44	here
U	Hankey Mary R—†	54	housewife	44	"
V	Hogan Paul X	54	pressman	22	"
W	Burns Catherine V—†	54	clerk	47	
X	Burns Howard	54	"	43	
Y	Burns Katherine—†	54	housewife	81	"
Z	Burns Marie L—†	54	clerk	49	
	1118				
A	Blakeslee Gertrude L—†	54	housewife	54	"
B	Blakeslee Howard E	54	clerk	55	
C	Poirier Alfred A	54	"	46	
D	Nanyok Antonette—†	58	housewife	51	"
E	Nauyok Domenic	58	retired	71	
E	Nauyok Helen—†	58	waitress	33	
G	Nauyok Olga—†	58	secretary	23	"
H	Anzalone Louis	58	clerk	29	"
K	Anzalone Martha—†	58	housewife	28	Cambridge
L	McEachern John K	58	ironworker	46	2 Hillside av
M	McEachern Mary A—†	58	housewife	46	2 "
N	Cross Anne--†	59	"	29	300 Chestnut av
O	Cross Bernard A	59	mechanic	37	300 "
P	Marquard John	59	agent	33	here
R	Marquard Sylvia—†	59	housewife	29	"
S	Carroll Claire—†	59	"	24	"
T	Carroll Ralph	59	broker	25	
U	Kuhlman Dorothy—†	59	housewife	25	"
V	Kuhlman Francis	59	manager	29	"
W	Lockberry Rosine—†	59	housewife	35	"
X	Lockberry Walter	59	carpenter	37	"
Y	Holmes Agnes—†	65	housewife	59	58 Glen rd
Z	Holmes Edmond G	65	retired	72	here

Page	Letter	Full Name.	Residence, Jan. 1, 1941.	Occupation.	Supposed Age.	Reported Residence, Jan. 1, 1940. Street and Number.

1119
Glen Road—Continued

A	Holmes Samuel S	65	retired	74	here
B	King Mark H	65	clerk	42	"
C	McLaughlin Edward J	65	cutter	46	"
D	Nickerson James K	65	engineer	51	
E	Paskell Alfred E	65	painter	30	
F	Paskell Mary H—†	65	housewife	70	"
G	Paskell William	65	artist	74	
H	Schulz Ann E—†	65	saleswoman	22	"
K	Dorrwachter Anna—†	70	housewife	40	"
L	Dorrwachter Paul	70	steward	42	"
M	Dolan Delia—†	71	at home	56	107 Forest Hills
N	Taylor Elizabeth—†	71	housekeeper	49	6 Glenside av
O	Kozlowski Amelia—†	71	housewife	52	252 Athens
P*	Kozlowski Kostanti	71	cook	49	259 "
R	Tarella Helen—†	71	stitcher	29	259 "
S	Farrell Cornelius	71	pressman	33	here
T	Farrell Jeremiah	71	retired	65	"
U	Farrell Mary L—†	71	housewife	31	"
V	Leo Mary—†	75	at home	77	
W	Stanger John S	75	agent	49	
X	Stanger Leonora—†	75	housewife	43	"
Y	Ward Joseph M	75	manager	49	··
Z	Ward Ruth F—†	75	housewife	35	"

1120

A	Gallagher Joseph G	75	clerk	26	Watertown
B	Mundie Catherine—†	75	housewife	58	Dorchester
C	Mundie William R	75	retired	68	"
D	Buchanan George W	79	expressman	69	11 Chilcott pl
E	Buchanan Hazel F—†	79	housewife	36	11 "
F	Hall Marjorie A—†	79	bookkeeper	21	11 "
G	Raymo Arthur S	82	operator	51	here
H	Raymo Maude L—†	82	housewife	54	"
K	Shire Abraham	82	operator	32	"
L	Shire Anna—†	82	secretary	35	"
M	Shire Sadie M—†	82	housewife	66	"
N	Shire Weded—†	82	"	32	
O	Wells Barbara—†	82	stenographer	51	"
P	Schole Catherine—†	83	housewife	60	"
R*	Schole Herman	83	retired	65	

Glen Road—Continued

s	Keane Helen—†	83	housewife	41	here
T	Keane Patrick	83	policeman	41	"
U	McLaughlin Catherine—†	83	housewife	55	"
V	McLaughlin Catherine—†	83	secretary	32	"
W	McLaughlin Joseph	83	"	23	
X	McLaughlin Theresa V—†	83	stenographer	26	"
Y	Nesky Claire E—†	85	"	23	"
Z	Nesky Edward P	85	factoryhand	23	"

1121

A	Nesky Winifred M—†	85	laundress	43	"
B	Rider Daniel	85	clergyman	51	"
C	Rider Ida F—†	85	housewife	50	"
D	Rider Lois—†	85	student	20	
F	Gravely James	85	clerk	22	
E	Gravely James A	85	machinist	49	"
G	Cross Gladys E—†	86	hygienist	34	"
H	Cross Violet—†	86	housewife	60	"
K	Wilbur Howard	86	teacher	46	
L	Wilbur Mildred—†	86	housewife	43	"
N	Hubbard Catherine A—†	91	"	59	
O	Hubbard Joseph M	91	guard	63	
P	Hubbard Mary V—†	91	teacher	37	"
R	Brougham John H	91	"	27	12 Lincoln
S	Brougham Patricia T—†	91	housewife	26	6 Brighton

Glenside Avenue

T	Mason Mary—†	6	housewife	40	Hingham
U	Mason Warren S	6	salesman	42	"
V	Breslin Frank J	6	manager	52	here
W	Breslin Margaret—†	6	housewife	46	"
X	Dwyer Bridget—†	6	at home	71	"
Y	Dwyer Helen E—†	6	housewife	52	"
Z	Dwyer John F	6	draftsman	34	"

1122

A	Curley Bessie M—†	8	housewife	37	"
B	Curley Michael F	8	guard	46	
C	Boyle Anastasia—†	8	housewife	70	"
D	Boyle Thomas F	8	retired	74	
E	Fontaine Arthur	8	accountant	34	"
F	Fontaine Mildred—†	8	housewife	29	"

Page.	Letter.	Full Name.	Residence, Jan. 1, 1941.	Occupation.	Supposed Age.	Reported Residence, Jan. 1, 1940. Street and Number.

Glenside Avenue—Continued

	G	Gulishek Helen—†	8	housekeeper	50	here
	H	Talbot Elizabeth—†	14	housewife	51	"
	K	Talbot Felix	14	salesman	51	"
	L	Talbot John	14	clerk	21	
	M	Talbot Leo	14	salesman	23	"
	N	Hardiman Isabel—†	14	housewife	35	37 St John
	O	Hardiman Joseph C	14	salesman	38	37 "
	P	Karcher Dorothy—†	14	housewife	30	here
	R	Karcher John C	14	investigator	32	"
	S	Drews Carrie—†	14	housewife	50	"
	T	Drews Gladys—†	14	attorney	24	"
	U	Drews John	14	factoryhand	26	"
	V	Drews Paul	14	"	21	
	W	Munson Jean—†	14	housewife	32	"
	X	Munson Luther H	14	clerk	35	"
	Y	Burke Margaret—†	14	housewife	26	371 Metropolitan av
	Z	Burke Thomas F	14	meter reader	35	371 "
		1123				
	A	Glennon Margaret—†	14	secretary	31	371 "
	B	Creighton Arthur J	16	chauffeur	33	here
	C	Creighton Margaret E—†	16	housewife	32	"
	D	McPherson Joseph	16	chauffeur	40	"
	E	McPherson Margaret—†	16	housewife	43	"
	F	Waters Emily F—†	16	"	40	
	G	Waters Thomas J	16	clerk	40	
	H	Schwender Harriet F—†	16	housewife	41	"
	K	Schwender Harriet F—†	16	bookkeeper	22	"
	L	Meehan Joseph F	16	yardman	46	"
	M	Meehan Julia H—†	16	housewife	42	"
	N	Reardon Anne G—†	16	stenographer	32	"
	O	Doherty Katherine—†	16	housewife	39	5 Hampstead rd
	P	Doherty Lester T	16	shipper	38	5 "

Green Street

	S	Johnson Albert H	151	chauffeur	35	here
	T	McNulty Annie E—†	151	at home	84	"
	U	LeBlanc Edgar A	151	cutter	38	"
	V	*LeBlanc Estelle R—†	151	housewife	28	"
	X	Fox Esther—†	153	"	23	
	Y	Fox Harwood	153	carpenter	30	"

Page.	Letter.	FULL NAME.	Residence, Jan. 1, 1941.	Occupation.	Supposed Age.	Reported Residence, Jan. 1, 1940. Street and Number.

1124
Green Street—Continued

c	Daum Arthur J	159	laborer	35	3395½ Wash'n
d	Daum Daniel M	159	"	65	3395½ "
e	Daum Edward C	159	busboy	21	3395½ "
f	Daum Emmet J	159	laborer	24	3395½ "
g	Daum Evelyn C—†	159	housewife	23	3395½ "
h	Daum Francis E	159	laborer	33	3395½ "
k	Daum William J	159	clerk	22	3395½ "
l	Walsh Maurice	159	laborer	49	3395½ "
m	Duncanson Frederick W	159	"	48	36 Oakdale
n	Duncanson Lulu—†	159	housewife	37	36 "
o	Gatturna Elizabeth J—†	159	"	35	31 Boynton
p	Gatturna Thomas G	159	laborer	42	31 "
r	Budurtis Dominic A	159	proprietor	52	here
s	Budurtis Francis J	159	bartender	27	"
t	*Budurtis Mary B—†	159	housewife	52	"
x	French Hazel S—† rear	165	bookkeeper	27	"
y	Ryan James E "	165	carpenter	51	"
z	*Ryan Lydia—† "	165	housewife	51	"

1125

b	Donohue Francis H	171	laborer	54	
c	Donohue Mary C—†	171	housewife	39	"
d	Kelley Kathleen V—†	171	"	38	
e	Kelley Thomas F	171	chauffeur	41	"
f	Kelley Ellen B—†	171	housekeeper	58	"
l	Marden Mary E—†	177½	housewife	65	123 Brookside av
m	Marden Robert E	177½	clerk	63	123 "
n	Ellsworth Charles R	177½	mason	33	here
o	*Ellsworth Elizabeth—†	177½	housewife	66	"
p	*Ellsworth Thomas	177½	carpenter	64	"
u	Collins Anna M—†	185	beautician	43	"
v	Collins Jacob M	185	machinist	53	"
w	Collins Vito J	185	"	24	
x	Abberton Priscilla A—†	185	housewife	32	"
y	Abberton William A	185	printer	36	
z	MacDonald Alexander J	185	laborer	47	

1126

a	O'Keefe Winifred L—†	185	housewife	49	"
b	Bagley John T	185	factoryhand	23	9 Plainfield
c	Bagley Mary A—†	185	housewife	47	9 "
d	Abberton Alfred G	185	chauffeur	30	here

16

Page	Letter	Full Name	Residence, Jan. 1, 1941.	Occupation.	Supposed Age.	Reported Residence, Jan. 1. 1940. Street and Number.

Green Street—Continued

	E	Abberton John J	185	chauffeur	32	here
	F	Abberton Mary—†	185	housewife	55	"
	G	Hurley Louise L—†	185	"	37	"
	H	Hurley Thomas F	185	B F D	40	..
	K	Sullivan Lawrence	185	laborer	29	
	N	Dwyer Patrick J	191	counterman	40	"
	O	*McCarthy Kathleen A-†	191	housewife	44	"
	P	Moynihan John D	191	laborer	45	
	R	Morahan Alice T—†	191	housekeeper	25	"
	S	Morahan Mary K—†	191	housewife	64	"
	T	Morahan Richard	191	trackman	58	"
	U	*Pittore Arthur E	191	barber	42	
	V	*Pittore Concetta—†	191	housewife	38	"
	W	Donovan Bridget—†	191	"	50	
	X	Donovan Catherine R—†	191	at home	20	
	Y	Donovan Daniel J	191	janitor	59	"
	Z	*Gilday Sadie—†	191	housewife	24	5 Glen rd
1127						
	A	*Wagner Jason	191	machinist	58	5 "
	B	Wagner Wilfred	191	painter	54	5 "
	C	*Tukey Katherine E—†	191	housewife	37	here
	D	Tukey Robert D	191	cutter	37	"
	G	Dupuis Arthur J	197	painter	42	"
	H	Dupuis Lydia R—†	197	housewife	38	"
	K	Travis Joseph	197	clerk	21	
	O	Jan Quen	205	laundryman	38	"

Kenton Road

	U	Conlin Anna M—†	2	hairdresser	44	here
	V	Conlin Annie—†	2	housewife	67	"
	W	Conlin Elizabeth—†	2	nurse	37	"
	X	Timmons Emma—†	2	manager	32	"
	Y	Timmons Emma T—†	2	housewife	67	"
	Z	Anderson Edna M—†	18	clerk	30	
1128						
	A	*Mahoney Gerald	18	engineer	33	
	B	*Swanson Anna S—†	18	housekeeper	55	"
	C	Keating Francis	20	leatherworker	40	"
	D	Keating Margaret—†	20	typist	41	
	E	Morris Catherine—†	20	at home	60	

11—11   17

Kenton Road—Continued

F	Baker Herbert	20	student	22	here
G	Baker Rose—†	20	housewife	51	"
H	Barry Francis X	20	plumber	23	"
K	Barry Frederick L	20	clerk	56	
L	Barry Lawrence A	20	machinist	24	"
M	*Barry Mary E—†	20	housewife	51	"
N	Redden Francis P	20	salesman	41	"
O	Battis Melville	24	guard	68	
P	Becker Emma C—†	24	housewife	58	"
R	Becker Harold J	24	manager	31	
S	Becker Margaret—†	24	secretary	30	"
T	Becker Mary L—†	24	housewife	31	"
V	Collyer Frank	30	buffer	49	
W	Collyer Mabel—†	30	housewife	43	"
X	Collyer Walter	30	wrapper	23	
Y	Stier Charles J	30	painter	51	
Z	Stier Charles J	30	student	23	

1129

A	Stier Helen R—†	30	"	20	
B	Stier Marie G—†	30	housewife	53	"
C	Stier Marie G—†	30	teacher	24	
D	Harkins George M	34	artist	26	
E	Harkins Margaret P—†	34	secretary	24	"
F	Harkins Michael J	34	B F D	49	
G	Harkins Rose M—†	34	clerk	22	"
H	Harkins Veronica M—†	34	housewife	50	"
K	Harkins William A	34	student	21	"
L	Pergola Antonina—†	40	housewife	21	128 Trenton
M	Pergola Michael	40	upholsterer	24	63A Charter
N	*Pergola Philippa—†	40	housewife	43	63A "
O	Pergola Vincenzo	40	pedler	52	63A "
P	*Coppinger Bridget—†	40	housewife	35	here
R	Coppinger John J	40	laborer	37	"
S	O'Connell Mary A—†	44	housewife	52	"
T	O'Connell Ruth M—†	44	social worker	25	"
U	O'Connell William H	44	butcher	58	
V	O'Connell William T	44	student	23	
W	Smith Annie E—†	46	housewife	47	"
X	Smith James P	46	retired	71	
Y	White Alice—†	56	student	21	
Z	White Eleanor T—†	56	typist	26	

Page	Letter	Full Name.	Residence, Jan. 1, 1941.	Occupation.	Supposed Age.	Reported Residence, Jan. 1, 1940. Street and Number.

1130

Kenton Road—Continued

	Letter	Full Name	Residence	Occupation	Age	Residence 1940
	A	White Henry F	56	clerk	24	here
	B	White Henry P	56	gardener	60	"
	C	White Mary—†	56	housewife	68	"
	D	White Michael J	56	retired	70	
	E	*White William	56	instructor	60	"
	F	Connell Mary J—†	63	housewife	69	"
	G	Connell Thomas B	63	retired	80	
	H	White Gertrude F—†	64	secretary	35	"
	K	White Julia—†	64	student	25	
	L	White Mary H—†	64	hairdresser	40	"

Lourdes Avenue

	Letter	Full Name	Residence	Occupation	Age	Residence 1940
	M	Berghans Charles E	6–8	machinist	20	here
	N	Berghans Mary N—†	6–8	housewife	48	"
	O	Berghans William C	6–8	chauffeur	51	"
	P	Berghans William C, jr	6–8	machinist	22	"
	R	Kelly Martin	6–8	steamfitter	37	"
	S	Kelly Mary—†	6–8	housewife	38	"
	T	Ward William J	6–8	shipper	43	"
	U	Lennon James H	6–8	chauffeur	37	107 Albano
	V	Lennon Loretta C—†	6–8	housewife	34	107 "
	W	Miller Eleanor M—†	7	clerk	22	here
	X	Miller Margaret A—†	7	housewife	23	"
	Y	Miller William J	7	salesman	47	"
	Z	Freeman Mary—†	7	housekeeper	65	"

1131

	Letter	Full Name	Residence	Occupation	Age	Residence 1940
	A	Kalpowski Hilda—†	7	stenographer	35	"
	B	Tosko Helen A—†	7	housewife	30	"
	C	Tosko John	7	policeman	43	"
	D	Roche Dorothy G—†	10–12	clerk	33	
	E	Roche Edwin P	10–12	"	31	
	F	Spellman Bernard T	10–12	chemist	26	
	G	Spellman Edith L—†	10–12	housewife	27	"
	H	*Asvesta Pauline—†	10–12	stitcher	37	
	K	Marinos Christine P-†	10–12	housewife	29	"
	L	Marinos Peter A	10–12	chef	39	
	M	*Charchut Margaret M-†10–12		housewife	49	"
	N	Charchut Theodore	10–12	cook	50	
	O	Huether Frank J	13	upholsterer	46	"

Page.	Letter.	FULL NAME.	Residence, Jan. 1, 1941.	Occupation.	Supposed Age.	Reported Residence, Jan. 1, 1940. Street and Number.

Lourdes Avenue—Continued

	P	Huether Yvonne M—†	13	housewife	42	here
	R	Lindroth Esther G—†	13	stenographer	43	"
	S	Lindroth John E	13	decorator	38	"
	T	Lindroth Selma—†	13	housewife	66	"
	U	Mulkeen Anna J—†	13	"	47	
	V	Mulkeen Francis M	13	clerk	22	
	W	Mulkeen Martin F	13	motorman	48	"
	X	Lehan James F	16–18	salesman	43	"
	Y	Lehan Kathryn C—†	16–18	housewife	42	"
	Z	McDonald Anna M—†	16–18	secretary	32	"
		1132				
	A	Shea John E	16–18	bricklayer	35	"
	B	Shea Madeline R—†	16–18	housewife	35	"
	C	McDonald Joseph H	16–18	metalworker	47	"
	D	Gray Elizabeth E—†	17	housewife	40	"
	E	Gray Joseph	17	clerk	56	
	F	Rostron Ada—†	17	at home	63	
	G	Conroy Florence M—†	17	housewife	37	"
	H	Conroy James J	17	agent	42	
	K	*Dow Mary E—†	17	housewife	45	"
	L	Dow Warren P	17	boilermaker	38	"
	M	*Stanton George S	19	retired	55	
	N	Stanton Helen M—†	19	secretary	35	"
	O	*Stanton Mary D—†	19	at home	21	"
	P	*Stanton Mary E—†	19	housewife	56	"
	R	Alward Eugene H	19	operator	44	"
	S	Alward Nellie I—†	19	housewife	43	"
	T	O'Donnell Margaret M—†	19	"	34	
	U	O'Donnell Thomas	19	dispatcher	34	"
	V	Friberg Iris H—†	25	housewife	59	"
	W	Friberg Karen A—†	25	bookkeeper	34	"
	X	Welch David J	25	manager	25	20 Rosemont
	Y	Welch Evelyn C—†	25	nurse	22	Chelsea
	Z	Hall Esther—†	25	clerk	33	here
		1133				
	A	Hall Ruth—†	25		35	
	B	Gleason Edward J	25	"	27	"
	C	Gleason Julia J—†	25	housewife	29	"
	D	Malloy Anna K—†	25	"	32	
	E	Malloy John P	25	clerk	40	
	F	Davis Emma L—†	25	housewife	42	"

Page.	Letter.	Full Name.	Residence, Jan. 1, 1941.	Occupation.	Supposed Age.	Reported Residence, Jan. 1, 1940. Street and Number.

Lourdes Avenue—Continued

G	Davis Samuel	25	pharmacist	44	here
H	Hoban Irene E—†	29	inspector	22	23 Byron
K	Hoban Walter J.	29	laborer	24	19 Adams
L	Knowland Arthur K	29	clerk	36	47 Reyem Circle
M	Knowland Susanna M—†	29	housewife	32	47 "
N	*Farrell Ellen G—†	29	"	31	here
O	*Farrell Joseph C	29	baker	33	"
P	*Crawford Minnie—†	29	at home	85	"
R	*Page Ann—†	29	housewife	50	"
S	Page Charles E	29	foreman	55	
T	Mee Georgia M—†	29	housewife	25	"
U	Mee William H	29	nurse	31	
V	Burke Grace M—†	29	housewife	48	"
W	Burke Peter	29	steamfitter	62	"
X	Franke Helen T—†	33	housewife	24	"
Y	Franke William C	33	projectionist	25	"
Z	Huban Katherine A—†	33	at home	54	19 Jackson pl

1134

A	McCready Elizabeth A—†	33	housewife	25	here
B	McCready Thomas F	33	clerk	30	"
C	Russo Mildred P—†	33	housewife	30	269 Forest Hills
D	Russo Paul E	33	operator	33	269 "
E	Cosgrove Edmund F	33	salesman	30	here
F	Cosgrove Mariette A—†	33	housewife	29	"
H	Connors John	33	retired	64	"
K	Gibbons Anna—†	33	operator	24	"
L	Elkind Mollie I—†	42	housewife	29	"
M	Elkind Morris	42	manager	32	"
N	Vaughn Leonard E	42	mechanic	43	"
O	*Vaughn Mary O—†	42	housewife	43	"
P	DeLeon Irene M—†	42	"	39	
R	DeLeon Manuel F	42	supervisor	42	"
S	DeLeon Robert F	42	laborer	20	

Meehan Place

T	Ferrante Catherine—†	1	housewife	51	here
U	*Wagner Howard	1	operator	30	10 Union av
V	Wagner Mary E—†	1	housewife	24	10 "
W	Cawley Catherine—†	1	housekeeper	85	here
X	Hynes Ellen E—†	1	clerk	45	"

21

Meehan Place—Continued

Y	Hynes Louise R—†	1	secretary	23	here
z	Wagner Ruth C—†	2	housewife	23	406 Amory
	1135				
A	Wagner William	2	machinist	31	406 "
B	*Ellsworth Alban	2	carpenter	38	177½ Green
D	Kolf Helen—†	3	housewife	32	3236 Wash'n

Peter Parley Road

E	Drake John E	11	retired	71	here
F	Drake Margaret C—†	11	housewife	63	"
G	O'Neil Theresa M—†	15	"	50	"
H	O'Neil Thomas E	15	salesman	50	
K	Ormond Winifred T—†	15	teacher	44	
L	Lueth Elmer C	19	salesman	35	"
M	Lueth Marion L—†	19	housewife	35	"
N	Lueth Clara E—†	19	"	60	
O	Lueth Henry A	19	watchman	62	"
P	Hurley Mary J—†	25	housewife	58	"
R	Hurley Thomas F	25	plumber	66	
S	Kelly Annastasia—†	25	teacher	45	
T	Tobin John J	33	retired	76	"
U	Tobin Katherine A—†	33	housewife	69	"
V	Carlisle Elizabeth—†	33	operator	42	"
W	Nazzaro Edward N	33	manager	42	
X	Nazzaro Rose—†	33	housewife	38	"
z	Kenney Mary—†	35	"	50	
	1136				
A	Kenney Phillip	35	chauffeur	30	"
B	Kenney William A	35	agent	52	
c	Sullivan Angela—†	35	stenographer	20	"
D	Cuttle Ignatius H	37	attorney	50	"
E	Cuttle Katherine A—†	37	librarian	24	
G	Cuttle Loretta A—†	37	housewife	48	"
F	Connolly Bartholomew	37	operator	50	
H	Connolly Marian—†	37	housewife	49	"
K	Connolly Mary R—†	37	clerk	20	
M	Dana Lester H	45	broker	39	
N	Dana Rebecca H—†	45	housewife	65	"
O	Dana Samuel	45	realtor	70	"
P	*Houlihan Elizabeth—†	45	domestic	24	Canada

Page.	Letter.	FULL NAME.	Residence, Jan. 1, 1941.	Occupation.	Supposed Age.	Reported Residence, Jan. 1, 1940. Street and Number.

Peter Parley Road—Continued

R	Wilner Jacob S	49	broker	58	here
S	Wilner Marvin J	49	engineer	26	"
T	Wilner Rose C—†	49	housewife	49	"
U	Dennis Sarah W—†	53	clerk	52	
V	Holt Winifred M—†	53	housewife	38	"
W	Howatt Sarah L—†	53	"	62	
X	Howatt Welton M	53	merchant	66	"
Y	Burke Gerard F	57	copy writer	27	"
Z	Burke Margaret C—†	57	housewife	61	"

1137

A	Miller Agnes B—†	63	"	49	
B	Miller Alonzo	63	U S A	23	
C	Miller Edward J	63	manager	26	"
D	Miller Michael J	63	longshoreman	56	"
E	Miller Patricia A—†	63	clerk	20	
F	Carty Catherine M—†	67	stenographer	26	"
G	Carty Helen A—†	67	housewife	59	"
H	Carty John J	67	stenographer	34	"
K	Carty Rita H—†	67	clerk	21	"
L	Carty Stephen H	67	retired	75	
M	Flynn Grace—†	71	reader	22	
N	Flynn John L	71	clerk	55	
O	Flynn Leo L	71	student	20	
P	Flynn Mary—†	71	housewife	57	"
R	Flynn Rita M—†	71	operator	25	"
S	Sullivan James J	71	mechanic	58	"
T	Brown Clarence E	75	merchant	36	4 Pinckney
U	O'Brien Margaret—†	75	waitress	22	25 Forest Hills
V	O'Brien William T	75	salesman	50	25 "
W	Doherty Cornelius	75	operator	50	here
X	Doherty Francis	75	clerk	24	"
Y	Doherty Mary A—†	75	housewife	49	"
Z	Doherty Mary B—†	75	stenographer	22	"

1138   Robeson Street

A	Beatty Jeannette D—†	2	housewife	38	here
B	Beatty Patrick J	2	pharmacist	38	"
C	Doyle Alice M—†	2	housewife	35	"
D	Doyle Joseph P	2	clerk	35	
E	Desjardins Agnes—†	4	stitcher	58	

Page.	Letter.	FULL NAME.	Residence, Jan. 1, 1941.	Occupation.	Supposed Age.	Reported Residence, Jan. 1, 1940. Street and Number.

Robeson Street—Continued

	F	*Desjardins Alexander	4	shoemaker	58	here
	G	Desjardins Gilbert	4	foreman	29	"
	H	Hayes Catherine—†	4	nurse	59	"
	K	Woelfel Frank	4	baker	63	"
	L	Madden Andrew J	4	dentist	52	
	M	Madden Lillian—†	4	inspector	55	"
	N	Costello Blanche E—†	8	housewife	52	"
	O	Costello Coleman J	8	mechanic	54	"
	P	Costello Marie J—†	8	stenographer	29	"
	R	Gorman Louise B—†	8	housewife	26	"
	S	Gorman Robert J	8	accountant	30	"
	T	Sullivan Cornelius J	8	mechanic	57	"
	U	Sullivan Joseph	8	packer	25	
	V	Sullivan Julia M—†	8	housewife	49	"
	W	Curley Peter	11	inspector	52	"
	X	Janes Bertha—†	11	housekeeper	39	"
	Y	Geehan Margaret M—†	12	saleswoman	42	"
	Z	*Geehan Mary—†	12	housewife	72	"

1139

	A	*Higgins Annie G—†	12	"	36	
	B	Higgins Michael J	12	salesman	42	"
	C	Harris Alice S—†	12	stenographer	26	"
	D	Harris Arthur N	12	bartender	28	"
	E	Harris Sophia—†	12	housewife	45	"
	F	Harris William J	12	printer	49	"
	G	Beyer Mary N—†	16	social worker	58	"
	H	Storer Morris B	16	teacher	37	"
	K	Jones Ralph J	18	salesman	21	N Carolina
	L	Jones Veda A—†	18	housewife	57	here
	M	Jones Viola S—†	18	manager	23	"
	N	Greyser Gladys—†	18	housewife	32	"
	O	Greyser Morris	18	instructor	35	"
	P	Koven Lois—†	18	clerk	25	"
	R	Scott Elsie—†	18	housewife	33	527 Beacon
	S	Scott John B	18	draftsman	31	527 "
	T	Taylor Clara—†	22	housewife	29	Quincy
	U	Taylor Edward A	22	inspector	30	"
	V	Irbin Erma M—†	22	bookkeeper	37	here
	W	Irbin Paul	22	machinist	30	Cambridge
	X	Mirankens Antonette—†	22	housewife	63	here
	Y	Mirankens Charles	22	machinist	67	"

Page.	Letter.	Full Name.	Residence, Jan. 1, 1941.	Occupation.	Supposed Age.	Reported Residence, Jan. 1, 1940. Street and Number.

Robeson Street—Continued

	z	Garvey Mary T—†	22	housewife	25	here
1140						
	A	Garvey Stephen J	22	electrician	29	"
	B	Kelly Delia A—†	22	housewife	56	"
	c	Kelly Thomas	22	motorman	60	"
	D	Sheehan Esther B—†	26	housewife	41	"
	E	Sheehan John J	26	clerk	42	
	F	Douglas Herbert W	26	salesman	36	"
	G	Douglas Madeline—†	26	housewife	63	"
	H	Connolly John	26	clerk	32	
	K	Connolly Margaret—†	26	housewife	65	"
	L	Connolly Mary—†	26	hairdresser	37	"
	M	Krug George B	30	shipper	31	
	N	Krug Ruth F—†	30	housewife	32	"
	o	Tumavicus Bartholomew	30	chauffeur	52	"
	P	Tumavicus Jadviga M—†	30	housewife	48	"
	R	Yurenas Gertrude—†	30	secretary	22	"
	s	Yurenas Irene—†	30	teacher	25	
	T	Higgins Charles F	30	foreman	44	
	U	Higgins Charles F, jr	30	clerk	22	
	V	Higgins Eleanor—†	30	housewife	43	"
	w	Murphy Thomas	30	retired	81	
	X	Murphy Timothy J	30	bookkeeper	35	"
	z	Roche James J	34	motorman	54	"
1141						
	A	Roche James T	34	messenger	21	"
	B	Roche John T	34	metalworker	25	"
	D	Schneider Anna E—†	34	milliner	46	
	E	Schneider Maria M—†	34	housewife	79	"
	F	Doherty James P	38	baker	34	"
	G	Doherty John E	38	blacksmith	37	"
	H	Doherty Mary M—†	38	housekeeper	27	"
	K	Baldwin Edward	38	manager	26	20 Caton
	L	Baldwin Mary B—†	38	clerk	25	2 Paul Gore ter
	M	Reagan Catherine—†	38	housewife	55	2 "
	N	Reagan William S	38	accountant	24	2 "
	o	Connell Mary M—†	38	secretary	51	here
	P	Wilkinson Gertrude N—†	38	"	43	"
	R	Witham Annie—†	39	housewife	35	"
	s	Witham John	39	mechanic	32	"
	T	Thomas Clifton H	39	checker	34	

Page.	Letter.	Full Name.	Residence, Jan. 1, 1941.	Occupation.	Supposed Age.	Reported Residence, Jan. 1, 1940. Street and Number.

Robeson Street—Continued

	u	Thomas Ruth M—†	39	nurse	28	here
	v	Riley Eugene A	39	clerk	44	"
	w	Riley Ottyl F—†	39	housewife	45	"
	x	Manning Dorothy—†	39	"	41	
	y	Manning Thomas F	39	manager	50	"
	z	Lombard Edward W	44	retired	47	
		1142				
	a	MacDonald Bessie—†	44	housekeeper	58	"
	b	Keenan Alice—†	45	secretary	41	"
	c	Keenan Frank L	45	checker	56	"
	d	Loughman Annie—†	45	at home	80	
	e	Loughman Annie—†	45	housewife	50	"
	f	Loughman Arthur	45	laborer	22	
	g	Loughman Clement	45	bartender	25	"
	h	Loughman Clement I	45	bookkeeper	50	"
	k	Barrett Catherine L—†	48	housewife	46	"
	l	Barrett Edward F	48	student	22	
	m	Barrett John G	48	"	25	
	n	Barrett John N	48	teacher	55	
	o	Barrett William L	48	student	23	
	s	Jacobson Anna—†	54	housewife	48	"
	t	Jacobson William	54	contractor	49	"
	u	Levine Charlotte—†	54	bookkeeper	29	"
	v	Swift Veronica—†	54	housekeeper	27	"
	w	Bortnick Phillip	54	teacher	35	
	x	Bortnick Rose K—†	54	housewife	34	"
	y	Cook Gertrude—†	58	at home	70	
	z	Cook Laura G—†	58	"	45	
		1143				
	a	Mandelstam Annie—†	63	housewife	39	"
	b	Mandelstam Harry	63	attorney	43	"
	c	Hark Anna—†	63	housewife	34	"
	d	Hark Jacob	63	merchant	35	"
	e	*Snee Betty—†	63	housekeeper	25	60 Crawford
	f	Selib Gertrude—†	69	housewife	51	here
	g	Selib Morris L	69	manufacturer	54	"
	h	Moody Mary A—†	69	clerk	23	6 Gordon
	k	Moody Wesley P	69	agent	24	6 "
	l	Rothstein Anne B—†	71	housewife	31	here
	m	Rothstein Morris	71	manufacturer	37	"

Rockvale Circle

Page	Letter	Full Name	Residence, Jan. 1, 1941.	Occupation	Supposed Age.	Reported Residence, Jan. 1, 1940. Street and Number.
	N	Sargent Alice A—†	28	housewife	32	here
	O	Sargent John S	28	mechanic	28	"
	P	Allaire Adele M—†	28	housewife	29	"
	R	Allaire Leon H	28	welder	41	
	S	Carr Edward H	28	ironworker	44	"
	T	Carr Mary H—†	28	housewife	42	"
	U	Walsh Helen E—†	32	"	34	
	V	Walsh Richard J	32	salesman	28	"
	W	Kopf Grace E—†	32	housewife	40	"
	X	Kopf Harry J	32	policeman	43	"
	Z	Finney Helen G—†	36	saleswoman	45	"
		1144				
	A	Enos Charles	36	printer	42	
	B	Nugent Marie I—†	36	"	44	
	C	Nugent Virginia M—†	36	entertainer	23	"
	D	Bohane Cornelius	36	retired	74	
	E	Bohane Katherine—†	36	at home	76	
	F	Watt Margaret E—†	36	housewife	33	"
	G	Watt William T	36	chauffeur	37	Brookline
	H	Roy Anna F—†	39	housewife	33	here
	K	Roy George J	39	fireman	35	"
	L	Maguire James H	39	policeman	31	"
	M	Maguire Mary M—†	39	housewife	26	"
	N	Burr Dorothy A—†	39	"	23	18 Durham
	O	Burr Thomas W	39	mortician	24	18 "
	P*	Crehan Kathleen A—†	40	housewife	39	152 Williams
	R	Crehan William J	40	policeman	47	152 "
	S	Keefe Mildred E—†	40	housewife	48	9 Bowdoin
	T	Young Arthur W	40	executive	35	3 Draper
	U	Young Frederick H	40	letter carrier	41	3 "
	V	Young Harry A	40	retired	67	3 "
	X	Murphy Christina—†	43	at home	65	40 Reyem Circle
	Y	Tanner Alfred C	43	laborer	30	40 "
	Z	Tanner Marjorie—†	43	housewife	30	40 "
		1145				
	A	Barteaux Edward H	43	clerk	50	
	B	Barteaux Margaret A—†	43	supervisor	42	"
	C	Souza Frank T	43	clerk	40	"
	D	Cunningham Helen D—†	43	housewife	21	24 Beecher
	E	Cunningham James J	43	machinist	26	24 "

Rockvale Circle—Continued

F	Marceaux Claude A	44	welder	26	here	
G	Marceaux Marjorie S—†	44	housewife	22	"	
H	Griffin Horace E	44	policeman	40	"	
K	Griffin Mildred E—†	44	housewife	40	"	
L	McGarry Bernard G	44	clerk	29		
M	McGarry Marie E—†	44	housewife	26	"	
N	Krapohl Gertrude A—†	47	"	39	43 Reyem Circle	
O	Krapohl Henry W	47	bookbinder	44	43 "	
P	Banks Charles W	47	photographer	32	here	
R	Banks Margaret C—†	47	housewife	27	"	
T	Whitten Antoinette—†	48	"	34	"	
U	Whitten Edward A	48	clerk	34		
V	Foley Flora G—†	48	housewife	33	"	
W	Foley Timothy R	48	clerk	42	"	
X	Martin Anna D—†	48	stenographer	27	"	
Y	Martin Annie M—†	48	housewife	62	"	
Z	Martin James J	48	polisher	62		

1146

A	Martin Mary T—†	48	teacher	30	"	
B	Rheault May—†	51	saleswoman	28	"	
C	Rheault Noel	51	operator	27	"	
D	Palombo Frances J—†	51	housewife	30	"	
E	Palombo Joseph J	51	policeman	37	"	
F	O'Connor Dorothy J—†	51	housewife	22	"	
G	O'Connor John J	51	plumber	27		

Rocky Nook Terrace

H	Kelley John G	6–8	foreman	43	here	
K	Kelley Mary J—†	6–8	housewife	41	"	
L	Whalen Helen—†	6–8	clerk	36	"	
M	Carr Mary—†	6–8	housewife	40	"	
N	Carr Thomas H	6–8	examiner	41	"	
O	Greenwood Ernest	10–12	waiter	52		
P	Greenwood Richard	10–12	engineer	25	"	
R	*Greenwood Pauline—†	10–12	housewife	46	"	
S	Cestoni Dava—†	10–12	"	43		
T	Cestoni Domonic J	10–12	chemist	25		
U	Cestoni Settimio	10–12	merchant	54	"	

Page.	Letter.	FULL NAME.	Residence, Jan. 1, 1941.	Occupation.	Supposed Age.	Reported Residence, Jan. 1, 1940. Street and Number.

Rocky Nook Terrace—Continued

v	Ryan Francis G	11	accountant	28	Maryland
w	Ryan Isabelle—†	11	housewife	20	"
x	Clougher Eleanor V—†	11	clerk	22	here
y	Clougher Mary A—†	11	housewife	41	"
z	Clougher Timothy	11	painter	42	"
	1147				
a	Luff Anna—†	11	housewife	61	"
b	Perola Henry	14–16	mechanic	30	24 Beech
c	Perola Necia R—†	14–16	housewife	27	24 "
d	Kelley Lillian G—†	14–16	"	52	here
e	Kelley Luke J	14–16	retired	63	"
f	Hunter Alfred	15	chauffeur	54	"
g	Hunter Mary—†	15	housewife	46	"
h	Lane Prudence—†	15	nurse	48	14 Rocky Nook ter
k	McPherson Arthur T	15	merchant	48	14 "
l	McPherson Victoria V—†	15	housewife	48	14 "
m	Masaschi Joseph L	17	printer	42	here
n	Moraschi Winifred—†	17	stenographer	42	"
o	Peterson Anna M—†	17	housewife	61	"
p	Peterson Carl A	17	mechanic	68	"
r	Peterson Carl R	17	"	24	

Rowen Court

s	Foss Charles W	1	painter	65	254 Mass av
t	Foss Fairy K—†	1	housewife	65	254 "
u	Suhr Frederick R	3	laborer	29	here
v	Suhr Helen M—†	3	housewife	30	"
w	Tucker Elizabeth—†	3	"	26	"
x	Tucker Henry J, jr	3	janitor	26	"
y	Hovling Helga—†	3	housewife	35	"
z	Letasz Florence L—†	5	"	27	Somerville
	1148				
a	Letasz John	5	machinist	31	"
b	*Kane Edward	5	retired	78	here
c	Kane Margaret—†	5	factoryhand	43	"
d	*Kane Mary—†	5	housewife	63	"
e	Lagsdin Bertha M—†	5	"	27	3117 Wash'n
f	Lagsdin John E	5	painter	27	3117 "
g	*Lagsdin Mildred E—†	5	housewife	51	3117 "

29

Page.	Letter.	Full Name.	Residence, Jan. 1, 1941.	Occupation.	Supposed Age.	Reported Residence, Jan. 1, 1940. Street and Number.

Sigourney Street

	H	Bardzilowski John	12	U S N	20	13 Dracut
	K	Bardzilowski Stanley	12	pressman	22	13 "
	L	*Bardzilowski Stephania—†	12	housewife	45	13 "
	M	*Bardzilowski Walter	12	foreman	57	13 "
	N	Sims Joseph L	12	carpenter	33	35 Buttonwood
	O	Hubley James C	24	mechanic	57	here
	P	Hubley Mary I—†	24	housewife	54	"
	R	English Mary E—†	25	at home	66	"
	S	Paris William H	25	caretaker	65	"
	T	Diab Rose—†	26	at home	48	281 Forest Hills
	U	Gibran Horace J	26	U S A	21	201 Harris'n av
	V	*Gibran Nicholas	26	carpenter	59	201 "
	W	*Gibran Rose—†	26	stitcher	46	201 "
	X	Gibran Susan—†	26	stenographer	20	201 "
	Y	*Guerrila Joseph	26	salesman	40	281 Forest Hills
	Z	Rubin Anna M—†	32	housewife	53	here
1149						
	A	Rubin Esther—†	32	teacher	25	
	B	Rubin Israel G	32	merchant	54	"
	C	Rubin Samuel	32	musician	24	"
	D	*Barr Anna—†	56	housewife	74	"
	E	Barr Sarah—†	56	bookkeeper	35	"
	F	Barr Sydney	56	attorney	30	"
	G	Lofchie Alfred	56	mechanic	25	"
	H	Lofchie Harry	56	"	45	
	K	Lofchie Lena—†	56	housewife	33	"
	L	Dowling Caroline L—†	64	"	61	
	M	Dowling Katherine L—†	64	teacher	29	"
	N	Dowling Paul E	64	"	31	
	O	Dowling William T	64	retired	69	
	P	Dowling William T, jr	64	clerk	22	

Union Avenue

	A	Anderson Carl H	4	chauffeur	35	50 Burnett
	S	Anderson Pauline—†	4	housewife	21	50 "
	T	DelCorso Joseph	4	manufacturer	23	101 Alabama
	U	Starr Mary—†	4	housewife	46	here
	V	*Dolan Mary—†	4	at home	76	"
	W	Groves J Hiram	4	retired	67	"
	X	Pieterz Madeline—†	4	at home	52	

Page.	Letter.	FULL NAME.	Residence, Jan. 1, 1941.	Occupation.	Supposed Age.	Reported Residence, Jan. 1, 1940. Street and Number.

Union Avenue—Continued

	z	Reardon Helen—†	5	housewife	39	12 Posen
1150						
	A	Reardon Thomas J	5	laborer	43	12 "
	B	Martin Loretta—†	5	packer	21	160 Williams
	C	Hough Everett	5	painter	36	2 Meehan pl
	D	Hough Mary—†	5	housewife	30	2 "
	E	Franck Emma P—†	5	at home	73	here
	F	*Franck Peter S	5	shoemaker	91	"
	G	Ferris Dorothy E—†	5	laundress	28	3387 Wash'n
	H	*Ferris Frank	5	winder	41	3387 "
	K	Caldwell Florence—†	5	housekeeper	55	here
	L	Cole Charles A	5	retired	67	"
	M	McDonald Michael	5	painter	65	"
	N	*McKenzie Olive—†	5	housewife	53	"
	O	Herman Anna M—†	5	"	39	
	P	Ferdinand George	6	laborer	30	
	R	Ferdinand Mary—†	6	housewife	31	"
	S	Chioccola Angelina—†	6	"	32	
	T	Chioccola Armand J	6	operator	30	"
	U	Coolidge Charlotte—†	6	housewife	36	"
	V	Coolidge Wesley	6	porter	36	
	W	*Quinn Catherine O—†	8	housewife	42	"
	X	*Quinn Isaac O	8	laborer	48	"
	Y	LeMay Joseph	8	chauffeur	43	Springfield
	z	LeMay Margaret—†	8	housewife	38	here
1151						
	A	*McCarthy Margaret—†	8	domestic	34	"
	B	Campanella John B	8	laborer	28	35 Barry pl
	C	Campanella Sadie—†	8	housewife	24	35 "
	D	*Thompson Estalla A—†	9	"	33	here
	E	Thompson James A	9	chauffeur	37	"
	G	Buinicki Florence—†	9	waitress	26	"
	F	*Buinicki Ignatz	9	millhand	50	"
	H	*Zaldoks Emily—†	9	cleaner	50	89 Wachusett
	K	Zaldoks John	9	operator	21	89 "
	L	Buckley Catherine A—†	10	at home	76	here
	M	Buckley Mary F—†	10	"	73	"
	N	Flate Eleanor E—†	10	stenographer	21	"
	O	Flate Nickolas	10	manufacturer	65	"
	P	Guinta Antonette—† 1st r	10	housewife	50	"
	R	Guinta Dominic 1st "	10	factoryhand	27	"

Page.	Letter.	FULL NAME.	Residence, Jan. 1, 1941.	Occupation.	Supposed Age.	Reported Residence, Jan. 1, 1940. Street and Number.

Union Avenue—Continued

s	Foye Arthur	2d " 10	chauffeur	21	Concord
T	Foye Elsie—†	2d " 10	seamstress	43	here
U	Parlon Catherine A—†	12	saleswoman	62	"
V	Parlon Mary—†	12	housewife	67	"
W	Fleming Anna—†	12	"	33	
X	*Fleming Michael	12	laborer	38	
Y	Desharnais Juliett—†	13	housewife	34	"

1152

A	Desharnais Wilfred	13	janitor	40	
B	*Dick Elizabeth—†	13	housewife	48	"
C	Dick William	13	waiter	52	
D	Mihovan Mary—†	13	housewife	25	"
E	Mihovan William	13	cook	28	
F	Rafford Exilda V—†	14	at home	38	"
G	*Rafuse Jeanette—†	14	bousewife	37	14 Rochdale
H	Rafuse Robert B	14	painter	38	14 "
K	Keaveney Henry M	17	compositor	36	here
L	Keaveney Margaret G—†	17	housewife	39	"
M	Leonard Mary C—†	17	clerk	45	"
N	Delaney Dennis J	19	chauffeur	43	"
O	Delaney Elizabeth H—†	19	housewife	40	"
P	Bryant Florence—† '	19	"	56	
R	Bryant George	19	draftsman	55	"
S	White Ella M—†	19	at home	58	
T	McCloud Edward	19	clerk	25	
U	McCloud Florence—†	19	housewife	45	"
V	Mahoney John J	19A	U S N	22	
W	Paige Daniel F	19A	laborer	39	
X	Paige Margaret R—†	19A	housewife	31	"
Y	Connor Lottie E—†	19A	at home	54	
Z	*Bovard Allen	19A	gardener	39	"

1153

A	Bovard Bertha I—†	19A	operator	32	"
B	Fuller Mary E—†	19A	housewife	24	"
C	Fuller Warren E	19A	operator	35	"
D	*Zazaretti Angelina—†	20	housewife	49	"
E	Zazaretti Catherine—†	20	factoryhand	22	"
F	Zazaretti Joseph	20	chef	53	
G	Zazaretti Michael	20	U S N	25	
H	Zazaretti Viola—†	20	factoryhand	20	"
K	Strickland Barbara A—†	21	housewife	24	"

Union Avenue--Continued

	L	Strickland Harry G	21	cleaner	28	here
	M	Card Ernestina—†	21	at home	63	"
	N	Small Eva J—†	21	housewife	36	"
	O	Small Solon B, jr	21	chemist	34	
	P	Fabi Constantino	22	laborer	48	
	R	*Fabi Rosina—†	22	housewife	50	"
	S	*O'Brien Helen T—†	22A	"	40	
	T	O'Brien John J	22A	merchant	21	"
	U	*O'Brien Thomas J	22A	retired	49	
	V	Hutchinson Nellie B—†	22A	housewife	39	"
	W	Hutchinson Patrick J	22A	laborer	42	
	X	Dean Ernest F	22A	machinist	33	"
	Y	Dean N Shirley—†	22A	housewife	32	"
	Z	Wilson Lois—†	22A	attendant	20	"

1154

	C	Smiddy Anna—†	24	housewife	27	"
	D	Smiddy William	24	checker	37	"
	E	*Bowen Donald	25	retired	69	1 Vine av
	F	*Bowen Hannah—†	25	housewife	68	1 "
	G	Bowen Margaret—†	25	bookbinder	33	1 "
	H	Bowen Michael H	25	"	31	1 "
	K	Dever Eveline A—†	25	at home	57	here
	L	Manning James T	26	shipper	26	3215 Wash'n
	M	Manning Mildred—†	26	housewife	24	3215 "
	N	Kosey Leonora—†	26	"	52	here
	O	Kosey Stanley	26	painter	52	"
	P	Hernon Ann C—†	27	teacher	23	"
	R	Hernon Catherine—†	27	student	20	
	S	Hernon Mary P—†	27	teacher	25	
	T	Hernon Thomas J	27	electrotyper	52	"
	U	Greenleaf Albert	28	chauffeur	24	"
	V	Greenleaf Marion—†	28	housewife	23	"
	W	Corbett Dominic A	rear 30	guard	49	
	X	Corbett Margaret A—† "	30	housewife	46	"
	Y	*Hughes William	32	operator	60	1 Regent pl

1155

	A	Brinkman John	33	auditor	28	22 Marmion
	B	Brinkman Mary—†	33	housewife	23	22 "
	C	Keough Albert	33	steelworker	24	here
	D	Keough William	33	"	21	"
	E	Keough William P	33	chauffeur	68	"

Union Avenue—Continued

F	Betts Cecil R	35	mechanic	50	here
G	Betts Lila M—†	35	housewife	49	"
H	Betts Merton R	35	baker	24	"
K	Groves Blanche K—†	37	housewife	42	"
L	*Groves George H	37	carpenter	45	"
M	*Groves George R	37	baker	22	"
N	Groves Nelda J—†	37	operator	20	"
O	Barnaby Adolph	40	salesman	22	"
P	Barnaby Charles	40	laborer	54	
R	Barnaby Mary—†	40	housewife	51	"
S	Barnaby Rita—-†	40	at home	24	
T	Sinacola Margaret M—†	41	housewife	43	"
U	Sinacola Michael J	41	chauffeur	33	"
V	Chiarenza Calogero	42	retired	52	
W	Chiarenza Charles P	42	pressman	26	"
X	*Chiarenza Maria C—†	42	housewife	53	"
Y	Connolly Joseph T	43	floorman	23	"
Z	Connolly Rose M—†	43	housewife	23	"

1156

A	Nye Frances L—†	43	housewife	62	"
B	Nye George L	43	painter	59	
C	Nye Wallace W	43	"	31	
D	Kelley Florence A—†	43	housewife	34	"
E	Kelley James J	43	window washer	37	"
F	*Weschrob Mary F—† rear	43	housewife	42	"
G	Weschrob Richard A "	43	painter	45	
H	Maguire Daniel "	43	laborer	38	
K	*Maguire Julia S—† "	43	housewife	37	"
L	Crawford Anna M—† "	43	"	21	
M	Crawford Walter J "	43	chauffeur	21	"
N	Lundbergh Carl R	46	machinist	22	"
O	Lundbergh Elizabeth H-†	46	housewife	55	"
P	*Lundbergh Ralph F	46	laborer	64	
R	Doran Mae—†	48	stitcher	46	
S	Martin Katherine—†	48	dressmaker	51	"
T	Maloney Delia—†	48	housewife	47	"
U	Maloney Francis	48	mechanic	27	"
V	Maloney James J	48	foreman	62	
W	Bennett Alfred	49	laborer	52	
X	Bennett Mary T—†	49	housewife	48	"
Y	Kelley Annie M—†	49	"	75	

Page.	Letter.	Full Name.	Residence, Jan. 1, 1941.	Occupation.	Supposed Age.	Reported Residence, Jan. 1, 1940. Street and Number.

Union Avenue—Continued

	z	Kelley Annie M—†	49	cashier	35	here
1157						
	A	Larkin Catherine—†	49	at home	23	
	B	Paige Anna A—†	58	housewife	33	"
	c	Paige Annie M—†	58	"	69	
	D	Paige Frederick	58	retired	72	
	E	Paige George L	58	laborer	36	
	F	Lederman Barbara—†	60	laundress	72	"
	G	Wimbauer Anton	60	cooper	61	
	H	Wimbauer Antonia—†	60	nurse	35	
	K	Wimbauer Charles J	60	cooper	23	
	L	Wimbauer Frank	60	breweryworker	35	"
	M	Wimbauer Theresa—† .	60	housewife	59	"
	N	Manning Anna F—†	62	"	48	
	o	Manning Edward F	62	laborer	52	
	P	Manning Mary F—†	62	at home	20	
	R	O'Brien Arthur F	63	retired	73	
	s	Vincent Alice—†	63	at home	68	
	T	Fraser Catherine F—†	64	"	37	
	U	Fraser Robert B	64	metalworker	36	"
	v	Cogan Anna—†	64	housewife	23	"
	w	Cogan Joseph	64	chauffeur	25	"
	x	Glennon John J	64	plumber	52	64 Williams
	Y	Glennon Mary J—†	64	housewife	50	here

Washington Street

	z	Kuegel Florence L—†	3316	housewife	38	here
1158						
	A	Quattrochi Frances J—†	3316	"	45	
	B	Quattrochi Gregory M	3316	laborer	42	
	c	Samuel Charles	3316	"	25	
	D	Samuel Edward	3316	guard	60	
	E	Samuel Mary—†	3316	housewife	59	"
	F	Dunne Mary E—†	3318	"	40	
	G	Dunne Stephen G	3318	laborer	40	"
	H	Ladd Albert H	3318	carpenter	58	"
	K	Ladd Ida M—†	3318	housewife	61	"
	M	Rumsey Charles L	3320	cook	32	
	N*	Rumsey Mary L—†	3320	housewife	32	"
	o*	Campbell William F	3320	chauffeur	31	Somerville

Washington Street—Continued

P	Doiron Francis I	3320	salesman	29	131 Boylston
R	Doiron Mary A—†	3320	housewife	23	131 "
S	Hough Harold	3320	painter	39	here
T	Hough Harold J, jr	3320	laborer	21	"
U	Hough Philomena—†	3320	housewife	37	"
V	Buckley Cornelius J	3322	chauffeur	44	"
w*	Dauphinee Gladys L—†	3322	housewife	38	"
X	McCarren Dorothy E-†	3322	stenographer	22	"
Y	McCarren Edward F	3322	salesman	54	"
Z	McCarren Edward F, jr	3322	bookkeeper	21	"

1159

A	McCarren Mary E—†	3322	housewife	49	"
B	Barr Alice M—†	3322	"	36	
C	Barr Arthur E	3322	salesman	40	"
D	Prendergast Raymond C	3322	laborer	45	"
G	Craffey Dorothy M-† r	3326	housewife	35	121 Green
H	Craffey George "	3326	laborer	35	121 "
K	McCarthy Frederick J "	3326	carpenter	28	95 Howard av
L	Allen Ethel M—†	3328	at home	62	here
M	Allen Frances G—†	3328	housewife	38	"
N	Allen Frank A	3328	shipper	38	"
T	Goode Mary—†	3355	at home	55	
U	Hanlon Francis J	3355	laborer	21	
V	Hanlon Joseph M	3355	"	25	"
W	Cooper Andrew	3355	basketmaker	24	Salisbury
X	Lalibertie Jennie—†	3355	housewife	43	335 Highland

1160

C	Magliardite Emma—†	3377	"	51	here
D	Magliardite Joseph	3377	merchant	59	"
E	Moffitt Florence V—† r	3377	housewife	48	"
F	Moffitt James F "	3377	superintendent	51	"
G	Moffitt Louise L—† "	3377	clerk	24	
H	Magliardite Lena M—†	3379	housewife	28	"
K	Magliardite Peter	3379	laborer	33	
L	Graham Henry E	3379	"	29	
M	Graham Josephine E—†	3379	housewife	28	"
N	Romano Mario	3379	insulator	37	"
O	Romano Rose—†	3379	housewife	34	"
T	Lambrecht Annie-† rear	3381	"	50	
U	Lambrecht Catherine L—† "	3381	clerk	21	
V	Lambrecht Charles A "	3381	painter	56	

Page.	Letter.	Full Name.	Residence, Jan. 1, 1941.	Occupation.	Supposed Age.	Reported Residence, Jan. 1, 1940. Street and Number.

Washington Street—Continued

	Letter	Full Name	Residence	Occupation	Age	Reported Residence
	w	Lambrecht Charles A, jr	r 3381	chauffeur	29	here
	z	*Nash Elizabeth B—†	3385	housewife	48	"
1161						
	A	Nash Michael J	3385	laborer	53	
	C	Jellison John A	3387	gardener	69	"
	D	Ward James	3387	laborer	50	
	E	Ward Mary M—†	3387	housewife	43	"
	F	McLaughlin Eleanor L—†	3387	"	28	
	G	McLaughlin Leroy F	3387	ironworker	30	"
	H	Chesterfield John	rear 3387	mechanic	55	"
	K	Salzgeber Alma H—†	" 3387	seamstress	61	"
	L	Turley Mary—†	" 3387	"	28	28 Norfolk av
	M	Schofield Edna M—†	3389	housekeeper	26	here
	N	Schofield William H	3389	machinist	40	"
	O	*MacDougall Catherine A—†	3389	housewife	37	"
	P	*MacDougall John A	3389	roofer	43	"
	R	Grace Elizabeth A—†	3389	housewife	35	83 School
	T	*Blomquist Alma B—†	3395A	"	56	3389 Wash'n
	U	Blomquist Carl E	3395A	laborer	21	3389 "
	W	Riley Gertrude R—†	3395A	laundress	41	here
	X	Riley Helen M—†	3395A	marker	46	"
	Y	Kelly George J	3395A	laborer	44	"
	z	Kelly Nellie M—†	3395A	housewife	78	"
1162						
	D	MacMillan Edith—†	3399	housewife	42	12 Ophir
	E	MacMillan Everett H	3399	merchant	47	12 "
	F	Savage Arthur	3399	clerk	55	12 "
	H	O'Rourke Cecelia I—†	3401	housewife	29	3 Fountain Hill
	K	O'Rourke Francis J	3401	contractor	29	5 Glenvale ter
	L	Noble James E	3411	salesman	45	47 E Cottage
	M	Noble Mary V—†	3411	housewife	40	47 "
	N	DeCosta Amelia R—†	3411	"	33	2652 Wash'n
	O	DeCosta Clifford K	3411	operator	33	2652 "
	P	Lawler Thomas P	3411	doorman	23	198 W Seventh
	R	Lawler Virginia I—†	3411	housewife	24	198 "
	S	Longuemare Alfred R	3415	cablemaker	33	here
	T	Longuemare Florence M—†	3415	housewife	30	"
	U	*Nevins Mary C—†	3415	"	44	"
	V	Nevins Michael	3415	laborer	42	
	W	Willis George A	3417	steelworker	38	"
	X	Willis Sarah L—†	3417	housewife	33	"

Washington Street—Continued

Y	Rogers John J	3417	sorter	47	here
z	Rogers John W	3417	laborer	21	"

1163

A	Rogers Katherine A—†	3417	housewife	43	"
B	Rogers Kathleen C—†	3417	clerk	20	
D	LaFalce Catherine—†	3421	cleaner	20	"
E	LaFalce Charles	3421	presser	23	
F	LaFalce Frank	3421	aborer	51	"
G	LaFalce Josephine F—†	3421	housewife	22	12 Gartland
H	*LaFalce Mary—†	3421	"	54	here
K	LaFalce Rosario	3421	barber	25	"
L	Piatelli Augustus N	3425	clerk	20	"
M	*Piatelli Conchetta—†	3425	housewife	42	"
N	*Piatelli Leone	3425	retired	77	
O	*Piatelli Rosa—†	3425	housewife	75	"
P	*Pompeo Giuseppe	rear 3425	shoemaker	42	"
R	Timperri Julius	" 3425	laborer	24	Dedham
S	Smeglin Anthony	" 3425	supervisor	45	here
T	Smeglin Antonette–†	" 3425	housewife	43	"
U	*Piatelli Antonette–†	" 3425	"	34	"
V	Piatelli Thomas	" 3425	laborer	37	
Y	Browne Arthur W	3451	clerk	21	
z	Browne Burton L	3451	cutter	60	

1164

A	Browne Edith G—†	3451	housewife	52	"
B	Browne John T	3451	clerk	23	
C	Griffin Lila—†	3451	at home	60	

Williams Street

E	*Cipollone Albert	102	cabinetmaker	20	here
F	*Cipollono Anna—†	102	housewife	50	"
G	Cipollone Phillip	102	laborer	52	"
H	Benner Mildred—†	102	housewife	38	"
K	English Mary—†	102	at home	74	
M	Manning Bernard	104	instructor	31	"
N	Manning Esther—†	104	housewife	30	"
O	O'Brien Joseph D	104	chauffeur	38	"
P	O'Brien Katherine—†	104	housewife	40	"
U	Manning Margaret C—†	116	typist	20	
T	Manning Margaret H—†	116	hairdresser	41	"

Page.	Letter.	Full Name.	Residence, Jan. 1, 1941.	Occupation.	Supposed Age.	Reported Residence, Jan. 1, 1940. Street and Number.

Williams Street—Continued

	v	Dunleavy John J	116	bartender	31	here
	w	Gallagher Francis J	116	"	26	Lowell
	x	Sexton James L	116	policeman	43	here
	y	Sexton Mary F—†	116	housewife	41	"
		1165				
	a	Reïs August	120	waiter	63	
	b	Reis Charlotte—†	120	housewife	60	"
	c	Sakrison Alice—†	120	"	30	"
	d	Sakrison Herbert	120	engineer	30	"
	e	Whelan John W	120	teacher	29	
	f	Whelan Marguerite—†	120	housewife	28	"
	g	Dooley Mary J—†	124	"	31	
	h	Dooley Thomas J	124	contractor	36	"
	k	Strange Bertha M—†	124	housewife	42	"
	l	Strange Martin H	124	upholsterer	40	"
	m	Collins Alfred L	124	operator	37	..
	n	Collins Alice—†	124	housewife	35	"
	o	Barthold Anthony	128	laborer	52	
	p	Weed John	128	"	72	
	r	*Weed Maria—†	128	housewife	59	"
	s	Corrado Catherine—†	128	"	21	36 Burrell
	t	Corrado Vincent	128	salesman	26	36 "
	u	Doocey Edward	128	porter	25	21 Plainfield
	v	Doocey Helen—†	128	operator	24	21 "
	w	Doocey Mary—†	128	attendant	21	21 "
	x	Doocey Michael	128	retired	55	21 "
	y	Doocey Nora—†	128	housewife	52	21 "
	z	Doocey Rita—†	128	clerk	22	21 '
		1166				
	a	Tobin John	132	painter	35	Somerville
	b	*Tobin Mary—†	132	housewife	30	"`
	c	Hasson George E	132	operator	54	here
	d	Hasson Theresa S—†	132	housewife	50	"
	e	Oppenheim Berta—†	132	"	41	33 Boylston
	f	*Oppenheim Hugo E	132	chef	36	33 "
	g	Ritter Henry, jr	132	student	21	Cambridge
	h	Bender Anthony	136	pressman	53	here
	k	Bender Ursula—†	136	housewife	47	"
	l	O'Hara Catherine P—†	136	"	27	"
	m	O'Hara Edwin A	136	pharmacist	27	"
	n	O'Hara William J	136	guard	55	

Williams Street—Continued

o	Hergt Charles H	136	patternmaker	63	here
p	Hergt Sara—†	136	housewife	48	"
R	Winsemann Gertrude—†	140	"	45	Indiana
s	Winsemann William	140	machinist	45	"
T	Peterson Helen—†	140	housewife	33	35 Wrentham
U	Peterson Tage—†	140	machinist	31	35 "
V	Quinzani Joseph	140	retired	76	here
W	Salvi Angelo	140	manager	50	"
X	Salvi Rose—†	140	housewife	41	"
Y	Linden Frances R—†	144	"	30	
Z	Linden Robert F	144	chauffeur	30	"

1167

A	Struzziero Anne—†	144	housewife	27	75 Rossmore rd
B	Struzziero Joseph T	144	mechanic	30	75 "
C	Suplee Catherine—†	144	housewife	54	here
D	Suplee Dorothy—†	144	operator	24	"
E	Suplee George	144	chauffeur	27	"
F	Suplee James	144	shoeworker	52	"
G	*Geaney Bridie—†	148	housewife	34	"
H	Geaney James	148	metalworker	36	"
K	Galeota Anthony	148	engineer	29	
L	Galeota Julia—†	148	housewife	26	"
M	Gately Alice M—†	148	"	52	
N	Gately Francis H	148	plumber	22	"
O	Tyo Elfriede H—†	152–154	housewife	25	38 Sedgwick
P	Tyo Joseph A	152–154	clerk	30	38 "
R	Judge Anna V—†	152–154	housewife	28	here
S	Judge Henry M	152–154	chauffeur	28	"
T	Wilson Arthur J, jr	152–154	salesman	34	"
U	Wilson Josephine—†	152–154	housewife	32	"
V	Johnston George	156	operator	41	
W	*Johnston Mary—†	156	housewife	41	"
X	Morris Albert J	156	salesman	26	202 South
Y	Morris Anna M—†	156	housewife	24	9 Gartland
Z	Brown George A	160–162	waiter	54	here

1168

A	Brown Winifred M—†	160–162	housewife	52	"
B	Barry Mary E—†	160–162	"	44	
C	Barry Patrick D	160–162	salesman	54	"

Page.	Letter.	Full Name.	Residence, Jan. 1, 1941.	Occupation.	Supposed Age.	Reported Residence, Jan. 1, 1940. Street and Number.

Williams Street—Continued

| | D | Rodrigue Eleanor E–† | 160–162 | housewife | 40 | here |
| | E | Rodrigue Joseph F | 160–162 | salesman | 40 | " |

Woodside Avenue

	F	*Doiron Clarence	5	painter	38	here
	G	*Doiron Jessie B—†	5	housewife	35	"
	H	Elliott Alfred D	5	roofer	50	"
	K	Ennis Edward A	5	welder	25	107 Dor av
	L	Ennis Eileen R—†	5	stitcher	30	107 "
	M	Ennis Joseph C	5	carpenter	56	107 "
	N	Ennis Mary T—†	5	housewife	58	107 "
	O	Arnold Emile	7	houseman	51	here
	P	*Arnold Lillian B—†	7	housewife	42	"
	R	Mulvey Bridget T—†	7	"	67	"
	S	Mulvey James F	7	finisher	33	
	T	Mulvey Patrick C	7	mason	63	"
	U	Auclair Mary V—†	7	housewife	34	14½ Greenley pl
	V	Auclair Oscar W	7	chef	35	14½ "
	W	Oberle Louise F—†	9	clerk	34	90 Forest Hills
	X	*Voegtlin Ernest A	9	waiter	37	90 "
	Y	Voegtlin Marie J—†	9	housewife	36	90 "
	Z	Cecconi Carlo	11	chauffeur	21	81 Brookley rd

1169

	A	Cecconi Helen—†	11	bookbinder	22	81 "
	B	*Cecconi Polisana—†	11	housewife	56	81 "
	C	Connor Catherine E—†	13	"	46	here
	D	Redden Margaret A—†	13	"	48	"
	E	Redden Mary C—†	13	operator	25	"
	F	Kelley Daniel J	15	laborer	39	
	G	Kelley Ellen T—†	15	housewife	69	"
	H	Simmons James J	15	metalworker	53	"
	K	Ozol Alfred J	17	laborer	29	
	L	*Ozol Anna—†	17	housewife	55	"
	M	Ozol John	17	machinist	60	"
	O	Doyle Clarence T	17	clerk	35	
	P	Doyle Francis X	17	shipper	30	
	R	Doyle Mary E—†	17	housekeeper	40	"
	S	Emerson Clarence L	19–21	sexton	38	"

Page.	Letter.	Full Name.	Residence, Jan. 1, 1941.	Occupation.	Supposed Age.	Reported Residence, Jan. 1, 1940. Street and Number.

Woodside Avenue—Continued

т	Emerson Iréne O—†	19–21	housewife	37	here
U	*Aghababian Hyganoush—†	19–21	"	66	"
v	Aghababian Vahe	19–21	operator	30	"
w	Aghababian Zarie—†	19–21	housewife	24	"
x	Benson Lena—†	19–21	housekeeper	68	"
y	Aitken Alfred W	19–21	superintendent	47	"
z	Aitken Sylvia M—†	19–21	housewife	42	"

1170

A	Brickley John P	19–21	supervisor	36	"
B	Brickley Margaret M–†	19–21	housewife	32	"
c	Shortall Joseph	19–21	clerk	21	
D	Shortall Katherine—†	19–21	shoeworker	62	"

Ward 11—Precinct 12

CITY OF BOSTON

LIST OF RESIDENTS
20 YEARS OF AGE AND OVER

(NON-CITIZENS INDICATED BY ASTERISK)
(FEMALES INDICATED BY DAGGER)

AS OF

JANUARY 1, 1941

1200

Arborway

A	Lynch Jerome J	194	policeman	41	here	
B	Lynch Veronica—†	194	housewife	38	"	
C	McElaney Jessie—†	194	"	70	"	
D	McElaney Robert S	194	salesman	42	"	
E	Donahue Eleanor F—†	194	secretary	22	"	
F	Donahue Margaret—†	194	"	26	"	
G	Donahue Patrick J	194	operator	60	"	
H	Clarke Hazel M—†	198	clerk	42		
K	Clarke Margaret J—†	198	housewife	71	"	
L	Clarke Thomas J	198	merchant	72	"	
M	Shannon John F	198	laborer	51		
N	Dooley Alice R—†	198	student	20		
O	Dooley Walter L	198	inspector	45	"	
P	Lundgren Charles C	198	electrician	32	"	
R	Lundgren Charles W	198	manager	59	"	
S	Lundgren Ellen C—†	198	secretary	33	"	
T	Lundgren Irene M—†	198	teacher	29	"	
U	Lundgren Sarah—†	198	housewife	52	"	
V	Binkley Ethel—†	202	"	60		
W	Binkley Russell	202	auditor	60		
X	Barnes Mildred W—†	202	bacteriologist	36	"	
Y	McDonough Mary C—†	202	housekeeper	49	"	
Z	McGuire Catherine—†	202	at home	63	"	

1201

A	Riley Franklin	206	inspector	43	Fall River	
B	Riley Margaret—†	206	housewife	39	"	
C	Cronan William H	206	instructor	50	here	
D	O'Leary Arthur A	206	realtor	63	"	
E	O'Leary Arthur C	206	chauffeur	36	"	
F	O'Leary Gwendolyn C-†	206	at home	41		
G	O'Leary John E	206	policeman	38	"	
H	Jones Alice J—†	218	housewife	51	"	
K	Jones Francis J	218	clerk	54		
L	Jones Joseph F	218	teacher	25		
M	Jones Paul B	218	student	21		
N	Smith James P	218	clerk	59	"	
O	Dufault Winifred—†	224	seamstress	56	17 Whitten	
P	Dwyer Amelia—†	224	housewife	28	17 "	
R	Dwyer Richard C	224	engineer	29	17 "	
S	Lane Fred	240	repairman	41	Maine	

2

Page.	Letter.	FULL NAME.	Residence, Jan. 1, 1941.	Occupation.	Supposed Age.	Reported Residence, Jan. 1, 1940. Street and Number.

Arborway—Continued

	T	Lane Mary—†	240	housewife	42	Maine
	U	LaRonde Elizabeth—†	240	"	50	here
	V	*LaRonde James S	240	clerk	22	"
	W	LaRonde Romeo O	240	foreman	51	"
	X	Rogers Mary E—†	240	clerk	60	
	Y	Kilduff Agnes G—†	242	housewife	50	"
	Z	Kilduff Maria—†	242	at home	76	
1202						
	A	Kilduff William F	242	agent	52	
	B	Rooney Augustine J	248	salesman	49	"
	C	Rooney Katherine M—†	248	housewife	48	"
	D	Rooney Margaret L—†	248	student	22	
	E	Cleary Elizabeth—†	248	saleswoman	59	"
	F	Cleary Elizabeth H—†	248	housewife	47	"
	G	Cleary John H	248	teacher	55	
	H	Etling Ernest J	248	manager	47	"
	K	Etling Ernest J, jr	248	mechanic	23	"
	L	Etling Fred J	248	"	21	
	M	Etling Freda—†	248	housewife	43	"
	N	Ladd Katherine F—†	250	secretary	36	"
	O	Ladd Mary E—†	250	housewife	68	"
	P	O'Brien Mary E—†	250	"	40	18 Stockwell
	R	O'Brien Michael J	250	policeman	41	18 "
	S	Sullivan Ellen—†	250	housewife	42	here
	T	Sullivan Joseph	250,	operator	48	"
	U	Yates Alfred S	254	chauffeur	49	"
	V	Yates Pearl M—†	254	housewife	40	"
	W	Dolan Anastacia—†	254	"	58	
	X	Dolan Joseph	254	clerk	28	
	Y	Dolan Mildred M—†	254	agent	30	"
	Z	Dolan Thomas J	254	mechanic	68	"
1203						
	A	Bulman Francis D	258	architect	56	"
	B	Bulman John B	258	student	20	
	C	Bulman Margaret—†	258	housewife	51	"
	D	Bulman Margaret B—†	258	nurse	24	
	E	Bulman Mary C—†	258	stenographer	22	"
	F	Thompson John F	258	mortician	47	"
	G	Thompson Rose M—†	258	housewife	46	"
	H	Kelley Helen M—†	266	"	30	
	K	Kelley Joseph F	266	dispatcher	34	"

3

Arborway—Continued

L	Curry Arthur L	266	assessor	45	here
M	Curry Esther—†	266	housewife	42	"
N	Ward George V	270	clerk	49	"
O	Ward Mary—†	270	social worker	49	"
P	Egan Thomas	270	painter	52	
R	Egan Winifred—†	270	housewife	42	"
S	Halloran Joseph	270	constructor	60	"
T	Wall Anne—†	274	clerk	30	
U	Wall Jane—·†	274	housewife	70	"
V	Wall Jane C—†	274	bookkeeper	34	"
W	Wall Mary—†	274	"	31	"
X	Lavery Alice D—†	274	housewife	47	"
Y	Lavery Frank J, jr	274	agent	53	"
Z	McKinnon Catherine A-†	278	clerk	33	"

1204

A	McKinnon Clara M—†	278	"	42	
B	McKinnon Earl R	278	salesman	36	"
C	McKinnon John	278	retired	70	
D	McKinnon John A	278	engineer	46	"
E	Remsen Leard D	278	"	41	
F	Remsen Viola M—†	278	housewife	40	"

Atwood Square

G	Clark Helen—†	9	housewife	35	New York
H	Nugent Frank	9	laborer	53	here
K	Nugent Sarah E—†	9	housewife	48	"
L	MacDonald Mary R—†	9	housekeeper	48	"
M	Roche Evelyn C—†	11	housewife	33	797 Hyde Park av
N	Donohue Jeremiah	11	U S A	26	here
O	*Donohue John	11	laborer	56	"
P	Donohue Mary—†	11	housewife	40	"
R	O'Brien John	11	machinist	33	"
S	O'Brien May—†	11	housewife	29	"
T	*MacDonald Belinda—†	14	"	68	15 Atwood sq
U	MacDonald John	14	laborer	65	15 "
V	Kirrane William	14	woodworker	49	here
W	Kirrane William J	14	chauffeur	22	"
X	Beal Anna E—†	15	housewife	28	5 Walden
Y	Beal George E	15	baker	26	5 "
Z	Fitch Elsie—†	15	housewife	28	36 Dalrymple

1205
Atwood Square—Continued

A	Fitch Richard	15	welder	29	36 Dalrymple
B	*Connolly Margaret—†	15	housewife	52	24 Heath av
C	Granlund Margaret—†	15	"	22	24 "
D	Granlund Oscar	15	electrician	25	Norwood
E	Kent Florence—†	15	housewife	21	Revere
F	Kent Matthew	15	nurse	28	6 Myrtle
G	Sybertz Joseph H	18	shipfitter	24	209 Boylston
H	Sybertz Mary—†	18	housewife	21	209 "
K	Buchan Alexander	18	machinist	38	20 Atwood sq
L	Buchan Minnie—†	18	housewife	40	20 "
M	*Cabana Pauline—†	18	winder	49	here
N	Bragger Adelaide E—†	19	housewife	32	"
O	Bragger Joseph E	19	auditor	41	"
P	Bragger William F	19	butcher	33	..
R	LeBlanc Frederick	19	mechanic	35	"
S	Mahoney Agnes—†	19	housewife	25	"
T	Mahoney John	19	machinist	32	"
U	Eldridge Bernard	20	laborer	35	135 Carolina av
V	Eldridge Mary—†	20	housewife	28	135 "
W	*Healy Elizabeth—†	20	"	30	3 Emsella ter
X	Healy Martin	20	laborer	30	3 "
Y	Curran Catherine A—†	20	housewife	74	28 Rossmore rd
Z	Curran Joseph J	20	serviceman	35	Florida

1206

A	Salmon Flora—†	20	waitress	27	78 Call
B	*Frazier Mary—†	20	housewife	29	31 Jamaica
C	Frazier Ralph	20	serviceman	29	31 "
D	Traficanti Antonette—†	20	housewife	28	30 Northampton
E	Traficanti Nichols	20	salesman	34	30 "

Ballard Way

K	Wood Amanda—†	2	housewife	52	here
L	Wood Frederick	2	retired	69	"
M	Lee Dorothy C—†	2	clerk	31	"
N	Lee Phyllis A—†	2	secretary	21	"
O	McCarthy Mary H—†	2	waitress	63	
P	McCarthy Peter	2	retired	84	
R	Fenerty Anne E—†	3	housewife	43	"
T	Fenerty Edward L	3	policeman	43	"

5

Page.	Letter.	Full Name.	Residence, Jan. 1, 1941.	Occupation.	Supposed Age.	Reported Residence, Jan. 1, 1940. Street and Number.

Ballard Way—Continued

s		Fenerty Catherine—†	3	seamstress	48	here
u		Fenerty James	3	porter	53	"

Bower Terrace

v		Perkins Lillian S—†	1	housewife	42	here
w	*Valk Marie M—†	2	"	44	"
x		Kendall Albert F	3	chauffeur	26	63 Jamaica

Call Street

z	*Shaughnessy Kathleen—†	75	housewife	30	here
	1207				
a	Shaughnessy Michael	75	chauffeur	45	"
b	Kerle Frederick	75	shipper	28	
c	Kerle Mary—†	75	housewife	53	"
d	Kerle Paul	75	gardener	24	"
e	Mullen John H	75	laborer	47	
f	*Mullen Josephine—†	75	housewife	42	"
g	*McCartin Mary—†	77	at home	84	"
h	*Cunningham James	77	houseman	39	30 Newburn
k	Cunningham Kathleen—†	77	housekeeper	26	30 "
l	McNulty Adeline R—†	77	housewife	29	here
m	McNulty William C	77	textile worker	32	"
n	Folkins Ann—†	79	housewife	23	238 Lamartin
o	Folkins Charles W	79	cleaner	23	238 "
p	O'Brien Catherine—†	79	housewife	23	here
r	O'Brien Thomas P	79	mechanic	24	"
s	*Folkins Albert H	79	retired	66	21 Oakdale
t	Folkins Lola A—†	79	housewife	69	21 "
u	Stronach Gilbert	81	retired	74	28 Hall
v	Stronach Mary A—†	81	at home	70	28 "
w	Sheehan Dennis	81	laborer	28	here
x	Sheehan Sadie—†	81	boxmaker	28	"
y	Ciavaitteri Dominic	81	laborer	53	"
z	*Ciavaitteri Theresa—†	81	at home	74	
	1208				
a	*Hart Mary—†	83	housewife	37	22 Boynton
b	Hart Thomas A	83	laborer	39	22 "
c	Noone Gertrude J—†	83	housewife	28	here
d	*Moroney Christina—†	83	"	35	"

Page.	Letter.	FULL NAME.	Residence, Jan. 1, 1941.	Occupation.	Supposed Age.	Reported Residence, Jan. 1, 1940. Street and Number.

Call Street—Continued

	E	Moroney John J	83	checker	36	here
	G	Whitaker Bessie—†	85	housewife	41	32 Everett
	H	Whitaker Charles	85	painter	47	32 "
	K	Bennett Amy E—†	85	housewife	64	26 Ellsworth
	L	Bennett William H	85	laborer	64	26 "
	M	Mannion Anna—†	89	clerk	31	here
	N	Mannion Bartholomew	89	laborer	50	"
	O	Mannion Nora—†	89	housewife	51	"
	P	Grenon Edgar R	89	painter	25	"
	R	Grenon Mary L—†	89	housewife	24	"
	S	Struzzieri Anthony	89	chauffeur	22	"
	T	Struzzieri Carmella—†	89	housewife	62	"
	U	Struzzieri Dominic	89	mason	59	

Carolina Avenue

	V	Cadigan Laura M—†	7	housewife	47	here
	W	Hucksam Julius M	7	clerk	58	"
	X	Hucksam Robert	7	"	21	"
	Y	Hucksam Rose K—†	7	housewife	55	"
	Z	Hucksam Ursula—†	7	teacher	29	
1209						
	A	*Kechejian Andrew	7	manager	49	..
	B	*Kechejian Margaret—†	7	housewife	40	"
	C	Bowes Brian M	9	attendant	22	"
	D	Bowes Catherine—†	9	housewife	52	"
	E	Bowes John F	9	attendant	28	"
	F	Bowes Michael	9	chef	62	"
	G	Norton Jane M—†	11	housewife	39	9 Hall
	H	Norton Lawrence H	11	operator	40	9 "
	K	Sullivan Daniel J	75	"	61	here
	L	Sullivan George	75	clerk	23	"
	M	Sullivan John P	75	letter carrier	34	"
	N	Sullivan Margaret M—†	75	bookkeeper	29	"
	O	Sullivan Mary A—†	75	"	31	..
	P	Sullivan Mary J—†	75	housewife	61	"
	R	Sullivan Thomas A	75	laborer	33	
	S	Judge Ellen—†	75	at home	80	"
	T	Maloney Carolina M—†	75	"	65	Framingham
	U	Spencer Bridget M—†	75	"	69	here
	V	Spencer Ellen—†	75	..	68	"

Page.	Letter.	FULL NAME.	Residence, Jan. 1, 1941.	Occupation.	Supposed Age.	Reported Residence, Jan. 1, 1940. Street and Number.

Carolina Avenue—Continued

w	Tucker Bertha F—†	75	at home	67	New Jersey
x	Fitzgerald Mary E—†	75	housewife	53	here
y	Fitzgerald Mary E—†	75	stenographer	27	"
z	Fitzgerald William	75	clerk	24	"
	1210				
A	Naughton Catherine F—†	79	housewife	36	17 Woodlawn
B	Naughton John	79	chauffeur	35	17 "
C	Finneran John J	79	paperhanger	70	here
D	Finneran John M	79	shipper	30	"
E	Finneran Joseph H	79	chauffeur	39	"
F	Finneran Margaret M—†	79	housewife	65	"
G	Gray Mary M—†	79	stenographer	33	"
H	Crowley Bridget—†	79	housewife	49	"
K	Crowley John	79	motorman	55	"
L	Crowley John P	79	porter	24	
M	Crowley Mary—†	79	operator	21	"
N	Halligan Catherine L—†	89	housewife	53	"
O	Halligan James B	89	laborer	52	
P	Halligan Mary—†	89	housewife	83	"
R	Halligan Rita C—†	89	wrapper	20	
S	Leland William E	89	retired	65	
T	Kennedy Arthur	89	janitor	31	
U	Kennedy Elizabeth J—†	89	housekeeper	47	"
V	Kennedy Helen A—†	89	operator	41	"
W	Kennedy Peter	89	retired	75	
X	Cunniff Anne—†	95	housewife	36	"
Y	Cunniff William F	95	janitor	42	
z	Kay James M	95	rubberworker	29	"
	1211				
A	Kay Marjorie C—†	95	housewife	29	"
B	Pilibosian John P	95	salesman	28	64 Moreland
c	*Pilibosian Rose E—†	95	housewife	20	64 "
D	Brown Eugene M	101	contractor	37	here
E	Brown Madelyn T—†	101	housewife	37	"
F	Keegan George E	101	carpenter	34	"
G	Keegan Rita—†	101	housewife	32	"
H	Nicholson Evelyn—†	105	"	50	
K	Nicholson Robert A	105	laundryman	51	"
L	Lunn Charles B	105	dairyman	59	"
M	*Lunn Effie—†	105	housewife	57	"
N	Harvey Catherine—†	107	"	28	

Carolina Avenue—Continued

o	Harvey Frederick R, jr	107	foreman	29	here
p	Meehan Anne F—†	107	typist	23	"
r	Meehan Helen V—†	107	secretary	29	"
s	Meehan Katherine V—†	107	housewife	50	"
t	Meehan Margaret M—†	107	waitress	25	
u	Smith Luther R	109	porter	35	
v	Smith Mary A—†	109	housewife	39	"
w	Grenham Hazel E—†	111	"	25	99 Wachusett
x	Grenham Matthew J	111	ironworker	27	99 "
y	Buckley Helen F—†	111	housekeeper	66	here
z	Doonan Catherine T—†	111	clerk	50	"
	1212				
a	Doonan S Gertrude—†	111	"	50	"
b	Johnson Albert E	113	electrician	31	1 Highland
c	Johnson Jessie W—†	113	housewife	21	700 Hyde Park av
d	Birch Andrew J	113	foreman	59	85 Call
e	Birch Annie M—†	113	housewife	47	85 "
f	McDonough John	127	machinist	40	here
g	McDonough Margaret—†	127	housewife	40	"
h	Murphy James F	131	laborer	48	"
k	Murphy Nora—†	131	housewife	48	"
l	McDonough Ann—†	131	"	76	
m	McDonough Timothy	131	social worker	47	"
n*	McParland Anna—†	135	housewife	28	33 Woodman
o	McParland James	135	chauffeur	26	33 "
p	Sullivan John	135	"	45	33 "
r	Harrington Lawrence F	135	bartender	37	here
s	Dolan Gertrude T—†	137	housekeeper	47	14 Orchard
t	Donahue Catherine F—†	137	at home	75	here
u	Scafati Florence A—†	137	housewife	41	"
v	Scafati Palmer C	137	guard	40	"

Carolina Place

w	Ginty Anthony	1	laborer	56	here
x	Ginty Margaret—†	1	housewife	46	"
y	Geigis Ernest	1	machinist	46	"
z	Geigis Lucy—†	1	housewife	36	"
	1213				
	Devaney Rita—†	1	"	21	12 Oakview ter
a	Devaney Thomas J	1	chauffeur	23	12 "

Page.	Letter.	FULL NAME.	Residence, Jan. 1, 1941.	Occupation.	Supposed Age.	Reported Residence, Jan. 1, 1940. Street and Number.

Carolina Place—Continued

c	*Bode Martha—†	2	housekeeper	56	here
d	*Federico Josephine—†	2	housewife	50	"
e	Federico Peter	2	gardener	53	"

Child Street

g	Kane Lawrence E	8	shipper	27	here
h	*Kane Margaret J—†	8	housewife	27	"
k	Downey Anna M—†	8	"	64	"
l	Downey Francis	8	decorator	25	"
m	Downey John M	8	trainman	32	"
n	Downey Thomas S	8	clerk	29	
o	*Billingham Bridget—†	8	housewife	29	"
p	Billingham James P	8	chauffeur	34	"
r	Dezell Elizabeth C—†	10	housewife	27	"
s	Dezell James M	10	merchant	33	"
t	Dougherty Bernard G	10	mechanic	51	"
u	Dougherty Mary J—†	10	housewife	44	"
v	Tirrell Adeline R—†	10	"	27	
w	Tirrell James J	10	guard	41	
x	Tirrell John F	10	salesman	35	"
y	Costello James P	72	bartender	40	"
z	Costello Mary A—†	72	housewife	35	"
	1214					
a	Dunnet James	76	carpenter	42	"
b	Dunnet Sarah—†	76	housewife	39	"
c	Ruddell George J	78	finisher	45	
d	Ruddell Isabella T—†	78	housewife	44	"
e	Thomson Catherine—†	78	at home	78	
f	Cowie Elizabeth—†	80	housewife	64	"
g	Cowie Samuel	80	mason	66	"
h	McKenzie Russell	80	laborer	30	49 Walden
k	*McLaughlin Catherine—†	80	at home	60	6 Everett
l	Biggs Christine M—†	82	housewife	49	here
m	Biggs Herbert	82	butcher	45	"
o	Fitzgerald Egbert	106	attendant	30	75 Sedgwick
p	Skelton Elizabeth L—†	106	housewife	50	75 "
r	Skelton James W	106	finisher	56	75 "
s	Skelton Walter C	106	laborer	29	75 "
t	McDonald Annie F—†	108	at home	71	here
u	McDonald Mary J—†	108	"	82	"

Child Street—Continued

v	Roy Antoinette—†	110	housewife	46	here
w	Roy August	110	optician	21	"
x	Roy David L	110	clerk	51	"
y	Roy Joseph A	110	laborer	23	
z	Glennon Edith E—†	116	housewife	43	"
	1215				
a	Glennon John H	116	clerk	46	
b	Stewart William J	116	retired	53	
c	Smith Fred W	120	"	58	
d	Smith James	120	letter carrier	34	"
e	Smith Mary—†	120	housewife	53	"
f	Smith Walter A	120	letter carrier	62	"

Custer Street

g	Greeley Claire G—†	8	housewife	35	98 Rossmore rd
h	Greeley Henry I	8	chauffeur	41	98 "
k	*Grady Mary K—†	8	housewife	30	11 "
l	Grady Patrick J	8	watchman	30	11 "
m	Norton Helen V—†	8	housewife	44	here
n	Marshall Gordon V	10	reporter	25	16 Cheshire
o	*Marshall Ila M—†	10	housewife	23	16 "
r	McNulty Cyrus J	10	clerk	36	here
s	McNulty Irene T—†	10	housewife	41	"
p	McBride Katherine L—†	10	"	49	"
t	McBride Peter T	10	stonecutter	52	"
u	Umlah Marion—†	12	housewife	34	52 Custer
v	*McGrath Annie A—†	12	"	60	here
w	*McGrath Patrick L	12	retired	62	"
x	Cowles George N	14	timekeeper	34	"
y	*Cowles Katherine F—†	14	housewife	37	"
z	Sweeney Agnes—†	14	"	46	
	1216				
a	Sweeney John J	14	waiter	20	
b	Sweeney Michael	14	fireman	50	
c	Jakas Joseph R	16	baker	36	
d	Jakas Mary J—†	16	housewife	34	"
e	Bertrand Anna A—†	16	"	28	
f	Bertrand Francis J	16	chauffeur	32	"
g	O'Shea Catherine R—†	16	at home	26	
h	O'Shea James P	16	watchman	69	"

Page.	Letter.	Full Name.	Residence, Jan. 1, 1941.	Occupation.	Supposed Age.	Reported Residence, Jan. 1, 1940. Street and Number.

Custer Street—Continued

K	McDonnell John M	18	watchman	34	601 E Fourth
L	McDonnell Margaret M–†	18	housewife	29	Belmont
M	Ryan John H	18	metalworker	38	here
N	Ryan Nora C—†	18	housewife	41	"
O	McCarthy Anne E—†	18	"	44	"
P	McCarthy Maurice J	18	teamster	49	"
R	Campbell Ella—†	22	housewife	41	"
S	Campbell Francis	22	laborer	47	"
T	Brandy Catherine—†	24	housewife	74	Lawrence
U	Donnelly Elizabeth—†	24	"	73	50 Walk Hill
V	Duggan Emma M—†	26	at home	50	31 Ballard
W	Duggan Helen G—†	26	stenographer	45	31 "
X	Connelly Alice E—†	26	"	32	here
Y	Connelly Elizabeth—†	26	housewife	65	"
Z	Connelly Josephine A—†	26	nurse	35	"
	1217				
A	*Bittrolff Kathleen—†	28	housewife	30	"
B	Bittrolff Ralph J	28	salesman	31	"
C	Reardon James F	28	shipper	23	
D	Reardon Mary E—†	28	housewife	48	"
E	Reardon Stephen F	28	rubberworker	50	"
F	Carroll Edward J	32	butcher	46	
G	*Carroll Mary A—†	32	housewife	45	"
H	Horan Francis J	32	chauffeur	34	"
K	Horan Margaret M—†	32	housewife	30	"
L	Finnerty Bernice M—†	32	stenographer	22	"
M	Finnerty Daniel G	32	supervisor	53	"
N	Finnerty Daniel G, jr	32	waiter	20	
O	Finnerty Rosanna G—†	32	housewife	53	"
R	Curry Basil E	34	chauffeur	57	"
P	Duff Annie—†	34	housekeeper	56	"
S	Gavin John, jr	38	milkman	31	"
T	Gavin Phyllis—†	38	housewife	28	"
U	Gavin Catherine M—†	38	"	60	
V	Gavin John J	38	laborer	62	
W	Gavin William L	38	carpenter	28	"
X	*Logue Catherine—†	38	housewife	40	"
Y	Logue Edward	38	chauffeur	36	"
Z	Griffin John V	40	operator	30	"
	1218				
A	Griffin Loretta C—†	40	housewife	31	"

12

Custer Street—Continued

B	Griffin Daniel J	40	clerk	59	here
C	Griffin Elizabeth A—†	40	"	22	"
E	Griffin Mary—†	40	housewife	58	"
F	Griffin Mary P—†	40	clerk	32	
D	Griffin Mildred J—†	40	"	25	
G	Carey Christopher A	52	plumber	45	
H	Carey Mary J—†	52	housewife	45	"
K	Donovan Albert C	52	stenographer	34	16 Gilman
L	Donovan Anne M—†	52	housewife	35	16 "
M	Martin Anna J—†	52	"	39	here
N	Martin Joseph	52	carpenter	45	"
O	Marchant Edward F	52	painter	41	103 Farquhar
P	Marchant Pearl F—†	52	housewife	40	103 "

Goldsmith Street

R	Paolini Francis J	48	attendant	28	1629 Com av
S	Paolini Julia H—†	48	housewife	36	1629 "
T	Tighe Anna J—†	48	"	31	here
U	Tighe James P	48	steamfitter	32	"
V	*Dolan Mary A—†	48	housewife	38	"
W	Dolan Thomas	48	laborer	34	..
X	MacLean Earl D	48	chauffeur	37	"
Y	MacLean Rose E—†	48	housewife	36	"

Jamaica Place

Z	*Scoledge John	1	mechanic	43	here
	1219				
A	Scoledge Rose—†	1	housewife	42	" .
B	Lyons Elizabeth—†	2	"	68	
C	Lyons William J	2	retired	72	
D	Grady Catherine—†	7	housewife	32	"
E	Grady James J	7	bookkeeper	29	"
F	Shanney Elizabeth—†	7	"	50	..
G	Shanney Gertrude—†	7	housekeeper	56	"
H	Caldwell Kathleen—†	8	housewife	29	"
K	Caldwell Owen	8	carpenter	36	"
L	Casey Lillian C—†	8	housewife	27	Brookline
M	Casey Stephen	8	steelworker	27	6 Eldridge rd

13

Page.	Letter.	Full Name.	Residence, Jan. 1, 1941.	Occupation.	Supposed Age.	Reported Residence, Jan. 1, 1940. Street and Number.

Jamaica Street

o	Brodrick Catherine T—†	24	housekeeper	68	20 Bradfield av
p	Morton Mabel E—†	24	stenographer	57	here
r	Morton Mary—†	24	at home	86	"
s	Quilty Anna T—†	26	housewife	39	"
t	Quilty Michael J	26	shipper	51	
u	Fossa Charles F	28	mechanic	61	"
v	Fossa Frank J	28	clerk	56	
w	Fossa Mary E—†	28	"	59	
x	Dolan Catherine A—†	30	packer	62	
y	Dolan James J	30	fishcutter	67	"
z	Dolan Mary E—†	30	saleswoman	66	"

1220

a	McDermott Mary—† rear	30	clerk	35	3 Grotto Glen rd
b	Powell Alfred T "	30	machinist	61	286 Perham
c	Powell Sarah A—† "	30	housewife	62	286 "
d	Nickerson Elsie I—†	31	"	21	Winthrop
e	Malone Mary T—†	31	"	24	1339 Dor av
f	Malone William J	31	laborer	36	1339 "
g	O'Hare Catherine T—†	31	housewife	45	here
h	Blades Viva—†	31	cook	54	"
k	Connolly Sarah J—†	32	housewife	34	"
l	Connolly Thomas M	32	chauffeur,	35	"
m	Greene Joseph	33	laborer	36	"
n	Keaney Bartley J	33	"	46	
o	Keaney Bridget—†	33	housewife	43	"
p	Murray Catherine A—†	33	at home	50	
r	Murray Patrick J	33	guard	46	
s	Johnson David E	34	engineer	45	
t	*Johnson Mary A—†	34	housewife	36	"
u	Reilly Fergus W	35	watchman	61	"
v	Reilly Mary E—†	35	housewife	59	"
w	Clark Arthur G	35	serviceman	34	"
x	Clark Ruth V—†	35	housewife	32	"
y	Kelly Katherine—†	35	"	43	
z	Kelly William G	35	laborer	20	

1221

a	Kelly William S	35		45	
b	Anthony Francis M	36	"	55	
c	Glynn Catherine—†	36	housewife	47	"
d	Glynn Catherine M—†	36	at home	21	
e	Glynn Daniel M	36	clerk	26	

14

Jamaica Street—Continued

F	Glynn Eleanor R	36	factoryhand	20	here
G	Glynn Francis T	36	student	24	"
H	Glynn John J	36	laborer	27	"
K	Kinsman Elizabeth—†	37	stenographer	29	"
L	Cunningham Kieran P	37	fireman	36	"
M	*Cunningham Mary—†	37	housewife	28	"
N	Rock Thaddeus F	37	conductor	64	"
O	McNulty Catherine—†	37	housewife	60	"
P	McNulty Michael J	37	fireman	60	"
R	Fidler Janet E—†	38	housewife	37	"
S	Grant Edward R	38	electroplater	25	"
T	Grant Mary J—†	38	housewife	22	"
U	Doyle Kathleen—†	39	"	29	
V	Doyle Patrick J	39	laborer	31	
W	Moynihan Francis J	40	assembler	22	"
X	Moynihan John J	40	policeman	53	"
Y	Moynihan Katherine C—†	40	operator	20	
Z	Moynihan Mary F—†	40	housewife	43	"

1222

A	*Kelley Delia M—†	41	checker	42	
B	Kelley Mary T—†	41	housewife	45	"
C	Kelley Michael J	41	watchman	46	"
D	English Alfred J	43	metalworker	45	"
E	English Caroline G—†	43	housewife	44	"
F	English Mary M—†	43	bookkeeper	48	"
G	English William J	43	clerk	47	"
H	Power John R	44	foreman	51	
K	Power Leonora P—†	44	housewife	47	"
L	Flynn John W	45	foreman	50	
M	Ouilette Hazel M—†	47	nurse	41	"
N	Ouilette Paul D	47	bookbinder	23	"
O	Daley Catherine L—†	47	at home	50	
P	O'Brien Annie M—†	rear 47	"	68	
R	Jefferson Alice—†	" 47	stenographer	22	"
S	Jefferson Clara—†	" 47	housewife	50	"
T	Jefferson Jeannette—†	" 47	stenographer	20	"
U	Carey John F	" 47	clerk	22	32 Bardwell
V	Carey Margaret F—†	" 47	housewife	21	32 "
W	Bosse Idell M—†	48	"	36	here
X	*Gordon Bridget M—†	48	"	37	"
Y	Gordon John J	48	chauffeur	39	"

Page.	Letter.	Full Name.	Residence, Jan. 1, 1941.	Occupation.	Supposed Age.	Reported Residence, Jan. 1, 1940. Street and Number.

Jamaica Street—Continued

z	Murphy George J	48	foreman	33	here
	1223				
a	Murphy Mary F—†	48	housewife	32	"
b	Kelleher Daniel J	49	laborer	22	7 Sunset
c	Kelleher Norah A—†	49	housewife	46	10 Rockdale
d	Kelleher Patrick	49	gardener	50	7 Sunset
e	Shone Catherine E—†	53	housewife	56	here
f	Shone John W	53	policeman	64	"
g	Feeley Martin	55	mechanic	40	"
h	*Keane Ellen—†	56	housewife	40	"
k	Keane Patrick J	56	chauffeur	49	"
l	Cady John J	58	"	45	
m	Cady Mary J—†	58	at home	75	
n	Cady Rose M—†	58	housewife	39	"
o	McGoldrick James J	59	B F D	45	
p	McGoldrick Louise A—†	59	housewife	45	"
r	Keane Helen F—†	59	"	31	
s	Keane William T	59	foreman	35	
t	Birkbeck Lillian K—†	59	housewife	22	"
u	Birkbeck William L	59	manager	25	"
v	Keane Julia A—†	61	saleswoman	47	"
w	Keane Lenore B—†	61	"	33	
x	Keane Marion A—†	61	housekeeper	37	"
y	McGann Margaret—†	61	domestic	67	"
z	*Lawler Catherine T—†	62	housewife	48	"
	1224				
a	Lawler John F	62	student	23	
b	Lawler Patrick J	62	custodian	52	"
c	Lawler William A	62	chemist	22	"
d	*Hackett Clifford J	62	salesman	31	"
e	*Hackett Cornelia M—†	62	saleswoman	38	"
f	*Hackett Dora G—†	62	student	28	
g	Mitchell Mary D—†	62	stenographer	39	"
h	Connolly Mary—†	62	housewife	54	"
k	Connolly Patrick J	62	chauffeur	56	"
l	Carney Annie F—†	63	at home	71	
m	Kendall Mary E—†	63	teacher	39	
n	Kendall Rose L—†	63	housewife	68	"
o	Gately Frank J	64	chauffeur	49	"
p	Gately Margaret M—†	64	student	20	
r	Gately Mary J—†	64	housewife	49	"

16

Page.	Letter.	Full Name	Residence, Jan. 1, 1941.	Occupation.	Supposed Age.	Reported Residence, Jan. 1, 1940. Street and Number.

Jamaica Street—Continued

s	Sullivan Eugene P	65	plumber	50	here
t	Sullivan Louise M—†	65	secretary	21	"
u	Sullivan Margaret M—†	65	housewife	45	"
v	Lanagan Anna G—†	67–69	"	41	
w	Lanagan William J	67–69	mechanic	49	"
x	Linehan Bart J	67–69	agent	46	
y	Linehan Margaret L–†	67–69	housewife	46	"
z	Murphy Katherine V–†	67–69	"	44	
	1225				
a	Murphy Morgan C	67–69	policeman	48	"
b	Deamon Charles W	68	serviceman	24	Medford
c	Deamon Ernest L	68	U S A	21	"
d	*Deamon Gertrude C—†	68	housewife	58	"
e	Deamon Samuel	68	mechanic	50	"
f	Quilty Catherine T—†	68	housewife	67	here
g	Quilty Martin W	68	cleaner	35	"
h	Quilty Thomas H	68	repairman	77	"
k	Gleason M Louise—†	68	housewife	75	"
l	Schaab Henrietta—†	68	"	68	
m	Healy John M	70	letter carrier	35	"
n	Healy Katherine M—†	70	housewife	36	"
o	Healy Charles P	70	clerk	27	
p	Healy Florence T—†	70	"	30	
r	Healy Joseph E	70	"	43	
s	Healy Mary A—†	70	housewife	73	"
t	Healy Ruth E—†	70	clerk	33	
u	Landrigan John J	71	inspector	41	"
v	Landrigan Mary E—†	71	housewife	43	"
w	Goddette Marion—†	71	writer	43	
x	Lee Annie F—†	72	housewife	78	"
y	Lee Thomas F	72	laborer	56	
z	*Peyton Catherine F—†	73	housewife	51	"
	1226				
a	Peyton Hubert J	73	laborer	25	
b	Peyton John J	73	foreman	52	
c	Peyton John T	73	student	22	
d	Peyton Kathleen P—†	73	"	20	
f	Chioccola Giovanni	73	shoemaker	61	"
g	Chioccola Louis	73	architect	33	"
h	DeFazi Carlo	73	pharmacist	55	"
k	Harkins John J	rear 74	policeman	38	"

11—12   17

Jamaica Street—Continued

L	Harkins Julia—†	rear 74	housewife	60	here	
M	Harkins Michael	" 74	retired	69	"	
N	Harkins Michael F	" 74	student	22	"	
O	Glynn John	" 74	clerk	45		
P	Glynn Lillian E—†	" 74	housewife	42	"	
R	Fopiano Agnes M—†	" 74	"	38		
S	Fopiano Jerome	" 74	laborer	52		
T	Shaw Helen G—†	75	clerk	40	"	
U	*Johnson Mary I—†	75	housewife	58	68 Weld Hill	
V	Johnson Olive M—†	75	factoryhand	28	68 "	
W	Turpinat Doris E—†	75	housewife	21	68 "	
X	Turpinat M Scott	75	laborer	25	68 "	
Y	Gately Mary F—†	77	housewife	35	here	
Z	Gately William H	77	laborer	54	"	
	1227					
A	Madden Catherine L—†	79	housewife	70	"	
B	Madden Vincent P	79	mechanic	28	"	
C	Lane Doris A—†	80	housewife	38	"	
D	Lane John C	80	chauffeur	42	"	
E	Quinn Catherine—†	81	housewife	38	"	
F	Quinn Martin	81	laborer	40		
G	Martell Gordon S	81	mechanic	39	"	
H	Martell Stasia—†	81	housewife	41	"	
K	Montgomery John F	81	installer	41		
L	Montgomery Pauline F—†	81	housewife	40	"	
M	Sullivan Frieda—†	82	"	37		
N	*Clougherty Gertrude S—†	83	"	40		
O	Clougherty Mark J	83	clerk	45		
P	McGarry Lillian R—†	83	operator	36	"	
R	McGarry Margaret L—†	83	clerk	31	"	
S	Leonardi Alice—†	83	housewife	26	50 Rossmore rd	
T	Leonardi Charles E	83	salesman	27	50 "	
U	Andrews Emma—†	85	housewife	32	here	
V	Andrews Peter J	85	carpenter	32	"	
W	Chaulk Harold R	85	painter	32	"	
X	McLellan Alexander	85	bookkeeper	40	"	
Y	*McLellan Daniel	85	retired	81	"	
Z	Fallon Delia—†	85	housewife	45	"	
	1228					
A	Fallon James H	85	clerk	25		
B	Bell Josephine B—†	86	domestic	49	"	

Jamaica Street—Continued

c	Freeman Rita M—†	86	stenographer	27	here
d	Gebhard Kathleen R—†	86	waitress	24	175 Hunt'n av
e	Kopp Albert T	86	laborer	55	here
f	Kopp Ellen G—†	86	housewife	54	"
g	Kopp Theodore	86	laborer	20	"
h	Flaherty Alice—†	87	nurse	28	Brockton
k	Flaherty William F	87	seaman	30	Maine
l	Howe Anna—†	87	clerk	30	here
m	Howe Henry M	87	"	36	"
n	Howe Laura E—†	87	housewife	61	"
o	O'Flaherty Patrick J	87	electrician	48	8 Hall
p	Gallagher Bridget—†	88	at home	72	here
r	Lake Agnes M—†	88	housewife	33	"
s	Lake Arthur F	88	chauffeur	33	"
t	Corkery Margaret E—†	90	at home	77	
u	McCarthy Bridget A—†	91	housewife	65	"
v	McCarthy Joseph A	91	clerk	25	
w	McCarthy Patrick	91	chauffeur	65	"
x	Dempsey Annie M—†	91	housewife	49	"
y	Dempsey James	91	chauffeur	54	"
z	Dempsey James A	91	laborer	24	
	1229				
a	Dempsey Joseph D	91	clerk	22	
b	Mellett Barbara R—†	91	"	23	
c	Mellett Coleman J	91	woolhandler	50	"
d	Mellett Kathleen—†	91	stenographer	21	"
e	Mellett Mary C—†	91	housewife	50	"
f	Mellett Mary H—†	91	secretary	25	"
h	Kelly Joseph M	93	longshoreman	48	"
k	Moore Anna M—†	93	housewife	40	"
l	Moore Harold T	93	policeman	39	"
m	Sutherland Ann S—†	93	inspector	27	"
n	Sutherland John E	93	laborer	24	
o	Sutherland Mary J—†	93	attendant	23	"
p	Sutherland William E	93	laborer	53	"
r	*Reynolds Ernest S	93	technician	30	11 Woodman
s	Swaine Hedley S	93	engineer	41	11 "
t	*Swaine Mary R—†	93	housewife	39	11 "
u	Strecker Louis	94	machinist	67	here
v	Strecker Mary E—†	94	housewife	64	"
w	*Donohue Ellen—†	96	"	41	"

Jamaica Street—Continued

x	Donohue James F	96	laborer	39	here
y	McGilvery Elizabeth—†	96	housewife	58	"
z	McGilvery James	96	fireman	68	"
	1230				
a	Powers Mary B—†	96	housewife	53	"
b	McComish Mary J—†	96	"	41	28 Fawndale rd
c	McComish William	96	electrician	41	28 "
d	McGarry George T	100	"	39	27 Stedman rd
e	McGarry Susanne—†	100	housewife	41	27 "
f	Snavely Ida M—†	100	"	32	here
g	Snavely Walter S	100	clerk	41	"
h	Danvers Eleanor G—† rear	100	housewife	35	"
k	Danvers Raymond T "	100	chauffeur	34	"
l	Hogan John A "	100	serviceman	39	"
m	Gilleo Margaret M—†	102	operator	33	
n	Gilleo Margaret V—†	102	housewife	54	"
o	Downing Alice M—†	104	"	25	
p	Downing James A	104	shipper	27	
r	Sheehan Dennis	104	retired	65	
s	Sheehan James	104	laborer	27	
t	Sheehan Katherine—†	104	housewife	60	"

Lee Street

u	Sullivan Daniel J	15	clerk	35	here
v	Sullivan Mary M—†	15	housewife	35	"
w	O'Connor Daniel W	15	guard	47	"
x	O'Connor Dora A—†	15	housewife	48	"
y	*Barrett Annie M—†	15	"	41	
z	*Barrett Edward	15	sexton	47	
	1231				
a	McGann Ann—†	15	housewife	22	27 Leyland
b	McGann Thomas P	15	coppersmith	24	27 "
c	Gordon John R	15	attendant	25	here
d	Gordon Louise R—†	15	bookkeeper	23	"
e	Sullivan John P	15	laborer	33	"
f	Sullivan Mary—†	15	housewife	74	"
g	Sullivan Mary A—†	15	shoeworker	38	"
h	McAvoy Francis A	17	attendant	23	"
k	McAvoy Laughlan	17	designer	32	
l	McAvoy Pauline—†	17	housewife	63	"

Page.	Letter.	FULL NAME.	Residence, Jan. 1, 1941.	Occupation.	Supposed Age.	Reported Residence, Jan. 1, 1940. Street and Number.

Lee Street---Continued

M	*McAvoy William P	17	retired	70	here
N	Fitzgerald Edward W	19	operator	32	"
O	Fitzgerald Josephine M-†	19	housewife	27	"
P	Matthes George H	20	fireman	65	
R	Matthes Joanna E—†	20	housewife	68	"
S	Matthes Joseph D	20	teacher	30	
T	Matthes Julia E—†	20	"	33	
U	Matthes Mary C—†	20	"	36	
V	DeCourcy Hannah—†	21	housewife	85	"
W	DeCourcy Paul	21	chemist	43	
X	Dolan James B	21	retired	75	
Y	Ward Mary—†	23	at home	41	"
Z	Connare Catherine G—†	25	housewife	23	156 South
	1232					
A	Connare James L	25	printer	24	156 "
B	Fitzgerald Catherine G—†	26	housewife	45	Medford
C	Fitzgerald Raymond H	26	operator	41	"
D	Coelsch Katherine B—†	27	housewife	47	here
E	*Coelsch Otto L	27	shoecutter	49	"
F	Coelsch Ruth D—†	27	artist	20	"
G	Fiske Mary—†	27	housewife	24	19 Mosgrove av

Saint Joseph Street

L	Ayer Margaret R—†	20	teacher	34	Somerville
M	*Beaton Margaret—†	20	domestic	53	here
N	Burke Angela—†	20	teacher	26	"
O	Burke Mary A—†	20	"	37	"
P	Burns Mildred F—†	20	"	33	
R	Curley Helen A—†	20	..	40	"
S	Delany Dorothy R—†	20	"	39	74 Union pk
T	Donohoe Marion J—†	20	"	41	here
U	Downing Margaret—†	20	"	42	"
V	Duffy Irene C—†	20	..	31	"
W	Fagan Grace A—†	20		29	Framingham
X	Fitzgerald Mary E—†	20	"	77	here
Y	Galvin Julia A—†	20	"	46	"
Z	Hines Catherine T—†	20	"	41	"
	1233					
A	Keefe Margaret A—†	20	"	52	
B	Kelleher Margaret L—†	20	"	50	

Page.	Letter.	FULL NAME.	Residence, Jan. 1, 1941.	Occupation.	Supposed Age.	Reported Residence, Jan. 1, 1940. Street and Number.

Saint Joseph Street—Continued

	c	Kelly Alice G—†	20	teacher	66	here
	d	MacInnes Elizabeth R—†	20	"	38	"
	e	Marconi Marie L—†	20	"	33	"
	f	*McKenzie Cecilia—†	20	"	30	
	g	McLaughlin Katherine J-†	20	"	53	
	h	Merrigan Anna J—†	20	"	34	
	k	Moynihan Mary—†	20	"	50	"
	l	Murphy Alice T—†	20		27	Lynn
	m	Murray Frances—†	20		22	here
	n	O'Gorman Agnes M—†	20	"	51	"
	o	Power Mary A—†	20	"	64	"
	p	Ring Julia V—†	20		52	"
	r	Sheehy Alice—†	20		24	Framingham
	s	Siebert Esther D—†	20	"	31	here
	t	*Sullivan Bridget—†	20	domestic	36	Cambridge
	u	Tegan Margaret C—†	20	teacher	29	here
	v	*Tracey Helen—†	20	cook	27	"
	w	Walsh Mary M—†	20	teacher	27	"
	x	Nolan Annie B—†	36	housewife	46	"
	y	Nolan Peter	36	operator	58	
	z	Ahlstrom Joanne—†	38	housewife	43	"
		1234				
	a	Ahlstrom Oscar R	38	machinist	49	"
	b	Wells Cora G—†	38	clerk	45	
	c	Blazo Blanche—†	38	housewife	45	"
	d	Blazo Irma—†	38	accountant	22	"
	e	Niss Hyman	39	pharmacist	30	"
	f	Niss Ruth—†	39	housewife	29	"
	g	Hayes Benjamin	39	mechanic	52	"
	h	Hayes Florence—†	39	housewife	47	"
	k	Connaughton Bernard	39	gardener	56	"
	l	Connaughton Louise—†	39	saleswoman	22	"
	m	Lyon Frank	39	cook	46	
	n	Lyon Marie—†	39	housewife	43	"
	o	Lyon Paul	39	U S A	21	
	p	Finburgh Louis J	39	salesman	53	"
	r	Finburgh Mary—†	39	housewife	57	"
	s	Colpas Beulah—†	39	"	56	Brookline
	t	Colpas Mary—†	39	"	27	here
	u	Colpas Phillip	39	painter	32	"
	v	Haskell George	40	manager	35	"

22

Page.	Letter.	Full Name.	Residence. Jan. 1. 1941.	Occupation.	Supposed Age.	Reported Residence, Jan. 1, 1940. Street and Number.

Saint Joseph Street—Continued

w	Haskell Julia—†	40	housewife	37	here
x	MacDonald Catherine A–†	42	"	37	"
y	MacDonald William J	42	salesman	45	"
z	*McCarthy John	42	woolworker	45	"
	1235				
a	Cronin Mary—†	43	housewife	27	"
b	Cronin Walter	43	roofer	29	
c	Dermody Annie E—†	43	seamstress	67	"
d	Lucas Mary—†	43	housewife	65	"
e	Maynes Catherine J—†	43	at home	40	
f	Jex James C	43	retired	80	
g	Jex Rita—†	43	housewife	55	"
h	L'Heureux William	43	retired	74	"
k	Jordan Frances—†	43	secretary	40	"
l	Jordan Nellie—†	43	housewife	64	"
m	Grady Frances M—†	43	"	25	21 Hutchinson
n	Grady William J	43	salesman	26	9 Rowe
o	Davis Emanuel	43	policeman	51	here
p	Davis Sadie—†	43	housewife	57	"
r	Cotter Jámes	47	manager	36	"
s	Cotter Margaret—†	47	housewife	36	"
t	Lundborn Ada—†	47	"	72	
u	Lundborn Raymond E	47	custodian	45	"
v	*McDonald Catherine—†	49	housewife	38	"
w	McDonald William J	49	operator	45	"

Saint Rose Street

x	Collins Helen A—†	47–49	operator	23	here
y	Collins John	47–49	laborer	68	"
z	Collins John F	47–49	letter carrier	33	"
	1236				
a	Collins Josephine N—†	47–49	housewife	64	"
b	Collins James C	47–49	laborer	36	
c	Collins Marcella V—†	47–49	housewife	36	"
d	Gilroy Thomas	47–49	clerk	21	"
e	*Keough John J	47–49	laborer	38	
f	Keough Nora—†	47–49	housewife	45	"
g	*Roche Christine—†	51	"	35	30A Jamaica
h	Roche James	51	laborer	34	30A "
k	Burnside Metta S—†	53	housewife	44	here

Saint Rose Street—Continued

L	Burnside Nelson E	53	teacher	43	here
M	Coleman Anna—†	53	housewife	29	"
N	Coleman James	53	seaman	34	"
O	Coleman John P	53	butcher	32	
P	Coleman Martin J	53	mechanic	29	"
R	English James M	55	watchman	62	"
S	Fogarty Frederick C	55	proprietor	54	"
T	Fogarty Mary A—†	55	housewife	53	"
U	*Tulk Caroline—†	55	"	58	
V	Tulk Dorothy—†	55	"	29	
W	*Tulk Edwin	55	retired	73	
X	*Tulk Phyllis—†	55	seamstress	36	"
Y	Tulk Victor L	55	clerk	28	
Z	Sheeran Margaret—†	55	"	45	

1237

A	Scanlon Frances—†	59	housewife	35	"
B	Scanlon William	59	motorman	35	"
C	*Scott Catherine—†	59	housewife	42	"
D	Scott William	59	assembler	46	"
E	Barnard Alan	59	welder	28	24 Cranston
F	Barnard Helen—†	59	housewife	26	24 "
G	Hohmann Agnes L—†	63	"	34	98 Fisher av
H	Hohmann Joseph N	63	clerk	34	98 "
K	McCluskey Joseph V	65	teamster	45	here
L	McCluskey Mary R—†	65	housewife	47	"
M	Costello Catherine—†	65	"	22	"
N	Costello William	65	laborer	28	"
O	*Donaghy Annie—†	69	housewife	37	Newton
P	Donaghy Hugh	69	laborer	58	6 Weld Hill
R	Dolan Mary A—†	69	housewife	69	here
S	Dolan William F	69	retired	70	"
T	Rowen Catherine D—†	69	housewife	29	"
U	Rowen Joseph E, jr	69	clerk	31	"
V	Kelly Paul R	71	operator	28	47 Custer
W	Kelly Veronica M—†	71	saleswoman	28	24 "
X	Sullivan Ellen J—†	71	housewife	43	here
Y	Sullivan John J	71	policeman	46	"
Z	Sullivan Mary E—†	71	clerk	20	"

1238

A	LaReau Albert F	71	repairman	24	Newton
B	LaReau Andrew J	71	engineer	34	819 Beacon

Page.	Letter.	FULL NAME.	Residence, Jan. 1, 1941.	Occupation.	Supposed Age.	Reported Residence, Jan. 1, 1940. Street and Number.

	c	Swanton William	75	clerk	41	here
	D	*Slyne Nora—†	75	housewife	33	"
	E	*Slyne P Stephen	75	manager	37	"
	F	Caliri Isabelle L—†	75	stenographer	27	20 Creighton
	G	Caliri Peter J	75	operator	27	24 Arcadia
	H	Hunkeler Julian	79	manager	49	here
	K	Hunkeler Mary—†	79	housewife	40	"
	L	Sullivan Mary E—†	79	seamstress	50	"
	M	Twiss Barbara—†	79	clerk	22	
	N	Twiss Evelyn—†	79	housewife	44	"
	O	Twiss Evelyn—†	79	saleswoman	20	"
	P	Twiss William	79	chauffeur	49	"
	R	Wright Beatrice—†	83	teller	20	
	S	Wright Helen—†	83	housewife	45	"
	T	Deery Catherine—†	83	"	49	
	U	Deery Joseph T	83	engineer	53	
	V	*Briggs Irene—†	83	housewife	22	"
	W	Briggs James N	83	mechanic	21	"
	X	Murphy Elizabeth—†	87	cashier	44	
	Y	Murphy James	87	salesman	32	"
	Z	Miller Frederick A	87	baker	68	
		1239				
	A	O'Neil Eunice M—†	87	stenographer	20	"
	B	Lanning Herman J	87	chauffeur	68	"
	C	Doyle Elizabeth H—†	91	housewife	31	71 Williams
	D	Doyle Thomas J	91	accountant	32	71 "
	E	Harrington James P	91	painter	42	here
	F	McAvoy Anna E—†	91	housewife	48	"
	G	McAvoy Francis T	91	engineer	52	"
	H	McAvoy Francis T, jr	91	inspector	24	"
	K	McAvoy James H	91	student	21	"
	L	Dahood Gabriel	95	cutter	47	
	M	*Dahood Rita—†	95	housewife	38	"
	N	O'Donnell Charles E	95	clerk	33	419 S Hunt'n av
	O	O'Donnell Florence N—†	95	housewife	33	419 "
	P	Dowd Ella G—†	99	"	46	here
	R	Dowd Patrick J	99	chauffeur	47	"
	S	Murphy Elizabeth B—†	99	housewife	47	"
	T	Murphy Eugene F	99	student	23	
	U	Murphy Eugene J	99	clerk	57	
	V	Murphy Katherine A—†	99	operator	25	

25

Page.	Letter.	FULL NAME.	Residence, Jan. 1, 1941.	Occupation.	Supposed Age.	Reported Residence, Jan. 1, 1940. Street and Number.

Saint Rose Street—Continued

	w	MacEachern Margaret–†	103	housewife	37	75 Forest Hills
	x	MacEachern Robert	103	electrician	36	75 "
	y	Donovan E Alice—†	103	operator	37	here
	z	Donovan Eliza A—†	103	housewife	75	"
		1240				
	a	Donovan Helen A—†	103	investigator	34	"
	b	Donovan Joseph F	103	retired	33	
	c	Tobin Dorothy—†	107	housewife	28	"
	d	Tobin John	107	clerk	29	
	e	Gillooly Catherine A—†	107	housewife	49	"
	f	Gillooly Margery C—†	107	at home	22	
	g	Gillooly Peter J	107	salesman	49	"
	h	Gillooly Richard P	107	student	20	
	k	Baatz Cecelia M—†	109	dressmaker	56	"
	l	Baatz Louise M—†	109	bookkeeper	55	"
	m	Baatz Anna C—†	109	housewife	44	"
	n	Baatz Carl J	109	manager	53	"
	o	Walsh Barbara—†	111	housewife	40	"
	p	Walsh David	111	retired	80	
	r	Walsh Thomas	111	electrician	40	"
	s	Morton Charles	111	chauffeur	52	"
	t	Morton Mary J—†	111	housewife	53	"
	u	Malone Anna M—†	115	"	36	
	v	Malone Laurence M	115	mechanic	37	"
	w	Laing Donald	121–123	"	40	"
	x	Laing Gladys G—†	121–123	housewife	31	"
	y	Finnegan Alice M—†	121–123	"	41	
	z	Finnegan John T	121–123	supervisor	51	"
		1241				
	a	Bailey Abigail R—†	131	teacher	50	
	b	Bailey Margaret M—†	131	student	20	
	c	Carroll Margaret—†	131	investigator	45	"
	d	Cronin Mary A—†	131	at home	65	

South Street

	k	Billing Maud E—†	67	waitress	49	Cambridge
	l	Broderick Francis P	67	physician	64	here
	m	Broderick Francis P, jr	67	architect	35	"

Page.	Letter.	FULL NAME.	Residence, Jan. 1, 1941.	Occupation.	Supposed Age.	Reported Residence, Jan. 1, 1940. Street and Number.

N	Broderick Lorraine A—†	67	at home	22	here	
o	*Letteney Elizabeth A—†	67	cook	50	Somerville	
s	Kearney Florence M—†	70	housewife	48	here	
T	Kearney John P	70	inspector	44	"	
u	Kelly James F	rear 70	chauffeur	21	"	
v	Kelly Mary A—†	" 70	laundress	52	"	
w	Kelly Rose A—†	" 70	housewife	50	"	
x	Kelly Thomas J	" 70	policeman	51	"	
y	Flynn Catherine—†	71	housekeeper	78	"	
z	*Walsh Thomas B	71	retired	96	..	

1242

A	Hilton Eleanor G—†	71	housewife	36	"	
B	Hilton Lewis J	71	clerk	36		
c	Riley Mary E—†	71	housewife	77	"	
D	McCall Ellen—†	72	"	70		
E	McCall Joseph P	72	clergyman	34	"	
F	McCall Mary E—†	72	at home	48		
G	McCabe Francis	74	mechanic	42	"	
H	McCabe Mary A—†	74	housewife	37	"	
K	Jennings Lewis E	74	instructor	55	Pennsylvania	
L	*Morris Gladys—†	74	clerk	31	here	
M	Morris John F	74	laborer	56	"	
N	Morris John J	74	engineer	29	"	
o	Morris Julia M—†	74	housewife	52	"	
P	Keaney Bridget T—†	74	"	40		
R	Keaney John J	74	chauffeur	41	"	
s	Fenerty Margaret H—†	75	housewife	51	"	
T	Fenerty Mary C—†	75	stenographer	20	"	
u	Fenerty William P	75	mechanic	51	"	
v	*McCarthy Annie—†	75	cook	66	".."	
w	McCarthy Catherine—†	75	at home	54		
x	Gambon Catherine—†	rear 75	housewife	76	"	
y	Gambon Christopher	" 75	retired	75		
z	Bellingham Catherine V	" 75	at home	63		

1243

A	Lynch Ellen F—†	" 75	"	69	"	
B	Gaffney Mary E—†	76	housewife	44	"	
c	Gaffney Thomas F	76	fireman	48		
D	Holland Ellen M—†	76	at home	67		
E	King Hannah M—†	76	housewife	64	"	

South Street—Continued

F	King Margaret M—†	76	teacher	30	here
G	Flaherty John F	76	porter	44	"
H	Flaherty Margaret E—†	76	housewife	51	"
K	O'Leary William A	76	laborer	33	"
L	Collins Frank E	77	dentist	56	
M	Collins Theresa A—†	77	housewife	56	"
N	Lordan Joseph P	78	guard	31	
O	Lordan Madelene M—†	78	housewife	28	"
P	Cahill Helen T—†	78	waitress	28	
R	Cahill John J	78	electrician	68	"
S	Cahill Margaret J—†	78	at home	30	
T	Cahill William E	78	laborer	32	
V	Dolan Eliza F—†	79	housewife	79	"
W	Dolan Sadie L—†	79	cashier	53	
X	Murdock Edward F	80	chauffeur	42	"
Y	Murdock Margaret K—†	80	housewife	43	"
Z	Bradley Edward J	80	laborer	39	
	1244				
A	*Bradley Mary A—†	80	housewife	37	"
C	Chaoing Peter	81	laundryman	41	"
D	Burke John J	82	janitor	60	8 Custer
E	Burke John J, jr	82	shipfitter	24	8 "
F	Burke Mary E—†	82	stenographer	21	8 "
G	Burke Mary M—†	82	housewife	53	8 "
H	Burke Thomas W	82	policeman	26	8 "
M	Cowan Alice J—†	84	housewife	46	here
N	Cowan Walter J	84	policeman	47	"
R	Lennon Frank V	86	salesman	55	807 Centre
S	Lennon Grace D—†	86	teacher	48	here
T	Lennon Margaret J—†	86	housewife	84	"
U	Harrington Fred R	86	laborer	58	Canton
V	Harrington John F	86	retired	71	here
W	Harrington Maude A—†	86	housewife	67	"
	1245				
B	Casey Catherine M—†	97	social worker	23	"
C	Casey William J	97	clergyman	68	"
D	Flynn Maurice J	97	"	45	
E	Magner Eliza—†	97	housekeeper	61	"
F	Parsons John L	97	clergyman	38	"
G	Riley Edward J	97	"	44	
H	Ryan Lawrence M	97	"	34	
K	Walsh Julia—†	97	domestic	33	"

Verona Street

L	Cohen Matthew	12	milkman	23	28 Greenock
M	Cohen Mildred N—†	12	housewife	26	28 "
N	Donovan Mary E—†	12	"	66	16 Verona
O	Donovan William A	12	retired	64	16 "
P	Niland Marie C—†	12	housewife	46	here
R	Niland William J	12	operator	50	"
S	Langer Curtis O	12	breweryworker	40	"
T	Langer Emma G—†	12	housewife	38	"
U	Frye Virginia M—†	12	"	27	
V	Frye William C	12	lather	32	"
w	*Foley Delia M—†	12	housewife	34	220 Fairmount av
X	Foley Martin J	12	repairman	40	779 E Fourth
Y	Kawana John L	16	armorer	40	here
Z	*Shaw Lauretta—†	16	housewife	70	"

1246

A	*Shaw Marion R—†	16	bookkeeper	32	"
B	Erickson Anna—†	16	housewife	65	"
C	Erickson Edward	16	musician	62	"
D	Erickson George W	16	retired	68	
E	Rankin Bertha G—†	16	housewife	32	"
F	Rankin James H	16	collector	33	"
G	Shea Daniel	16	laborer	53	82 Carolina av
H	*Shea Julia A—†	16	housewife	57	82 "
K	Baker Anne M—†	16	"	28	here
L	Baker John D	16	chauffeur	40	"
M	Whalen Anna M—†	16	housewife	29	"
N	Whalen Ronald T	16	upholsterer	34	"

Woodman Street

O	Coffey Catherine—†	3	housewife	26	546 Dor av
P	Coffey James	3	ironworker	32	103 Cataumet
R	Owens Catherine M—†	3	at home	84	here
S	Owens Susan—†	3	"	74	"
T	Aldred Margaret—†	5	clerk	30	"
U	Aldred William	5	usher	30	"
V	Hailer Catherine A—†	5	housewife	27	"
W	Hailer Joseph B	5	chauffeur	27	"
X	Cronin Arline T—†	8	housewife	30	"
Y	Cronin Michael J	8	clerk	37	"
Z	Walsh Elizabeth—†	8	"	20	Brookline

2

Page.	Letter.	Full Name.	Residence, Jan. 1, 1941.	Occupation.	Supposed Age.	Reported Residence, Jan. 1, 1940. Street and Number.

1247

Woodman Street—Continued

A	Walsh Francis	8	salesman	23	Brookline
B	Walsh Rose—†	8	housewife	53	"
C	Barsky John F	9	painter	38	50 Holbrook
E	Powers James E	9	clerk	22	here
D	Powers Lawrence J	9	retired	65	"
F	Powers Theresa—†	9	housewife	61	"
G	*Strycharski Frank	9	painter	39	
H	Strycharski Helen—†	9	housewife	34	"
K	Barrett Edward F	10	clerk	35	
L	Barrett Helen L—†	10	nurse	26	
M	Barrett James L	10	seaman	29	
N	Barrett Margaret—†	10	clerk	33	
O	Foley Theresa—†	10	housekeeper	28	"
P	Houlihan Barbara—†	11	housewife	46	26 Clive
R	Houlihan William J	11	porter	46	26 "
S	Howe Ralph	11	operator	34	California
T	Blodgett Clifford P	11	attendant	28	28 Whitford
U	Spencer Anna M—†	11	housewife	54	28 "
V	Spencer William H	11	tree surgeon	42	28 "
W	Lavin Mary—†	11	housewife	50	31 Sedgwick
X	Sullivan Mary—†	11	clerk	54	51 "
Y	MacFarlane Alexander	15	packer	22	here
Z	MacLean Mary E—†	15	housewife	48	"

1248

A	MacLean Neil	15	carpenter	50	"
B	Reilly Joseph P	15	U S A	20	
C	Reilly Margaret P—†	15	bookkeeper	22	"
D	Reilly Mary J—†	15	housewife	50	"
E	Reilly Patrick G	15	chauffeur	51	"
F	Mosel Alexander	15	laborer	40	46 Goldsmith
G	Mosel Margaret—†	15	housewife	35	46 "
H	McDowell Eva M—†	21	"	48	here
K	McDowell John	21	clerk	48	"
L	Higgins Helen—†	21	housewife	31	"
M	Higgins Patrick J	21	bartender	33	"
N	O'Donnell Francis L	21	baker	30	
O	O'Donnell Mary J—†	21	wrapper	28	
P	Franz Corinne—†	21	housewife	40	"
R	Franz George J	21	draftsman	42	"
S	Glennon Joseph M	21	foreman	48	

Woodman Street—Continued

T	Glennon Mildred—†	21	housewife	42	here
U	Roscoe Charles	21	floorlayer	34	"
V	Roscoe Mary—†	21	housewife	36	"
W	McCarney Edith—†	23	"	37	
X	McCarney Francis	23	chauffeur	36	"
Y	McCarney Alice—†	23	operator	36	
z*	McCarney James	23	retired	70	

1249

A	McCarney John	23	"	75	
B	McCarney Rose—†	23	bookkeeper	38	"
C	Dolan Pauline—†	27	housewife	24	88 McBride
D	Dolan Robert	27	shipper	27	254 Arborway
E	Cullen Hugh	27	fireman	41	here
F*	Cullen Margaret—†	27	housewife	34	"
G	Greenhall Winifred—†	27	at home	67	"
H	Barry Mary E—†	31	housewife	51	"
K	Barry William J	31	laborer	59	
L*	O'Connor James	31	gardener	50	"
M*	O'Connor Katherine J—†	31	housewife	47	"
N	O'Connor Patrick J	31	porter	49	
R*	Powers Angus L	33	laborer	44	"
P*	Powers Katherine—†	33	housewife	43	"
S	George Mildred—†	33	clerk	32	
T	Gilleo George J	35	laborer	32	
U	Gilleo Margaret—†	35	housewife	29	"
V	Roden Bridget A—†	35	"	56	
W	Roden Eleanor M—†	35	clerk	24	

Ward 11—Precinct 13

CITY OF BOSTON

LIST OF RESIDENTS
20 YEARS OF AGE AND OVER

(NON-CITIZENS INDICATED BY ASTERISK)
(FEMALES INDICATED BY DAGGER)

AS OF

JANUARY 1, 1941

JOSEPH F. TIMILTY, *Chairman*
FREDERIC E. DOWLING, *Secretary*
WILLIAM A. MOTLEY, JR.
FRANCIS B. McKINNEY
HILDA HEDSTROM QUIRK
Listing Board.

CITY OF BOSTON PRINTING DEPARTMENT

1300

Boynton Street

A	Mahoney Arthur L		mechanic	35	here
B	Mahoney Eleanore B—†		housewife	30	"
C	Welch Mary—†		adjuster	24	"
D	Welch Thomas B		clerk	20	
E	Welch Thomas J		operator	52	
F	Sullivan Daniel L	5	engineer	38	
G	Sullivan Susan—†	5	housewife	38	"
H	Mayberry Elwin	9	clerk	25	58 Westland a'
K	Mayberry Irene—†	9	housewife	26	58 "
L	McNamee Beatrice M—†	10	"	24	Blackstone
M	McNamee Joseph E	10	clerk	24	
N	*LaBonte Anastasia—†	10	housewife	38	here
¹N	LaBonte Gerard	10	letter carrier	42	"
O	Lynch Annie—†	10	housewife	65	"
P	Lynch Edward J	10	laborer	79	
R	Lynch Helen—†	10	operator	34	
S	Lynch Mary—†	10	"	38	
T	Lynch Rose—†	10	attendant	26	"
U	Boyd Charles F	11	retired	50	
V	Boyd Mary D—†	11	maid	47	
W	Lennon Joseph	11	carpenter	55	"
X	*Lennon Margaret—†	11	housewife	47	"
Y	Connell John V	14	laborer	26	
Z	Connell Mary—†	14	housewife	49	"

1301

A	Connell Michael J	14	chauffeur	50	"
B	Connell Michael J, jr	14	clerk	20	
C	Thompson Catherine M—†	14	housewife	37	"
D	Thompson Edward G	14	buyer	35	
E	Marshall Chester G	14	proofreader	51	"
F	*Marshall Harriet E—†	14	at home	91	
G	Marshall Harriet W—†	14	housewife	42	"
H	Gavin Ann—†	15	"	58	
K	Gavin Edward	15	retired	50	
L	Gavin John	15	clerk	22	
M	Gavin Mary—†	15	at home	23	"
N	O'Reilly Katherine—†	15	housewife	27	22 Dalton
O	O'Reilly Thomas J	15	bartender	37	22 "
P	Holton Margaret E—†	15A	housewife	28	5 Lamartine
R	Holton Richard M	15A	clerk	29	5 "

Page.	Letter.	FULL NAME.	Residence, Jan. 1, 1941.	Occupation.	Supposed Age.	Reported Residence, Jan. 1, 1940. Street and Number.

Boynton Street—Continued

	s	Hogarty Michael	17	shipper	38	here
	t	Hogarty Nellie—†	17	housewife	36	"
	u	Ford Catherine—†	17	"	40	"
	v	Ford John J	17	machinist	44	" '
	w	Cahill Mary F—†	17	seamstress	54	"
	x	Fallon Jennie M—†	17	operator	49	
	y	Fallon William F	17	laborer	59	
		1302				
	a	Delaney Anna B—†	18	housewife	53	"
	b	Delaney Charles J	18	caretaker	23	"
	c	Delaney William D	18	machinist	52	"
	d	Fitzgerald John G	18	laborer	33	
	e	*Fitzgerald Mary E—†	18	housewife	32	"
	f	Delaney Anna E—†	18	"	27	
	g	Delaney Joseph E	18	laborer	27	
	h	Cawley Bartholomew	20	"	20	
	k	*Cawley Bridget—†	20	housewife	53	"
	l	Cawley James	20	laborer	58	
	m	Cawley James M	20	clerk	23	"
	n	Duffy Thomas	20	laborer	45	40 McBride
	o	*Clifford Agnes—†	20	housewife	34	here
	p	Clifford Jeremiah	20	mechanic	36	"
	r	Rock Anthony	20	carpenter	54	"
	s	Rock Anthony	20	manager	23	
	t	Rock Edward	20	laborer	26	
	u	Rock Margaret—†	20	housewife	52	"
	v	Rock Mary—†	20	at home	20	
	w	Dailey Edward G	21	bricklayer	32	"
	x	Dailey Mary J—†	21	housewife	29	"
	y	Murphy Charles L	21	assembler	42	"
	z	Murphy Mary F—†	21	housewife	45	"
		1303				
	a	Pulaski Joseph	21	chauffeur	36	Cambridge
	b	Pulaski Margaret—†	21	operator	34	here
	c	Reilly Agnes E—†	21	waitress	37	"
	d	Reilly Margaret—†	21	at home	74	"
	e	Cleary Edward	22	roofer	31	34 Hall
	f	Cleary Mary V—†	22	housewife	30	34 "
	g	Trowbridge Alice—†	22	waitress	29	here
	h	Trowbridge Dorothy—†	22	packer	23	"
	k	Trowbridge Ernest	22	machinist	20	"

3

Boynton Street—Continued

	L	*Trowbridge Sarah—†	22	housewife	56	here
	M	Flahive John	22	laborer	42	"
	N	*Flahive Rosanne—†	22	housewife	42	"
	O	*Rogers Grace—†	23	"	33	
	P	Rogers Henry P	23	technician	37	"
	R	*Fitzgerald Dorothy G—†	23	housewife	26	38 Wensley
	S	Fitzgerald Robert E	23	shipper	30	38 "
	T	Shufeldt Dorothy—†	23	maid	21	Maine
	U	LaPointe Joseph A	23	carpenter	55	here
	V	LaPointe Laura A—†	23	waitress	20	"
	W	*LaPointe Loretta M—†	23	housewife	42	"
	X	O'Hanley Mary—†	23	hostess	28	
	Y	*McPhee Jeanette—†	25	housewife	32	"
	Z	*McPhee Joseph D	25	barber	35	
		1304				
	A	Duggan Annie T—†	25	housewife	42	"
	B	Duggan Michael F	25	engineer	43	
	C	Moylan Elizabeth—†	25	housewife	42	"
	D	Moylan Thomas	25	letter carrier	50	"
	E	Gavin Martin F	26	salesman	34	
	F	Gavin Mary C—†	26	housewife	33	"
	G	Toolin Elizabeth—†	29	"	34	31 Bardwell
	H	Toolin Patrick	29	fireman	35	31 "
	K	Matthews Marion F—†	29	housewife	39	here
	L	Matthews Owen J	29	watchman	43	"
	M	McGonigle Genevieve—†	29	housewife	26	"
	N	McGonigle William	29	laborer	31	
	O	Reardon John F	30	fireman	60	
	P	Reardon Mary H—†	30	housewife	45	"
	R	Dee Catherine—†	30	at home	67	55 Paul Gore
	S	Whitehead Hiram D	30	chauffeur	40	55 "
	T	Whitehead Mary—†	30	housewife	37	55 "
	U	*Parsons Andrew J	30	porter	51	50½ Ballard
	V	*Parsons Jessie—†	30	housewife	43	50½ "
	W	*Bergquist Mary—†	31	"	37	here
	Y	Knight Catherine F—†	33	"	49	"
	Z	Knight Harold R	33	chauffeur	40	"
		1305				
	A	Cuddy Agnes—†	33	housewife	41	"
	B	Cuddy Joseph	33	painter	45	
	C	Monahan Margaret—†	34	housewife	49	"

Page.	Letter.	FULL NAME.	Residence, Jan. 1, 1941.	Occupation.	Supposed Age.	Reported Residence, Jan. 1. 1940. Street and Number.

Boynton Street—Continued

D	Monahan Michael	34	janitor	51	here
E	Monahan Thomas	34	clerk	21	"
F	Welsh Joseph W	34	lineman	49	"
G	Welsh Mary—†	34	housewife	47	"
H	Kelleher Beatrice—†	34	"	43	30 Newbern
K	Kelleher David	34	laborer	46	30 "
L	Donovan Joseph P	35	salesman	35	37 Dunster rd
M	Donovan Mary A—†	35	housewife	28	21 Highland av
N	Manning Walter P	35	carpenter	52	here
O	Carley Helen C—†	37	checker	24	"
P	Carley Mary—†	37	housewife	53	21 Atwood sq
R	Henderson Eugenie E—†	37	housekeeper	24	here
S	Jenkins Charles W	37	retired	71	"
T	Jenkins Elizabeth W—†	37	housewife	56	"
U	Jenkins John W	37	U S A	25	"
V	Barr Florence M—†	38	housewife	23	62 Grampian way
W	Barr Harold C	38	shipper	29	62 "
X	Murray Evelyn—†	38	housewife	21	29 Holman
Y	Murray William	38	chauffeur	27	94 Parker Hill av
Z	Sullivan John J	38	clerk	56	here
	1306				
A	Sullivan Margaret M—†	38	housewife	57	"
B	Ledwith Evelyn—†	38	"	34	
C	Ledwith Thomas J	38	papercutter	35	"
D	Gill Alice—†	38	housewife	27	"
E	Gill John	38	chauffeur	33	"
F	Ulrich Florence—†	38	housewife	38	"
G	Ulrich William A	38	machinist	45	"
H	McElhinney Bernard L	39	accountant	27	"
K	McElhinney Mary V—†	39	housewife	27	"
L	*Daneault Angelina—†	39	dressmaker	41	"
M	Daneault Herve	39	plasterer	45	"
N	*Flanagan Bridie—†	39	housewife	33	"
O	Flanagan Edward	39	laborer	40	
P	Foley Patrick H	39	pressman	28	"
R	Foley Stella—†	39	housewife	25	"
S	Flynn Daniel	39	foreman	36	
T	Flynn Marguerite—†	39	housewife	33	"
U	Bernstein Anna—†	39	"	34	
V	Bernstein Louis	39	merchant	28	"
W	*Bores William	42–44	laborer	60	

5

Boynton Street—Continued

x	Carmody Margaret—†	42–44	housewife	54	here
y	Costello James	42–44	fireman	36	"
z	Gilmore Frank	42–44	pipelayer	40	"
	1307				
a	*Landenberger Henry	42–44	chef	46	35 Boylston
b	*Landenberger Mary—†	42–44	housewife	55	35 "
c	Conway Francis J	43	ship joiner	44	30 "
d	*Conway Mary—†	43	housewife	35	30 "
f	*Doyle Bridget—†	43	"	54	here
g	*Doyle Edward J	43	clerk	26	"
h	Smith Howard J	43	shoeworker	46	"
k	Smith Olive—†	43	housewife	42	"
l	Harold Anne—†	43	"	35	
m	Harold Richard C	43	longshoreman	35	"
n	Denaro Dominic	43	salesman	30	"
o	Denaro Dorothy—†	43	saleswoman	27	"
p	Velleca Anthony L	53	laborer	44	
r	Velleca Dorothy—†	53	housewife	42	"
s	*Velleca Nicholas	53	retired	66	
t	Bohan Catherine—†	53	secretary	21	"
u	Bohan John	53	counterman	23	"
v	Skelly Hugh	53	retired	65	
w	*Skelly Rose—†	53	at home	70	
z	Alexanian Richard	54	cutter	37	
	1308				
a	*Alexanian Rose—†	54	housewife	29	"
b	Kelly Charles	54	chauffeur	29	"
c	Kelly Elizabeth L—†	54	waitress	24	
d	*Kelly John	54	gardener	52	"
e	Kelly John	54	laborer	26	
f	Kelly Mary—†	54	operator	30	"
g	*Kelly Mary E—†	54	housewife	50	"
h	Akmekjian Emust—†	54	"	47	
k	Akmekjian Sarkis	54	cobbler	47	
l	Sharbetian Byron	54	cabinetmaker	26	"
m	Godfrey Charles	58	salesman	26	24 Forest Hi
n	Godfrey Helena—†	58	clerk	22	24 "
o	White Charles	58	guard	31	here
p	White Ellen—†	58	housewife	25	"
r	Palmer Alice—†	58	"	36	"
s	Palmer Anthony	58	bartender	42	"

Boynton Street—Continued

T	Carroll John E	58	pharmacist	32	here
U	Carroll Winifred—†	58	housewife	25	"
V	Sullivan Adeline—†	58	"	28	"
W	Sullivan Joseph F	58	chauffeur	27	"
X	Snow Effie M—†	58	housewife	39	"
Y	Snow John T	58	policeman	38	"
Z	Gulledge Agnes E—†	66	housewife	28	29 Lourdes av
	1309				
A	Gulledge Harry	66	floorman	27	here
B	Reynolds Agnes—†	66	at home	51	Waban
C	*Cohen Ella—†	66	"	60	Chelsea
D	Cohen Tela—†	66	seamstress	27	"
E	Klass Helen—†	66	housewife	30	"
F	*Klass Meyer	66	salesman	42	89 Chandler
G	Klass Simon	66	shoeworker	32	here
H	White Ellen—†	66	at home	77	"
K	White John	66	policeman	37	"
L	Kerr Agnes E—†	66	housewife	28	43 Boynton
M	Kerr Robert	66	janitor	45	43 "
N	Coletta Helen—†	66	housewife	28	here
O	Coletta Patrick	66	accountant	31	"
P	Hall Geraldine F—†	66	housewife	29	"
R	Hall John H	66	repairman	35	"
S	Hough Albert A	68	painter	46	
T	Hough Mary A—†	68	housewife	47	"
U	Cotugno Jennie—†	72	"	42	
V	Cotugno Joseph	72	laborer	47	
W	Cotugno Matthew	72	machinist	24	"

Call Street

Z	Paulson Martha A—†	74	housewife	34	here
	1310				
A	Paulson Mills J	74	painter	37	
B	Ricci Albert J	74	repairman	28	"
C	Ricci Josephine L—†	74	housewife	27	"
D	Fleming Alice F—†	74	"	33	
E	Fleming Charles E	74	cutter	34	
F	Nolan Mary A—†	78	at home	68	"
G	Nolan Thomas J	78	retired	83	W Newton
K	Connare Julia A—†	80	housewife	54	here

Page.	Letter.	FULL NAME.	Residence, Jan. 1, 1941.	Occupation.	Supposed Age.	Reported Residence, Jan. 1, 1940. Street and Number.

Call Street—Continued

	Letter	FULL NAME	Res.	Occupation	Age	Reported Residence
	L	Connare Julia A—†	80	inspector	33	here
	M	Goode Francis J	80	laborer	24	"
	N	Goode Teresa—†	80	housewife	64	"
	O	Goode Teresa—†	80	stenographer	22	"
	P	Mulhern Isabelle—† rear	80	housewife	45	"
	R	Mulhern Matthew J "	80	carpenter	46	"
	S	Murphy Daniel J	82	collector	41	"
	T	Murphy Mary—†	82	housewife	42	"
	U	MacKay Harriet E—†	86	"	45	"
	V	MacKay Joseph A	86	operator	47	
	W	MacKay Joseph A, jr	86	U S A	20	"
	X	MacKay Theodore	86	clerk	23	"
	Y	DeCoste Francis E rear	88	inspector	32	227 Amory
	Z	DeCoste Louise V—† "	88	housewife	32	here
		1311				
	A	Sullivan Harold F	90	custodian	42	"
	B	Sullivan Mary E—†	90	housewife	40	"
	C	Danco Gertrude C—†	90	"	22	
	D	Danco Salvatore J	90	chauffeur	27	"
	E	Graham DeWitt T	90	"	50	
	F	Munafo Ida—†	90	housewife	27	"
	G	Munafo Leo N	90	mechanic	27	"
	H	O'Brien Beatrice E—†	94	housewife	34	"
	K	O'Brien Philip F	94	machinist	36	"
	L	Estabrook Margaret E—† r	94	waitress	27	
	M	Estabrook Perley W "	94	chauffeur	31	"
	N	Barnes Ellery C "	94	laborer	28	Maine
	O	Barnes Isabel—† "	94	housewife	24	"
	R	Hatch Eleanora C—†	96	"	28	here
	S	Hatch Frank L	96	porter	34	"
	T	Miller Charles W	96	packer	30	"
	U	Miller Lena—†	96	housewife	65	"
	V	Miller Virginia D—†	96	"	26	
	Y	Brunette Arthur W	98	draftsman	32	"
	Z	Brunette Dorothy M—†	98	housewife	29	"
		1312				
	A	*Dumont Armand	98	plasterer	36	"
	B	*Dumont Jeanne—†	98	housewife	30	"
	C	Molway Eleanor I—†	99	"	21	67 W Walnut pk
	D	Molway Francis R	99	laborer	22	67 "
	E	Gill Delia R—†	99	matron	41	here

8

Page.	Letter.	FULL NAME.	Residence, Jan. 1, 1941.	Occupation.	Supposed Age.	Reported Residence, Jan. 1, 1940. Street and Number.

Call Street—Continued

	F	Gill Ellen—†	99	housewife	78	here
	G	Gill William T	99	retired	80	"
	H	Binns Rose—†	102	housekeeper	37	"
	K	*Letourneau Henry	102	carpenter	41	"
	L	*Letourneau Sadie—†	102	housewife	38	"
	M	Dwyer Louise A—†	104	"	49	
	N	Dwyer William J	104	machinist	28	"
	O	*Drouin Germaine—†	104	housewife	33	"
	P	*Drouin Romeo	104	plasterer	34	"
	S	Tosti Antonio	110	mason	52	41 Rossmore rd
	T	Tosti John A	110	laborer	22	41 "
	U	Tosti Mary—†	110	housewife	44	41 "
	V	Flynn Catherine N—†	110	"	47	here
	W	Flynn John F	110	inspector	47	"
	X	Flynn John W	110	clerk	20	"
	Y	Flynn Owen W	110	machinist	23	"
	Z	Maginnis Joseph P	110	clerk	26	
1313						
	A	Maginnis Mary L—†	110	teacher	29	
	C	Gibson Helen G—†	111	housewife	30	"
	D	*Gibson Margaret M—†	111	at home	64	"
	E	Gibson William B	111	plumber	31	
	F	Glennon Sadie E—†	111	housewife	60	"
	G	Teehan John	111	clerk	22	"
	H	Volpe Arthur D	133	chauffeur	38	7 Everett
	K	Volpe Rose L—†	133	housewife	34	7 "

Child Street

	N	Flynn Anthony	21	manager	40	here
	O	*Flynn Mary—†	21	housewife	29	"
	P	Reilly James P	21	student	22	"
	R	McIsaac Angus A	21	carpenter	57	"
	S	McIsaac Margaret—†	21	housewife	56	"
	T	Shewan George	21	electrician	28	"
	U	Shewan Margaret—†	21	housewife	50	"
	V	LaRonde Frank	25	clerk	31	
	W	LaRonde Regina—†	25	housewife	27	"
	X	Hanley Annie—†	25	"	43	
	Y	Hanley John	25	laborer	49	
	Z	Hanley Thomas	25	"	23	

1314
Child Street—Continued

	A	Flaherty Delia—†	25	housewife	43	here
	B	Flaherty Patrick	25	waiter	53	"
	C	Stevens David	29	clerk	64	78 Woodlawn
	D	Stevens Mary—†	29	housewife	60	78 "
	E	Galvin Catherine M—†	29	"	64	here
	F	Galvin Mary K—†	29	clerk	25	"
	G	Galvin Thomas J	29	retired	65	"
	H	Galvin Thomas J, jr	29	laborer	27	
	K	Corney George W	29	operator	57	"
	L	Corney Rose A—†	29	housewife	58	"
	M	Marchese Annamae—†	33	"	31	183 Bourne
	N	Marchese Vincent	33	carpenter	38	183 "
	¹N	McCann Elizabeth—†	33	at home	50	here
	O	Haralambides George	33	clerk	43	23 Goldsmith
	P	Haralambides Mary—†	33	housewife	30	23 "
	R	Sullivan Elizabeth F—†	37	"	28	263 Chestnut av
	S	Sullivan Humphrey V	37	dispatcher	29	263 "
	T	Lucey Annie M—†	37	maid	48	here
	U	Walsh Marie J—†	37	housewife	52	"
	V	Walsh Thomas F	37	foreman	56	"
	W	Davis Emma C—†	37	housewife	47	"
	X	Davis Frederick C	37	chemist	46	"
	Y	Ring Ellen E—†	41	housewife	59	49 Jamaica
	Z	Ring Helen C—†	41	clerk	20	49 "

1315

	A	Ring Thomas F	41	factoryhand	26	49 "
	B	Ring William B	41	engineer	67	49 "
	C*	Martin Dora B—†	41	housewife	35	here
	D*	Martin Thomas F	41	dairyman	36	"
	E	Keohane John	41	laborer	37	"
	F	Keohane Mary—†	41	housewife	35	"
	G	Kelledy Lawrence A	45	electrotyper	48	"
	H	Kelledy Mary—†	45	housewife	43	"
	K	Cornell Lawrence W	45	laborer	43	
	L	Walsh Hazel F—†	45	housewife	44	"
	M	Walsh Patrick J	45	foreman	45	"
	N	McDougall Mary—†	45	housewife	33	79 Brookley r
	O	McDougall Timothy	45	printer	32	79 "
	P	Welsh Florence—†	49	housewife	36	here
	R	Welsh William	49	chauffeur	36	"

Child Street—Continued

s	Toland Michael	49	repairman	62	here
t	Flynn Margaret—†	49	housewife	53	"
u	Flynn Patrick J	49	packer	50	"
v	Kearney Harriet H—†	53	clerk	23	
w	Kearney Margaret T—†	53	at home	55	
x	Gately Catherine—†	53	housewife	70	"
y	Gately John	53	electrician	36	"
z	Gately Louise—†	53	typist	38	

1316

a	Goggin Catherine—†	53	maid	31	
b	Goggin Elizabeth—†	53	"	33	
c	McColgan Helen M—†	57	housewife	39	"
d	Mullaney Mary V—†	57	"	43	
e	Mullaney Patrick J	57	laborer	47	
f	Sullivan John J	57	chauffeur	56	"
g	Sullivan Josephine—†	57	secretary	20	"
h	Brennan Philip	61	laborer	31	
k	*Lehane Beatrice—†	61	housewife	27	"
l	Lehane John J	61	gardener	32	"
m	*Gallagher Kathleen—†	61	housewife	27	"
n	Gallagher William J	61	manager	31	"
o	Hart John	61	U S A	30	
p	McWhinnie Mary E—†	61	matron	65	..
r	McWhinnie Victoria M—†	61	waitress	22	
s	Watts Charles R	61	houseman	40	"
t	McGann Edward J	65	clerk	34	
u	McGann Florence—†	65	housewife	32	"
v	Hines John F	65	salesman	38	24 St Peters
w	Hines Mary E—†	65	housewife	24	24 "
x	Post Elizabeth J—†	65	"	57	here
y	Post John L	65	merchant	58	"
z	Kiernan Margaret A—†	69	housewife	46	"

1317

a	Kiernan Patrick	69	letter carrier	46	"
b	Noonan Alice—†	69	housewife	34	"
c	*Noonan Patrick	69	mechanic	33	"
d	Walsh John J	69	operator	50	..
e	Walsh Mary A—†	69	housewife	47	"
f	Walsh Mary A—†	69	packer	21	
g	Walsh William H	69	student	24	
h	*Bury Agnes—†	73	housewife	58	"

Page.	Letter.	FULL NAME.	Residence, Jan. 1, 1941.	Occupation.	Supposed Age.	Reported Residence, Jan. 1, 1940. Street and Number.

Child Street—Continued

K	Madden Joseph V	73	policeman	42	here
L	Madden Mary J—†	73	housewife	41	"
M	Gallacher Emily—†	73	"	41	"
N	Gallacher John	73	sexton	42	
O	Hynes Mary A—†	77	housewife	37	"
P	Hynes Michael	77	bartender	40	"
R	Sexton Alice—†	77	clerk	22	
S	Sexton Anna—†	77	hairdresser	24	"
T	Sexton Delia—†	77	at home	63	..
U	Riley Charles A	77	plumber	64	
V	Riley Eleanor—†	77	housewife	53	"
W	Glynn Delia—†	81	"	52	
X	Glynn Joseph	81	clerk	22	
Y	Glynn Mary—†	81	cashier	20	
Z	Glynn Michael	81	operator	53	

1318

A	Connolly Elizabeth M—†	81	housewife	59	"
B	Connolly John J	81	watchman	62	"
C	Connolly John J, jr	81	U S N	24	
D	Connolly Margaret M—†	81	clerk	26	
E	Gately Mary—†	81	housewife	40	"
F	Gately Thomas F	81	laborer	40	
G	Griffen William	81	"	60	
H	Gulley Leo E	85	printer	31	
K	Gulley Mary C—†	85	housewife	29	"
L	Dunning John J	85	mechanic	43	"
M	Dunning Margaret N—†	85	nurse	47	
N	*Gaffey John	85	carpenter	42	"
O	*White Mary—†	85	housekeeper	68	"
P	*McKenney Douglass A	85	foreman	37	Belmont
R	McKenney Josephine—†	85	housewife	36	"
S	King Edward	95	clerk	39	here
T	King Marguerite—†	95	housewife	39	"
U	Connare Frances—†	95	"	31	"
V	Connare John	95	clerk	31	
W	O'Neill Edmund J	95	pipefitter	38	"
X	*O'Neill Mary S—†	95	housewife	39	"
Y	Porter Catherine—†	97	"	67	
Z	Porter John	97	laborer	63	

1319

A	Porter John, jr	97	seaman	26	

Page	Letter	Full Name.	Residence, Jan. 1, 1941.	Occupation.	Supposed Age.	Reported Residence, Jan. 1, 1940. Street and Number.

Child Street—Continued

B	Poplaska Stella—†	rear 103	factoryhand	24	here
C	*Tarucewich Constance—†	" 103	at home	47	"
D	Korman Anna M—†	" 103	housewife	43	"
E	Korman Frances M-†	" 103	saleswoman	22	"
F	Korman Leo. C	" 103	shipper	47	"
G	Zakur Alice—†	105	housewife	22	64 Newburg
H	Zakur William	105	electrician	30	64 "
K	Driscoll Catherine—†	105	housewife	60	here
L	Driscoll Edmund F	105	gardener	29	"
M	Driscoll Frederick J	105	laborer	31	"
N	Driscoll Gerald T	105	"	25	
O	Driscoll John J	105	janitor	71	
P	Driscoll John J, jr	105	bartender	35	"
R	Driscoll Lillian—†	105	waitress	37	
S	Driscoll Paul A	105	watchman	33	"
T	Noonan Ellen T—†	109	housewife	73	"
U	Oser Albert	109	chauffeur	33	"
V	Oser Louise—†	109	housewife	30	"
W	*Ferrari Hazel—†	113	"	28	
X	Ferrari Robert	113	cook	30	
Y	Curley Chester	115	chauffeur	28	"
Z	Curley Grace—†	115	housewife	27	"
	1320				
A	Fellowes Albert E	115	repairman	52	"
B	Fellowes Albert E, jr	115	clerk	21	"
C	Fellowes Charles H	115	electrician	25	59 St Rose
D	Fellowes Mary E—†	115	housewife	52	here
E	Graham Mary—†	117	at home	22	20 Atwood sq
F	Walsh Delia—†	117	housewife	65	here
G	Walsh Hugh	117	seaman	30	"
H	Walsh John	117	mason	65	"
K	Walsh John F	117	chauffeur	37	"
L	Walsh Paul T	117	welder	28	
M	Walsh Thomas P	117	teacher	32	
R	Hajenlian Agnes—†	123	housewife	33	"
S	Hajenlian Maren	123	laborer	55	

Hall Street

U	Foley Daniel J	8	clerk	34	here
V	Foley Dorothy M—†	8	housewife	34	"

13

Hall Street—Continued

w	Davis Hilda M—†	8	housewife	41	Norwood
x	May Charlotte N—†	8	nurse	31	"
y	*Kelly Mary A—†	8	housewife	55	here
z	*Kelly Thomas F	8	gardener	60	"
	1321				
a	Findlay Bridget M—†	9	housewife	50	"
b	*Findlay Nellie—†	9	at home	85	
c	Findlay William E	9	shoeworker	48	"
d	Maloney Elizabeth M—†	9	housewife	47	85 Call
e	Maloney William M	9	clerk	63	85 "
f	Conway Margaret R—†	9	manager	38	here
g	Foley Mary A—†	9	at home	85	"
h	Watson Elizabeth V—†	12	"	67	"
k	Watson Mary J—†	12	"	71	
l	Bennett John C	12	auctioneer	29	"
m	Bennett John K	12	manager	55	
n	Bennett Raymond L	12	merchant	20	"
o	Bennett Stella M—†	12	housewife	48	"
p	Libby Blanche E—†	13	"	52	"
r	Libby Eileen M—†	13	"	26	"
s	Libby Woodrow W	13	salesman	27	"
t	Williams Cora E—†	13	housewife	37	21 Rosemary
u	Williams George R	13	clerk	38	21 "
v	Winchenbach Katherine-†	13	housewife	70	21 "
w	Winchenbach Lester F	13	foreman	38	21 "
x	Cronin Ellen M—†	15	housewife	70	here
y	Hanley Edward F	15	U S A	23	"
z	Wood Francis A	15	executive	43	"
	1322				
a	Wood Teresa D—†	15	housewife	43	"
b	Barron John	16	retired	69	
c	Barron Mary J—†	16	housewife	50	"
d	Salmon Lawrence M	16	laborer	32	
e	Kelley Marion C—†	16	housewife	55	"
f	Kelley William J, jr	16	laborer	22	
g	Kelley William J	16	salesman	52	"
h	MacDonald Angus J	16	plumber	23	
k	*MacDonald Annie—†	16	housewife	42	"
l	MacDonald John R	16	clerk	22	
m	MacDonald Joseph A	16	steamfitter	52	"
n	MacDonald Vincent H	16	student	20	

Hall Street—Continued

o	Brennan Joseph M	17	cable splicer	44	here
p	Brennan Marie F—†	17	housewife	44	"
r	Cronin Andrew L	17	salesman	40	"
s	Cronin Winifred A—†	17	housewife	40	"
t	Kelley David E	19	supervisor	34	"
u	Kelley Agnes L—†	19	housewife	26	"
v	Harney Mary—†	19	laundress	68	"
w	Keough Winifred—†	19	housewife	60	"
x	Nyhan Agnes L—†	19	"	49	
y	Nyhan Margaret T—†	19	clerk	20	..
z	Nyhan Patrick J	19	polisher	48	

1323

a	Nyhan Thomas A	19	clerk·	22	
b	Lydon John	21	laborer	56	
c	Lydon Joseph T	21	composer	29	"
d	Lydon Margaret—†	21	housewife	56	"
e	Lydon Margaret T—†	21	"	23	
f	*Collins Louise A—†	21	"	35	
g	Collins Paul S	21	painter	34	
h	Shea John	21	retired	70	
k	Shea Mary—†	21	housewife	70	"
l	Harkins Catherine M—†	22	waitress	20	
m	*Walsh Mary A—†	22	housewife	53	"
n	*Walsh Patrick J	22	laborer	52	
o	Durant Beatrice M—†	22	saleswoman	20	"
p	Durant Emil	22	shoeworker	60	"
r	Durant Georgina A—†	22	housewife	51	"
s	Mouratian Abraham P	22	clerk	48	
t	Mouratian Alice—†	22	housewife	37	"
u	Russo Saverio	24	laborer	34	
v	Russo Victoria—†	24	housewife	26	"
w	Ratta Francesco	24	laborer	44	
x	Ratta Saveria—†	24	housewife	36	"
y	Russo Bruno	24	chauffeur	32	"
z	Russo Joseph	24	retired	69	

1324

a	Prestera Antonio	24	gardener	47	"
b	Prestera Frances J—†	24	housewife	41	"
c	Prestera Marion T—†	24	bookkeeper	21	"
d	Truitt Ernest L	25	superintendent	38	"
e	Truitt Helen M—†	25	housewife	45	"

Page.	Letter.	FULL NAME.	Residence, Jan. 1, 1941.	Occupation.	Supposed Age.	Reported Residence, Jan. 1, 1940. Street and Number.

Hall Street—Continued

F	Fraser Estella R—†	25	housewife	39	here
G	Fraser John M	25	manager	37	"
H	Hogan Delia—†	28	seamstress	62	10 Woodman
K	Hogan Joseph F	28	laborer	27	10 "
L	Manning Annie—†	30	housewife	82	here
M	*McLaughlin John J	30	retired	66	"
N	Leahy Clara I—†	31	housewife	40	33 Hall
O	O'Connor Virginia I—†	31	"	20	33 "
P	Shurety Francis J	31	teamster	46	here
R	Shurety Mary G—†	31	stitcher	44	"
S	Grover Edward G	31	salesman	52	"
T	Murtagh Alexander B	32	watchman	35	"
U	Murtagh Katherine—†	32	housewife	38	"
V	*Hebert Elizabeth A—†	32	"	41	"
W	Hebert Leon J	32	woolpacker	40	"
X	McInnis Alley E	32	carpenter	28	"
Y	McInnis Helen A—†	32	housewife	26	"
Z	Winchenbach Roscoe L	32	laborer	51	
	1325				
B	Sargent James F	33	clerk	34	
C	Sargent Julia M—†	33	housewife	33	"
D	Fennelly Bridget A—†	33	"	23	1127 Dor Av
E	Fennelly Lawrence J	33	laborer	24	1127 "
F	Kilrow Bertha—†	34	shoeworker	34	here
G	Kilrow Walter	34	seaman	31	"
H	Mulvey Martha—†	34	shoeworker	25	"
K	Dowling Thomas F	34	chauffeur	44	"
L	Poole Edward E	34	retired	70	
M	Poole Mary E—†	34	housewife	67	"
O	Davis Bertha C—†	35	packer	31	
P	Davis Emil A	35	machinist	34	"
R	O'Connor Mary E—†	35	housewife	69	"
S	O'Connor Michael	35	retired	69	
T	O'Connor Thomas M	35	laborer	34	
U	Changelian Haig	35	tailor	36	
V	Changelian Virginia—†	35	housewife	28	"
W	Mulrey Alice T—†	36	at home	65	
X	Mulrey Annie E—†	36	housewife	77	"
Y	Mulrey Timothy	36	retired	73	
Z	Mulrey William H	36	"	78	

Letter	Full Name.	Residence, Jan. 1, 1941.	Occupation.	Supposed Age.	Reported Residence, Jan. 1, 1940. Street and Number.

1326
Hall Street—Continued

Letter	Full Name.	Residence, Jan. 1, 1941.	Occupation.	Supposed Age.	Reported Residence, Jan. 1, 1940. Street and Number.
E	Glennon John T	36	guard	55	here
C	Glennon Margaret—†	36	dressmaker	58	"
D	Glennon Mary T—†	36	at home	87	"
F	Glennon William H	36	custodian	55	"
	McDonald Elizabeth—†	36	at home	52	
	McDonald Joseph	36	student	22	
	Case Sabina L—†	40	housewife	40	"
H	Case William W	40	mechanic	44	"
K	Splaine James J	40	laborer	62	
L	Splaine Mary E—†	40	inspector	36	"
M	Splaine William J	40	operator	35	
N	Credit Alice M—†	40	housewife	33	"
O	Credit George J	40	laborer	36	
P	Kapravy Andrew	41	painter	43	
R	Kapravy Jennie—†	41	housewife	28	"
S	*Gill Christine—†	42	"	29	
T	Gill Thomas J	42	bartender	33	"
U	Strecker Louis E	42	machinist	38	"
V	Strecker Sarah T—†	42	housewife	34	"
W	Woodman Mary—†	42	"	25	
X	Maloney John	43	laborer	43	
Y	Maloney Julia E—†	43	housewife	33	"
Z	Feeley Helen S—†	45	"	46	

1327

Letter	Full Name.	Residence, Jan. 1, 1941.	Occupation.	Supposed Age.	Reported Residence, Jan. 1, 1940. Street and Number.
A	Feeley James E	45	laborer	47	
B	Greene Gertrude M—†	45	operator	42	
C	Ordway Clara M—†	45	housewife	57	"
D	Ordway George A	45	chauffeur	57	"
E	Cleary Agnes M—†	45	housewife	41	"
F	Cleary Thomas G	45	metalworker	35	"
G	*Branley Catherine—†	47	housewife	36	"
H	Branley Joseph	47	operator	48	
K	*Crocker Ananias C	47	carpenter	38	"
L	*Crocker Florence A—†	47	housewife	35	"
M	Keegan Bridget T—†	47	"	43	
N	Kelly Anna—†	48	clerk	21	
O	Kelly John J	48	laborer	43	
P	Kelly Mary F—†	48	housewife	43	"
R	*Richards Bertha—†	48	"	44	

Hall Street—Continued

s	*Richards Stanley	48	carpenter	45	here
T	Keaney Coleman	48	laborer	48	"
U	*Keaney Ellen F—†	48	housewife	47	"
v	Fennelly Rita M—†	49	"	27	
w	Fennelly William C	49	merchant	27	"
x	Barter George A	49	porter	41	80 South
Y	Barter Isabella—†	49	housewife	37	80 "
z	Short Anna A—†	49	"	36	here

1328

A	Short George T	49	steamfitter	37	"
B	Faherty Anne—†	50	housewife	62	"
c	*Faherty John J	50	laborer	27	
D	Faherty Martin F	50	clerk	25	
E	*Noseworthy Gertrude—†	50	housewife	32	"
F	Noseworthy Robert G	50	engineer	39	
G	Glennon James J	50	printer	21	"
H	Glennon Margaret T—†	50	housewife	53	"
K	Glennon Thomas J	50	fireman	54	
L	Glennon Thomas P	50	messenger	23	"
M	Glennon William E	50	student	25	"
N	Placido Mary E—†	54	housewife	41	11 Woodside a
o	Placido Terence S	54	receiver	44	11 "
P	Coffey Jennie—†	54	housewife	60	here
R	Coffey Walter	54	watchman	65	"
s	Mason John T	54	foundryman	38	"

Lee Street

U	*Dever Fanny—†	32	housewife	62	here
v	Dever James	32	laborer	30	19 Kenney
w	Dever John A	32	"	32	here
x	Dever Margaret—†	32	operator	24	"
Y	Dever Philip	32	clerk	26	"
z	Dever Susan—†	32	inspector	20	"

1329

A	Blye John T	34	laborer	62	
B	McLaughlin Mary B—†	34	housewife	65	"
c	Dickie Ellen A—† rear	34	"	60	
D	Dickie Norman "	34	plumber	60	
E	McManus Joseph F	37	cleaner	27	
F	McManus Michael J	37	clerk	22	

Page	Letter	Full Name.	Residence, Jan. 1, 1941.	Occupation.	Supposed Age.	Reported Residence, Jan. 1, 1940. Street and Number.

Lee Street—Continued

	G	McManus Robert D	37	clerk	26	here
	H	*McManus Rose A—†	37	housewife	57	"
	K	McManus Thomas D	37	laborer	28	"
	L	McManus Mary F—†	37	operator	25	
	M	McManus Michael J	37	bartender	61	"
	N	Connolly Barbara—†	37	housewife	57	"
	O	Connolly Barbara—†	37	clerk	27	"
	P	Maloney John T	38	engineer	47	
	R	Maloney Kathleen H—†	38	housewife	42	"
	S	Maloney John	41	letter carrier	42	"
	T	Maloney Marie—†	41	housewife	30	"
	U	Packenham Daniel	42	electrician	50	"
	V	Packenham James	42	cleaner	22	

McBride Street

	Y	Barnard Alfred D	7	sorter	42	24 Cranston
	Z	Barnard Arthur C	7	retired	72	24 "
1330						
	A	Barnard Eunice—†	7	housewife	66	24 "
	B	Barnard Margaret—†	7	"	36	61 Marion
	D	Reno Elmer E	9	retired	44	here
	E	Reno Sarah M—†	9	housewife	54	"
	F	Tucker Dorothy F—†	9	maid	30	"
	G	Tucker Robert T	9	laborer	26	
	H	Harrold Agnes M—†	9	housewife	38	"
	K	Harrold Arthur W	9	longshoreman	39	"
	L	McShea Mary—†	9	housekeeper	70	"
	N	Tosi Henry J	11	laborer	34	20 Hall
	O	Tosi Irene V—†	11	housewife	30	20 "
	R	Leupold Frances—†	17	stenographer	38	here
	S	Tarpey Annie G—†	17	housekeeper	60	"
	T	Goldrick Ellen—†	22	"	65	"
	U	Goldrick Helen—†	22	clerk	30	
	V	Goldrick Hugh	22	machinist	32	"
	W	Goldrick James	22	clerk	33	
	X	Goldrick John	22	chauffeur	33	"
	Y	Goldrick Joseph	22	dairyman	24	"
	Z	Goldrick Martha—†	22	stenographer	28	"
1331						
	A	Goldrick Thomas	22	laborer	26	

McBride Street—Continued

	Letter	FULL NAME	Residence Jan. 1, 1941	Occupation	Supposed Age	Reported Residence Jan. 1, 1940
	c	Godvin James J	25	teamster	57	here
	d	Godvin Julia A—†	25	housekeeper	71	"
	e	Godvin Martin L	25	setter	65	"
	f	Godvin Mary V—†	25	housekeeper	60	"
	g	Aghjayan Malikof	27	meatcutter	46	"
	h	Dunning Delia—†	27	housewife	46	"
	k	Dunning John	27	watchman	46	"
	l	Murray Elizabeth M—†	27	housekeeper	66	"
	m	Goode Johanna M—†	29	housewife	29	"
	n	Goode Stephen A	29	shipper	30	
	o	McCormick Michael	30	machinist	46	"
	p	Murray Mary A—†	•30	housekeeper	48	"
	r	Lyons Elizabeth—†	34	housewife	59	"
	s	Lyons William A	34	stonecutter	60	"
	t	Doyle Cecelia V—†	37	collector	61	"
	u	Doyle Katherine M—†	37	housekeeper	65	"
	v	Phillips Albert E	39	chauffeur	46	"
	w	Phillips Edward L	39	metalworker	20	"
	x	Phillips Lillian C—†	39	housewife	42	"
	y	*Daley Eugene	40	longshoreman	37	"
	z	Daley Frances—†	40	housewife	38	"
		1332				
	a	Ryan Lena—†	46	cashier	21	"
	b	Ryan Margaret—†	46	housewife	46	"
	c	Ryan Mary—†	46	clerk	23	
	d	Ryan Patrick	46	foreman	47	
	e	Donavan Joseph P	46	chauffeur	42	"
	f	Donavan Julia—†	46	housewife	46	"
	g	Coffey James	46	electrician	36	"
	h	Coffey Joseph	46	bricklayer	48	"
	k	Coffey Margaret—†	46	housekeeper	71	"
	l	Coffey Margaret—†	46	operator	46	"
	m	Coffey Mary—†	46	housekeeper	49	"
	n	Murray Joseph F	47	metalworker	49	"
	o	Murray Sarah J—†	47	housewife	43	"
	p	Martin Edward	49	chauffeur	21	"
	r	Martin Henry G	49	brakeman	56	"
	s	Martin Margaret—†	49	housewife	57	"
	t	Fitzgerald Helen M—†	50	bookkeeper	32	"
	u	Fitzgerald Timothy	50	clerk	35	"
	v	Phillips Josephine A—†	54	housekeeper	68	"

Page.	Letter.	Full Name.	Residence, Jan. 1, 1941.	Occupation.	Supposed Age.	Reported Residence, Jan. 1, 1940. Street and Number.

McBride Street—Continued

w	Galvin Catherine A—†	54	furrier	70	here
x	Galvin Elizabeth A—†	54	housekeeper	63	"
y	Phillips Chester M	rear 54	laborer	28	"
z	Phillips Dorothy—†	" 54	housewife	27	"

1333

a	MacMillan James A	55	conductor	64	"
b	MacMillan Leo S	55	attendant	26	"
c	MacMillan Mary A—†	55	housewife	56	"
e	*Adams Mary—†	60	"	36	
f	Adams Roger	60	assembler	35	"
g	Campbell Agnes—†	60	housewife	28	"
h	Campbell Lawrence	60	chauffeur	29	"
l	McCann James	63	laborer	57	
m	Brennan Mary—†	63	nurse	34	
n	Kellett Mary J—†	rear 64	housewife	36	"
o	Kellett Owen	" 64	laborer	39	
p	Ruane Mary K—†	68	housewife	33	"
r	Ruane William J	68	plasterer	36	"
s	Cahalane Anna—†	68	housewife	38	"
t	Cahalane Dennis	68	repairman	40	"
u	Morrissey John P	68	laborer	30	
v	Morrissey Mary H—†	68	housewife	28	"
w	Cunningham Henry T	69	repairman	47	"
x	Doody Edward P	69	retired	78	
y	Doody Mary A—†	69	housewife	63	"
z	Doody Mary C—†	69	stenographer	35	"

1334

a	Bolton Agnes—†	71	housewife	50	"
b	Bolton Frederick	71	machinist	52	"
c	Bolton Granville	71	clerk	25	
d	Casey Bessie A—†	71	housekeeper	77	"
e	McKinnon Hannah—†	74	housewife	75	"
f	McKinnon Thomas S	74	retired	70	
g	Fox Thomas	75	laborer	50	
h	Fennessy Isabelle—†	76	housewife	34	"
k	Fennessy William	76	bracer	35	
l	Cunniff Annie—†	79	housewife	52	"
m	Cunniff Esther A—†	79	nurse	22	
n	Cunniff John	79	laborer	29	
o	Cunniff John J	79	"	54	
p	Cunniff Marguerite—†	79	clerk	26	

McBride Street—Continued

R	Hamilton Gertrude J—†	80	housewife	24	116 Chestnut av
s	Hamilton John W	80	sorter	25	116 "
T	Festa May—†	80	beautician	37	88 Hemman
U	Karas Peter	80	cleaner	50	23 Granfieldav
v	Dockray Rose A—†	82	housewife	70	here
w	Dockray Thomas F	82	retired	72	"
x	Caulfield John T	82	chauffeur	44	Brookline
Y	Caulfield Rose A—†	82	housewife	48	27 Robinwood av
z	Nolke Dorothy S—†	82	saleswoman	23	27 "

1335

A	Flynn Mary E—†	85	housewife	28	here
B	Flynn Patrick C	85	chauffeur	32	"
c	*Wencus Anna—†	85	housewife	44	"
D	Wenens Helen S—†	85	clerk	22	"
E	Weneus Joseph J	85	machinist	24	"
F	*Wencus Joseph W	85	longshoreman	52	"
G	Connolly Margaret–† rear	85	housekeeper	82	"
H	Coleman John J "	85	salesman	39	"
K	Coleman Patrick F "	85	laborer	69	"
L	Lant Dorothy—† "	87	housewife	31	"
M	Lant Weston F "	87	engineer	34	
N	Strong William T	88	carpenter	63	"
o	Smith George	89	clerk	28	
P	Smith Henry	89	U S A	28	
R	Smith Hjalmar	89	retired	68	
s	Smith Matilda—†	89	housewife	63	"
T	Boyd Edward A	92	salesman	26	"
U	Boyd Ina—†	92	housewife	24	"
v	Lehrer Anna M—†	92	"	35	"
w	Lehrer William R	92	engineer	44	"
x	Lawlor Alice L—†	95–97	housewife	46	"
Y	Lawlor Henry J	95–97	constable	60	"
z	Lawlor John F	95–97	fireman	59	

1336

A	Sizer Anna G—†	95–97	maid	50	
B	Kyle Helena—†	96	housekeeper	54	"
c	Walsh Julia—†	96	fitter	55	"
E	Hammill Margaret–†	107–109	housekeeper	75	"
F	McConville Mary C-†107–109		clerk	22	"
G	Owen Margaret—†	107–109	maid	41	
H	Barbour Charles	110	shipper	24	

22

Page.	Letter.	FULL NAME.	Residence, Jan. 1, 1941.	Occupation.	Supposed Age.	Reported Residence, Jan. 1, 1940. Street and Number.

McBride Street—Continued

	K	Barbour Elizabeth—†	110	housewife	62	here
	L	Barbour John	110	student	26	"
	M	Barbour Robert	110	painter	67	"
	N	Barbour Ruth—†	110	clerk	24	
	o	Barbour Woodrow	110	"	22	
	P*	Carson Allan	116	plasterer	38	"
	R	Carson Delia—†	116	housewife	33	"
	s	Keough Mary—†	116	"	42	
	T	Keough Patrick F	116	chauffeur	39	"
	u	Howard Mary—†	116	housekeeper	68	"
	v	Howard Robert	116	laborer	36	"
	w	Walsh David I	117	clerk	22	
	x	Walsh Joseph. F	117	"	28	
	y	Walsh Katherine L—†	117	"	39	
	z	Walsh Mary G—†	117	secretary	34	"
1337						
	A	Boughter Catherine—†	120	housewife	31	"
	B	Boughter Edward	120	chauffeur	33	"
	c	Sayers Edward A	120	laborer	34	
	D	Sayers Mary—†	120	housewife	33	"
	E	Falconette Susan—†	123	laundress	37	133 Call

Rosemary Street

	F	Norton Catherine F—†	8	housewife	39	here
	G	Norton John F	8	inspector	50	"
	H	Anderson Harry	8	bellhop	35	"
	K	Anderson Isabelle—†	8	housewife	36	"
	L	Anderson Nora—†	8	at home	71	
	M	Dolan William T	8	retired	71	
	N	Gibbons Mary F—†	8	housewife	70	"
	o	Gibbons Richard	8	retired	70	
	P	Shea Dorothy J—†	8	housewife	31	"
	R	Shea Michael J	8	policeman	30	"
	s	Mahony Dennis	8	metalworker	47	"
	T	Mahony Ellen—†		housewife	43	"
	u	Johnston Helen G—†		at home	65	
	v	Johnston Thomas F	8	photographer	35	"
	w	Barrett Nora L—†	12	housewife	58	"
	x	Barrett Thomas	12	retired	55	
	y	Fahey Mary—†	12	at home	65	"

Page.	Letter.	FULL NAME.	Residence, Jan. 1, 1941.	Occupation.	Supposed Age.	Reported Residence, Jan. 1, 1940. Street and Number.

Rosemary Street—Continued

z	*Leonard Delia—†	12	housekeeper	68	here
	1338				
A	MacAdam Mary A—†	12	at home	67	
B	Murch Gertrude—†	12	"	51	
C	Lyons Anna M—†	12	"	56	
D	Lyons Mary A—†	12	secretary	26	"
E	Lyons Thomas M	12	clerk	21	
F	Hughes Thomas	16	retired	78	
G	Sullivan Edward	16	chauffeur	21	"
H	Sullivan John J	16	clerk	25	
K	Sullivan Margaret—†	16	housewife	45	"
L	Sullivan Patrick J	16	boilermaker	47	"
M	McCarthy John J	16A	guard	50	
N	McCarthy Mary—†	16A	housewife	47	"
O	Keady John P	16A	chauffeur	55	22 Spaulding
P	Keady Martha J—†	16A	housewife	45	22 "
R	McDonough Catherine H—†	20	teacher	33	here
S	McDonough Frank B	20	operator	69	"
T	McDonough Joseph B	20	accountant	24	"
U	McDonough Nora A—†	20	housewife	64	"
V	Dolan James A	20	counterman	34	"
W	Dolan John J	20	clerk	32	
X	Dolan Michael E	20	merchant	74	"
Y	Dolan Nellie—†	20	housewife	66	"
Z	O'Leary Dorothy M—†	20	stenographer	23	"
	1339				
A	O'Leary John J	20	cooper	61	
B	O'Leary Margaret E—†	20	stenographer	24	"
C	O'Leary Mary B—†	20	housewife	54	"
D	Costello Jennie A—†	22	"	41	
E	Costello John J	22	operator	42	"
F	*Mitchell Delia M—†	22	housewife	34	"
G	Mitchell John J	22	laborer	44	
H	Hudson Edward R	22	B F D	40	
K	Hudson Harriet—†	22	housewife	41	"
L	Coleman Anna M—†	26	"	39	
M	Coleman Martin J	26	policeman	44	"
N	Gillen Joseph	26	timekeeper	26	6 St Marks rd
O	Ryder Esther J—†	26	saleswoman	21	here
P	Ryder Mary T—†	26	at home	47	"
R	Hennessey James	26	laborer	62	"

24

Rosemary Street—Continued

s	Smith Florence—†	26	egg candler	24	here
t	Smith May—†	26	at home	50	"
u	Smith Virginia—†	26	operator	23	"

South Street

x	Millett Clara—†	rear 110	housekeeper	76	16 Akron
y	Millett Matilda—†	" 110	at home	64	16 "
z	Crane Alice—†	112	saleswoman	26	here
	1340				
c	Alvarez Anna—†	120	housewife	36	"
d	Alvarez Ralph W	120	chauffeur	42	"
e	Balmforth Harry	120	cook	55	
f	Killion John J	120	merchant	39	"
g	Killion Ruth G—†	120	housewife	33	"
	1341				
c	Norton Josephine A—†	150	"	21	
d	Norton Lawrence H, jr	150	clerk	23	
e	Downing Charles D	150	waiter	23	
f	Downing Delia E—†	150	housewife	52	"
g	Downing John T	150	chauffeur	24	"
h	Kaine Agnes M—†	150	stenographer	29	"
k	Korman Frank A	150	clerk	41	"
l	Korman Ignatius F	150	salesman	49	"
m	Korman Rose M—†	150	saleswoman	36	"
n	Korman Rose V—†	150	housewife	73	"
p	Woodard Vernard C	156	clerk	33	76 Mt Hope
r	Woodard Victoria A—†	156	housewife	31	here
s	Coyne Mary A—†	156	"	68	"
t	Coyne Thomas	156	retired	59	"
u	O'Donnell Gerald R	156	welder	39	"
v	*Singer Annie—†	156	housewife	34	51 Seaverns av
w	*Singer Thomas	156	painter	33	51 "
x	Pappas Eugenia—†	156A	housewife	36	Wakefield
y	Pappas Steve	156A	merchant	52	"
z	McGarry Doris—†	156A	housewife	26	564 Centre
	1342				
a	McGarry Francis	156A	salesman	33	564 "
b	Flynn Catherine A—†	156A	housewife	69	here
c	Flynn Margaret R—†	156A	clerk	33	"
d	Flynn Mary A—†	156A	operator	40	"

Page.	Letter.	FULL NAME.	Residence, Jan. 1, 1941.	Occupation.	Supposed Age.	Reported Residence, Jan. 1, 1940. Street and Number.

South Street—Continued

E	Caulfield Catherine J—†	156A	housewife	40	here
F	Caulfield Patrick	156A	laborer	46	"
H	Carter Henry W	156A	operator	56	"
K	Carter Mary E—†	156A	housewife	53	"
L	Perrault Elmer E	158	retired	67	"
M	Perrault Lucille G—†	158	clerk	28	"
N	Perrault Lucy C—†	158	housewife	64	"
O	Jackley Mary—†	158	"	45	59 Tower
P	Jackley Mary T—†	158	clerk	20	here
R	Jackley Theodore	158	operator	47	59 Tower
S	Grady Marie E—†	158	housewife	60	here
T	Grady Peter F	158	clerk	60	"
U	Havey Catherine V—†	158	housekeeper	40	"
V	Havey Joseph	158	clerk	42	..
W	Hynes Margaret H—†	158	shoeworker	40	"
X	Hynes Michael	158	watchman	71	"
Y	Dillon Helen M—†	158	saleswoman	40	"
Z	Dillon James H	158	retired	67	

1343

A	Dillon Mary T—†	158	housewife	66	"
B	Gray Etta C—†	158	housekeeper	38	"
C	Gray Hugh	158	retired	71	..
	Walker Leonard	158	operator	52	

Williams Street

E	Tierney Catherine T—†	3	housewife	60	here
F	Tierney Frances M—†	3	waitress	24	"
G	Tierney Gertrude V—†	3	saleswoman	22	"
H	Tierney Timothy F	3	laborer	62	
K	Lyon Edward	3	"	45	
L	Lyon John	3	milkman	30	"
M	Lyon Rita—†	3	housewife	26	"
N	Madden Dennis R	5	laborer	24	
O	Madden Helen L—†	5	saleswoman	40	"
P	Madden James R	5	chemist	33	
R	Madden Johanna M—†	5	housewife	67	"
S	Madden John J	5	plumber	68	
T	Madden Thomas E	5	salesman	22	"
U	Madden William M	5	laborer	28	

1

Ward 11—Precinct 14

CITY OF BOSTON

LIST OF RESIDENTS
20 YEARS OF AGE AND OVER

(NON-CITIZENS INDICATED BY ASTERISK)
(FEMALES INDICATED BY DAGGER)

AS OF

JANUARY 1, 1941

JOSEPH F. TIMILTY, *Chairman*
FREDERIC E. DOWLING, *Secretary*
WILLIAM A. MOTLEY, JR.
FRANCIS B. McKINNEY
HILDA HEDSTROM QUIRK

Listing Board.

CITY OF BOSTON PRINTING DEPARTMENT

1400

Brookley Road

A	Reiser Irene—†	2	housewife	25	here
B	Reiser Joseph	2	chauffeur	35	"
C	Reiser Mary—†	2	housewife	62	"
D	Connolly Hugh	2	painter	49	
E	Connolly Lillian—†	2	housewife	51	"
F	Connolly Lily—†	2	clerk	20	
H	O'Donnell Bella—†	4	housewife	68	"
K	O'Donnell William	4	retired	80	"
L	*Kurlauskis Annie—†	41	housewife	55	402 E Seventh
M	Kurlauskis Annie—†	41	waitress	22	402 "
N	*Kurlauskis Anthony	41	laborer	57	402 "
O	Spillane Mary—†	41	housewife	39	here
P	*Spillane Thomas	41	laborer	36	"
R	Lopez Carmen—†	41	housewife	53	"
S	Lopez Celia—†	41	"	23	
T	Lopez Henry	41	cook	21	
U	Coleman Mary—†	42	housewife	39	"
V	Coleman Peter	42	laborer	36	
W	Hogan Emily—†	42	housewife	36	"
X	Hogan William	42	laborer	37	
Y	Vogel Charles	42	chauffeur	20	"
Z	Vogel Louis A	42	"	56	

1401

A	Vogel Pauline G—†	42	attendant	23	"
B	Vogel Ruth F—†	42	housewife	30	"
C	Vogel Sarah F—†	42	"	58	
D	Vogel William F	42	manager	24	"
E	Shaw Elmer A	46	salesman	27	Watertown
F	Shaw Margaret—†	46	housewife	27	"
H	Damato Anthony	46	manufacturer	20	41 Brookley r
K	Damato James	46	chauffeur	53	41 "
L	*Damato Margaret—†	46	housewife	49	41 "
M	Damato Mary—†	46	housekeeper	22	41 "
O	West Florence—†	48	housewife	36	here
P	West Herbert	48	machinist	34	"
R	McBride Mary—†	50	housewife	42	"
S	McBride Michael	50	chauffeur	42	"
T	Burgess John A	50	"	51	30 Kenton r
U	Burgess Mabel G—†	50	waitress	42	30 "
V	Wilkinson Annie—†	50	housewife	61	here

Brookley Road—Continued

w	Wilkinson Arthur	50	clerk	32	here
x	Wilkinson Robert	50	U S A	26	"
y	Wilkinson William	50	clerk	33	"
z	Glennon John	52	repairman	36	"
	1402				
A	Glennon Mary—†	52	housewife	36	"
B	Mulry Annie—†	52	"	50	
c	Mulry John T	52	chauffeur	51	"
D	Talanian Keham K	52	meatcutter	33	"
E	Talanian Mary C—†	52	housewife	29	"
F	DeCourcy Julia—†	55	"	40	
G	DeCourcy Thomas	55	laborer	40	
H	Kruse Eileen—†	55	housewife	30	"
K	Kruse Stephen	55	machinist	30	"
L	VanStry Katherine—†	55	housewife	32	"
M	VanStry Leonard	55	clerk	31	"
N	Stanton Helen R—†	55	housewife	25	"
o	Stanton James L	55	painter	29	
P	Koenig Bridget—†	55	housewife	27	"
R	Koenig Robert	55	merchant	27	"
s	Bury Fred	55	operator	28	204 Lamartine
T	Bury Grace—†	55	housewife	28	204 "
U	Mankiewicz Anna—†	59–61	"	49	here
v	Mankiewicz Edward	59–61	shipper	23	"
w	Mankiewicz William	59–61	mechanic	50	"
x	Calnan Mary M—†	59–61	housekeeper	60	New York
Y	Dooley Alice A—†	59–61	housewife	24	Cambridge
z	Dooley Andrew J, jr	59–61	cashier	23	"
	1403				
A	Moynihan Daniel	59–61	policeman	27	here
B	Moynihan Lila—†	59–61	housewife	27	"
c	Morse Italia F—†	62–64	"	26	"
D	Morse William S	62–64	laborer	31	"
E	Irvine George	62–64	mechanic	40	"
F	Irvine Lillian—†	62–64	housewife	39	"
G	O'Connell Helen—†	62–64	"	34	
H	O'Connell John J	62–64	mechanic	34	"
K	Murphy Margaret—†	63–65	housewife	41	"
L	Murphy Miles V	63–65	fireman	45	
M	Oldfield Mary E—†	63–65	housewife	62	"
N	Oldfield Mary E—†	63–65	operator	26	

Brookley Road—Continued

o	Oldfield Nellie—†	63–65	clerk	24	here
p	Oldfield William	63–65	machinist	62	"
r	Miller Henry	63–65	"	35	183 Sydney
s	Miller Minerva—†	63–65	housewife	36	183 "
t	Stewart Falba—†	67–69	"	41	here
u	Stewart Frank E	67–69	foreman	48	"
v	Broderick Anna—†	67–69	housewife	39	"
w	Broderick Patrick	67–69	waiter	39	
x	Boates Mary A—†	67–69	operator	31	
y	Boates Mary T—†	67–69	housewife	73	"
z	Oberlander Mildred A—†	67–69	"	33	

1404

a	Oberlander Milton E	67–69	chauffeur	36	"
b	Rehill Edward W	71–73	letter carrier	39	"
c	Rehill Margaret M—†	71–73	housewife	39	"
d	Turner John R	71–73	pharmacist	34	295 Lamarti
e	Turner Rose M—†	71–73	housewife	44	295 "
f	Clifford James T	71–73	retired	52	here
g	Lundgren Anne L—†	71–73	housewife	25	"
h	Lundgren Everett	71–73	serviceman	29	"
k	Powers Margaret M–†	76–78	housewife	45	"
l	Powers William H	76–78	clerk	47	
m	Hoban Joseph A	76–78	steamfitter	44	"
n	Kerr Catherine—†	76–78	housewife	40	"
o	Kerr Thomas J	76–78	steamfitter	42	"
p	Brock Karl H	76–78	electrician	51	Brookline
r	Gastonguay Marie A–†	76–78	milliner	42	"
s	Shannon Anne A—†	79–81	housewife	28	4073 Wash'i
t	Shannon Hugh J	79–81	clerk	33	4073 "
u	Galvin Mary—†	79–81	housewife	31	11 Fessende
v	Galvin Maurice	79–81	machinist	31	11 "
w	Russell Eleanor—†	79–81	housewife	22	Newton
x	Russell William	79–81	mechanic	27	30 Elmwoo
y	Creedon Daniel J	80–82	restaurateur	33	here
z	Creedon Genevieve—†	80–82	housewife	33	"

1405

a	Webster Catherine—†	80–82	"	49	
b	Webster William E	80–82	clerk	43	"
c	Burke John	80–82	teacher	27	
d	Burke Rose—†	80–82	housewife	65	"
e	Devlin George	84–86	watchman	54	"

Brookley Road—Continued

F	Devlin Nora—†	84–86	housewife	43	here
G	Cahill James E	84–86	salesman	25	Brookline
H	Cahill Madeline V—†	84–86	housewife	27	"
K	Alther Margaret L—†	84–86	"	32	105 Regent
L	Alther Robert J	84–86	fireman	35	82 "
M	Fox Catherine—†	92–94	housewife	29	here
N	Fox Michael J	92–94	carpenter	36	"
O	Kelly Anne M—†	92–94	housewife	27	109 Rossmore rd
P	Kelly Patrick	92–94	engineer	36	109 "
R	Garabedian Betty—†	92–94	housewife	35	here
S	Garabedian Giragos	92–94	artist	40	"
T	Conway Helen—†	96–98	housewife	42	"
U	Conway John L	96–98	mechanic	42	"
V	Wilson William F	96–98	clerk	31	
W	Curtin Rose J—†	96–98	housewife	37	"
X	Curtin William L	96–98	salesman	42	
Y	Hayes Agnes—†	96–98	housewife	24	"
Z	Hayes Chester F	96–98	salesman	26	"

1406   Burnett Street

A	Dean Annie L—†	8	housewife	65	here
B	Dean Edward	8	laborer	27	"
C	Dean Ruth—†	8	at home	21	"
D	McDonough Bessie—†	8	housewife	38	"
E	McDonough Martin J	8	porter	39	
F	Brown Ethel M—†	8	housewife	39	"
G	McDonnell Mary—†	10	domestic	37	
H	McNulty Francis J	10	chauffeur	38	"
K	McNulty James P	10	machinist	35	"
L	McNulty Mary—†	10	at home	70	"
M	Devine Eleanor—†	10	housewife	20	177 Milton
N	Devine William	10	repairman	20	177 "
O	LaBonte Helen—†	10	housewife	47	here
P	LaBonte Paris	10	chauffeur	42	"
R	Prendergast Chester	10	laborer	29	"
S	Webster Frederick	10	"	49	..
T	Masters Helen—†	14	housewife	30	"
U	Masters John	14	laborer	31	"
W	Jordan Charles	18	"	34	24 Fawndale rd
X	Jordan Ruth—†	18	housewife	30	24 "

Burnett Street—Continued

Y	Jay Allan J	18	painter	28	35 Boynton
z	Jay Mary A—†	18	housewife	29	35 "
	1407				
A	*Rodenhizer Edward	18	mechanic	48	here
B	Rodenhizer Geraldine—†	18	housewife	31	"
c	McGeown Catherine—†	20	"	29	20 Mansur
D	McGeown Philip	20	coppersmith	30	20 "
E	Downey Lena—†	20	at home	58	180 Heath
F	Fitzgerald Gertrude—†	20	housewife	28	180 "
G	Fitzgerald James E	20	chauffeur	30	180 "
H	Young Elizabeth A—†	20	housewife	58	here
K	Young William P	20	operator	62	"
L	Dowd John W	32	"	29	26 Union av
M	Dowd Mary T—†	32	housewife	28	26 "
N	Cook Louis J	32	laborer	33	here
O	Cook Mary A—†	32	housewife	33	"
P	Pike Albert J	32	salesman	43	17 Spalding
R	Pike Margaret—†	32	housewife	43	17 "
S	Hutchinson Clayton	34	mechanic	36	here
T	Hutchinson Emma G—†	34	housewife	35	"
U	Hoyt Laura L—†	34	at home	55	1 Crosby sq
V	Franke Lilla—†	34	housewife	48	128 Heath
W	Franke Otto	34	engineer	56	128 "
X	*MacDonald Gladys M—†	36	housewife	32	here
Y	MacDonald John M	36	laborer	38	"
z	*Connors Mary—†	36	housewife	70	"
	1408				
A	*Connors Thomas J	36	laborer	56	
B	Kelly Patrick	36	"	38	
c	Rennie Jeanne—†	36	housewife	46	"
D	Rennie William	36	machinist	44	"
E	Noll Elmer B	38	clerk	30	
F	Noll Rita F—†	38	housewife	25	"
G	Embree Boyd	38	milkman	34	"
H	*Embree Maudena—†	38	housewife	26	"
K	Sholes Anne—†	42	"	22	4294 Wash'
L	Sholes Marie M—†	42	stenographer	24	here
M	Sholes Rosalie—†	42	at home	48	"
N	Sholes Warren J	42	inspector	25	84 Tower
O	Mandeville Caroline J—†	44	housewife	35	here
P	Mandeville Edward R	44	chauffeur	37	"

Burnett Street—Continued

R	Mandeville Mary A—†	44	at home	74	here
S	Mandeville William J	44	laborer	39	"
T	Tyler Bertha M—†	50	housewife	72	"
U	Tyler Ezra A	50	retired	68	"
V	Bean Frank	51–51A	machinist	41	N Hampshire
W	Bean Lura—†	51–51A	housewife	40	"
X	Moloney Ida—†	51–51A	"	30	here
Y	Moloney Raphael J	51–51A	plumber	39	"
Z	Peterson Beatrice M—†	55	housewife	47	"

1409

A	Peterson Charles L	55	plumber	61	
B	Peterson Charles L, jr	55	shipper	23	
C	Peterson Virginia A—†	55	clerk	25	"
D	Callahan John J	56	retired	70	814 Parker
E	O'Brien Annie—†	56	at home	63	here
F	O'Brien Catherine—†	56	housewife	30	814 Parker
G	O'Brien Francis	56	assembler	20	here
H	O'Brien John H	56	shoemaker	28	"
K	Lundsgaard Borghild—†	57	housewife	54	"
L	Lundsgaard Emil	57	operator	59	
M	Lundsgaard John	57	instructor	31	"
N *Vandersnoek Aberdiena—†	58–60	housewife	57	"
O	Vandersnoek Cornelius	58–60	gardener	54	"
P	Martin Henry, jr	58–60	repairman	33	New York
R	Martin Mary—†	58–60	housewife	24	"
S	Silva Anthony J	58–60	retired	69	here
T	Silva Theresa D—†	58–60	at home	69	"
V	Fandel Catherine M—†	59	secretary	30	"
W	Fandel Louisa—†	59	at home	73	
X	Cook Frances E—†	61	housewife	28	"
Y	Cook Russell	61	machinist	30	25 Leland
Z	Eaton William T	61	"	70	here

1410

A	Peterson Margaret F—†	61	housekeeper	71	"
B	McArthur Daniel	61A	retired	62	44 Johnson
C	Middleton Harold J	61A	welder	22	here
D	Rath Rose A—†	61A	housekeeper	47	"
E	Hathaway Dorothy—†	62	housewife	25	Dedham
F	Hathaway Francis	62	laborer	29	"
G	Hill George	62	clerk	51	"
H	Priesing Edwin T	62	"	39	here

Page.	Letter.	Full Name.	Residence, Jan. 1, 1941.	Occupation.	Supposed Age.	Reported Residence, Jan. 1, 1940. Street and Number.

Burnett Street—Continued

K	Schiff Mary—†	62	at home	34	here
L	*Johnson Anna—†	62	"	34	"
M	Johnson Paul M	62	painter	34	"
O	Burke Loretta—†	65	operator	29	
P	Burke Mary—†	65	housewife	60	"
R	Burke Ellen—†	65	"	32	
S	Burke John	65	operator	32	..

Forest Hills Street

U	Pratt George O	269	physician	30	Maine
V	Pratt Gertrude—†	269	housewife	31	"
W	Eells James	269	salesman	40	11 Rocky Nook ter
X	Eells Marion—†	269	saleswoman	36	11 "
Y	*Cemoch Benjamin	269	merchant	38	New York
Z	*Cemoch Sara—†	269	housewife	35	"
	1411				
A	Farrell Evelyn—†	269	clerk	23	Hull
B	Farrell Mary—†	269	housewife	50	"
C	Farrell Michael	269	chauffeur	56	"
D	Keller George	269	proprietor	32	22 Crowell
E	Keller Rose—†	269	housewife	27	68 Capen
F	Regan Mabel E—†	269	proprietor	40	here
G	Haskins Benjamin M	277	operator	48	24 Bournedale rd
H	Saunders Jessie—†	277	housekeeper	41	24 "
K	Duffy Anna—†	277	bookkeeper	22	here
L	Duffy Catherine M—†	277	stitcher	31	"
M	Duffy Lawrence J	277	operator	25	"
N	McCollum Annie—†	277	housewife	54	"
O	*McCollum Otis L	277	chauffeur	69	"
P	Riley Mary F—†	277	at home	61	48 Walden
R	Byrd John H	277	proofreader	40	here
S	Byrd Sadie J—†	277	housewife	40	"
T	Brooks Gussie—†	281	"	38	80 Rossmore rd
U	Brooks John J	281	chauffeur	44	80 "
V	*Gibran Mary K—†	281	at home	55	here
W	Parent Amelia D—†	281	housewife	47	"
X	Parent Irene—†	281	waitress	37	"
Y	Parent Victor R	281	policeman	48	"
Z	Kelley Anne M—†	285–287	housewife	37	"

8

1412
Forest Hills Street—Continued

A	Glenn Adeline E—†	285–287	housewife	45	101 Rossmore rd
B	Glenn Albert E	285–287	laborer	49	101 "
C	Vaughan Michael D	285–287	carpenter	42	here
D	Vaughan Nellie—†	285–287	housewife	38	"
E	Donovan John J	289	clerk	25	15 Buswell
F	Donovan Kathleen C—†	289	housewife	25	15 "
G	Peterman Emily D—†	289	"	49	here
H	Peterman John H	289	accountant	50	"
K	Merrill Grace L—†	289	nurse	59	"
L	Merrill Katherine—†	289	housewife	23	22 Union ter
M	Merrill Sumner	289	artist	33	here
N	Weeks Annie E—†	289	at home	79	"
O	Petersen Adeline—†	295	"	82	"
P	Petersen Martin	295	machinist	45	"
R	*Terkelsen Sofie—†	295	at home	77	
S	Jayer Edward	295	electrician	32	"
T	Jayer Ethel—†	295	clerk	31	"
U	*Kelliher Nora A—†	295	housewife	56	"
V	Kelliher William	295	chauffeur	64	"
W	McCarrick Margaret—†	297	housewife	36	"
X	McCarrick Thomas	297	letter carrier	41	"
Y	Smith Elsie—†	299	nurse	30	110 Call
Z	*Smith Leslie	299	carpenter	30	110 "

1413

A	*Smith Ralph	299	"	32	110 "
B	Fernandes Dorothy—†	299	stenographer	28	here
C	Fernandes Evelyn—†	299	saleswoman	23	"
D	*Fernandes Virginia—†	299	housewife	59	"
E	Dalton Frederick	301–303	laborer	28	"
F	Dalton Josephine—†	301–303	at home	70	
G	Dalton Margaret—†	301–303	stenographer	30	"
H	Hurley Mary—†	301–303	housewife	36	"
K	Hurley Michael	301–303	laborer	41	
L	Russo Antonio	301–303	"	28	
M	Russo Cosimo D	301–303	U S A	24	
O	Russo Marie C—†	301–303	clerk	30	
N	Russo Mary G—†	301–303	housewife	56	"
P	Russo Natalie—†	301–303	clerk	29	
R	Russo Philomena—†	301–303	stenographer	22	"
S	Lutz Beatrice A—†	307	housewife	47	"

Forest Hills Street—Continued

t	Lutz Walter J	307	policeman	45	here
u	Gilday Edward	307	laborer	21	"
v	Gilday Frank H	307	foreman	55	"
w	Gilday Lucy A—†	307	housewife	55	"
x	Tyo Agnes G—†	307	"	55	
y	Tyo Doris M—†	307	at home	27	
z	Tyo John A	307	carpenter	62	"
	1414					
a	Tyo Leo B	307	clerk	22	
b	Fleming John J	311–313	foreman	38	"
c	Fleming Sarah—†	311–313	housewife	36	"
d	*Cummings Anna V—†	311–313	"	32	
e	Cummings Paul J	311–313	clerk	35	
f	Campbell Bessie M—†	311–313	housewife	43	"
g	Campbell Charles J	311–313	operator	44	"
h	Campbell Charles J	311–313	U S A	21	
k	Harrington Helen—†	315	housewife	37	"
l	Harrington James	315	shipper	47	
m	Harrington Thomas	315	painter	38	
n	Tivnan Martin F	315	manager	48	"
o	Tivnan Mary A—†	315	student	20	
p	Tivnan Winifred M—†	315	housewife	51	"
r	Walsh Eleanor—†	315	"	39	
s	Walsh Thomas W	315	mechanic	41	"
t	Hickey Catherine—†	319	housewife	37	"
u	Hickey Thomas H	319	policeman	43	"
v	*Sullivan Margaret—†	319	housewife	73	7 Bailey
w	Sullivan Mary E—†	319	"	34	Weymouth
x	Sullivan Timothy J	319	policeman	43	7 Bailey
y	Daley Catherine—†	319	housewife	26	28 Pleasant
z	Daley John	319	electrician	27	28 "

1415   Gartland Street

a	Dewey Arthur L	5–7	chauffeur	40	here
b	Dewey Margaret—†	5–7	housewife	36	"
c	Coulman Dorothy C—†	5–7	"	28	"
d	Coulman Frederick E	5–7	chauffeur	34	"
e	Foster Eileen T—†	5–7	housewife	26	"
f	Foster Joseph E	5–7	proprietor	27	"

Gartland Street—Continued

G	Strassel Anna C—†	8	housekeeper	41	here
H	Andriassi Joseph	8	operator	38	"
K	*Andriassi Rose—†	8	housewife	35	"
L	Giangrande Carmello	8	contractor	43	"
M	Giangrande Mary S—†	8	housewife	49	"
N	Gatturna Frances V—†	9–11	"	49	
O	Gatturna John H	9–11	cutter	52	
P	Casale Anthony B	9–11	machinist	50	"
R	Casale Catherine F—†	9–11	clerk	22	
S	Casale Josephine J—†	9–11	housewife	43	"
T	Mahood Elizabeth M—†	9–11	"	26	
U	Mahood William J	9–11	guard	32	
V	Donnelly Barney F	10	attendant	43	"
W	Donnelly Nellie M—†	10	housewife	38	"
X	DiRado Angelo	12	laborer	46	New York
Y	*Pace Mary—†	12	housewife	56	here
Z	Pace Thomas J	12	laborer	24	"

1416

A	McMasters Neil B	14	superintendent	39	69 Montebello rd
B	McMasters Theresa L—†	14	housewife	36	69 "
C	Bingham Harry S	14	carpenter	67	here
D	*Bingham Julia—†	14	housewife	54	"
E	Lemont Alexander	14	baker	58	"
F	Lemont Mary—†	14	housewife	52	"
G	Irbine Ruth B—†	17	"	34	
H	Irbine Thomas L	17	chauffeur	32	"
K	Haddock Christina M—†	17	housewife	35	"
L	Haddock Leroy G	17	supervisor	42	"
M	Fatersek Anna—†	17	housewife	49	8 Danville
N	*Fatersek Dora—†	17	at home	81	8 "
O	Fatersek John R	17	teacher	26	8 "
P	Fatersek Joseph S	17	laborer	59	8 '
R	Fatersek Mary A—†	17	bookkeeper	29	8 "
S	Hurley John E	20	retired	75	here
T	Hurley Nora A—†	20	at home	84	"
U	Morrissey Emily C—†	20	housekeeper	47	"
V	Elliot Alexander	21	retired	72	
W	Getz Henry J	21	welder	44	
X	Getz Sallie E—†	21	cashier	41	"
Y	Ferreira Anna J—†	21	housewife	49	9 Woodside av
Z	Ferreira George E	21	clerk	49	9 "

11

1417
Gartland Street—Continued

A	Lovett Frederick J	21	attendant	56	here
B	Lovett Frederick J, jr	21	U S N	20	"
C	Lovett Mary A—†	21	operator	26	"
D	Lovett Sarah A—†	21	housewife	54	"
E	*Duck Dorothy A—†	25	"	30	Weymouth
F	Duck Frank J	25	guard	44	"
G	Smith Lillian I—†	25	housewife	55	here
H	Smith William W	25	retired	67	"
K	*Kalenderian Agavni—†	25	housewife	50	15 Oneida
L	Kalenderian Bert	25	printer	30	15 "
M	*Kalenderian Gerard	25	jeweler	32	15 "
N	*Kalenderian Ossanna—†	25	printer	24	15 "
O	Donaldson Catherine M—†	27–29	housewife	45	here
P	Donaldson James J	27–29	pipefitter	47	"
R	O'Neill Edward W	27–29	laborer	22	85 Savin Hill av
S	O'Neill Mary A—†	27–29	housewife	49	85 "
T	O'Neill Mary G—†	27–29	clerk	24	85 "
U	Horgan Catherine M-†	27–29	housewife	53	here
V	Horgan Joseph	27–29	carpenter	65	"
W	Bishop Alice V—†	32	housewife	32	"
X	Bishop Arthur J	32	clerk	32	
Y	Tomasello Natalie A—†	32	housewife	27	"
Z	Tomasello Ross	32	clerk	30	

1418

A	D'Agostino Antoinette—†	32	housewife	30	"
B	*D'Agostino Frank	32	barber	36	162 South
C	Pagano Antonio	32	"	62	here
D	Pagano Augustine—†	32	"	34	"
E	Pagano Mary—†	32	housewife	54	"
F	Quinn Catherine M—†	33	"	70	
G	Quinn Cecelia A—†	33	stenographer	32	"
H	Quinn Michael P	33	retired	65	
K	Curry Gladys P—†	33	housewife	39	"
L	Curry John P	33	embalmer	38	"
M	Butler Louise T—†	33	housewife	28	Revere
N	Butler Patrick	33	bartender	33	107 Appleton
O	Kelly Joseph	35–37	mechanic	39	here
P	*Kelly Margaret—†	35–37	housewife	36	"
R	Murray Ethel C—†	35–37	collector	20	47 Millwood
S	Murray Nora E—†	35–37	housewife	55	47 "

Page	Letter	Full Name	Residence, Jan. 1, 1941.	Occupation.	Supposed Age.	Reported Residence, Jan. 1, 1940. Street and Number.

Gartland Street—Continued

	T	Murray Ruth C—†	35–37	cashier	22	47 Millwood
	U	Bond Charles H	35–37	packer	23	here
	V	Bond Charles L	35–37	engineer	47	"
	W	Bond Elizabeth V—†	35–37	housewife	45	"
	X	Thistle Francis C	36	carpenter	44	"
	Y	Thistle Helen M—†	36	housewife	28	"
	Z	Fitzgibbons Jeremiah J	36	repairman	30	"

1419

	A	Fitzgibbons Margaret—†	36	housewife	30	"
	B	Cotter Adelle R—†	36	"	41	
	C	Cotter Jeremiah J	36	chauffeur	43	"
	D	Semple David	40	machinist	59	"
	E	Semple Elizabeth C—†	40	housewife	58	"
	F	Semple Winifred M—†	40	bookkeeper	27	"
	G	Kelly Michael J	40	houseman	51	"
	H	McCormack Dorothy E—†	40	stenographer	22	"
	K	McCormack Lillian—†	40	housewife	45	"
	L	O'Donoghue Nora R—†	40	accomodator	51	"
	M	Hilland Elizabeth—†	40	housewife	54	"
	N	Hilland Thomas J	40	machinist	58	"
	O	McCann John	40	operator	64	"
	P	*Kairis Nellie—†	43	housewife	54	8 Nira av
	R	*Kairis Peter P	43	tailor	57	8 "
	S	Siltis John	43	baker	28	8 "
	T	O'Brien Anna A—†	43	housewife	43	here
	U	O'Brien John J	43	finisher	45	"
	V	Harrold Fred P	43	clerk	38	"
	W	Harrold Margaret—†	43	housewife	36	"
	X	*Lynch Ellen G—†	44	"	37	
	Y	Lynch John A	44	laborer	39	
	Z	Sarkisian Hachig	44	machinist	55	"

1420

	A	Sarkisian Louise—†	44	housewife	43	"
	B	*Ronan Mary C—†	44	"	38	
	C	Ronan Thomas P	44	baker	37	

Kenton Road

	D	*Connolly John F	7	laborer	35	3411 Wash'n
	E	*Connolly Patricia N—†	7	housewife	29	3411 "
	F	Stevens Alice B—†	7	"	46	36 School

Kenton Road—Continued

G	Stevens Edward W	7	laborer	48	36 School
H	Mahoney Michael J	7	teamster	63	21 Anita ter
K	Mahoney Thomas J	7	laborer	29	21 "
L	Martin George H	7	milkman	25	21 "
M	Martin Margaret J—†	7	housewife	24	21 "
N	Corscadden John J	9	molder	60	here
O	Corscadden Mary F—†	9	housewife	58	"
P	Feeney Mary E—†	9	secretary	25	"
R	McDonald Eileen P—†	9	stenographer	23	"
S	Nihill Anna L—†	11	operator	34	
T	Nihill Eugene F	11	U S A	22	
U	Nihill John M	11	"	27	
V	Nihill Josephine F—†	11	housewife	57	"
W	*Carnabuce Cosmo	19	presser	38	3425 Wash'n
X	Carnabuce Nancy—†	19	housewife	30	3425 "
Y	*Cammarata Anna—†	19	"	44	here
Z	Cammarata Rocco	19	cobbler	21	"
	1421				
A	Cammarata Therese—†	19	wrapper	23	
B	Cammarata Vincent	19	candymaker	50	"
C	Walsh Elizabeth M—†	23	housewife	37	"
D	Walsh John T	23	pedler	42	"
E	*Walsh Mary—†	23	at home	63	81 Chestnut
F	McAllister Agnes—†	31	housewife	63	here
G	McAllister John	31	engineer	66	"
H	Hartnett Edith R—†	35	housewife	44	"
K	Hartnett John W	35	buffer	49	
L	Curley Alice I—†	35	stenographer	31	"
M	Curley Arthur	35	accountant	45	"
N	O'Meara Irene A—†	35	housewife	36	"
O	O'Meara Stephen H	35	policeman	44	"
P	Glennon Mary A—†	39	housewife	78	"
R	Glennon Thomas H	39	operator	70	
S	Glennon William M	39	accountant	36	"
T	Glennon William P	39	retired	76	

Lotus Street

V	*Kelly Annie M—†	19	housewife	50	here
W	Kelly Michael F	19	porter	50	"
X	Kelly Thomas	19	mechanic	28	"

Page.	Letter.	Full Name.	Residence, Jan. 1, 1941.	Occupation.	Supposed Age.	Reported Residence, Jan. 1, 1940. Street and Number.

Lotus Street—Continued

Y	Fisichella Caroline—†	19	assembler	23	here
z	Fisichella Salvatore	19	clerk	26	"

1422

A	Edstrom Rose R—†	33	housewife	24	"
B	Edstrom William F	33	chauffeur	27	"
c	*Maggioli Attillio	33	sausagemaker	44	"
D	*Maggioli Theresa—†	33	housewife	38	"
E	Pignat Antonio	33	laborer	55	
F	*Pignat Ida—†	33	housewife	44	"
G	Pignat Joseph	33	tilesetter	60	"
H	Pignat Yolanda—†	33	stenographer	20	"
K	Randon Isadore F	33	laborer	22	"
L	Randon Peter J	33	"	56	
M	Vicenzi John	33	tilesetter	56	"

Meehan Street

o	Puleo Dominic	11	carpenter	43	here
P	*Puleo Mary—†	11	housewife	41	"
R	Sciaba Anthony	11	barber	42	"
s	*Sciaba Victoria—†	11	housewife	35	"
T	*Gravina Anthony	11	barber	32	
u	Gravina Catherine—†	11	housewife	32	"
v	Trennie Carl	13	carpenter	31	"
w	Trennie Johanna—†	13	housewife	25	"
x	Uminski Henry J	13	technician	21	"
Y	Uminski John P	13	machinist	48	"
z	*Uminski Josephine—†	13	housewife	44	"

1423

A	Mirabello John	13	tailor	47	
B	*Mirabello Nancy—†	13	housewife	33	"
c	Leveroni Louise—†	15	housekeeper	60	"
D	*DeSalvatore Domenic	15	shoemaker	69	"
E	*DeSalvatore Josephine—†	15	housewife	68	"
F	DeSalvatore Louis	15	boilermaker	35	"
G	DeSalvatore Pasquale	15	retired	28	

Plainfield Street

K	Ogletree Frances—†	9	housewife	40	10 Plainfield
L	Ogletree Raymond C	9	fireman	48	10 "

15

Page.	Letter.	FULL NAME.	Residence, Jan. 1, 1941.	Occupation.	Supposed Age.	Reported Residence, Jan. 1, 1940. Street and Number.

Plainfield Street—Continued

M	*Pedersen Esther M—†	10	housewife	55	185 Green
N	Pedersen Ruth—†	10	operator	20	185 "
O	*Pedersen Thomas	10	engineer	50	185 "
P	Andrew Alma C—†	10	at home	84	here
R	Andrew Gustave E	10	laborer	51	"
S	Blanchard Fred H	10	retired	62	"
T	Blanchard Fred H, jr	10	chauffeur	42	"
U	Blanchard Margaret—†	10	housewife	42	"
V	Collins Mary—†	11	"	41	..
W	Collins Raymond L	11	laborer	34	"
X	Lynch John J	11	cashier	37	Cambridge
Y	Harkins Agnes—†	11	saleswoman	22	here
Z	Harkins Edward J	11	chauffeur	56	"
	1424				
A	Harkins Harold	11	"	24	
B	Harkins Lena M—†	11	housewife	50	"
C	Harkins Marion—†	11	clerk	21	
E	Higgins Catherine—†	19	housewife	38	"
F	Higgins Michael A	19	chauffeur	42	"
G	*Higgins Rose—†	19	at home	72	
H	Shuckrowe Margaret E—†	21	housewife	66	"
K	Shuckrowe Timothy C	21	retired	68	
L	Quinn Flora—†	21	housewife	34	"
M	Quinn Joseph M	21	laborer	36	
N	Quinn Michael	21	caretaker	65	"
O	Craven Bridget—†	21	housewife	53	6 Williams
P	Craven Malachi	21	laborer	56	6 "
S	Marino Mary—†	29	housewife	22	here
T	Marino Michael	29	chauffeur	26	80 Linden
U	Lindholm Karl	29	proprietor	45	here
V	*Lindholm Mary—†	29	housewife	45	"
W	Werner Appolina—†	29	at home	75	"
X	Werner Frances—†	29	clerk	42	
Y	Werner John C	29	accountant	40	"
Z	Matukas Frank	31	salesman	28	"
	1425				
A	Matukas Helen—†	31	housewife	25	"
B	Walsh Annie A—†	31	"	52	
C	Walsh Chester R	31	bookbinder	29	"
D	Walsh John A	31	chauffeur	54	"
E	Siblo Mildred—†	31	housewife	30	"

16

Plainfield Street—Continued

F	Siblo Robert A	31	foreman	34	here
G	*MacPherson Annie M—†	33	housewife	50	"
H	MacPherson Duncan	33	carpenter	49	"
K	Horgan Catherine A—†	33	housewife	38	"
L	Horgan James F	33	shipper	43	"
M	Murphy Elizabeth B—†	33	at home	46	
N	Magee Charles A	33	mechanic	59	"
O	Magee George A	33	laborer	24	
P	Magee Rose—†	33	housewife	52	"

Rossmore Road

R	Cody Ellen—†	2	housewife	64	here
S	Cody James	2	chauffeur	30	"
T	Stover Herbert W	2	plasterer	31	96 Lawn
U	Stover Rita J—†	2	housewife	25	here
V	Lasko Alice—†	2	"	21	"
W	Lasko Stanley	2	embosser	26	"
Y	Haberle Sophie—†	9	at home	74	
Z	O'Neil Arthur H	9	chauffeur	30	"
	1426				
A	O'Neil Helen A—†	9	housewife	28	"
B	MacLeod Alice R—†	9	operator	33	"
C	MacLeod Donald D	9	laborer	41	
D	Maisey Maude C—†	9	at home	59	
E	Dellacamera Helen—†	10	housewife	31	"
F	Dellacamera Ralph	10	chauffeur	34	"
G	Johnson Marie—†	10	at home	35	
H	Desto Joseph	10	barber	34	
K	Desto Martha—†	10	housewife	31	"
L	Kerin Anne—†	11	cashier	21	
M	Kerin Nora M—†	11	cook	52	
O	McGonagle Cecelia—†	11	housewife	45	"
P	McGonagle Edward	11	laborer	22	
R	McGonagle James	11	student	20	
S	McGonagle John	11	painter	24	
U	Bennett Florence—†	12	housewife	22	"
V	Bennett Gordon	12	auctioneer	24	"
W	Jacobson Carl	12	molder	27	
X	Jacobson Edith—†	12	housewife	26	"
Y	Busconi Mary—†	14	at home	34	

Page.	Letter.	FULL NAME.	Residence, Jan. 1, 1941.	Occupation.	Supposed Age.	Reported Residence, Jan. 1, 1940. Street and Number.

Rossmore Road—Continued

z	*Busconi Pauline—†	14	at home	56	here
	1427				
A	*Digiovine Adeline—†	14	housewife	38	"
B	Digiovine Robert	14	laborer	46	
C	Copponi Anthony	16	operator	30	"
D	Copponi Phoebe—†	16	housewife	29	"
E	Copponi John	16	laundryman	31	"
F	Copponi Joseph	16	laborer	33	
G	Copponi Luigi	16	"	64	
H	*Copponi Virginia—†	16	housewife	64	"
K	DeAngelis Edith—†	16	operator	21	"
L	*DeAngelis Mary—†	16	housewife	49	"
M	DeAngelis Ugo	16	waiter	23	
N	DeAngelis Valentina—†	16	operator	25	
O	Kelley Edward J	19	shipper	24	
P	Kelley Marguerite—†	19	packer	22	"
R	Kelley Mary—†	19	housewife	54	"
S	Salvi Louis	19	merchant	52	"
T	Salvi Louise—†	19	housewife	54	"
U	Salvi Peter	19	clerk	21	
V	Drake Gertrude R—†	19	housewife	32	"
W	Drake James M	19	diemaker	34	"
X	Burrill George L	21	meatcutter	61	153 Northampton
Y	Lewko Helen—†	21	housewife	33	here
Z	Lewko Peter P	21	chef	24	"
	1428				
A	Ray Eleanor—†	21	housewife	24	"
B	Ray Sylvester A	21	chauffeur	23	"
C	LaGuardia Anthony	21	barber	40	
D	*LaGuardia Cesare	21	retired	66	
E	LaGuardia Eleanor—†	21	housewife	24	"
G	Quigley Catherine—†	26	"	64	
H	Quigley Harry P	26	mechanic	56	"
K	Scipione Domenic	27	barber	32	
L	Scipione Helen—†	27	housewife	30	"
M	*Scipione Mary—†	27	"	58	
N	*Scipione Vincent	27	laborer	56	
O	*Scipione Anthony	27	"	40	
P	*Scipione Lucy—†	27	housewife	38	"
R	*Boyle Kathleen—†	28-30	domestic	30	"
S	Byrne Agnes M—†	28-30	housewife	37	"

Rossmore Road—Continued

	T	Byrne James J	28–30	clerk	45	here
	U	Byrne Margaret—†	28–30	housewife	38	"
	V	Byrne William J	28–30	meatcutter	38	"
	w*	Rutledge Leonora—†	28–30	housewife	32	Canada
	x*	Rutledge Peter	28–30	laborer	37	"
	Y	Ahern Annie A—†	34	at home	37	3527 Wash'n
	z	Mullen Gladys M—†	34	housewife	37	here
1429						
	A	Mullen Thomas J	34	gardener	40	"
	B	Kelly Michael J	34	watchman	35	"
	C	Mitchell Mary A—†	34	housewife	46	"
	D*	Mitchell Thomas	34	laborer	43	
	E*	Waring Essie A—†	35	housewife	45	"
	F	Waring Hazen H	35	machinist	48	"
	G	Waring Waldo J	35	clerk	23	
	H	McEleney Daniel J	35	salesman	37	"
	K	McEleney Velma—†	35	housewife	33	"
	L	Kuczin Anna—†	35	secretary	22	"
	M	Kuczin Anna V—†	35	housewife	46	"
	N	Kuczin Walter A	35	mechanic	46	"
	O	Barth Paul	41	foreman	25	42 Huron Circle
	P	Barth Phyllis—†	41	housewife	20	42 "
	R	Armstrong Agnes—†	41	"	33	69 Heath
	S	Armstrong David	41	counterman	36	69 "
	T	Davis Fay M—†	41	housewife	51	161 South
	U	Davis Walter H	41	machinist	24	161 "
	V	Whitsell Alice E—†	41	at home	71	New York
	w	Buckley Francis L	41	salesman	36	here
	x*	Buckley Mildred—†	41	housewife	37	"
	Y*	Duerden Dorothy C—†	41	operator	43	85 Lamartine
	z	George Frederick	41	chauffeur	28	here
1430						
	A	George Jennie—†	41	housewife	21	"
	B*	Maxwell Sarah E—†	41	operator	48	"
	c*	Williamson Peter	41	laborer	38	
	D	Lennon Bartholomew	46	engineer	60	
	E	Lennon Bartholomew J	46	chauffeur	21	"
	F	Lennon Margaret—†	46	housewife	62	"
	G	Lennon Martin	46	painter	23	
	H	Lennon Mary—†	46	clerk	26	"
	K	O'Leary Gertrude—†	46	waitress	27	102 Brown av

Page.	Letter.	Full Name.	Residence, Jan. 1, 1941.	Occupation.	Supposed Age.	Reported Residence Jan. 1, 1940. Street and Number

Rossmore Road—Continued

L	Crowley Joseph	46	bartender	38	44 Whalen
M	*Crowley Winifred—†	46	housewife	24	44 "
N	MacBeth Mary C—†	46	cook	49	44 "
O	MacCleary Ethel—†	46	housewife	48	1156 Com a
P	MacCleary Oakley P	46	fireman	63	1156 "
R	Cavanaugh James T	47	retired	53	here
S	Cavanaugh Nora A—†	47	housewife	55	"
T	Crowley Julia J—†	47	matron	42	"
U	*Feeley Mary—†	49-51	housewife	42	"
V	Feeley Patrick	49-51	longshoreman	45	"
W	Chislett Frank	49-51	checker	38	
X	Chislett Mabel—†	49-51	housewife	58	"
Y	*Chislett Phyllis—†	49-51	domestic	24	41 Russett r
Z	*Gabalin Elizabeth C—†	49-51	housewife	44	here

1431

A	Gabalin Evelyn C—†	49-51	stenographer	22	"
B	Gabalin Peter J	49-51	woodworker	52	"
C	McCormack George H	50	carpenter	48	3 St James p
D	McCormack William T	50	fireman	58	here
E	Potter Catherine A—†	50	housewife	55	"
F	Potter George H	50	guard	33	"
G	May Bessie M—†	50	housewife	42	"
H	May Daniel H	50	cabinetmaker	43	"
K	May Daniel H, jr	50	oiler	23	"
L	Anderson Rebecca M—†	50	domestic	47	Dedham
M	Shields Cornelius	53-55	retired	79	here
N	Shields Cornelius M	53-55	laborer	35	"
O	Shields Elizabeth—†	53-55	housewife	29	"
P	Shields Lawrence	53-55	shipper	39	"
R	*Kelley Phyllis—†.	53-55	housewife	32	97 Brook a
S	Kelley Stephen	53-55	steamfitter	42	97 "
T	Nabreski Edward	54	operator	30	86 Rossmor
U	Nabreski Eileen—†	54	housewife	27	86 "
V	Cawley Frances—†	54	housekeeper	43	here
W	Sullivan Mary E—†	54	saleswoman	53	"
X	Feeney Bridget—†	58	housewife	34	"
Y	Feeney James	58	chauffeur	35	"
Z	Fallon Mary—†	58	housewife	32	"

1432

A	Fallon Timothy	58	chauffeur	34	"
B	Koziewicz Alice—†	58	bookkeeper	25	"

Rossmore Road—Continued

c	Koziewicz Helen—†	58	housewife	48	here
d	Koziewicz Jennine—†	58	domestic	23	"
e	Koziewicz Josephine—†	58	bookkeeper	26	"
f	Koziewicz Michael	58	shoemaker	60	"
g	Morton Douglas	59	fireman	45	
h	*Morton Elmira—†	59	housewife	43	"
k	Morton Victor	59	U S A	21	
l	Cash Gertrude C—†	59	housewife	35	"
m	Cash Thomas L	59	assembler	40	"
n	Broadley Frank J	59	chauffeur	42	"
o	Broadley Marie—†	59	housewife	42	"
p	*Gauthier Eugene	59	retired	79	
r	Carabuci Joseph	61	boilermaker	40	"
s	Carabuci Josephine—†	61	housewife	34	"
t	Sheedy Albert	61	musician	33	
u	Sheedy Mary E—†	61	housewife	32	"
v	Stanton Joseph F	61	laborer	34	
w	Stanton Ruth L—†	61	housewife	27	"
x	*O'Sullivan Barbara—†	61	"	33	
y	O'Sullivan John	61	chauffeur	33	"
z	*Kennedy Nora—†	61	housewife	33	"
	1433				
a	Kennedy William	61	foreman	35	
b	Aldred Charles	61	fireman	30	
c	Aldred Mary—†	61	housewife	30	"
d	Ward Henrietta—†	65	"	28	
e	Ward Richard	65	machinist	31	"
f	Schaaf John	65	assembler	29	"
g	Schaaf Marion—†	65	housewife	26	"
h	Marco Grace A—†	65	"	28	
k	Marco Joseph P	65	woodcarver	29	"
l	Kas Andrew J	65	manufacturer	32	"
m	Kas Lottie—†	65	housewife	32	"
n	Kroll Catherine—†	65	"	20	
o	Kroll Victor J	65	welder	25	"
p	Vater Annie—†	65	housewife	30	15 Varney
r	Vater Clarence J	65	clerk	30	15 "
s	Heffernan Catherine T—†	66-68	housewife	47	here
t	Heffernan Dorothea A—†	66-68	stenographer	23	"
u	Heffernan James H	66-68	carpenter	47	"
v	*McKeown Daniel	66-68	retired	70	

Page.	Letter.	FULL NAME.	Residence, Jan. 1, 1941.	Occupation.	Supposed Age.	Reported Residence, Jan. 1, 1940. Street and Number.

Rossmore Road—Continued

w	McKeown Joseph D	66–68	chauffeur	27	here
x	*McKeown Mary—†	66–68	housewife	70	"
y	McKeown Mary A—†	66–68	operator	24	"
z	McKeown Philip	66–68	accountant	36	"
	1434				
a	Reilly Margaret—†	66–68	at home	70	73 Wenham
b	Murphy Catherine—†	71	housewife	30	21 Worcesters
c	Murphy James	71	clerk	30	21 "
d	O'Donnell Mary—†	71	housewife	34	65 Burnett
e	O'Donnell William	71	fireman	33	65 "
f	Morelli Guy	71	shipper	31	here
g	Morelli Mary—†	71	clerk	28	"
h	Lister John W	71	plasterer	30	7 Copeland p
k	Lister Lillian A—†	71	housewife	30	7 "
l	Schaaf George P	71	draftsman	28	here
m	Schaaf Lillian—†	71	housewife	24	"
n	Masone Beatrice—†	71	"	22	13 Ottawa
o	Masone Samuel	71	painter	23	166 W Third
p	Goldberg Irving	75	salesman	24	here
r	Goldberg Lillian—†	75	operator	21	"
s	Cameron Gertrude L—†	75	housewife	27	9 Bancroft
t	Cameron John	75	plasterer	34	9 "
u	Thomas Genevieve—†	75	housewife	21	173 Minot
v	Thomas Maurice S	75	cleanser	23	84 Harvard
w	Runge John	75	shipfitter	25	652 Hunt'u a
x	Runge Rita F—†	75	housewife	22	652 "
y	Harnish Rose—†	75	"	36	here
z	Harnish Warren	75	carpenter	38	"
	1435				
a	Kell Collin F	75	painter	46	3831 Wash'n
b	Kell Gertrude C—†	75	housewife	35	3831 "
c	Bradley Florence G—†	78	"	38	here
d	Bradley Joseph F	78	mechanic	50	"
e	O'Mara John	78	typist	50	"
f	O'Mara Julia—†	78	housewife	39	"
g	Donohue Cecelia E—†	78	"	48	86 Rossmore
h	Donohue Edward J	78	clerk	54	86 "
k	Ford Anna—†	79–81	stenographer	21	here
l	*Ford Delia—†	79–81	housewife	54	"
m	Ford John	79–81	clerk	26	"
n	*Ford Patrick	79–81	operator	64	

Rossmore Road—Continued

o	Ford Thomas	79–81	chauffeur	32	here
p	Ford William	79–81	clerk	28	"
r	Gardner Dorothy—†	79–81	stenographer	20	"
s	Gardner George	79–81	policeman	43	"
t	Gardner Naomi—†	79–81	housewife	46	"
u	Ewasko Boleslaw	79–81	machinist	40	"
v	Petkus Joseph	79–81	mechanic	46	"
w	Petkus Pauline—†	79–81	housewife	40	"
x	*Fitzgerald Helena—†	82	"	38	
y	*Fitzgerald William F	82	manager	33	"
z	Dennery Helen L—†	82	housewife	34	"
	1436				
a	Dennery Waldo S	82	buyer	37	
b	Thomas Melvina—†	82	housewife	31	"
c	Thomas Millard	82	chauffeur	30	"
d	Murray Agnes—†	83–85	housewife	52	46 Boylston
e	Murray George W	83–85	waiter	49	46 "
f	Murray George W, jr	83–85	salesman	24	46 "
g	Dennis David	83–85	artist	31	here
h	Dennis George W	83–85	student	22	"
k	*Dennis Rose—†	83–85	housewife	57	"
l	McDonough Ellen—†	83–85	housekeeper	56	"
m	Wallace John J	83–85	hostler	43	"
n	Ray Joseph M	86	chauffeur	29	"
o	Ray Rose A—†	86	housewife	28	"
p	McCarthy James A	86	clerk	31	109 Williams
r	McCarthy Nora T—†	86	housewife	31	109 "
s	Carey Gladys—†	86	"	27	7 Glade av
t	Carey Paul	86	fireman	26	7 "
u	*Suderis Marcella—†	87–89	cook	45	here
v	MacMillan Arthur H	87–89	manager	28	"
w	MacMillan Geraldine—†	87–89	housewife	30	"
x	Green John	87–89	merchant	45	"
y	Green Mary B—†	87–89	housewife	41	"
z	Kukstis Albert	90	U S A	21	
	1437				
a	*Kukstis Anthony	90	meatcutter	47	"
b	*Kukstis Dana—†	90	housewife	47	"
c	Wilson Harry	90	manager	49	"
d	Wilson Julia E—†	90	housewife	42	"
e	Tribuna Anthony	90	salesman	38	"

Rossmore Road—Continued

F	Tribuna Wanda—†	90	housewife	34	here
G	Barrett Anna—†	91–93	"	38	"
H	Barrett James	91–93	chauffeur	38	"
K	Stelfox Dorothy—†	91–93	housewife	30	"
L	Stelfox Harold A	91–93	woodworker	25	"
M	Ingraham Frank T	91–93	mechanic	53	"
N	Ingraham Helen E—†	91–93	housewife	50	"
O	Weincus John	94	machinist	45	"
P	*Weincus Josephine—†	94	housewife	43	"
R	Weincus Stanley	94	machinist	26	"
S	Morrison Julia—†	94	housewife	40	447 Walnut av
T	Morrison Vincent T	94	plumber	40	447 "
U	Callanan Joseph F	94	photographer	39	here
V	Callanan Kathleen A—†	94	housewife	39	"
W	Green Anna L—†	94	nurse	39	"
X	O'Day James P	94	policeman	43	"
Y	Whitston Patrick	95–97	shipper	36	"
Z	Whitston Rita—†	95–97	housewife	26	"
	1438				
A	Francis Florence M—†	95–97	"	31	
B	Francis John W	95–97	foreman	29	
C	Gray Martha E—†	95–97	at home	81	
D	Gray William M	95–97	retired	81	
E	Paige Jerome O	95–97	salesman	28	"
F	Krauchunas Anna—†	95–97	housewife	50	"
G	*Krauchunas George	95–97	boilermaker	50	"
H	*Hasiuk George O	98	laborer	45	
K	Hasiuk Magdalena—†	98	cook	45	
L	Lako Catherine—†	98	housewife	25	"
M	Lako William	98	florist	30	"
N	*Hardiman Della—†	98	housewife	30	3 Alpine
O	Hardiman Kieran	98	cook	36	3 "
P	Murray James	98	operator	40	3 "
R	Donohue James	98	welder	60	here
S	*Donohue Mary—†	98	housewife	45	"
T	Joyce Festus V	99–101	engineer	39	"
U	*Joyce Mary A—†	99–101	housewife	31	"
V	Geary Edward J	99–101	boilermaker	31	39 Ballard
W	Geary Mary M—†	99–101	housewife	24	39 "
X	Welch Catherine—†	99–101	"	37	here
Y	Welch John	99–101	meter reader	40	"

Rossmore Road—Continued

z	Doherty Alice—†	102–104	at home	68	here
	1439					
A	Doherty Anne T—†	102–104	clerk	36	
B	Hynes John J	102–104	policeman	36	"
C	Hynes Mary F—†	102–104	housewife	34	"
D	Baltusis Agnes A—†	102–104	"	34	
E	Baltusis Joseph F	102–104	pressman	35	"
F	Liaknickas Mary—†	102–104	housewife	28	"
G	Liaknickas Peter J	102–104	laborer	29	
H	Povilaitis Adela—†	102–104	housewife	54	"
K	Povilaitis Frank	102–104	molder	56	
L	Maloney Olga—†	103–105	housewife	32	"
M	Maloney Thomas F	103–105	laborer	33	
N	Carey Margaret M–†	103–105	housewife	29	"
O	Carey Thomas J	103–105	carpenter	29	"
P	Kilduff Mary—†	103–105	housewife	43	"
R	Kilduff Thomas	103–105	inspector	43	"
S	Molloy Josephine—†	106–108	housewife	35	319 Forest Hills
T	Molloy Thomas M	106–108	foreman	34	319 "
U	Norton John F	106–108	clerk	30	here
V	Norton Margaret—†	106–108	housewife	30	"
W	Walsh Eleanor C—†	106–108	secretary	33	"
X	Walsh Josephine E–†	106–108	housewife	59	"
Y	Ahern Charles F	107–109	checker	32	7 Tiverton rd
z	Ahern Irene A—†	107–109	housewife	31	7 "
	1440					
A	*Daley Ellen J—†	107–109	"	32	20 Olmstead
B	Daley James H	107–109	manager	28	38 Orchard
C	DeMuth Henry	107–109	chauffeur	30	23 Newark
D	DeMuth Mary—†	107–109	housewife	27	23 "

Shurland Street

E	Dorrer Mary M—†	6	housewife	46	here
F	Dorrer Otto	6	collector	48	"

Stedman Street

G	*Caswell Helen—†	9	housewife	32	here
H	Caswell Wesley	9	chauffeur	33	"
K	Feeley John H	9	mechanic	55	"

Stedman Street—Continued

L	O'Connell Mary—†	9	operator	46	here
M	O'Connell William J	9	counterman	20	"
N	Colofrancesco Daphne—†	9	housewife	29	"
O	Colofrancesco Paul	9	laborer	31	"
P	Pierantoni Mabel—†	9	stenographer	24	"
R	*Pierantoni Margaret—†	9	stitcher	53	"
S	Skenderian Alice—†	11	housewife	25	128 Williams
T	Skenderian Emil	11	machinist	30	128 "
U	Scharks Annie—†	11	housewife	49	3149 Wash'n
V	Scharks Frances—†	11	clerk	22	3149 "
W	Scharks Leonard	11	watchman	54	48 Worcester
X	Scharks Mary—†	11	clerk	20	3149 Wash'n
Y	Hergt Louisa G—†	11	housewife	39	here
Z	Hergt Raymond W	11	operator	45	"

1441

	Hergt Susan E—†	11	waitress	63	
	Hergt William C	11	operator	55	"
	Lynch Mary—†	40	at home	50	
	Lynch Pauline—†	40	"	56	"
	Vogel Jean—†	40	housewife	21	74 Circuit
	Vogel Louis A, jr	40	counterman	28	74 "

Washington Street

K	Campbell Emily—†	3464	housewife	52	here
L	Campbell Patrick	3464	plasterer	54	"
M	Carmody William F	3464	laborer	63	"
N	McNulty Charles	3466	painter	45	
O	McNulty Elizabeth—†	3466	housewife	41	"
P	McNulty Mary—†	3466	clerk	20	"
R	Caines Lillian—†	3474	operator	40	40 Stedman
S	Hagan Anna—†	3474	housewife	42	here
T	Hagan Daniel	3474	salesman	53	"
U	Hagan Joseph	3474	shipper	22	"
V	Lavie Anna M—†	3476	housewife	45	"
W	Lavie Anna M—†	3476	waitress	21	
X	Lavie Francis W	3476	machinist	22	"
Y	Lavie John J	3476	electrician	48	"
Z	Lavie John J, jr	3476	clerk	23	

1442

L	Puleo Doris—†	3500	housewife	35	"

Washington Street—Continued

		FULL NAME.	Residence, Jan. 1, 1941.	Occupation.	Supposed Age.	Reported Residence
	M	Puleo Vincent	3500	chauffeur	49	here
	N	Cassali Louis	3502	retired	78	"
	O	Cassali Mary—†	3502	at home	54	"
	P	Scagnoli Helen—†	3502	housewife	43	"
	R	Scagnoli Henry	3502	bartender	56	"
	S	Scagnoli Walter	3502	chauffeur	21	"
	U	Devaney Elizabeth—†	3504	housewife	42	"
	V	Devaney John	3504	merchant	20	"
	W	Devaney Joseph	3504	salesman	47	"
	X	Creedon John	3504	laborer	64	
	Y	Creedon Mary—†	3504	housewife	60	"
1443						
	B	VanTassell Annie—†	3508	at home	82	
	C	VanTassell Florence—†	3508	stenographer	46	"
	D	VanTassell Hilda—†	3508	housewife	45	"
	E	VanTassell Richard	3508	chauffeur	25	"
	F	VanTassell William	3508	laborer	22	
	H	McArthur Florence W-†	3510	at home	61	"
	K	McArthur Walter H	3510	chauffeur	37	"
	L	Mercer William L	3510	laborer	59	
	M	McGrath Elizabeth—†	3510	housewife	75	"
	N	McGrath Peter	3510	retired	75	"
	O	Shea Joseph	3510	laborer	31	94 Call
	P	Shea Mary—†	3510	housewife	29	94 "
	R	Moran Mary—†	3512	"	47	here
	S	Philbin Gladys—†	3512	"	21	"
	T	Philbin Joseph	3512	operator	24	"
	V	Kenney William	rear 3514	laborer	66	
	W	Patigian Hampertzoun"	3514	barber	45	
	X	Patigian Isabelle—† "	3514	housewife	36	"
	Y	Hubbard Leroy	3516	laborer	47	
	Z	Hubbard Leroy, jr	3516	chauffeur	22	"
1444						
	A	Hubbard Marion—†	3516	housewife	45	"
	B	Dolan Alfred	3516	clerk	37	
	C	Dolan Freda—†	3516	housewife	35	"
	F	Kennedy James	3526	machinist	43	"
	G	Mullen Joseph F	3526	welder	34	
	H	Murdock Mary—†	3526	housekeeper	60	"
	L	O'Connor Mary A—†	3528	housewife	43	"
	M	Cavallerie Charles	3528	salesman	40	"

Washington Street—Continued

N	Cavalierie Gertrude A—†	3528	housewife	32	here
R	Swartz Leo	3532	chauffeur	25	"
S	Swartz Louise—†	3532	housewife	23	"
T	Donnelly Joseph P	3532	chauffeur	43	"
U	Donnelly Mary E—†	3532	housewife	42	"
V	Richie Charles	3534	laborer	27	
W	Richie Jennie—†	3534	housewife	23	"
X	Quintaglie Mary—†	3534	"	32	..
Y	Quintaglie Peter	3534	laborer	48	"
Z	Ward James	3534	"	51	"

1445

A	Ward Mary M—†	3534	housewife	44	"
B	Donovan Elizabeth—†	3536	"	24	"
C	Donovan Paul F	3536	clerk	27	"
D	Phinney Florence—†	3536	housewife	27	"
E	Phinney Lester F	3536	chauffeur	25	"
F	Matthews Irene—†	3536	housekeeper	35	"
H	Peters Angie—†	3540	at home	78	..
K	Peters Charles L	3540	laborer	56	
L	Peters George	3540	U S A	22	
M	Peters Ruth—†	3540	housewife	49	"
N	Grankewicz Marion C—†	3540	"	24	
O	Grankewicz Stanley	3540	mechanic	30	"
S	Smith Irene—†	3542	housewife	30	"
T	Smith James	3542	laborer	34	
U	Smith James	3542	watchman	59	"
V	Smith Sarah—†	3542	housewife	57	"
W	Foley Odlie—†	3542½	"	29	"
X	Flynn Mary E—†	3544	cook	60	161 Warren av
Y	Flynn Susan—†	3544	housewife	54	49 Middlesex
Z	Fisher William	3544	attendant	43	here

1446

A	Wright Bessie—†	3544	housewife	47	"
B	Bates Helen—†	3544½	"	21	12 Hutchins
C	Bates Warren	3544½	electrician	24	12 "
D	Donohue Ruth—†	3544½	housewife	28	13 Chandler
E	Sullivan Daniel	3544½	clerk	41	here
F	Sullivan John	3544½	mechanic	36	"
G	Delaney George	3544½	chauffeur	23	"
H	Delaney Helen—†	3544½	housewife	20	"
K	O'Hara Frances J—†	3546	at home	70	67 E Brookline

Page.	Letter.	Full Name.	Residence, Jan. 1, 1941.	Occupation.	Supposed Age.	Reported Residence, Jan. 1, 1940. Street and Number.

Washington Street—Continued

	L	Rehill Mary—†	3546	housekeeper	68	here
	M	Harding Evelyn—†	3546	waitress	33	133 Lamartine
	N	Sutton Charles E	3546	laborer	29	1264 Dudley
	O	Sutton Evelyn—†	3546	housewife	23	19 St Germain
	P	Keefe Gertrude—†	3546	"	46	246 Hyde Park av
	S	Keefe Lawrence	3546	mechanic	23	246 "
	R	Keefe Lawrence J	3546	"	46	246 "
	V	Fegan Albert	3555	U S A	20	here
	W	Fegan Edward	3555	laborer	23	3544 Wash'n
	X	Fegan Josephine—†	3555	housewife	44	here
	Y	Fegan Walter	3555	mechanic	54	"
	Z	Magee Charlotte—†	3555	housewife	30	"

1447

	A	Magee Thomas	3555	laborer	33	
	B	Cushman George W	3557	millwright	36	"
	C	Cushman Virginia—†	3557	housewife	31	"
	D	Conway Charles E	3557	laborer	40	
	E	Conway Johanna—†	3557	housewife	29	"
	F	Cicavi Josephine—†	3557	domestic	53	"
	K	Russo Catherine—†	3559	housewife	45	"
	L	Russo Mary—†	3559	at home	85	
	M	Russo Anthony	3559	barber	22	
	N	Russo John	3559	"	54	
	O	Russo Mary—†	3559	waitress	23	
	P	*Brassell Mary—†	3563	at home	80	"
	R	Casey James T	3563	clerk	22	
	S	Casey John	3563	chauffeur	52	"
	T	Casey Julia V—†	3563	housewife	48	"
	U	Casey Mary A—†	3563	at home	21	
	V	Casey James J	3567	chauffeur	49	"
	W	Casey Mary—†	3567	at home	87	
	X	Casey Timothy	3567	guard	56	"
	Y	McDonald James J	3571	retired	61	126 Blue Hill av
	Z	McDonald James P	3571	chauffeur	31	126 "

1448

	A	McDonald Rose—†	3571	housewife	26	126 "
	B	Connolly Esther—†	3571	"	30	231 Dudley
	C	Connolly James B	3571	guard	36	231 "
	D	MacCullough Charles	3573	janitor	40	here
	E	Ryan Frances—†	3573	housewife	28	"
	F	Ryan Raymond	3573	laborer	42	"

Page.	Letter.	FULL NAME.	Residence, Jan. 1, 1941.	Occupation.	Supposed Age.	Reported Residence, Jan. 1. 1940. Street and Number.

Washington Street—Continued

G	Hulme Frederick J	3573	printer	21	here
H	Hulme George H	3573	chauffeur	47	"
K	Hulme Margaret—†	3573	housewife	28	"
L	Hulme Mary—†	3573	"	45	"
M	Lawrence Bertha—†	3585	"	29	138 George
N	Lawrence Calvin	3585	mechanic	35	138 "
P	Peterson George H	3587	laborer	49	here
O	Shurety Mary—†	3587	housekeeper	67	"

1449   Williams Street

A	Ferrara Anthony J	62	engineer	33	here
B	Ferrara Juliette—†	62	housewife	30	"
C	Bonsanti Domenic	62	shoemaker	56	"
D	Bonsanti Euphemia T—†	62	bookkeeper	25	"
E	Bonsanti Madeline—†	62	housewife	53	"
F	Karchunes Alexander	62	attendant	30	5043 Wash'n
G	Karchunes Eva—†	62	housewife	28	5043 "
H	Burke Nora M—†	64	"	39	67 Brighton av
K	Burke Stephen F	64	superintendent	39	67 "
L	Deuterio Albert	64	mechanic	32	here
M	Deuterio Anna—†	64	housewife	60	"
N	Deuterio Joseph	64	pipefitter	62	"
O	Jones Helen—†	64	housewife	31	1990 Col av
P	Jones William E	64	painter	31	1990 "
R	Shields Joseph	66	laborer	42	33 Wachusett
S	Shields Nora—†	66	housewife	37	33 "
T	Welby James	66	manager	30	here
U	Welby Mary—†	66	housewife	29	"
V	Hession John	66	mechanic	55	"
W	Davin Catherine—†	68	housewife	49	"
X	McGrath Arthur	68	laborer	29	
Y	McGrath Katherine—†	68	housewife	26	"
Z	White Bridget—†	68	"	38	
	1450				
A	White James J	68	laborer	45	
B	Gale Bruce L	69	mechanic	27	"
C	Gale John L	69	operator	54	
D	Gale Lorraine—†	69	bookkeeper	20	"
E	Gale Margaret M—†	69	housewife	30	"

Page.	Letter.	Full Name.	Residence, Jan. 1, 1941.	Occupation.	Supposed Age.	Reported Residence, Jan. 1, 1940. Street and Number.

Williams Street—Continued

	F	Gale Mary E—†	69	housewife	58	here
	G	Foye Edward	70	machinist	30	108 Linden Park
	H	Foye Frederick A	70	writer	28	108 "
	K	Foye Mary A—†	70	housewife	61	108 "
	L	McCarthy Hannah—†	70	"	49	here
	M	Burke Catherine—†	70	"	27	"
	N	Burke Patrick	70	longshoreman	32	"
	O	Dillon Catherine—†	71	clerk	23	
	P	Dillon Edith I—†	71	housewife	43	"
	R	Hulme John P	71	chauffeur	41	"
	S	Kachele Charles F	71	salesman	54	"
	T	Kachele Doris—†	71	clerk	26	
	U	Kachele Grace—†	71	housewife	52	"
	V	Kachele Paul	71	salesman	24	"
	W	Barry Dorothy—†	71	housewife	23	263 Chestnut av
	X	Barry John P	71	shipper	30	263 "
	Y	Graves Catherine—†	72	housewife	67	82 Paul Gore
	Z	Graves Joseph E	72	mechanic	63	82 "
		1451				
	A	Johnson Mary K—†	72	bookkeeper	33	82 "
	C	Beatty Margaret—†	72	housekeeper	34	31 Robeson
	D	Hayes Catherine A—†	72	"	58	31 "
	E	McDermott John J	74	clerk	38	here
	F	McDermott Patrick	74	retired	80	"
	G	McDermott Rose—†	74	clerk	42	"
	H	McDermott Susan—†	74	housewife	73	"
	K	Regan Theresa—†	74	"	80	
	L	Regan William F	74	inspector	45	"
	M	Regan William J	74	retired	79	
	N	Dunbar James	74	plumber	65	
	O	Dunbar Jeanette—†	74	housewife	88	"
	P	Dunbar Mary E—†	74	embosser	48	"
	R	Howe Edna M—†	74	clerk	25	
	S	Stewart George G	74	"	22	"
	T	Stewart Jessie M—†	74	housewife	62	"
	U	Stewart Jessie M—†	74	clerk	23	
	V	Doyle Dorothy—†	75	housewife	28	"
	W	Doyle William F	75	retired	38	
	X	Sullivan Catherine—†	75	housewife	59	"
	Y	Sullivan Catherine J—†	75	clerk	29	
	Z	Sullivan Mary E—†	75	"	32	

1452
Williams Street—Continued

A	Kachele Antonette—†	75	housewife	31	here
B	Kachele Charles E	75	salesman	32	"
C	Edstrom Bernard	91	finisher	25	"
D	Edstrom Mary—†	91	housewife	25	"
E	Pasquale Sabbatino	91	supervisor	58	"
F	Pasquale Santa—†	91	housewife	53	"
G	MacEwan Alfred	91	plumber	39	"
H	MacEwan Ella—†	91	housewife	73	"
K	MacEwan Marjorie—†	91	beautician	31	"
L	MacEwan Ruby J—†	91	housewife	24	"
M	Catogge Anna L—†	91	stitcher	41	
N	Catogge Camella—†	91	housewife	28	"
O	Catogge Joseph R	91	draftsman	45	"
P	Catogge Mary R—†	91	housewife	71	"
R	Catogge N Mary—†	91	stenographer	33	"
S	McMackin Mary—†	97	housewife	53	"
T	McMackin Rose—†	97	"	80	
U	McMackin William J	97	laborer	53	
V	Jensen Carl J	97	chauffeur	47	"
W	Jensen Marie—†	97	housewife	44	"
X	McFarlin Frank E	97	attorney	42	"
Y	McFarlin John J	97	chauffeur	45	"
Z	McFarlin Katherine M—†	97	housewife	28	"

1453

B	D'Entremont Agnes—†	109	"	27	
C	D'Entremont Bernard R	109	painter	27	
D	Quigley Frances—†	109	housewife	30	"
E	Quigley Frank	109	mechanic	36	"
F	Whitston Anne—†	109	housewife	27	65 Rossmore rd
G	Whitston William K	109	porter	31	65 "
H	Shalline Anna—†	109	housewife	33	here
K	Shalline Moritz	109	painter	37	"
L	O'Toole Martin J	109	chauffeur	29	62 Williams
M	*O'Toole Mary—†	109	housewife	27	62 "
N	*Coyne Agnes—†	109	"	32	here
O	Coyne Patrick	109	manager	34	"
P	McDonagh Frank T	111	draftsman	35	"
R	McDonagh Loretta T—†	111	housewife	35	"
S	Krouse Anna M—†	111	nurse	55	
T	Wilson Beatrice—†	111	housewife	56	"

Page.	Letter.	FULL NAME.	Residence, Jan. 1, 1941.	Occupation.	Supposed Age.	Reported Residence, Jan. 1, 1940. Street and Number.

Williams Street—Continued

U	Wilson James T	111	paperhanger	67	here
V	Walsh Lillian M—†	111	housewife	33	"
W	Walsh William A	111	painter	33	"
X	Murphy Catherine—†	113	housewife	54	"
Y	Murphy David	113	laborer	58	
Z	Murphy David F	113	U S A	30	
	1454				
A	Murphy John J	113	technician	28	"
B	Murphy Mary C—†	113	nurse	24	
C	Hoey Nellie—†	115	housewife	24	"
D	Hoey Robert	115	clerk	25	"
E	Haggerty James	115	steamfitter	22	55 Seaverns av
F	Haggerty Lucy—†	115	housewife	23	55 "
G	Hartford Matilda—†	117	"	27	192 Fairmount av
H	Hartford Myron	117	cutter	28	192 "
K	Doyle Sarah—†	117	housekeeper	49	here
L	Ruane Francis	117	laborer	23	"
M	McCalmont Agnes—†	117	housewife	63	"
N	McCalmont Paul	117	machinist	25	"
O	Calloe Fred	˙121	waiter	47	
P	Calloe Irene—†	121	housewife	37	"
R	Foran Ellen E—†	121	"	50	
S	Foran John	121	machinist	22	"
T	Foran Michael J	121	manager	51	"
U	Carroll Helen V—†	121	housewife	31	"
V	Carroll Peter H	121	laborer	31	
W	Murphy Daniel J	123–125	fireman	66	
X	Murphy Katherine—†	123–125	housewife	70	"
Y	*Gatulis Annie—†	123–125	"	45	Worcester
Z	*Gatulis Charles	123–125	repairman	49	Brookline
	1455				
A	Gatulis Frank	123–125	clerk	21	"
B	Gatulis Helma—†	123–125	housewife	23	Quincy
C	Gatulis William	123–125	machinist	25	Brookline
D	Tuohy Margaret—†	123–125	housewife	36	here
E	Tuohy Patrick	123–125	laborer	41	"
F	Mitchell Margaret-†	127	housewife	30	"
G	Mitchell Thomas	127	meatcutter	33	"
H	Hanney Esther M—†	127	teacher	34	
K	Hanney Joseph J	127	meatcutter	64	"
L	Hanney Joseph L	127	chauffeur	33	38 Newbern

11—14

Page.	Letter.	Full Name.	Residence, Jan. 1, 1941.	Occupation.	Supposed Age.	Reported Residence, Jan. 1, 1940. Street and Number.

Williams Street—Continued

	M	Hanney Mary A—†	127	housewife	62	here
	N	Pihl Elna—†	127	"	44	"
	o	*Pihl Sofus A	127	painter	45	"
	P	O'Malley John	131	laborer	35	
	R	O'Malley Margaret A—†	131	housewife	28	"
	s	Iskra Anthony	131	policeman	44	"
	T	Iskra Anthony A	131	chauffeur	23	"
	u	Iskra Nora G—†	131	housewife	40	"
	v	Bryan Arthur G	131	chauffeur	30	"
	w	Bryan Pauline M—†	131	housewife	24	"
	x	Gainor James J	135	bookbinder	45	"
	y	Gainor Nora—†	135	housewife	44	"
	z	Labrie Elizabeth—†	135	"	29	211 Park Drive
1456						
	A	Labrie Leon	135	clerk	28	211 "
	B	Stowell Frederick H	135	manager	44	125 Southern av
	C	Stowell Ruth V—†	135	housewife	41	125 "
	D	Karkutt Howard J	139	attendant	28	here
	E	Karkutt Mary M—†	139	housewife	29	"
	F	Lester Agnes—†	139	"	38	"
	G	Lester James	139	laborer	38	"
	H	*Ahlin Alice—†	139	housewife	32	1665 Com av
	K	*Ahlin George	139	foreman	31	1665 "
	L	Donahue Margaret–†	143–145	housewife	40	here
	M	Donahue Patrick J	143–145	policeman	44	"
	N	Bailey Helen—†	143–145	housewife	32	"
	o	Bailey Joseph C	143–145	policeman	38	"
	P	Schwelm Frederick	143–145	engineer	24	Somerville
	R	Schwelm Mary—†	143–145	housewife	23	127 Marcella

1

Ward 11—Precinct 15

CITY OF BOSTON

LIST OF RESIDENTS
20 YEARS OF AGE AND OVER

(NON-CITIZENS INDICATED BY ASTERISK)
(FEMALES INDICATED BY DAGGER)

AS OF

JANUARY 1, 1941

JOSEPH F. TIMILTY, *Chairman*
FREDERIC E. DOWLING, *Secretary*
WILLIAM A. MOTLEY, JR.
FRANCIS B. McKINNEY
HILDA HEDSTROM QUIRK
Listing. Board.

CITY OF BOSTON PRINTING DEPARTMENT

1500
Bremen Terrace

A	*Cappuccio Mary—†	3	at home	55	here
B	Cerrato Louis	3	tailor	46	"
C	*DiGregorio Emanuella—†	3	housewife	70	"
D	*DiGregorio Manuel	3	retired	70	
E	DiGregorio Allesio	5	contractor	41	"
F	DiGregorio Christine—†	5	housewife	37	"
G	Burke Margaret L—†	6	"	48	
H	Burke Thomas F	6	mechanic	49	"
K	Flynn Arthur T	7	manager	48	..
L	Flynn Frances C—†	7	housewife	45	"

Forest Hills Avenue

M	Josselyn Martha M—†	1	housewife	75	here
N	Josselyn Walter H	1	sexton	75	"

Hyde Park Avenue

U	Mitchell Bridie M—†	8A	at home	61	here
V	Mitchell William J	8A	salesman	34	"
W	Volk Laura—†	8A	saleswoman	32	. "
X	O'Donnell Margaret—†	10	housewife	44	"
Y	Lyons Laura—†	10	"	33	
Z	*Lyons Martin P	10	checker	43	"

1501

C	Brownlow Genevieve M-†	14A	housewife	52	"
D	Brownlow Josephine E—†	14A	governess	22	"
E	Brownlow Louis A	14A	sorter	50	
F	Alley Anna—†	14A	at home	42	"
G	Hackett Peter	14A	engineer	45	..
H	Hackett Thomas	14A	retired	74	
K	Yocas Mary—†	14A	housewife	39	"
L	Yocas Paul	14A	laborer	53	"
M	Delaney Ellen F—†	14½	housewife	61	18 Tower
N	Delaney Joseph A	14½	retired	73	18 "
O	Donahue Bridget—†	14½	housewife	58	here
P	Donahue Francis J	14½	usher	21	"
R	Nash Harold E	14½	dentist	47	"
U	Connolly May—†	20	housekeeper	38	"
V	Ryan Esther V—†	20	housewife	51	1041 Hyde Park av

2

Hyde Park Avenue—Continued

	w	Ryan James	20	laborer	20	1041 Hyde Park av
	x	Ryan Joseph C	20	molder	51	1041 "
	y	Ryan Frank J	22	mechanic	53	here
	z	Ryan Nora—†	22	housewife	40	"
1502						
	A	Reardon Catherine J—†	22	"	31	246 Hyde Park av
	B	Reardon John J	22	shipper	31	246 "
	E*	Kiely Bridget—†	28	housewife	42	11 Kent
	F	Kiely Lawrence	28	laborer	48	11 "
	G	Pettinato Mary—†	28	housewife	31	here
	H	Pettinato Salvatore R	28	sorter	34	"
	K	Carmichael Francis F	30	attorney	38	"
	L	Carmichael Pauline M—†	30	housewife	35	"
	M	Bell Mary A—†	30	"	41	
	N	Bell Richard G	30	conductor	41	"
	O	Kwong Charlie	32	laundryman	62	"
	P	Marshall Leon	34	baker	56	
	R	Marshall Winona—†	34	housewife	46	"
	S	Harson Grace K—†	34	"	52	
	T	Malcolm David M	34	porter	62	

Lennoco Road

	v	Koch Chreston	1	foreman	41	here
	w	Koch Grace N—†	1	housewife	37	"
	x	Leahy Mabel E—†	5	"	53	"
	y	Burke Myrtle G—†	6	operator	28	
	z	O'Donnell Minnie E—†	6	housewife	54	"
1503						
	A	O'Donnell William J	6	clerk	62	
	B	Francis Anna W—†	9	housewife	31	"
	C	Francis Richard T	9	laborer	35	
	D	Leonard Mary—†	9	clerk	31	

Morton Street

	F*	Babineau Mary H—†	29	maid	28	here
	G	Baker Winifred—†	29	dietitian	45	"
	H	Barbone Jennie L—†	29	nurse	26	Quincy
	K	Bayner Jean C—†	29	"	24	here
	L*	Bernard Letitia M—†	29	"	26	"

Page	Letter	Full Name.	Residence, Jan. 1, 1941.	Occupation.	Supposed Age.	Reported Residence, Jan. 1, 1940. Street and Number.

Morton Street—Continued

	M	Blake Dorothy H—†	29	nurse	33	here
	N	Bowes Gertrude E—†	29	seamstress	60	"
	O	Bradley Celia V—†	29	nurse	38	14 Lakeville r
	P	Brown Martha G—†	29	attendant	23	here
	R	Clutt Mabel—†	29	maid	41	"
	S	Cole Gladys O—†	29	nurse	45	"
	T	Cullihall May—†	29	"	39	"
	U	Doddis Leta B—†	29	attendant	27	437 Cambridg
	V	Flannery Mary K—†	29	nurse	33	here
	W	Garland Georgia M—†	29	attendant	26	"
	X	Guthrie Margaret—†	29	nurse	30	"
	Y	Handrahan Catherine—†	29	"	31	Cambridge
	Z	Hatt Geraldine M—†	29	"	23	Watertown

1504

	A	Henchall Gertrude—†	29	"	36	here
	B	Johnson Myrtle L—†	29	"	31	"
	C	Kennedy Mary—†	29	domestic	31	"
	D	LaPierre Delia—†	29	nurse	25	"
	E	Larkin Estelle—†	29	"	29	"
	F	Lennox Janet—†	29	"	24	Medford
	G	Lomasney Helen—†	29	attendant	26	52 Dix
	H	Lydon Mary—†	29	maid	39	here
	K	*Lynch Edward	29	gardener	65	"
	L	Lynch William J	29	fireman	40	"
	M	*McConnell Norma M—†	29	nurse	28	
	N	*McGuirk Elizabeth T—†	29	"	27	"
	O	McMahon Lucy—†	29	domestic	41	"
	P	Megerian Gladys—†	29	nurse	23	Cambridge
	R	*O'Connor Mary—†	29	maid	51	here
	S	O'Connor Mary A—†	29	nurse	29	"
	T	O'Dowd Agnes J—†	29	"	23	"
	U	*Paradis Louisette R—†	29	attendant	21	Somerville
	V	Park Phyllis—†	29	nurse	38	753 Saratoga
	W	Ramponi Florence I—†	29	"	29	here
	X	St George Elodie—†	29	waitress	47	Lowell
	Y	Sampson Jacqueline—†	29	attendant	21	N Hampshire
	Z	Schofield Virginia E—†	29	nurse	30	here

1505

	A	Seabury Jean A—†	29	attendant	20	Somerville
	B	Sewall Joanne E—†	29	nurse	29	Brookline
	C	Stanley Olive M—†	29	"	34	here

Page.	Letter.	FULL NAME.	Residence, Jan. 1, 1941.	Occupation.	Supposed Age.	Reported Residence, Jan. 1, 1940. Street and Number.

Morton Street—Continued

D	Stubbs Robert E	29	physician	22	Chelsea
E	Suhr Marguerite—†	29	maid	29	Arlington
F	Swedborg Ernest W	29	houseman	44	Hingham
G	*Trainor Gertrude A—†	29	nurse	31	here
H	Wedge Sarah H—†	29	"	43	"
K	Williams Walter	29	fireman	42	106 Maverick
L	Williamson Edith—†	29	nurse	44	here
M	Wright Alicia D—†	29	"	23	"
N	Ziury Anna M—†	29	"	32	"
P	Shadman Alonzo J	rear 41	physician	63	"
S	Carroll Anna C—†	81	housewife	38	"
T	Carroll John F	81	printer	45	"
U	Sullivan John J	81	operator	61	
V	Sullivan Margaret V—†	81	housewife	55	"
W	McGinley Catherine M—†	85	at home	75	
X	McGinley Evelyn G—†	85	"	70	

1506

B	Driscoll Gerald T	113	clerk	36	"
C	Munroe Mary E—†	113	housewife	66	"

Orchard Hill Road

D	Killoran Mary K—†	40	housekeeper	28	here
E	McDonald Elizabeth M—†	40	secretary	28	"
F	McDonald John F	40	attorney	73	"
G	McDonald John F, jr	40	student	24	
H	McDonald Mary E—†	40	housewife	66	"
K	*Green Mary M—†	41	"	39	
L	Green William F	41	chauffeur	51	"
M	Handy Frank	41	foreman	72	"
N	O'Toole Thomas	41	bartender	33	"
O	Stober Louis	41	counterman	57	"
P	Minton Annie F—†	45	housewife	70	"
R	Minton John M	45	clerk	30	"
S	Killion Edward J	50	florist	44	
T	Killion Josephine—†	50	at home	68	"
U	Jordan Andrew R	55	inspector	44	20 Bardwell
V	Jordan Helen G—†	55	housewife	38	20 "
W	Murphy Edward F	59	clerk	38	here
X	Murphy Helen M—†	59	housewife	38	"
Y	Tracy John F	59	bricklayer	43	"

Orchard Hill Road—Continued

z	Tracy Margaret—†	59	housewife	65	here
	1507				
A	Tracy Michael	59	retired	70	
B	Tracy Thomas J	59	compositor	45	"
C	Flaherty Bartley J	62	carpenter	50	"
D	Flaherty Mary A—†	62	housewife	49	"
E	Glynn John	62	clerk	30	
F	Lewis Arthur J	63	broker	38	"
G	Lewis Margaret C—†	63	housewife	39	"
H	Tansey Ann—†	63	"	69	
K	Tansey Ann T—†	63	secretary	30	"
L	Tansey Joseph L	63	physician	29	"
M	Tansey Mary J—†	63	secretary	40	"
N	Pew Emma J—†	64	at home	82	
O	Pew Sally A—†	64	supervisor	59	"
P	Story Marie B—†	64	nurse	66	
R	MacQueen John	66	salesman	41	
S	MacQueen Laura—†	66	housewife	32	"
T	Travers Ellen M—†	67	"	43	
U	Travers Helen R—†	67	stenographer	20	"
V	Travers Joseph E	67	chemist	46	
W	Corrigan Delia—†	68	housewife	62	"
X	Corrigan Edward S	68	agent	25	
Y	Corrigan John J	68	mechanic	28	"
Z	Corrigan Peter J	68	engineer	66	
	1508				
A	Miles Agatha—†	71	housewife	51	"
B	Miles Edmond J	71	engineer	49	"
C	Looney Dennis J	72	superintendent	34	"
D	Looney Rosalie A—†	72	housewife	34	"
E	Ford Mary M—†	74	"	54	
F	Ford William J	74	proprietor	56	"
G	Lang John H	75	repairman	46	"
H	Lang Mary E—†	75	housewife	47	"
K	Lang Mary F—†	75	clerk	23	

Tower Street

P	Corrigan Clara P—†	11	housewife	43	here
R	Sentance Agnes—†	11	"	50	"
S	Sentance Evelyn C—†	11	clerk	21	"

Page.	Letter.	Full Name.	Residence, Jan. 1, 1941.	Occupation.	Supposed Age.	Reported Residence, Jan. 1, 1940. Street and Number.

Tower Street—Continued

T	Sentance Joseph W	11	blacksmith	52	here
U	Stanton Mildred M—†	11	bookkeeper	20	"
V	Stanton Mildred M—†	11	housewife	41	"
W	Stanton Thomas J	11	salesman	43	"
X	Stanton Thomas J, jr	11	clerk	22	
Y	Treadwell Emma C—†	15	housewife	74	"
Z	Treadwell Emma G—†	15	teacher	49	
	1509				
A	Travers Edwin J	15	laborer	25	
B	Travers James F	15	clerk	28	
C	Travers Louise A—†	15	cashier	23	
D	Travers Louise P—†	15	housewife	52	"
E	Travers Martin J	15	sealer	60	
F	Murray Catherine C—†	15	stenographer	29	"
G	Murray Catherine F—†	15	housewife	62	"
H	Murray Michael	15	gateman	65	"
K	Murray Ruth M—†	15	typist	20	"
L	Wipperman Mary—†	16	housekeeper	63	"
M	Wipperman Victoria—†	16	"	50	"
N	Leonard Mary—†	16	"	85	
O	Leonard Mary A—†	16	bookkeeper	50	"
P	Leonard Thomas J	16	clerk	49	"
R	Lawlor Margaret—†	16	housewife	40	"
S	Lawlor Thomas	16	carpenter	39	"
T	Young Ralph R	17	underwriter	31	"
U	Young Wilhelmina J—†	17	housewife	30	"
V	Healey Dorothea C—†	17	operator	25	"
W	Healey Irene M—†	17	secretary	27	"
X	Healey John J	17	merchant	65	"
Y	Healey Maria J—†	17	housewife	60	"
Z	Healey Marie G—†	17	secretary	26	"
	1510				
A	Kaine Elizabeth—†	17	housewife	54	"
B	Kaine Paul E	17	mechanic	30	"
C	Kaine Richard A	17	"	27	"
D	Glickman Frances—†	18	manager	45	14 Woodlawn
E	Glickman Murray	18	"	23	14 "
F	Hines Elizabeth—†	18	housekeeper	77	here
G	Kelley James E	18	clerk	49	"
H	Kelley John J	18	laborer	47	"
K	Kelley Mary E—†	18	operator	38	"

Tower Street—Continued

L	McKinney Katherine—†	18	housekeeper	64	here
M	Mahler Laura—†	18	housewife	31	200 Hyde Park av
N	Mahler Warren	18	cutter	34	200 "
O	Field Isabelle—†	20	operator	49	here
P	Field William C	20	baker	34	"
R	Coyne Margaret—†	20	housekeeper	74	"
S	Curran John	20	laundryman	34	25 Seaverns av
T	Leslie Albert	20	shipper	43	16 Chipman
U	Leslie Rosemary—†	20	housewife	46	16 "
V	Webster Ella—†	20	housekeeper	75	16 "
W	Fiske Nan L—†	23	housewife	54	8 Fowle
X	Fiske Robert L	23	auditor	53	8 "
Z	McGillicuddy Daniel F	23	inspector	52	19 Heath av
	1511				
A	McGillicuddy Daniel F, jr	23	packer	24	19 "
B	McGillicuddy Helen—†	23	stenographer	26	19 "
C	McGillicuddy John	23	student	22	19 "
D	McGillicuddy Mary—†	23	housewife	52	19 "
E	Harvey Anna E—†	24	"	40	here
F	Harvey Seward T	24	policeman	45	"
G	Burgess Emma B—†	24	housekeeper	71	"
H	Hartshorn Mary E—†	24	"	71	
K	Weiler Walter	24	retired	66	
L	Gay Clement S	24	agent	67	
M	Gay Roberta L—†	24	housewife	67	"
N	Walter Ethel M—†	25	housekeeper	31	"
O	Walter Frank J	25	ironworker	67	"
P	Walter Mary J—†	25	housewife	66	"
R	Doidge Clara M—†	25	"	68	
S	Liddell William	25	retired	70	
T	Garrity Katherine T—†	26	clerk	34	
U	Garrity Mary A—†	26	housekeeper	35	"
V	Broderick John J	26	bartender	27	"
W	Broderick Mary A—†	26	housewife	60	"
X	Broderick Patrick	26	retired	72	"
Y	Nolen Catherine E—†	26	housekeeper	50	69 Tower
Z	Splaine Margaret T—†	26	inspector	35	69 "
	1512				
A	Splaine Nellie A—†	26	housekeeper	38	69 "
C	Rowen Katherine E—†	27	typist	49	here
D	Rowen Mary G—†	27	housewife	54	"

Page.	Letter.	FULL NAME.	Residence, Jan. 1, 1941.	Occupation.	Supposed Age.	Reported Residence, Jan. 1, 1940. Street and Number.

Tower Street—Continued

E	Rowen Thomas J	27	plumber	47	here
F	*Boylan Irene M—†	31	housekeeper	40	Arlington
G	Simmons Letha E—†	31	"	84	here
H	Tosi Alfreda—†	31	bookkeeper	45	"
K	Mulligan Alexandrine—†	31	housewife	73	"
L	Mulligan Mary E—†	31	teacher	43	
M	Mulligan Thomas J	31	salesman	39	"
N	Pelky Louis	31	"	40	
O	Bird Harriett A—†	32	housewife	50	"
P	Bird William T	32	foreman	60	
R	Vierra Everett F	32	accountant	44	"
S	Vierra Katherine A—†	32	housewife	38	"
T	Donahue Sarah G—†	32	housekeeper	65	"
U	Kiely Eugene F	33	freighthandler	41	Dedham
V	Kiely Marguerite M—†	33	housewife	33	"
W	Bird Alfred J	33	student	21	here
X	Bird Frances M—†	33	secretary	25	"
Y	Bird Louis A	33	chauffeur	57	"
Z	Bird Mary A—†	33	bookkeeper	26	"

1513

A	Bird Olla M—†	33	housewife	52	"
B	Bird Rose C—†	33	organizer	23	"
C	McCann Edward	37	retired	72	"
D	McCann Joseph J	37	painter	31	
E	McCann Mary J—†	37	housekeeper	35	"
F	McCann Mary E—†	37	housewife	31	132 Hyde Park av
G	McCann William T	37	laborer	36	132 "
H	Martin Nellie—†	37	waitress	38	here
K	Muldoon Delia—†	37	housekeeper	40	"
L	Jacobs Frances—†	38	stenographer	22	"
M	Jacobs Frank C	38	inspector	76	"
N	Jacobs Frank C, jr	38	fireman	47	
O	Jacobs Grace L—†	38	dietitian	20	
P	Jacobs Hazel M—†	38	housewife	48	"
R	Jacobs Harriet H—†	38	"	38	
S	Jacobs Henry I	38	inspector	45	"
T	McMorrow Anna L—†	39	housewife	66	"
U	McMorrow Joseph M	39	baker	31	
V	Field Anita G—†	39	operator	25	"
W	Field Bernadette M—†	39	stenographer	25	"
X	Field Susan A—†	39	housewife	68	"

Tower Street—Continued

	Y	Towle Thomas M	39	retired	70	here
	z	Davey Colin L	40	caretaker	39	"
		1514				
	A	Davey Helen—†	40	housewife	40	"
	B	Bowie Annie—†	40	bookkeeper	23	110 Cedar
	C	Bowie Charlotte—†	40	housewife	58	110 "
	D	Bowie Harrison	40	engineer	26	110 "
	E	Bowie Mary—†	40	beautician	20	110 "
	F	Bowie Thelma B—†	40	housewife	30	Maine
	G	Bowie William	40	cutter	33	"
	L	Cullivan Evelyn—†	41	housekeeper	43	here
	M	Cullivan Russell	41	clerk	36	"
	N	Cullivan Simon	41	welder	59	"
	O	Dunn Margaret M—†	41	housewife	47	"
	P	Dunn Mary E—†	41	housekeeper	22	"
	R	Dunn Michael J	41	chauffeur	55	"
	S	Finnegan Patrick J	41	jeweler	65	
	T	Rich George	43	agent	59	
	U	Rich Lillian—†	43	housewife	41	"
	V	Maloney Ellen—†	43	"	46	
	W	Maloney Matthew	43	chauffeur	49	"
	X	Massey Mary—†	43	buyer	21	
	Y	Massey Nora—†	43	housewife	54	"
	z	Massey Thomas	43	gardener	24	"
		1515				
	A	*Cronin Kathleen—†	44	maid	27	Somerville
	B	Long Isabelle—†	44	housewife	65	here
	C	Long William P	44	commissioner	65	"
	D	Madden Anna—†	46	teacher	32	"
	E	Madden Margaret E—†	46	housewife	52	"
	F	Fitzpatrick Julia M—†	47	teacher	51	
	G	Fitzpatrick Thomas B	47	realtor	49	
	H	Finnegan Helen—†	47	stenographer	24	"
	K	Hickey Mary J—†	47	housewife	48	"
	L	Hickey Michael J	47	milkman	54	"
	M	Hale Edward F	47	counterman	25	"
	N	Hale Helen M—†	47	attendant	26	"
	O	Hale M Louise—†	47	clerk	28	
	P	Hale Mary A—†	47	housewife	64	"
	R	Geehan John J	48	manager	37	20 Jamaicaway
	S	Geehan Madeline—†	48	housewife	37	20 "

Page.	Letter.	FULL NAME.	Residence, Jan. 1, 1941.	Occupation.	Supposed Age.	Reported Residence, Jan. 1, 1940. Street and Number.

Tower Street—Continued

T	O'Brien Elizabeth C—†	48	housewife	65	here
U	O'Brien Helen A—†	48	teacher	36	"
V	McComish Anna—†	49	stenographer	20	"
W	McComish Katherine—†	49	secretary	23	"
X	McComish Rose—†	49	housewife	54	"
Y	Phelan Agatha—†	49	"	48	
Z	Phelan James H	49	carpenter	52	"

1516

B	Lewis Annie—†	52	housewife	48	"
C	Lewis George S	52	architect	35	"
D	Cassidy Annie—†	52	housewife	50	"
E	Cassidy Michael	52	retired	66	
F*	Keanevy Margaret M—†	52	housekeeper	81	"
G	Donegan Catherine—†	55	housewife	60	"
H	Donegan Robert	55	auditor	36	
K	Clements Esther—†	57	housekeeper	42	"
L	Downey Arthur A	57	surveyor	30	"
M	Downey Helen M—†	57	seamstress	40	"
N	Barstow Marie—†	57	saleswoman	41	"
O	Fitzgerald Margaret—†	57	housekeeper	68	"
P	Scott Bernard J	59	supervisor	63	"
R	Scott Katherine E—†	59	housewife	61	"
S	Brady Bernard	61	retired	78	
T	Lowry David	61	chauffeur	52	"
U	Lowry David F	61	engineer	24	
V	Lowry Margaret—†	61	housewife	51	"
W	Knowlton Aaron L	62	chauffeur	53	18 Tower
X	Knowlton Cora A—†	62	housewife	52	18 "
Y	Knowlton Jessie M—†	62	secretary	30	18 "
Z	Sybertz Lillian T—†	62	housewife	21	18 "

1517

A	Sybertz Paul A	62	metalworker	22	18 "
B	O'Leary Anna L—†	62	housekeeper	56	here
C	O'Leary Gertrude A—†	62	secretary	49	"
D	O'Leary Katherine T—†	62	bookkeeper	53	"
E	Connors Ellen M—†	63	housewife	44	"
F	Connors John J	63	machinist	45	"
G	Rogers George	63	"	41	
H	Rogers Sadie—†	63	housewife	37	"
K	Cochran Alice E—†	63	beautician	58	"
L	Cochran Charles	63	operator	70	"

Tower Street—Continued

M	Cochran Grace M—†	63	housekeeper	54	here
N	Rose Alfred H	66	letter carrier	54	"
O	Rose Virginia—†	66	stenographer	30	"
P	Harrison Jennie G—†	66	housewife	47	"
R	Harrison Reginald B	66	mechanic	51	"
S	Beyer Agnes K—†	66	housewife	50	"
T	Beyer Doris M—†	66	operator	22	"
U	Beyer John L	66	draftsman	50	"
V	Beyer Leonard J	66	attendant	26	"
W	Beyer Rita—†	66	housewife	23	"
X	Kerr Margaret—†	66	housekeeper	82	"
Y	MacDonald Louis	67	metalworker	45	"
Z	Toohy Anna—†	67	housewife	65	"

1518

A	Toohy Thomas M	67	printer	62	"
B	Andrews Susan M—†	69	housewife	61	49 Tower
C	Andrews Wallace A	69	laborer	60	49 "
D	McCann Edward F	69	salesman	43	37 "
E	McCann Mary A—†	69	housewife	31	37 "
F	Donaghy Edward J	70	teacher	35	here
G	Donaghy Frances—†	70	housewife	34	"
H	McCarron Catherine—†	70	housekeeper	60	"
K	Paige Laura—†	70	housewife	47	"
L	Paige Wilfred	70	jeweler	47	
M	McMorrow Louise—†	70	operator	53	"
N	Grady Mary—†	71	housewife	39	"
O	Grady Walter	71	clerk	38	
P	Regan Francis	71	laborer	23	
R	Scanlon Elizabeth F—†	71	housewife	37	"
S	Scanlon William F	71	installer	42	
T	Connolly John F	71	clerk	44	
U	Connolly Margaret A—†	71	housewife	41	"
V	Dolan Frank J	73	chauffeur	46	"
W	Dolan Julia A—†	73	housewife	46	"
X	Bosse Henry	73A	student	21	N Hampshire
Y	Durepo Ora—†	73A	housekeeper	60	here
Z	Laquier Raoul	73A	student	20	N Hampshire

1519

	Green James	73A	custodian	51	here
A	Green Mary W—†	73A	housewife	43	"
C	Simpson Chester N	75	chauffeur	42	"

Tower Street—Continued

D	Simpson M Elizabeth—†	75	housewife	37	here
E	Connolly Anna M—†	75	housekeeper	27	"
F	Connolly Thomas H	75	conductor	61	"
G	Connolly Thomas J	75	laborer	36	
H	Nicholson Catherine—†	75	clerk	47	
K	Nicholson John	75	baker	44	
L	Nicholson John	75	technician	21	"
M	Karas Bessie—†	76	housewife	23	"
N	Karas Peter	76	counterman	30	"
O	Reveliotes Demosthines K	76	retired	67	
P	Corkery Ellen—†	77	housewife	53	"
R	Corkery Paul	77	clerk	21	
S	Mello Joseph L	78	attendant	25	"
T	Mello Marie A—†	78	clerk	30	
U	Messer Lillian A—†	78	"	38	
V	Murphy Agnes T—†	78	housewife	45	"
W	Murphy John L	78	plumber	50	"
X	Finn James S	78	manager	33	171 Green
Y	Flynn Delia T—†	78	housewife	46	here
Z	Flynn Dennis M	78	foreman	52	"
	1520				
A	Kelliher Thomas J	78	manager	37	171 Green
B	Leonard Anne N—†	78	cook	26	here
C	Leonard Francis J	78	attendant	25	876 Albany
D	O'Brien Ellen—†	79	clerk	38	here
E	O'Brien Mary—†	79	housewife	68	"
F	Gill Harold W	81	bookkeeper	26	"
G	Gill Ruth—†	81	housewife	23	"
H	Conaty Rose—†	83	checker	50	
K	Waters Catherine—†	83	housewife	59	"
L	Waters Elizabeth—†	83	secretary	23	"
M	Waters John M	83	machinist	21	"
N	Ross David J	83	clerk	34	
O	Ross Sadie L—†	83	housewife	34	"
P	Porter Katherine M—†	84	"	22	
R	Porter William R	84	engineer	23	"
S	Kearns Angelina—†	84	housewife	68	"
T	Kearns Thomas H	84	retired	69	
U	Glynn Anne T—†	85	nurse	27	
V	Glynn Gertrude—†	85	housewife	54	"
W	Glynn Jacob F	85	student	24	

Tower Street—Continued

x	Glynn William J	85	chauffeur	53	here
y	Lord Addie E—†	86	housekeeper	72	"
z	Lord Kathleen B—†	86	housewife	35	"

1521

A	Lord Robert	86	printer	37	"
B	Dimock Nelson	87	salesman	52	20 Tower
C	Dimock Phyllis—†	87	saleswoman	48	here
D	Light Evelyn—†	87	"	30	"
E	Light Walter C	87	clerk	24	"

Union Terrace

F	Clarke Dorothy V—†	16	housekeeper	26	here
G	Clarke John O	16	superintendent	56	"
H	Knox Helen—†	16	housewife	30	Virginia
K	Tierney Helen M—†	18	"	33	here
L	Tierney John J	18	brakeman	37	"
M	Flaherty Anna L—†	21	buyer	47	"
N	Flaherty Annie—†	21	housewife	74	"
O	Flaherty James F	21	policeman	44	"
P	Flaherty John M	21	plumber	45	"
R	*Saulite Caroline—†	22	housewife	77	"
S	*Saulite Jacob	22	retired	75	"
T	O'Brien Henry M	22	upholsterer	26	16 Union ter
U	O'Brien Marjorie J—†	22	housewife	23	16 "
V	O'Roak Glenn R, jr	22	millhand	20	here
W	O'Roak Marguerite—†	22	waitress	47	"
X	Shippee Addie—†	22	houseworker	55	"
Y	Byrne Daniel J	29	engineer	42	"
Z	Byrne Nellie B—†	29	housewife	39	"

1522

A	Della Salla Elia	29	laborer	29	N Hampshire
B	*Della Salla Elia	29	retired	84	here
C	Della Salla Emilio	29	shoeworker	52	"
D	Della Salla Emma—†	29	housewife	46	"
E	Della Salla Justina—†	29	clerk	41	
F	*Della Salla Theresa—†	29	at home	79	
G	Giordano Silvio	29	manager	52	"
L	Sharpe Alice M—†	60	housewife	55	39 Union ter
M	Sharpe William W	60	manager	52	39 "

14

Page.	Letter.	FULL NAME.	Residence, Jan. 1, 1941.	Occupation.	Supposed Age.	Reported Residence, Jan. 1, 1940. Street and Number.

1523
Weld Hill Street

	F	Donaghy George	6	engineer	41	here
	G	*Donaghy Sarah J—†	6	housewife	39	"
	H	*Williamson Annie—†	8	"	41	"
	K	Williamson Archibald	8	gardener	43	"
	L	Fennessey Agnes E—†	12	buyer	29	
	M	Fennessey Anne L—†	12	social worker	31	"
	N	Fennessey Charles A	12	bartender	63	"
	O	Fennessey Charles W	12	salesman	29	"
	P	*Fennessey Mary A—†	12	at home	77	
	R	Doidge Mary—†	12	"	46	
	S	Shea Eleanor A—†	14	agent	26	
	T	Shea Flora M—†	14	"	31	
	U	Shea John F, jr	14	clerk	29	
	V	Shea Mary C—†	14	stenographer	23	"
	W	Downey Alice C—†	16	housewife	59	"
	X	Downey John J	16	B F D	59	"
	Y	Downey John J	16	clergyman	27	"
	Z	Long Dorothy A—†	16	teacher	31	

1524

	A	Long Mary A—†	16	housewife	62	"
	B	Long Thomas F	16	foreman	65	"
	C	D'Entremont James A	16	clerk	23	80 Kittredge
	D	D'Entremont Ruth E—†	16	housewife	21	80 "
	E	Meyer Helen A—†	18	"	37	here
	F	Meyer Paul	18	laborer	37	"
	G	English Joseph E	18	lather	46	71 Glen rd
	H	English Margaret E—†	18	housewife	77	71 "
	K	English Mary M—†	18	operator	42	71 "
	L	English William T	18	laborer	34	71 "
	M	Dicey Marie E—†	18	hygienist	35	here
	N	Brown Bradford O	20	foreman	61	"
	O	Brown Elizabeth G—†	20	housewife	59	"
	P	Collings Edna C—†	20	at home	42	
	R	Driscoll Ellen—†	20	housewife	67	"
	S	Driscoll John	20	retired	70	
	T	Driscoll Michael J	20	engineer	35	
	U	Smith Bertha G—†	20	matron	48	
	V	Smith Florence—†	20	clerk	65	
	W	Grethe Fannie L—†	24	at home	46	
	X	Oberg John G	24	carpenter	37	"

15

Page.	Letter.	FULL NAME.	Residence, Jan. 1, 1941.	Occupation.	Supposed Age.	Reported Residence, Jan. 1, 1940. Street and Number.

Weld Hill Street—Continued

Y	*Walsh Delia—†	24	at home	65	here
z	Walsh John W	24	mechanic	39	"
	1525				
A	Walsh Mildred—†	24	housewife	36	"
B	MacDougall Fred P	24	salesman	42	"
C	*MacDougall John W	24	retired	84	
D	MacDougall Mary A—†	24	at home	78	
E	*Harrington Agnes L—†	26	housewife	35	"
F	Harrington Timothy J	26	wool sorter	37	"
G	Martin John J	26	laborer	37	
H	Martin Therese—†	26	housewife	38	"
K	Ahern Edward C	28	printer	34	61 Wenham
L	Plunkett Margaret M—†	28	at home	63	61 "
M	Laporte Agelos	28	molder	49	here
N	Laporte Aldea A—†	28	housewife	34	"
O	Wilson Anne P—†	28	"	39	12 Amherst
P	Wilson Robert G	28	investigator	35	12 "
R	MacDonough Elva R—†	36	housewife	38	5 Bostonia av
S	MacDonough James T	36	salesman	50	5 "
T	Kelly Eileen A—†	36	housewife	34	168 Hyde Park av
U	Kelly John F	36	machinist	39	168 "
V	Faulkner Annie—†	36	housewife	70	here
W	Faulkner Clarence A	36	retired	71	"
X	Pemberton Faunce G—†	38	housewife	37	46 Woodlawn
Y	Pemberton Theodore	38	florist	37	46 "
Z	Moran Eleanor M—†	38	housewife	32	here
	1526				
A	Tanner Mauretta M—†	38	"	27	
B	Tanner Randolph H	38	plumber	32	
C	Downey James J	40	clerk	45	
D	Downey Katherine M—†	40	housewife	44	"
E	Doyle Ellen—†	40	"	46	"
F	Doyle James	40	mechanic	23	"
G	Doyle Patrick	40	laborer	56	
H	LeMay Anthony C	40	guard	33	
K	LeMay Theresa D—†	40	housewife	32	"
L	Stanton Margaret F—†	44	at home	78	
M	Waters John H	44	laborer	49	"
N	Waters Mary E—†	44	housewife	49	"
O	Bowen Harriet F—†	44	at home	69	
P	Dugan Annie F—†	44	"	80	"
R	Hassett Josephine H—†	44	housewife	42	76 Bourne

6

Weld Hill Street—Continued

Page.	Letter.	FULL NAME.	Residence, Jan. 1, 1941.	Occupation.	Supposed Age.	Reported Residence, Jan. 1, 1940. Street and Number.
	s	Hassett Walter R	44	salesman	42	76 Bourne
	t	Barnicle Mary A—†	48	housewife	58	here
	u	Barnicle Peter	48	carpenter	60	"
	v	Birmingham Catherine—†	48	dressmaker	87	"
	w	Neary Mary A—†	48	housewife	75	"
	x	Corcoran Bridget J—†	48	"	58	
	y	Corcoran Frank R	48	salesman	28	"
	z	Corcoran John J	48	machinist	59	"
1527						
	a	Corcoran Margaret E—†	48	bookkeeper	30	"
	b	Corcoran Mary L—†	48	secretary	24	"
	c	Moynihan James J	50	operator	38	"
	d	Moynihan Julia J—†	50	housewife	38	"
	e	McGrath Joseph M	50	clerk	51	
	f	McGrath Margaret J—†	50	housewife	49	"
	g	McGrath Thomas M	50	usher	21	
	h	Folsom Agnes B—†	50	at home	73	
	k	Kearin Harold J	50	cutter	48	
	l	Kearin Luella—†	50	housewife	45	"
	m	Farr Eva M—†	52	"	38	
	n	Farr Glenn W	52	machinist	40	"
	o	Knight Evelyn T—†	52	at home	60	
	r	Corcoran Helen M—†	52	operator	52	
	s	Carlson August	54	retired	91	
	t	Lang Carl J	54	"	85	
	u*	Wilholm Gustava—†	54	housekeeper	74	"
	v	Broderick John J	54	manager	42	"
	w*	Broderick Mary T—†	54	housewife	33	"
	x	Svenson Frances M—†	54	"	34	
	y	Svenson George J	54	auditor	37	"
	z	Ferrie Daniel J	60	salesman	52	75 Seymour
1528						
	a	Ferrie Mary A—†	60	housewife	49	75 "
	b	Ferrie Rita F—†	60	stenographer	20	75 "
	c	Fallon Edward F	60	clerk	22	here
	d	Fallon Mary J—†	60	housewife	45	"
	e	Fallon Thomas J	60	collector	53	"
	f	Fallon Thomas J, jr	60	"	23	
	g	Fallon William F	60	clerk	21	
	h	Campbell Anna T—†	64	housewife	40	"
	k	Campbell George C	64	chauffeur	41	"
	l	Doyle Irene M—†	64	housewife	33	"

Weld Hill Street—Continued

M	Doyle Maurice F	64	salesman	35	here
N	Ciccolo Rosario	64	cutter	26	"
O	Perry Bertha N—†	66	housewife	43	"
P	*Kelly Patrick	66	laborer	42	
R	*Nickerson Margaret S—†	66	housewife	38	"
S	Nickerson Morton W	66	laborer	38	
T	Sayers Stanley P	68	blacksmith	56	"
U	Sayers Susan—†	68	housewife	48	"
V	Savill Annie E—†	68	"	66	5 Carlford rd
W	Savill Horace E	68	mattressworker	60	5 "
X	Savill Josephine F—†	68	housewife	28	5 "
Y	Savill Sidney A	68	clerk	29	5 "
Z	Savill Vincent	68	baker	28	19 Gay Head

1529

A	*Mahoney Bridget T—†	70	housewife	30	here
B	Mahoney Peter P	70	laborer	39	"
C	Browne Catherine—†	70	housewife	29	24 Fawndale rd
D	Browne Daniel	70	clerk	30	24 "
E	Doherty James	70	laborer	44	172 Hyde Park av
F	Doherty Mary A—†	70	housewife	33	172 "
G	Doherty Phillip	70	laborer	33	172 "
H	Gerety Elizabeth—†	74	housewife	70	here
K	Gerety John	74	retired	79	"
L	McLaughlin Katherine—†	74	housekeeper	72	"
M	Colgan Irene E—†	74	clerk	32	"
N	Colgan James J	74	retired	70	
O	Colgan Margaret J—†	74	stenographer	28	"
P	Colgan Mary C—†	74	housewife	39	"
R	Brady Elizabeth A—†	74	operator	45	
S	Monahan John F	76	leatherworker	29	"
T	*Monahan Mary A—†	76	housewife	29	"
U	Brauneis Frederick	76	draftsman	49	"
V	Brauneis Henry	76	carpenter	38	"
W	Brauneis Lillian K—†	76	housewife	36	"
X	Sowkow Anne L—†	76	hairdresser	23	76 Weld

Woodlawn Street

Y	Wilcox Alfred T	3	serviceman	35	here
Z	Wilcox Anna—†	3	housewife	31	"

1530
Woodlawn Street—Continued

A	McCabe Edward J	3	inspector	36	here
B	McCabe Evelyn R—†	3	housewife	30	"
C	O'Donnell Dorothy D—†	5	"	28	Worcester
D	O'Donnell John L	5	salesman	28	"
E	McGarry Helen E—†	6	housewife	35	here
F	McGarry Stephen T	6	inspector	35	"
G	*Armfelt Anna E—†	6	housekeeper	63	Quincy
H	Boutin Amelia B—†	6	nurse	39	here
K	*Nelson Martha E—†	6	housewife	37	"
L	Nelson Walter G	6	carpenter	40	"
M	Dosch Albert E	6A	rigger	45	
N	Dosch Sarah V—†	6A	housewife	50	"
O	Strickland Eldon M	7	chauffeur	37	5 Woodlawn
P	Strickland Madeline M—†	7	housewife	28	5 "
R	Ahern James F	8	laborer	44	19 Stellman rd
S	Ahern Nora M—†	8	housewife	44	19 "
T	*Cox Frances M—†	8A	"	52	108 Neponset av
U	Hunt Dorothy C—†	8A	hairdresser	33	108 "
V	*Nelson Elsie E—†	8A	housewife	40	here
W	Nelson Gustav A	8A	mechanic	40	"
X	Bellew Agnes M—†	9	housewife	65	12 Sagamore
Y	Callahan Eveleen E—†	9	"	37	12 "
Z	*Judge John C	9	stableman	65	here

1531

A	*Judge Mary J—†	9	housewife	62	"
B	Conway John H	11	retired	71	
C	Conway John H, jr	11	waiter	49	
D	Conway William F	11	laborer	29	"
E	Ollen Helen—†	11	housewife	56	"
F	Ollen Stanley	11	laborer	23	"
G	Blackwood Alice M—†	11½	secretary	28	Brookline
H	Blackwood Cyril J	11½	accountant	28	"
K	O'Leary Arthur J	12	laborer	29	here
L	O'Leary Charles M	12	mechanic	65	"
M	O'Leary Edward F	12	laborer	21	"
N	O'Leary Mary A—†	12	housewife	54	"
O	Bradley Sarah—†	12	clerk	60	"
P	Conrad James	12	manufacturer	51	Florida
R	Walodse Elsie—†	12	secretary	34	here
S	Walodse Selma—†	12	bookkeeper	36	"

Woodlawn Street—Continued

	Letter	Full Name	Res.	Occupation	Age	Reported Residence
	T	Walsh Evelyn S—†	14	housewife	36	here
	U	Walsh Thomas P	14	agent	35	"
	V	Goode Gerard J	14	mechanic	21	217 Gardner
	W	Goode James M	14	laborer	26	217 "
	X	Goode Mary A—†	14	housewife	61	217 "
	Y	Goode Mary E—†	14	packer	28	217 '
	Z	Goode Owen	14	laborer	65	217 "
1532						
	A	Goode Rita K—†	14	stenographer	23	217 "
	B	Walsh Anna T—†	14	clerk	32	here
	C	Walsh David R	14	laborer	23	"
	D	Walsh Ellen T—†	14	housewife	63	"
	E	Walsh Mary A—†	14	stenographer	34	"
	F	Walsh Rose E—†	14	"	30	
	G	Driscoll John J	15	laborer	48	
	H	*Driscoll Theresa B—†	15	housewife	48	"
	K	Corey Clara G—†	16	"	58	
	L	Corey James W	16	painter	63	"
	M	Corey Mary T—†	16	waitress	21	"
	N	Delaney Phyllis A—†	16	housewife	24	Brookline
	O	Delaney William E	16	superintendent	35	18 Tower
	P	Megerditchian Ervant D	16	printer	53	here
	R	Morris Ann C—†	16	housewife	52	"
	S	Clarke Elizabeth—†	17	"	51	4 Linden av
	T	Clarke Thomas W	17	clerk	48	4 "
	U	Cochrane Anna C—†	17	housewife	37	2944 Wash'n
	V	Cochrane Joseph M	17	laborer	40	2944 "
	W	Sullivan Edward T	19	chauffeur	39	here
	X	Sullivan Margaret C—†	19	housewife	39	"
	Y	Connors Catherine T—†	19	"	38	"
	Z	Connors James E	19	carpenter	40	"
1533						
	A	Durkin Dominick	19	gardener	31	Peabody
	B	Durkin Sheila—†	19	housewife	28	52 Chestnut
	C	Johnson Lillian A—†	19	"	25	41 Philbrick
	D	Johnson Robert A	19	manager	28	41 "
	E	Strick Arthur	20	mechanic	38	here
	F	*Strick Helen—†	20	dressmaker	38	"
	G	McPhee Catherine T—†	20	housewife	33	"
	H	McPhee Joseph F	20	clerk	46	"
	K	Bradley Anna M—†	20	housewife	44	22 Parker

Wocdlawn Street—Continued

L	Bradley Lawrence A	20	policeman	46	22 Parker
M	Small Ellen B—†	20	at home	63	Salem
N	Delaney Mary C—†	25	housewife	29	here
O	Delaney Patrick J	25	custodian	34	"
P	Broderick Joseph M	25	driller	24	"
R	Broderick Theresa—†	25	housewife	53	"
S	Broderick Thomas	25	ironworker	55	"
T	Dunn Benedict J	25	retired	85	
U	Smith Bernice R—†	25	housewife	39	"
V	Smith Ernest B	25	chauffeur	40	"
w	*Gourley Christine S—†	27	housewife	49	"
X	Gourley John S	27	chauffeur	39	"
Y	Dolan Ellen E—†	27	clerk	29	
Z	Dolan Mary A—†	27	"	34	
	1534				
A	Dolan Peter F	27	laborer	36	
B	Gilleo Catherine F—†	27	housewife	30	"
C	Gilleo John F	27	chauffeur	34	"
D	Murray Mary—†	29	housewife	55	"
E	Murray Mary E—†	29	stenographer	21	"
F	Murray Patrick	29	mechanic	54	"
G	Murray Ruth M—†	29	nurse	20	
H	Regan Francis A	29	clerk	46	
K	Regan Julia A—†	29	housewife	46	"
L	Allan Edith G—†	29	"	55	
M	Allan Elaine D—†	29	clerk	20	"
N	Fitzpatrick Blanche E—†	30	housewife	37	"
O	Fitzpatrick George A	30	salesman	45	"
P	Lonergan Bertha M—†	30	clerk	44	
R	Lonergan Susan A—†	30	housewife	64	"
S	Noble Clinton A	30	carpenter	45	"
T	Noble Durwood B	30	porter	22	
U	Noble Nellie S—†	30	housewife	43	"
V	Backoff Doris M—†	30	binder	26	
w	Backoff William E	30	shoeworker	33	"
X	Maloof Anna—†	31	housewife	44	46 Woodlawn
Y	Maloof George	31	clerk	46	46 "
Z	Maloof Mary F—†	31	student	20	46 "
	1535				
A	Desmond Jerome J	31	bartender	51	here
B	Desmond Josephine E—†	31	housewife	48	"

Page.	Letter.	FULL NAME.	Residence, Jan. 1, 1941.	Occupation.	Supp'sed Age.	Reported Residence, Jan. 1, 1940. Street and Number.

Woodlawn Street—Continued

c	Desmond Lillian T—†	31	saleswoman	23	here
d	Desmond William J	31	U S A	21	"
e	McCarthy Anna M—†	32	housewife	29	"
f	McCarthy John F	32	mechanic	36	"
g	Haddad Elizabeth—†	32	clerk	32	
h	Haddad Joseph	32	chauffeur	33	"
k	*Pazaree Barbara A—†	32	housewife	55	"
l	Pazaree Charles D	32	machinist	56	"
m	Pazaree Charles J	32	"	24	
n	*Fallon Mary C—†	34	housewife	33	"
o	Fallon Peter J	34	shipper	30	"
p	Stone Frances M—†	34	at home	50	Revere
r	Kelley Elsie I—†	34	packer	27	here
s	LaPlante Daniel P	34	plumber	29	"
t	LaPlante Mabel M—†	34	housewife	29	"
u	Johnson Clyde A	34	draftsman	34	"
v	Johnson Eva R—†	34	housewife	24	"
w	Gaulitz Marie C—†	35	"	33	
x	*Gaulitz Olaf R	35	painter	32	
y	Hobson Joseph P	37	clerk	37	
z	Hobson Theresa M—†	37	housewife	35	"

1536

a	Corcell Angela A—†	37	hairdresser	25	532 Hyde Park av
b	Cummings Edward J	37	chauffeur	28	532 "
c	Cummings Theresa R—†	37	housewife	27	532 "
d	Mintz Elizabeth B—†	38	"	31	3235 Wash'n
e	Mintz Julius	38	operator	39	3235 "
f	Duerden Albert H	38	deckhand	48	189 Bourne
g	Duerden Annie M—†	38	housewife	34	189 "
h	Johnson John J	38	clerk	34	29 Gartland
k	Johnson Laura M—†	38	housewife	28	29 "
l	*Backman Ida L—†	39	operator	52	here
m	*Bayers Sophia—†	39	housewife	63	"
n	McFarland John A	39	watchman	64	"
o	Fay Nellie E—†	39	housewife	31	"
p	Fay Robert C	39	attendant	29	"
r	Jones Lenetta—†	40	housewife	47	Braintree
s	Jones Neal D	40	starter	43	"
t	*Milton Sanford H	40	painter	37	here
u	Milton Svea E—†	40	housewife	32	"
v	Mooers Daniel T	40	salesman	35	"

22

Page.	Letter.	Full Name	Residence, Jan. 1, 1941.	Occupation.	Supposed Age.	Reported Residence, Jan. 1, 1940. Street and Number.

Woodlawn Street—Continued

w	Mooers Elizabeth I—†	40	housewife	34	here
x	Harrington Catherine—†	41	"	30	26 Caton
y	Harrington Timothy P	41	fisherman	34	26 "
z	O'Dowd Patrick J	41	cutter	36	77 Wenham
	1537				
a	Fitzgerald Alice A—†	42	dressmaker	44	142 Thornton
b	Fitzgerald Mary R—†	42	maid	20	142 "
c	Fitzgerald Richard E	42	painter	71	142 "
d	Fitzgerald William F	42	machinist	20	142 "
e	Butler Edward J	44	stenographer	26	here
f	Butler Elizabeth M—†	44	"	28	"
g	Butler Martin B	44	clerk	27	"
h	Evans Bridget—†	44	cleaner	52	"
l	Beardsley Robert F	46	chauffeur	35	32 Newbern
m	Beardsley Ruth M—†	46	housewife	32	32 "
n	Burke Annie J—†	46	"	49	52 Woodlawn
o	Burke Mary V—†	46	bookkeeper	23	52 "
p	Burke William M	46	operator	21	52 "
r	Arpin Mary A—†	47	houseworker	49	here
s	Gorman Doris M—†	47	at home	20	"
t	Gorman Ella M—†	47	housewife	59	"
u	Gorman Richard E	47	timekeeper	22	"
v	DeRoche Arthur J	47	salesman	35	Cambridge
w	DeRoche Mary—†	47	housewife	35	"
x	Collins Bridget M—†	47	"	72	here
y	Collins Timothy A	47	machinist	70	"
z	Linso Elizabeth F—†	48	housewife	34	"
	1538				
a	Nicholson Elizabeth F—†	48	"	58	··
b	Nicholson Harold W	48	laborer	20	"
c*	Doherty Catherine—†	49	housewife	30	52 Brookley rd
d	Doherty John	49	cleaner	28	52 "
e	Doherty Joseph	49	laborer	60	here
f	Doherty Mary—†	49	housewife	55	"
g	Lewis Albert C	49	salesman	28	63 Walk Hill
h	Lewis Bridget T—†	49	housewife	26	here
k	Doherty Cecilia V—†	49	operator	23	"
l	Doherty James A	49	chauffeur	27	"
m	Doherty John T	49	laborer	24	
n	Doherty Mary E—†	49	stenographer	30	"
o	Feeney Elizabeth F—†	51	housewife	46	"

Woodlawn Street—Continued

P	Feeney James J	51	laborer	59	here
R	Feeney John P	51	counterman	22	"
S	O'Rourke Charles L	51	laborer	22	"
T	O'Rourke Katherine—†	51	housewife	48	"
U	O'Rourke Katherine V—†	51	at home	21	
V	O'Rourke William J	51	clerk	25	
W	Howley Agnes—†	51	housewife	38	"
X	Howley Joseph P	51	laborer	40	"
Y	Wilkins Helen M—†	52	housewife	29	4 Rockdale
Z	Wilkins Walter H	52	chef	33	4 "

1539

A	Wilmarth Bernice D—†	52	housewife	40	Haverhill
B	Wilmarth Irvin R	52	patternmaker	35	"
C	Cawley Patrick J	52	chauffeur	36	here
D	*Cawley Winifred J—†	52	housewife	39	"
E	Barnett Ethel M—†	54	"	33	"
F	Barnett John J	54	riveter	30	
G	Kelley Anna—†	54	housewife	36	"
H	Kelley James	54	steamfitter	38	"
K	Mullen Mary E—†	54	housewife	44	"
L	Griffin Evelyn M—†	55	saleswoman	23	"
M	Nihill Daniel J	55	marbleworker	65	"
N	Nihill Margaret F—†	55	housewife	51	"
O	Cunningham Harriet A-†	55	"	36	
P	Cunningham Thomas F	55	operator	25	"
R	Sloan George W	55	longshoreman	38	"
S	Sloan Mary E—†	55	housewife	35	"
T	*Steponkus Anna M—†	56	"	49	
U	Steponkus William B	56	machinist	20	"
V	Carney Charles W	56	laborer	41	
W	Carney Rose M—†	56	housewife	39	"
X	Dufour Fred	56	clerk	61	
Y	Stafford Antoinette M—†	56	housewife	47	"
Z	Stafford Walter S	56	salesman	48	"

1540

A	O'Brien James P	59	conductor	69	"
B	O'Brien Margaret M—†	59	housewife	61	"
C	O'Brien William F	59	machinist	20	"
D	*Spruin William F	59	electrician	53	"
E	*Kelly Ruby B—†	59	cashier	32	
F	*Noonan Clyde F	59	usher	21	

Woodlawn Street—Continued

G	*Noonan Cyril R	59	machinist	27	here
H	*Noonan James B	59	clerk	57	"
K	*Noonan Loretta C—†	59	housewife	55	"
L	*Kerrigan Anna M—†	59	"	33	327 Hyde Park av
M	Kerrigan Daniel	59	chauffeur	42	327 "
N	*Callahan Bertha J—†	60	housewife	44	here
O	Callahan James A	60	bricklayer	46	"
P	Day David J	60	painter	57	"
R	Day Elizabeth M—†	60	housewife	41	"
T	Iverson Oscar A	63	carpenter	47	"
U	McGilvray Albert J	63	neonworker	26	"
V	McGilvray Catherine—†	63	housewife	66	"
W	McGilvray Edward	63	laborer	65	
X	McGilvray George	63	clerk	35	"
Y	McGilvray Isabelle S—†	63	typist	37	"
Z	Smith Evelyn R—†	63	teacher	30	

1541

A	McNulty Frank J	64	engraver	54	"
B	McNulty Madeline F—†	64	housewife	40	"
C	Storey Gertrude E—†	64	"	38	
E	Laing George	65	machinist	40	"
F	Laing Isabelle J—†	65	housewife	42	"
G	Walsh Bernard F	65	operator	54	"
H	Walsh Delia F—†	65	housewife	53	"
K	Walsh Francis B	65	machinist	25	"
L	Walsh Mary R—†	65	operator	23	"
M	MacDonald Archibald A	66	ironworker	50	"
N	MacDonald Margaret M-†66		housewife	49	"
O	*Wylie Margaret M—†	66	clerk	27	
P	*Griffin Helen—†	68	housewife	37	"
R	Griffin John F	68	laborer	34	
S	Dolan Margaret A—†	68	housewife	65	"
T	Dolan William F	68	clerk	62	
U	*Chetwynd Etta B—†	69	housewife	39	"
V	*Chetwynd Mitchell L	69	mechanic	40	"
X	Cronin Katherine—†	69	attendant	56	"
Y	Cronin William	69	laundryman	50	"
Z	Kirby Hannah M—†	70	housewife	66	"

1542

A	Kirby Jeremiah F	70	inspector	32	"
B	Kirby Kathleen H—†	70	stenographer	27	"

Page.	Letter.	FULL NAME.	Residence, Jan. 1, 1941.	Occupation.	Supposed Age.	Reported Residence, Jan. 1, 1940. Street and Number.

Woodlawn Street—Continued

	c	Burke Catherine E—†	72	assembler	47	Weymouth
	D	Kearney Daniel H	72	carpenter	49	here
	E	Kearney Daniel H, jr	72	U S A	22	"
	F	Kearney Johanna T—†	72	housewife	49	"
	G	Cunniff Martin	74	merchant	47	"
	H	Cunniff Mary E—†	74	housewife	47	"
	K	Cunniff Michael J	74	chauffeur	57	"
	L	McLoughlin Joseph P	76	laborer	45	
	M	McLoughlin Katherine M—†76		housewife	44	"
	N	*Kirby Anna B—†	76	"	34	
	o	Kirby William E	76	foreman	37	
	P	Donovan Joseph E	77	electrician	38	"
	R	Donovan Nora A—†	77	housewife	38	"
	s	Bermingham Bridget A—†	77	"	55	
	T	Bermingham Mary C—†	77	typist	28	
	U	Bermingham Phillip E	77	laborer	23	
	v	Mehrhoff George F	77	agent	36	
	w	Mehrhoff Mary G—†	77	housewife	28	"
	x	Greene James F	78	laborer	20	"
	Y	Greene John P	78	"	56	
	z	Greene Joseph W	78	clerk	21	

1543

	A	Greene Mary—†	78	housewife	50	"
	B	Kilday Dennis J	78	plumber	40	"
	c	Wagner Elsie V—†	78	housewife	50	68 Rockdale
	D	Wagner William J	78	operator	49	68 "
	E	Kirkpatrick Doris E—†	78	housewife	28	Somerville
	F	Kirkpatrick Lemuel A	78	machinist	38	"
	G	Brennan Clare F—†	80	secretary	35	here
	H	Brennan Margaret J—†	80	"	38	"
	K	Conway Maurice B	83	guard	71	"
	L	Harrington Mildred L—†	83	clerk	41	

Ward 11—Precinct 16

CITY OF BOSTON

LIST OF RESIDENTS
20 YEARS OF AGE AND OVER

(NON-CITIZENS INDICATED BY ASTERISK)
(FEMALES INDICATED BY DAGGER)

AS OF

JANUARY 1, 1941

JOSEPH F. TIMILTY, *Chairman*
FREDERIC E. DOWLING, *Secretary*
WILLIAM A. MOTLEY, JR.
FRANCIS B. McKINNEY
HILDA HEDSTROM QUIRK

Listing Board.

CITY OF BOSTON PRINTING DEPARTMENT

1600

Anson Street

A	Cunningham Loretta C—†	9	housewife	36	here
B	Cunningham William F	9	milkman	40	"
C	Cain Patrick E	9	retired	72	"
D	Cunningham Catherine J-†	9	clerk	44	
E	Cunningham Mary E—-†	9	"	52	
F	Madden Bernard W	11–11A	retired	42	
G	Madden Delia—†	11–11A	housewife	70	"
H	*Cronin Bridget T-†	11–11A	"	40	
K	Cronin Timothy	11–11A	fireman	45	"
L	Horgan John A	11–11A	clerk	30	108 School
M	Clay Rose A—†	11–11A	housewife	37	here
N	Allen Kathleen—†	12	"	47	"
O	Allen Samuel J	12	metalworker	48	"
P	Dufresne Cara J—†	12	housewife	69	"
R	Dufresne Edward P	12	machinist	75	"
S	LaPointe Emma E—†	12	at home	67	
T	Crowell Hazel—†	12	factoryhand	24	"
U	Crowell Laura—†	12	housewife	49	"
V	Getz Mildred B—†	13	"	25	210 Amory
W	Egan Patrick	13	retired	81	here
X	McEachern Elizabeth J—-†	13	housewife	46	30A Jamaica
Y	Shea James R	13	attendant	20	here
Z	Shea Mary J—†	13	housewife	47	"

1601

A	Getz Henry F	13	breweryworker	29	210 Amory
B	Monagle Barney J	14	laborer	50	here
C	*Monagle Margaret M—†	14	housewife	50	"
D	Glennon Delia H—-†	14	"	72	"
E	Glennon Thomas J	14	retired	74	"
F	*Morrissey Bessie M—-†	15	housewife	45	85 Call
G	*Morrissey John J	15	laborer	50	85 "
H	Spellman Margaret—†	15	housewife	39	here
K	Spellman Thomas J	15	cleaner	44	"
L	McLachlan Agnes—†	15	housekeeper	72	"
M	*Gardiner Elizabeth E—†	16	housewife	60	"
N	Gardiner Hugh A	16	welder	34	
O	Gardiner Hugh F	16	laborer	61	
P	Gardiner Rose M—†	16	clerk	31	
R	*Long Ethel L—†	17	housewife	28	"
S	Long Francis E	17	supervisor	28	"

T Fennell John J	17	fireman	45	here
U Fennell Sarah E—†	17	housewife	44	"
V Foley Michael	17	retired	78	"
W Connolly Annie F—†	18	housekeeper	63	"
X Lynch Mary J—†	18	at home	60	"
Y *Lynch Catherine—†	18	housewife	33	"
Z *Lynch Patrick J	18	laborer	33	
1602				
A Reardon Mary B—†	19	housewife	37	"
B Nash George	19	painter	24	408 Amory
C Parker Nelson	19	laborer	30	Quincy

Arborway

K Morgan Catherine—†	350	housewife	75	here
H Morgan James F	350	attorney	41	"
L McGowan Ellen J—†	352	teacher	39	"
M Sullivan John P	352	supervisor	38	"
N Sullivan Marjory D—†	352	housewife	38	"
P McCarthy Harold T	356	engineer	37	
R McCarthy Helen A—†	356	housewife	30	"
S O'Connor Daniel G	356	clerk	32	
T O'Connor Daniel J	356	retired	76	"
U Greer Beatrice E—†	358	clerk	35	
V Leveroni Edna M—†	358	student	20	
W Leveroni Frank J	358	attorney	61	
X Leveroni Heloise R—†	358	clerk	22	"
Y Leveroni Louise—†	358	housewife	60	"
Z Leveroni Vivian—†	358	clerk	27	
1603				
A Kelley Agnes M—†	360	housewife	55	"
B Kelley Ferdinand T	360	auditor	26	
C Donahue Dorothy T—†	362	housewife	45	"
D Downey Agnes G—†	362	at home	54	
E Downey Arthur T	362	retired	64	
F Downey Dorothy T—†	362	housewife	41	"
G Downey Ella T—†	362	housekeeper	75	"
H Downey Joseph T	362	clerk	38	"
K Sullivan Patrick	362	retired	82	
L Kirby Cecelia R—†	364	stenographer	41	"
M Kirby Mary A—†	364	housekeeper	46	"

Arborway—Continued

N	McMorrow John J	364	broker	41	71 Stanley
o	McMorrow Margaret M—†	364	housewife	37	71 "
P	Collins Ann C—†	366	clerk	35	here
R	Kelly Anna C—†	366	housewife	64	"
s	Kelly Edward T	366	assessor	70	"
T	Kelly Mary A—†	366	secretary	25	"
U	Kelly Philip R	366	manager	30	"
V	Kelly Ruth M—†	366	student	21	
w	Curry Madeline J—†	368	teacher	49	"
x	Curry Mary L—†	368	housewife	60	"
Y	Joyce Agnes M—†	370	at home	65	
z	Joyce Ellen F—†	370	"	63	

1604

A	Kenney John T	370	attorney	70	"
B	Kenney John T, jr	370	realtor	30	
C	Kenney Mary A—†	370	teacher	28	
D	Mullen Thomas H	370	retired	70	
E	Connors Katherine G—†	374	at home	60	
F	Holland Louise—†	374	teacher	24	
G	Holland Margaret A—†	374	housewife	59	"
H	Syderman Abraham	376	manufacturer	76	"
K	Trimbach Laura A—†	376	housekeeper	56	"
L	Killion Margaret F—†	384	at home	57	"
M	Troy Sarah E—†	384	housewife	52	"
N	Troy William A	384	editor	54	
o	Troy William A, jr	384	student	20	
P	Robinson Leo	388	manager	33	"
R	Robinson Maurice	388	agent	28	
s	Robinson Rose—†	388	housewife	65	"
T	Robinson Samuel	388	salesman	26	"
U	Godfrey Margaret E—†	392	at home	55	"
V	O'Brien Lois G—†	392	housewife	47	"

Hampstead Road

w	Egan Adelaide D—†	1	housewife	29	here
x	Egan Francis J	1	manager	30	"
Y	McNaughton Clarita—†	1	at home	45	19 Thomas
z	Donovan John J	1	contractor	34	here

1605

A	Donovan Noreen—†	1	housewife	33	"

Hampstead Road—Continued

	Letter	Full Name	Residence Jan. 1, 1941	Occupation	Supposed Age	Reported Residence Jan. 1, 1940 Street and Number
	B	Walsh Delia A—†	3	housewife	49	here
	C	Walsh Kathleen M—†	3	clerk	27	"
	D	Walsh Martin J	3	painter	53	"
	E	McAuliffe Michael J	3	salesman	39	"
	F	O'Brien Madeline R—†	3	stenographer	24	"
	G	Walsh Frederick J	3	investigator	37	"
	H	Walsh Helen F—†	3	at home	54	
	K	Walsh John O	3	salesman	52	"
	L	Walsh William H	3	clerk	51	"
	M	Kelly Rita P—†	5	housewife	25	9 St Peter
	N	Kelly Thomas J, jr	5	contractor	28	9 "
	O	Flanagan James J	7	porter	62	here
	P	Flanagan Joseph T	7	agent	29	"
	R	Flanagan Mary J—†	7	housewife	62	"
	S	Flanagan Mary J—†	7	typist	25	
	T	Hines Bridget G—†	9	housewife	73	"
	U	Hines Helen R—†	9	teacher	34	
	V	Hines Sarah A—†	9	stenographer	40	"
	W	Hines William J	9	machinist	52	"
	X	Leach William M	9	chauffeur	36	Rhode Island
	Y	Makant Mabel—†	9	saleswoman	48	"
	Z	McGinnis Isabelle—†	9	at home	59	"
1606						
	A	Warner Norman E	9	salesman	32	Waltham
	B	White Emily G—†	14	housewife	42	here
	C	White Emily J—†	14	bookkeeper	20	"
	D	Finan Helen J—†	14	teacher	26	"
	E	Finan Helena J—†	14	housewife	58	"
	F	Finan Mary C—†	14	at home	27	
	G	Finan William D	14	student	24	
	H	Finan William F	14	retired	68	
	K	Carney Dorothy C—†	15	housewife	25	"
	L	Carney William F	15	statistician	27	70 Fletcher
	M	Hechinger Beatrice M—†	15	housewife	47	here
	N	Hechinger Herbert A	15	editor	59	"
	O	Lane Catherine E—†	15	housewife	41	"
	P	Lane James M	15	clerk	48	"
	R	Clemont Beatrice—†	16	secretary	38	"
	S	Clemont Joseph R	16	foreman	40	
	T	Jackson Joseph G	16	manager	50	"
	U	McGann Margaret—†	16	housekeeper	58	Somerville

Hampstead Road—Continued

v	Batic Marion L—†	16	housewife	30	here
w	Batic Michael	16	floorlayer	42	"
x	Bittihoffer Catherine—†	16	dietitian	53	"
y	Bittihoffer Thomas	16	student	20	
z	Desmond Maud—†	16	clerk	30	

1607

a	Desmond Robert	16	mechanic	32	"
b	Larkin Mark	16	contractor	36	"
c	Lydon James	16	student	28	"
d	*Harney Helen T—†	24	housewife	39	2 Roseclair
e	Harney James J	24	custodian	49	2 "
f	Byrne Catherine F—†	24	at home	67	here
g	Sullivan John J	24	retired	69	"
h	Sullivan Mary E—†	24	housewife	53	"
k	Hutchinson Catherine—†	27	"	64	"
l	Hutchinson John M	27	operator	29	"
m	Hutchinson Rita—†	27	housewife	26	"
n	Kenny Bernard	27	letter carrier	63	"
o	Kenny Mildred—†	27	nurse	28	"
p	Galvin Josephine G—†	27	housewife	35	48 Spring Park Ave
r	Galvin William P	27	chemist	29	48 "
s	McMahon James	27	laborer	63	48 "
t	McMahon Rebecca—†	27	at home	58	48 "
u	McPhee Joseph	27	chauffeur	31	206 South
v	McPhee Mary—†	27	housewife	68	206 "
w	McPhee Rita—†	27	stenographer	20	206 "
y	Shea Bridget M—†	35	housewife	74	here
z	Shea Pauline F—†	35	teacher	39	"

1608

a	Shea Thomas J	35	contractor	80	"
b	Cohan John A	36	broker	36	
c	Cohan Margaret M—†	36	examiner	39	"
d	Cohan Mary T—†	36	housewife	70	"
e	Cohan T Francis	36	letter carrier	41	"
f	Costello John M	36	retired	67	
g	Costello Leo J	36	broker	31	
h	Costello Mary J—†	36	housewife	67	"
k	Costello Paul J	36	fireman	28	
l	Leary Henry F	36	teacher	30	
m	Hall Louis	37	watchman	59	"
n	*Hall Ragnhold—†	37	housewife	45	"

Page.	Letter.	Full Name.	Residence, Jan. 1, 1941.	Occupation.	Supposed Age.	Reported Residence, Jan. 1, 1940.
						Street and Number.

Hampstead Road—Continued

	O	Arnold Eugene C	37	musician	44	here
	P	Arnold Josephine—†	37	housewife	45	"
	R	Quinn Helen F—†	37	clerk	33	240 Arborway
	S	Thompson Edith O—†	37	"	23	here
	T	Thompson Mary A—†	37	housewife	65	"
	U	Thompson Ruth M—†	37	manager	28	"
	Y	Klueber Elizabeth M—†	40	housewife	53	"
	Z	Klueber Gertrude R—†	40	secretary	29	"
1609						
	A	Klueber Joseph A	40	contractor	63	"
	B	Klueber Mary J—†	40	clerk	26	"
	C	Post Gertrude—†	40	nurse	40	
	D	Scott Gertrude—†	40	"	30	
	E	Meleedy Francis	43	retired	78	
	F	Meleedy Mary L—†	43	secretary	42	"
	G	Meleedy Rose A—†	43	typist	27	
	H	Meleedy Teresa U—†	43	designer	40	
	K	Ronan Frederick J	43	supervisor	42	"
	L	Ronan James W	43	operator	56	
	M	Ronan Mildred C—†	43	at home	38	
	N	Green Anna—†	44	bookkeeper	40	"
	O	Green John	44	architect	39	"
	P	Green Mary—†	44	saleswoman	41	"
	R	Glennon James G	44	clergyman	41	"
	S	Glennon Maria—†	44	housewife	69	"
	T	Glennon Marie C—†	44	teacher	36	
	U	Glennon Thomas	44	retired	71	
	V	Glennon Thomas P	44	electrician	38	"
	W	Blackstock Honora M—†	47	at home	22	61 Brook
	X	Sullivan Joseph B	47	pilot	30	61 "
	Y	Blomberg Alma C—†	47	at home	72	here
	Z	Blomberg Edith M—†	47	"	67	"
1610						
	A	Blomberg Emma M—†	47	clerk	69	
	B	Blomberg Hilma L—†	47	at home	78	
	C	Francis Ida B—†	47	"	63	
	D	Griffith Irma—†	47	"	61	"
	E	McLaughlin Anne D—†	48	teacher	34	9 Hampstead rd
	F	McLaughlin Henry P	48	"	54	9 "
	G	McLaughlin Mary A—†	48	"	52	9 "
	H	Reardon Alice—†	50	stenographer	20	73 Jamaica

Hampstead Road—Continued

K	Reardon Catherine—†	50	stenographer	20	73 Jamaica
L	Reardon Charles W	50	operator	40	73 "
M	Reardon Mary M—†	50	housewife	40	73 "
N	Fogarty Arthur G	51	engineer	40	here
O	Fogarty Mary C—†	51	housewife	43	"
P	Mooney Lawrence L	51	draftsman	36	17 Kingsbury
R	Amnotte John J	51	welder	28	17 Seaverns av
S	Amnotte Mary F—†	51	housewife	24	17 "
T	McIntyre Mary E—†	51	"	44	5 Thomas
U	McIntyre Robert E	51	clerk	22	5 "
V	Keating Elizabeth P—†	52	housewife	63	98 St Rose
W	Keating John J	52	mechanic	53	98 "
X	Keating Marion E—†	52	secretary	36	98 "
Y	Fitzgerald Elizabeth J—†	54	housewife	53	here
Z	Fitzgerald Mary L—†	54	teacher	24	"
	1611				
A	Fitzgerald Mortimer F	54	printer	58	"
B	Cain Joseph F	56	accountant	46	319 Faneuil
C	Cain Viola W—†	56	housewife	39	319 "
D	Ramsdell Catherine B—†	56	"	45	here
E	Ramsdell Catherine M—†	56	student	20	"
F	Ramsdell Robert	56	proprietor	47	"
G	Whalen Andrew	59	janitor	60	
H	Whalen Anna—†	59	stenographer	26	"
K	Whalen Eileen—†	59	"	23	"
L	Whalen Esther—†	59	clerk	28	
M	Burke Agnes—†	59	housewife	52	"
N	Burke Athena—†	59	clerk	24	
O	Burke William T	59	retired	62	
P	Murray Helen G—†	59	clerk	42	
R	Murray Mary A—†	59	housewife	74	"
S	Murray William H	59	retired	75	"
T	Gaff Thomas	60	student	25	Maine
U	Peacock Deane S	60	teacher	47	here
V	Peacock Deane S, jr	60	salesman	22	"
W	Peacock Eleanor—†	60	stenographer	20	26 Newbury
X	Peacock Ruth—†	60	housewife	43	here
Y	Gambon Andrew	61	accountant	48	"
Z	Gambon Christopher	61	student	21	"
	1612				
A	Gambon Nellie—†	61	housewife	50	"

8

Hampstead Road—Continued

B	O'Brien Mary F—†	61	housewife	40	here
C	O'Brien William P	61	retired	70	"
D	O'Brien William P, jr	61	pharmacist	42	"
E	Marshall Joseph P, jr	61	clerk	33	"
F	Marshall Margaret—†	61	housewife	40	"
G	Brown Catherine M—†	67	"	31	
H	Brown Gerald F	67	polisher	31	
K	Reynolds Charles A	67	student	20	
L	Reynolds Ellen—†	67	housewife	60	"
M	Reynolds James D	67	machinist	60	"
N*	Leonard Anne—†	71–73	housewife	47	"
O	Leonard Patrick	71–73	clerk	50	"
P	Barry Lillian M—†	71–73	housewife	45	39 Hampstead rd
R	Barry Thomas A	71–73	salesman	44	39 "
S	Rogers Thomas M	71–73	retired	73	39 "
T	Mascone Claire—†	75–77	housewife	33	here
U	Mascone Fred J	75–77	attorney	39	"
V	Glynn Annette—†	75–77	clerk	38	"
W	Glynn Catherine—†	75–77	"	26	
X	Glynn John J	75–77	retired	75	
Y	Glynn Stephen	75–77	repairman	35	"
Z	Fischer Albert A	76	wigmaker	71	"
	1613				
A	Fischer Bertha A—†	76	housewife	68	"
B	Gibbons Edward J	79	clerk	57	
C	Gibbons Ellen E—†	79	housewife	51	"
D	Charbonneau Delima—†	79	at home	73	
E	Genereux Harvey	79	repairman	43	"
F	Genereux Priscilla E—†	79	housewife	37	"

Rosemary Street

G	Mahony Isabella H—†	7	housewife	34	here
H	Mahony James C	7	printer	35	"
K	Mahony Michael W	7	metalworker	42	"
M	Barry Mary A—†	9	stenographer	58	"
N	Campbell Charles	9	carpenter	68	"
O	MacDonald Ella J—†	9	housewife	67	"
P	MacDonald Mary T—†	9	stenographer	41	"
R	Ginty Anthony	11	longshoreman	58	"
S	Ginty Margaret T—†	11	housewife	54	"

Page.	Letter.	Full Name.	Residence, Jan. 1, 1941.	Occupation.	Supposed Age.	Reported Residence, Jan. 1, 1940. Street and Number.

Rosemary Street—Continued

T	Fallon Anna—†	15	housewife	30	here
U	Fallon Patrick J	15	breweryworker	32	"
V	Dolan Catherine—†	15	housewife	44	"
W	Dolan Thomas	15	chauffeur	21	"
X	Dalton Edward G	17	bartender	38	"
Y	Dalton Margaret M—†	17	housewife	37	"
Z	McCarthy Anna E—†	17	teacher	32	

1614

A	McCarthy Elizabeth—†	17	dietitian	22	
B	McCarthy Helen J—†	17	teacher	27	"
C	McCarthy Joseph T	17	salesman	25	"
D	McCarthy Julia A—†	17	housewife	65	"
E	McCarthy Margaret E—†	17	stenographer	36	"
F	McCarthy Mary F—†	17	"	38	"
G	*Keneavy Agnes T—†	19	housewife	42	"
H	*Keneavy Martin J	19	laborer	46	
K	*Moore James	19	"	50	
L	Schneider Ellen A—†	19	housewife	45	"
M	Schneider William H	19	clerk	45	
N	Wentworth John D	19	diemaker	22	"
O	Wentworth Mary A—†	19	waitress	52	
P	Shields Catherine V—†	21	housewife	42	"
R	Shields Columbus M	21	lamplighter	41	"
S	Burke Bridget—†	21	at home	82	11 Woodman
T	Cauley Patrick	21	laborer	55	11 "
U	Riley Annie T—†	21	housewife	54	11 "
V	Riley Timothy J	21	retired	72	11 "
W	*Doherty John	25	laborer	35	here
X	*Haveron Bridget—†	25	housewife	53	"
Y	McLaughlin Joseph	25	laborer	40	"
Z	Dolan Lillian N—†	25	housewife	43	"

1615

A	Dolan Thomas F	25	B F D	45	
B	Murnaghan Daniel	25	laborer	37	
C	*Green Anna H—†	27	housewife	46	"
D	Green Joseph	27	engineer	45	"
E	Hanley Mary E—†	27	at home	70	
F	Monaghan Eleanor M—†	27	housewife	37	"
G	Monaghan Thomas J	27	mechanic	26	"
H	Walsh Edward F	27	painter	46	135 Williams
K	Walsh Kathleen J—†	27	housewife	43	135 "

10

Page.	Letter.	FULL NAME.	Residence, Jan. 1. 1941.	Occupation.	Supposed Age.	Reported Residence, Jan. 1. 1940. Street and Number.

Rosemary Street—Continued

	L	Cole Cecelia J—†	29	housewife	43	here
	M	Cole John J	29	laborer	50	"
	N	Cole Martin J	29	houseman	45	42 Carolina av
	O	Nixon Annie M—†	29	housewife	52	here
	P	Nixon Catherine M—†	29	secretary	26	" .
	R	Nixon Edward G	29	clerk	25	"
	S	Nixon Frederick W	29	"	21	
	T	Nixon John J	29	janitor	60	
	U	Neale Frances S—†	29	housewife	55	"
	V	Neale Walter F	29	watchman	60	"
	W	Dick Joseph A	33–35	signalman	61	"
	X	Dick Mary B—†	33–35	housewife	50	"
	Y	Dick Renoch	33–35	engineer	23	"
	Z	Barrett Sarah—†	33–35	housewife	73	"

1616

	A	McGuinnis Francis	33–35	chauffeur	46	"
	B	Nash John	33–35	laborer	64	"
	C	Roche Catherine A—†	33–35	housewife	43	30 Boynton
	D	Roche Virginia E—†	33–35	operator	20	here

Saint Mark Street

	F	Baird Euphemia—†	7	housewife	40	here
	G	Baird William	7	salesman	42	"
	H	*Arena Amelia—†	9	housewife	43	"
	K	Arena Liborio	9	barber	54	

Saint Rose Street

	M	Daly Mary F—†		housewife	43	here
	N	Daly Parker		wardman	63	"
	O	McCloskey Joseph L		carpenter	53	Newburyport
	P	*Herman Sally—†		cook	27	42 Woodlawn
	R	*Twohig Elizabeth—†		housekeeper	35	here
	S	*Twohig Mary—†	5	cook	33	"
	T	Bartsch Gustave	10–12	salesman	47	"
	U	Bartsch Joseph E	10–12	attendant	21	"
	V	Bartsch Mary F—†	10–12	housewife	46	"
	W	Kelly Elizabeth A—†	10–12	"	38	
	X	Kelly William	10–12	engineer	40	
	Y	Rochefort Helen T—†	10–12	housewife	44	"

Page.	Letter.	FULL NAME.	Residence, Jan. 1, 1941.	Occupation.	Supposed Age.	Reported Residence, Jan. 1, 1940. Street and Number.

Saint Rose Street—Continued

z	Rochefort Henry	10–12	chauffeur	48	here
	1617				
A	Rochefort Mary C—†	10–12	packer	22	
B	Fleming Delia A—†	14–16	housewife	71	"
C	Fleming James F	14–16	cutter	36	
D	Fleming Lillian F—†	14–16	clerk	30	
E	Fleming Mary A—†	14–16	"	45	
F	Brooks Delia J—†	14–16	housewife	64	"
G	Brooks James	14–16	machinist	36	"
H	Brooks Mary F—†	14–16	clerk	25	
K	Meade Gertrude—†	14–16	"	25	
L	Meade John	14–16	photographer	26	"
M	Crowell Margaret M—†	14–16	housewife	62	"
N	Crowell Mary—†	14–16	clerk	26	
O	Crowell Michael F	14–16	motorman	65	"
P	Mitchell Mary E—†	18–20	at home	81	
R	Mullaney Lillian M—†	18–20	housewife	49	"
S	Grogett Bessie—†	18–20	"	33	
T	Groggett Richard	18–20	mechanic	39	"
U	Peters Anna—†	18–20	housewife	49	"
V	Peters Ernest	18–20	shipper	58	
W	Peters Ernest	18–20	clerk	21	
X	Foley Henry	22–24	retired	75	
Y	McDermott Agnes—†	22–24	at home	68	
Z	Snyder Francis C—†	22–24	accountant	33	"
	1618				
A	Snyder Helen—†	22–24	housewife	31	"
B	Cronin Catherine—†	22–24	"	57	
C	Cronin John	22–24	painter	57	
D	Cronin Joseph	22–24	shipper	26	
E	Cronin Mary—†	22–24	stenographer	20	"
F	Harrington Catherine—†	26–28	housewife	59	"
G	Harrington Catherine V—†	26–28	clerk	25	
H	Harrington James	26–28	student	23	
K	Harrington John	26–28	operator	55	
L	Carey Gertrude—†	26–28	housewife	36	"
M	Carey John	26–28	policeman	42	"
N	Cohane Cornelius	26–28	operator	65	
O	Cohane Cornelius Y	26–28	gardener	29	"
P	Cohane Mary—†	26–28	housewife	66	"
R	Dunn George F	30–32	laborer	26	

12

Page.	Letter.	FULL NAME.	Residence, Jan. 1, 1941.	Occupation.	Supposed Age.	Reported Residence, Jan. 1, 1940. Street and Number.

Saint Rose Street—Continued

	s	Dunn Margaret M—†	30–32	housewife	57	here
	t	Dwyer Harry B	30–32	salesman	38	"
	u	Dwyer Mary—†	30–32	housewife	28	"
	v	Kelley Catherine J—†	30–32	clerk	43	
	w	Kelley Mary E—†	30–32	"	45	
	x	Kelley Patrick J	30–32	laborer	37	
	y	Quinn Anne—†	30–32	secretary	22	"
	z	Quinn Annie K—†	30–32	housewife	57	"
1619						
	a	Quinn Edward	30–32	laborer	59	
	b	Quinn Francis	30–32	clerk	24	"
	c	Frazier Arthur W	34–36	chauffeur	41	"
	d	Frazier Francis	34–36	"	43	
	e	Frazier Margaret H—†	34–36	housewife	43	"
	f	Hanberry John	34–36	salesman	22	"
	g	Hanberry Mary C—†	34–36	housewife	49	"
	h	Hanberry William F	34–36	policeman	49	"
	k	Horan Mary A—†	34–36	housewife	64	"
	l	Horan Patrick J	34–36	retired	62	"
	m	Harrington Catherine—†	38	housewife	31	"
	n	Harrington John	38	mechanic	39	"
	o	Lesbirel Lenore—†	38	housewife	43	"
	p	McGraw Lucy M—†	42	housekeeper	59	"
	r	McGraw Margaret—†	42	saleswoman	47	"
	s	Honey Anna T—†	46	housewife	35	"
	t	Honey Joseph A	46	manager	49	"
	u	*Griffin John J	48	retired	48	
	v	Griffin Margaret C—†	48	secretary	48	"
	w	Griffin Sadie R—†	48	clerk	45	
	x	*Griffin Sarah C—†	48	housewife	77	"
	y	Grady Charlotte—†	50	teacher	28	11 Com av
	z	Mitchell Ethel—†	50	housewife	45	here
1620						
	a	Mitchell William	50	clerk	37	"
	b	Lynch David W	50	costumer	65	"
	c	Lynch Eleanor M—†	50	secretary	26	"
	d	Lynch Helen—†	50	housewife	60	"
	e	Lynch Kathleen M—†	50	clerk	23	
	f	Hutton Helen—†	54	housewife	55	"
	g	Hutton Helen—†	54	clerk	26	
	h	Hutton John	54	motorman	54	"

13

Saint Rose Street—Continued

K	Hutton John	54	clerk	24	here
L	Curley Mary J—†	58	housekeeper	58	"
M	Phelan Timothy	58	retired	81	"
N	Carroll Joseph B	62	clerk	27	
O	Carroll Margaret F—†	62	housewife	27	"
P	Bridges Ellen—†	62	"	75	
R	Bridges Michael F	62	toolmaker	81	"
S	Carroll Alice M—†	62	clerk	22	
T	Carroll Daniel J	62	guard	62	
U	Carroll Eileen—†	62	clerk	23	
V	Carroll Mary E—†	62	housewife	60	"
W	Healy Ethel—†	66	"	33	
X	Healy Thomas A	66	shipper	36	"
Y	*Kelly Eileen—†	66	housewife	30	19 Greenville
Z	Kelly Patrick J	66	gateman	31	19 "
	1621				
A	Huber Ann—†	70	housewife	37	here
B	Huber John	70	chauffeur	42	"
C	Murray Edward	70	laborer	29	14 Woodlawn
D	Babb Charles H	70	machinist	42	here
E	Babb Mabel E—†	70	housewife	41	"
F	Sargent F Milton	74	brewer	37	"
G	Sargent Mary M—†	74	housewife	43	"
H	Walsh Bartholomew	74	laborer	36	
K	Walsh Margaret—†	74	housewife	34	"
L	*Carr Nellie—†	74	"	31	
M	Carr Patrick J	74	laborer	41	
N	Sasche Emily J—†	78	housewife	32	"
O	Sasche Walter	78	accountant	40	"
P	Walsh Margaret—†	78	housekeeper	59	"
R	Brazia Anne—†	78	clerk	23	"
S	Brazia Leo	78	machinist	63	"
T	Grogan John	82	salesman	35	"
U	Maguire James H	82	"	36	
V	Maguire Madeline—†	82	housewife	34	"
X	Harrington James J	94	manager	76	"
Y	Harrington Margaret M—†	94	housewife	44	"
Z	Young Elizabeth—†	98	"	41	Quincy
	1622				
A	Young Harold E	98	booker	37	"
B	Malloy Alice M—†	98	at home	27	here

Page.	Letter.	Full Name.	Residence, Jan. 1, 1941.	Occupation.	Supposed Age.	Reported Residence, Jan. 1, 1940. Street and Number.

Saint Rose Street—Continued

c	Malloy John	98	mason	58	here
d	Gast Clara—†	98	housewife	55	"
e	Gast Paul	98	retired	63	"

South Street

g	Comerford Matthew E	133	painter	50	here
h	Glynn Alice—†	133	laundress	46	"
k	Leonard Albert F	133	shipper	57	"
l	Leonard Elizabeth—†	133	housewife	50	"
m	Gorman Bessie—†	141	"	43	
n	Gorman Edward J	141	carpenter	44	"
o	Gorman Gerard J	141	counterman	21	"
p	Lyons James A	141	chauffeur	55	"
r	Lyons James J	141	clerk	20	
s	Lyons Nellie—†	141	housewife	46	"
t	Traynor Mary A—†	141	"	54	
u	Traynor Mary A—†	141	clerk	23	
v	Traynor Matthew J	141	machinist	28	"
w	Traynor Paul A	141	clerk	26	
x	Traynor Susan H—†	141	"	22	
y	Buckley Patrick J	145	laborer	52	
z	Mullen Bridget M—†	145	housewife	49	"
	1623				
a	Mullen Peter J	145	laborer	49	
b	Flynn Annie A—†	145	housewife	67	"
c	Benjamin Frank J	145	manager	25	14 Colborne rd
d	O'Brien Helen B—†	145	housewife	24	here
e	*O'Brien William T	145	clerk	28	"
f	Johnson Catherine A—†	149	housewife	66	"
g	Johnson Edward F	149	letter carrier	42	"
h	Johnson Elizabeth M—†	149	housewife	42	"
k	Gately Margaret C—†	149	"	43	
l	Gately Thomas L	149	repairman	52	"
m	Clancy Ellen E—†	149	operator	28	"
n	Clancy Joseph P	149	starter	42	
o	Clancy Mary E—†	149	housewife	70	"
p	LeVie Forrest C	153	chauffeur	29	"
r	LeVie Frances E—†	153	housewife	30	"
s	Mullen Eleanor M—†	153	bookkeeper	26	"
t	Mullen Helen—†	153	housewife	65	"

15

South Street—Continued

u	Mullen Thomas J	153	motorman	54	here
v	*Duffy Catherine J—†	153	housewife	45	"
w	Duffy Edward	153	wool grader	45	"
x	Cheney Barbara E—†	159	nurse	27	
y	Emery Prudence M—†	159	housewife	53	"
z	Emery William D	159	foreman	53	
	1624				
a	Waible Hilda T—†	159	at home	39	"
a¹	Waible Joseph A	159	retired	75	
b	Waible Leo J	159	salesman	45	"
c	Favaloro Anna M—†	159	housewife	45	"
d	Favaloro Felix	159	retired	60	
e	Hamrock Edward F	159	clerk	27	
f	McGee Mary E—†	159	stitcher	48	
g	McGee William C	159	manager	34	"
h	Greeley Mary E—†	159	housewife	82	"
k	Greeley Thomas F	159	chauffeur	59	"
l	Cooke Horace S	159	machinist	33	12 Goldsmith
m	Cooke Margaret—†	159	housewife	40	12 "
n	Cruickshank Alice H—†	161	secretary	25	87 Atherton
o	Cruickshank James G	161	repairman	30	2 Eliot pl
p	Gaddish Delia A—†	161	waitress	62	here
r	*Gaddish Margaret A—†	161	at home	57	"
s	Galvin Mary C—†	161	operator	28	"
t	Murray Anne—†	161	housewife	69	"
u	O'Neil Geraldine F—†	161	typist	21	
v	O'Neil Margaret V—†	161	housewife	47	"
w	Cabot Charles R	161	musician	25	
x	Dwyer Arthur G	161	"	29	
y	Dwyer Clarence J	161	salesman	27	"
z	Dwyer Theresa M—†	161	housewife	51	"
	1625				
a	Bowles Helen M—†	161	"	28	
b	Bowes James J	161	policeman	30	"
c	Luppold Bernard L	161	shoecutter	57	"
d	Luppold Katherine F—†	161	housewife	55	"
f	Curtis Edith M—†	163	"	21	
g	Curtis Walter L	163	winder	36	"
h	Gormley John J	163	clerk	50	61 Hill Top
k	Gormley Mary G—†	163	housewife	45	49 Bournedale rd
l	Duff Jemima M—†	163	"	41	here

M	Duff William G	163	manager	39	here
N	Foley Michael	163	porter	53	"
O	Foley Nellie J—†	163	housewife	50	"
P	Leonard John J	163	shipper	25	
R	Leonard Mary F—†	163	housewife	23	"
S	Flanagan Frederick L	163	machinist	35	"
T	Flanagan Marguerite F-†	163	housewife	34	"
V	Flynn Margaret—†	165	"	79	
W	Flynn William H	165	technician	38	"
X	Smith Anna G—†	165	housewife	36	"
Y	Smith Walter J	165	repairman	48	"
Z	Reynolds Catherine T—†	165	housewife	32	"

1626

A	Reynolds John J	165	foreman	35	
B	Gaddish Catherine A—†	165	housewife	48	"
C	Gaddish Michael F	165	student	20	
D	Gaddish Michael J	165	laborer	59	"
E	*Harney Ellen L—†	165	at home	45	12 Brown ter
F	Brannelly John J	165	bartender	41	here
G	*Brannelly Margaret M—†	165	housewife	39	"
H	Wanders Agnes M—†	165	stenographer	20	"
K	Wanders William J	165	motorman	45	"
O	Dillen Melvin J	171	electrician	56	"
P	MacFarland John H	171	laborer	53	
R	*Rounds Rebecca S—†	171	housekeeper	63	"
T	Smith Carl E	185	pressman	38	180 W Canton
U	Smith Helen M—†	185	housewife	34	178 "
V	Frank I Robert	185	physician	35	here
W	Frank Vera W—†	185	housewife	31	"
X	*Walker Alfred W	185	chauffeur	57	"
Y	*Walker Catherine A—†	185	housewife	60	"
Z	Stebbins Mary C—†	185	"	48	315 Cornell

1627

A	Stebbins Robert O	185	policeman	49	315 "
B	Weldon Katherine—†	185	at home	76	315 "
C	Morgan Anne G—†	185	housekeeper	50	here
D	Morgan Helen G—†	185	teacher	46	"
E	Morgan Michael H	185	operator	63	"
F	Walker Florence—†	185	housewife	66	"
G	Walker Thomas	185	clerk	36	
H	*Harris Stella—†	190	housewife	36	"

Page.	Letter.	FULL NAME.	Residence, Jan. 1, 1941.	Occupation.	Supposed Age.	Reported Residence, Jan. 1, 1940. Street and Number.

South Street—Continued

K	Harris Walter R	190	knitter	38	here
L	McCarthy Margaret E—†190		housewife	30	"
M	McCarthy William J	190	machinist	42	"
N	Barry Charles F	190	clerk	28	
O	Barry Eleanor G—†	190	at home	26	
P	Barry Gertrude L—†	190	housewife	44	"
R	Barry Joseph P	190	clerk	52	
S	Barry Joseph W	190	welder	29	
T	Barry Marie E—†	190	examiner	24	"
U	Mudge Margaret E—†	195	clerk	32	
V	Mudge Mary B—†	195	housewife	68	"
W	O'Hara Mary V—†	195	clerk	35	
X	Kelley Henry A	195	retired	74	
Y	Kelley Mary F—†	195	housewife	70	"
Z	Curtis Carmella H—†	195	operator	34	"

1628

A	Curtis Frank A	195	retired	75	
B	Curtis Maud A—†	195	housewife	62	"
C	Curtis Mildred M—†	195	clerk	27	
D	Curtis Milo C	195	salesman	37	"
E	Larson Gustave F	195	chauffeur	36	"
F	Larson Lillian M—†	195	housewife	34	"
G	Collins Dennis J	195	laborer	49	
H	Collins Helen M—†	195	clerk	29	"
K	Collins Patrick W	195	laborer	51	
L	Golden Dorothy J—†	195	clerk	29	
M	Morrison Edna L—†	195	operator	27	
N	Morrison Elsie M—†	195	housewife	58	"
O	Morrison James	195	motorman	62	"
P	Ging Cecilia—†	196	housekeeper	42	"
R	Ging George W	196	letter carrier	40	"
S	Ging John J	196	"	34	
T	Purtell Anna A—†	196	secretary	48	"
U	Purtell Thomas	196	retired	76	"
V	Thompson John J	196	engineer	62	
W	Thompson Mary J—†	196	operator	28	
X	Thompson Theresa F—†	196	housewife	61	"
Y	Thompson Theresa F—†	196	secretary	26	"
Z	Lestrange Thomas	198	shipper	45	"

1629

A	MacIntyre John	198	clerk	38	

Page.	Letter.	Full Name.	Residence, Jan. 1, 1941.	Occupation.	Supposed Age.	Reported Residence, Jan. 1, 1940. Street and Number.

	B	MacIntyre Margaret—†	198	stenographer	34	here
	C	Kenney Catherine—†	198	housewife	48	"
	D	Kenney Dennis F	198	operator	51	"
	E	Hines John J	198	repairman	45	"
	F	Hines Mary C—†	198	housewife	45	"
	G	Wittig Carl L	199	superintendent	49	"
	H	Wittig Marjorie A—†	199	housewife	47	"
	K	Geary Inez M—†	199	"	43	6 Gordon
	L	Geary Martin J	199	repairman	46	6 "
	M	Garrity Mary E—†	199	housewife	29	here
	N	Garrity Thomas A	199	mechanic	43	"
	o	O'Brien Daniel F	199	adjuster	27	42 Neponset av
	P	O'Brien Frederick J	199	toolmaker	23	42 "
	R	O'Brien Margaret J—†	199	cashier	53	42 "
	S	O'Brien Mary R—†	199	secretary	28	42
	U	Smith Fred E	199	shoeworker	60	here
	V	Smith Gertrude—†	199	"	50	"
	W	Bradley Helen—†	200	housekeeper	45	"
	X	Connaughton Catherine—†200		housewife	43	"
	Y	Connaughton John J	200	gardener	52	"
	Z	Crehan John J	200	operator	43	"
		1630				
	A	Potter Dorothy—†	200	housewife	32	38 Kittredge
	B	Potter William E	200	foreman	30	38 "
	c	*Barrett Margaret—†	202	housewife	36	here
	D	*Barrett Patrick M	202	laborer	36	"
	E	Linehan Anna M—†	202	housewife	38	"
	F	Linehan John J	202	salesman	40	"
	G	Morris John	202	operator	62	"
	H	Morris John F	202	laborer	29	
	K	Morris Nora—†	202	housewife	58	"
	L	Morris Thomas	202	laundryworker	23	"
	N	Diggins Dennis	204	shipper	22	
	o	Diggins Helen—†	204	secretary	27	"
	P	Diggins John	204	laborer	57	
	R	Diggins Joseph	204	chauffeur	20	"
	S	Diggins Julia—†	204	presser	29	
	T	*Morgan Catherine—†	206	housewife	60	"
	U	Morgan Michael	206	laborer	60	
	V	Morgan William	206	"	22	
	W	Brown Donald E	206	plumber	31	

South Street—Continued

x	Brown Margaret M—†	206	housewife	32	here
y	Richardson Clyde	206	diemaker	27	Braintree
z	Richardson Helen L—†	206	housewife	23	"

1631

b	Strecker Frank A	211	machinist	34	94 Jamaica
c	Strecker Mary A—†	211	housewife	28	79 McBride
d	*Valanzola Louise—†	211	"	37	here
e	Valanzola Urbano	211	barber	41	"
f	*Doherty Bridget—†	211	housewife	34	"
g	Doherty William H	211	baker	31	
h	Plummer Clifford W	211	retired	68	
k	*Martineau Olivette—†	212	housewife	37	"
l	Martineau Philip H	212	architect	37	"
m	Hawkins Catherine J—†	212	housewife	47	"
n	Hawkins Joseph	212	chauffeur	21	"
o	Hawkins Patrick J	212	operator	48	
p	Foley Bridget—†	214	housewife	50	"
r	Foley Daniel	214	student	31	
s	Foley Edward	214	chauffeur	22	"
t	Foley Timothy	214	salesman	52	"
u	Dolan James J	214	"	45	
v	Euscher Fred	214	chauffeur	36	"
w	Euscher Rae—†	214	housewife	35	"
x	Nagle Helen T—†	215	"	31	624 Cummins H'w'y
y	Boucher James J	215	watchmaker	33	here
z	Boucher Pearl M—†	215	housewife	30	"

1632

a	Morrissey John	215	die setter	33	"
b	Morrissey Mary J—†	215	housewife	31	"
c	Hutchinson Catherine E—†	217	"	37	
d	Hutchinson Michael A	217	porter	45	
e	Gibbons Sarah—†	217	at home	69	
f	Hemeon Dorothy H—†	217	entertainer	24	"
g	Hemeon Helen V—†	217	housewife	45	"
h	Hemeon Ralph H	217	carpenter	23	"
k	Early John P	217	clerk	21	
l	*Early Mary—†	217	housewife	44	"
m	Early Peter	217	laborer	48	
n	Connolly James	218–230	clerk	23	
o	Connolly Mary J—†	218–230	stenographer	29	"
p	Connolly Peter	218–230	laborer	67	"

R	Hanley Helen—†	218–230	housewife	38	here
S	Hanley William	218–230	manager	44	"
T	Lund John	218–230	photographer	44	"
U	Lund Mary D—†	218–230	housewife	38	"
V	Healey Catherine—†	218–230	at home	65	
W	Norton Catherine C–†	218–230	housewife	33	"
X	Norton Kenneth	218–230	clerk	32	
Y	Wesley Sarah—†	218–230	housekeeper	74	"
Z	Adams Anna T—†	218–230	housewife	60	"

1633

A	Adams Grace C—†	218–230	stenographer	34	"
C	Griffin Daniel S	218–230	accountant	45	"
D	Griffin Irma—†	218–230	housewife	29	"
E	Keenan Dennis L	218–230	chauffeur	28	"
F	Bain Christine—†	218–230	housewife	41	"
G	MacQueen Mary—†	218–230	nurse	43	
H	Lamb Frances C—†	218–230	teacher	54	"
K	Drinkwater Louise–†	218–230	domestic	25	Dedham
L	McLellan Grace—†	218–230	housewife	71	12 Abbot
M	McLellan Herbert S	218–230	broker	52	12 "
N	MacFayden George	218–230	letter carrier	31	here
O	MacFayden Thomas	218–230	watchman	58	"
P	Hartung Centa G—†	218–230	clerk	35	"
R	Hartung Crescentia B—†	218–230	housewife	60	"
S	Clifford Agnes C—†	218–230	"	37	
T	Clifford Charles W	218–230	salesman	50	
U	Faulkner James M	218–230	guard	36	
V	Faulkner Leonora—†	218–230	housewife	36	"
W	Hill Louise—†	218–230	forewoman	37	"
X	Patterson Mabel J–†	218–230	clerk	30	
Y	Silvia Eleanor J—†	218–230	housewife	27	"
Z	Silvia Roscoe O	218–230	salesman	28	

1634

A	McLaughlin Beatrice—†	218–230	nurse	24	3 Bishop
B	McLaughlin Victor	218–230	janitor	63	here
C	Swanson Alice—†	218–230	nurse	30	3 Bishop
D	Ripley Arthur	218–230	manager	51	here
E	Ripley Lillian—†	218–230	housewife	37	"
F	Chase Ivy B—†	218–230	nurse	44	"
G	Falt Gertrude H—†	218–230	teacher	36	
H	McGinnis Ellen—†	218–230	housewife	50	"

Page.	Letter.	Full Name.	Residence, Jan. 1, 1941.	Occupation.	Supposed Age.	Reported Residence, Jan. 1, 1940. Street and Number.

South Street—Continued

K	McGinnis Patrick	218–230	operator	47	here
L	Hopewell Mary E—†	218–230	housewife	60	"
M	Hopewell Nehemiah	218–230	cook	61	"
N	Kennedy Alice H—†	218–230	housewife	37	3 Chilcott pl
O	Kennedy Thomas	218–230	policeman	40	46 Creighton
P	Palmer Gertrude H–†	218–230	clerk	61	here
R	Palmer Harriet S—†	218–230	"	59	"
S	Shaw Roderick N	218–230	salesman	54	200 Wood av
T	Shaw Sadie R—†	218–230	housewife	46	200 "
U	Rogers James	218–230	chauffeur	62	here
V	Rogers Marie—†	218–230	clerk	27	"
W	MacDonald John A	218–230	janitor	57	"
X	MacKay Charles	218–230	"	55	
Y	MacKay Margaret E—†	218–230	housewife	23	"
Z	MacKay Minnie L–†	218–230	"	50	

1635

A	Canfield Mabel A—†	218–230	nurse	46	
B	Sheridan Abbie B—†	218–230	"	46	
C	Keigher John	218–230	machinist	44	"
D	Keigher Margaret—†	218–230	housewife	38	"
E	Dillon Margaret—†	218–230	stenographer	28	"
F	Norton David	218–230	contractor	51	"
G	Norton Mary F—†	218–230	housewife	43	"
H	Burnham Dorcas M—†	218–230	"	69	
K	Burnham Loretta—†	218–230	"	26	
L	Burnham Wilbur F	218–230	clerk	28	
M	McCann Joseph	218–230	laborer	23	
N	McCann Rose—†	218–230	housewife	44	"
O	McTernan Alice—†	218–230	bookkeeper	51	"
P	McTernan Mary A–†	218–230	housekeeper	66	"
R	Killeen Catherine H—†	218–230	housewife	37	"
S	Killeen Edward C	218–230	policeman	38	"
T	Watson Alice L—†	218–230	housewife	72	"
U	Watson Fred A	218–230	retired	82	
V	Watson Gladys—†	218–230	secretary	41	"
W	McCafferty Annie R—†	218–230	housewife	31	"
X	McCafferty Hugh J	218–230	machinist	35	"
Y	Bowman Edna M—†	218–230	housewife	32	"
Z	Bowman Harold L	218–230	accountant	35	"

1636

A	Magner Thomas	218–230	foreman	47	

South Street—Continued

B	Prendergast Daniel J	218–230	agent	60	here
C	Prendergast Rose M—†	218–230	housewife	50	"
D	Sullivan Helen M—†	218–230	clerk	50	24 Colonial av
E	Sullivan Mary E—†	218–230	operator	28	24 "
F	Clougherty Margaret—†	218–230	housewife	49	here
G	Clougherty Michael F	218–230	salesman	52	"
H	McNally John W	218–230	accountant	33	"
K	McNally Mary B—†	218–230	housewife	26	"
L	Antman Burdella—†	218–230	"	46	
M	Antman Ernest	218–230	salesman	37	"
N	Carey Margaret H–†	218–230	nurse	30	
O	Carey Sarah C—†	218–230	stenographer	29	"
P	Carey Sarah J—†	218–230	housewife	68	"
R	Dove Joseph	218–230	printer	64	
S	Pierce Frank S	218–230	agent	70	
T	Pierce Olive N—†	218–230	housewife	69	"
U	Heil Marion—†	218–230	stenographer	39	"
V	Whiting Edith—†	218–230	clerk	39	"
W	Parker Everett	218–230	custodian	50	"
X	Parker Frances F—†	218–230	housewife	60	"
Y	VanBlack Anna A–†	218–230	"	44	
Z	VanBlack Roy H	218–230	starter	46	
	1637				
A	Tobey Fred S	218–230	reporter	32	
B	Tobey Rolph E	218–230	builder	51	
C	Hickey Lucena M–†	218–230	housewife	41	"
D	Hickey Richard	218–230	policeman	44	"
E	Walker Charles	218–230	chauffeur	67	"
F	Walker Ethel C—†	218–230	housewife	65	"
G	Nickerson Harold E	218–230	policeman	45	87 Fort av
H	Nickerson Helen B–†	218–230	housewife	44	87 "
K	Hazoun Adama—†	218–230	"	57	here
L	Hazoun Alfred	218–230	student	27	"
M	Hazoun Jacob	218–230	salesman	59	"
N	Dergans Alfred	218–230	"	27	New York
O	Dergans Olga—†	218–230	housewife	25	"
P	DeVite Mary—†	218–230	at home	51	"
R	Duddy Agnes L–†	218–230	housewife	60	here
S	Duddy John F	218–230	retired	59	"
T	Cronin Charles F	218–230	manager	59	"
U	Cronin Mary G—†	218–230	storekeeper	61	"

South Street—Continued

	Letter	Full Name	Residence Jan. 1, 1941	Occupation	Supposed Age	Reported Residence Jan. 1, 1940
	v	Galvin James	218–230	retired	51	here
	w	Karam Charles	218–230	agent	28	"
	x	Karam George	218–230	"	35	"
	y	Karam Soha—†	218–230	housewife	62	"
	z	Karam Theodore	218–230	investigator	29	"
1638						
	A	McNabb Helen—†	218–230	housewife	55	"
	B	McNabb Mary F—†	218–230	stenographer	30	"
	C	McNabb Myrtle E—†	218–230	"	24	..
	E	O'Donnell Margaret F–†	219	housewife	42	"
	F	O'Donnell Patrick R	219	salesman	21	"
	G	Pearl Frances—†	219	housewife	35	"
	H	Pearl Louis W	219	manager	37	..
	K	Lee Isabelle R—†	221	housewife	32	"
	L	Lee Joseph W	221	chemist	31	
	M	Pearl Anne—†	221	teacher	24	
	N	Pearl Harold	221	accountant	38	"
	O	Pearl Louis	221	mechanic	40	"
	P	Pearl Marianne—†	221	housewife	60	"
	R	Maguire Lena—†	221	hostess	24	20 Spalding
	S	Maguire Paul L	221	clerk	26	20 "
	T	Downey Margaret—†	223	housewife	55	54 "
	U	Downey William F	223	chauffeur	57	54 "
	v	Bell Catherine—†	223	cleaner	67	here
	w	Bell John F	223	chauffeur	41	"
	x*	Gibbs Anna C—†	223	housewife	43	"
	Y	Gibbs George J	223	painter	41	
	z	Gibbs Richard J	223	longshoreman	46	"
1639						
	A	Kaufman Lena—†	225	housewife	55	239 West
	B	Kaufman Max	225	storekeeper	65	239 "
	C	McCorry Agnes L—†	225	housewife	39	here
	D	McCorry James E	225	ironworker	42	"
	E	Pallamary Dorothy M–†	225	housewife	54	"
	F	Pallamary Michael J	225	investigator	52	"
	G	Pallamary Mildred M—†	225	stenographer	20	"
	K	Brucker Arnold E	234	clerk	26	..
	L	Brucker Emma—†	234	housewife	63	"
	M	Brucker Louis	234	chef	60	
	N	Dailey Catherine A—†	238	housewife	39	"
	R	Dailey William F	238	testman	41	

o	Dailey James F	238	retired	66	here
p	Dailey Mary A—†	238	housewife	65	"

Spalding Street

s	Savage Bernard	7	student	20	here
t	Savage Emily W—†	7	housewife	56	"
u	Savage James P	7	meatcutter	67	"
v	Savage John	7	clerk	21	
w	Hill Anna—†	7	at home	51	
x	Owens Bridget—†	7	"	75	"
y	Walker Arvin R	7	ironworker	48	83 Bickford
z	Mee Catherine—†	8–10	domestic	55	here
	1640				
a	Mee Margaret—†	8–10	cashier	47	
b	Mee William H	8–10	laborer	21	
c	Mee William J	8–10	operator	55	
d	*Scully Annie—†	8–10	housewife	63	"
e	Scully John	8–10	clerk	21	
f	Scully Patrick J	8–10	laborer	61	
g	Smith Dorothy I—†	8–10	saleswoman	22	"
h	Smith Gladys M—†	8–10	clerk	20	
k	Smith John C	8–10	machinist	51	"
l	Smith John C, jr	8–10	laundryworker	23	"
m	Smith Margaret H—†	8–10	housewife	50	"
n	McManus Helen—†	9	"	40	
o	McManus Michael	9	laborer	46	
p	Kelly Ann—†	11	housewife	33	"
r	Condry Genevieve—†	11	saleswoman	47	"
s	Condry Julia E—†	11	"	48	
t	Condry Mary E—†	11	housewife	77	"
u	Crowley Jane—†	11	at home	65	"
v	Geary Julia—†	11	"	70	New York
w	Crotty Constance G—†	12	housewife	28	110 Sycamore
x	Crotty John P, jr	12	draftsman	30	110 "
y	McGonagle Helen G—†	12	housewife	46	here
z	McGonagle James E	12	clerk	46	"
	1641				
a	McGonagle Joseph G	12	student	20	
b	Walsh Joseph	12	clerk	37	
c	Lemieux Henry F	12	chauffeur	30	"

Page.	Letter.	Full Name.	Residence, Jan. 1, 1941.	Occupation.	Supposed Age.	Reported Residence, Jan. 1, 1940. Street and Number.

Spalding Street—Continued

	D	Lemieux Rita A—†	12	housewife	32	here
	E	*Anderson Ada—†	13	at home	62	"
	F	Blomquist Knute R	13	painter	77	"
	G	Blomquist Regina—†	13	housewife	59	"
	H	Sayce Catherine C—†	13	"	52	
	K	Sayce Edna—†	13	waitress	20	"
	L	Sayce Francis W	13	foreman	53	"
	M	*Werner August	13	laborer	49	"
	N	*Werner Pauline—†	13	housewife	52	"
	O	Dee Anthony J	15	bricklayer	39	"
	P	Dee Theresa M—†	15	housewife	38	"
	R	Drummey Dorothy—†	15	"	32	44 Weld Hill
	S	Drummey William	15	cashier	33	44 "
	T	Hatje E Jean—†	15	stenographer	30	44 "
	U	Bullen Albert W	15	retired	66	here
	V	Bullen Catherine—†	15	seamstress	63	"
	W	McMurrough Frank E	16	installer	51	"
	X	Allen Mae—†	16	housewife	23	16 Angell
	Y	Allen Richard	16	metalworker	24	12 Anson
	Z	Schnieder Josephine—†	16	housewife	51	here
1642						
	A	Schnieder Lorenz	16	retired	71	"
	B	*Costello Catherine—†	17	housewife	33	"
	C	Costello John	17	laborer	38	
	D	*Beatty Eilleen—†	17	housewife	33	"
	E	Beatty John	17	ironworker	34	"
	G	Malone Charles E	19	clerk	27	"
	H	McGloin Francis P	19	"	27	
	K	McGloin Mary A—†	19	domestic	55	"
	L	O'Donnell Julia A—†	19	housewife	35	"
	M	O'Donnell Michael J	19	longshoreman	35	"
	N	Norton John	19	trackwalker	34	"
	O	*Norton Mary—†	19	housewife	30	"
	P	Norton William	19	shipper	38	"
	R	Burke Eleanor M—†	20	housewife	24	Watertown
	S	Burke Francis E	20	shipper	24	"
	T	Evans George T	20	laborer	39	here
	U	*Evans Sally—†	20	housewife	38	"
	V	Dempsey Dennis	20	laborer	50	"
	W	Dempsey Jennie—†	20	housewife	49	"

Page	Letter	FULL NAME.	Residence, Jan. 1, 1941.	Occupation.	Supposed Age.	Reported Residence, Jan. 1, 1940. Street and Number.

Spalding Street—Continued

	x	*Hutchinson Mary—†	22	housewife	32	82 St Rose
	y	Hutchinson Thomas	22	caretaker	28	82 "
	z	Bernard Helen M—†	22	housewife	37	120 Day
1643						
	A	Bernard John E	22	dairyworker	38	120 "
	B	McHugh Patrick	22	laborer	45	here
	C	McHugh Sabina—†	22	housewife	43	"

View South Avenue

	D	McCarthy John J	4–6	freighthandler	49	here
	E	McCarty Mary E—†	4–6	housewife	48	"
	F	Harding John J	4–6	manager	47	"
	G	Harding Nora T—†	4–6	housewife	47	"
	H	Dillon Agnes—†	4–6	waitress	27	
	K	Dillon Elizabeth—†	4–6	housewife	50	"
	L	Dillon James	4–6	printer	55	
	M	Fitzgerald Catherine—†	5–7	housewife	43	"
	N	Fitzgerald Patrick	5–7	laborer	45	
	O	Fitzgerald Beatrice—†	5–7	housewife	50	"
	P	Walsh Catherine—†	5–7	"	46	
	R	Walsh John	5–7	laborer	48	
	S	Shiers Forrest J	5–7	accountant	24	"
	T	Shiers Forrest W	5–7	operator	53	".."
	U	Shiers Nellie M—†	5–7	housewife	53	"
	V	Shiers Richard G	5–7	student	20	
	W	Brennan Alice—†	8–10	housewife	39	"
	X	Brennan William F	8–10	salesman	43	"
	Y	*Johanson Anna—†	8–10	housewife	60	"
	Z	Johanson Arthur	8–10	engineer	25	
1644						
	A	Johanson Carl O	8–10	carpenter	59	"
	B	Johanson Walter	8–10	engineer	27	
	C	Coady David J	8–10	salesman	30	"
	D	Coady Evelyn—†	8–10	housewife	30	"
	E	Gerke Albert	9–11	manager	57	"
	F	Gerke Charles	9–11	carpenter	28	"
	G	Gerke Eleanor—†	9–11	housekeeper	32	"
	H	Gerke George	9–11	timekeeper	32	"
	K	Morrison Edward	9–11	attendant	50	"

Page.	Letter.	FULL NAME.	Residence, Jan. 1, 1941.	Occupation.	Supposed Age.	Reported Residence, Jan. 1, 1940. Street and Number.

View South Avenue—Continued

L	Gallivan Catherine—†	9–11	housewife	48	here
M	Gallivan Stephen	9–11	fireman	56	"
N	O'Brien Daniel V	9–11	salesman	26	"
o	O'Brien John H	9–11	"	24	
P	O'Brien Kathleen—†	9–11	operator	22	"
R	O'Brien William T	9–11	superintendent	64	"